D1600847

The Battle for the Catholic Past in Germany, 1945–1980

Were Pope Pius XII and the Catholic Church in Germany unduly singled out after 1945 for their conduct during the National Socialist era? Mark Edward Ruff explores the bitter controversies that broke out in the Federal Republic of Germany from 1945 to 1980 over the Catholic Church's relationship to the Nazis. He explores why these cultural wars consumed such energy, dominated headlines, triggered lawsuits and required the intervention of Foreign Ministries. He argues that the controversies over the church's relationship to National Socialism were frequently surrogates for conflicts over how the church was to position itself in modern society – in politics, international relations and the media. More often than not, these exchanges centered on problems perceived as arising from the postwar political ascendancy of Roman Catholics and the integration of Catholic citizens into the societal mainstream.

Mark Edward Ruff is Professor of History at Saint Louis University in Missouri. He is the author of *The Wayward Flock: Catholic Youth in Postwar Germany, 1945–1965* (2005), and co-editor of *Die Katholische Kirche im Dritten Reich* (2011). He is the recent recipient of research fellowships from the ACLS, NEH and the Alexander-von-Humboldt Foundation. He is also a pianist and church organist.

The Battle for the Catholic Past in Germany, 1945–1980

Mark Edward Ruff

Saint Louis University, Missouri

CAMBRIDGE
UNIVERSITY PRESS

CAMBRIDGE
UNIVERSITY PRESS

University Printing House, Cambridge CB2 8BS, United Kingdom

One Liberty Plaza, 20th Floor, New York, NY 10006, USA

477 Williamstown Road, Port Melbourne, VIC 3207, Australia

4843/24, 2nd Floor, Ansari Road, Daryaganj, Delhi – 110002, India

79 Anson Road, #06–04/06, Singapore 079906

Cambridge University Press is part of the University of Cambridge.

It furthers the University's mission by disseminating knowledge in the pursuit of
education, learning, and research at the highest international levels of excellence.

www.cambridge.org
Information on this title: www.cambridge.org/9781107190665
DOI: 10.1017/9781108116107

First published 2017

Printed in the United States of America by Sheridan Books, Inc.

A catalogue record for this publication is available from the British Library.

Library of Congress Cataloging-in-Publication Data
Names: Ruff, Mark Edward, author.
Title: The battle for the Catholic past in Germany, 1945–1980 / Mark Edward
Ruff (St. Louis University, Missouri).
Description: Cambridge, United Kingdom ; New York, NY : Cambridge
University Press, 2017. | Includes bibliographical references and index.
Identifiers: LCCN 2017012155 | ISBN 9781107190665 (hardback)
Subjects: LCSH: Catholic Church – Germany – History – 1933–1945 –
Historiography. | National socialism and religion – Germany – Historiography.
| Catholic Church – Foreign relations – Germany – Historiography. | Germany –
Foreign relations – Catholic Church – Historiography. | Pius XII, Pope, 1876–
1958 – Public opinion. | World War, 1939–1945 – Religious aspects – Catholic
Church – Historiography. | Christianity and politics – Germany (West) –
History. | Germany (West) – Politics and government – 1945–1990. | BISAC:
HISTORY / Europe / General.
Classification: LCC BX1536 .R84 2017 | DDC 282/.430904–dc23
LC record available at https://lccn.loc.gov/2017012155

ISBN 978-1-107-19066-5 Hardback

Additional resources for this publication at www.cambridge.org/9781107190665

To Lynnae

Contents

Illustrations

Acknowledgments

Spanning eleven years, two continents, six nations and seventy-seven archives, this work could never have come to fruition without the assistance of scholarly communities on both sides of the Atlantic. Dependent as we are on the generosity of others, this work is ultimately a reflection of the recollections, documentary collections, insights, wisdom and encouragement of hundreds, some no longer with us.

My four collective years of full-time research and writing were made possible by a Research Fellowship from the Alexander-von-Humboldt Foundation from 2006 to 2008, an ACLS Research Fellowship from 2011 to 2012, and an NEH Research Fellowship from 2012 to 2013. In conjunction with the ACLS, the Humanities Institute at the University at Buffalo graciously hosted me for portions of the spring semester in 2011. Smaller grants from the Cushwa Center for the Study of American Catholicism at the University of Notre Dame, the Humboldt Foundation, the Exzellenzcluster Religion und Politik at the Westfälische Wilhelms-Universität in Münster, the Mellon Research Fund at Saint Louis University, the Summer Research Award Fund at Saint Louis University and travel funds from the Department of History made possible shorter research sojourns between 2008 and 2016. I would like to thank Wilhelm Damberg of the Ruhr-Universität-Bochum for generously serving as my host during my years as a Humboldtianer and for providing me with an office and logistical support. I would like to thank Christine Pudlowski and Kelly Goersch, departmental administrators in the History Department, for helping me navigate the salient bureaucratic hoops.

Since the vast majority of my source material consists of letters, diaries and telegrams, many straight from attics, basements and personal libraries, my debts to archivists, scholars and Zeitzeugen are prodigious. I would like to begin by thanking the staffs of all of seventy-seven archives, nearly 500 persons in all, for responding so courteously to my ever-persistent requests. They all deserve special acknowledgment, and only limitations of space prevent me from mentioning all by name.

I launched my research by spending nearly seven months at the Historisches Archiv des Erzbistums Köln. I have returned here multiple times and would like to thank Ursula Brendt, Josef van Elten, Raimund Haas, Ulrich Helbach, Wolfgang Schmitz[†] and Brigitte Torsy. On so many occasions, the staff there made the impossible possible. Raimund Haas drove me to the house of Narzissa Stasiewski, who made available the papers of her deceased brother, Bernhard Stasiewski, in Ittenbach bei Königswinter.

The staff at the Archiv des Erzbistums München-Freising proved exceptionally helpful, and I would like to thank Volker Laube, Peter Pfister, Guido Treffler and Michael Volpert. Clemens Brodkorb at the Archiv der Deutschen Provinz der Jesuiten steered me through the papers of Ludwig Volk, SJ. Gotthard Klein at the Diözesanarchiv Berlin not only made available to me all of the relevant holdings but spent dozens of hours in conversations about my project. Andreas Burtscheidt, Petra Cartus, Christoph Kösters, Karl-Joseph Hummel and Erik Gieseking at the Kommission für Zeitgeschichte went beyond the call of duty as did Heinz Terhorst at the archive of the Zentralkomitee der Deutschen Katholiken. Sabine Zolchow at the Archiv der Akademie der Künste in Berlin likewise provided invaluable assistance.

In Switzerland, I would like to thank Ursula Ruch at the Schweizerisches Literaturarchiv, who provided so many helpful pointers about the Rolf Hochhuth papers. In the United States, I would like to thank the staff at the Catholic University Archives and, in particular, Maria Mazzenga and William John Shephard, who repeatedly went out of their way to assist me.

I am extremely indebted to many of my Zeitzeugen for answering my requests for information, meeting with me to discuss their work and generously providing access to their personal papers. Rolf Hochhuth met with me over dinner in Berlin; his first wife, Marianne (Heinemann) Sideri, hosted me over coffee at her home in Basel. Ernst-Wolfgang Böckenförde met with me twice in Freiburg im Breisgau over lunch. Rudolf Morsey hosted me for lunch twice in Neustadt an der Weinstrasse and met with me on many occasions to answer queries about subject matter in which he is the unsurpassed expert. On this side of the Atlantic, Angelika Kühn met with me in Oak Park to discuss her parents' role in these historical controversies. Thomas Brechenmacher provided me with copies of Konrad Repgen's papers on his historical controversy with Klaus Scholder. John Conway met with me in Vancouver, Canada, several times to discuss his experiences in Germany in the 1960s. Without their support, this project would never have been possible.

I would like to thank so many colleagues in Germany for their kindness in providing commentary on my ideas, lectures, articles and chapters. These include Riccardo Bavaj, Wilhelm Damberg, Ulrike Ehret, Thomas Großbölting, Andreas Henkelmann, Nicolai Hannig, Michael Kißener, Klaus Große Kracht, Rosel Oehmen-Vieregge, Christian Schmidtmann, Norbert Trippen†, Sylvia Tschopp, Rudolf Uertz and Andreas Wirsching. In Switzerland, I would like to thank Urs Altermatt, Catherine Bosshart, David Luginbühl, Franziska Metzger and Nadine Ritzer. I would like to give special recognition to Christoph Kösters, Gotthard Klein and Rudolf Morsey, who provided me with incisive commentary and helped fact-check the entire manuscript.

In North America, I would like to thank several distinct groups for their feedback on my chapters. I would like to thank the members of the German Historians Workshop in St. Louis and, in particular, Dirk Bönker, Sace Elder, Jennifer Miller, Warren Rosenblum, Jonathan Sperber, Corinne Treitel and S. Jonathan Wiesen. The members of two writing groups at Saint Louis University, Ellen Crowell, Claire Gilbert, Amber Johnson, Ian McReady-Flora, Pascale Perraudin, Ruben Rosario-Rodriguez and Amy Wright, provided me with invaluable help in rendering this manuscript more intelligible to a nonspecialist audience. So too did Ted Bromund, Mark Riebling, Eric Sears and my neighbor, Charles Fremont. I would also like to thank my departmental colleagues, including Douglas Boin, Flannery Burke, Phil Gavitt, Lorri Glover, James Hitchcock, Filippo Marsilli, George Ndege, Hal Parker, Jennifer Popiel, Steve Schoenig, SJ, Eric Sears, Silvana Siddali, Damian Smith and Luke Yarbrough, for their feedback. My thanks go to Victoria Barnett, Suzanne Brown-Fleming, John Connelly, Charlie Gallagher, SJ, Michael Geyer, Derek Hastings, Matthew Hockenos, Kevin Spicer and Jeff Zalar for their insights and leads on sources. David Stoddard and Elaine Marschlik helped me in the preparation of the electronic manuscript. Joseph Reidy, Alaric Powell and Beth Petitjean, serving as research assistants, made sundry helpful comments. John Conway and Guenter Lewy not only read through nearly the entire manuscript but made available to me documents from their personal collections. Finally, I would like to thank the two anonymous readers for Cambridge University Press whose suggestions made this a better manuscript along with my three editors, Lew Bateman, Michael Watson and Julie Hrischeva.

On a personal note, I would like to thank many close friends for their gracious hospitality. Margit and Tom Lindsay welcomed my wife and me at the Cologne airport and extended their friendship through many meals, afternoon teas and wonderful conversations. Wim and Annelie Damberg provided us a second home in Münster and the finest of Westphalian cuisine as did Thomas Großbölting. Christoph Kösters provided wonderful hospitality in Ittenbach. Gotthard Klein and Andreas Wirsching invited us to their homes in Berlin and Sixnitgern multiple times. Franziska Metzger arranged lodging for us in Fribourg while Nadine Ritzer kindly granted us use of her apartment in Bern for an entire summer. Jürgen Enninger and Christian Mutzel repeatedly found accommodations for us in Munich. Winfried Delitzsch helped us locate housing in Berlin and hosted us many times in Bremen and Lausanne. Christof Morrissey did the same for us in Berlin.

My deepest thanks go to my family, who has accompanied me on this long eleven-year journey. My two sons, Micah and Xavier, were born in 2008 and 2011 and remind us of the joys of childhood that are more important than scholarly monographs. I would like to thank my two brothers, Michael and Matthew, my sister-in-law Justine and my father, Roger Ruff. Sadly, my mother, Elaine Ruff[†], was unable to see this book appear in print, having passed away in January 2016 after a ten-month struggle with gallbladder cancer.

But the greatest recognition must go to my dear wife, Lynnae, who has been with me nearly every step of the way. She has lived through the peaks and valleys as well as the blood and sweat from unceasing transatlantic voyages, archival forays and draft revisions. She reminds me of life's delicacies and necessities – fine tea and fruitful conversation. It is to my loving wife that this book is dedicated.

Note on Translations

All translations, unless otherwise indicated, are my own.

Introduction

On February 20, 1963, Rolf Hochhuth, an unknown thirty-two-year-old house editor at the German publishing conglomerate Bertelsmann unleashed a scandal on the stage of the Free People's Theater in West Berlin. Under the direction of Erwin Piscator, a former Communist who had spent the Nazi years in Moscow and New York, the Berlin theater company premiered Hochhuth's debut play, *The Deputy*. The title referred to the recently deceased pontiff, Pius XII, who had sat on the papal throne from 1939 until 1958 – right through the cataclysmic Second World War. The work made headlines by accusing the pope of refusing to speak out publicly against Nazi genocide; one of its major characters even denounced Pius as "a criminal."[1]

The Deputy immediately set off a firestorm. It was denounced in a written statement by prominent members of Germany's Christian Democratic Party, who asked the German Foreign Office to monitor the reaction overseas. Within 100 days, Hochhuth received thousands of angry letters and even death threats. New productions triggered riots in Switzerland later in 1963, demonstrations in New York City in 1964 and bombings in Rome in 1965. For years, hundreds of newspapers world-wide kept their readers abreast of the scandal that refused to die. Not least because of this notoriety, *The Deputy* shot to the top of the German best-seller list and brought in so much in sales that the once-hard-up author, his wife and his young son took refuge in the tax haven of Switzerland.[2]

Without a doubt, the imbroglios over the Roman Catholic response to National Socialism were at their most dramatic in the immediate aftermath of *The Deputy*'s premieres on more than sixty stages in twenty countries. But they were part of a longer tradition of criticism that extended back to the immediate postwar years and has continued nearly unabated to this day. Exposing, debating and denying the church's alleged sins of commission and omission during the Nazi years spawned a cottage industry of best sellers, incendiary articles, provocative magazine covers, inflammatory pamphlets, radio broadcasts, television scoops and dense scholarly tomes.

This book excavates the lost but vital causes of these historical controversies. Focusing on the era from the end of the Second World War until 1980, it historicizes these debates about the church's relationship to National Socialism. Why did these cultural wars emerge when they did in West Germany? Why did they consume such energy, dominating headlines, triggering lawsuits and even requiring the intervention of foreign ministries? Why did the Catholic Church – and not the Protestant churches – emerge as the subject of critical scrutiny, even though scholars now recognize that German Protestant churches collaborated more and resisted less? Why was the picture of the Catholic Church painted in black and white by critics and defenders, even though recent scholarship leaves little doubt that the conduct of the more than 210 million individual Catholics throughout Europe was remarkably diverse, running the gamut from collaboration and capitulation to resistance and martyrdom? Finally, why did the critical take on the church's past meet with increasing popular acceptance from the early 1960s onward?

These and other questions may all be answered by the central finding of this book. The controversies over the church's relationship to National Socialism were frequently surrogates for a larger set of conflicts over how the church was to position itself in modern society – in politics, international relations, the media and the public sphere. Wrangling over these issues is typically associated with the Second Vatican Council, a gathering of thousands of bishops, cardinals and laity from 1962 to 1965 at St. Peter's Basilica over how to engage with the modern world. In fact, the often-tumultuous process of postwar political reconstruction in the Federal Republic of Germany led to a series of confrontations in the decades preceding the council over the role Catholics and their institutions were to play in their respective societies.

In West Germany, these proxy wars were, more often than not, centered on problems perceived as arising from the postwar political ascendency of Catholics and the integration of Catholic citizens into the mainstream of their society. As they pursued agendas anchored in confessional priorities, opposing memories invariably resurfaced of a violent century in which divisions between Catholics and Protestants had been woven into everyday life. Fueling these conflicts were divergent understandings of what had been done both by Catholics and to Catholics during the frequent intervals of political upheaval between 1870 and 1949.

As Catholic and Protestant political and intellectual leaders reflected on what it meant to live together under the same political roof, their attention was inevitably directed back to those years and eras of confessional conflict jarring ecclesiastical life ever since German unification in 1871 under Bismarck. At the heart of these was an undeniable reality: Germany had been and remained a majority Protestant nation. This reality had fueled an era of persecution that lasted until 1878, the Kulturkampf, in which an alliance of liberals and Protestant conservatives, citing alleged Catholic backwardness and treasonous loyalties to Rome, drastically curtailed Catholic civil liberties, landing more than 1,800 priests in jail. The need to defend the church led in 1870 to the founding of what for nearly two-thirds of a century was Germany's major Catholic political party, the Center Party. For decades, many Catholic political leaders were accordingly driven by an implacable hostility toward confessional and ideological enemies. The ranks of ideological enemies expanded to include the socialist movement, which by the turn of the century had become Germany's most rapidly growing and formidable force.

These antipathies softened but by no means disappeared in the twentieth century. Even though the Center Party became a major player in the fractured parliamentary politics of the German Empire and the even more troubled Weimar Republic from 1918 through 1933, Catholic religious and political leaders still saw themselves as a minority under siege. Faced with partisan hostility and political gridlock, they sought international treaties to guarantee their civil and religious liberties. In short succession, the Vatican signed treaties with the states of Bavaria in 1924, Prussia in 1929 and Baden in 1932. Only one treaty was still missing, one that the fractured politics of the era had apparently left beyond reach: a comprehensive concordat with the entire German nation.

And yet in a widely heralded signing ceremony held in the Vatican on July 20, 1933, the seemingly impossible happened. Representatives of the German government and the Vatican put their pens to a document that promised to resolve thorny questions of church-state relations that had bedeviled countless previous governments. Two noteworthy personages put the finishing touches on what forever became known as the Reichskonkordat. Representing the Vatican was Cardinal Secretary of State Eugenio Pacelli, who long before becoming pontiff and taking the name Pius XII in 1939 had earned a reputation as a Germanophile. Signing for the new German government was notorious Vice Chancellor Franz von Papen, an opportunistic Catholic aristocrat and renegade from the Center Party who as much as any other figure was responsible for Hitler's appointment as chancellor on January 30, 1933.

No other event loomed as large in so many of the historical controversies that raged through the early 1980s over the church's role in the politics of the Nazi era. This treaty guaranteed Catholics the freedom to practice their faith but also forbade the church from taking part in politics directly. Its ratification was made possible only through the infamous Enabling Act of March 24, 1933, which had granted Hitler full dictatorial powers. Even though a number of bishops and cardinals had issued earlier pronouncements forbidding the flock from joining the Nazi party, all of the delegates from the Center Party and the Bavarian People's Party, a fellow Catholic party, made the fatal error of voting for this legislation. Five days later, the bishops jointly rescinded their earlier prohibitions on joining the Nazi party, believing Hitler's promises that the new German Reich would rest on a Christian foundation. On April 10, 1933, Pacelli formally met with von Papen to launch negotiations for a Reichskonkordat. The treaty was concluded just fifteen days after the Center Party, facing the arrest of its officials, voted to dissolve itself on July 5, 1933. The Nazis began violating its terms almost immediately, launching wave after wave of persecution against the church. Former Center Party politicians thus had little choice but to join the Nazi party, go into exile abroad, join the resistance against Hitler or remain quiet at home in what they called "inner emigration."

The lessons later drawn from this unfortunate chain of events provided the tinder for future historical controversies about the church's sins of commission and omission during the Third Reich. Putting the timing of the treaty under the microscope and questioning whether the Nazi government had used the Reichskonkordat as a bargaining chip to persuade the Center Party to vote for the Enabling Act, critics would come to excoriate this treaty as a "criminal agreement" and a "pact with the devil." Sapping resistance, they argued, it was a sign of Catholic collusion. But many Catholic politicians and churchmen drew very different lessons. The Reichskonkordat, many argued, had provided protection for a church under siege. It could continue to do so for the beleaguered church in the Soviet zone of occupation were it legally binding in the post-Nazi era.

Looking back to what had gone awry in 1933, a cadre of former Center Party leaders helped found at the close of the war a new political party, the Christian Democratic Union, better known by its acronym, the CDU.[3] These politicians, some straight from the resistance against Hitler, opted to open up the fledgling party to Protestants. A small number of Protestants came on board, most like their Catholic counterparts convinced that rechristianizing Germany represented the only way to overcome the bitter legacies of the Nazi and Weimar eras. Not least because it was now open to people from both confessions, the CDU, in turn, became the dominant party in the Federal Republic of Germany, which was created in 1949. Its leader was former Center Party politician and septuagenarian Konrad Adenauer, who in serving as chancellor from 1949 until 1963 found his name given to the entire era.

But the CDU was correctly perceived as Catholic-dominated, its success made possible by changes in the confessional landscape of West Germany. At the close of the Second World War, Germany was carved up by the victorious Allies. Protestant strongholds in the east were given over to Poland and the Soviet Union; the creation of the new East German state in 1949 severed more than sixteen million Protestants from the German mainland. Catholics in the western Federal Republic thus were not as small a minority as they had been in the German nation before 1945. They comprised just under 45 percent of the population in 1949, up from 36 percent for the German Reich in 1937.[4] Attending mass at far higher rates than Protestants attended church, practicing Catholics were much more likely to cast their votes for the CDU than for the rival liberal, socialist and Communist parties. Because of their dominant role in the CDU, they took a leading role in the government of the Federal Republic. And hence the polarized reaction. Dissenters spoke out harshly against what they believed to be the all-pervasive "clericalism" of the new republic. Many politically active Catholics, in contrast, worried well through the 1950s that their foes might launch another assault on their religious freedoms and, in the worst case, another Kulturkampf were they to regain power.

The resentments and fears from both sides that went along with this changing of the guard between 1945 and 1963 provided much of the energy as well as the raw materials for the explosive controversies about the church's past. In the majority of cases, these controversies served as a referendum on the church's relationship to the Christian Democratic Union and its politics. This connection was made all the easier since many of those leading the charge into the Catholic past were themselves members of or had close ties to one of the three major West German political parties. These included Christian Democrats in the CDU and its Bavarian sister-party, the Christian Socialist Union (CSU); Social Democrats in the Social Democratic Party (SPD), West Germany's oldest party with a rich heritage dating back to 1869; and liberals in the Free Democratic Party (FDP), a new party created in 1947 out of the wreckage of liberal parties from the Weimar era.

It is tempting to let nostalgia for the 1950s leave a false perception of political harmony. According to myths arising in the 1970s, Germans had put politics aside after the upheavals of National Socialism to raise families, housing, living standards and production levels. The reality was the reverse: the Adenauer era was one of partisanship and protest.

There were more megaphones, police wagons and demonstrators en masse on the streets than during the heyday of the counterculture in the late 1960s.[5] The leaders of the Christian, socialist and liberal political parties were driven by the need to please their fired-up electoral bases whose beliefs and tactics all too often remained anchored in ideologies of confrontation from the second half of the nineteenth century. Polarizing the political landscape further was the specter of the Communist party, which oversaw a budding police state in the East and was banned in the West only in 1956. Since the parties continued to officially promote or counter agendas of secularism, any political discussion whose subject was the Catholic Church was likely to become supercharged and engulfed in waves of protest.

The specific triggers for the controversies about Catholic conduct during the Third Reich were battles over how to draw lines between church and state, whether or not to segregate public schools by religion, and whether and how to rearm Germany. Other controversies broke out over the church's hostility to liberalism and socialism, its adherence to natural law teachings, and its alleged refusal to fully embrace an ethos of democracy. These issues had bedeviled the political parties in the Weimar Republic, but one of the most grueling fights was spawned by the question of whether the Reichskonkordat from 1933 was still legally binding in the Federal Republic of Germany. This question had to be resolved by Germany's highest court, the Constitutional Court, which declared the treaty from 1933 to still be the law of the land – though only after a landmark trial in June 1956 before a packed courthouse and a full German press corps, thousands of pages of expert opinions and historical treatises delving into this treaty's origins and the creation of rival research teams.[6]

The process of delving into the Roman Catholic past thus followed a fundamentally different trajectory than the broader discussions of National Socialism in West German society. The former, anchored in the political conflicts and street protests of the first decades of the Federal Republic, began earlier – long before the student rebellions of the late 1960s.[7] There was no era of silence in the 1950s about the Catholic Church's past; the well-publicized controversies from the late 1940s onward about the validity of the Reichskonkordat ensured this.[8] The latter, in contrast, tended to begin in the early 1960s and was driven by eye-catching events like renewed war crimes trials that directed public attention to anti-Semitism and genocide.[9] The result was a wave of scholarly, educational and commemorative initiatives that continue to this day, all of which have been well documented in the vast literature on how Germans came to terms with the Nazi past.[10]

Once launched in the 1950s, the public debates over the Catholic Church's past took on a momentum of their own. Each round of accusations generated powerful counter-punches by church defenders, who typically responded by attacking their opponents in the press and by publishing documents from the Nazi era intended to exonerate the church. To explain the ferocity of the ensuing conflagrations, this book reconstructs the political, ecclesiastical and intellectual networks with which church critics and defenders waged these struggles. Some were long-lasting formal institutions, others ad hoc working groups or simple friendships. Most of these culture warriors came to see these networks as a necessity because it was exceptionally difficult to wage these wars single-handedly. These networks controlled levers of funding, regulated access to historical documents and served as a gateway to the international media at a time when most documents lay under lock and key and a modern scholarly infrastructure with its ubiquitous conferences and research centers was in its infancy.

The range of participants crossed national boundaries and included luminaries in all three major German political parties; professors on both sides of the Atlantic; international journalists; eminent public intellectuals; Communist propagandists from East Germany; and Jewish, Protestant and Catholic religious leaders, including the highest-ranking Vatican officials and even Pope Paul VI. The activities of these networks, many anchored in the parties or the church, decisively shaped the trajectory of the ensuing historical controversies. Understanding themselves as combatants in a larger struggle against ideological foes, network members were quick to ascribe disreputable motives and a heightened significance to the activities of "the other side" and "our ideological opponents" long into the 1970s.

This book accordingly brings to light the less savory side of these altercations – the involvement of the East German state, attempts by the Vatican and diocesan authorities to fire or demote church critics employed by religious institutions, lawsuits, public denunciations and efforts to prevent critical voices from being heard on radio and television and in newsmagazines and newspapers throughout Germany and in the United States. The timing of these controversies was pivotal. By the late 1950s and early 1960s, the mass media in both the United States and the Federal Republic of Germany began to adopt a new self-understanding as critical organs upholding the right to dissent. Journalists decried these attempts to muzzle contrary voices. Seeing the past and present of the Catholic Church as a topic about which every man and woman had the right to speak, they were outraged by the reiteration of church teachings under which "error" had "no right to exist." The debates about the

Catholic past during the Third Reich in Germany were thus transformed into a broader plea for free expression, civil liberties and a democratization of society.

This book centers on clashes in courtrooms and the courtroom of public opinion. But at its heart, it is a work of intellectual history, with elements of political, social and cultural history serving as an essential backdrop. It is influenced by the extensive literature on the history of memory that has blossomed within the past twenty years.[11] For most participants in these controversies who had been born before 1925, traumatic experiences from 1933 to 1945 shaped how they opted later in life to delve into the church's past. For this reason, each chapter features short biographies of the major participants in these controversies.

The difficulty, however, lies in the fact that hundreds of individuals and groups from almost every major Western nation as well as the Eastern bloc advanced public criticisms and defenses of Catholic conduct during the Third Reich. Their arguments sprang from a vast array of religious and political agendas. Since it would be impossible to recount the arguments of every individual speaking out on these subjects between 1945 and 1980, this book concentrates on seven controversies that generated the greatest heat, each one of which is the focus of one of this book's seven chapters.[12] All but two had deep roots in the political controversies raging in the Adenauer era. Each debate also had a ripple effect, piquing curiosities or awakening passions, particularly when moral or theological positions were at stake. The networks used the expertise accumulated in prior struggles to launch new investigations. Stinging defeats, particularly in the eyes of the public, had a way of mobilizing soldiers for the next battles. One could not let criticisms go unanswered.

While these chapters generally run chronologically, they do so imperfectly. Several of these controversies were waged simultaneously; others had roots in different eras of the past. Each chapter entails jumping back into the past, sometimes to multiple eras – the 1920s, the Nazi era, the immediate postwar era and the Adenauer era. These leaps back and forth in time are necessary to show how traumatic experiences in the lives of individual participants in these debates led them to return to these eras of bloodshed, sacrifice and suffering.

The first chapter analyzes the emergence of more than ten documentary histories of the Catholic Church under National Socialist rule between 1946 and 1949. It features two early chroniclers, both clerics who were ardent enemies of National Socialism. Walter Adolph was the editor of the Berlin diocesan newspaper and the author of dozens of books and articles about the church under Nazi rule. Johannes Neuhäusler was the author of seven books about the church struggle, including his

900-page, two-volume magnum opus *Cross and Swastika*. Until his arrest and incarceration in Dachau in 1941, he had run an illegal courier service to statesmen and dignitaries abroad, smuggling out reports of Nazi anti-clerical measures to the Vatican. Both clerics penned their works in response to criticism of the church's conduct coming from Communists, foreign journalists and the western Allies. These encounters reignited potent nationalist sentiment still lingering from the First World War, since rule by foreign occupiers – and the prospect of denazification tribunals, war crimes trials and reparations payments – summoned the ghosts of the Treaty of Versailles. Crucially, these church defenders waged their battles against church critics using tactics drawn from their struggle with Nazi overlords. The conspiratorial milieu once sorely needed to wage the fight for survival against a brutal dictatorship reemerged as the means to fight conflicts over the past. As a result, a differentiated memory of the church under National Socialism was quickly shorn of its nuance.

The second chapter hones in on the landmark court case that, more than any other event, awakened interest in the church's past. This was the trial from June 4–8, 1956, before West Germany's highest court, the Constitutional Court in Karlsruhe, over whether the Reichskonkordat from 1933 remained legally binding. Arising out of a long-standing struggle over whether public schools could be segregated by confession, this trial set the tone for subsequent battles over the past. It raised the questions that would haunt church defenders for years to come. It divided researchers into rival camps and teams. Each side in the case had to assemble networks of legal experts, politicians, journalists and a smattering of historians to launch and promote research into the legality and history of the concordat. On the one side were Catholics in the CDU and CSU; on the other were liberals in the FDP and socialists in the SPD, most of whom were Protestants. These divisions would persist for decades.

The third chapter examines how these networks continued to influence the discussions about the church's past in the aftermath of the court's verdict from March 1957. With many legal questions remaining open and public interest in the church's role in 1933 awakened, a growing number of young historians began to plumb the relationships between church and state both for the end of the Weimar Republic and the Federal Republic. Fusing these criticisms was the young German Catholic constitutional theorist Ernst Wolfgang-Böckenförde, who in early 1961 published a landmark article in the Catholic magazine *Hochland* analyzing Catholic missteps in 1933 and drawing explicit analogies with the inadequate democratic spirit of the Adenauer years in Germany. The subsequent controversy served as a watershed. It catalyzed the founding of the Association for Contemporary History (*Kommission für Zeitgeschichte bei der katholischen Akademie in Bayern*), a Catholic historical association charged with documenting the charged historical terrain of the first half of the twentieth century. The networks that helped build and support this association of professional historians included some of the same politicians, diplomats, historians, clerics and journalists who had spearheaded the fight before the Constitutional Court in 1956. Future battles over the Catholic past thus lay neatly along the ideological fault lines of the early Federal Republic.

The fourth chapter analyzes how another controversy over the church's past grew out of hot-button issues during the Adenauer era. The man leading the charge against the church was not a left-wing German politician but an American Catholic sociologist and pacifist, Gordon Zahn. This intensely devout middle-aged American academic had spent the 1956–1957 academic year in Germany on a Fulbright fellowship, where he witnessed major debates about German rearmament. In a talk in September 1959 at Mundelein College, a small Catholic college in Chicago, Zahn accused the church of having supported Hitler's predatory wars against Poland and the Soviet Union in clear violation of Catholic just-war teachings. His criticisms were triggered not only by the hierarchy's strong support for West German rearmament and atomic diplomacy but by what he regarded as the "super-patriotism" of American Catholic politicians and the American hierarchy during the Cold War. After generating headlines in the Chicago press, Zahn's talk became the subject of an international melee in which the German Foreign Office, its consulate in Chicago, the German bishops and the Vatican were involved. At the core was a transatlantic network assembled in part by Walter Adolph, who helped enlist the services of more than a dozen high-ranking Catholic officials to take on Zahn.

The fifth chapter analyzes the international furor generated by Rolf Hochhuth's play *The Deputy*. Whereas almost-identical criticisms of the pontiff ventured in the 1940s and 1950s had failed to stick, this debut work of a young Protestant did more than anything else to direct public attention to the conduct of the church during the Third Reich. Spearheading the charge against the playwright in Berlin was once again Walter Adolph, who fresh from the battles against Gordon Zahn assembled a new team to defend the beleaguered pontiff. Their counter-strikes transformed a debate ostensibly about the silence of the wartime pope into something more injurious to their cause – a debate about freedom of expression, civil liberties and tolerance, when in the early to mid-1960s societal attitudes on these subjects were fundamentally shifting.

The sixth chapter analyzes the response to the publication of *The Catholic Church and Nazi Germany* by the American political scientist Guenter Lewy in 1964. A Jewish refugee from Nazi Germany who had been inspired by the findings of Gordon Zahn, Lewy returned to Germany in the early 1960s to carry out his research. He argued that the church had offered resistance to National Socialism only when its immediate interests were at stake; the ideological affinities between Nazism and Catholicism had led church officials to seek cooperation with the Nazi government. His work was almost immediately translated into German and excerpted week by week over two months the following year in *Der Spiegel*, Germany's leading newsmagazine. Angered that an American citizen had offered up a comprehensive and critical monograph before Catholic historians were able to complete their own accounts, Johannes Neuhäusler as well as Jesuit historian Ludwig Volk moved to ensure that diocesan archives across Germany restricted access to their holdings. Future Lewys might paint an inaccurate and incomplete portrayal of the church, they feared, and as a result the archival doors were often closed to those not yet deemed reliable.

The seventh chapter turns to the last major controversy over the Roman Catholic past for nearly two decades. This was a showdown between 1977 and 1979 on the pages of Germany's leading daily newspaper and historical quarterly. Waging this duel were two academics, Protestant church historian Klaus Scholder and the Catholic historian at the helm of the Association for Contemporary History, Konrad Repgen. This debate not only raised divisive questions of historical methodology. It reopened the confessional and political divide over the Reichskonkordat from the battle before the Constitutional Court in 1956.

This debate concluded in 1980 with no resolution. For the next fifteen years, debates over the Catholic past remained at something of a standstill but never reaching the intensity of earlier decades. This changed in the late 1990s, once culture wars centered largely on Pope Pius XII reignited in the United States and Great Britain and spread to Germany, triggering a new burst of polemic and scholarship sometimes referred to as the Pius Wars.[13]

This book shows how historical images of the Catholic Church's past arose and were immediately contested. It argues that the overwhelming majority of those sculpting these images were driven by present-minded concerns, even where almost all sincerely professed their commitment to principles of historical objectivity. Their lines of inquiry were accordingly shaped by traumatic experiences during the Third Reich, religious convictions, political agendas, social pressures and, above all, the need to combat ideological adversaries. Though the ensuing debates often centered on the legitimacy of the historical methodologies employed, at the heart of these controversies between 1945 and 1980 were the perceived ideological baggage of the combatants and the present-minded manner in which leading questions had been framed.

Since the ideological and confessional fault lines that originally animated these debates are largely a thing of the past, it is this author's hope that the time is finally ripe to historicize these thirty-five years of strife over the church's conduct during these twelve years of revolution, dictatorship, war and genocide. Doing so not only sheds light on how political parties, religious leaders and intellectuals crafted narratives about the past to justify their own visions of what the church's role was to be in the fledgling West German state and modern society. It allows a past so often painted in black and white to be restored to the shades of gray that better correspond to the messiness of the religious experience under a brutal and ultimately anti-Christian dictatorship.

1   The First Postwar Anthologies, 1945–1949

In the weeks and months after the Nazi regime was vanquished on May 8, 1945, veterans of the church's struggle against National Socialism with literary inclinations, political agendas and pastoral challenges set out to tell the story of the church under National Socialist rule.[1] The German bishops commissioned a documentary history in their first annual meeting in Fulda in late August. In a short span of four years, more than a dozen anti-Nazi stalwarts from citadels of Catholic religious and intellectual life like Freiburg, Münster, Munich, Berlin and Cologne published dozens of books and articles bearing testimony to the struggles from which they had just emerged seemingly triumphant.[2] In recounting persecution, they were joined by activists from the Confessing Church, the oppositional Protestant church-body created in 1934 to halt the Nazification of the Protestant churches.[3]

In their portraits of their churches, these veterans of the church struggle chose to paint in black and white rather than in the hues of gray that better corresponded to their own firsthand experiences and recollections of the tumultuous era between 1933 and 1945. They painted a picture of a church unified in resistance and in solidarity with its leaders. As one of the earliest chroniclers, Johannes Neuhäusler, a Bavarian cathedral canon and auxillary bishop, was to put it: the resistance "was there" for the entire twelve years of the National Socialist dictatorship and in the years of its coming to power from 1923 to 1933. It was "strong and tough for high and low, for Pope and Bishops, for the clergy and the people, for single persons and entire organizations."[4]

Yet these same authors were well aware that there was another side to Catholic witness during the previous twelve years. They knew firsthand which churchmen and lay leaders had offered support for the regime or equivocated in their opposition. They could easily point to the weak links in the chain of resistance. They knew – how could they not? – that the church had lost its decisive battles against the National Socialist juggernaut, its resistance notwithstanding. The Catholic political parties had been banned, most ancillary organizations disbanded, the religious press emasculated or dissolved, the denominational schools stripped of their religious character and thousands of priests sent to concentration camps. Faced with this reality, these earliest chroniclers of the past, mostly veterans of the resistance against National Socialism, turned back to skills honed in the conspiratorial milieu so necessary for the struggle against a tyrannical state. They left their accounts riddled with errors, some the result of haste, others of deliberate manipulations.

This chapter focuses on two ingredients that led these authors to filter out contrary evidence from their embryonic accounts during these crucial early weeks, months and years. The first was a shift prompted by signals by Pope Pius XII in the summer of 1945 in the willingness (or, rather, unwillingness) of the German bishops to discuss openly and critically the guilt of the German nation and their church. The second was a series of encounters with critics who were beginning to raise mistrustful questions about what the churches had actually done in the Third Reich. The ranks of the skeptics included Communist ideologues as well as an inchoate smattering of foreign journalists, opposition politicians and solitary critics embittered by their failure to have received greater support from the hierarchy in their opposition to the National Socialist regime. These often-humiliating public encounters between those in the vanguard of the church struggle and their emerging critics reignited potent nationalist sentiment and summoned ghosts from the Treaty of Versailles at a time when Germany lay under foreign occupation. To counter allegations of collective German guilt and take the edge off Allied policies of denazification and war crimes trials, Catholic and Protestant leaders in a rare moment of ecumenism sought to convince sympathetic occupation officials as well as their co-religionists abroad that the churches had done all that they could to resist the evils of National Socialism.

This story starts in Fulda at a meeting of the German bishops conference to explain why a team commissioned to compile the official history failed to produce even a barebones documentary and statistical history. It then heads southwest to Freiburg to tell of the genesis of a ten-volume documentary series. The compiler was Reinhard Schneider, the distinguished Catholic poet, novelist and pacifist from Freiburg whose works had been banned by the Nazis.

Our setting then moves to Munich and Rome to detail the ideological battles behind what would come to be considered the definitive account of the Catholic Church struggle.[5] This was the 800-page magnum opus, *Cross and Swastika*, by Johannes Neuhäusler, who spent more than four months in Nazi concentration camps because of his role in coordinating Catholic resistance efforts across Germany. Neuhäusler's twin volumes would sell out two editions of 20,000 copies in less than seven months.[6]

Our venue then shifts to Berlin to examine a crusade against critics in the eastern and western zones of Germany by one of the most prolific apologists, Walter Adolph, a pugilistic journalist-priest from proletarian Berlin. Adolph used his positions as head of the diocesan press and editor-in-chief of the Berlin diocesan newspaper to produce scores of books, newspaper articles and editorials commemorating the Catholic martyrs of the Third Reich. This chapter concludes in Cologne with a look at the last major documentary edition from the immediate postwar era, a collection that because of its late publication date in 1949 never received the attention it deserved.[7]

The Failed Effort by the German Bishops to Produce a Documentary History

In the summer of 1945, German church leaders found themselves in a delicate position. After twelve years of persecution and war, they faced enormous pastoral challenges. Germany's cities and towns had been reduced to piles of rubble. Millions of men were lost, displaced or in prisoner-of-war camps; civilians faced merciless shortages of food. Seeking a leadership role in reconstructing and rechristianizing Germany, church leaders had to be able to explain the catastrophe to their flock. But as they knew well, Catholics as well as Protestants were about to be implicated in the denazification and war crimes tribunals being set up to punish the crimes of the regime and remove Nazis from positions in state and society.

At the same time, the bishops were aware that many Germans laid the blame not on themselves but on the Allies and their policies like denazification deemed punitive.[8] Sensing an opening, the German churches stepped forward as spokesmen for the defeated German nation.[9] They were the only sizeable non-leftist institutions left in Germany with their moral authority intact, and they duly played this up in their encounters with the victorious Allied occupiers. In laying out their opposition to denazification and war crimes trials, they made sure that the Allies first received brief accounts of their protest and opposition during the Nazi years.[10]

Emphasizing their moral authority was the best card available for them, for they had good reason to believe that rekindling interest in the church struggle in the victorious Allied nations might lead occupation officials to soften their policies toward Germany. During the darkest hours of persecution, influential churchmen in the Vatican and Protestant ecumenical organizations like the World Council of Churches had taken up the cause of the German churches. Some like the Anglican bishop George Bell and Pope Pius XII had been participants in the plots assembled by the German resistance to assassinate Hitler.[11] They had succeeded in spreading awareness in Great Britain and the United States about the clamps on religious freedom in Germany. From offices in Geneva, London, New York and the Vatican, they had promoted the publication of scores of accounts detailing the ongoing church struggle. These had appeared beginning in 1934 and continued through 1941 when the United States entered the war. Some had taken the form of firsthand memoirs, others of documentary editions.[12] These had not been intended to be nuanced historical works; they had been designed to rouse fellow Christians to action. No doubt for this reason, they came to serve as templates for the scores of documentary histories produced during the years of occupation.

Some of these churchmen – like Bell – had become advocates of a softer peace settlement already in 1944 and remained so even after the discovery of the concentration camp horrors in the spring of 1945 led passions to run high in favor of retributive justice. Pope Pius XII had even gone on record in his Christmas address of 1944 as opposing any notion of collective guilt of the German nation.[13] He reiterated this message at the close of a widely heralded and headline-grabbing address to the College of Cardinals on June 2, 1945, in which he famously denounced National Socialism as a "satanic ghost."[14] After providing detailed information about the courage and sacrifice of Catholics who had suffered and died for the faith in concentration camps like Dachau, Pius spoke out for a peace settlement "worthy of the name." He urged that hatred and mistrust give way to wiser and more objective decision-making and brotherly understanding.

Pius's unequivocal words of support for the German nation and church altered how the bishops chose to reflect on their immediate past. In the weeks after German surrender on May 8, some of the bishops, clearly shaken by reports of concentration camp horrors and allegations of collective German guilt being aired on Allied radio broadcasts, cinematic newsreels and placards, were questioning whether they should have been more outspoken in their opposition to the crimes of National Socialism.[15] Not yet knowing of Pius' course, the eleven bishops from northwestern Germany put together around June 5 the draft of a petition to Pius XII that attempted to explain their relative "silence."[16] Their draft made clear that the bishops had been divided during the war over the likely consequences of a more activist stance. But it also did not deny that they bore at least some responsibility for these atrocities because of their reticence.

By their meeting on August 21–23, 1945, in Fulda, the bishops had received the text of Pius' address from June 2 and changed their tone accordingly. In the first pastoral letter from the postwar era that they issued at the close of the conference, they would admit only that many Germans "from our ranks as well" had let themselves be "beguiled by the false teachings of National Socialism" and remained "indifferent to the crimes against human freedom and dignity."[17] Some, they noted, had "abetted the crimes" or become criminals themselves.[18]

Clearly, most of the bishops no longer intended to dwell on what the church might have done differently. In line with Pius' recounting of Catholic defense and sacrifice against the satanic spirit of National Socialism, they instead gave themselves the task of documenting their resistance. They did so on the first day of their meeting and – tellingly – directly after discussing a petition to the Allied occupation authorities calling for a swifter import of food, improved security, better conditions for German POWs, exemptions for the bishops to travel between the occupation zones and the resettlement of Catholic refugees from the East in predominantly Catholic regions in the West. Agreeing to a suggestion by the new powerful chairman, Archbishop Joseph Frings of Cologne, they commissioned a massive survey of the damage inflicted by twelve years of National Socialism.[19] They issued a call to collect and publish all of their petitions and letters of protest from the years of repression.[20]

It took just weeks for chancery officials in Cologne to send out questionnaires to statistically assess nationwide the scope of persecution. By late September 1945, diocesan officials across Germany were asked to provide detailed information about the numbers of parishioners who had died during the war or were serving as POWs, of clergy who had perished or been fined, incarcerated or given warnings by Nazi authorities and of the amount of church property confiscated by the Nazis.[21] Later in October, the Cologne chancery issued another request for documentary evidence, a call it reiterated twice in April 1946.[22] It sought copies of pastoral letters, leaflets, brochures, newspaper articles, letters from the front, information about the confiscation of monasteries, the Nazis' euthanasia program, verbal and physical attacks on clergy and lay leaders, censorship and the dissolving of ancillary organizations.

Laity and clergy from dioceses in northern and western Germany duly filled out their questionnaires and sent in scores of documents. But they had no inkling that their efforts were about to be literally relegated to the scrap heap of history. Since the Cologne chancery had been destroyed in an Allied bombing raid, the arriving documents had to be stored in makeshift buildings. Short of space, the clerical assistants were forced to take these reams of newspaper clippings, letters and communiques home. In a fatal blow to Frings' hopes of compiling an official documentary record, a clerical assistant died with piles of documents still on his desk at home.

Figure 1.1 The chancery building for the Archdiocese of Cologne was utterly destroyed in an Allied bombing raid. Its employees had to be relocated to makeshift buildings, and as a result documents for a history of the church under Nazi rule were lost. Courtesy of Karl Hugo Schmölz, © Archiv Wim Cox, Köln [MR1].

His widow, not knowing of their importance amid a severe paper shortage, sold what must have looked like scrap paper to a second-hand dealer.[23]

Even had their initiative not wound up apparently being sold down the Rhine River, Frings and his fellow bishops had greatly underestimated the difficulties in compiling a comprehensive documentary history and statistical data while church archives lay in ruins and the church suffered from a shortage of paper and personnel. Starting in 1953, the church would delegate this task to professional historians. It went first to a church historian from Berlin, Bernhard Stasiewski and, after it had become clear by the 1960s that he was making little headway, to the Association for Contemporary History.[24] Even with its team of researchers, it took this historical association until 1985 and 1998, respectively, to bring these two projects – a documentary history of the church between 1933 and 1945 and a statistical analysis of priests facing Nazi terror - to fruition.[25]

Reinhold Schneider and the Documentary Editions from Freiburg

Because this attempt to provide a comprehensive national account had been scrapped, the more than twenty-five works on the Protestant church struggle and sixteen on the Catholic one that appeared in print in

Germany alone between 1945 and 1949 came by default to serve as a collective history of the churches under Nazi rule. That so many volumes appeared in such a short period of time indicates how urgent the chanceries and dignitaries perceived the need to be. And indeed, in the coming decades, they found use not just in parish libraries but in restitution hearings over church property confiscated by the Nazis, denazification tribunals, war crimes trials and the case before the Constitutional Court in 1956 over the validity of the Reichskonkordat.[26]

Of these local initiatives, the ten-volume series out of Freiburg took shape just days after German surrender.[27] The architect was a distinguished fifty-year-old Roman Catholic pathologist and professor, Dr. Franz Büchner, who issued the only public denunciation of the Nazi euthanasia program by a medical professional – a courageous lecture from November 1941 titled "The Hippocratic Oath."[28] Having miraculously escaped arrest and determined to place Germany back upon a Christian foundation, he reached out immediately after the cessation of hostilities to a group of Protestants with ties to the Confessing Church and the military resistance against Hitler.[29] On May 11, 1945, he also met with Archbishop Conrad Gröber of Freiburg, whom he described as "the strongest and most recognized authority of the immediate postwar era" for the German nation and, not least, for the French occupying authorities. Gröber, he boasted, had survived the collapse of the Third Reich "like a rock."[30]

For Büchner, confessional fragmentation was the culprit behind the great national calamity. Insisting that Roman Catholics and Protestants needed to work together to avoid reestablishing sectarian parties like the Catholic Center Party, he proposed to the archbishop plans for an interconfessional book series jointly edited by officials from the Confessing Church and bearing the title *Christian Germany, 1933–1945.* The purpose, he told Gröber, was not merely to awaken the Christian consciousness of "our people." It was to "prove" to the outside world – and specifically to the victorious Allies – that there had been another Germany, one acting from a Christian conscience during the years of terror and persecution.[31]

Having received the archbishop's enthusiastic assent, Büchner immediately rounded up publishers and editors. The publisher was an easy choice – the storied Freiburg-based Catholic Herder publishing company. To head up the Protestant volumes, he recruited the Freiburg Professor Constantin von Dietze, member of the Confessing Church and friend of Carl Goerdeler, a leading fighter in the resistance against Hitler.[32] To edit the Catholic volumes, he approached on May 13 the poet and literary giant Reinhold Schneider, who later in the 1940s came to be revered as the "conscience of the nation."[33] During the war,

Schneider had produced a corpus of sonnets, prayers and short texts intended as "spiritual resistance."[34] He had escaped an arrest warrant for high treason and deployment on the West Wall only by taking refuge first in a hospital and then a Protestant monastery.[35]

But Schneider was desperately ill, having undergone surgery just five days earlier.[36] He also harbored misgivings. He insisted that his had been a solitary crusade; his voice of protest had not been joined by a chorus of the bishops. Frustrated that the bishops had not yet owned up publicly for their sins of omission, Schneider went so far as to send the bishop of Mainz, Albert Stohr, on August 7, 1945, his draft of a pastoral letter to be read aloud from pulpits across Germany.[37] It was written, he informed Stohr, to touch the heart and shake the conscience.[38] At its heart stood the words "mea culpa" and the belief that confessing sin was the only path to spiritual renewal. The spiritual and emotional punch of his draft notwithstanding, Schneider never received a formal answer: the bishops were obviously adhering to the papal line in their de facto rejection of his entreaties. In retrospect, this was a milepost in his path toward a rupture with the bishops and the Catholic mainstream, as it would be for a small number of other critics coalescing under the umbrella of left-wing Catholicism.

So why did Schneider agree to serve as the formal editor for this series of volumes when he seems to have disagreed with its premise that the church had consistently and forcefully raised its voice against the demonic force of National Socialism?[39] No doubt to placate his conscience, he refused to allow his name to be mentioned as editor.[40] But at the same time he also saw the series as an opportunity to add a note of dissent. In his foreword published on January 24, 1946, he recapitulated some of the same themes from his draft pastoral letter that had not been taken up by the bishops. Already in his third sentence, he expressed his wish that the "voice of truth, conscience and responsibility" had not been so solitary and that those suffering in God's kingdom had found visible companionship. "We wish from our hearts," he lamented in a sentence that extended over a half page, that "the men and bodies" could have resolved to protest the injustice that was more or less an open secret.[41]

But it was his radical hope of planting Christianity back on German soil that best explains his willingness to serve as a series editor. For Schneider, the voices of truth to be featured in each volume of this series were witnesses to the dedication of the German people to its true lord, Jesus Christ. Yet these voices of witness – popes, philosophers and bishops – could seldom be heard beyond Germany's borders. The picture of Germany abroad was "more desolate than the actual reality." In appending a minimum of commentary, he and his fellow editors sought to let the voices of witness speak for themselves as proof of the existence of "another Germany" whose faithful had risked life and limb in the struggle against a satanic ideology. Out of the blood of German martyrs, Schneider prophesied, the church would renew itself and, in turn, the German nation.[42]

Almost all of the series held fast to this vision of the historical register as the vehicle for spiritual uplift and national renewal, and none more so than the edition of Bishop Clemens Graf August von Galen's sermons of protest. Appropriately titled "Bishop von Galen Speaks: An Apostolic Struggle and Its Echo," its editor included in its appendices eleven documents discussing potential reprisals against the outspoken cleric who had denounced the Nazi program of euthanasia. All eleven were from either the local Gauleiter Dr. Alfred Meyer, who had committed suicide on April 11, 1945, or the Reich Propaganda Ministry. The eighth volume modestly titled "Highlights" featured the last writings of four Christians just before their executions in the second half of 1944 during the furious wave of recriminations following the failed assassination plot against Hitler.[43] They spoke of their fidelity to the kingdom of God in spite of pressure to renounce their faith, their calmness in the face of death and their glimpses of the gate to eternity.

The devout would have instantly recognized the story narrated through these documents. These were accounts of the early church, the suffering of its faithful, the light of its martyrs and its ultimate triumph over state-sanctioned paganism and a modern-day Nero. Most faithful readers would have immediately grasped their political message, which dove-tailed almost perfectly with the goals of Christians active in the CDU. Through their resilience against persecution, the modern-day martyrs, or those like von Galen who had prepared themselves for martyrdom, had paved the way for the establishment of a state founded on Christian visions – just as in ancient Rome.

As the publication of this series stretched on from January 1946 into mid-1947, there was one volume that strayed noticeably from this depiction of saintliness. The thickest and thorniest and with the lengthiest foreword of all the documentaries, this was a collection of pastoral letters, sermons and private letters of protest to state authorities by the mercurial Freiburg archbishop Conrad Gröber, known not so charitably to some in his archdiocese as "Conrad the Sudden."[44] Gröber was one of the first ecclesiastical patriarchs to find his name entered into the annals of collaboration and resistance.[45] While Gröber had protested the boycott of Jewish stores and the Nazis' policies of euthanasia both privately and publicly, there was a side to his conduct of which he preferred not to be reminded. He had not only effused about the Nazi party in 1933 and

1934. He and six members of his chancery had also served as "supporting members" of the SS from 1934 until his expulsion in 1937 apparently on direct orders of SS chief Heinrich Himmler. Gröber claimed that he had lent his support to the SS because of its reputation as the only "respectable" organization within the Nazi party.[46] Albert Hartl, a mendacious SS intelligence chief and turncoat priest defrocked and excommunicated in 1934, told American investigators in 1947 that Gröber had yielded to blackmail, hoping to keep an affair with a half-Jewish mistress hidden.[47]

With knowledge of his tainted past widespread in his archdiocese, it naturally did not take long for characterizations of Gröber as a "brown bishop" (this pejorative term for collaborators referred of course to the color of Nazi uniforms) to be flung in front of the larger public. Word first seeped to the general public through radio reports about the Nuremberg trials. But the real thorns in Gröber's side were reports from the Hessian-born journalist Wilhelm Karl Gerst, the first in a series of stinging gadflies who would persist in their criticism through the 1960s and 1970s. As implausible as it might seem, Gerst was both a practicing Roman Catholic pacifist and an unyielding Communist and intelligence operative doing the bidding of handlers in East Berlin.[48] Guided by the belief that Communism and Catholicism could be symbiotic, Gerst had been alternatively praising bishops like von Galen for their selective acts of heroism and lambasting them for their capitulations on the pages of the *Frankfurter Rundschau*.[49] It was only a matter of time before he turned his fire against the archbishop from Freiburg, who in late September 1946 rather feebly claimed that attacks on his past no longer fazed him after all he had been through with the Nazis.[50]

Though not published on Gröber's direct initiative, Konrad Hofmann's volume, *Pastoral Calls of Archbishop Gröber to His Time*, from 1947 could not appear in print soon enough for the archbishop. The apologetic purposes jump off almost every page of the introduction. Hofmann alluded to the archbishop's troubled past but took obvious pains to avoid incriminating details like his status as a supporting member of the SS. Readers were informed that reasons of state had led the church to annul its prohibitions on joining the Nazi party in March 1933. Gröber had affirmed the new state, insofar as it appeared to be built on a Christian foundation, in order to "reduce mistrust" from both sides.[51] Roman Catholics had a duty to submit to the legitimate governing authorities – and the Nazis, as everyone knew, had come to power legally.[52] The archbishop so loved the fatherland and the German people that he could not bear to see his Catholic flock left outside the walls of the new state.[53] Yet in spite of this, this modern Jeremiah and "fighter for truth" had discerned early on that the Nazi movement was going to lead to an orgy of violence and immorality – and hence his fervent protests against the materialism and anti-Christian spirit of the Nazis.[54]

This volume also anticipated the coming flash point of the immediate postwar era as far as the politics of past and present were concerned for the church. This was the conflict over confessional segregation in the public schools. This question was intimately connected with the fate of the Reichskonkordat signed by representatives of the Vatican and Hitler's government, which had explicitly provided for the maintenance of confessionally segregated schools. Readers thus learned that Gröber had been a champion of the Christian ethos of the schools and had served in Rome as an advisor for the German bishops during treaty negotiations.[55] Hofmann's breakdown of the goals for which the archbishop had fought during the Third Reich – opposing materialism, maintaining denominational schools, cultivating good relations with the Vatican, upholding treaties like the Reichskonkordat and laying a Christian foundation for the new state – read as a set of talking points for representatives of political Catholicism looking to Christianize government and society.[56] The stage was set for the politics of the Catholic past and present to come together.

Johannes Neuhäusler and the Emergence of *Cross and Swastika*

The most weighty and influential of all postwar documentary histories were Johannes Neuhäusler's twin volumes, *Cross and Swastika*. This eight-hundred-page fusion of the historical, political, spiritual and apologetic was the culmination of the author's remarkable odyssey begun just after Hitler's appointment as Chancellor on January 30, 1933, and continued well after the German surrender into the summer of 1945. Launched and concluded in Munich, his journey spanned two continents, including North America, two concentration camps, a luxury mountain hotel in the Italian Alps, an American internment facility in Capri and sojourns in the Vatican and Naples.

More than any of the volumes trickling out of Freiburg, *Cross and Swastika* served as a snapshot of its author and his more than twelve-year spiritual and political pilgrimage. It was a fittingly blurry portrait, since Neuhäusler was obviously no ordinary eyewitness to the church struggle. He was in charge of coordinating the episcopate's national defense and resistance activities. He was not only a special envoy who delivered protests to a Bavarian state government hijacked by thugs and negotiated with the police and Gestapo to secure the release of Catholic political prisoners.[57] He was an intelligence operative who gathered detailed information about the regime's anti-clerical and anti-Christian measures and disseminated it to leading churchmen in neighboring countries and the Vatican. Through couriers with close ties to the German military resistance, he dispatched hundreds of reports to Eugenio Pacelli, the Vatican Cardinal Secretary of State and soon-to-be pontiff. After monitoring his phone and mail and finding nothing, the Gestapo paid him the highest of backhanded compliments. It dubbed him the "most dangerous man in the Munich chancery" and swooped in to put him out of commission on February 4, 1941.[58]

Neuhäusler's secretive modus operandi, so suited to his conspiratorial work from 1933 to 1941, naturally carried over into the postwar era. His reconstruction of the historical record from the Nazi era in *Cross and Swastika*, in turn, bore the subterfuge of the ecclesiastical and political underground. Which information to choose, how to present it, how to deal with evidence of ecclesiastical support for the Nazis? All were questions that preoccupied him between 1933 and 1941 and again in his postwar documentaries and reflections – and cloak and dagger shaped his answers.

Why was Neuhäusler selected to bear the cross? Character certainly played a role. Already as a young boy on a farm near Dachau, Johannes had a reputation for stubborn independence that exceeded even that ascribed, usually only half in jest, to the obdurate peasantry of Bavaria.[59] But for one so notoriously not a team player, he was remarkably well connected.[60] From 1918 through 1932, he had served first as the financial secretary and then the president of the Ludwig-Missions-Verein in Munich, an organization to spread the faith worldwide. Given the tasks of raising money and aligning the Bavarian chapter more closely to the Vatican, he traveled constantly to parishes throughout the archdiocese and even as far as Rome and Chicago.[61] This meant scores of new contacts, including two future pontiffs: Angelo Roncalli, the future Pope John XXIII, and Eugenio Pacelli.[62] It also led to a promotion on November 10, 1932, as a cathedral canon for the archdiocese.

The fateful moment came just months later during the first meeting of the Munich chancery after the appointment of Hitler as German chancellor. After telling those at the meeting to prepare for a bracing struggle, Cardinal Michael Faulhaber placed the burden of coordinating defense and resistance on his newly minted cathedral canon.[63] Neuhäusler suddenly found himself in a stronger position than just about anyone in the German Catholic hierarchy to capture the crudeness and cruelty of the Nazi war against the church.[64] He met regularly with bishops, parish priests, nuns, monks, abbots, schoolteachers and leaders

Figure 1.2 Johannes Neuhäusler in 1927. AEM NL Neuhäusler Nr. 421.

of lay organizations from across Germany who gave him copies of pastoral letters, anti-Catholic propaganda from Nazi newspapers, threatening letters from state authorities and secret state ordinances.[65] He was given firsthand reports of the dissolution of monasteries and nunneries, the confiscation of the assets of Catholic organizations, brutal attacks on Catholic youth groups by members of the Hitler Youth and above all arrests of fellow Catholics.

Probably more than any other person in the German Catholic hierarchy, Neuhäusler became aware of the internal tensions that surfaced during the confrontation with National Socialism. With tears in his eyes, he told the American journalist Dorothy Thompson in 1934 about "all the corruption and dissension that Nazism was sowing even among the Catholic orders, where one brother was denouncing another."[66] With such knowledge, it was little wonder that Pacelli gave him the task of bringing back a wayward colleague to the fold in 1938. Neuhäusler was to engineer a confrontation with Cardinal Theodor Innitzer, the archbishop of Vienna, who had issued a declaration endorsing the Anschluss and concluded it with the line "Heil Hitler!" Pacelli asked Neuhäusler to send his closest confidante, the Munich lawyer Josef Müller, to Vienna to disabuse the cardinal of his enthusiasm. Müller was to drum into him lessons excruciatingly wrung out of the church struggle in Germany.[67] Neuhäusler prepared the talking points based on recent experiences with his superior, Cardinal Faulhaber. Müller was to tell Innitzer that Faulhaber too had been seduced by Hitler, in particular after a private meeting from 1936 in which the German leader had vaunted his resolve to destroy Communism. Faulhaber had needed to be corrected and returned to the tougher line he had pursued years earlier. Müller duly carried out the job, relaying to Innitzer the damage caused by Faulhaber's missteps – but it required a "challenging" meeting of nearly three hours.[68]

Neuhäusler's main task, however, was to dispatch up-to-date information about the church struggle to high-ranking church officials abroad. Pope Pius XI beseeched the three German cardinals and Bishops von Galen, Konrad von Preysing of Berlin and Faulhaber to send reliable reports, recognizing that accurately reporting chicanery in foreign news-papers and radio stations like Vatican radio could put a dent into Nazi persecution. Neuhäusler complied, distilling the information he collected into detailed biweekly and weekly reports destined for the Roman desks of Pacelli, Ludwig Kaas and Robert Leiber, SJ, an influential German Jesuit adviser to Pacelli.[69] Whereas Leiber hid some of the reports in a library inside a codex with a false front, Pacelli committed much of their content to memory and had others carried out of the Vatican, some to a container to which he alone had the key.[70]

As it was impossible for Neuhäusler to travel abroad every two weeks to deliver his reports to high-ranking Vatican officials like Pacelli and Leiber, Neuhäusler had to rely on a select group of approximately ten trusted couriers, most clerics.[71] His chief courier, Josef Müller, however, was not. like Neuhäusler, he was the son of Bavarian peasants. Two schoolmates witnessed him using an oxcart to transport dung and jokingly called him the "Ochsensepp," a nickname that would stick and later be rendered into English as "Joe the Ox."[72] Müller teamed up with Neuhäusler in the summer of 1933 in the course of a lengthy stroll in the English garden in Munich, and the pair subsequently met nearly every day in Müller's law office.[73]

Neuhäusler could not have known that through Müller he was about to enter the world of cloak and dagger. Müller was serving in another even more dangerous capacity: he was exploiting his position in the military intelligence branch of the German army to serve as a messenger to Rome for the resistance to Hitler. He gradually introduced Neuhäusler to a number of conspirators in the German resistance, including the

Figure 1.3 Johannes Neuhäusler was called by Cardinal Michael Faulhaber to coordinate Catholic efforts to combat Nazi persecution of the church. AEM NL Neuhäusler Nr. 430.

Lutheran theologian Dietrich Bonhoeffer, with whom he met several times in late 1940 and early 1941 before his arrest.[74] In turn, Neuhäusler introduced Müller to high-ranking officials in Rome, including Leiber and Pankratius Pfeiffer, the Salvatorian father known as the Roman Oskar Schindler.[75]

The information provided by Neuhäusler and Müller apparently helped persuade Pius XII to support a high-risk operation, one that according to one high-ranking British official "went to the outer limits of what was possible for a Pope."[76] The German military opposition was drawing up plans for a coup in 1939 and early 1940: it would likely have assassinated Hitler. Pius was to serve as an intermediary between the Western Allies and these resistance circles that included now famous names such as Hans Dohnanyi, Hans Oster, Wilhelm Canaris and, not least, Müller himself. Though the German invasion of France and the Benelux countries dashed the plotters' hopes, Neuhäusler was clearly kept abreast of their plans, later claims of ignorance notwithstanding.[77] In a confidential statement, he wrote that Müller "reported to me in rather great detail already back then after each respective trip to Rome what he had negotiated with the contact-man of the Holy See and with his English and American contacts."[78]

Neuhäusler's reports not only provided material for broadcasts on Vatican Radio. They also served as the basis for a book published in Belgium in 1937; *Brown Bolshevism* earned its author, Dr. Florent Peeters, forty months in the concentration camp Oranienburg.[79] Even more significantly, they provided much of the content for the massive 500-page tome *The Persecution of the Catholic Church in the Third Reich*, published simultaneously in London and New York in 1940.[80] This volume, which saw a second edition, served as a translation of a German compendium of documents detailing the Nazis' war against the church, many of which later found their way into *Cross and Swastika*.

These volumes bore the obvious hallmark of Neuhäusler, even if he learned of their publication only after his release from captivity in 1945. For one, the incidents described, which included physical assaults and arrests, had disproportionately taken place in Bavaria. Their heavy reliance on Bavarian source material also did not escape the attention of the Gestapo. According to Neuhäusler, the appearance of *The Persecution of the Catholic Church in the Third Reich* in 1940 was the real reason underlying his arrest on February 4, 1941.[81] He had been arrested once before on December 19, 1933, for allegedly having violated new bans on assembly; reports of his arrest circulated as high as Cardinal Secretary of State Eugenio Pacelli.[82] But he had only been held overnight. This time, the Gestapo determined to shut him down for good.[83] He was interrogated six times over three months in Gestapo prisons in Munich and Berlin, sent to the notorious Sachsenhausen concentration camp and beaten so badly that an old acquaintance failed to recognize him three months later.[84]

On July 11, 1941, he was transferred to Dachau, where the overwhelming majority of priests were incarcerated. To his astonishment, he was given the protected status of a "special prisoner."[85] The physical abuse ceased, and he received the same rations as his SS guards. He was interned not in the main barracks but in a foreboding-looking prison known as the Bunker looking out to a bleak courtyard used for public executions. He discovered that his cell doors were not locked during the day, and in the spartan cells next to him were two familiar faces, Michael Höck, the editor of the Munich diocesan newspaper, and the Confessing Church leader, Martin Niemöller. The three were allowed to mingle and even celebrate communion together.[86]

The ranks of the comparatively privileged prisoners swelled in the coming years, particularly during the last months of the war, as "special prisoners" from all across Europe, including cardinals and former heads of state, were placed in the same prison in Dachau. Finally on April 24, 1945, the Gestapo, under orders from above, transported the prisoners to the mountains of northern Italy. No doubt it was intending to liquidate all 139 special prisoners, but its plans were foiled at the last minute. The Gestapo chieftain responsible for carrying out the executions committed suicide, and the American army liberated all of the prisoners in a rescue operation that generated international headlines.[87] Neuhäusler and the other German prisoners were transported to Paris and to the island of Capri to be interrogated by American officers about abuses in the concentration camps. Their revelations, they discovered later, were used to prepare for upcoming war crimes trials in Nuremberg.[88] Neuhäusler also was permitted to make two trips from Capri to Rome with Josef Müller, with whom he had just been reunited. He had a widely publicized audience with Pope Pius XII on May 23, 1945, and the opportunity on June 3 to read on Vatican radio the German translation of Pius' address to the College of Cardinals from the day before.[89]

Neuhäusler, Niemöller and Müller were then flown to Naples for a press conference on June 5.[90] They were joined by several other high-ranking Germans and Austrians.[91] The opportunity to present a heartwarming picture of the "other Germany" before approximately thirty-five British and American journalists, however, turned into a public relations debacle. All five were asked questions by American and British journalists about the churches' resistance to National Socialism and, above all, about their current stances toward democracy and how to rebuild Germany politically.[92] The reporters asked Niemöller, who had served as a naval commander in World War I, to confirm rumors that he had volunteered for service in the German Navy in 1939 from his concentration camp cell. Niemöller not only verified these claims but stated that he had been ignorant of most concentration camp atrocities. Worse yet, and here he was backed up in this statement by Neuhäusler and the other four, he stated that Germany was "unfit for democracy."

The damage to the churches' image abroad seemed staggering once the next day's headlines made hay out of these revelations. The reporter for the *New York Times* concluded his story, "Freed Pastor Says Germany Is Unfit for Democracy: Four Anti-Nazis Agree," with the observation that all of the interviewed "agreed that they were unable to live under a democratic government as we know it."[93] As one American occupation official, Marshall Knappen, put it with only some degree of overstatement: "a bewildered public, conditioned by the biased reports of the war years, hastily drew the conclusion that all Germans were Nazis at heart." He added: "Even the preachers minimized the atrocities and were willing to fight for Hitler."[94] Finally and less than two weeks after this fiasco, Neuhäusler was allowed to return to Munich on June 16.[95]

Every one of these stopovers in the first half of 1945 – Dachau, northern Italy, Capri, the Vatican and Naples – was bound up with the genesis of *Cross and Swastika*, but precisely how remains open to question. Neuhäusler, as he would do on so many other occasions, gave conflicting and even misleading accounts of these dramatic events even in the months directly after they occurred. Even his accounts of how and why he came to write his magnum opus varied significantly, and it is safe to say that a faulty memory was not the issue for this meticulous former intelligence operative. Rather, he altered his accounts of his and his church's past to serve political and ideological ends. At their best, these alterations were designed to protect the faithful; at their worst, they were mendacious.

In the opening paragraph of *Cross and Swastika*, Neuhäusler claimed that he had begun writing the first lines before he was evacuated from Dachau in late April 1945.[96] This claim might seem to stretch credulity: how could a concentration camp inmate begin work on a book, even a small work initially intended to be no more than eighty pages?[97] There is an easy answer. Special prisoners like Neuhäusler and Niemöller received privileges unknown to the normal inmates, so many in fact that Karl Barth disparaged them publicly. They were, Barth alleged, "Salon Dachauer" who enjoyed the normal rations of the privileged few in the Dachau Bunker: pipe smoking and even the occasional glass of wine.[98] As grotesque as this characterization was, Neuhäusler had indeed been granted permission to take walks outside, receive visitors including his nearly twenty nephews, use the SS bath house, go to the theater and, most crucially for our story, receive books and pursue his "scholarly interests."[99] His friend and fellow inmate Martin Niemöller had been granted a typewriter.

Neuhäusler's single-paragraph description, however, leaves open key questions.[100] How did he retain his notes, brief as they were since he relied on a system of stenographic shorthand, after being transported into buses headed for an uncertain fate? Did guards pass them on to family members, did he keep them on his person, or were they discovered when the camp was liberated?

Neuhäusler's account also does not explain why he chose to pen this work when it was unclear whether he would even survive his incarceration. It seems most logical to conclude that at this early stage, Neuhäusler intended for *Cross and Swastika* to serve primarily spiritual purposes. It was to be a martyrology and account of human suffering, for which there was a rich tradition. It was also to be a voice of prophecy. It reiterated the exhortations of the Old Testament prophets, showing how God had led foreign invaders to destroy the promised land of a chosen people because of its falling away from God. Proclaiming the triumph of the cross over the swastika – the symbol of the new Baal – Neuhäusler's tomes served as a call to repentance and a return to the Lord.[101]

He seemed to have conceived of *Cross and Swastika* in a more overtly political light once he and his fellow special prisoners were liberated from the resort hotel in the mountains and lakes of Northern Italy where they had spent their final, uncertain days of captivity. His two sojourns in the Vatican seem to have provided the crucial impulses. During his visits on May 3 and May 23, he learned how his documents, once published, had aroused foreign interest in the church struggle. "German circles in Rome" – and here he presumably meant Leiber and Kaas – told him of the need for new "white papers" to document Nazi persecution and Catholic resistance.[102] Neuhäusler quoted them as claiming that white papers that reprinted copies of state laws, the bishops' pastoral letters and the like would help "rescue our honor, at least in Catholic circles."[103]

This view was shared by Pope Pius XII, who ever since his years as the nuncio to Germany was known for his sympathies toward Germany. In his audience with Müller and Neuhäusler on May 23, 1945, the pontiff reportedly told them that "we have to say something for the German people" for "all are speaking about the collective guilt of the German people."[104] Pope Pius XII apparently asked both former couriers for documentation to show "how valiantly Germans, priests and laity had resisted National Socialism" and for statistical data on the number of priests who had suffered in concentration camps. Müller duly provided him with this information, which Pius inserted directly into his influential address to the College of Cardinals on June 2, 1945, in which he unequivocally denounced National Socialism as a "satanic ghost."[105]

Branding itself just as deeply into Neuhäusler's psyche was the press conference in Naples just days later on June 5, 1945. He repeatedly cited this fiasco as the moment of genesis, his earlier papal audiences and scribbles from his last months in Dachau notwithstanding.[106] Needless to say, he skirted over its most embarrassing details. He made no mention of how he and his friends had just put their feet in their mouths through their intemperate comments about the Germans' lack of fitness for democracy. In his preface to *Cross and Swastika* dating from January 27, 1946, moreover, he claimed that the correspondents had repeatedly asked for "a depiction of the National Socialist struggle against the church," a query nowhere to be found in their write-ups of this press conference.[107] Neuhäusler also stated that the journalists had specifically asked about the "German resistance" to National Socialism. "Where then was the resistance to National Socialism?" he quoted them as demanding.[108] Ostensibly hostile questioning from foreign journalists clearly aggravated a deeply aggrieved nationalism, one that had even led him during his incarceration to refer in his diaries to the "loss" of cities like Paris and Aachen to the Allies.[109] In a fundraising letter from 1950 as part of his efforts for clemency for Nazi war criminals, he brought this injured patriotism to a head: Germany needed to be freed "from the guilt complexes imposed upon it."[110]

Neuhäusler thus returned from this press conference to Germany convinced that the German nation remained under attack even after Nazi surrender. Determined to fight back, he intervened on behalf of Germans who had been penalized by denazification boards because of their membership in the Nazi party.[111] In November 1945, he testified before the War Crimes Tribunal on behalf of the defense in the trials of Dachau camp officials and guards.[112] Having been interrogated by American lawyers in Capri for his knowledge of concentration camp atrocities, he was aware that the Americans had war crime trials in the works that went beyond the International Military Tribunal's trial of the major Nazi offenders, which had not been concluded by the time *Cross and Swastika* went to press in the spring of 1946.

He and Faulhaber instinctively knew the best way to fight back: they flashed their seemingly impeccable moral credentials before the occupiers. The Vatican took up one of Neuhäusler's cases involving a former Nazi party member barred from practicing his craft as a journalist because of his tainted past. It began its letter to the U.S. personal representative to the Vatican from November 24, 1945, by citing Neuhäusler's "courageous opposition to Nazism" and confinement in Dachau.[113] But the two Munich church leaders still wanted to make documentary proof available to the public – and to the American occupiers. And hence just nine months after Neuhäusler returned to work full-time as a cathedral canon, they published the 800-plus pages of *Cross and Swastika*.

Faulhaber appended a foreword, in which he defiantly asserted that "one cannot speak of a general collective guilt" since the bishops and some laity had raised their voices in protest against injustice and immorality.[114] The task of collecting, editing and writing fell on Neuhäusler, who had but a sole research assistant – his nephew.[115]

Lending *Cross and Swastika* its power of persuasion, at least to those not in the know, was its sheer mass of documentary evidence and firsthand recollections. It read as an authoritative legal brief. It was an overwhelming compilation of transcribed documents, pastoral letters from the bishops, newspaper articles and fact-filled documents from the Nazi party, the Gestapo and chanceries across Germany. These documents, some in their entirety or in excerpted form, and Neuhäusler's own firsthand recollections served as the undergirding of *Cross and Swastika*. That enough emerged unscathed from bombing raids to fill out the volumes' eight hundred pages serves as testimony to the author's canniness in finding hiding places in monasteries and churches.

In 1947, Neuhäusler launched in earnest a crusade to assist convicted Nazi war criminals, one he pursued as late as 1969, even knowing fully that many were unrepentant.[116] He, in turn, used *Cross and Swastika* to put the brakes on what appeared to him to be overzealous prosecutors bent on revenge. In its pages, he told of the head doctor at an SS military hospital who, realizing that the National Socialist ideology amounted to a house built on sand, saw the cross of Christ as the only way out for him and his young wounded soldiers.[117] Years later, he publicized his encounters at Dachau with SS men sentenced to death, telling of his role in the redemption of one such prisoner just before his death by firing squad.[118] After testifying in a war crimes trial from 1958 against the sadistic Sachsenhausen guard Wilhelm Schubert, who had helped "work him over" on May 14, 1941, Neuhäusler provided him with a copy of *Cross and Swastika* to bring about an inner transformation.[119] This testimony, the KNA, the Catholic wire service agency, reported, "immediately" allowed the newly penitent Schubert to confess his guilt. For Neuhäusler, it seems, prodigal sons needed the opportunity to return home to the church.

But both he and Faulhaber had to negotiate a tightrope in extending a hand to former party members who had long seen the church as an ideological enemy and convincing the Allies that the churches had offered enough resistance to these same party members. Neuhäusler's solution? He was going to let others take up the question of armed resistance to Hitler and its world of conspiracies, sabotage, revolution and uprisings. On his pages, only the "ideological-religious" resistance would come into question.[120] And here, laity, clergy, bishops and popes had marched lock and step against a long line of abuses – violations of the Reichskonkordat, euthanasia, sterilization, the persecution of the orders and Jews, the muzzling of the press, dechristianization, the Führer, the government and the party.

In a swipe at the journalists he encountered at Naples, Neuhäusler cautioned that resistance could not be offered "as many hotheads expected" or as "outsiders, perhaps those living safely abroad with no expertise and responsibility, urged or dictated." One page later, he intensified his criticisms of what he dubbed "know-it-alls," "150 percent-critics" and "either-or-politicians."[121] Any decent journalist, he stated, had to either lay down his pen to carry out passive resistance or flee abroad to live as a "free man" and enlighten the world about the Third Reich: no one should underestimate the challenges of carrying out resistance in a brutal police state.[122] As proof, he cited his experiences from 1933 through 1941 with visitors to his office just released from Nazi concentration camps. Visibly uncomfortable by questions about conditions in the camps, these former prisoners had been required to sign statements threatening them with arrest should they reveal any information about their incarceration and camp life.[123]

What also allowed Neuhäusler to deflect potential criticisms from both Allied critics and former Nazis was a patriotic claim. The anti-Christian Nazi ideology of paganism, he insisted, had been the worst enemy of the German people and the Roman Catholic Church its true defender. The two volumes of *Cross and Swastika* accordingly told first of the Nazi efforts to topple the cross and then documented the efforts of popes, bishops, clergy and laity to keep it standing. After the destruction of the twisted cross of the Nazis, Neuhäusler asserted, it was now time to reestablish and once again honor the cross of Christ so that "Germany should live" and "something better and new could arise out of the rubble of houses, the people and hearts."[124] Rechristianization, in sum, would lead to national renewal.

But Neuhäusler also negotiated this tightrope between critical foreigners and patriotic Germans through a technique straight out of the playbook of a skilled intelligence operative. He presented evidence rife with omissions and manipulations. He naturally did not tell stories of collaboration, cowardice or intranecine strife to which he was privy from his work in coordinating resistance. In ambiguous documents that showed evidence of both support for the Nazi regime and opposition, he cut out passages professing support, leaving out the ellipses that would have indicated the cuts. Virtually every pastoral letter (those letters penned by the bishops and read aloud from the pulpits in their dioceses) featured in Neuhäusler's volumes contained tendentious cuts, usually around potentially embarrassing statements.[125] Elsewhere, he did insert ellipses to indicate cuts – but as a rule only in passages with no potentially embarrassing material.[126]

More than a decade later and while putting together his own documentary collection, the young historian Hans Müller, himself a devout Catholic, discovered this cut-and-paste job, albeit not to its full extent since not all of the originals were yet publicly available. He publicly took the author to task.[127] Documents, he alleged in 1961, had been "cleansed" in front of unsuspecting readers. Forced to respond, Neuhäusler wrote to Müller privately three years later to insist that he had always respected the love of truth but had been in a rush while putting together his book. He regretted that his cuts and slight changes had left a contrary impression.[128]

Publicly, however, Neuhäusler never issued a mea culpa. The sermons and pastoral letters, he insisted, were too lengthy to be reproduced in their entirety. Even for volumes of more than 800 pages, cuts needed to be made.[129] Nor were there any changes in his modus operandi. Just three years later in 1967, he published a three-hundred-paged semi-autobiographical account, *Hammer and Anvil*. These memoirs of sorts laid out his role in the ecclesiastical resistance and his arrest, imprisonment and release. But once again, entire portions were rife with distortions, telling omissions, slightly altered facts and dates and implausible word-for-word reconstructions of conversations that had taken place years earlier.[130]

So why did he distort his evidence – and continue to do so even after critics like Müller were finding the cover-up as morally damning as the original sins? Retracing the zigzags and rifts he had witnessed between 1933 and 1941 would have been at odds with his larger theological message that the church had stood united in its struggle against Nazi paganism. Like most high-ranking clerics, he assumed – and mistakenly continued to assume – that keeping dirty laundry hidden would protect the spiritual welfare of the flock. He was also painfully cognizant of how revelations from the past could be used for political mudslinging. He merely had to look at the battles in the press and in his own party in 1946 engulfing Josef Müller who had returned from Rome to Munich to cofound the CSU.[131] Allegations that Müller had been a bridge-builder to National Socialism in 1932 and 1933 threatened to derail his political aspirations. He was hauled before a denazification tribunal. Neuhäusler was forced to write confidential letters defending his friend, who was eventually exonerated.

Neuhäusler also refused to reveal the close ties between Pope Pius XII and the resistance circles centered in the counterintelligence branch of the army. Since most Germans regarded the conspirators in the army as traitors, his reticence is understandable in the immediate postwar era.[132] As late as 1952, Müller was publicly accused of treason by a rival in the CSU.[133] Neuhäusler, however, maintained a steely silence even after critics like Rolf Hochhuth assailed Pope Pius XII in the 1960s and 1970s for his silence in the face of Nazi genocide – and his refusal to come forward with potentially exculpating evidence is difficult to explain. Both he and Müller knew more than just about any high-ranking ecclesiastical figure in Germany about the scale and scope of ecclesiastical and papal resistance to Hitler. Though Müller was much more forthcoming than Neuhäusler about his role in these conspiracies, neither ever publicly revealed what Müller told Harold Tittmann, an American diplomat to the Vatican, on June 3, 1945, one day after Pius' address to the College of Cardinals. Müller asserted that "his anti-Nazi organization had always been very insistent that the Pope should refrain from making any public statement singling out the Nazis and specifically condemning them and had recommended that the Pope's remarks should be confined to general-ities only." He added that "if the Pope had been specific, Germans would have accused him of yielding to the promptings of foreign powers and this would have made the German Catholics even more suspected than they were and would have greatly restricted their freedom of action in their work of resistance to the Nazis."[134]

The best explanation for Neuhäusler's reticence later in life seems the simplest: Neuhäusler, like so many intelligence agents, was determined to take his secrets with him to the grave.[135] In his defense of the church lingered the spirit of the conspiratorial anti-Nazi underground.

Walter Adolph and the Commemoration of Catholic Martyrs

If Johannes Neuhäusler was apt to wage his campaigns on behalf of the ecclesia with slyness and subterfuge, his counterpart in Berlin, Walter Adolph, maintained his postwar defense of the church with the delicacy of a heavyweight fighter dishing out rapid-fire punches. For this chain-smoking, fast-talking journalist-priest, the mission of apology was inse-parable from the brawny manner of delivery. In his memoirs, he made clear that his blunt manner was an outgrowth of formative experiences as a young Catholic in proletarian Berlin deflecting blows from left and right.[136] Born in 1902, he was raised on the tough streets of Kreuzberg, a hardscrabble quarter in a city where faithful Catholics were no more than 10 percent of the population. He encountered anticlerical prejudice from high-school teachers steeped in the rational axioms of liberal Protestantism, left-wing classmates disrupting school prayers and mocking religious instruction, street-mates clustering in freethinker associations and disaffected youth gravitating toward organized Communist clubs and brigades.

Out of necessity, this teenager contemplating the priesthood learned to fight back, often physically, against ideological adversaries.[137] In one act of bravado, he hung up Center Party election posters in his neighborhood in the chaotic aftermath of the monarchy's collapse in 1918 – and was promptly beaten up by a tough from a rival party.[138] Showing further mettle, he and a friend infiltrated a raucous assembly of more than a thousand freethinkers, where he rose to voice his defense of the church and its sacraments.[139] At a rally of *völkisch* right-wingers led by a Freikorps leader from the Baltic, he stepped in to rebut accusations that religion in Germany could draw sustenance only from German springs and not from Rome.[140]

Just as instrumental in launching him into the public arena were his early stations as a priest. In 1930, little more than three years after his ordination, Adolph became the Secretary of Catholic Action, then led by the charismatic Erich Klausener, Sr., who also served as the chief of the Prussian police.[141] In 1932, Klausener gave him the task of revitalizing the Berlin diocesan newspaper, which had been moribund since its heyday under Dr. Carl Sonnenschein, another child of the Catholic working class known for his love of a good fight.[142] Having studied journalism at the University of Berlin for four semesters, Adolph mastered a technique central to his craft – writing polemics against ideological foes on both left and right that moved seamlessly between past and present. This was a necessity in the polarized media landscape of the late Weimar Republic, in which virtually every newspaper operated with political imperatives like those seen today in the blogging world or Fox News.

Adolph also established lasting connections with prominent Berlin Catholics who would become a fulcrum of support against the National Socialism onslaught and against ideological offensives from the left through the late 1960s. This network of patrons and allies included the politician Heinrich Krone, who had been the Acting General Secretary of the Center Party and was now a delegate in the CDU, a confidant of Adenuaer and a liaison to various governmental ministries in the Federal Republic.[143] It also consisted of Klausener's wife and son, Erich Klausener Jr., who would follow in Adolph's footsteps to become a priest, editor of the Berlin diocesan newspaper and head of the diocesan publishing house, the Morus Verlag.[144]

It was the cold-blooded murder of the patriarch of the Klausener clan on June 30, 1934, in the course of the Röhm purge that awakened in Adolph a calling guiding him through the 1960s. He took it upon himself just weeks later to commemorate the Roman Catholic martyrs of the National Socialist era, defying Gestapo censors to print a commemorative edition of the diocesan newspaper on behalf of the deceased.[145] Once the shackles of censorship were removed in 1945, Adolph was free to devote himself more fully to this calling. He reconstituted the diocesan newspaper. Its first issue of December 2, 1945, contained an extensive feature on the journey of Bernard Lichtenberg, a Berlin priest who after two years of imprisonment died en route to Dachau after having led prayers for the Jews during an evening prayer service.[146] In the coming years and decades, he put the finishing touches on dozens of commemorative articles and three books profiling martyrs, including one on Klausener.[147] He spearheaded the effort to build a church to memorialize Catholic victims, Maria Regina Martyrum.[148] His efforts came to fruition in 1963, when this stark monument to the dead was consecrated near the site of the Nazi prison in Berlin-Plötzensee, the execution grounds for 2,891 political opponents, including members of the Kreisauer Kreis and the conspirators of July 20, 1944. Amid such commemorations, he also found time to record the deeds of the living. In 1948, he published a documentary of the writings and protests of his bishop and cardinal, Cardinal Konrad Graf von Preysing.[149] He also occasionally reprinted documents from the Nazi era in the diocesan newspaper.[150] They were, as a staff writer noted, not dusty scraps from the past but "extraordinarily important to life," having been kept as secrets under the Nazi terror state.[151]

Even so, the contrast with Neuhäusler was immense – and, perhaps fittingly, the rough-mannered son of the Berlin working class and the stiff-necked child of the Bavarian peasantry moved in worlds apart, their common interests in bringing to light the Catholic resistance to National Socialism notwithstanding. Though they were certainly abreast of each other's initiatives and vendettas, one will be hard pressed to find much evidence of communication between the two.[152] Their lenses on the past differed. Neuhäusler, who only narrowly escaped martyrdom himself, tended to focus on the exploits of the living. Adolph, who seems to have largely been let alone by the enforcers of the Nazi police state, was haunted by the journeys of the dead.

How do we explain Adolph's greater dedication to commemorating martyrs and the feats of his bishop in these early postwar years? And how do we account for the fact that, his well-deserved reputation as a fearsome apologist notwithstanding, he was also keenly aware of the limitations of at least one of the martyrs he profiled? In his original draft of his booklet

Figure 1.4 An undated photo of Walter Adolph, Berlin priest, vicar general and journalist. Courtesy of the Diocesan Archive of Berlin, BN 46,07 und 46,08.

on Klausener, he had called attention to Klausener's sympathies for the National Socialist movement.[153] Describing a meeting between Klausener, the Berlin Bishop Nikolaus Bares, the vicar general, Paul Steinmann and himself on June 24, 1934, Adolph had noted: "Klausener went to bat time and again for the Third Reich. In his zeal and with the dedication with which he defended the cause of the National-Socialist regime, he completely overlooked how the bishop became increasingly silent and swallowed his hymns of praise (to the Nazi regime) like bitter pills."[154] For this published version, however, Adolph excised these sentences, telling his readers instead that Klausener's name had now been entered into the ranks of the Berlin martyrs next to their patrons, St. Peter and St. Otto.[155]

Explaining these seeming paradoxes steers us to two interrelated factors – the lessons Adolph drew from the confrontation with National

Socialism he witnessed and participated in and the challenges facing him on the front lines of the Cold War in Berlin between 1945 and 1961. He recognized that the diocese of Berlin, its martyrs notwithstanding, had suffered less from Nazi intrusions than other dioceses.[156] This was also true for him personally. The worst setback to his career took place in 1936, when he was sacked from his position as the head of the Catholic press department in the Reich press chamber to which he had been appointed in December 1933.[157] He attributed his diocese's relative good fortune not just to the fact that Berlin's status as the capital of the Third Reich had caused the regime, sensitive to critical reporting from foreign journalists, to spare it from the worst attacks. He also credited it to Bares' successor as bishop of Berlin, Konrad Graf von Preysing, who "did not shy from issuing public protests."[158]

Von Preysing is generally recognized as the most consistently outspoken opponent of the Nazi regime among the German bishops. From 1936 to 1939, Adolph was his right-hand man, penning many of his letters of protest.[159] They were an unlikely pair, the Bavarian nobleman and the brusque priest from Kreuzberg smarting under his status as an outsider in a hierarchy dominated by the rural sons of Catholic Germany. But both were frustrated by Cardinal Adolf Bertram's tepid response to the Nazi juggernaut.[160] As a courier between von Preysing and Cardinal Adolf Bertram of Breslau, the head of the Fulda Bishops Conference, Adolph learned of differences of opinion between the bishops over how to fend off the parries of the regime. During one trip to Breslau, he had to persuade a reluctant Cardinal Bertram to allow Pope Pius XI's encyclical of protest, *Mit brennender Sorge*, to be read from pulpits across Germany.[161] From these experiences, he drew an unequivocal lesson: the best defense was a good offense. The mistake of the bishops lay in their lack of temerity; fighting the anticlericalism of totalitarian regimes required defiance.

These were no mere academic lessons for a publicist in a diocese straddling four zones of occupation and, after 1949, two states. Adolph's worst suspicions of the Communists were confirmed, as policies of religious toleration pursued by the Soviet occupation authorities and SED in 1945 and 1946 gave way to a crackdown on the freedom of the churches between 1947 and 1949.[162] With extra paper provided on occasion by the Americans, his newspaper, the *Petrusblatt*, was circulated not just in Berlin but for a time in other dioceses in the Soviet zone. Its unbridled anti-Communism aroused the hackles of the authorities. On April 1, 1949, they banned it from all regions outside of Berlin.[163] Adolph was forced to watch Eastern zone newspapers and radio stations exploit and replay the reproofs of Western intellectuals of their own political, cultural and religious institutions. Hence, he kept his misgivings about the conduct of men like Klausener private. To have done otherwise would have corroborated every accusation of the East German state against its "clerico-Fascist" enemy.

Adolph also looked on as two acquaintances were kidnapped by Russian officers from their houses in West Berlin and imprisoned. One was Bernhard Stasiewski, a mild-mannered priest and gifted linguist from Berlin. Starting in 1954 and thanks to Adolph's efforts, Stasiewski would receive funding from the Federal Ministry of the Interior to compile a documentary history of the church under Nazi rule.[164] Stasiewski had served as a translator in Poland under the German Army. Coming under suspicion after the war for espionage, he was accosted at his home on July 19, 1946, by two agents in civilian clothes and driven away by

Figure 1.5 Bernard Stasiewski, a priest from Berlin, was kidnapped from his home in West Berlin by Russian agents. He was given federal funds between 1954 and 1958 to research and write a history of the Catholic Church under National Socialism. Overwhelmed by the task, he never completed the project. Courtesy of Raimund Haas.

a Russian officer. After more than a year in prison, he reappeared emaciated at a train platform in 1947, half his prior weight.[165]

Such struggles on this fault line between East and West also help explain why Adolph not only focused more intensely on martyrs but was also outwardly more bellicose than counterparts in Southern Germany. Not just the Soviet zone of Berlin but the working-class neighborhoods of the west like his native Kreuzberg were the stage for a joust between Catholics and Communists over rituals, symbols and political sway. The latter were determined to commemorate "their" martyrs of concentration camps like the Communist Party leader Ernst Thälmann, murdered in Buchenwald in 1944.[166] They cloaked their often-checkered pasts in an anti-Fascist veil, proclaiming their willingness to die for a just society.

From the outset, Adolph's hermeneutic of martyrdom and documentary exposés bore the imprint of this contest with propaganda shills. Adolph's pantheon of ecclesiastical resisters was thus illustrated in a language often less theological than journalistic and political. Bernhard Lichtenberg was described as a "fighter of Christ," who through his "unflinching and dauntless way which knew no compromise and retreat," soon earned the enmity of the National Socialist state.[167] Just as the Communists recounted the deeds of their saints to bludgeon Western liberalism, so too did Adolph increasingly after 1948 use Catholic martyrs as a weapon against Eastern totalitarianism.

"What did our martyrs die for?" asked Adolph in his book from 1953, *In the Shadows of the Gallows*. They died "for the freedom of conscience and faith, for the freedom of the church, for the value and worth of the individual human being, for the rule of law and for the fact that God's law should rule the public and private life of our people, that the state respect the boundaries of its power and that in our people truth, love, justice and peace should reign." In a jab at the German Democratic Republic, he added, "For millions of our brethren, the end of the Third Reich was not the day of freedom but the beginning of renewed persecution."[168] An exposé from September 1949 of anticlerical quotations from the diaries of the Nazi ideologist Alfred Rosenberg was preceded by a sharply worded article against the Orwellianism of the Communist masters in the East. Though Hitler was dead, the writer opined, his spirit still lived on. Lies had become the political weapon of choice; in the name of religious freedom, the church was being persecuted.[169]

Adolph politicized his account to such an extent that the activities of their anti-Christian persecutors on occasion eclipsed the deeds of the Christian martyrs themselves.[170] Nearly half of his booklet from 1953, *In the Shadow of the Gallows*, provides details of Nazi plans for the persecution of the church and gruesome description of the interrogation methods of the Gestapo and the People's courts. Only the last fifteen pages – less than a fifth – contained eulogies and explanations of the spiritual significance of the martyrs' suffering.

At the same time, Adolph lashed out against dissenters from the West, whose take on the past lent itself to easy exploitation by Communist propagandists. In a case that would come back to haunt fellow Catholics in the mid-1950s and again in the early 1960s, Adolph used the *Petrusblatt* to combat a team of two brothers beginning a tooth-and-nail struggle against the hierarchy. Johannes and Josef Fleischer were Catholic pacifists from Baden, the latter having just undergone a most extraordinary ordeal.[171] He escaped from a prison cell in 1945 as the sole surviving Catholic conscientious objector in Germany during the Second World War. Josef Fleischer had latched on to the prohibition against killing found in the Fifth Commandment – killing could only take place upon God's direct orders, he insisted. He cited this in his dogged decision to refuse conscription into the Wehrmacht, even though several brothers had already seen combat, one perishing five days into the invasion of Poland.[172] After refusing to enlist, he was arrested in May 1940.[173] While awaiting his hearing in an army investigative center in Berlin-Tegel, he was visited by a high-ranking Catholic military chaplain wearing a uniform laced with swastikas. This visitor asked him in the strongest terms to swear the oath of allegiance to Hitler "so that he might give unconditional obedience to the Führer and participate wholeheartedly in his war," advice Fleischer refused to heed.[174] But in what was nothing short of miraculous, he was declared clinically insane, sparing him a death sentence and the martyrdom he was willing to embrace.

In January 1947, Johannes Fleischer took up his brother's cause on the pages of the Berlin newspaper *Der Tagesspiegel* and used it as an opportunity to deliver a broadside against the German Catholic hierarchy.[175] Contrasting the bishops' conduct with that of Martin Niemöller and Josef Müller, he argued that what the German bishops called Christianity had as little to do with Christianity as National Socialism with true socialism. Their protests, "which are now filling entire volumes," had been mere "paper protests." They had no effect because the bishops had failed to prevent the faithful from making compromises with National Socialism. In sanctioning such sacrileges as oaths of allegiance to Hitler, the bishops had betrayed the essence of Christianity. It was an argument sure to rankle Adolph. In discussing his brother's willingness to take up the cross to follow Christ, Fleischer had impinged on that category most central to Adolph: martyrdom.

Walter Adolph's response to Johannes Fleischer prefigured future defense strategies that like those of Neuhäusler were partially born out of the struggle against Nazi overlords. Adolph turned to the religious press to deliver public protests, and this time with no fear of retribution or censorship, at least in the Western zones of Berlin. In the *Petrusblatt*, Adolph denounced Fleischer's allegations as an incipient "stab-in-the-back legend."[176] He tarred his adversary as a "fanatic." He called for publishing more documents from the Third Reich to prove to the world the church's resistance to National Socialism. Fleischer, he argued, had refused to let sources and historical events speak for themselves. These tactics – *ad hominem* attacks and calls for upholding Rankean norms of historical objectivity – remained a mainstay of his approach to critics in the coming decades, including Gordon Zahn and Rolf Hochhuth.

The Origins of *Cologne Documents*

When compared with the volumes published in Freiburg, Munich and Berlin, Wilhelm Corsten's 350-page anthology *Cologne Documents* from the spring of 1949 seemed an afterthought.[177] Though well constructed, it never found a place in the historical canon. Nor did it find much of a popular audience, perhaps because it exclusively consisted of documents with no commentaries: its introduction spanned one meager page. Its intended focus on the archdiocese of Cologne minimized interest from other regions of Germany. It also appeared in print after several waves of criticism against the church's conduct during the Third Reich had subsided. Of its limited edition of 2,000 copies, 120 had to be given away. Looking back in 1962, the author himself lamented that it had been "airbrushed out of existence."[178]

His material came from the archdiocese's call to the flock for documentary evidence of Nazi persecution. Though much of this material had been lost, enough material survived to fill out the pages of this anthology, and not all of it was flattering to churchmen. One woman wrote to the chancery to tell how her priest had criticized her efforts to keep her children out of the Hitler Youth.[179] Her actions, she was told, violated her maternal duty and would make it impossible for her children to establish a career.

Corsten, an ordained priest who had served as a secretary to the Cologne cardinal, Karl Joseph Schulte, naturally did not print this letter. His decision underscored one of the central challenges facing defenders of the church's past. Calls for testimony about the church struggle risked awakening those with less flattering tales to tell. The process of working through the past would unfold dialectically: claims of heroic resistance evoked counterclaims of cowardice and collaboration. If Corsten had not been aware of such stories before, he was now.

Appearing in print as the western zones of Germany were transitioning from rule by the Western occupiers to the Federal Republic, Corsten's anthology bore hallmarks of the political battles erupting. By late 1948 and early 1949, the fight over the schools had emerged as the most significant flash point in the battles over the new West German constitution. Corsten's volume accordingly dedicated page after page to the battles over the schools in the Nazi era in which the Catholic forces suffered defeat after defeat. He also had nonpartisan reasons for doing so. He presented his evidence of Nazi persecution chronologically, but the number of documents appearing for any given year depended on the extent to which the Nazi state pursued its vendetta against the church. The richest documentation stemmed from 1934 to 1937, years which saw the seizure of monasteries, attacks on the moral and sexual conduct of priests and assaults on the religious character of the public schools. Though ignored, his volume heralded pending controversies over the schools.

Conclusions: The Persistence of the Conspiratorial Milieu

The editors and authors of the volumes streaming out of Freiburg, Munich, Berlin and Cologne thus filtered out evidence that hinted at support, possible collaboration, capitulation or cowardice by ecclesiastical leaders. While they often did so for pastoral reasons, their reasons for presenting a picture of a united religious front were more often than not political: they sought to counter criticisms that could damage the church's moral standing at this hour of national rebirth.

In Germany, ironically, homegrown critics of the first hour were few in number and minimal in influence. Overwhelmingly identifying as victims, most Germans had come to detest Allied war crimes trials and denazification initiatives.[180] Insinuations of guilt, either of German church or nation, were more likely to come from the Allies or the far left of the political spectrum. To no surprise, criticism from Communists or probing journalists injected a defensive, if not apologetic, character into the DNA of these earliest documentary collections. Such allegations, real and imagined, had left their authors, mostly middle-aged churchmen on the middle rungs of the hierarchy, with hair-trigger responses – and above all outrage that the church after twelve years of persecution could once again find itself the target of barbs and slings. This meant that early chroniclers like Neuhäusler turned back to the past only when they had to – and usually in response to unflattering revelations about the past and present of prominent churchmen. It was no accident that his later books, *What Was It Like in Dachau?*, *The Seed of Evil*, and *Hammer and Anvil*, appeared on the heels of confrontations with Leonhard Roth, Rolf Hochhuth and Guenter Lewy, respectively.[181]

In keeping with this defensive tone, apologists like Adolph and Neuhäusler deployed a series of somewhat-dubious tactics. These included creating informal networks, holding closed-door meetings to plan punitive steps against critics, denouncing critics publicly and, for Neuhäusler, distorting the historical record. Such strong-armed measures were derived from the struggle against a police state but not in the obvious way. It might be tempting to conclude that men like Adolph and Neuhäusler were merely imitating the tactics of their former oppressors. Rather, these churchmen never completely broke away from the closeted, conspiratorial milieu that had been requisite for the struggle against a brutal dictatorship.

Such formative experiences in the underground during the Third Reich created a playbook for how to respond to future critics. When ideological adversaries surfaced with allegations, these apologists fell back on techniques they knew best. They worked behind the scenes to confound; they strove to keep dissenters as far as possible from the Roman Catholic public sphere – or at least make them pay a steep price for entry. In a case that would later generate national headlines in 1962, Neuhäusler would apply such tricks to a priest and fellow Dachau survivor, Father Leonhard Roth.[182] Both clerics had become embroiled in a public controversy over Neuhäusler's alleged refusal to allow a memorial chapel to be built on the grounds of the Dachau concentration camp. The English press picked up the story, and Roth was transferred away from Dachau and by all indications committed suicide in late June 1960 in the Austrian Alps. Three-quarters of a year later, Neuhäusler sent an article to all of the diocesan newspapers indicating that Roth had been imprisoned not because of resistance activities but because of his homosexuality.[183] The renegade priest had indeed been caught in a Gestapo sting operation.[184]

Not surprisingly, alliances forged during the years of persecution and occupation with many left-wing Catholics and Protestant churchmen broke down as soon as Allied allegations of collective German guilt receded.[185] Left-wing critics like Reinhold Schneider, who sought a moral reckoning instead of mythmaking, quickly found themselves estranged from the hierarchy. Establishing himself as an ardent opponent of Adenauer's policies of rearmament until his untimely death in 1958,

Schneider would briefly make common cause with "crypto-Communist" groups and, in turn, be exposed and pilloried by Walter Adolph's newspaper, the Berlin *Petrusblatt*.[186] But many influential Protestant churchmen, including mavericks like Martin Niemöller, also found themselves at odds with Adenauer's agenda. As confessional tensions rose in the 1950s, church leaders would find themselves at odds over the most divisive open question hearkening back to the Third Reich: the Reichskonkordat. The legal and moral question marks hanging over it would ensure that the spotlight would in the years to come be largely directed at the Catholic Church's past during the Third Reich – and not at their Protestant cousins.

2   The Battles over the Reichskonkordat, 1945–1957

On June 4, 1956, the nine justices of West Germany's highest-ranking court, the Constitutional Court, began five days of highly anticipated hearings in the southwestern city of Karlsruhe. A packed assembly of reporters and fifteen law professors who had submitted written briefs in the prior months had gathered inside the court's palatial 1880s villa. They were there to hear or take part in one of the most ferociously complex cases facing the court since its creation in 1951. In its potential impact, this case was on a par with *Brown vs. Board of Education*, which had been decided by the United States Supreme Court little more than two years before.

The justices were taking up a case that had undergone significant transformation during the previous two years. It began as a showdown over segregation in public schools. It evolved into a case centered on the validity of laws and international treaties from the Nazi era. On March 12, 1955, the federal government in Bonn, led by CDU Chancellor Konrad Adenauer, had filed a lawsuit against the northwestern state of Lower Saxony, then governed by the SPD.[1] The federal government sought to have the court strike down a state school law that had gone into effect there on October 1, 1954.[2] Lower Saxony was trying to dismantle a system of "denominational schools," which had no equivalent in the United States or Great Britain.

Under this system, parents had the right to send their children to public schools, thousands of which existed across the country, officially billed as exclusively Catholic or Protestant. They could also request new ones be built. Lower Saxony's law not only made it virtually impossible to create such schools. It put so many restrictions on existing denominational schools that within weeks of the law's passage, the state education ministry converted more than three-quarters of them into a competing model. This was the interconfessional school, one that for decades had provided schoolchildren with Christian religious instruction but as its name suggested was open to teachers and students of both faiths.

48

That this rift over education would land before West Germany's equivalent of the US Supreme Court was the result of the centuries-old confessional divide between Catholics and Protestants, one suddenly potent again in the early 1950s. Lower Saxony, an overwhelmingly Protestant state, was also home to a small Catholic diaspora as well as a Catholic enclave between Osnabrück and Oldenbourg. Ironically, more Protestant than Catholic schools had been affected by the conversion of denominational into interconfessional schools.[3] But it was almost entirely Catholic churchmen, laity and politicians who raised their voices in protest. With few exceptions, Protestant churchmen remained silent or, like Martin Niemöller, who was now the church president of Hesse-Nassau, openly supported the interconfessional schools.[4] Within four months of the federal government's motion, Hesse and Bremen, two majority-Protestant states governed by the Social Democrats, joined their brethren from the north in their fight before the court.

The lack of vocal Protestant support for the denominational schools meant that Catholic leaders within the CDU and the ecclesia had to resort to a tactic that amounted to a confessional Pandora's box. They argued that the Reichskonkordat from July 20, 1933, remained binding for the Federal Republic, the successor state to Nazi Germany in the west. Adenauer's government claimed that Lower Saxony's new school law specifically violated Article 23 of this treaty, which guaranteed the existence of existing denominational schools and the right to create new such schools should the parents request them.[5] The government of Lower Saxony not only rejected this claim. It argued that this treaty from 1933 was no longer binding at all upon the individual states of the Federal Republic. Education, it insisted, was a state and not a federal issue, noting that other German states like Bremen had already gone ahead and created systems of interconfessional schools in blatant violation of Article 23 and not been subjected to any sort of penalty.[6]

The governments of Bremen and Hesse raised an even more fundamental claim that struck at the legal foundation of this pact between the Vatican and Hitler's government. The Reichskonkordat, they alleged, had been illegitimately concluded under international law.[7] It had not been ratified by any organ of parliament. Its ratification was made possible only through the infamous Enabling Act from March 24, 1933, best known for having given Hitler full dictatorial powers. This act also contained a lesser-known provision that allowed the Reich government to sign treaties with foreign governments over issues like denominational schools that would normally be ratified by the parliament. It stated that "treaties of the Reich with foreign states that affect matters of Reich legislation do not require the approval of legislative bodies."[8] Both the Hessian and Bremen governments went still further and argued that the Enabling Act itself was unconstitutional. It had not been properly ratified by the upper house of the German Parliament, the Reichsrat. It had been voted into law only after the Nazi government had thrown into jail a significant number of parliamentary delegates from the opposition.[9] As a result, any international treaties ratified through it – like the Reichskonkordat – were null and void.

Before the court, then, was a series of monumental issues. Had the Reichskonkordat been properly concluded in the spring and summer of 1933 from a legal standpoint? Did it remain valid even after the collapse of the Nazi regime and, if so, for whom? Did it apply only to the federal government or the individual states as well? And did Lower Saxony's school law violate its provisions guaranteeing denominational schools?

This mammoth case led opposing teams of lawyers, politicians and historians to explore the Catholic Church's responsibility for the disastrous events of the first half of 1933. All knew that passing the Enabling Act had required a two-thirds vote in the German Reichstag. Since the Social Democratic Party would not budge in its opposition and most Communist delegates already had been sent off to prison, one of the two major Roman Catholic parties, the Center Party, had emerged as the swing vote. In spite of initial misgivings, the party had capitulated, all of its delegates voting for the legislation. Its about-face from March 1933 raised suspicions that it had entered into a quid pro quo with Hitler. According to this theory, later known as the "linkage theory," Center Party delegates had supported the Enabling Act in exchange for the Reichskonkordat.[10] They could not resist Hitler's gift horse – the guarantee of denominational schools. This was the realization of a dream that had gone unfulfilled for decades because of the implacable opposition of the socialists and liberals.

Why did politicians of the 1950s ascribe such importance to this case, knowing that skeletons from the Catholic past would be exhumed before state parliaments, the Constitutional Court and the press corps? The argument here is simple: drawing attention to the Catholic Church's relationship to the National Socialist state became a weapon in the struggles over how to draw lines between church and state. On trial was the commitment of the major political parties to an ethos of democracy and the Catholic Church's role in transitions from democratic to authoritarian systems of government. Liberal and socialist opponents of the Reichskonkordat saw this treaty as a totalitarian intrusion into a democratic republic that threatened to corrode fundamental rights and liberties only recently regained. Its supporters, on the other hand, saw it as a guarantee of religious liberties for a beleaguered confessional minority, since even in the Federal Republic, Catholics still constituted a minority.

The fight over the Reichskonkordat and the schools thus quickly evolved into a larger debate about civil liberties and tolerance. For Catholics active in their parishes, the forced conversions of the denominational schools into interconfessional schools resembled the tactics of the Nazis during their war against the church in the 1930s. For opponents, schools segregated by confession were themselves agents of intolerance and exclusion. These debates unfolded at a time when contemporaries were unsure whether the Federal Republic under Adenauer was a state built on a solid democratic foundation or still mired in the authoritarianism of the German past.

Summoning ghosts from the Nazi era, the fight over the Reichskonkordat and the schools would divide those looking back at the past into two distinct camps, paralleling the ideological fault lines of the early Federal Republic. It reignited smoldering confessional tensions between Roman Catholics and Protestants that had been temporarily put aside during the Nazi years and in the joint postwar fight against denazification and war crimes trials. It would also weave questions of tolerance and liberty into the fabric of historical controversies about the past from the very outset.

This chapter traces the steps from the battles in the Weimar Republic over public schools to the courtroom in Karlsruhe. It unfolds in six distinct episodes. It begins by looking back to those battles in the Weimar Republic that led prominent German Catholics to promote a comprehensive treaty with the Vatican. It also examines how the Nazis violated this treaty, including its provisions guaranteeing denominational schools. Secondly, it examines how the schools and the Reichskonkordat threatened to derail the work of the Parliamentary Council on drafting the new West German constitution that became known as the Basic Law. For its third episode and to explain why Lower Saxony passed its school law and Adenauer opted to litigate, this chapter shifts its focus to schoolhouses in the early 1950s. Fourth, it traces the origins of two competing networks waging the fight before the court. On the one side stood the governments of Lower Saxony and Hesse, the latter led by the SPD Minister President Georg August Zinn. Spearheading the other side was the Cologne prelate, Wilhelm Böhler, who put together a team to defend the validity of the Reichskonkordat. Fifth, this chapter looks at the public relations battles fought by these networks. Finally, it heads to Karlsruhe for the oral hearings in June 1956, where it remains until the court announced its verdict on March 26, 1957.

The Battle over Denominational Schools, 1871–1945

The defense of denominational schools was deeply embedded in the psyche of German Catholics. Fighting interconfessional education was a rallying cry for Roman Catholic politicians and bishops who could evoke the memory of at least four separate conflicts with the state prior to 1945. The fate of denominational schools had indeed emerged as a flash point at every moment of political transition – in Prussia in the 1850s, during the Kulturkampf of the 1870s, in the opening months of the Weimar Republic in 1919 and 1920, during the Nazi era and again during the years of occupation and the early years of the Federal Republic.[11] To be sure, conservative Protestants – and here it was often orthodox Lutherans – were angered as well by encroachment of the state on their confessionally pure fortresses.[12] But for Catholics, a minority under repeated assault from liberals, socialists and National Socialists, educational autonomy was a litmus test for the rights of the church.

The revolutionary transitions at the dawn and twilight of the Weimar Republic provided golden opportunities for those who sought to settle the questions of denominational schools and church-state relations once and for all.[13] Militant secularizers sought to sweep away clerical influences, leaving church defenders to try to anchor the right to denominational schools in constitutions and treaties. In November 1918, the left-wing Socialist deputy, co-founder of the USPD (the breakaway SPD faction) and newly appointed head of the Prussian Ministry of Culture, Adolph Hoffmann, ordered that all traces of religion, including crosses, bibles, catechism instruction and prayers, be expunged from classrooms in the state of Prussia, the republic's largest state.[14] Reminiscent of measures just imposed in the Soviet Union, Hoffmann's fiat seemed to herald a renewed Kulturkampf. It triggered massive protests and galvanized Catholic voters. Though his measures were quickly retracted, Catholics, liberals and socialists remained at loggerheads over this issue throughout the Weimar era, and the status of confessional schools was left in legal limbo. The Weimar constitution called for a comprehensive school law to resolve this question, but no such legislation could ever secure passage in the notoriously fractured Weimar parliament.[15] Several states, including Bavaria in 1924, Prussia in 1929 and Baden in 1932, thus attempted to bypass this impasse by directly negotiating treaties with the Vatican. But to the dismay of ecclesiastical leaders, only the Bavarian concordat actually included regulations directly affecting the schools.

Here were the essential ingredients in the Catholic response to attacks on school choice through the mid-1950s: striving to enshrine the right to denominational schools in treaties and constitutions and protesting

Figure 2.1 The signing of the Reichskonkordat on July 20, 1933, in
Rome. At the center is Cardinal Secretary of State Eugenio Pacelli, who
would become Pope Pius XII in 1939. At the far right is Rudolf
Buttmann, a member of the Reich Ministry of the Interior whose
papers would play an important role in the debates about the
Reichskonkordat's origins. Courtesy of Getty Images.

violations, often through large public demonstrations. This strategy bore
the unmistakable thumbprint of Eugenio Pacelli, who first as nuncio to
Germany from 1919 through 1929 and then as Cardinal Secretary of
State strove to bring about a comprehensive Reichskonkordat. One of its
principal architects, he regarded the treaty from July 20, 1933, as
a crowning achievement and, as pontiff from 1939 to 1958, defended it
to the utmost.[16]

The concordat, contrary to the promise of its name, proved to be
a fount of discord. Inciting controversy was not just its seven articles
dealing with education. Though guaranteeing the freedom to practice
the faith publicly and upholding the three existing state concordats,
others of its remaining twenty-seven articles required new bishops to
swear a loyalty oath to the President of the Reich, mandated Sunday
prayers for the German Reich and forbade the clergy from holding
political office and working on behalf of political parties.[17]

A number of prominent German Catholics, including bishops, theologians and lay leaders, greeted the signing of the Reichskonkordat

on July 20, 1933, with cascades of enthusiasm.[18] Since 1919, Catholic
political leaders had been struggling to work out a comprehensive concordat between the German nation and the Vatican. With Hitler now able
to bypass the parliament in ratifying treaties, the stalemate had been
apparently ended. He appeared to give freely what in the Weimar government with its welter of parties and factions had been impossible. Article
23 contained an indisputable guarantee for the existence of current
denominational schools and the right to create new ones where the
parents requested them.[19]

Feelings of relief and euphoria were palpable. As late as January 15,
1934, the *Bayerische Volkszeitung* reprinted a collective statement from
the Catholic clergy in Nuremberg under the headline "The
Denominational School Guaranteed in the Reichskonkordat of the
Führer Is the School of the Catholic German Child."[20] The local clergy
were quoted as calling for church and state to work together and to
educate children through denominational schools to become "valuable
coworkers in the German *Volksgemeinschaft*" – that community of the
German people so extolled by Nazi ideologists. More than two decades
later, a young legal scholar and budding historian, Ernst-Wolfgang
Böckenförde, wondered whether the cascades of enthusiasm and willingness to work with the new regime had been the result of misplaced
priorities. To him, it seemed that the desire to protect schoolchildren had
displaced any commitment to democratic values and processes.[21]

Even more fundamentally, the Reichskonkordat failed to live up to
its billing as a guarantee of denominational schools. Within weeks of
its ratification, Nazi party leaders wedded to visions of a "people's
community" free of confessional and class divides began violating the
terms of the Reichskonkordat, including its guarantees for denominational schools. Already by January 1934, the party leadership in
Middle Franconia launched a campaign to drive students from the
denominational into the interconfessional schools under the slogan
"One people, one youth, one school."[22] But such campaigns failed
to persuade most parents to abandon these bulwarks of confessional
education.[23] Recognizing the failure of propaganda alone to bring
about the desired exodus, party leaders imposed more draconian
measures. In some states, Nazi party leaders with the assistance of
bureaucrats like the opportunistic Hanover jurist Helmut Bojunga
dissolved denominational schools altogether and converted them into
confessionally mixed schools.[24] Prussia, the largest state in Nazi
Germany whose territory not coincidentally included much of the
future state of Lower Saxony, abolished its denominational schools
in 1939, as did Bavaria and Württemberg.[25] Even in states where

denominational schools continued to exist, Nazi party leaders launched a campaign to minimize religious influences in the schools. They ordered crucifixes and the picture of saints removed from classrooms. They reduced the time available for teaching religion, often replacing clergy with lay teachers.[26]

For the faithful, there was one recourse – to protest – and the Reichskonkordat provided the legal framework from which to do so.[27] For Pacelli, this was the intent from the outset. Only a comprehensive international treaty could defend the rights of twenty-three million German Catholics against likely intrusions from Hitler's government.[28] The bishops thus repeatedly used the Reichskonkordat as the legal basis for their appeals and petitions to the Nazi state.[29] In his encyclical from 1937, *Mit Brennender Sorge*, Pope Pius XI famously honed in on how the Nazis had breached the concordat in assaulting denominational schools.

Looking back, Pope Pius XII insisted that the Reichskonkordat had prevented far worse things from happening.[30] This belief was a mainstay of his address to the College of Cardinals on June 2, 1945, the one to which Josef Müller had contributed so heavily.[31] Indeed, fears of new violations of ecclesiastical sovereignty may have spelled the decisive

Figure 2.2 Pope Pius XII at his desk in 1949. The Reichskonkordat was at the center of his life's work. Courtesy of Getty Images.

reason why the pontiff so vigorously defended not only his course of action during the years of Nazi tyranny but the continued validity of his handiwork in the postwar era.[32] It is clear that the pontiff believed that the division of Germany into four zones had drastically increased the like-lihood that old ideological opponents – liberals, socialists and Communists – would find themselves in the driver's seat and attack what he regarded as the rights and privileges of the church.[33] In any case, maintaining the German concordats remained the Holy Father's "principal concern," jotted the new nuncio to Germany and bishop of Fargo, North Dakota, Aloisius Muench, in his diary after his first meeting with the pontiff.[34] The Reichskonkordat was, in the words of the West German ambassador to the Vatican, at the center of his life's work and his legacy to the next pontiff.[35]

The Battle over "Parents' Rights," 1945–1949

"Holding on to denominational schools is worth a fight." These words of Pope Pius XII were relayed by Father Ivo Zeiger, SJ, to Cardinal Frings in an impromptu visit on September 8, 1945.[36] Zeiger was a close and powerful confidant of Pius XII and the leader of the Vatican Mission in Kronberg, the future home of the nunciature. Taking their cue from the determined pontiff, the bishops made the beleaguered denominational school a focus of their internal discussions, letters, conversations with Allied officials and petitions to the occupation authorities.[37]

On this hot-button issue, the bishops and laity used coded language that all would have understood, much as the different sides in the abortion controversy in the United States encapsulate their positions as "the right to life" or "free choice." They used the code words "the right of the parents" or "parents' rights" as their mantra, referring to the right of the parents to choose denominational schools for their children. Although this term dated back to battles over the schools at the start of the Weimar Republic, it resonated powerfully in the immediate postwar era to parents who remembered all too well the claims of the Nazis that it was the state – and not the parents – that possessed the right to determine the education of German children.[38]

It is doubtful, however, that either Zeiger or Pius XII foresaw that their fight over parents' rights would set in motion a chain of events that would over time precipitate a full-fledged reexamination of the Catholic role in the catastrophic events of 1933. The bishops understood full well that this fight would lead to excursions into the immediate past but no doubt believed that these forays would be restricted to the interval from 1936 to 1939 when the Nazi war against religious schools was at its peak. For them, in fact, reminding the Allied occupation authorities of the church's resistance during these years of the church struggle could only help realize their educational agenda. Two weeks after Frings received his message from Pius, one of the German bishops – either Wilhelm Berning of Osnabrück or Lorenz Jaeger of Paderborn – stated bluntly to a representative of the British occupation that the socialists now running the show in parts of the British zone were pursuing the same tactics as Hitler in converting denominational into interconfessional schools.[39] The pressure worked, for the British decided to subject the matter to a vote in 1946, and the results showed massive support for the denominational schools in heavily Roman Catholic regions.[40]

But this was at best a lull. Prompting the resumption of the battle was the fact that work on a new German constitution once again was thrusting prickly questions of church-state relations into the open.[41] At a constitutional convention held in August 1948 to piece together a first draft at the historic chateau on the southeastern Bavarian island, Herrenchiemsee, Catholic representatives had shied away from forcing the issues of the schools and the Reichskonkordat.[42] But these matters resurfaced after delegates from all major political parties assembled at the Museum König in Bonn between September 1, 1948, and May 8, 1949, to transform this rough draft into a final binding document.[43] At this constitutional convention known as the Parliamentary Council, individual politicians from the reconstituted Center Party and the newly formed CDU insisted that the new constitution contain specific guarantees for denominational schools.[44]

Almost overnight, the denominational schools became a test case over how to define religious freedom in the new republic. But defining the churches' educational rights proved polarizing. The more expansive definitions laid out by some of the Catholic delegates reactivated ideological fault lines that had fractured Weimar coalitions.[45] In the one camp was a loose alliance of Communists, socialists and liberals. The Communists were opposed to any and all religious education in public schools and sought to merge, by force if necessary, Catholic and Protestant schoolchildren into "unity" schools resembling those of the Nazis.[46] The socialists and liberals remained hostile to schools segregated by confession but generally accepted that religion should remain a required subject for public schoolchildren. In the other camp sat delegates from the right-leaning German Party, eminences from the Catholic hierarchy and many – though crucially not all – of the Roman Catholic delegates in the CDU and reconstituted Center Party.[47]

Acting as a liaison between the bishops and the laity was the Cologne cathedral canon and prelate Wilhelm Böhler, an expert in the schools whose forte lay in putting together first-rate operational teams and working groups. Having served as the General Secretary for the Catholic School organizations between 1920 and 1935 before pressure from the Nazis caused him to step down, Böhler had been plucked by Frings in May 1946 from his parish in Essen-West to serve as the expert adviser for political affairs for the West German church. Periodic bouts of illness notwithstanding, Böhler would serve as a forcible political broker until his death in 1958. As revered as he was in some circles, he also became a polarizing presence, his political thrusts giving rise to turf-battles with the nunciature and jealousies in Rome.[48]

The showdown in the Parliamentary Council laid bare rifts over not just specific agenda items but underlying principles. Böhler, the newly appointed Michael Keller of the diocese of Münster, and Catholic delegates like Adolf Süsterhenn and Helene Weber placed at the heart of the Catholic defense of denominational schools a specific understanding of natural law. This was the deeply rooted Catholic moral and legal tradition and key ingredient in the struggles before the court and in subsequent controversies over the Catholic past.[49] It was not difficult for these champions of denominational schools to anchor the right to them in natural law teachings and frame it as one of "parents' rights." In their reservoir of teachings was Pope Pius XI's encyclical from 1929, *Divini Illius Magistri*, which argued that the inalienable right of the parents to educate their children proceeded directly from God and that it was the state's duty to protect this parental right.[50] For Cardinal Frings, democracy was a system in which the state upheld the rights of the individual and communities granted by natural law, including the rights of the family over education; without parental rights, democracy would remain "nothing more than a shell."[51] According to nuncio Muench, forced mergers of Catholics and Protestants into "unity schools" were totalitarian and trampled on the rights of parents to "educate their children according to the dictates of their conscience."[52]

Such choices of words left little doubt that the twelve years of struggle with National Socialism had given natural law such primacy in the postwar era. For the bishops and founders of the Christian Democratic Union, Nazism had been the result of the de-Christianization of society and an ethos of materialism.[53] They accordingly saw their task as re-Christianizing politics and society, and aligning constitutions along the principles of natural law represented the way to do so. For founders of the CDU like Hans Peters, a constitutional expert from Berlin, natural law had provided a foundation for resistance against National Socialism as powerful as that laid by the Reichskonkordat; its neglect had paved the way for the catastrophe of 1933.[54] Peters now battled authorities in the

Soviet zone over the right to denominational schools, appealing to the Reichskonkordat to secure the claim.[55] Fittingly, Peters would defend the Reichskonkordat's validity and the right to denominational schools in a lengthy brief to the Constitutional Court and again in the oral hearings in Karlsruhe.[56]

Seeing denominational schools as the best means to re-Christianize society, Catholics in the CDU and church hierarchy accordingly sought to alter the draft constitution under revision at the Parliamentary Council in a manner consistent with natural law principles. They found two ways to secure what they called "the right of the parents" in the new republic, and they were not mutually exclusive. The first – and most direct – was to insert a clause guaranteeing this right directly into the text of the constitution.[57] The other was to add an article stipulating that the Reichskonkordat remained in force and that its Article 23 guaranteed denominational schools.

The first approach drew immediate fire from delegates on the other side of the aisle. FDP leader and future president of the Federal Republic Theodor Heuss argued that including a clause guaranteeing "the right of the parents" would make a mess of the German school system, particularly in regions where countless refugees from the East had upset traditional and delicate confessional balances.[58] Others like the SPD lawyer Georg August Zinn disputed that establishing a right of the parents over education was a proper extension of natural law.[59] He argued that it was the duty of the state to promote tolerance; the church's extension of natural law to the sphere of education infringed on the rights of freethinkers.[60] More fundamentally, delegates like the law professor and leader of the SPD caucus in the Parliamentary Council Carlo Schmidt insisted on drawing a more stringent separation between church and state like those found in the United States and France.[61] Well aware that the Christian Democrats sought to renew state and society through Christian principles, these delegates were allergic to anything resembling a Christian state or the "clericalization" of politics.[62]

The second tack ran up against an additional hurdle – the reality that the ultimate legal status of the Reichskonkordat was still in dispute. The Allies had declared the international treaties signed by the Third Reich to be null and void, since the state that had signed them – the Third Reich – had ceased to exist. But they seemed to have made an exception for the Reichskonkordat – or had they? They decided that it would remain "technically binding" but reserved the right to declare it invalid in the future.[63] Such uncertainty rubbed off on political opponents and even on some bishops, who questioned whether this treaty had any place in the post–Third Reich era because of its dated provisions.[64] The

Reichskonkordat, for instance, contained a provision requiring new bishops to swear a loyalty oath to the Reich President or Reich governor, positions made defunct by the collapse of the Nazi state. Muench admitted that this provision could "call the entire Reichskonkordat into question."[65]

Recognizing parental rights and the Reichskonkordat was galling enough for the opposition, who outnumbered denominational school supporters by three votes in the Parliamentary Council. But more objectionable was a threat first made by Bishop Keller of Münster in a meeting on December 14 between representatives of both churches and representatives to the Parliamentary Council from all of the major parties save the Communists. Of the bishops, Keller was arguably the staunchest advocate of natural law. Territorial changes within his diocese had strengthened his convictions.[66] His diocese included the Catholic enclave south of Oldenbourg, which in 1946 had been placed in the overwhelmingly Protestant and SPD-dominated state of Lower Saxony. Speaking for himself but in the belief that the bishops were of like mind, Keller warned that the church would reject the new constitution in its entirety were "the rights of the parents" not included.[67] He plunged the CDU into an unexpected political crisis two months later when he resorted to even more egregious browbeating: the German bishops would urge Catholic delegates to reject the Basic Law altogether were this right not included.[68]

Such threats appear to have been the straw that broke the camel's back for those already hostile to the Catholic educational agenda. They responded by using one of the most powerful weapons available to them – excoriating the church for its allegedly tainted past. Between January and May 1949, three prominent figures from the FDP and SPD publicly placed responsibility for Hitler's consolidation of power on this treaty from July 1933. The first was the jurist Hermann Höpker-Aschoff, an FDP delegate and future president of the Constitutional Court from 1951 through 1954. As a Prussian DDP delegate decades earlier, he had taken part in the negotiations over the Prussian concordat with the Vatican. Secretary of State Pacelli later described him as one of "the most dogged opponents" of its school provision.[69]

Höpker-Aschoff attacked the Reichskonkordat in an article in *Die Zeit* on January 6, 1949.[70] This pact, which he incorrectly alleged to be the first of a series of international treaties with the new Nazi state, had allowed Hitler's regime to gain international respect and consolidate its power at home. In the Parliamentary Council's steering committee charged with working out the kinks in the often-contradictory drafts brought to it by six subject committees, Höpker-Aschoff additionally declared that "the so-called Reichskonkordat of 1933" had been concluded by "a band of criminals with the intention all along of not adhering to it."[71] Its naïve Catholic sponsors, he inferred, had been duped.

This argument became part of the standard arsenal of church criticism. But in its immediate political impact, it paled in comparison to the devastating criticism hurled by SPD delegate and Hessian Minister of Justice Georg August Zinn less than two weeks later. If there was a foil to Böhler in the coming ten years, it was this engineer's son from a Protestant-dominated state known for its progressive system of education.[72] Just forty-seven years old during most of the negotiations in early 1949 and ten years younger than Böhler, Zinn came of age during the turbulent Weimar era.[73] He became a leader in the democratic defense organization founded in 1924, the *Reichsbanner*. In 1928, he was elected to the Kassel city council, where knock-down, drag-out fights were more than a figure of speech. He used his new law practice to defend victims of National Socialist violence, including beleaguered Jews. To no surprise, he remained ever suspect to Nazi rulers, something that his retreat to private life could not alter. He barely and miraculously escaped arrest after the failed assassination attempt on Hitler on July 20, 1944, his persecutors unable to locate him on the front where he was serving as a sergeant. Almost immediately after his release from an American POW camp, he reentered politics. He rose in status to become one of the most influential architects of the Basic Law. In the process, he cultivated networks of like-minded colleagues from within the FPD and the SPD, including Adolf Arndt, the future house lawyer of the SPD.[74]

As a member of the drafting committee (*Redaktionsausschuss*), Zinn appeared before the Parliamentary Council on January 20, 1948, to argue against including in the Basic Law paragraphs pertaining to the church from the Weimar constitution. He also opposed a paragraph stipulating that existing treaties between the states and the churches still in force on May 8, 1945, should remain so unless replaced with new accords.[75] This latter paragraph was an unmistakable reference to the concordats from Prussia, Baden and Bavaria. But for Zinn, these were intimately connected to the Reichskonkordat, which he called no "glorious chapter" for the church. With its provision calling for prayers for the Reich, he argued, it had no place in a new republic.

But at this point the normally methodical Zinn unexpectedly escalated his criticisms. He stunned committee members by calling attention to Catholic luminaries' enthusiasm for the new state after the Reichskonkordat had been signed. The abbot of Maria Laach, Ildefons Herwegen, had proclaimed in 1933 that the Catholic Church could become a model for the new Nazi state. The Westphalian aristocrat and

Figure 2.3 Two opponents of the Reichskonkordat gather in Bonn for the proclamation of the Basic Law on March 24, 1949. On the left is the SPD delegate and future Minister President of Hesse Georg August Zinn. On the right is the SPD delegate and future Minister President of Lower Saxony Hinrich Kopf, whose school law of October 1, 1954, would trigger the showdown before the Constitutional Court in June 1956. Courtesy of Getty Images.

member of the resistance executed in 1944, Ferdinand Freiherr von Lüninck, had boasted that the church had been fighting the spirit of individualism, liberalism and humanitarian thought for five centuries. The church had not protested sharply against Nazi attacks even in the religious and political realm. Indeed, bishops like the Austrian Cardinal Innitzer had effused about National Socialism as late as 1938. The ideological affinities between two totalitarian institutions, Zinn strongly implied, had sapped the spirit of ecclesiastical resistance.

Zinn's outburst touched on the chief fear gnawing away at opponents through the hearing in Karlsruhe in 1956: the Reichskonkordat was a totalitarian intrusion that could only corrode the substance of democracy. For Zinn, the spirit of National Socialism had too heavily infused this treaty for it to enter the new constitution; even the paragraphs from the Weimar Constitution were too tainted by the past.[76] In closing his report, Zinn cited the cautionary words of Father Paul Jungblut, a Catholic priest from the Black Forest who had recently sent him an address highly critical of both the Reichskonkordat and ecclesiastical conduct under National Socialism.[77] The Reichskonkordat was full of Nazi poison, what he called "the rape of the individual." Those who had gladly imbibed of it would die of it, including holy powers like the church.

Zinn's "very impertinent speech" caught the flabbergasted CDU-CSU delegates, six of eight of whom were Protestant, so completely off guard that the chair was forced to abruptly adjourn the meeting.[78] Only one of the two Catholic delegates, Johannes Brockmann of the reconstituted Center Party, had been able to muster up even a barebones rejoinder, and he could only feebly underscore the resistance of the recently deceased bishop of Münster, Clemens August Graf von Galen.[79] Once picked up by the media, Zinn's barrage unleashed furious exchanges in the daily press. Johannes Neuhäusler and Zinn traded volleys on the pages of the *Süddeutsche Zeitung*, while Wilhelm Karl Gerst published a polemic denouncing the Reichskonkordat as yet another exercise in "clerico-fascism."[80] The SPD politician Johannes Meerfeld found himself in a heated exchange with Böhler in the press over which institution – the SPD or the Catholic Church – had carried out more resistance to National Socialism.[81]

The effect of these allegations against the church from the left was profound. Several key Catholic leaders from Berlin, including Walter Adolph as well as the CDU politicians Heinrich Krone and Hans Peters, recognized that in the long term they would be unable to rebut allegations from the left without help from professional historians. In 1953, Krone succeeded in appropriating federal funds from the Interior Ministry for a documentary overview of the Catholic Church under National Socialism. Gustav Kafka, a political adviser in the Central Committee of German Catholics, later stated that this initiative arose out of the desire to counter the efforts of the SPD to "portray itself as the nearly sole source of resistance to National Socialism."[82]

But this project did not turn out as hoped. Their first choice to carry out the work on this project was overloaded with other commitments.[83] Since the pool of available well-trained Catholic researchers was abysmally small, Adolph turned instead to the church historian he knew from

Berlin, the mild-mannered Bernhard Stasiewski and former Soviet captive.[84] He would be a fateful choice. His heart never fully in the task to begin with, Stasiewski would be overwhelmed by the mountains of documents he encountered in his four years of full-time research between 1954 and 1958. By the time of the Hochhuth and Lewy controversies in 1963 and 1965, the project still lay on his desk.

In the short term, Zinn's criticisms succeeded in torpedoing efforts to include the "right of the parents" into the new constitution.[85] Skeptical of natural law principles to begin with, Konrad Adenauer, the pragmatic future German chancellor, forced the bishops to back down.[86] Unwilling to jeopardize the constitution and allow the bishops to inflict irreparable harm upon their church, he informed Frings on February 7, 1949, that the CDU-CSU caucus had been unable to insert "parents' rights" into the constitution because of determined opposition. But it had worked out a compromise that guaranteed religious instruction and, it was implied, the treaty's validity.[87]

It seems that Böhler and Süsterhenn helped concoct this back-door stratagem.[88] Their proposed Article 123 allowed for treaties concluded by the German Reich "concerning matters within the legislative competence of the states" to remain in effect – a not terribly subtle reference to this treaty of 1933.[89] Since it applied to the entire German Reich, it trumped the rights of the individual states. The federal system created by the founding fathers intended to reserve certain areas of authority, including educational and cultural policy, to the states, albeit with exceptions. From the very outset, this compromise put the federal government on a collision course with the states. Between 1945 and 1951, a number of overwhelmingly Protestant states – Berlin, Hesse, Hamburg, Schleswig-Holstein and Bremen – passed school laws openly contravening Article 23 of the Reichskonkordat in the belief that the demise of Hitler's regime had rendered the treaty invalid.[90]

To make Article 123 palatable to the SPD and the FDP, Böhler and Süsterhenn were forced to accept several caveats. These treaties had to be "and continue to be valid under general principles of law." They could be replaced with new treaties or be terminated for other reasons. Its murkiest phrase, which stated that these treaties were "subject to all rights and objections of interested parties," caused untold head-scratching, even for the church's A-team of lawyers.[91] It was not clear whether the category of "interested parties" referred to the states, individual persons or the federal government.[92] Some took this supreme example of legal gobbledygook to mean that the "interested parties" needed to submit a list of potential objections to the treaty, including their doubts that the Reichskonkordat had been legally concluded.[93] But to whom were these objections to be presented? It was clear to almost all, including Böhler and Süsterhenn, that the validity of the Reichskonkordat would eventually be decided by the courts.[94]

These compromises led to an upwelling of frustration beginning the last frantic week of the Parliamentary Council's session in early May.[95] On May 2, 1949, the Cologne diocesan press, presumably at the behest of Böhler, published excerpts from an angry letter to the German bishops from February 20 from Pope Pius XII, who announced that he was watching the path toward the new constitution with "growing concern."[96] This phrase was an unmistakable allusion to the "burning concern" with which his predecessor, Pope Pius XI, had opened his famous anti-Nazi encyclical from 1937.[97] Pius XII now rebuked the opposition in the FDP and the SPD as the "imitators of a broken state system," whose "disreputable characteristics" included the "systematic disregard of constitutional religious rights and the blatant breach of treaties."[98] The bishops chimed in with a final note of discord on May 23, just as the finished constitution was ceremoniously presented to the German people. They had an uncompromising pastoral letter read from the pulpit decrying the absence of parental rights as a "rape of our Christian parents' conscience" and a failure to "respect the convictions of Christian citizens."[99] Largely written by Böhler but given a sharper wording by Keller, it made full acceptance of the new constitution contingent on its inclusion of rights and principles derived from natural law. The bishops could regard the new constitution only as provisional.[100]

Such lines in the sand may help explain the remarks of Thomas Dehler, the sharp-tongued and controversy-loving future head of the FDP. As a delegate in the Parliamentary Council he had been present at one of the two meetings between Zinn and Adenauer.[101] Like Zinn, Dehler boasted an impeccable past during the Third Reich. He enjoyed ties to liberal resistance groups and had protected his Jewish wife from the clutches of the Gestapo.[102] But unlike his more measured friend, the volatile Dehler had a knack for inflammatory rhetoric even to the detriment of his political career. In the coming fifteen years, he would repeatedly inject explosive elements into the debates about the church's past. In a speech delivered in Bayreuth on July 11, 1949, two months *after* the ratification of the Basic Law, he received a round of applause by challenging the myth of church resistance carefully cultivated by leading CDU politicians and clergy. The churches, he stated, were not the great opponents of National Socialism "as they would have it."[103] The Reichskonkordat, he strongly implied, had made Hitler's regime internationally "respectable" when even Mussolini had distanced himself from the new state to his north.

Figure 2.4 FDP politician and Reichskonkordat opponent Thomas Dehler, known for his fiery rhetoric, delivers a speech in 1950. Courtesy of Getty Images.

With Dehler's entrance into the arena, all but one of the ingredients for future conflict were in place. There were bishops and a pontiff unwilling to yield on the denominational schools and the Reichskonkordat, politicians from the SPD and FDP determined to buck his wishes, a fractured political landscape that continued to resemble that of the Weimar Republic in all its volatility, bitter memories of persecution and a polarizing treaty whose legal status remained up in the air.

Missing was a press corps capable of sustaining lengthy forays into the Catholic past. *Die Zeit*, which was not yet the critical organ it would become by the late 1950s, sold fewer than 81,000 copies at the tail end of the severe paper shortage in 1950.[104] The press, like society as a whole, was weary of settling scores from the Nazi era. Denazification tribunals were winding down; pressure was growing to grant war criminals amnesty. Few non-Communist politicians, as a result, saw much to be gained from future sallies against the allegedly tainted past of the Roman Catholic Church. Even Zinn worked to keep the controversy muted, at least temporarily. At the explicit request of Adenauer, he deleted the derogatory references to Ildefons Herwegen, the Austrian bishops and von Lüninck in the official stenographic version of his remarks before the Parliamentary Council.[105] The reaction in the public arena, not surprisingly, amounted to little more than a few letters to the editor, a far cry from the thousands of letters and editorials penned on the subject later in the 1950s and 1960s.[106]

For this to change, the press had to capture the popular imagination on a byzantine subject. German radio and the major newspapers had broadcast debates between leading politicians and summarized the key bones of contention. But the speakers expostulated over the relationship between the rights of the parents, schools, churches and state at such an abstract level that even some of them admitted that the man on the street would not understand their chatter.[107] This would start to change by the mid-1950s. Day-to-day conflicts breaking out in the classrooms and playgrounds of individual denominational schools would suddenly make the issue real to average German citizens in confessionally mixed battleground states. They put the heat on politicians, who sent the issue before the courts.

Schoolyard Fights and the Law, 1949–1955

After 1949, conflicts erupted at schoolyards and statehouses throughout Germany.[108] The resettlement of twelve million expellees from the former German East placed newcomers cheek by jowl with longstanding residents of other confessions. State borders had also been altered, combining administratively regions with proud but rival traditions of public schooling like North Baden with its interconfessional and North Württemberg with its denominational schools. Staring local school administrators, church leaders and state politicians in the face were two volatile questions: should they mandate a particular school type, and if so, which model?

The ensuing constitutional fight in the new state of Baden-Württemberg ended in an affirmation of the educational status quo in 1953.[109] But what brought the entire matter to combustion elsewhere was the reality that it was unclear what actually constituted a "denominational school."[110] In some villages, denominational schools excluded all teachers and children from the other denomination. But in others, they contained little more than curricula drawn up by pedagogues and teachers exclusively from one denomination. This confusion in theory reflected the necessities of practice. In many sparsely populated rural areas, elementary school pupils either attended schools reserved for children of the other faith or, in the words of one opponent, faced alternative treks "against wind and weather."[111] Many were one- or two-room schools often derided as "dwarf schools." One such newly created denominational school located outside Bielefeld was originally home to forty-two students who had been promised four classes and teachers. In just three weeks, thirty-nine left, having discovered that there was only one teacher and classroom for eight grades.[112] Even so, as late as 1956, 52 percent of German elementary schools fit the category of "dwarf schools," and their numbers were rising.[113]

Opponents of denominational schools naturally gave dwarf schools failing grades because of their curricular shortcomings.[114] But they also did so because confessional minorities complained of discrimination. Reports of children being ignored, teased, bullied or beaten up became the subject of open assemblies and newspaper exposés.[115] By the second half of 1954, opponents claimed that children at segregated schools suffered from psychological distress, an argument seized from the recently concluded case from across the ocean, *Brown vs. Board of Education*.[116]

Adding fuel to the flames were fears that Roman Catholics had undertaken an offensive to convert existing interconfessional schools into denominational fortresses. In Rheinland-Pfalz, Mainz bishop Albert Stohr called on Catholic parents on Protestant terrain to send in requests for new denominational schools, even though the Protestant churches there had made it clear they wished to maintain the old models.[117] Opponents like the Protestant physicist and SPD member Karl Bechert, who later attended the hearings at Karlsruhe, were enraged by the manner in which some school conversions trampled on the rights of the Protestant minority. In the village of Drais near Mainz, a two-classroom interconfessional school was converted into a Catholic denominational school after petitions were submitted by parents of 89 of its 94 Catholic schoolchildren. The local Protestant pastor was to be granted the use of a schoolroom to offer religious instruction to the four remaining Protestant pupils. The school director reneged on the agreement, tossing the clergyman out of the building with a battery of insults.[118] Bechert also strongly implied that parents who submitted petitions did so only because of pressure by church authorities. He cited passages from prayer books and hymnals that asked parents to own up at confession if they had not requested denominational schools for their children. He quoted threats of fire and brimstone voiced in slogans like "He who doesn't send his children to denominational schools won't go to heaven."[119]

These schoolyard fights allowed memories of the past to collide and two competing narratives of intolerance to emerge.[120] It took a widening confessional rupture in the early to mid-1950s to bring this about.[121] As Catholic leaders like Bishop Keller publicly excoriated the perils of interconfessionalism, some local guardians of the flock took their admonitions to extremes.[122] They demanded segregation not just in secondary schools but in technical schools, universities and even graveyards.[123] In a notorious and widely publicized incident, Bishop Julius Döpfner of Würzburg consecrated a sugar factory in the small Lower Franconian city of Ochsenfurt and refused to allow Protestant clergy to give a secondary blessing.[124] Protestant opponents saw in this mania for purification the zeal of the Counter-Reformation and Thirty Years' War.[125] They allowed reports of encroachments on Protestant parishes in Spain, Colombia and Italy to sustain their worst fears of a renewed Catholic onslaught flowing from the Marian year of 1954.[126] For Protestant bishop of Hanover Hanns Lilje, the Reichskonkordat was being used for "a strategic major offensive" to overrun the Protestant heartland of Northern Germany.[127]

Such overblown fears reflected the changing confessional balance in the West. Professor Ulrich Scheuner, a professor of law at the University of Bonn, went so far as to claim that the Federal Republic, a "rump state" in his estimation, was no longer Protestant. Ignoring the fact that it still held a slight Protestant majority, he insisted that it was a de facto "Catholic nation" in light of the "specific weight of both confessions."[128] Scheuner was correct on only one count: Catholics were indeed more likely than Protestants to be faithful to their church and take seriously political and cultural pronouncements from the pulpit.

Catholic intolerance thus was the elephant in the room for those behind Lower Saxony's school law passed on September 14, 1954. Drafted by the SPD and supported by the FDP, parties overwhelmingly dominated by Protestants, this law declared the interconfessional schools the norm. To eliminate the possibility of "dwarf schools," it stipulated that confessional schools could be created only with a minimum of 120 students. They could not be "substantially" smaller than the others.[129] Within weeks, state officials moved to convert denominational to interconfessional schools outside of the Oldenburg region. Yet in a setup that infuriated Catholics, the state secretary who oversaw many conversions was Helmut Bojunga, the same Nazi official who had shuttered Catholic schools in the late 1930s and now wore the garb of an SPD functionary.[130] The bishops of Hildesheim, Osnabrück and Münster, all with parishes in Lower Saxony, openly protested. Their calls for a school strike set more than 60,000 Catholics on to the streets and led more than 40,000 children to boycott the schools.[131] A number of Catholics took to calling the interdenominational schools in Lower Saxony "N S Unity Schools." This was a pun in German. They put in capital letters the N and S from the proper noun *Niedersachsen*, the German name for Lower Saxony, but the N and S were also, of course, the standard acronym for National Socialism. In so doing, they gave a nod to the National Socialist school struggle of the late 1930s in which the Nazis had taken children out of confessional schools and placed them in interconfessional ones often further afield.[132]

Here was the specter of a renewed church struggle from the 1930s and a Kulturkampf, in which Protestant liberals were once again wielding their cudgel against a religious minority.[133] As Keller and the bishops of Hildesheim, Paderborn and Osnabrück put it in a sharply worded letter to SPD Minister President of Lower Saxony Hinrich Kopf, minority rights in a democracy and the freedom of conscience were inalienable: the SPD law represented a clear violation of these rights.[134] Looking over zonal borders into the Communist East, they saw something even worse – a state war against the churches, outlawing religious instruction in public schools altogether.

Protestant and Catholic Church leaders who had made common cause over the Nazi past through joint opposition to war crimes trials and denazification thus parted ways over the school conflict. In the constitutional struggles in 1948 and 1949 over the schools, Protestant churchmen had deferred to the Roman Catholic ecclesia, if unenthusiastically. Between 1954 and 1956, however, the position of prominent Protestant leaders had changed. Martin Niemöller openly spoke out against the Catholic Church's position on the schools just as he had done on controversial questions of rearmament.[135] A group of eight prominent Protestant Church leaders met secretly in Bonn in November 1955 to conclude that a decision by the Constitutional Court in favor of the federal government's position would be "undesirable."[136]

The consequences of these ruptures: for more than a decade, headlines would focus on the Catholic Church's role in 1933 and 1934 and its bridge-builders to National Socialism and not on Protestant agents of *Gleichschaltung* from the same era like the German Christians. Allegations that Catholic denominational schools were agents of intolerance were set to be carved into debates about the National Socialist past. And these probes into the past were invariably present-minded, since the immediate political goals of Catholic leaders – legal and constitutional guarantees for denominational schools – had not changed.

The Networks Form, 1955–1956

Six months elapsed before Adenauer signed off on a motion to have the Constitutional Court adjudicate the case. He made the decision to litigate reluctantly.[137] The issue of "parents' rights" remained an annoying distraction to him, and he did not wish to alienate Protestants in the interconfessional CDU whom he saw as indispensable for future electoral successes.[138] But he could also not ignore the unrelenting pressure from the papal nuncio, the bishops and, probably most crucially, his Catholic base fired up by the wave of strikes and demonstrations.[139] Indeed, this mobilization of the Catholic milieu – petitions to politicians by Catholic parents' organizations, strikes, marches, a coordinated campaign by the Catholic press – became a template for future Catholic action over the Reichskonkordat later in 1956 and again in 1963 during the Hochhuth controversy.[140]

From his office in the Catholic Office in a beautiful southside neighborhood of Bonn with splendid architecture from the Wilhelmine era, Böhler emerged as one of the masterminds behind the defense of the Reichskonkordat before the court.[141] He doubtlessly believed that the superior resources available to the church and federal government would give his side a leg up. He had at his disposal close ties to church officials, the nuncio, the CDU-CSU, the network of Catholic ancillary organizations and, not least, the Catholic press and, in particular, the Catholic wire-services organization, the KNA. Through his expertise in the schools, he had little difficulty in putting together a first-rate team of educational and constitutional experts like Hans Peters to deliver no fewer than nine expert opinions to the court in less than a year. In fact, he had begun commissioning legal opinions already on May 11, 1949, having anticipated this showdown before the courts already just days after the Parliamentary Council had concluded its draft of the Basic Law.[142]

Böhler and his allies also believed that they could exploit the composition of the Constitutional Court, which was divided into two bodies, or senates. His close ally Adolf Süsterhenn pointed out that the Second Senate was more likely to be conducive to the arguments of their side than the First – or "red" – Senate, six of whose twelve members were SPD members.[143] According to Süsterhenn, seven of the twelve members of the Second Senate stood "positively close" to the CDU; the majority of these were "faithful Catholics," whose legal positions were derived from natural law teachings.[144]

Figure 2.5 Prelate Wilhelm Böhler spearheaded Catholic efforts to defend the validity of the Reichskonkordat. Courtesy of the Historisches Archiv des Erzbistums Köln.

This was wishful thinking. They overlooked the fact that influential justices like Gerhard Leibholz did not fit this billing.[145] They also had not reckoned with the entry of Bremen and Hesse into the fray, and the latter proved a game-changer. Since 1950, Hesse's minister president was none other than Georg August Zinn, Süsterhenn's old *bête noire* from the Parliamentary Council who continued to insist that the Reichskonkordat lacked all moral authority.[146] Zinn had lost none of his determination to see an end to this totalitarian intrusion into a democratic republic, or what he took to calling the "Hitler-Konkordat."[147] The Hessian state had refused to recognize the legitimacy of this treaty since 1946, he pointed out. An unfavorable decision by the court, he argued, would threaten Hessian autonomy.[148] Zinn was equally determined to see his state of Hesse become a counterweight to the CDU-dominated federal government. This meant turning it into a "social-democratic model state" and reining in what he saw as Adenauer's heavy-handed compulsion toward centralization.[149] This, when combined with deep commitments to state sovereignty and social-democratic educational ideals, gave Zinn plenty of reasons to join the state of Lower Saxony in its fight against the Reichskonkordat.

In an echo of his tactics from January 20, 1949, Zinn used his position at the top of the state chancery to oversee a defense that in its quality and audacity went far beyond the legalities concocted by Lower Saxony. Between August 1955 and January 1956, he brought on board the brilliant SPD crown jurist Adolf Arndt to serve as the lead counsel (*Prozessbevollmächtiger*). Arndt was a devout Protestant deeply influenced by the teachings and example of Swiss-born Confessing Church Reformed theologian Karl Barth.[150] Arndt was no stranger to the controversy, having little more than a year earlier publicly taken issue with Süsterhenn's claim that the fight over the schools represented a new Kulturkampf.[151] He shared his adversary's belief that his side had little chance of success in light of the confessional composition of the court.[152] He too recognized a crucial weakness: his team had yet to prove that the Enabling Act had been illegally and illegitimately concluded and that the church was aware of this.[153] These were questions for the historian, and to answer them, Arndt recruited a thirty-four-year-old rising star. This was Karl Dietrich Bracher, a young Protestant from Stuttgart married to the niece of Dietrich Bonhoeffer and committed to rehabilitating the men of the resistance against Hitler.[154]

Bracher was a political scientist, classicist and historian wrapped into one. Having been captured by the American army in Tunisia in 1943 and undergone a process of "reeducation" for three years at the POW camp in Concordia, Kansas, Bracher now made it his life's goal to direct the spotlight on how citizens could so quickly jettison democratic institutions in favor of authoritarian or totalitarian models.[155] In 1955, he published a landmark study on the dissolution of the Weimar Republic, one that exploded like a bomb on the West German political landscape.[156] Bracher focused on the ruinous transfer of power from the parliament to authoritarian leaders in the last years of Weimar.[157] He argued that transitional figures like the Roman Catholic Center Party Chancellor Heinrich Brüning, who had governed from 1930 to 1932, had paved the way for the Nazi takeover in 1933. Brüning's generous use of the emergency powers granted under Article 48 of the Weimar constitution permanently sullied the democratic order. These were autocrats, not democrats.

Bracher agreed to put together an expert opinion, for which he like all of the others was paid handsomely.[158] He was the only non-lawyer to be commissioned, and the young political scientist was the beneficiary of a documentary windfall engineered by Zinn and his team as part of a scramble for evidence from the Nazi era. At the end of the Second World War, the British army had captured the records of the German Foreign Ministry, including those pertaining to the negotiations over the Reichskonkordat from the first half of 1933.[159] Already by 1953, word had spread back to Germany about this treasure trove stored in a repository in Whaddon Hall in Buckinghamshire, not far from London, where academic teams were already preparing these documents for eventual publication. Recognizing the centrality of these documents to the case before the court and to West German relations with the Vatican and frustrated by the inability to find much of anything useful in the records of the Vatican Nunciature in Germany, the German Foreign Office secured permission to send one of its officials from London to skim through potentially relevant documents in June 1955.[160] Discovering records of indisputable significance for the court, the Foreign Office struck a deal with its British counterparts: seventeen binders of documents were to be lent to the Constitutional Court in Karlsruhe.[161] The German parties quickly learned about this arrangement, and the FDP issued a formal query to the German parliament in late November 1955 to discern whether the documents relevant to the Reichskonkordat could be made available to its researchers for the upcoming case before the Constitutional Court.[162]

Federal Minister for Foreign Affairs Heinrich von Brentano responded affirmatively. In fact, the documents were scheduled to arrive in the Foreign Office on January 5 and to the court in Karlsruhe on January 12.[163] The Hessian government quickly applied for and received permission. The court, in turn, granted the chancery less than two weeks to view what amounted to twenty-seven binders of documents at the Karlsruhe courthouse.[164] This was a deliberately narrow window, since the documents were scheduled to be sent back to London.[165] In mid-February 1956, Zinn, several officials from his official office in Wiesbaden and at least one official from the Lower Saxon capital of Hanover traveled to Karlsruhe for a viewing.[166] Equally determined to show that the Enabling Act from March 24, 1933, was unconstitutional, the Hessian government applied to the Federal Minister of the Interior on March 29, 1956, for permission to inspect its cache of relevant documents in the National Archives (*Bundesarchiv*) in Koblenz.[167]

Zinn's team discovered several smoking guns in these troves of official correspondence from 1933. It encountered the full text of the Reichskonkordat, which, unbeknownst to most, including apparently Dehler, contained a secret supplement allowing for the conscription of clerics into the army in the event of universal conscription and general mobilization.[168] It came across an admission by the Vatican that it never would have been able to conclude a concordat without the help of the Nazis: the parliamentary governments of Weimar would have rejected its terms out of hand.[169]

Zinn's team not only included these nuggets in its official statement to the court. It passed them on to an eager press.[170] It forwarded copies of documents on to Bracher, who exploited them in his expert opinion. The Reichskonkordat, he insisted, was the next pivotal stage of democratic erosion, the process that he had just laid out in his magnum opus. Bracher noted that the Reichskonkordat was made possible only by the passage of the Enabling Act on March 24, 1933. But he also observed that the elections from March 5, 1933, which gave the Nazis a plurality of 43.9 percent of the vote and enabled the passage of the Enabling Act, had been anything but free elections. Intimidation, deceit, violence, the brutalization of Communists in prisons – all had facilitated the Nazi gains.[171] The legal basis of the Reichskonkordat was thus utterly questionable. The implication of his argument was clear: to grant the legitimacy of the Reichskonkordat was to retroactively sanction the annihilation of democracy. And equally devastatingly, Bracher raised the "linkage argument," the claim that the Center party had signed off on the Enabling Act in exchange for a comprehensive Reichskonkordat guaranteeing confessional schools. His claim found its way into the written submission from the state of Hesse from April 30 and into exchanges in the oral testimony in Karlsruhe.[172] Böhler was so troubled by this "linkage argument" that he immediately sought out four highly respected former Center Party politicians who assured him that it was not true.[173]

Bracher's expert opinion was presented to the court in May 1956. It immediately set off shock waves to treaty defenders who described it as "dangerous."[174] Along with the briefs compiled by Zinn's team, it exposed the Achilles' heel of Böhler's ensemble: it was short of documentary evidence from 1933 and had no professional historians to examine what little it had gathered. This was already the case back in February 1952, when Böhler was contacted by Herbert Groppe, a young law student working on a dissertation on the thorny issues stemming from the "Bremen clause" and Article 123 of the Basic Law. Seeking additional documentary materials on the question of the Reichskonkordat, he needed five follow-up letters, a trip to Bonn and a strong recommendation from Auxillary Bishop Walter Kampe from the diocese of Limburg to get Böhler, who had fallen ill, to comply with his increasingly desperate requests.[175] Böhler could provide him only with a paltry assortment of twelve newspaper articles, the earlier legal opinions from 1949 and transcripts of letters from Cardinal Frings from 1948.[176]

The situation improved only marginally in 1956. Böhler's principal assistant from the historical side was Ernst Deuerlein, a somewhat-volatile thirty-five-year-old historian, jurist and political speechwriter for the CSU whose leg had been amputated after Stalingrad.[177] This Middle Franconian native and onetime activist in the Catholic youth movement had found his interest in the subject piqued by the school controversy that had broken out in Baden-Württemberg in 1953. Deuerlein had taken issue with statements made by FDP Minister President Reinhold Maier and now argued positions that were the very opposite. He maintained that signing a concordat had not been a sudden temptation waved before them by Hitler only in the spring of 1933 but a goal of the German ecclesia almost from the very outset of the Weimar Republic.[178]

This argument became the foundation for his subsequent book, *Das Reichskonkordat*, which appeared in print at the start of June 1956, less than one month before the start of the hearings in Karlsruhe.[179] Honing in on the series of concordats that had been already signed by the individual states and the Vatican prior to 1933, he hoped to demolish arguments that maintained that the Reichskonkordat had grown from a Nazi embryo. Its core principles, he insisted, were those of the Weimar Republic and not the National Socialist era; its content had changed but little.[180]

Deuerlein was the first to make extensive use of the papers of Rudolf Buttmann, a high-ranking Nazi official in the Reich Interior Ministry who had taken part in the negotiations with the Vatican in 1933.[181] But he was also crunched for time, having had little more than five months of full-time work to put together 381 pages. He began writing in December 1955 but was freed up from his day job at the CSU only in January 1956.[182] This belated sabbatical was made possible after Böhler intervened directly with Franz-Josef Strauss, an influential CSU politician.[183] Deuerlein lacked research assistants, and to make matter worse was unable to travel to Karlsruhe to view the documents from the German Foreign Office. He was forced to rely instead on archival materials that Böhler and his associates had been amassing.[184] To no surprise, his scholarship was sloppy, a clutter of factual and interpretative errors so extreme that the first round of published copies had to be destroyed.[185] He had also approved a series of substantial cuts just as the improved version was going into print, leaving it splattered with errors of printing and layout.[186]

Each side thus had access to different pieces of the historical puzzle that was the signing of the Reichskonkordat. The Hessian government had received the records from the German Foreign Office, Böhler's team the papers from the Interior Ministry. Even so, the Hessians had gained the advantage, judged by the fact that Bracher's work generated far more headlines.

The Public Relations Wars, 1955–1956

But spearheading a massive legal defense was in many ways the least of Böhler's worries. He had to oversee a colossal public relations effort involving all of the pillars of the milieu – the Catholic press, the lay organizations, political networks in the CDU-CSU and governmental ministries. The public relations campaign went hand in hand with a no-less-important aim: winning over to his side the judges on the court who were certain to follow the controversy in the press. Böhler was soon consumed with the tasks of writing letters, holding meetings, convening formal conferences and even asking a group of nuns to pray for a favorable outcome.[187] As enthusiastic and confident as he had been when the suit against Lower Saxony was first announced, these unrelenting demands brought the sixty-four-year-old cleric repeatedly to the point of physical collapse.[188]

Böhler's opponents were no less active, and what emerged was a vigorous public relations competition waged in German newspapers, radio, governmental ministries, parliamentary floors and political rallies. The Reichskonkordat, its prehistory, its connection to the Enabling Act and its implication for civil liberties and freedom of conscience were suddenly a focus of intense public debate.[189] In one instance, Hessian radio broadcast an extensive report on a speech delivered at the SPD's annual party convention by Adolf Arndt. This airing prompted a demand for equal time for representatives of the federal government from Walter Kampe.[190] In another instance, the *Hessische Zeitung* reported on Zinn's briefs to the Constitutional Court with the headline "The Concordat Was Hitler's Weapon against Jews."[191]

Böhler delivered several public relations coups in May and June 1956. Not content with piecemeal reporting, he published revised portions of some of the legal briefs with Catholic publishing houses just prior to the hearing in Karlsruhe.[192] The Federal Press Office in Bonn agreed to purchase and distribute 600 copies of Deuerlein's book.[193] Copies were to be sent to prominent CDU and CSU politicians, including Adenauer and Strauss, all Ministries of Culture, the bishops, prominent Catholic law professors, all diocesan newspapers – and, most significantly, to all of the judges on the Constitutional Court itself.[194] The German Catholic wire services, the KNA, sent out to its subscribers a massive hundred-page special report on the Reichskonkordat, including a detailed description of its prehistory derived almost exclusively from Deuerlein's work in progress.[195] Newspapers had the option of printing easily digestible excerpts that could conveniently fill a third or a quarter of a page.

The most attention-grabbing move, however, came from a group of more than twenty SDP and FDP delegates led by Adolf Arndt. They took advantage of a parliamentary instrument known as the "large query," in which a group of delegates, typically those in the minority, posed a formal question or set of questions to the government.[196] The government was required to issue a written response and hold a debate in the German parliament. Their "large query" consisted of four polemical questions that asked whether the government was "aware" that the decision to go to court was "awakening concern in some Protestant circles" and violating principles of federalism.[197]

The ensuing debate on May 30, 1956, opened the parliamentary floor to the heaviest hitters from all major political parties, who made clear that the issues at hand were no longer the teachers, children and curricula inside schoolhouse gates. The FDP delegate and former member of the Parliamentary Council Hans Reif hurled out the "linkage argument."[198] Adolf Cillien, a Protestant CDU delegate from Lower Saxony representing the government's position, temporarily turned away from a discussion of the Reichskonkordat to urge tolerance for religious convictions deemed unpopular.[199] Even more so than the oral hearings at Karlsruhe, where the focus remained on legalities, the hours of high-level debate at the Bundestag in Bonn left little doubt about what these fighters perceived the political and ideological stakes to be – the Roman Catholic Church's place in a democratic state and society.[200] The Reichskonkordat was indeed shaping up as the test case of how to draw lines between church and state. For opponents reflecting on its historical ballast, it was a matter of redrawing them like those in the United States.[201]

Both sides made missteps, and it is probably most accurate to regard the outcome of this public relations battle as a draw. Böhler's side was the beneficiary of the bluster and bumbles of one of Zinn's closest allies, Thomas Dehler. Now the leader of the FDP, Dehler had generated headlines for more than a year by calling for a suspension of the Reichskonkordat from 1933 and negotiations for a new treaty.[202] Since 1949, Dehler's party had been in a ruling coalition with the CDU-CSU. But by late February 1956, this coalition came to an abrupt end over concerns that Adenauer's CDU had been crippling the small liberal and conservative parties by co-opting their politicians into the Christian Democratic behemoth.[203] A visibly agitated Dehler took to the podium to address an overflowing crowd at an FDP rally in Hamburg on March 4. In an off-the-cuff eruption, he denounced Adenauer's alleged contempt for the parliament in terms like "Gleichschaltung" and "the seizure of power," evoking the violent dawn of the Nazi era.[204] Dehler proceeded to quote from Höpker-Aschoff's criticism of the concordat from 1949 as the work of a "band of criminals" and proceeded to fulminate against what he now excoriated as the "criminal concordat." Attempting to make political hay out of documents from Karlsruhe furnished to him by Zinn, who had become a close friend, Dehler claimed that that they proved that Catholics had speculated about establishing "a clerical-Fascist state in Germany with Hitler."[205] When later pressed for proof by the KNA, Dehler could merely stammer that National Socialism had originated in Bavaria. He sputtered that Cardinal Faulhaber had once sung a paean to Hitler, hoping to reach a deal with the man Dehler called a "criminal" leader.

Overnight, Dehler became an object of national scorn. His mortal sin: in assailing the concordat, he had committed an act of blasphemy against its architect, Pope Pius XII. For the German political establishment, Pius XII remained an untouchable icon because of his efforts on behalf of the defeated German nation in the late 1940s. It was bad enough that the national press, including the Hamburg-based newsweekly *Der Spiegel*, almost uniformly condemned Dehler's impertinence and tactlessness.[206] The KNA even circulated an article detailing a lament by Cardinal Frings, who had just met with the pontiff earlier that week. Had he heard these "outrageous attacks by a leading political figure in Germany" before his papal audience, Frings stated, he "would have had to direct his eyes to the ground in shame."[207] The riotous reception Dehler received one week later at the Hackerkeller, a renowned Munich beer hall, arguably represented something worse – a nadir (and, in reality, one of several) of his postwar political career. His stump speech before hundreds of Bavarian beer drinkers was drowned out by a deafening chorus of boos, hisses, jeers and whistles. Dehler had to flee, and it took a commando squadron of a hundred policemen to escort him out safely, according to one newspaper account.[208] The milieu had served its function well. The faithful had expressed their outrage, Dehler had been silenced, and this response became a stencil for the future defense of the pontiff's honor, one to be pulled out of the drawer seven years later against Rolf Hochhuth.

Dehler's fiasco aside, there were signs that the tide in the mainstream press was going to turn against the Catholic cause in the coming decade. Three days after the close of hearings in Karlsruhe, *Der Spiegel* showed that it was becoming an emerging player. It published a multi-page article on the history of the Reichskonkordat subtitled "Secret Joys," a reference to Hitler's jubilation at his gains from this treaty.[209] This article was obviously the product of months of research. The authors provided extensive quotations from documents from the German Foreign Office. In at least one instance, they cut and pasted directly from Deuerlein's work.[210] But there was an increasingly critical and strident tone to their work. Even if they still referred to Dehler pejoratively as a hothead, they quoted extensively from Höpker-Aschoff and Dehler and seemed to buy into their arguments. The authors pointed out how Roman Catholics had enthusiastically striven to ingratiate themselves with the new regime in order to attain the long-standing goal of securing denominational schools. The new documents, according to *Der Spiegel*, showed why the Holy See "so stubbornly clung to the 1933 concordat with its brown mortgage." The Vatican, it claimed, would never otherwise have received such extensive concessions from a land like Germany, which was two-thirds Protestant.

The Constitutional Court Decides, June 4, 1956–March 26, 1957

The five days of oral hearings before the Constitutional Court from June 4–8, 1956, were a master display of pomp and circumstance. According to one of the many journalists who had cascaded into Karlsruhe, never before had so many high-profile legal counsels and state dignitaries appeared before the court.[211] The proceedings were dominated by Adolf Arndt, who gave a virtuoso performance unequaled by the federal government's opposing counsels. Karl Bechert was not far from the mark when he remarked to Zinn after the close of the hearings that the Hessians were by far the best prepared and most acuminous delegation.[212]

Arndt ultimately grasped what others had not: the issue before the court had been fundamentally transformed since the federal government launched its case against Lower Saxony in March 1955. As important as the confessional balance in the schools was, it had been eclipsed by two larger issues – federalism and the legality of the decrees and legislation like the Enabling Act used by Hitler to make his dictatorship iron-proof.

The latter issue naturally spilled over onto the territory of the historian. Even though no historians took the docket at Karlsruhe, not even Karl Dietrich Bracher, it was clear to both sides that Bracher and the Hessian delegation were setting the terms for future historical research.[213] As Deuerlein would point out to Böhler, "it must be assumed that the discussion will continue along the lines laid out by Bracher."[214] This shift in focus before even the court was reflective of so many of the battles about the Catholic past. Begun as proxy wars, they inexorably took on a life of their own.

This recognition explains why Böhler and the Hessian government tangled in the press over the origins of the Reichskonkordat just six weeks after the hearings. In late July, the Hessian chancery put together a press statement claiming that Böhler had publicly insisted that the Reichskonkordat had been the result of long-lasting negotiations during the Weimar Republic and had been the brainchild of Hindenburg.[215] Hitler, the press statement claimed, had been, in fact, the driving force behind this treaty, which he saw as necessary for the urgent struggle against "international Jewry." Attempting to correct the record, Böhler insisted that the Hessians had distorted his words. He had stated that the treaty had been signed by von Papen "on the authority of Hindenburg."

And it was not just the treaty's origins that remained shrouded in intrigue. The court itself was no less fractured than the German parliament, and it took nearly ten months to wring out a decision, one apparently by a bare five-to-four majority.[216] While not all parties to the case were aware of this fissure, some clearly sought to exploit common bonds of religion. Following the hearings, Ernst Deuerlein had an extensive private telephone conversation with the Catholic justice close to the CDU and the author of the decision, Anton August Hennecka.[217] In a glaring breach of confidentiality, Hennecka apparently praised the historian's book in exceptional terms and informed him that the recognition of the concordat by the Second Senate of the court was a done deal.[218] Another of the nine justices also apparently told Deuerlein to expect a decision by late September or October.[219] "I would be pleased," Deuerlein gushed in a letter to Böhler, "if my work as well could contribute its part to a happy decision in Karlsruhe."[220]

But Deuerlein learned from Hennecka in late October that the court had deadlocked.[221] Word too reached Pope Pius XII that the court had failed to reach a verdict.[222] By early December, the alarmed pontiff pondered a more drastic step. He considered having a statement issued threatening a suspension of all of his obligations under the terms of the Reichskonkordat were the delays in Karlsruhe to continue.[223] This was no empty bluster. Under the terms of Article 11 of the Reichskonkordat, the Vatican was obligated to respect all current diocesan borders; any alterations required the approval of the Reich government. Any unilateral papal changes to the German diocesan borders along the borders with Poland and East Germany that could take effect were the concordat to be suspended thus had the potential to upset the foreign policy of the Federal Republic, since the Bonn government had refused to recognize the legitimacy of the East German state and the borders with Poland.[224] In fact, a letter drafted but never sent to the vice president of the Second Senate of the Constitutional Court spoke directly about this possibility.[225] Such threats spread consternation in the German Foreign Office. Fearing that any such statement by the Holy See could be construed as blackmail and become fodder for the opposition press, one of the concerned diplomats, Wilhelm Grewe, contacted Hans Kutscher, a justice who had just joined the Second Senate.[226] Grewe, however, learned that these political concerns were not going to play any role in the court's deliberations. The diplomats' verdict: the Holy See should desist from any further pressure and let the matter lie.

This sage advice was indeed followed but did not stop a final round of shenanigans. Less than a week before the court announced its verdict in late March 1957, Aloisius Muench's concordat expert, Bernhard Hack, traveled to Karlsruhe to meet with justice Willi Geiger, whom Muench described in his diary as "a good Catholic."[227] Geiger, Muench learned, was "at odds" with a group of justices who were "not friendly to the church." This report did not augur well, as Muench was soon to learn when he and the German public received the court's decision.[228]

The court's eighty-eight-page verdict, announced on March 26, 1957, was the result of painful compromises. The court took on directly some of the issues raised by the plaintiffs and defense, sidestepped others and left others couched in a befuddling mumbo jumbo. With some sleight of hand, the nine judges declared that the Konkordat had been legally concluded. Though the Enabling Act was inoperative under the provisions of the Weimar Constitution, this law had to be seen as "a stage in the revolutionary justification for the national-socialist tyranny."[229] In a masterstroke of obfuscation, the justices labeled Hitler's budding dictatorship a "new division of powers" (eine neue Kompetenzordnung) and noted that it had already met with international recognition. Even before Pacelli signed his name to this treaty, Hitler's government had concluded treaties with other international powers through the powers vested in it by the Enabling Act.[230] The court stated further that one could not affirm the existence of a "new division of powers" and a priori deny the acts of state passed by it. Such acts could be declared null and void only if their content ran contrary to established principles of justice and law. "From this vantage point," the justices stated, "no objections could be raised against the Reichskonkordat." Because of three facts – the Allies did not declare this treaty null and void, the Federal Republic was the successor state to the German Reich and Article 123 allowed for past treaties to remain in force until new ones were concluded – its legality remained beyond dispute.[231]

But Böhler's joy in reading the verdict was short-lived. In an assertion of states' rights, the court ruled that the federal government could not legally force the states to uphold the school clause of the Reichskonkordat, since the Basic Law had given the individual states sovereignty over education. The court was therefore not even in a position to determine whether Lower Saxony's school law had violated Article 23 of the Reichskonkordat.[232] The court accordingly threw out the motion by the federal government. Arndt's appeal to federalism had carried the day. The federal government had lost its case over the schools, even as – in a masterstroke of irony – the question mark hanging over the concordat's legal status disappeared.[233] The Reichskonkordat remains in force to this day, and Lower Saxony finally put the vexing school question to rest by signing its own concordat with the Holy See on February 26, 1965.[234]

In contrast to the US Supreme Court, the German Constitutional Court neither issued dissenting opinions nor indicated which justices had dissented. Muench and Hack easily found a way around this hurdle. Hack met with at least two of the Roman Catholic justices, Willi Geiger and Ernst Friesenhahn.[235] By March 30, he reported back to Muench that four Catholic justices had dissented and, more crucially, furnished his superior with an unsigned copy of the dissent.[236] According to the journalist Frederic Spotts, Friesenhahn himself gave Hack a copy of the dissenting opinion he had coauthored with Geiger and another justice, Julius Federer.[237] Muench considered "inducing" the Catholic monthly magazine *Herder Korrespondenz* to publish the unsigned dissent.[238] The majority of the justices, it seems, were none too pleased by this breach of the court's regulations.[239] They forced Muench to return his copy of the dissenting opinion, which was kept under lock and key until 1979.[240]

Conclusions

There is an immediate conclusion to be drawn out of this landmark case: emerging out of day-to-day skirmishes over denominational schools, the battles over the Reichskonkordat in the mid-1950s reached the intensity they did because they were proxy wars for two larger, interrelated questions. How were the legal lines between church and state to be drawn, and how was the church to position itself politically and ideologically in a democratic society? There was no simple answer that all could agree upon in the tumultuous years. The ensuing skirmishes from the late 1940s through the mid-1950s over these two questions took place directly over the ideological fault lines of the early Federal Republic between liberals, Catholics, socialists and communists. These were the old fault lines from the Weimar Republic.

That partisan lineups and networks first addressed these questions on a national stage would leave its mark on research coming down the pipeline on the churches in the Nazi era. The most obvious impact was found in the choice of subject matter. Since the denominational schools and the Reichskonkordat were both seen as uniquely Catholic causes, historical attention would remain disproportionately riveted on the Catholic Church's response to National Socialism – and not on that of the Protestant churches. Most prominent Protestants did not have a dog in either fight or had come to side against the Catholic positions.

The debates about school segregation, moreover, were moored in motifs of religious intolerance and religious liberty. These themes too would become embedded in future research about the church's past. How could they not? They were so deeply rooted in personal and collective memories of traumatic pasts, including the eras of National Socialism, the Kulturkampf and the Counter-Reformation. Pointing out examples of persecution and injustice thus repeatedly forced uncomfortable parallels to the surface during the first decade of the Federal Republic. Was not Lower Saxony violating the Reichskonkordat and the religious liberty of German Catholics in much the same way as had the National Socialists? Was not the Roman Catholic Church through its surrogate, the CDU-CSU, trampling on the rights of Protestants?

The impact of these hearings went even beyond the choice of subject and how it was framed. The open debates on the floor of the parliament in Bonn and in the courtroom in Karlsruhe required those speaking out on the subjects to classify their fellow speakers as coming from "their side" or "the other side." For participants in historical debates in coming years and decades, even those who were not politicians, such dichotomies became hard-and-fixed mental categories. When newcomers to the field appeared, the alarm was almost immediately sounded. Friend or foe?

The result was predictable. The arguments deployed for and against the Reichskonkordat first in the Parliamentary Council in 1949, again in the lead-up to Karlsruhe and finally during the oral hearings would hardly change in coming decades, no matter how much new empirical evidence was unearthed in archives and libraries across Europe. Defenders continued to assert that the Reichskonkordat had safeguarded Catholic rights and prerogatives, a mainstay of defense that went back to Pope Pius XII. Critics held on to the "linkage argument." In 1977, Protestant church historian and FDP member Klaus Scholder made it a centerpiece of his massive two-volume, 1,200-page history *The Churches and the Third Reich*.[241] The "linkage argument" continues to be given credence in works from this century.[242]

For champions of the Reichskonkordat, there was an irony impossible to miss. By taking the disputed issues of the schools and treaty to the court, they provided politicians, journalists and historians of a more critical ilk with the grist they needed to assail the church's role in both past and present. In a classic illustration of how even the best-laid of plans can boomerang, they unwittingly helped demythologize the narratives of resistance so carefully crafted between 1945 and 1949. The historical controversies about to unfold in the coming seven years were all directly inspired or influenced by this landmark case from 1956. For those keen on hearing about the church's role in 1933, the hearings in Karlsruhe were not the climax but the prelude.

3   Generation Gaps and the Böckenförde Controversy

In the first week of February 1961, a reassessment of the Catholic Church's conduct in 1933 hit like a bolt of lightning.[1] Bearing the title "German Catholicism in 1933: A Critical Examination," it came in the form of a meticulously constructed critique of the church's role in the politics of past and present.[2] This article not only argued that Catholic loyalties to republican forms of government had been – and remained – suspect. It marshaled an array of devastating quotations from cardinals, bishops, theology professors and lay presidents who in 1933 had enthusiastically urged their fellow Catholics to support and help build the fledgling Nazi state.[3]

The unexpected parentage of this article sent out immediate shock waves. Had this twenty-four-page analysis of past and present shown the provenance of the Protestant-SPD intellectual milieu, as had mostly been the case in the controversies over the validity of the Reichskonkordat, it would likely have been typecast as party propaganda and remained in the pigeonhole reserved for the confessional and political opposition to Adenauer's CDU. But it came instead from the pen of a thirty-year-old Roman Catholic who had already earned a Ph.D. in law, was nearing completion of a second Ph.D. in history and would go on to enjoy a renowned career as a constitutional theorist, law professor and Constitutional Court justice. Stunningly, it appeared on the pages of the highly respected Roman Catholic journal *Hochland*, a publication known for its intellectual gravitas.

This article by the young Ernst-Wolfgang Böckenförde became the subject of discussion in dozens of leading newspapers and magazines during the subsequent two years. *Der Spiegel* exalted that it was the "orthodox magazine Hochland" that was devoting its "pious pages" to an author who was "mercilessly scratching at a Catholic wound that was still festering."[4] Earning him reprimands and acidulous remarks from prominent names in the ecclesia and political Catholicism, this article spawned a historical controversy so charged that it helped alter the institutional landscape of research into the Catholic past. It catalyzed the founding twenty months later in September 1962 of the Association for Contemporary History, a Catholic historical association charged with documenting and analyzing modern German Catholicism to the present day.

Why did the controversy launched by Böckenförde's article prove a watershed? Why did this watershed occur in 1961 and not in 1956 during the fight before the Constitutional Court? It might be tempting to attribute this to renewed war crimes trials forcing politicians, journalists and intellectuals to wrestle with the responsibility for National Socialism's rise and crimes. But driving the response to Böckenförde's article was something very different: the politics at the close of the Adenauer Era. The interval between 1957 and 1962 was one of political and religious transition, the dawn of the Second Vatican Council, the start of the ferment of the "long sixties." Many in the political opposition were embittered from a string of recent political defeats; those in power, while celebrating the accomplishments of Christian Democratic rule, equally feared future losses. Such passions spilled over into the politicized networks that had been created to wage the battle in Karlsruhe and remained determined to carry out research into the church's past from 1933 before ideological rivals could beat them to the punch.

At precisely this moment, these networks were seeing an influx of newcomers into their ranks. These were mostly intellectuals in their twenties and thirties – what many now call the "generation of 1945" because of the formative role that the collapse of National Socialism from that year played in changing their worldview.[5] Out of these conversion experiences, many emerged committed to laying a stronger foundation for liberal democracy and convinced that the church had a central role to play in this process.[6] But they did not agree on its role. Had the church helped restore illiberal impulses from the past that had led to the catastrophe of 1933? Or had it built a foundation for renewal through its commitment to Christian Democracy?

How the conflicting answers to these questions culminated in the controversy generated by Böckenförde's bolt from the blue is the subject of this chapter. It begins by describing how newcomers began transforming the network originally set up by Prelate Wilhelm Böhler in Bonn to wage the fight over the Reichskonkordat in 1956. Second, it describes how a handful of left-wing and younger Catholics, taking their cues from the criticisms voiced at Karlsruhe, began to delve into the Catholic past. Third, it examines how Ernst-Wolfgang Böckenförde developed his criticism in response to public controversies over church-state relations. Fourth, it analyzes why his criticism, though also drawing on motifs broadcast during the battles over the Reichskonkordat and the denominational schools, created a far greater firestorm than reproaches from other activists on the left. Finally, it examines how this controversy gave a boost to efforts to institutionalize research into the Roman Catholic past and helped establish lasting mechanisms of exclusion and inclusion.

The Lingering Impact of the Reichskonkordat Hearings on Historical Research

It was with good reason that the diplomatic and political strategies pursued by Catholics in Rome, Berlin and Weimar in the first half of 1933 remained in the crosshairs of critics long after the oral hearings in Karlsruhe. The status of denominational schools in individual states like Lower Saxony remained up in the air and served as a continued irritant even after the court's verdict in March 1957. More significantly, the *Sturm und Drang* from Karlsruhe had piqued curiosity. Just days before the hearings in Karlsruhe began on June 6, 1956, Böhler learned that two prominent German academics were intent on publishing all of the motions, briefs, expert opinions, transcripts of the oral arguments and the verdict.[7] One of the two co-editors, Friedrich von der Heydte, a right-wing CSU functionary and expert in constitutional law, approached both the CDU politician Adolf Süsterhenn and Böhler for assistance, insisting that it was paramount that this publication come from "their side."[8]

Although Böhler had shown interest in a more modest project of this sort back in November 1955, he offered only lukewarm support for the project in 1957 and 1958.[9] As comprehensive documentation, the ensuing publication was set to contain the political scientist Karl Dietrich Bracher's expert opinion and claims of a link between the Center Party's support for the Enabling Act and Hitler's promise of a comprehensive Reichskonkordat.[10] But Böhler's lukewarm support made no dent in the two editors' plans. Though their materials eventually comprised more than 1,800 total pages in the smallest of fonts and the press in Munich was forced to publish them piecemeal; twelve installments, bundled into four separately bound volumes, appeared in print over the next two years.[11]

To be sure, much of what was contained in these four volumes was so abstruse that few without legal training could have made heads or tails of it. There were other proposed publications in the immediate aftermath of Karlsruhe, however, that raised heartbeats for Böhler and Ernst Deuerlein, who had just authored a book on the Reichskonkordat's origins. In the June 1956 issue of its highly regarded quarterly historical journal, the seven-year-old Institute for Contemporary History in Munich published an incisive six-page analysis of a document from 1933 that had been long assumed destroyed.[12] Adolf Arndt had handed a copy to the nine justices during the oral hearings and made it available to the general public. It was a rough sketch of the minutes of the fateful Center Party meeting held on the afternoon and early evening of March 23, 1933, about voting for the Enabling Act. Raising Deuerlein's hackles was the fact that the article's author, Erich Matthias, a young political scientist close to the SPD, specifically used it to give credence to the linkage thesis.[13] Two months later, Deuerlein reported back to Böhler with an even greater reason for worry. He had learned that Bracher and the head of the Institute for Contemporary History in Munich were planning to disseminate to the general public the documents from the German Foreign Office used for the hearings in Karlsruhe. What Bracher intended to do with these documents, Deuerlein wrote, "needs no further explanation."[14]

There was a larger reason why scholars like Bracher (who was following up his magisterial tome on the collapse of Weimar with a groundbreaking analysis of the Nazi seizure of power in 1933) would indeed remain fixated on the whirl of intrigues, plots and deals believed to have characterized the collapse of political Catholicism.[15] It was a factor not unique to research into the Catholic past: scholarly energies, still driven by the question of why democracies perished, were converging on the cataclysmic events of 1933. At this point in the mid-1950s, it was less risky for German scholars to focus on how dictatorships began than on how they actually operated. Those analyzing the latter typically relied on frameworks of totalitarianism emphasizing deadly structures and minimizing individual agency.[16] Memories of denazification remained raw, and tribunals from the immediate postwar era had illustrated how millions could potentially be implicated were the spotlight directed back at what happened once the Nazi regime gained power. It was safer to dissect the missteps of men at the helm in early 1933, some like Paul von Hindenburg and the former Center Party leader, Ludwig Kaas, long in the grave.

For those keen on defending the church's conduct in 1933, however, this meant several problems. One lay in the fact that some Catholics at the steering wheel were still alive and generating headlines. Heinrich Brüning, the Center Party chairman from 1930 to 1932, had fled Germany in 1934. He was living in self-imposed exile in the remote hills and woods of Norwich, Vermont, just across the river from Dartmouth College. His seventy-fifth birthday on November 26, 1960, was covered extensively in the German press.[17] Brüning, however, had maintained a public silence on his time as chancellor. He had promised but refused to publish memoirs, heightening the mystery about his party's relationship to the Vatican.[18]

Franz von Papen, the chief engineer of Hitler's appointment as chancellor in January 1933, was proving an even greater public embarrassment.[19] For most Catholic politicians in the CDU, he remained a renegade and a disgrace. The new and ostensibly liberal pope, John XXIII, however, reappointed him in 1959 to the symbolic post of a papal chamberlain. He did so in spite of the fact that Pope Pius XII, aware of Papen's fateful responsibility for Hitler's coming to power, had stripped him of this title in 1939. Von Papen's return to the limelight made it more likely that scholars and journalists would question the extent to which prominent Catholics, in having given their blessing to a dictatorship, bore responsibility for what was to come.

The other major problem, as Böhler correctly perceived, was that defenders of the church's diplomacy and politics of 1933 were ill prepared to mount an effective response to the discovery and release of potentially unflattering documents from dusty archives. For one, his side was handicapped by the nature of the debate. It was playing defense, and it was far easier for opponents to haul out smoking guns than for defenders to systematically map out the historical circumstances informing controversial treaties and decisions. For another, his team was running up against a weakness with deep roots in the German university landscape. Since the nineteenth century, the historical profession in Germany had been overwhelmingly dominated by Protestants. Of the eighty-five chairs in history, six were exclusively reserved for Catholics under the terms of the concordats – and the holders of those few Catholic chairs tended to be dismissed as second-rate.[20] And so Böhler put forward a justifiable lament: where are our professors who could hand out dissertation topics on topics like the Reichskonkordat to their graduate students?[21]

The only solution to this competitive disadvantage, Böhler realized, lay in more systematic planning. His team was all too aware that the slapdash historical surveys his side had produced so far were barely scratching the surface. This recognition served as the driving force behind a hodgepodge of blueprints for working groups, research agendas and think tanks.[22] New intergenerational historical teams were to bring together senior professors and younger blood; a new historical institute, its exact contours still undefined, was to parlay research into publications.

But even the earliest of these plans and sketches from September 1956 – just two months after the close of the oral hearings – showed a juggling act between two commitments, a tension endemic to many think tanks of today.[23] On the one hand, these scholarly networks were to

advance political agendas; on the other, they were to distinguish themselves through their objective historical methodology. The agenda found
on these early blueprints thus was unabashedly political. Their opening
sentence cited "negotiations over church-state relations like concordat
questions, school problems and *Kirchenpolitik*" as the impetus.
Their second paragraph called for research into the nineteenth and first
half of the twentieth century to gain "reference points for our own
decisions" and to gain "strength and consolation for our own battles of
our time." And yet one of the first to respond affirmatively to these plans,
the future head of the Catholic Academy in Bavaria, saw in these plans the
potential to create a Catholic counterpoint to the Institute for
Contemporary History.[24] This was an indication that he too believed
that Catholics would have to put their scholarly mettle on display.
In fact, this new institution would serve as proof that Catholics were
capable of leaving the defensive fortress of the Kulturkampf era and
making sense of the church's new missionary and political role in the
modern world.[25] At a time when Catholic educational achievement
clearly lagged, this was the credo of overcompensation, the belief that
Catholics would need to not only master the tools of the historical trade
but wield them even more skillfully than Protestant competitors.

The sources of this tension between academic rigor and political
engagement are not difficult to locate: circulating blueprints was
a mixture of academics, political consultants and politicians. It was members of Böhler's team mounting the defense of the Reichskonkordat who
put forward the first set of plans. It included Ernst Deuerlein; Leo Just,
a history professor at the University of Mainz; and Alfons Kupper,
Böhler's leading associate on the concordat case.[26] As this trio grew to
a semiformal network of ten between meetings on December 20, 1956,
and February 22, 1957, these tensions, if anything, grew more pronounced. Kupper put together a list of fourteen themes for research
explicitly geared to the political needs of the present.[27] All touched in
some way on the Reichskonkordat, its prehistory, the phases of negotiations between 1920 and 1933, Catholic conceptions of the state or the
wrangling over the schools in Weimar. And yet, the plans explicitly
stipulated, these topics were also to be approached free of apology and
polemic, regardless of how the decision of the nine justices in Karlsruhe
turned out.[28]

This diverse group of recruits included several professors as well as the
fifty-two-year-old historian Bernhard Stasiewski. Attending was Hans
Peters, the CDU politician and lawyer at Karlsruhe who also served as
the head of the venerable Catholic academic society, the Görres Society.
At the meeting on February 22, however, Peters declared himself to be

Figure 3.1 The young historian Rudolf Morsey in the 1950s as he
was beginning his research into the collapse of the Center Party.
Courtesy of Rudolf Morsey.

opposed to the entire enterprise of contemporary history. This ethos was
fundamentally at odds with that of other group members. For Rudolf
Morsey, a twenty-eight-year-old aspiring professor born in 1927, making
sense of the recent past was precisely the reason to attend. The
Westphalian native had been steered to the group (and to Böhler) by his
undergraduate mentor, Georg Schreiber, while studying history at the
university in Münster.[29] Schreiber was a former Center Party member
and onetime Professor of Church History at Münster until he lost his
chair in 1935 to Joseph Lortz, the Catholic historian and Nazi party
member known for cascades of enthusiasm for the Nazi movement.[30]
Schreiber turned his house in Münster into a gathering place for academics and former Center Party politicians. Ever the elder statesman, he
set the undergraduate in his mid-twenties on to the topic to which he

had been a firsthand witness: the collapse of the Center Party in the first half of 1933.[31]

This topic would consume Morsey's energies for decades. Like most historians of his era, he prioritized political and diplomatic history. He was a single-minded empiricist, wont to reserve final judgment on larger questions of causality until he could conclusively analyze all available sources.[32] He became relentless in his pursuit of diaries, diplomatic dispatches, meeting protocols, letters, briefings – in short, any written evidence that could shed light on the collapse in 1933.

Such an approach earned him Deuerlein's suspicions. Deuerlein was troubled by the fact that Morsey was unwilling to rule out the possibility that Hitler and the Center Party leader Ludwig Kaas might have hammered out a deal in their secret meeting of March 22, 1933, the latter possibly offering votes for the Enabling Act in exchange for the Reichskonkordat.[33] As it turned out, Morsey did renounce publicly and explicitly the linkage argument – albeit in 1977, having never found in the course of decades of exhaustive research the conclusive proof he had sought.[34] This was one of the few instances in the battles over the Catholic past where careful consideration of factual evidence compelled a participant to abandon a key theory or hypothesis.

The meeting on February 22, 1957, also made clear just how difficult the pursuit of such written sources would be. Kupper had hoped that team members could ideally visit all state and church archives. His zeal was dashed by a report by Stasiewski, now two years into his research on the church in the era of National Socialism. Stasiewski pointed out that conditions in most diocesan archives were poor.[35] He revealed a crucial truth: access to the relevant sources was given personally and hinged on whether diocesan officials or archivists were willing to trust individual users. The members discussed an underappreciated alternative: private archives. But as Stasiewski pointed out from hard-won experience, using private collections like those of Johannes Neuhäusler and Cardinal Faulhaber was equally daunting, even for insiders wearing clerical collars.

This meeting was the second and last of this working group operating out of Böhler's office in Bonn. Böhler died in July 1958, while others in the group moved on to other endeavors. But four of its members – Deuerlein, Morsey, Kupper and Stasiewski – were trained historians and provided a locus for future networks committed to launching research into the past. Kupper quickly authored a series of articles on the Reichskonkordat in the renowned Jesuit journal *Stimmen der Zeit*, baby steps toward his ultimate goal of a comprehensive history of the Reichskonkordat.[36] He also procured microfilmed copies from London of the German Foreign Office holdings on the Reichskonkordat.[37]

But it was Morsey who brought the most crucial forensic evidence from 1933 to the attention of the public. He possessed a unique standing in the profession, one borne out of his unlikely participation in crisscrossing historical networks. He began work in the Bonn-based *Commission for the History of Parliamentarianism and the Political Parties*, then headed by the historian and his graduate advisor, Werner Conze.[38] Morsey found there an ongoing collaborator in the same Erich Matthias who was viewed somewhat askance in Böhler's circle for his close ties to the SPD and willingness to entertain the "linkage argument."[39] But Matthias was also a highly regarded profiler of the collapse of Social Democracy in 1933, a project that offered incisive comparisons with Morsey's subject material. Their edited volume, *The End of the Parties: 1933*, was their postmortem of the leading Weimar political parties from the conservatives to the Communists. Their autopsy, which included numerous appended documents, stemmed from the premise that the National Socialist victory, Hitler's own magnetism notwithstanding, was not inevitable. It resulted from fatal miscalculations, human weakness and, in some cases, a Pollyanna dismissal of the true danger lurking behind the Nazi masses.[40] This widely reviewed volume emerged as the most cited of all those published by the *Commission for the History of Parliamentarianism and the Political Parties*, so much so that it was reprinted in paperback form in 1984.[41] Morsey's account of the collapse of the Center Party, in turn, became a classic.

Morsey's short article in the September 1960 issue of *Stimmen der Zeit* created just as many waves.[42] This article never would have come to fruition without the help of a former Center Party politician whom Morsey met in 1958 in the house of Georg Schreiber.[43] Johannes Schauff had been an implacable opponent of the Nazi Party and the Enabling Act who had spent most of the Nazi years in exile. Already in 1934 while on board a ship to Brazil, Schauff was determined to see the Center Party's death throes become the subject of scholarly research. This resolve only grew after his return to Europe in 1949 and hearing aspersions directed at former Center Party leaders.[44] Intent on refuting the "linkage argument" that had surfaced in the battle before the Constitutional Court, he hoped to put together a collection of the diaries and speeches of his former party leader, Ludwig Kaas.[45] Schauff himself had purchased Kaas' old house in northern Italy after the former party leader's death in 1952. In early 1960, he made a remarkable discovery in Kaas' old desk – fragmentary diary-like jottings in Kaas' handwriting from April 7–20, 1933.[46] These described how Kaas by chance met Franz von Papen in the dining car of a train on the morning of April 8,

1933. They also revealed Kaas' decision "out of inner conviction" to work constructively on building and consolidating the new state.[47]

Schauff passed these on to Morsey with whom he had developed a strong working relationship. What happened next became a recurring dynamic during the coming months and years, and there were already hints of this in *Der Spiegel*'s exposé on the Reichskonkordat from June 1956. Portions of the national press, looking to make sensation out of substance, plucked sober scholarship from staid scholarly journals and edited volumes and paraded it to a seemingly insatiable audience. Revelations within Morsey's two seminal publications – his sober article in *Stimmen der Zeit* and co-edited volume on the end of the Weimar Republic – thus provided fodder for *Der Spiegel's* reporters. Just two weeks after Brüning's seventy-fifth birthday, *Der Spiegel* published an article on December 7, 1960, titled, "Reichskonkordat: Hitler applauded."[48] The Vatican harbored dark secrets, the article's opening line suggested. It likened the Third Reich to a giant flypaper trap. It was not Papen but the gaunt priest Kaas who "lured the mistrustful Vatican diplomats to the sticky glue of the Third Reich" and had bowed to the "upstart Hitler."

There were good reasons for why *Der Spiegel* was turning to this explosive subject: well-educated younger Germans were showing a growing appetite for a reckoning with the Nazi past. In the winter semester of 1959/1960, Morsey joined forces with a cadre of freshly minted Ph.D.s including Hans Buchheim, Karl Otmar von Aretin, Kurt Sontheimer and Martin Broszat, the latter two destined to become giants in their fields.[49] This team collectively delivered more than a hundred lectures on the theme of "overcoming the past" to overflowing crowds in Catholic student parishes throughout Germany.[50] Their standing-room-only lectures could not have escaped attention from a new and more aggressive cadre of journalists and editors, themselves often only a few years removed from their studies. The press corps itself was starting to change and adopt a more critical attitude toward institutions like the church to which many journalists had once given wide berth.[51] These younger journalists were already discovering windows into the crimes of National Socialism. These included Anne Frank's diaries, the testimony of victims and perpetrators at the war crimes trials in Ulm from July 28 through August 29, 1958, and William Shirer's landmark indictment, *The Rise and Fall of the Third Reich*, published in October 1960.[52]

From former statesmen and Center Party members from 1933, however, Morsey's recent work was more apt to reap a harvest of private grumbling, public criticisms and corrections – and not only because of its use by *Der Spiegel*.[53] From his home in Vermont, Heinrich Brüning wrote to Heinrich Krone that he was "aghast" at the fact that the Jesuit journal *Stimmen der Zeit* would reveal the deeds centered on Kaas.[54] Brüning expressed his hope that his negotiations with Pacelli would never be published. More ominous was a corrective of sorts in the December issue of *Stimmen der Zeit* from Robert Leiber SJ, the private secretary and adviser to Pacelli.[55] Leiber cast doubt on some of Morsey's claims, putting the onus for the ignominious collapse on the Center Party and not the Vatican.[56] Not wishing to jeopardize this influential Jesuit's potential as a historical source and interview subject, Morsey opted to not respond directly to Leiber's rebuttal.[57]

Such responses gave an idea of the difficulties in store for those younger scholars who rightly suspected that there was more to the recent past than had been depicted in the documentaries put together by the likes of Adolph and Neuhäusler just after the close of the war. These younger scholars had to negotiate a wall of silence. Too many witnesses were reluctant to speak out publicly about 1933 or to make available their written records of the past. How would they finance their research, find sources and publish their findings, particularly when some presses were reluctant to touch the subject? To no small extent, the answer to all of these questions hinged on their ability to exploit personal or family connections or to tap into the ecclesiastical and scholarly networks taking shape between 1956 and 1962.

Left-Wing Catholic Networks

But which connections and which networks? These younger intellectuals and scholars were coming of age in a badly fractured confessional and political landscape in which networks tended to fall along political, confessional and ideological lines. Members often spoke of "our side" and "the other side," and these fronts tended to be synonymous respectively with the CDU-CSU and the opposition in the FDP and SPD, Protestants, lapsed or irregular Catholics and secular voices better represented in the latter. A smattering of Catholic intellectuals, however, fit perfectly into neither group. These were the "left-wing Catholics," a moniker frequently affixed to church dissidents by adversaries from within the faith and sometimes used as a tool of self-identification by voices of critical dissent themselves.[58] They could certainly point to a rich tradition of dissent. In the 1950s, dissenters like the journalist Walter Dirks had gained notoriety for their public clashes with the hierarchy and leading lay organizations over West German rearmament. As a result, they found themselves standing largely outside the world of organized Catholicism and its formal edifices like the Central Committee of

German Catholics. Many such nonconformists subsequently bemoaned their marginalized status, the writer Heinrich Böll famously doing so in his acerbic novel from 1963, *The Clown*.[59]

What remained uncertain was how individual representatives of the younger generation of German Catholics (generally speaking, those born after 1925) challenging orthodoxies about their church's past would position themselves. Would they find themselves relegated to the ranks of the left-wing Catholic dissenters, or would they find themselves accepted into the mainstream, institutionalized world of German Catholicism? Would they find their way to the CDU-CSU? Or would they take the unthinkable step of joining the SPD, an unacceptable proposition for so many in the hierarchy and in the flock so long as the party refused to abjure the Marxism of its official platform? There is a simple answer here: members of this cohort split ranks. The side that they gravitated toward – or formally joined – would strongly determine success with sources, witnesses and publications.

For a thirty-year-old Catholic elementary school teacher from the Ruhr, Hans Müller, the path to "the other side" and the SPD stemmed from a personal conversion story.[60] Born in 1928, he was a true believer and zealous Hitler Youth member. In 1945, he launched a desperate last-ditch defense with the *Volkssturm*, anticipating a heroic death at the hands of American troops invading his home territory. Aware of the senseless-ness of any such sacrifice, his commanding officer urged him to desert, undoubtedly saving his life in the process. His future wife, whose liberal-leaning father had opposed the Nazi regime, in turn helped steer him away from Nazi values.

He opted to become a historian, a critical voice learning from the errors of the immediate past. He became the lead assistant on the Karlsruhe trial project co-directed by von der Heydte. While editing the twelve install-ments of trial documents, Müller began exhuming newspaper and maga-zine clippings, letters and reports from diocesan archives in Münster, Aachen, Limburg, Paderborn and even Breslau. He began work on a critical documentary history of the relationship between the church and National Socialism from 1930 to 1935, a tome that would eventually consume more than 400 pages.[61] Had the Nazi state given up its cultural and political crusade against the church, he concluded, the church and Nazi state could have easily lived together symbiotically. The gap between them on many questions of state and politics was not as large as com-monly assumed.[62]

While compiling documents for his anthology, the young Müller began to notice discrepancies between the originals and the versions redacted more than a decade earlier by Johannes Neuhäusler in *Cross and*

Swastika. Müller set out to straighten the record. In 1961, he pointed out these tendentious errors in a review article in the respected journal *Politische Studien*.[63] But he encountered some of the same difficulties as others on the Catholic left trying to effect political and cultural change within the mother-church. In 1960 and 1961, he attempted to publish documents pertaining to the Bishops' Declaration of March 28, 1933, which had lifted restrictions on Catholic entry into the Nazi party and its ancillary organizations.

After two rejections, he chose to publish these in the *Working Papers of Catholic Laity* (*Werkhefte Katholischer Laien*), a low-budget publication of the marginalized Catholic left with poor layout, dismal fonts, cheap paper, approximately 2,000 subscribers and a correspondingly dim reputation in the Roman Catholic mainstream.[64] In many respects, this hybrid between a magazine and a newsletter was emblematic of the fate of left-wing Catholicism during the 1950s and early 1960s. It had clashed with the hierarchy and the representatives of mainstream lay Catholicism over virtually every hot-button issue of the 1950s including rearmament, the rights of conscientious objectors and the obligation of Catholics to vote for the CDU-CSU. In 1958, the embittered editors had begun taking up the question of the Nazi past, linking the church's role in 1933 to political mentalities lingering into the present.[65] Like Böckenförde would do little more than two years later, the author, Paul Weinberger, had honed in on affinities in structure and ideology that had led prominent Catholics to embrace National Socialism in 1933. It would be false to assume, Weinberger wrote, that "everything was different today and that one had learned from the past."[66]

But at least initially, these nonconformists on the Catholic left wound up on the losing side of their battles. To add insult to injury, they often found themselves pilloried by mainstream Catholic leaders.[67] Such defeats left these activists with a distinct sense of marginalization, particularly since they recognized they were pitted against networks with more money and influence. Themes of nonconformity thus came to infuse subsequent controversies over the Catholic past like those soon to be launched by American sociologist and pacifist Gordon Zahn. Their hopes of extracting lessons from the Catholic past from 1933 to 1945 often took on the trappings of an insurgency. The networks hastily built to counter these agitators, in turn, often adopted tactics of a counterinsurgency.

The Böckenförde Controversies, 1945–1961

For some overzealous defenders of the church's political alignments in past and present, Ernst-Wolfgang Böckenförde became a poster child for the young rebel insurgency.[68] Born in 1930, he was of the generation of intellectuals who came to be known as the "generation of 1945."[69] He leaned slightly left in his political orientation, even joining the SPD in 1967 – an unthinkable step for orthodox Catholics of an integralist ilk. He raised many of the same criticisms as those militant nonconformists, albeit in a more cerebral and less strident tone. For the former bishop of Berlin and cardinal of Munich, Julius Döpfner, Böckenförde belonged with Hans Müller, Gordon Zahn, Paul Weinberger and the writer Carl Amery on a list of "nonconformist Catholics" with "questionable ecclesiological tendencies" he presented to the Fulda Bishops Conference on August 24, 1963.[70]

But pigeonholing this young intellectual into the category of nonconformity, as some of his less informed and more intemperate critics did, glosses over one inconvenient fact. It was not only young critical intellectuals like the young Catholic ethicist Robert Spaemann who provided a nexus for the discussion of ideas and their transmission to the public.[71] It was his steadfast Catholic family from Westphalia. If others of the nonconformist left saw themselves with some justification as outsiders, Böckenförde was to no small extent an insider, and this made his critique all the more piercing.

So how did a talented graduate student emerge from a devout family to publish a systematic set of reflections that challenged Catholic orthodoxies on church-state relations and the Nazi past? And how did he decide to burrow into the church's past from 1933? Ernst-Wolfgang Böckenförde's focus on things cerebral may have been facilitated by a childhood accident in 1943 in which he lost a leg, leaving him unable to devote energies to physical activities like hiking more typical of the teenage experience in the immediate postwar era.[72] More decisive was undoubtedly his family, an incubator of an unusual mixture of devotion and critical intellectual reflection. His father was a master forester working near Arnsberg in the hills of the Catholic Sauerland, a region renowned even in other Catholic regions of Germany for its unusually dense ensemble of religious rituals, processions, festivals and organizations. He was not the lumberjack vivid in the North American imagination but a high-ranking civil servant and intellectual who regularly read publications like the *Rheinischer Merkur* and the Catholic journal *Hochland*.[73] The latter was edited by Ernst-Wolfgang Böckenförde's uncle, Franz-Josef Schöningh, one of the co-founders of the Munich daily newspaper *Die Süddeutsche Zeitung*.[74]

With such intellectual openness, ongoing questions of church and state were a staple of household and dinnertime conversation, and these were in no short supply. As a fourteen-year-old, Böckenförde witnessed the collapse of the Third Reich and intently watched the rebirth of the German civil administration and political order on the orders of the military government. These seminal events spurned his interest in law and constitutional order.[75] Already as a teenager, he was troubled by the attempts by leading Roman Catholics to establish natural law as the fundamental principle of the moral and legal order in this process of reconstruction.[76] Could the acceptance of a constitution ultimately hinge on the inclusion of the "right of the parents," as Bishop Michael Keller insisted in February 1949.

Böckenförde would have repeated occasion to encounter Keller's staunch views. He chose to study law in Münster, a university town and seat of Keller's bishopric with a reputation throughout Germany for the unusual richness of its voluntary organizations and religious life. For anti-Catholics, Münster was the embodiment of clerical autocracy.[77] Fitting this reputation to a T, Keller was known for his highly politicized pastoral letters, which functioned as scarcely veiled voter directives. They were read from the pulpit of every parish in the diocese, reminding the voters of the ideological and religious issues at stake in upcoming elections and usually concluding with the exhortation to vote "Christian," a not-so-delicate reminder that good Christians did not vote for the Social Democrats. Other bishops issued similar pastoral letters, but Keller made his rejection of the SPD more explicit than most. In an uncompromising address in 1957, he stipulated that no true Catholic could vote for the SPD in good conscience.[78] In a private letter to the Archbishop of Salzburg, he went even further, noting that it was his personal belief that it would be a form of "suicide" for faithful Catholics to support the SPD.[79]

But as he began a doctoral program in history in Munich under the direction of Professor Franz Schnabel, Böckenförde discovered a compelling counterpoint to Keller's integralism. He attended a speech by the renowned Adolf Arndt at the Technical University in Munich less than one year after the SPD house-lawyer had dominated the oral exchanges in Karlsruhe.[80] Arndt's richly nuanced benchmark address anticipated the SPD's new course unveiled in its Godesberger Program from 1959 famously renouncing Marxism.[81] Speaking out against the yawning ideological fissures in the German political landscape, Arndt observed that the German parties increasingly resembled religious institutions. The CDU, he noted, threatened to degenerate into a "church party." Arndt urged that ideology and political mission be decoupled from each other.[82] Insisting that democratic socialism and Christianity could find grounds of compatibility, Arndt sought to allay doubts about

Figure 3.2 Bishop Michael Keller of Münster speaks with the young historian Rudolf Morsey in the 1950s. Courtesy of Rudolf Morsey.

the genuine commitment of Social Democracy to a democratic ethos. In so doing, he hoped not only to make the SPD palatable to Catholic voters but also to fundamentally rethink the relationship between church and state. Tolerance for different values was the order of the day.

Though not convinced by all of Arndt's arguments, Böckenförde described the lecture as having "reinforced" his own resolve to work toward what became a fundamental goal – gaining the church's approval and recognition of a pluralistic society.[83] If Arndt's principles could be realized, Böckenförde wrote to Arndt, there would no longer be cause for the steady stream of electoral sermons and pastoral letters from the bishops and for Catholics not to vote for the SPD, should they agree with its platform.[84]

Both Keller and Arndt delivered their pronouncements and overtures to Catholic voters in the summer of 1957 during the lead-up to the federal elections of September. It was in this context of overheated rhetoric and ideological jockeying that Böckenförde found himself given an opportunity to put his reflections on the role of the church in a democratic society into print in *Hochland*.[85] The invitation came from Franz-Josef Schöningh, and the topic fit perfectly into the course his uncle had been steering for this venerable journal ever since the American military government granted him a license to resurrect it in 1946. During the Weimar era, *Hochland* had become known for its willingness to wrestle with metaphysical questions in many of its articles.[86] But after the war, Schöningh also deemed it imperative to discuss pressing historical and ideological questions of the day. Tellingly, these did not include a reckoning with Germany's Nazi past. It was probably no coincidence that between 1941 and 1943, Schöningh had served as a government official in the General Government of Poland overseeing the transfer of property as the Nazis carried out the massacres and deportation of the Jewish population during these phases of the Final Solution.[87]

Schöningh had his eye instead on safer constitutional questions. Which constitutional forms would provide the bedrock for the new republic? Like Böckenförde, he was skeptical of the church's role in politics. In 1957, he went so far as to consciously provide a forum to the loyal opposition within the church. In the forward to the fiftieth anniversary edition of *Hochland* that same year, he explained why he was allowing the presence of more critical voices in his journal. He sought to offer "justifiable resistance" to the increasingly visible tendency of "binding the universal, international (*völkerverbindend*) church to one party and narrowing itself to the horizon" of that same party.[88]

After receiving a draft of his nephew's article, Schöningh urged him to make his criticism more incisive, his argumentation more expansive, his style less austere.[89] The twenty-seven-year-old complied, noting that a "puritanical" style and way of thinking was true to his austere Westphalian disposition.[90] His uncle's admonitions notwithstanding, his article still retained a tone of sobriety, and this would remain true for his article four years later about German Catholicism in 1933. That both of his incisively argued critiques would arouse such passion could not be attributed to sensation-seeking or incendiary rhetoric; it lay in the arguments themselves and the evidence backing them up.

Several arguments undergirded Böckenförde's debut article, "The Ethos of Modern Democracy and the Church," appearing in the October 1957 issue of *Hochland*.[91] He maintained that the insistence on upholding teachings and principles derived from natural law reflected a larger indifference to the proper forms of government. Roman Catholics could adapt to any form of state, be it democracy, monarchy or even dictatorships, so long as it was based on a Christian footing: decisive was only whether principles derived from natural law were likely to be upheld. This observation was obviously a criticism of what appeared to be the dominant feature of the political landscape of the Federal Republic – the tight links between Christian Democracy and the church that politicians like Thomas Dehler or the political scientist Thomas Ellwein were excoriating as "clericalism."[92] But Böckenförde's article reflected deeper anxieties that the Federal Republic might be a democracy without democrats and whose republican allegiances were fickle. It was driven by lingering fears about the "tyranny of the majority." Was the Catholic Church truly committed to an ethos of democracy and willing to countenance minority rights?

Böckenförde's solution? The church needed to assume a new role of a lobby, one that would seek to influence *all* political groups and parties in a bid to disseminate religious and moral values. The ecclesia was to stay out of political fights as much as possible, leaving this work to the faithful. This strategy might lead to short-term loss: it required affirming a pluralistic society not formally anchored in Christian institutions. But it offered the chance to secure Christian values more enduringly by freeing it from political coalitions that were by definition transitory. To promote this message less than one month after the electoral triumph of the CDU in the elections of September 1957, Schöningh proposed sending off-prints to all delegates in all political parties in the parliament.[93] Böckenförde rejected this idea. This problem, he concluded, first needed to be tackled within the church itself – and not by outsiders with an ax to grind.[94]

Böckenförde's article nonetheless served its purpose. At odds with the "Catholic mainstream," it unleashed tremors among concerned laity and clergy who perceived it as "rebellious."[95] Its appearance in the venerable *Hochland* was sufficient to rouse a concerned Gustav Kafka from his desk in the Division of Civic Affairs in the Central Committee of German Catholics. Wary of the fact that Böckenförde was a former pupil of Carl

Schmitt, the controversial German legal theorist with a compromised past from the Nazi era, Kafka tried to gain more information about the author.[96] He contacted the Münster cathedral canon, Heinrich Tenhumberg, who sent back a somewhat detailed portrait two days later.[97] Böckenförde, in an opinion that would be shared by all who would come to know him, was a young man of impeccable integrity. But an acquaintance had described him as "somewhat too intellectual, or rather a one-sided young academic."[98] Tenhumberg urged entering into a discussion, since "the one-sidedness and errors must not be allowed to stay put."

Undoubtedly at Tenhumberg's behest, Hermann Josef Spital stepped forward in mid-January 1958 with a rebuttal in the Catholic weekly newspaper *Echo der Zeit*.[99] A young curate in his early thirties, Spital served as the secretary for Bishop Keller and would be appointed as the bishop of Trier in 1981. Within several weeks, Schöningh, Böckenförde, the managing editor at *Hochland* and Spital began hashing out the details for a formal exchange.[100]

Their extended back and forth unveiled points of contention that echoed arguments just made in the recent battles over the Reichskonkordat and denominational schools. Tellingly, both men were not far apart in age, and this would not be the last time that representatives of the so-called "generation of 1945" would come to diametrically opposed conclusions about how best to implant a democratic ethos. Spital's position was largely representative of the defensive posture endemic to Roman Catholicism in the early years of the Federal Republic.[101] For Spital, democracy remained as fragile as the CDU's recent electoral gains: the other political parties would exercise a "tyranny of the majority" once they had wrested political power from their ideological enemies through electoral gains.[102] The CDU-CSU's ideological rivals could easily deny minorities like Roman Catholics fundamental political and moral rights such as the "right of the parents," as had indeed been the case during the Nazi and Kulturkampf eras. The fight, then, was for religious liberty.

Böckenförde, in contrast, no longer saw Roman Catholics as a beleaguered minority. Eight years of rule by a CDU chancellor was proof of change. But their disagreement was over more than whether the glass was half full or empty. Democracy, for Spital, was not an ethical norm. Nor could it be. The form of a state, Spital implied, was ethically neutral. For Böckenförde, democracy necessarily assumed certain ethical norms – tolerance, openness and, above all, the willingness to grant others, even longstanding ideological foes from parties like the SPD, the opportunity to hold political power.

This exchange focused exclusively on the role of the Catholic Church in the present. It was Schöningh (ironically in light of his checkered past in Eastern Poland) who helped put Böckenförde on the path to a critical reassessment of the Catholic Church's conduct in 1933. For one, Schöningh drew an explicit analogy between the present and the past in his forward to the fiftieth anniversary edition of *Hochland* of 1957 containing his nephew's debut article. Warning of placing allegiance to political and ancillary organizations ahead of religious substance, Schöningh ruefully observed that "almost all Catholic organizations fell not after dogged resistance but like a house of cards from a single gust of wind."[103] This single sentence set off a kerfuffle and a call for document gathering about the fates of Catholic ancillary organizations.[104] On cue, the leadership of the League of German Catholic Youth (BDKJ), the organization with nearly a million members, published its own 240-page documentary history of Catholic youth organizations in the Nazi era – one, however, that also pointed out Catholic youth leaders' enthusiasm for the Nazi state in 1933.[105]

For another, Schöningh commissioned Böckenförde's controversial essay about 1933 in the summer of 1960 and approved it for publication in the late fall not long before his death in December.[106] This was an irresistible opportunity. Böckenförde's curiosity had been awakened by the polemics hurled in the spat over the concordat and especially by Dehler's alleged act of libel against the Holy Father back in 1956.[107] As Böckenförde began probing into the subject material, his findings took him aback.[108] He discovered an array of incriminating utterances by high-ranking church dignitaries, officials in prominent ancillary organizations and Roman Catholic intellectuals in Paul Weinberger's article "The Church and the Third Reich in 1933," which had appeared in the *Working Papers of Catholic Laity* in 1958.[109] Boasting of their willingness to work with the new state were academics like Joseph Lortz and Michael Schmaus, leaders of Catholic organizations like the Kolping organization for artisans, prominent members of the Catholic nobility and even the bishops. Böckenförde, reading Morsey's work on the collapse of the Center Party, also learned of this surge of enthusiasm following news of the Reichskonkordat in July 1933.[110]

The discovery of so many examples of spontaneous enthusiasm for the fledgling National Socialist regime left its mark on the young scholar.[111] It solidified a line of reasoning that would undergird his new article. Rendering Catholic leaders – and particularly those determined to realize organic conceptions of state and society – susceptible to the siren-calls of Fascism in 1933, he argued, was the reality that Catholic political thought for more than 200 years had been driven by an antipathy toward the

Enlightenment: Catholics had been saddled with an ambivalent relationship to the liberal state. Since the French Revolution, the modern state had pushed them out of their once dominant position of political and societal authority. Scarred by bitter experiences such as the German Kulturkampf of the 1870s, Catholics, when they did engage with the liberal political order, did so only to preserve their religious freedoms and secure longstanding goals derived from conceptions of natural law, not least of which was the right to establish and maintain confessional schools for Catholic schoolchildren. Under the neo-scholastic political teachings of Pope Leo XIII, allegiance to concrete state and constitutional forms was secondary to the degree to which natural law principles could be realized. Roman Catholic loyalty to republican forms of government such as the Weimar Republic thus remained suspect, since all forms of government in this neo-scholastic edifice were by definition transitory and little more than "historical contingencies." Hitler's promises to sign a concordat that would preserve the freedoms of the church and guarantee the existence of confessional schools proved to be a deadly temptation. Once the Nazis promised, however duplicitously, to help German Catholics realize goals unattainable under the Weimar Republic such as state guarantees for confessional schools, tepid Catholic support for liberal democracy evaporated almost overnight.

Böckenförde's discoveries reinforced his sense that he belonged to a "younger" generation of Catholics whose elders had not told the truth about the era of National Socialism. The truth, he concluded, had been "repressed."[112] But bringing the truth of Catholic conduct in 1933 to light meant risking a firestorm. For his article to be credible, Böckenförde would have to name names. Weinberger had only used initials in his exposé, although it had taken little imagination to decipher these. It was also utterly foreseeable that many of those prominent Catholics in the professoriate, ecclesia and world of organized lay Catholicism still alive would prefer to have their onetime words of support remain buried. For this reason, the controversial jurist and legal philosopher Carl Schmitt, who served as a mentor to the young Böckenförde in the 1950s, wagered that his mentee's exposé would never appear in print.[113] Schöningh himself, after reading a rough draft of this article, urged his nephew to cut back its first half listing names and expressions of enthusiasm and expand its second half explaining their unvarnished support.[114] In so doing, he would avoid "the impression of an after-the-fact denazification."

Böckenförde, however, chose not to alter his article's structure. Instead he adopted three additional "safety mechanisms."[115] He added potentially relativizing historical details in his footnotes. He asked the finest specialist available – Rudolf Morsey – to correct the page proofs, and the young historian duly did so.[116] He increased the number of offprints to forty and sent them (along with a few lines of apology) to many of those singled out for their expressions of enthusiasm.[117] He also sent offprints to two bishops, Keller and Julius Döpfner of Berlin, with the assurance that his article was not a broadside against the church but the launch of a painful but necessary discussion.[118]

This was all to little avail. The new issue of *Hochland* appeared in mailboxes, libraries and church reading rooms in early February 1961, and for the Catholic intellectual elite, Böckenförde's article was a bolt out of the blue. Böckenförde himself spoke of having unleashed a "mid-range earthquake." Less than two weeks after the article appeared in print, Morsey reported back that it was generating an enormous echo, particularly in southern Germany.[119] One week later, it had completely sold out, and *Hochland* had to quickly print off 3,000 additional copies to keep up with demand.[120] Within months, it was translated into English and published in the American Catholic journal *Cross Currents*.[121] It generated more than twenty-five commentaries bearing titles like "A 'Hochland' Legend" and "Führer's prelates" in well-regarded newspapers and magazines catering to a well-read and intellectual readership including *Der Spiegel*, *Echo der Zeit*, the *Süddeutsche Zeitung*, and the *Rheinischer Merkur*.[122]

Two of these stood out for their vitriol, leaving little doubt that Böckenförde's article had touched a nerve. Hans Peters launched an impassioned denunciation on the pages of the *Kölner* and *Bonner Rundschau* that disintegrated into personal attacks.[123] He dismissed Böckenförde as a "pseudo-scientist." He even placed quotation marks around the word "historian" when referring to his nemesis, excoriating "jurists who take the stage as historians." He "sharply condemned" Böckenförde's one-sided attempt to denigrate the resistance of the Catholic faithful.

The sharp-tongued historian Hans Buchheim went further. A veteran of the Eastern front born in 1922, Buchheim had been writing expert opinions for the Institute for Contemporary History in Munich since 1951, including one on the restitution of church property confiscated by the Nazis.[124] He was also researching the history of the Nazi police state, a project consistent with his interest in the structures of totalitarianism. But his work betrayed many of the inconsistencies of early scholarship about a regime only sixteen years defunct. Scholarship required objectivity, he argued – but only those who had experienced life under a totalitarian regime could actually understand it.[125]

Figure 3.3 An article by Ernst-Wolfgang Böckenförde, the future justice on Germany's highest-ranking Constitutional Court, set off a historical firestorm in 1961. Courtesy of Iris Fleßenkämper.

Such inconsistencies found their way into his criticism of Böckenförde's article, which in his estimation boiled down to a polemic against the German bishops. In his attack on Böckenförde, he took up a mantra also deployed by Peters, one that was a staple for many in the German historical profession looking back at the past: historical reconstruction of traumatic pasts required empathy.[126] Instead of standing in judgment over their subjects, historians needed to feel the sweat and pangs of delegates who for years had operated under the shadow of civil war. Buchheim accordingly penned an "empathetic" portrayal of the situation in 1933 in a rebuttal published in *Hochland*, which after the death of Schöningh in December 1960 had a new editor.[127] He was, however, less empathetic toward Böckenförde, whom he charged with "negligence," even describing one of his arguments as "blasphemous."

Böckenförde also received nearly a hundred personal letters, many laudatory, others critical and even excoriating. Julius Döpfner and

Michael Keller minced no words, directing their ire directly at Böckenförde's person: "I am truly concerned," Keller wrote, " – forgive me if I express this so openly – that, if you continue to go down this path, your love of the church could gradually become cold and you would feel one day to your own horror that the church is no longer your home."[128]

Böckenförde's article thus unleashed invective and personal criticism that went far beyond anything generated by Morsey and Weinberger in their wave of publications from the previous three years. Böckenförde and Weinberger had even singled out many of the same prominent Catholics in the ecclesia and academy. Yet Weinberger's exposé of Catholic complicity had been greeted with utter silence, the editorial team expecting a torrent of obloquy but receiving not a single response.[129] A similar process of cross-fertilization had also been at work between Morsey and Böckenförde. In his work on the collapse of the Center Party, Morsey drew directly on suggestions by Böckenförde in his essay from 1957 to explain a "certain disappearance of democratic substance" in the Center Party after the election of Kaas as party leader. The party, he wrote, could adapt to democratic or conservative "developments" and ultimately chose the latter, as it by no means saw "Fascism" as its a priori deadly enemy.[130]

Why Böckenförde's Article Became a Watershed

So why did Böckenförde's work and not that of pioneers like Weinberger or Morsey unleash such a seismic shift? It was certainly true that since the publication of Weinberger's article and the Ulm trials in 1958, many intellectuals and journalists were engaged in soul searching over the question of responsibility for National Socialism. But Morsey's publications had appeared in print only months before Böckenförde's article.

Making this watershed possible were factors more narrowly political and ecclesiastical. For starters, Morsey's account of the end of the Center Party appeared in an 800-page volume that critically eyed the collapse of all the political parties in Germany in 1933 – and not just the Center Party. Böckenförde's work lacked this potentially mitigating backdrop. It put forward a broader definition of the church, one that assumed a unity of the kind Neuhäusler had triumphantly asserted in *Cross and Swastika*. For Böckenförde, German Catholicism at the end of the Weimar Republic was "a social group bound together to a singular political will, one firmly united on a religious-ideological foundation and organized in numerous professional and class-based organizations." Consistent with this definition, Böckenförde directed greater fire against those at the apex of this hierarchy – the bishops – who enjoyed a "predominant position" in the aftermath of the Kulturkampf.[131] Morsey, in contrast, pointed the finger at the foibles and miscalculations of the Center Party politicians, most of whom, with the notable exception of Ludwig Kaas, were laity.[132] For many loyal Catholics, politicians from a disgraced Republic were fair game, but open criticism of the hierarchy was still taboo. As one outraged critic of Böckenförde summed it up on the pages of the *Deutsche Tagespost*: do the German bishops from 1933 have to be retroactively denazified?[133]

But for some endorsing Böckenförde's arguments, breaking the taboo – and what they regarded as a code of silence about the Nazi past – was precisely the point. In an article appropriately titled "The Taboos in Catholicism," the Austrian dramatist and cultural historian Friedrich Heer rejoiced in tearing down taboos, even if it meant reaping opprobrium from "taboo-representatives" within the church.[134] Heer and his fellow left-wing Catholic travelers embraced provocation, undoubtedly because their carps at the hierarchy from the second half of the 1950s onward had seemingly done little to change attitudes on social justice and war. It seems that Böckenförde's "extremely serious accusations" against the church reminded critics like the cathedral canon of Cologne, Josef Paulus, of such effrontery and that they reflexively pigeonholed him into the drawer reserved for left-wing church critics.[135] As a serious and principled young intellectual, Böckenförde was, in fact, opposed to anything resembling facile armchair moralizing, a point that he and the editors at *Hochland* found necessary to reiterate after the fact.[136] Deploring the strident ad hominem attacks found in Hans Peters' broadside on Böckenförde, Morsey wrote to the director of the Catholic Academy in Bavaria to call for a new approach for dealing with criticism: "It is unacceptable to work with suspicions instead of arguments."[137]

Böckenförde's portrait of enthusiastic Catholic politicians, academics and churchmen seeking to build bridges to National Socialism ran contrary to the self-understanding of the CDU as a party born out of resistance to National Socialism. And this factor seems to have been at the core of Professor Hans Peters' broadside. Peters had been a Center Party delegate to the Prussian parliament in the spring of 1933. By his own admission, he had been in contact with all of the German bishops in 1933. That same year, Peters also joined the Görres Society, an organization of Catholic academics with roots in the German Empire. He was elected its president in 1940, just one year before its dissolution on the orders of the high-ranking SS leader Reinhard Heydrich. In response, he delivered a courageous four-page letter of protest in 1941 to Wilhelm Frick, the Minister of the Interior.[138] In 1945, Peters became one of the co-founders of the CDU in Berlin. An outspoken defender of natural law, he defended the Reichskonkordat's validity before the justices of the Constitutional Court in 1956.

Peters' words, values and deeds thus served for Böckenförde as the perfect embodiment of Catholic "aspirations" and "conduct."[139] This meant complicity and "bridge-building" in 1933, resistance only later in the Third Reich. Not surprisingly, the critical mirror that Böckenförde held up to Peters was not to the elder statesman's liking. In his article from 1961, Böckenförde had singled out the Görres Society as one of the many orders, societies and ancillary organizations that had gone far beyond the norms of diplomatic caution in voicing its support for the National Socialist regime.[140] In a rebuttal published in the 1962 issue of *Hochland*, Böckenförde too made his criticism explicitly personal, quoting from his nemesis' speech before the Prussian parliament on May 31, 1933: "There definitely exists the possibility and chance for Catholics in the Third Reich to incorporate their worldview (into National Socialism) and we certainly have to work on this."[141]

Böckenförde's entire article was premised on the fact that Catholic acceptance of the Nazi regime stemmed, at least in part, from the Nazis' willingness to grant longstanding Catholic demands for specific ends like denominational schools derived from natural law principles. And natural law was the principle most dear to this aging constitutional theorist, the foundation on which national rebirth in 1945 rested.[142] For Karlsruhe, Peters had composed an expert opinion for the federal government and taken to the stand in defense of denominational schools and the Reichskonkordat. In his attack on Böckenförde, it seems that Peters was reliving the battle before the court, his scathing response more redolent of a closing statement in the adversarial setting of a courtroom than of a scholarly review. Peters reiterated his defense at Karlsruhe of the need for this treaty: it represented "the last chance" to allow the National Socialists at the helm of the new government "to develop into mannered human beings and decent partners." Peters even ventured a defense of the Enabling Act, whose validity was also an issue before the court. "The acceptance of this law under firm guarantee from the side of the government, but the strict rejection (of this law) as well seem to me even today to be both defensible."[143]

And here, Böckenförde had also done something that Morsey had categorically refused to do: draw lessons from the past and make them "applicable to the present and to the future."[144] For Morsey, the "sad final chapter" of the Weimar Republic had been "closed for good."[145] For Böckenförde, in contrast, this was emphatically not the case. As he was to put it in the final line of his article from 1961: "Or can one seriously say that the positions and political principles which led to the errors of 1933 have been overcome in the German Catholicism of today?"[146] And his critics took umbrage precisely with claims that Catholics would accept democracy only if it allowed them to realize principles derived from natural law. Cardinal Julius Döpfner of Berlin wrote him personally to say: "I cannot see in your work any objective depiction of the historical events of 1933 pertaining to the church. Rather, I am forced to come to the opinion that you select events and one-sided interpretations with the goal of confirming your pre-established, a priori and, in part, questionable theses about the church, the task of the hierarchy and the position of Christians in the world."[147] Bishop Keller of Münster expressed this view in even stronger terms, claiming that Böckenförde was trying to "prop up" with a thesis that "in this form and in my estimation cannot be reconciled with the teaching of the church."[148]

The timing here was critical, for 1961 was another election year. In the upcoming federal elections in September, the CDU's historic majority was at stake and the SPD was poised to make major gains. The present-mindedness in Böckenförde's approach thus made it far more likely that anticlerics in the two major opposition parties – the FDP and SPD – would latch on to his work. Morsey had written about the missteps of Center Party politicians, many of whom had died, gone into exile or retired from politics altogether. The reputations of those with still active careers in the CDU such as Helene Weber or Christine Teusch stood to take less of a hit, since in the initial intraparty vote on the Enabling Act they had been in the minority of twelve to fourteen refusing to grant Hitler dictatorial powers.[149] In contrast, some with unflattering quotations brought to light by Böckenförde had assumed or remained in high-ranking positions in the politics, society and ecclesia of the Federal Republic. Professor Jakob Hommes had just been appointed chancellor (*Rektor*) of the university in Regensburg in 1959. Michael Schmaus held the chair for dogmatic theology in Munich from 1945 to 1966 and had served as rector in 1951–1952.[150] Edmund Forschbach, who had served as a leader of the Catholic student fraternities in 1933, became a press secretary for Adenauer in 1955 and was still occupying a director post in the Ministry of the Interior.

Ironically, Böckenförde had sought to head off the possibility that his article might be used for political mudslinging or grandstanding. Böckenförde accordingly wrote to Herbert Wehner, a well-placed leader in the SPD, urging him not to exploit his article for propaganda purposes.[151] This was a discussion, he insisted, that needed to take place within the church itself. But he was too late. Already in February 1961, Bernhard Leverenz, the Minister of Justice in the northern state of Schleswig-Holstein and a loyal FDP man, sought to make political hay out of Böckenförde's revelation that the "constant anti-liberal stance of the Catholic church" had benefited National Socialism.[152] The SPD magazine *Vorwärts* also went on to publish a summary of his article.

It was, then, political and personal ties that helped determine whether these exposés of the Catholic past in 1933 became the subject of excoriation or serious reflection. Morsey had worked with Peters in the Böhler circle and with Buchheim in giving lecture tours at Roman Catholic student groups, and it was unlikely that they would publicly turn against a colleague who since 1958 had come to enjoy the support of the influential former Center Party delegate, Heinrich Krone. Krone was now the head of the CDU-CSU delegation in parliament and enjoyed the nickname "Papa Krone" thanks to his facility as a political broker.[153] Krone was aware of Morsey's plans to put together two reference works, one on the "Center Party and its Impact in the German Republic" and the other on the CDU-CSU and its "Ten Years in the Government" and "its Ten Years of Responsibility."[154] In Morsey's words, the latter volume could serve as a "solid foundation for the preliminary work for the next parliamentary election."[155]

More than a year later, the influential CDU leader distributed 400 offprints of Morsey's account of the Center Party collapse, a step that undoubtedly ensured that potential criticism from the ranks of the CDU-CSU was not publicly aired.[156] In January 1961, Morsey's work was also profiled in the official Bulletin of the Federal Press and Information Bureau, for it was also apparent that Morsey saw the present more sanguinely than his younger colleague, Böckenförde. [157] Writing nearly two decades later, Morsey made it clear that the Federal Republic was a success story. He gave credit to representatives of postwar political Catholicism who had drawn the relevant lessons out of the collapse of the Center Party and identified with democratic values.[158] To a significant extent, acceptance for critics of the church's conduct during the Nazi era fell along party lines. A decisive criterion was how they stood toward the politics and values of Adenauer's CDU.

The Creation of the Association for Contemporary History, 1960–1962

It was indeed party lines that helped shape mechanisms of inclusion and exclusion for younger scholars researching the Catholic past from the Nazi era. But inclusion into what? Exclusion from what? The controversy over Böckenförde's article unfolded just as Morsey, Schauff, Krone, Kupper and Karl Forster, the new head of the Catholic Academy in Bavaria, were planning a conference to bring together surviving Center

Party delegates from 1933 and a select group of younger scholars. Facing a paucity of written sources from 1933 (for obvious reasons, many written records had been destroyed in 1933), these planners realized that their best chance at discovering what had transpired in the meeting rooms of the Center Party in 1933 lay in persuading those politicians to share their recollections.

Johannes Schauff served as the master architect, hoping to use the conference to launch something more ambitious, the Catholic historical institute that had been in his mind for years. Such a major undertaking, he recognized, would take a village. But Schauff was, in the words of Morsey, a consummate networker who seemingly "knew everyone."[159] He accordingly tapped Karl Forster in early 1960, knowing that his new Catholic Academy – a window to the modern world – could provide organizational support and possibly even space for offices, books, documents and conferences.[160] Schauff also needed money. No doubt for that reason, he turned to Krone. Krone had helped arrange the funds for Bernhard Stasiewski's research and was the ideal person to provide a base of support within the CDU-CSU.[161] For scholarly expertise, Schauff brought on board Morsey, the best-versed researcher in the field. By October, they drew up a formal list of topics, speakers and just under seventy participants, including representatives from the state parliament, Bavarian People's Party and Center Party as well as clergy, historians, jurists, academics and politicians.[162]

But all of this was easier said than done. At several points in the lead-up in the late winter and early spring of 1961 and following the publications by Morsey and Böckenförde, it seemed that their plans might flounder because of the reluctance of some former Center Party leaders to enter into critical discussions with younger and presumably more critical historians. These former leaders included even Krone, whose misgivings, he informed Schauff, were piling up.[163] For him as well as Christine Teusch, a Center Party delegate in 1933 and Minister of Culture in Northrhine-Westphalia from 1947 until 1954, confidential discussion of this sensitive topic was impossible in front of more than sixty participants; optimal would be fifteen.[164] Both specifically objected to the presence of gentlemen too young to have taken part in the events to be discussed. By this, they meant historians on the list like Deuerlein and Morsey ostensibly too beholden to written documents from the past.[165] Ideal for Teusch was an exclusive gathering of former Center Party politicians.[166]

And yet for the team that Schauff had assembled, the costs of not going forward were too high. The controversy generated by Böckenförde's article had given greater urgency to the topic.[167] Doing nothing risked ceding the floor to church critics like Gordon Zahn, Adolf Arndt, Karl Dietrich Bracher, the professional anticleric Avro Manhattan and propagandists from the SED, all expressly mentioned by name in conference and historical institute blueprints.[168]

Faced with reluctant witnesses, Schauff, Morsey and Forster had to decide whom to invite and exclude. Forster penned an invitation intended to assuage fears.[169] He made no attempt to hide the fact that younger Catholics would be taking part in the conference. The "younger generation of Catholics," he pointed out, was "strongly interested" in gaining clarity about the course of events at the end of the Weimar Republic. But he also took pains to differentiate younger Catholics like himself or Morsey interested in "the full historical truth" from ideological opponents. Communist functionaries, he noted, were exploiting historical documents for their "unscrupulous propaganda." "Left-wing Catholic" arguments about "the political responsibility of Catholic Christians" were ripping events out of context and leading to "erroneous judgments." And hence those "intending harm" or "those not invited" were not to be allowed in. This was to be a closed-door gathering of only those with truly "something to contribute" – and even his letter of invitation was to be kept confidential.

In reducing the number of participants to approximately thirty, the planners left off the list those most likely to meet with disfavor.[170] Böckenförde was not invited, as much as Alfons Kupper had wished to include him.[171] Nor was he invited to a follow-up conference in September 1962, "The Political Activity of German Catholics, 1928–1934." Both Forster and Morsey opposed the second invitation, fearing – undoubtedly correctly – that the politicians, unsettled by Böckenförde's presence, would not have spoken freely.[172] No doubt for the same reason, Hans Müller, who had asked Forster for an invitation and whose name might have been familiar because of his work editing the proceedings from Karlsruhe, was kept out.[173]

But even these steps were not enough to persuade elder statesmen like Krone and Christine Teusch. Schauff had to intervene personally.[174] He met with an influential German Jesuit in Rome, Cardinal Augustin Bea, SJ, and, it seems, persuaded him to lend his support for the creation of a Catholic historical institution modeled after the Institute for Contemporary History in Munich.[175] After he sent a telegram to Teusch and a handwritten letter to Krone, the latter came on board.[176] Forster even persuaded him to contribute 2000 Deutschmark from the CDU-CSU caucus, Krone having done something similar for the new Catholic Academy in Bavaria.[177]

The conference took place on May 8 and 9 in the Burkardus House in Würzburg. Forster had to bar entrance to a reporter from *Der Spiegel*, who had shown up uninvited, having presumably learned about the conference through some misleading reports issued by the Bonn Press Service earlier in April.[178] The planners structured the conference around four lectures, two per day, including one by Morsey.[179] But they reserved just as much time for formal and informal discussions between the participants, where most of the action took place.[180]

Fireworks occurred on the second day following a lecture from a young historian not originally scheduled to attend. This was Konrad Repgen, who would quickly rise in stature to become the head of the new historical institute and its public face for decades.[181] Repgen was filling in for the overcommitted Hans Buchheim, who, though able to attend, lacked the time to prepare the scheduled lecture, "German Catholics and the State Crisis after 1930."[182] This topic was not yet Repgen's forte. He was completing a second dissertation (*Habilitation*) on papal diplomacy during the Thirty Years' War and preferred to turn the task over to a more qualified scholar, as interested as he was in the topic.[183] But as Morsey would admit in a blunt acknowledgment of the paucity of Catholic academics: there was nobody else to whom to turn.[184]

Repgen duly delivered his lecture, one eighteen pages in length and intended to spark discussion.[185] That it did, for in the ensuing free-for-all, Krone launched an attack on the absent Heinrich Brüning, who had been unwilling to leave Vermont to attend. One participant interpreted Krone's criticism as an attempt to shunt responsibility away from Kaas.[186] Krone responded that the time had not yet come to speak publicly about a conversation between Brüning and Pope Pius XI.[187] Repgen rose to contradict the senior CDU statesman with the rousing cry: "The truth must come to light!" With some understatement, Krone noted in his journal that evening that he had reaped the displeasure of some of the "young historians." But at the close of the conference, Krone reiterated his position. At a time of decisive struggle between East and West, he opined, those working through the past had to be extremely conscious of when and where to raise such difficult questions, particularly when the Vatican was involved. Otherwise, he insisted, such historical reconstructions would become tools of Communist propaganda.[188]

The Würzburg discussions provided the momentum for launching the Association for Contemporary History.[189] Constituted in the fall of 1962 after consultation with the Central Committee of German Catholics and the Catholic Office in Bonn, its two boards consisted of a mélange similar to that found at Würzburg – politicians, intellectuals, journalists and academics, some of whom had been involved in the concordat fight of the 1950s.[190] Of the seventeen members of its academic board of directors, just under half had taken part in the conference in Würzburg, including the historians Repgen, Morsey, Deuerlein, Stasiewski and Hans Buchheim.[191] Repgen would go on to be elected its first director (*Erster Vorsitzender*) in 1962.[192]

Though some individual members of the academic board of directors were members of the CDU or CSU, its ten-member board of trustees (*Kuratorium*) was more overtly colored by ties to politics and, to a much lesser extent, the ecclesia. It included Hans Berger, the ambassador to Denmark who from his previous high-ranking position in the legal wing of the German Foreign Office had played a significant role in transmitting communications in the imbroglio over the concordat. In its ranks was Prelate Wilhelm Wissing, Böhler's successor as head of the Catholic Office in Bonn; he was charged with cultivating ties between the ecclesia and the state. The board of trustees also included two CSU politicians in addition to the former Center Party politicians Johannes Schauff and – most surprisingly – Hans Peters.[193] Peters undoubtedly had been chosen because of his position as the head of the venerable society of Catholic academics, the Görres Society, even though his anger at Böckenförde's article had deepened his animosity toward contemporary history.[194]

Why did the composition of these two boards matter? The new historical association would show the same balancing act between partisan politics and impartial scholarship that had characterized scholarship from its "side" ever since Karlsruhe. This meant that the choice of topics was often dictated by the currents of politics. In the early years of the new Association for Contemporary History, this meant a disproportionate focus on the Reichskonkordat and the diplomacy and politics leading up to the fateful collapse of 1933. Approximately half of its documentary editions and monographs from its early years dealt with the period from 1930 to 1934.[195] One of its first proposed projects was to be a documentary edition edited by Alfons Kupper on the signing of the Reichskonkordat in 1933. In drawing on collections from various Reich ministries, this volume was intended to allow the discussion that had been going on since the deliberations in the Parliamentary Council in 1948–9 to move to a new level.[196]

More fundamentally, with this network of scholars and sponsors forged in the strife over the concordat in the mid-1950s and the early 1960s, the tone from these political and ideological struggles frequently carried over into the new institution. To be sure, not all of its members were bellicose partisans. Morsey continued to work with scholars from other sides of the political spectrum. But others like Deuerlein were hardened fighters with no hesitations about calling out the errors of fact and judgment by ideological foes. The same would become true of its new head,

Konrad Repgen, who would gain a reputation in the coming decades for his pugilism. Characteristic was a politicized way of thinking – a binary division into "our side" and "the other side" and a heightened sensitivity to ideological opponents' criticism.

The composition of the boards mattered for an additional reason: this new institution was a historical association – and not a historical institute. To non-Germans, this would seem to be a hair-splitting distinction, but the differences were, in fact, significant. Contrary to some initial hopes, the Association for Contemporary History did not become a carbon copy of the Institute for Contemporary History in Munich, which had its own building, paid director, professional archivists, paid team of researchers and paid secretarial staff. The association was instead a modest undertaking, one more in keeping with the model of historical associations dating back to the nineteenth century. It lacked its own building. Until 1972, it was officially based out of the newly created Catholic Academy in Bavaria, its finances overseen there. Its board members were all volunteers and dispersed across the Federal Republic. While the board of trustees did agree to hire an archivist in its first meeting on December 17, 1962, it was individual members of the association who took responsibility for overseeing particular publication projects.[197] It had no specialists in public relations in its ranks.

Relying primarily on volunteers who were either retirees or fully employed elsewhere had a deleterious impact on the new association's influence: it slowed down the pace of publications. Alfons Kupper published his documentary edition not as planned in 1962 but in 1969 after having twice broken down physically.[198] Though Cardinal Frings and Lorenz Jaeger of Paderborn had been prepared to grant him financing for either a Habilitation or full-time research into the origins of the Reichskonkordat, he had opted to enter the world of high school teaching, having a growing family to support.[199] Bernhard Stasiewski became a professor at the University of Bonn for modern church history in the fall of 1962. His major love remained the study of Eastern Europe and not questions of church and state during the Nazi era. His delays in putting together his documentary editions of the papers of the German bishops, in turn, became a major irritant.[200] His volumes were published only piecemeal beginning in 1968, and even these came to fruition only under duress and through significant help from others in the association.[201]

By this time, moreover, public interest in the Reichskonkordat had waned, even at historical institutions like the Institute for Contemporary History. Even already in 1962, it negatively reviewed a proposal for funding this volume on the Reichskonkordat that had been submitted to the Federal Ministry of the Interior.[202] The proposed research was no longer germane. The new Association for Contemporary History, by virtue of its personnel, administrative structures and painstaking insistence on detail, would simply not be in a position to respond immediately and fully to the criticism that would emerge in the first four years of its life from 1962 through 1966.

Conclusions

It was questions of church-state relations that in the late 1950s and early 1960s led a handful of mostly younger scholars to research the Nazi past they experienced either as children or teenagers. These were proxy wars, even if participants would have been reluctant to identify them as such; many with criticisms of the church's political tactics simply projected them back from the Federal Republic to the last years of Weimar. For Ernst-Wolfgang Böckenförde, this younger generation of German Catholics was aiming for nothing less than reshaping the political landscape of the Federal Republic. Reexamining attitudes from 1933 was about making the church's acceptance of democracy unconditional and no longer contingent on the extent to which parliaments were able to enact legislation consistent with Catholic natural law teachings. It was about making it possible for Catholics to vote for all political parties, including the SPD. His spotlight, by definition, shone exclusively on the Catholic and not the Protestant past.

Fittingly, many scholars found their interest in the church's past piqued by the legal battles over the Reichskonkordat. It is hardly surprising that the networks that took shape were often extensions or modified forms of those constructed for Karlsruhe. Emerging by 1962 was a rechristened network of former Center Party politicians, CDU officials, churchmen and younger scholars. On the other side were younger scholars from the Catholic left who found platforms in the well-respected journal *Hochland* or the dimly regarded *Working Papers of Catholic Laity*.

Younger scholars entering this terrain either chose sides or found themselves, willingly or not, put into a particular camp. Some on the Catholic left, pigeonholed into categories of nonconformity, earned the opprobrium of high-ranking officials in the ecclesia. In being excluded from the mainstream network of Catholic scholars, they lost out on two perks: a privileged access to sources and Catholic publishing houses. To no surprise, informal webs of assistance and support would emerge between those scholars left out. Böckenförde, as we shall see, would provide invaluable assistance to Gordon Zahn and develop a strong working relationship with Guenter Lewy. Themes of nonconformity would pervade future scholarship on the Catholic past.

But the new Catholic network was in many ways also disadvantaged and marginalized, at least in comparison with the Protestant-dominated mainstream historical profession. The numbers of active scholars were few, their resources comparatively scarce, its tone defensive. There were certainly reasons for this. The secular news media was eagerly taking up the issue of the church's past, the Hamburg newsweekly *Der Spiegel* discovering a particular knack for transforming the substantial into the sensational. The new network, lacking effective public relations experts, found itself ill-equipped to respond when the popular press exploited scholarly revelations.

The media indeed was to feast on a chain of stories between 1961 and 1965 that unfolded in rapid succession. Piece by piece, the building blocks of the heroic Catholic narratives sculpted by the likes of Johannes Neuhäusler and Walter Adolph were being chipped away, each chink more gouging than the last. Though still holding on to claims that asserted Catholics had "valiantly resisted Nazi pressure and proven to be the most convinced opponents of National Socialism," Böckenförde undercut myths of Catholic opposition in 1933. Gordon Zahn whittled away the idealized picture of the church's conduct during the Second World War. Rolf Hochhuth hollowed out the pontiff's moral authority. Guenter Lewy cut out what was left, arguing that Catholic resistance, too little too late, emerged only when the church's survival and interests were at stake.

All of this transpired before a mass, international audience. The new Catholic historical association, itself a work in progress, could muster little in response. The burden of defense would thus fall once again on those who had first taken up the charge in the immediate postwar era and created these narratives. These were veterans of the church struggle like Adolph and Neuhäusler who resumed the fight with weapons honed during the struggles against Nazi and Communist dictatorships.

4   Gordon Zahn versus the German Hierarchy

On September 2, 1959, Gordon Zahn, a soft-spoken and unassuming sociology professor at Loyola University, Chicago, unwittingly launched a transatlantic controversy that would consume him for the next three years. He delivered a fifteen-page paper at the annual gathering of the American Catholic Sociological Association, which was convening at neighboring Mundelein College, a small Catholic women's college on the north side of Chicago. Based on material he had gathered during a Fulbright year in Germany in 1956–1957, his thirty-minute presentation, "The Catholic Press and the National Cause," examined the support of German diocesan newspapers and journals for the German cause in the Second World War. Zahn spoke of the "critical failure" of the Catholic press in Germany to guide the flock. He argued that the Catholic press had become hyper-nationalistic, publishing articles such as "A Saintly Soldier," "We Play our Part in the War," and "War, School for Sacrifice," the last of which even likened the sacrifice of soldiers to that of Jesus on the cross. In his concluding remarks, Zahn asserted that the Catholic press had joined with the secular press "in the same crusade to create a total consensus in support of the national cause."[1]

But the talk made it clear that Zahn was setting his sights on bigger fish than the Catholic press. German Catholics as a whole, he observed, had given their nearly unconditional support for the Second World War, even though it was highly doubtful that Hitler's "predatory" wars met the criteria for a just war as laid out by centuries of Roman Catholic just war teachings. Zahn insisted that the Catholic hierarchy bore partial responsibility for this failure. Bishops and cardinals had urged young Catholics to "do their Christian duty" and serve wherever the military authorities might send them in the defense of Volk and the fatherland. Zahn could only conclude that, for the Catholic hierarchy as well, the nation came first. Having faced accusations for decades that Catholics were second-rate citizens with suspect loyalties, church leaders now sought to prove their patriotism in a belated but no less fervent effort at compensation. Against the informal "social controls" of their church and formal controls of the state, German Catholics who refused to serve or showed insufficient enthusiasm risked scorn, dishonor and death.

Zahn had reckoned with the possibility that his material might lead to a blow-up. A similar paper titled "Nationalism: The 'Heresy' of our Day" had been rejected by *Thought* magazine, *The Review of Politics* and *Cross Currents*.[2] But he had presented the same paper earlier in the year before a gathering of the Rosary College Pi Gamma Mu Chapter, where it had met with a favorable response from the Chicago-based sisters. The unspectacular venue at the ACSA – a meeting of Roman Catholic sociologists at a regional women's college – was hardly the site from which to start a transatlantic ruckus. Zahn's talk, weighted down with leaden academic prose, received a round of spontaneous and loud applause at the forum itself, even if not all audience and panel members were in full agreement with his conclusions.[3]

Yet Zahn blundered. Fearing adverse reactions should higher-ups in the chancery of the archdiocese of Chicago get wind of his talk and hear distorted versions of it, he furnished the public relations office at Mundelein College with not only a summary press release but also the full text of his paper with strict instructions to release it only just prior to his presentation.[4] The Public Relations Office dutifully sent pro forma reports later on September 2 to the local press, including the *Chicago Daily Tribune*, the *Chicago Sun-Times* and the *Chicago Daily News*. These daily newspapers cut and pasted from the full text provided by Mundelein College to provide grist for the readers of their early morning editions the next day. But they did so underneath attention-grabbing headlines such as "Hitler Backed by Catholics, Scholar Says," "Bishops Backed Hitler, Study Finds" and "Catholic Clergy in Nazi Germany Draws Criticism" that distorted Zahn's position that carefully distinguished between the support of the bishops for Hitler's wars and their support for the dictator himself.[5] After reading these articles after the morning session of the ACSA, Dick Leonard, a lifelong friend of Zahn and fellow sociologist, quipped: "Well, does Zahn still have his job?"[6]

Dick Leonard was more right than he knew. The publicity given to Zahn's criticism of the German church by the leading Chicago dailies set in motion a chain of events that Zahn never anticipated. Within months, a fracas on the streets of Catholic Chicago escalated into an international melee in which the German Foreign Office, its Consulate in Chicago, the German bishops and the Vatican were involved. At the core was a transatlantic network assembled in part by Walter Adolph, who helped enlist the services of more than a dozen high-ranking Catholic officials to take on Zahn. It successfully blocked publication of Zahn's scholarly articles and books at Catholic presses. It urged the archbishop of

Chicago and the president of Loyola University to consider removing Zahn from his position as a tenured professor.

The scope and size of the network arrayed against him would seem to be vastly out of proportion to the offense – criticism of the conduct of the German church hierarchy at a gathering of sociologists. As sensational as the headlines in the Chicago newspapers had been, even these had been buried on the back pages and received few column inches. Zahn was a little-known professor of sociology at a small Catholic university on the other side of the Atlantic. His previous articles on the subject had appeared in the pages of the New York–based *The Catholic Worker* and the Jesuit weekly *America* – all periodicals with a loyal following but hardly mainstream reading even for devout Catholics.[7]

So why did these defenders of the German church pick a fight with an obscure American professor, inadvertently plucking him into prominence? And why did their collision course run so long, hard and far – from Chicago to Bonn via Berlin and back to Chicago with a stopover in the Vatican? In a classic example of a proxy war, crashing together were the personal, the political and the religious, which for the more than one dozen combatants were forged out of bitter memories of dictatorship and war. For most participants, it entailed biographies hitting head-on. This clash opened up deep wounds from the Second World War, a conflict that came to be seen as a test of fundamental religious identities and understandings. Here too it is not difficult to draw lines of continuity from searing experiences in their pasts to their involvement in historical controversies decades later.

This chapter traces the personal, political and religious journeys that turned these men into adversaries. It begins by describing Zahn's religious odyssey from the 1930s through the mid-1950s. It then shows how his research during his Fulbright year in 1956–1957 was shaped by individuals who used him for their own ends during the tumultuous West German rearmament debates. It describes how a transatlantic network was created to counter his findings and prevent them from reaching the public. Finally, it analyzes how this network's tactics boomeranged, giving Zahn greater prominence than before and raising questions of freedom of expression.

The Roots of Gordon Zahn's Pacifism

How did a professor of sociology so outwardly unassuming that he was nicknamed Professor Sominex by his students become a pacifist warrior crusading against Catholic teachings on war and peace?[8] His odyssey was one steered by warfare, poverty and faith. Gordon Zahn was born out of wedlock in Milwaukee in 1918. His mother had refused to marry his biological father, an Irish American perhaps aptly named Roach heading off to the battlefields of France in the Great War.[9] He never had contact with his absentee biological father, and his working-class family struggled, moving repeatedly for cheaper rent.

Crippling poverty never prevented the precocious boy from excelling academically. He was a voracious writer who sharpened his talents as a wordsmith for his high school newspaper.[10] It was not uncommon for him to compose each day as many as six letters, personal and professional, some more than three pages long single-spaced. Another longtime friend observed: "Even in the parlor, he would sit and write. I never saw Gordon without a tablet and pen – or *The New Yorker*."[11]

His mother and stepfather were religiously inactive, refusing to send their children to the confessional schools ubiquitous in Milwaukee.[12] He was to comment later in life that had he been educated by nuns and brothers, he would never have joined the church, a bitter commentary on attitudes he encountered later in the ecclesia.[13] He came to his life in the church outside the family. His hard-up mother worked in a local bakery. Since paid child care was not an option, she had to leave her young son in the care of the Catholic owners who lived upstairs. Gordon established a close friendship with the devout family, whose daughter reintroduced him to the faith of his baptism and became his sponsor for his return to the church.[14]

Zahn was both a convert in the broadest sense and a theological auto-didact. Such converts and saints often make trouble for the faithful through their willingness to court controversy. Precisely because of the commitment to saintliness and witness, they are frequently unwilling to defer to hierarchical superiors. Their zeal lacks boundaries, limits often instilled by formal religious instruction. Indeed, Zahn, lacking a strong confessional upbringing and formal religious instruction, found his voca-tion of pacifism while privately studying the New Testament, although he admitted at least once that it also stemmed from revulsion from watching a friend hunt squirrels with a BB gun.[15]

However it emerged, the obligation to oppose war and any Christian participation in it served as the guiding force for his life.[16] Pacifism was his profession of conscience and faith, the commitment made at baptism not merely to imitate but to become another Christ.[17] Pacifists were to place allegiance to God before family, church or nation. They were to oppose all attempts to glamorize war, remove national symbols and flags from churches and place limits on patri-otism, even risking the defeat of the nation "if the only alternative is the serious violation of God's law."[18]

Since Zahn elevated the conscience to a higher rung than church teach-ings, he invariably opened up troubling questions of conformity and dissent. Two bitter disputes from his twenties left him with little doubt that he was a gadfly with a "propensity towards perversity."[19] Months after the United States entered into the Second World War, Zahn received his conscription papers. He pled his case before the local draft board as a Catholic pacifist, only to be confronted with the objections of the tribunal's priest who vehemently argued that no Catholic could rightfully be a conscientious objector.[20] Church tradition, it seems, hardly provided a solid framework for a religiously grounded pacifism. Confronted by seemingly contradictory passages from both the Old and New Testaments on the legitimacy of warfare and state-sanctioned violence, church leaders from Augustine and Aquinas wove them into what eventually came to be known as just war theory. While never receiving the official status of a dogma or even a doctrine, this body of thought allowed war to be waged legitimately should certain conditions be met. In the Augustinian formulation, war, when ordered by a legitimate authority, had to punish injustice, redress grievances and reinstate justice.[21] In the better-known Aquinian version, war had to be ordered by a legitimate authority, be for a just cause and serve the goal of reinstituting peace.

Either unaware of or undaunted by these centuries of tradition, Zahn sent registered letters to the archbishop of Milwaukee, explaining his refusal to serve in the military and beseeching him to support his bid for conscientious objector status. He received no response. He interpreted the lack of even a pro forma acknowledgment from the archdiocesan chancery as evidence that he was the sole American Catholic to take an active stance against military service. This illusion was immediately dispelled when the decision by the local draft board was overturned on appeal and he was whisked away by bus to the forlorn Catholic conscientious objectors' camp near Warner in densely forested central New Hampshire.[22]

The isolation of Camp Warner proved the crucial launching pad for Zahn's pacifist agitation.[23] There, he encountered Dorothy Day, the founder of the Catholic Worker movement, who, in his words, helped "light the torch."[24] This notorious pacifist during the First World War had been a Greenwich Village bohemian in the late 1910s and early 1920s before converting to Catholicism in late 1927. An advocate for social change, she launched the Catholic Worker movement. Lacking official status in the church, it was a lay undercurrent of intellectual ferment beneath the tightly run ship of American Catholicism.[25] Particularly for Catholics of little financial means seeking intellectual sustenance, her newspaper of the same name became a substitute for formal education. *The Catholic Worker* thus became a logical site for Zahn to publish his first critiques of Catholic conduct in the Second World War in the late 1950s.

Looking back more than twenty years later, Zahn shockingly concluded that the Civilian Public Service (CPS) camps were concentration camps even though they lacked barbed wire, guard dogs and gas chambers. "No matter how liberal the regulations or how relaxed the discipline," he claimed, "the first priority was to gather these potentially troublesome conscientious objectors into isolated work camps, safely out of sight and mind."[26] Most galling was the recognition that their voices of protest had gone completely unheard not only by secular American society but by the "designated spiritual leaders of the American Church."[27] The bishop of Manchester, New Hampshire, it seems, objected so strenuously to the presence of Catholic dissenters in his diocese that he urged the government to shutter the camp. His request was granted, and the camp's inmates were dispersed in 1944 to Quaker-run camps in Maryland and North Dakota.[28]

A second incident confirmed his awareness of his outsider status in his adopted church. In 1946, Zahn and Dick Leonard, a fellow pacifist whom he had most likely met at Camp Simon, enrolled at St. John's University, a Benedictine college located amid the lakes and gently undulating German Catholic heartland of central Minnesota. Zahn and Leonard had previously been denied entry to two Franciscan universities after openly touting their pacifism in their applications.[29] St. John's initially had no qualms about granting both full tuition remission and work-study jobs, the same deal granted to returning GIs.[30] In the mid-1940s, St. John's had a decidedly monastic feel – a student body of less than 500, few departments, few majors and only eight laity out of forty-three professors.[31] Important decisions tended to be made in the Benedictine chapter meetings at the St. John's abbey located on campus grounds. Its faculty was overwhelmingly German American. Even so, St. John's University had a reputation as a quirky if not progressive place. It was a nexus for Catholic intellectual inquiry and liturgical experimentation where, because of its ongoing social activism that verged on radicalism, even Dorothy Day could be a regular speaker.[32]

Jumping into campus life, Zahn penned articles for the university newspaper. He reported on lectures by Oliver Kapsner, a Benedictine professor freshly returned from service as a US Army chaplain in Germany. Kapsner, he stated, found "no evidence of direct persecution of the Catholic church under the Nazi regime."[33] But during their first and what was to be their last year at Collegeville, Minnesota, Zahn and Leonard became vocal about their pacifism.[34] Their zeal aroused the ire of a number of Benedictines at the abbey, fourteen of whom like Kapsner had served as military chaplains in the Second World War.[35] In an argument reprised in his analysis of the German hierarchy, Zahn claimed that the monks were compensating for their German heritage by trumpeting their patriotism, an argument that probably had some basis in fact.[36]

Their Benedictine adversaries objected not merely to their pacifism but also to their "spiritual pride" and "hypercritical attitude toward religion and the priesthood."[37] The president of St. John's University was also the abbot; all financial decisions ran through the abbey. At the start of the 1947–1948 academic year, a formal debate was convened in the abbey to determine whether their fellowships should be renewed. At the onset of their two days of deliberation, Zahn and Leonard were banished from the residence halls, a measure that forced them to camp in a university shuttle.[38] The verdict: the troublesome twosome was to withdraw for the academic year but be granted the possibility of returning the following academic year with a guaranteed tuition remission.[39]

The two immediately transferred to St. Thomas College, another small Catholic liberal arts college in Minnesota undergoing tremendous expansion through the GI bill. They came under the tutelage of a St. John's alumnus from 1936 eking out a living as a sociology instructor. Eugene McCarthy, the famous peace activist and future Democratic presidential candidate, had entered a novitiate at St. John's Abbey in 1942 but was dismissed within a year for the sin of "intellectual pride."[40] He taught at St. Thomas between 1946 and 1948, when he launched his storied political career as a Democratic-Farmer-Labor member of the US House of Representatives. After Zahn and Leonard graduated in 1951, the sophomore congressman plied the duo with jobs at his staff headquarters in Washington, a setup that gave them the financial liberty to pursue doctorates at nearby Catholic University.[41]

Both gravitated to lauded sociologist, pacifist and social activist Rev. Paul Hanly Furfey. Zahn put together a dissertation on the social backgrounds of conscientious objectors in the CPS camps and their relative support from their religious communities.[42] While his dissertation made use of basic statistical analysis, albeit marred by errors of arithmetic as his adviser duly noted, sociology at most Catholic universities in no way resembled the methodologically sophisticated discipline of today. Its practitioners primarily sought to elucidate Catholic social doctrine. They superimposed empirical data on to the church's rich tradition of social teaching and Catholic moral theology.[43] In a very broad sense, their function was that of Catholic public intellectuals who saw it as their duty to comment on the moral and religious issues of the day.

In this vein, Zahn submitted an article, "McCarthyism: A Catholic Issue," to the Catholic magazine *Sign*. He argued that American Catholics, in supporting Joseph McCarthy, were complicit in his prevarications. The faithful, he insisted, had a moral obligation to oppose such evils. Zahn's article was rejected. In an otherwise-polite response to the editor, he could not resist pointing out the failings of the American

Catholic press in fulfilling its proper function as a guardian of morals, a telling foretaste of the theme he advanced six years later.[44]

Zahn's Fulbright Year, 1956–1957

Aside from a one-year postdoctoral fellowship at Harvard, Zahn's academic career was until the mid-1960s almost completely bound to this narrow American Catholic world, albeit one where lay activity was exploding in size and richness.[45] Zahn's intended audience was Catholic; his articles appeared almost exclusively in Catholic journals and newspapers. From 1953 through 1966, he taught at Loyola University

Figure 4.1 and Figure 4.2 These photos of Gordon Zahn taken during his sojourn in Germany in 1956–1957 capture his soft-spoken and earnest nature. Courtesy of the University of Notre Dame Archives, CZHN-04463–01 and Michael Hovey, respectively.

Figure 4.1 and Figure 4.2 (cont.)

Chicago. He would likely have remained a relatively unknown professor of sociology had it not been for a Fulbright scholarship for the 1956–1957 academic year in Germany that radically altered the course of his career.

Zahn intended to research the fate of the Catholic peace movement (*Friedensbund deutscher Katholiken*, often referred to as the *FDK*) in the Third Reich. How had a vibrant movement of more than 40,000 members strong during the Weimar Republic gone so quickly into eclipse?[46] It quickly became clear to Zahn, however, that this original avenue of inquiry was fruitless. Not only were the records of this organization largely destroyed, but the behavior of German Catholics, he concluded, showed "an almost total conformity to the war demands of the Nazi regime."[47] There were few objections to the war effort in Germany and even fewer examples of conscientious objection.

Zahn accordingly shifted his focus to Catholic complicity in the war effort, a topic bound to land him in trouble. Scarcely ten years had elapsed since the close of the war, and he was relying on firsthand interviews to launch his research. A small number of contacts, mostly former members of the FDK scattered throughout Germany, helped him tap into loose associations of left-wing Catholics who had unsuccessfully opposed the rearmament program spearheaded by Adenauer's CDU and championed by the Catholic hierarchy.[48] Zahn's list of more than sixty sources with whom he carried out often-lengthy conversations neatly summarized in his logbook reads in places as a 1956 who's who of left-wing Catholicism. It included Walter Dirks, the publicist; Alfons Erb, the future head of the German branch of Pax Christi; Franziskus Stratmann, the Dominican luminary and peace activist at the helm of the FDK before the Gestapo arrested him in 1933; and Johannes Ude, the Austrian moral theologian and lifelong companion of the pacifist Father Max Josef Metzger, executed in 1944 on orders from the notorious Roland Freisler, the People's Court judge.[49] Nearly all of Zahn's leads bore points of view on rearmament at odds with those of the German hierarchy. Some enjoyed a semi-respectable status within the German Catholic mainstream, but others, utterly alienated from church authorities and in the camp of left-wing Catholics, repeatedly clashed with church authorities over the politics of past and present.

Upping the ante was a bitter debate that had broken out in the late spring and summer of 1956 between the major German political parties over whether military service was to be made mandatory.[50] Although the right to refuse military service had been enshrined in the West German constitution in 1949, it remained unclear under what circumstances individuals could exercise this right. In a preliminary hearing before the parliamentary defense committee on June 6, 1956, Johannes Hirschmann, SJ, a prominent Catholic Jesuit, argued that Catholic moral theology would not recognize as legitimate a pacifist who rejected all forms of military service, even if his appeal to conscience was grounded on his reading of seminal texts like the Sermon on the Mount. In accordance with Catholic tradition, he could stake his claim only on the assertion that a particular war was unjust. Hirschmann denigrated appeals to individual conscience; human conscience, he argued, was a priori fallible. Those who categorically rejected war needed to ask themselves not just whether they had examined their consciences thoroughly but also "whether they were even capable of deciding such a complex question through their conscience ... "[51]

By the time of Zahn's arrival, these questions had been provisionally settled and not in the way that the advocates of strong protections for conscientious objectors had hoped. The legislation that passed in July 1956 imposed such strict restrictions that Germany's Constitutional Court, the final arbiter of such matters, had to liberalize the law in 1960.[52]

NATO's decision to equip the Bundeswehr with atomic weapons added more fuel to the fire.[53] This step predictably pitted not only the SPD against the CDU-CSU but left-leaning Catholics against the hierarchy. Since the vast but loose body of church pronouncements on war and peace had never been stamped with the official seal of dogma or doctrine, positions taken on the subject were subjected to a different level of interpretation. A case in point was Pope Pius XII's Christmas address from 1956 delivered on the heels of the Soviet invasion of Hungary. This message seemed to deny Roman Catholic conscientious objectors the right to refuse conscription when freely elected governments passed legislation making military service mandatory in times of national emergency and when facing dangerous foes.

Since this statement lacked the binding authority of an infallible papal statement, the door had been left open for public debates not only on the actual papal position itself but also on the right of Roman Catholics to disagree publicly with papal positions that lacked the seal of infallibility.[54] Resenting what they regarded as attempts to stifle and censure, Roman Catholic dissenters naturally asserted their right to speak out freely on such questions, transforming the debate into one centering on civil liberties.[55] In one attention-drawing instance, fifty-one mostly left-leaning Catholic intellectuals in Germany issued in May 1958 a public declaration that took issue not only with the CDU's atomic strategy but with defamatory attacks on church critics by ecclesiastical figures. The petitioners appealed to the bishops "to provide religious protection to the freedom of conscience that was threatened."[56]

In interviewing Catholic activists reeling from defeat after defeat, Zahn strode into a raucous climate that was a mixture of idealistic fervor, pent-up frustration and a grim determination to settle the score with figures in the hierarchy who had by their account inflicted grave wrongs on peace enthusiasts. Within three weeks of settling into Würzburg, his home base for the duration of his Fulbright year, Zahn sought out a notorious left-wing peace agitator, Professor Franz Rauhut, the mention of whose name, according to Zahn, summoned up "the kind of shoulder-shrugging references one makes concerning people on 'the lunatic fringe.'"[57] Rauhut, a lapsed Catholic who nonetheless still identified with the fold, had been outraged by the hierarchy's position on rearmament and the introduction of the draft, which he saw as part of an ominous "German satellite-slavery towards the U.S." and "a crusading spirit towards the East."[58] Several weeks after meeting with Zahn, Rauhut was the featured speaker at a boisterous gathering that climaxed with beer bottles flying toward a Catholic priest daring to express contrary positions in defense of German rearmament.[59]

A scathing controversy in the spring preceding Zahn's arrival in Germany and involving some of these activists had a decisive bearing on his research. Some of the parties to this dispute, seeking public exculpation, provided Zahn with leads and tips that decisively altered his research and scholarship. The conflict centered on Johannes and Dr. Josef Franz Maria Fleischer, two pacifist brothers from southern Baden who had been waging a tooth-and-nail struggle with the hierarchy since crossing verbal swords with Walter Adolph in January 1947 over clerical support for the war.[60] Ever since, they had been bombarding high-ranking bishops and officials in the various diocesan chanceries with manifestos, tirades and articles excoriating the church. Harangues like "The Papal Bankruptcy" had appeared in alternative left-wing newspapers, since by the mid-1950s no Catholic publisher was still willing to print them.[61] A periodical headed by a Dominican provincial, Johannes claimed, had even been shut down after publishing one of his articles.[62] In response, Johannes opened the Catholic Peace Office, a mostly one-man operation that generated numerous complaints from annoyed diocesan officials and bishops across Germany.[63]

The two brothers were consummate outsiders. So too was the Saxon-born family patriarch, Dr. Paul Fleischer, a convert to Catholicism and Center Party delegate in the 1920s from Berlin.[64] Driving their crusade was their painful memories of the past. Josef had been imprisoned for refusing to swear a loyalty oath to Hitler and vividly recalled how a high-ranking military chaplain had visited him in prison and refused to support his status as a conscientious objector.[65] Assisted by their father in his eighties, the two brothers ratcheted up their efforts in February 1956 to coincide with parliamentary discussions of Catholic plans for a military chaplaincy in the new West German army.[66] In a manifesto sent to the Defense Ministry, Josef added details to his account of his browbeating.[67] He insisted that this enraged chaplain had shouted out that "such elements were to be exterminated" and "shortened by a head."

Crucially, Josef identified him as Georg August Werthmann, the head of the Catholic Military Bishop's Office in Bonn.[68] Werthmann was a figure gaining prominence. The Fulda Bishops Conference had charged him with erecting a Catholic military chaplaincy, and he was due to be appointed head in March 1956.[69] Working closely with NATO forces, Werthmann completed a course in the chaplain's school in Washington,

DC, in 1952 and drew up plans for the military chaplaincy as both a state and religious agency, a system that remains in place to this day.[70]

From 1936 through 1945, Werthmann had served as the right-hand man of Franz Justus Rarkowski, the choleric Catholic field bishop known for blustery nationalism and blunt exhortations to Catholic soldiers to keep up the fight.[71] Working with Werthmann to set up a military chaplaincy for the Wehrmacht, Rarkowski issued many calls to arms, writing typically in 1939 that "at stake is all that is the holiest, the most honorable, the dearest and the most precious things on earth."[72] Though Werthmann refrained from voicing any dissatisfaction with his superior during the war, what can only be assumed to be simmering frustration eventually boiled over. Two years after Rarkowski's death in 1950, he compiled unfavorable comments from former Center Party leader Ludwig Kaas, describing the gruff military bishop as "an unqualified, below average and insignificant personality," apparently a widely held view among those who knew him.[73] The short and squat Rarkowski was indeed an interloper despised by his fellow bishops, who excluded him from almost all of their meetings.[74] Over the objections of the German bishops, he had been appointed field bishop in 1933, presumably by Paul von Hindenburg. According to Werthmann, the friendship between the German president and Rarkowski was so close that the military chaplain was a frequent guest at his official state dinners.[75] Werthmann, by contrast, provided the German military chaplaincy during the war with a more spiritual presence than his superior. At great personal risk, he strove to enhance the presence of Catholic military chaplains in the Wehrmacht against Nazi encroachments, even receiving a warning in 1943 from the Ministry of Church Affairs for his courier service from the Bamberger Bishop to the Papal Nuncio, Cesare Orsenigo.[76]

Fleischer's sensational accusations were fodder for an eager German press in early 1956. The *Frankfurter Allgemeine Zeitung*, one of Germany's leading national newspapers, printed an article on March 6 detailing Fleischer's allegations, a report picked up by numerous other papers.[77] Reiterating Fleischer's original charges, Professor Rauhut delivered a widely publicized talk at the Würzburger "Society for Culture and Politics," the details of which were triumphantly held up in an article by the East Berlin newspaper *Die Weltbühne* as evidence of a revival of Nazi militarism in the Federal Republic.[78] The SPD in Bavaria pounced on these reports in an assembly in Munich in April, using them to question not only Werthmann's fitness for the position but also "restorative tendencies" in the military chaplaincy and the new West German military.[79] In what seemed a *coup de grâce*, Fleischer's allegations became the subject of an investigation by the West German parliament's defense committee in the early summer of 1956.

Yet Fleischer's cause went nowhere. The parliamentary committee charged with the investigation declared the case baseless.[80] Werthmann never recounted setting foot in Tegel prison. By his own admission, Josef Fleischer had not been face-to-face with Werthmann since the war, leaving the reliability of his memory sixteen years later open to question.[81] In another public statement from February 1956, he flatly contradicted his own account, identifying Rarkowski – and not Werthmann – as the visitor to his prison cell.[82] After receiving rather ominously phrased letters from legal officials in the Munich chancery, the Munich SPD retracted its earlier statements.[83] Confronted with the discrepancies in Fleischer's new version, Rauhut issued a public declaration of regret that took back his original indictment of Werthmann. After "new" information renewed his doubts about Werthmann's alibis, he rescinded this declaration. Following renewed pressure, he reissued his declaration of regret several weeks later.[84] Werthmann bluntly concluded that Josef Fleischer, who in spite of all of this persisted in identifying Werthmann as his clerical nemesis, was nothing less than a full-fledged psychopath.[85]

How did this muddled conflict between an eccentric conscientious objector and the highest-ranking Roman Catholic military chaplain in the Federal Republic have such a powerful bearing on the controversy that would engulf Zahn three years later? His interest piqued by the treatment meted out to the aberrant pacifist, Zahn met once with Johannes, Paul and Josef Fleischer and twice with Werthmann.[86] Though the meeting with the Fleischer family revealed only mundane insights, Werthmann – to Zahn's great surprise and delight – proved exceptionally cooperative, even though Zahn made no attempt to hide his pacifist research agenda in their meetings. In fact, Werthmann went out of his way to assist Zahn in what were unmistakable efforts at exculpation.[87] He suggested to his American guest that Rarkowski may have been the clergyman who visited Fleischer.[88] He personally chauffeured Zahn by car to a meeting with Heinrich Kreuzberg, the Wehrmacht military chaplain responsible for the prison ministry at Tegel prison and tending to Fleischer.[89] Kreuzberg's leads ultimately steered him to the widow of an Austrian peasant and family man, Franz Jägerstätter, who had been executed for refusing to swear the oath of allegiance to Hitler and join the army. This tipoff led Zahn to the village of St. Radegund in Upper Austria and turned the heroic young conscientious objector into the subject of *In Solitary Witness*, the book that made Zahn's career and led to Jägerstätter's canonization in 2007.[90]

In what was likely posthumous revenge against his onetime clerical superior, Werthmann lent Zahn copies of Rarkowski's pastoral letters extolling the war effort. He continued to send the American academic incriminating documents, including copies of chaplains' magazines from the war years, as late as December 1961, even though he was well aware of the controversy that had broken out at Mundelein College more than two years earlier.[91] Before receiving these sermons and letters, Zahn had only snippets from the Catholic diocesan press from nine bishoprics that he could obtain via interlibrary loan with which to work, a laughably thin source base when compared to the scholarship of coming decades. To protect his source, Zahn desisted from mentioning Werthmann by name in his book, *German Catholics and Hitler's Wars*, even though he recounted in some detail the controversy between him and Fleischer.[92] These documents provided Zahn with what he regarded as the most damning evidence of Catholic complicity in the war effort.[93] Rarkowski, Zahn noted, enjoyed the status of a bishop. That his fellow bishops refused to repudiate his extreme show of support for Hitler's predatory wars, he concluded, stemmed from their own faith in the Nazi war effort.[94]

Yet Zahn's stay had earned him enemies. Several power players came to perceive him as part of a coterie of peacemongers that included Fleischer and three Würzburg professors – even though he had treated these left-wing agitators with a distinct reserve during his visits.[95] But this was not known to Bernhard Stasiewski, Johannes Neuhäusler and Walter Adolph, whom Zahn sought out as authors and compilers of the history of the church under Nazi rule and interviewed in the late spring and early summer of 1957. All came away with their hackles raised. Stasiewski wrote in his journal that the American sociologist seemed to be a "rather confused pacifist enthusiast."[96] After guiding him to his basement to view the documents he had stashed away, Neuhäusler apparently proceeded to lecture the youthful academic about the harsh realities of living under a dictatorship.[97] Adolph claimed to have expressed his doubt to Zahn "that he as an American would succeed in accurately evaluating the atmosphere in a totalitarian state, and the behavior of Christians who must live in it."[98]

It is not surprising that all of these future opponents read Zahn's talk in Chicago through the lens of the Cold War at its apex in Central Europe and the escalating confrontations between left-wing Catholics and the German hierarchy. Not only had the young American academic expressed agreement with the left-wing positions in the debates about rearmament and the rights of conscientious objectors. He had publicly attacked the church's stance in the Cold War. In a sermon from October 1956, Cardinal Frings of Cologne had praised the nobility of soldiers, whose virtues were an ideal preparation for Christian thinking: "To be a part of this soldier class means subordination."[99] Two years later, Zahn attacked "these troubling signs" on the pages of *The Catholic Worker*, warning about sermons from "prominent" churchmen, many Catholic, who were "pointing to the military dead of the two world wars as worthy ideals for the youth of today to follow." The same passages had already been excoriated by the East German press.[100]

The Battle Lines Are Drawn

But in 1957, Adolph and Neuhäusler naturally did not foresee the splash that their curious American visitor's findings would make. For these to jump across the pond took the intervention of two sets of newcomers from Europe still emotionally vested in the German church. After reading about Zahn's talk in the Chicago newspapers, a Hungarian immigrant married to a German doctor sent word to Otto Roegele, the editor of the Catholic newspaper *Rheinischer Merkur*.[101] Roegele contacted Heinrich Köppler, the General Secretary of the Central Committee of German Catholics, who forwarded the letter to Gustav Kafka, a specialist in church-state relations who had completed his Habilitation in Graz in law and was searching for professorial positions.[102] Kafka was an Austrian citizen, an outcast during the Nazi era because of his Jewish ancestry.[103] Shortly after the Anschluss, he fled to France and the Netherlands, but the Gestapo tracked him down after the German invasion in 1940.[104] The People's Court sentenced him to five years in a correctional facility in Graz, from which he escaped in the spring of 1945. Assuming his position in Bonn in 1956, he earned a reputation as an ardent defender of the application of Catholic natural law traditions in politics and a relentless critic of the SPD.[105] Our current task, he wrote, is to ensure that "we are not being brought into emergency situations."[106]

News of Zahn's talk spread to Walter Adolph through a different channel. Several days after his conference presentation, Zahn was given the name and address of a woman extremely upset by what she had read in the Chicago newspapers.[107] He promptly wrote Mrs. Heinz Kühn in Oak Park, Illinois, but never received a reply.[108] She and her husband instead forwarded his letter across the Atlantic to the Berlin general vicar. Less than one week later, Zahn was stunned to find leaping from the front page of *The New World*, the Chicago archdiocesan newspaper, in downtown kiosks the reproaching headline, "Support of Hitler by Catholic Bishops Is Labeled 'Untrue': Dr. Zahn's Findings Contested."[109]

What had happened? Regina and Heinz R. Kühn were two young devout German Catholic émigrés. But Heinz was racially mixed, according to Nazi codes. His Protestant father from Solingen had married his young Jewish secretary from East Prussia while serving in the German embassy in Bern in 1919. After they divorced in 1925, the six-year-old Heinz and his sister were raised by their father, sent to Protestant state schools – but also baptized Catholic.[110] Their mother also converted to Catholicism and fled to England in the late 1930s; two aunts, however, perished in the Holocaust. Heinz survived only by toiling for the State Labor Service, constantly fearing round-ups and deportation.

Only after the war did Kühn's Catholic faith flower. He had long been troubled by the fact that members of his youth organization, *Neudeutschland*, "all too often fed on the same spiritual streams that nourished the ideologies of the Nazis."[111] He put in an application to become a priest, but his bid was nixed by Cardinal von Preysing who cited a welter of career changes and two marriage engagements that had gone awry.[112] Kühn went to work instead for Walter Adolph as a journalist for the *Petrusblatt*, later becoming its co-editor. He compiled a short volume commemorating Catholic martyrs from the Nazi years and visited the United States in 1950 to study mass communication techniques under the Cultural Exchange Program.[113] One year later, he returned to America for good, together with his new wife and two young daughters.[114] Because of his limited English, he could only find work loading beer cases on trucks in Milwaukee, but as his grasp of American English improved, a succession of better-paying white-collar jobs followed, including a public relations position with the American Dental Association.[115] Although his literary output shifted to English with articles printed in *The New World, Commonweal* and *America*, he retained a strong interest in the German church, hoping to write an article for *America* on the history of the Berlin diocesan newspaper.[116]

Ordinarily calm and collected, Kühn was outraged by Zahn's allegations against the German Catholic press. His daughter observed that she had only twice seen him so perturbed: the other instance involved unwarranted criticisms of Franz Kafka.[117] Without having read Zahn's actual paper, Kühn put the wheels into motion. Notifying associates at *The New World* about his displeasure, they interviewed him, quoting him as saying that Zahn had no grasp of the situation of the Catholic press under Hitler.[118] But Kühn was not done: he dialed up his friend Monsignor Dr. Gerhard Fittkau, a fellow émigré and gifted linguist working in the Bronx. Finally having received Zahn's paper, which he concluded was "a bloody disgrace," he implored Fittkau: "And now the Schweinehund

Figure 4.3 Heinz and Regina Kühn immigrated to Chicago with their two young daughters in 1951. A diocesan journalist in West Berlin, he took umbrage at Gordon Zahn's depiction of the Catholic press during the Second World War. Courtesy of Angelika Kuehn.

wants a public apology. The German bishops should demand a public apology and retraction. See what you can quickly do."[119]

Kühn got more than he asked for. Of Zahn's antagonists, Fittkau proved most persistent and noxious. He operated so clandestinely that even Zahn did not know the identity of this chief adversary for several months.[120] One of Kühn's daughters recalled him as a rather sinister figure, a humorless cleric garbed in dark apparel incapable of small talk or lighthearted banter with the children.[121] In his many lengthy letters about Zahn, vitriol dripped off the pages. Zahn was a "fanatic totally fixed in his views," he was a "rabble-rouser who had made respectable in the Western world the traveling Communist legend of an crusading episcopate enthusiastic for war," his conclusions were "poison," his thesis "monstrous," his "indictment" of the church "outrageous." He carried on "arrogant and fanatical rabble-rousing with fuzzy pseudo-religious and pseudo-sociological arguments" and "some fanatical adepts parrot the voice of their deceitful master."[122] It is no surprise that this man of rhetorical extremes was the network member who most frequently initiated meetings, drew in new conspirators and wielded the cudgel.

But as Dorothy Day pointed out to Zahn, episodes of horrifying suffering also shaped Fittkau's behavior.[123] Like Rarkowski, Fittkau hailed from Ermland in East Prussia, a fact that may explain his sympathies for the former field bishop.[124] Ermland had been a beleaguered Catholic enclave in a Protestant fortress. Its German inhabitants had experienced horror after horror between 1945 and 1946. It was one of the first German regions to be overrun by the Red Army, an experience that fundamentally altered Fittkau. In a trenchant bestseller that had just been translated into English, *My Thirty-third Year*, he recounted the horrors that ensued after the Soviet army ravaged his small East Prussian village of Süssenberg, where he had just been installed as pastor.[125] The Russians raped untold numbers of women and young girls and deported townspeople to camps in the Russian north, where scores died, including nearly Fittkau himself. Adding to his anguish was that his beloved region had been carved up and annexed by the Poles and Russians. After his release and convalescence, Fittkau went to work for the bishop of Ermland, Maximilian Kaller, himself a refugee known as the "bishop of the homeless." Kaller had been dismissed by the new Polish bishop of Ermland Cardinal August Hlond, who claimed that Pope Pius XII had given him the authority to fire his German predecessor. Kaller passed away in 1947, and five years later, Fittkau set up shop in New York as the executive director of the American branch of the St. Boniface Society, where he ministered to German immigrants and harbored thoughts of writing a biography of his revered Bishop Kaller.[126]

Why did Fittkau and the Kühns take such a keen interest in the reprimands of an obscure American sociologist? Sensitive as they were to the fragile image of Germany in the United States, Fittkau and Adolph had immediate reasons for worry. Through the second half of the 1950s, many individual Catholics and national Catholic charities like the National Catholic Welfare Conference had sent financial donations and care packets to Berlin Catholics. One of Fittkau's main tasks in the Bronx headquarters of the St. Boniface Society was raising money to rebuild damaged German churches.[127] Both may well have been anxious that Zahn's critique, if publicized widely, might lead donations to dry up. An associate of Kafka's feared that the airing of passages from Zahn's lecture by a New York City television station shortly before Adenauer's visit to New York City might dampen enthusiasm for the Catholic chancellor.[128] Another had qualms that Zahn's arguments could damage Kennedy's election chances in November 1960, although by all accounts Zahn was a loyal Democrat who presumably voted for Kennedy.[129]

Zahn's rebuke of the Catholic wartime press was also tantamount to a personal insult for Adolph and Kühn, the two diocesan journalists. During the Nazi era, Adolph bore the slings and arrows from the Nazi press office. In the late 1940s and early 1950s, both battled the increasingly onerous restrictions from East German authorities in a diocese that straddled zonal boundaries.[130] Zahn's criticisms of the Catholic press made a mockery of their often-valiant efforts to preserve the *Petrusblatt* against totalitarian intrusions. His reprimand of the bishops for not having reined in Rarkowski was an undeniable affront to the memory of Adolph's bishop and hero, Cardinal Graf von Preysing, the most forceful advocate for a tougher course against the Nazis among the bishops. "I can remember exactly how the bishop from Berlin back then, Dr. Konrad Graf von Preysing, rejected the hyper-enthusiasm of the Military Bishop Rarkowski with sharp criticism," Adolph wrote to a new recruit in the campaign against Zahn, Father Placidus Jordan.[131] Before entering the Benedictine Order, Jordan had gained a name for himself as Max Jordan, the German American radio pioneer in the 1930s and 1940s at NBC, longtime correspondent for the NCWC News Services and German sympathizer.[132]

Equally vexing to Fittkau was Zahn's insistence that the conformist pattern of behavior shown by German Catholics during the Second World War was just as present among Roman Catholics in the United States. In a subsequent talk delivered in March 1960 for a symposium on "The Catholic Viewpoint on War and Peace" sponsored by the Graduate Student Council at Catholic University, Zahn excoriated the acquiescence of American Catholics in the atomic diplomacy of its government.[133] This issue rankled Adolph on the front lines of the Cold War in West Berlin. East German newspapers had long printed accusations exposing what they snidely called "clerico-Fascism," the alleged "league" between the church and Fascism. As part of a much more aggressive campaign against the churches between 1957 and 1961, the GDR government unleashed an avalanche of more than fifty anti-clerical publications.[134] One ninety-page brochure from November 1959 bearing the title "Preachers of Atomic Death" showed a bishop at an altar surrounded by applauding helmeted soldiers as an atomic missile soared above a crucifix under a purple Lenten sky. It trumpeted quotations from Franz Rarkowski similar to those Zahn had unearthed.[135]

Reminding Zahn of the extensive Communist arsenal of allegations of clerical support for Hitler's war plans, Adolph dreaded the propaganda frenzy that would ensue were this Eastern anti-clerical onslaught to be reinforced by the scholarship of Western critics.[136] Kafka shared these fears, having discovered from contacts in Würzburg that Zahn had "surely" made his way to most of the opponents of rearmament and atomic weaponry in the Bundeswehr.[137] No less than Dorothy Day, a staunch anti-Communist herself, admonished Zahn for his insensitivity to this reality.[138]

It was with good reason that Adolph and Fittkau were more apt to dwell on the likely political fallout from Zahn's talks and sidestep his frontal challenge to Catholic moral theology. In an article published in *The Catholic Worker* in 1958, Zahn argued that Catholic just war teachings led only to "the dead end of moral bankruptcy," since "even 99,000 out of every hundred thousand" modern wars will "certainly" be unjust.[139] For Zahn, the conclusion was obvious: "a complete refusal to take active part in such unjust wars . . . ." This "grim prospect of a retreat to the catacombs as the alternative to participation in an unjust war" meant martyrdom. Christians, he opined, had forgotten that the price of discipleship was never intended to be easy.[140]

Zahn's call for nonviolent forms of resistance to state-sanctioned wars undeniably challenged a deeply rooted ethic of obedience. But in raising the question of martyrdom, Zahn struck at a hermeneutic central to the lifework of Adolph and Kühn, both authors of works on Catholic martyrs from the Third Reich. For Zahn, it was crucial that Austrian conscientious objector Franz Jägerstätter, whom he labeled a martyr-saint, was a social deviant who openly defied the Nazis on the issue of conscription.[141] Jägerstätter the peasant, Zahn noted, had placed his fealty to God higher than his commitment to his wife, children and bishop. Such martyrs, he lamented, were now unfairly disparaged as fanatics, even though martyrs from bygone centuries with personalities no doubt equally extreme were revered in storybooks, stained-glass windows and *The Lives of the Saints*. Zahn's understanding of martyrdom was diametrically opposed to that of Adolph and Kühn, who generally extolled neither the motives nor the deviance but rather the suffering of the Catholic *Blutzeugen*, victims of the Nazi onslaught remaining true to faith and church. But the issue of martyrdom was not an issue that Adolph and Kühn were willing to address head-on. It would have meant taking on the old question of why there had been so little apparent Catholic resistance to National Socialism. More importantly, embracing Zahn's position – modern wars were unjust and Christians had the duty to resist the calls for war from secular and religious leaders even to the point of self-sacrifice and death – would have completely undermined the stance of the hierarchy in its struggle against Communism. Adolph had little choice but to dismiss Zahn as an "ideologue with little grasp of reality."[142]

Personality and biography played an equally determinative role in these battles. The leading soldiers, equally matched in tenacity, were converts and outsiders. It is hardly surprising that these qualities that lent themselves suitably to opposition against the American, Nazi and Communist regimes would be turned against each other. What united these men was a history of suffering: all had experienced privation or persecution during the wartime years because of their faith and found solace in that same faith. But these adversaries applied divergent lessons out of their own experiences of suffering and persecution to the politics of the present. Drawing on their own experiences with Communist dictatorships, Adolph, Fittkau and Kühn believed it imperative for the church to be eternally vigilant against anticlerical and totalitarian regimes. Zahn, in contrast, believed that open dialogue, whatever critical questions it might raise, provided the only hope for reforming faulty moral theologies of war and peace.

Adolph's Network versus Gordon Zahn

These men thus entered into battle with different tactics. Fittkau made an explicit point of operating under cover. As he put it, "For Mr. Zahn, every type of confrontation, even if it annihilates him scholarly, is a welcome opportunity to gain more publicity for himself."[143] Kafka likewise argued that telegrams of letters of protest would merely turn Zahn into a "martyr for academic freedom."[144] But Adolph was incapable of such restraint; the lesson from the Third Reich was that the best defense is a good offense. Zahn, in contrast, sought to make use of a critical public sphere, engaging his opponents openly in a spirit of dialogue unmarred by ad hominem attacks. He strove to maintain a dispassionate academic tenor in his writings, though even he could become strident and paranoid when backed to the wall. After he sounded off about Fittkau's conduct, Dorothy Day rebuked him: "We have enough fighting pacifists around here . . . ."[145] Zahn hid the documents gathered during his stay in Germany at friends' homes in Milwaukee, fearing targeted break-ins ordered by church officials.[146] He contacted the State Department, terrified that his enemies could jeopardize the future of educational initiatives like the Fulbright program.[147]

Such specific forebodings were absurd, but the reasons for his larger apprehension were not unwarranted. As Zahn was about to find out, his adversaries boasted more powerful connections than his scattered circle of defenders. Adolph, Kafka and Fittkau emerged as the point men in the campaign against Zahn, frequently coordinating efforts.[148] Zahn had naively forwarded a copy of his paper to Kafka, who arranged for a hasty translation that he passed on to the bishops.[149] Fittkau forwarded excerpts from Zahn's talk to Archbishop Jaeger of Paderborn, who apparently raised the issue of the troublesome American at the Fulda Bishops Conference in September.[150] Though refraining from official steps, the bishops entrusted the matter to Julius Döpfner, bishop of Berlin and Adolph's ecclesiastical superior.[151] Cardinal Wendel of München, the German military bishop, brought on board Johannes Neuhäusler.[152] Kafka also coordinated efforts with Karl Fürst von Löwenstein, president of the Central Committee of German Catholics.[153]

The network against Zahn gave itself three tasks: surveying the damage to the image of the German Catholic Church in the United States, the Federal Republic and the German Democratic Republic; countering Zahn's arguments in newspapers and scholarly publications; and preventing publication of further articles and books by Zahn. The first two were the simplest to accomplish but required the occasional assistance of the federal government in Bonn and the German Foreign Office, a sign of how closely church and state could be intertwined.

Members of this network began by launching several offensives in Chicago and Rome that made Zahn's life at Loyola perfectly miserable. Put on the defensive by Kühn's allegations, Zahn attempted to publish a rebuttal in the pages of *The New World*. His requests were stonewalled by the editor, Monsignor John M. Kelly, who accused him of "academic irresponsibility."[154] Zahn had little option but to meet with the chancellor of the Archdiocese, who took his side.[155] Ordered to print Zahn's rejoinder, Kelly appealed directly to German American Archbishop Albert Meyer. But Meyer, according to Zahn, "was determined that anyone attacked in *The New World* be given a fair chance to answer the attack."[156]

Handed a second defeat, Kelly printed Zahn's letters but defiantly tacked in a lengthy counterpoint prepared by Adolph in Berlin and translated by Kühn.[157] The following week, Kelly published a supportive letter from Paul Mundy, a sociologist at Loyola and Zahn's close friend. But he added to it a withering critique by Placidus Jordan of a post-mortem smear of "the memory of great leaders and martyrs of the faith in Catholic Germany."[158] Zahn, he stated, had "utterly fail(ed) in his attempt" to understand this small portion of the Catholic Church struggle.

Having realized that Meyer and the Chicago Chancery were protecting Zahn, Fittkau decided to pay him and President James Maguire of Loyola a personal visit to warn them of the worldwide consequences of Zahn's "rabble-rousing campaign" against the German bishops. He showed up unannounced at the office of the cardinal's personal secretary and managed to secure an appointment for the next morning after telling him that the meeting concerned a matter of great importance for the entire German episcopate and for Archbishop Meyer personally.[159] Zahn later learned that "this gentleman of the cloth" had identified himself at this meeting the next day as a personal representative of the German bishops. Fittkau told his Chicago audience that Zahn was not engaging in academic tomfoolery but playing with fire. Pointing out that his talk could and would be exploited by anti-clerical forces, Fittkau gleefully held up an article highlighting the nefarious use made of Zahn's theses in the *Voice of Freedom*, a rabidly anti-Catholic nondenominational Christian news-monthly that he had discovered just the day before in a Polish seminary.[160] This publication reminded him of the worst Nazi propaganda organs like *Der Stürmer* and the *Schwarze Korps*.[161] But as destructive as he found Zahn's theses to be, Maguire rejoined, his hands were tied: Zahn was a tenured professor with academic freedom.[162]

Complaining bitterly about this recourse to what he sneeringly referred to as "academic fools' freedom," Fittkau attempted to turn up the heat on the Loyola president.[163] He dispatched a letter that asserted that "the prestige of your University as an outstanding Catholic institution will suffer not only in the eyes of the German hierarchy and the German Catholic people if you do not find a way to disassociate the name of Loyola University from Zahn's violent pacifist campaign at the expense of the Church in Germany."[164] He also voiced his frustrations about Meyer's and Maguire's tepid response in a nine-page letter to Adolph.[165] Adolph gave a copy to Bishop Döpfner just before his departure for Rome, where he and Meyer were due to be elevated to the rank of cardinal.[166] After the ceremony, Döpfner pulled aside both Cardinal Meyer and President Maguire, who had accompanied the Chicago archbishop to the Holy City. The Berlin cardinal attempted to make clear to the Chicago duo the harm that Zahn's arguments could do to the church "especially in areas like Poland and Nicaragua."[167]

Fittkau and Adolph remained unconvinced that these two top-level Chicago clerics had done enough to rein in the errant sociologist. They evidently concluded that only pressure from the top of the Jesuit hierarchy in Rome would bring about a change of course. The German bishops had already decided against taking any significant official steps in their meeting at Fulda in September and again at the West German Bishops Conference in December.[168] And so in late January 1960, Fittkau sent a letter to Augustin Bea, SJ, the noted German biblical scholar just appointed to the rank of cardinal by Pope John XXIII.[169] At the Second Vatican Council, Bea would emerge as an ecumenical champion and architect of Nostra Aetate, the landmark document that repudiated Christian anti-Judaism. Yet contrary to his liberal image today, the eminent Jesuit was actually better known then as a theological conservative determined to uphold theological orthodoxy. On more than one occasion in the preceding decades, he reprimanded and extracted apologies from wayward German professors.[170]

And so it was hardly difficult for Fittkau to win him over to the cause. Fittkau told him that Zahn's employer was Loyola University and that the Jesuit magazine *America* had included a short and not unfavorable summary of Zahn's talk in its September issue.[171] Professor Zahn, Bea insisted in a letter to Döpfner, should be "forbidden from further such activities under threat of being fired. It is truly not acceptable that today when we have to defend ourselves with all our forces against atheism and materialism our own comrades in faith stab us in the back."[172]

Bea made good on these words. He contacted the editorial leadership at *America* to express his displeasure about its positive mention of Zahn's talk.[173] While avoiding any steps that would give Zahn additional publicity, he "made it clear" to the Jesuit provincial in the United States that the leadership of both *America* and Loyola University were to express their regret for their actions to the German bishops.[174] Such pressure forced the hand of both *America* and the university leadership. The editor of *America* personally apologized to Döpfner: "May I, on this occasion, stress to Your Eminence (as I have already declared to His Eminence Cardinal Bea), how much *America* regrets that the allusion which this Review made to the Zahn thesis in our issue of September 26, 1959, however short and indirect, not only lent itself to unfortunate misinterpretations but also incurred the very real danger of exploitation by the Communists in the East zone to the detriment of the Church in Germany."[175]

Maguire was also forced to grovel. He wrote Döpfner that he was "grieved" to learn of the embarrassment Zahn's address at Mundelein had caused the German bishops. He added that Zahn had just assured him that "every effort will be made to disassociate the university from his personal views."[176] In a private meeting, Maguire informed Zahn that he "could expect little support from the University if the affair broke open in Rome."[177] He insinuated that Zahn should refrain from publishing such incendiary material. The Loyola University leadership thus made it understood throughout its northside campus that Zahn was persona non grata. A colleague of Zahn in the Sociology Department, Ralph Gallagher, SJ, helped block publication of his paper on the pages of the *American Catholic Sociological Review*, which was publishing the conference proceedings from the ACSA conference in 1959 with financial assistance from Loyola University.[178] Student journalists at the university newspaper were given to understand that no mention was to be made of Zahn, his scholarly work and his other activities on campus.[179]

Nor did the hubbub die down soon. Pungent criticisms of Zahn's work continued to appear in Catholic newspapers and magazines on both sides of the Atlantic.[180] It was not until 1965 that a German-language publisher issued his book, *German Catholics and Hitler's Wars*, which had appeared in 1962 in the United States.[181] After the University of Massachusetts Boston offered Zahn a better-paying job with more research support in 1966, Loyola University refused to match the offer even partially – and he opted to leave.[182] Zahn had become persona non grata in a notable swath of international Catholicism. Bea could thus judge his measures a success: "Father Graham (the editor of America) has in the meantime come to see that Americans often deal with such questions simplistically and that they are lacking in historical thought. The success of the entire matter will thus be that they become more cautious over there."[183]

Further Battles

Yet it was the proverbial double-edged sword that members of this network wielded in taking on this "fanatical" pacifist. Though Zahn and his handful of supporters were outnumbered and outgunned, his adversaries generally registered successes only when operating in secret. Adolph's rebuttal in the pages of *The New World* illustrated the potential perils of bellicose public attacks and transparently apologetic arguments. In the set of talking points that Kühn had translated in a weekend and published in *The New World*, Adolph attempted to gainsay Zahn's claim that German Catholics should have known that the Second World War did not fall under traditional Catholic definitions of a just war. He argued that the

German public, aware only of the arguments that Hitler's regime presented to it, could not have known in 1939 that the war against Poland was unjust. It saw the war as an extension of legitimate foreign policy goals – undoing the "burden" of the Treaty of Versailles and protecting beleaguered German minorities in Poland. The "stubborn attitude" of the Polish secretary of state, Adolph averred, "facilitated Hitler's gamble." The German public knew nothing of a war of annihilation.[184]

Adolph transformed the defense of German Catholicism into a defense of the German nation, an argument sure to lose in the court of international public opinion. In Chicago with its large Polish population with fresh memories of German atrocities in the Second World War, it was a nonstarter. As Placidus Jordan noted with regret, Germany enjoyed few sympathies in the larger world.[185] Noting these problems, Kühn excised several paragraphs in which Adolph had described how the German army "was drawn into the war on September 1, 1939 in good faith and with the firm conviction of fighting and dying for the fatherland." He told Adolph to send his German version to "nobody here in America."[186]

Kühn's deft editing probably spared Adolph some embarrassment, but the same cannot be said for an ill-fated endeavor launched by Kafka and Neuhäusler. In late November 1959, Neuhäusler wrote to an official in the Press and Information Office of the German government in Bonn to inform him of Zahn's attacks against the hierarchy and to ask for federal help.[187] Was it not in the greater German public interest, he asked, to counter these attacks on German Catholics by subsidizing a reprint of *Cross and Swastika* and translation into English? The official in Bonn, a certain Dr. Zöller, called the German Foreign Office, which contacted its consulate in Chicago, asking it to monitor the situation.[188] It took the Chicago consulate more than a month to respond, by which time it had also received the transcript of a letter from Fittkau to Neuhäusler that claimed that Zahn had succeeded in winning the "overwhelming majority" of the Catholic intelligentsia in Chicago over to his side.[189]

By the time the Foreign Office in Bonn forwarded on a copy of the Chicago consulate's report that stated that Zahn's talk – the subject of two paltry newspaper articles – had failed to resonate with the Chicago public, Kafka and Zöller had already taken measures into their own hands.[190] The West German bishops commissioned Kafka in December 1959 to gather documentary materials from the Third Reich for use by trustworthy Catholic scholars.[191] At the behest of Zöller, Kafka's recently formed *Arbeitsgemeinschaft kirchliche Presse e.V* hosted an assembly of a hundred Catholic journalists in the Great Hall of the Foreign Office in Bonn, where Kafka delivered a report titled "Gordon Zahn and the Catholic Religious Press in the Second World War."[192] The event was sponsored by the Federal Press Office, which distributed the clunky translation of Zahn's Chicago address to the journalists. They were to use it to unearth additional documents from the Nazi era to print articles defending the Catholic press's conduct in the wartime years.[193] The gala event was initially deemed a resounding success. Zöller basked in having gleaned from Catholic press circles how Zahn had supposedly hauled in bits of information from the trio of left-wing Würzburg professors.[194]

To Kafka's chagrin, however, the home press of one of the participants, *Die Deutsche Tagespost* of Würzburg, reprinted Zahn's talk in its entirety.[195] Under fire from outraged readers, the editor justified his decision to print the talk, claiming that it was better for a newspaper friendly to the church to publish Zahn's work before the secular press, and, in particular, the controversy-loving and increasingly anticlerical newsweekly *Der Spiegel*, got a hold of this "dynamite."[196] It was through the publication in the *Deutsche Tagespost* that the secular national press, and, in particular, *Der Spiegel*, was tipped off to the details of Zahn's talk.[197] *Der Spiegel* contacted numerous individuals as well as the German affiliate of the American press with which Zahn planned to publish his book.[198] Although Zahn had wanted to send the Hamburg newsweekly a copy of his talk, the possibility that a *Spiegel* exposé might jeopardize publication of his monograph dissuaded him from doing so.[199]

It was easier for Zahn's opponents to block publication of his book. For in forwarding his talk from Mundelein to Kafka, Zahn unwittingly alerted his critics to his monograph in progress. One footnote, intended for the commentator at the ACSA, referred to *German Catholics and Hitler's Wars*. Zahn originally intended to publish it with Helicon Press, a Baltimore-based Catholic publishing house whose editor shown a strong interest in the manuscript and published his work before.[200] Helicon, however, had a German affiliate in Düsseldorf that became the target of ecclesiastical pressure once Zahn's adversaries realized the connection between the two presses.[201] Zahn learned, presumably from his editor at Helicon, that Cardinal Frings had threatened to cut its contracts with Helicon's affiliate, which published school textbooks for the archdiocese of Cologne.[202] In a letter to Döpfner, the editor of its German affiliate openly admitted to attempting to block publication of Zahn's book with Helicon.[203]

The pressure from its German affiliate effectively sealed the fate of Zahn's book with Helicon.[204] Frustrated by the growing delays, Zahn opted to publish his book with Sheed and Ward, a publishing outfit in London and New York that in spite of its reputation as an "established" Catholic house received the book with open arms.[205] Like Zahn, Frank Sheed was a religious seeker who rediscovered as a young man the Catholic faith into which he had been baptized as an infant. Though temperamentally averse to being pinned down on one side or another on the religious spectrum, this Australian native and his English wife, Maisie Ward, did have deep sympathies for Dorothy Day's Catholic Worker movement as well as the French Worker-Priest movement.[206] As a result of Sheed and Ward's marketing, sales and connections, *German Catholics and Hitler's Wars* was reviewed in a significantly larger number of scholarly journals and Catholic periodicals internationally. At the same time, a devastating assessment by Robert Graham, SJ, an associate editor of *America*, whom Fittkau had brought in to help block publication of the book in the United States with Catholic publishing houses, backfired.[207] In printing five letters including one that lambasted Graham's review as "unjust and immature," the editor laconically observed that "rarely has a critical review been so vehemently challenged as this one."[208]

Zahn's book also caught the eye of the left-liberal Rowohlt Verlag, the publisher of *The Deputy*, which in the wake of the Hochhuth scandal declared its interest in bringing out Zahn's work in German translation.[209] But his monograph did not appear in a German-language edition until 1965 since Zahn insisted on publishing it with a Catholic press. After trying unsuccessfully in 1962 to persuade the editor of the Kösel Verlag, the publisher of *Hochland*, to publish a German translation, Ernst-Wolfgang Böckenförde finally secured publication with the Austrian branch of the Styria Verlag.[210] Even then, an introduction penned by Franziskus Stratmann had to be left out. Under pressure from Bernhard Stasiewski, Stratmann's provincial in the Dominican order forbade him from appending his name to the introduction, fearing that the book would evoke a similar controversy to that launched by Hochhuth's play.[211] Until then, most exposure to Zahn's arguments in Germany came through either critical reviews, mostly in the diocesan press, of Zahn's talk from Chicago or excerpts in the dimly regarded *Working Papers of Catholic Laity*.[212] It is perhaps for this reason – some publicity is better than none at all – that Zahn somewhat sardonically wrote to the head of the KNA to express his gratitude for reprinting the Graham review in German translation.[213]

A comprehensive critical scholarly response to Zahn's arguments was late in coming, since there was no established German scholar who could provide a thorough-going rebuttal based on substantial archival evidence. Stasiewski's work was not forthcoming. Kafka and Adolph had little choice but to turn to a young theology student from Freiburg, Karl Aloys Altmeyer, who had completed a sizeable senior thesis on the Catholic press in the Nazi era.[214] Financial hardship had forced him to give up any doctoral aspirations, but still hoping for some larger recognition for his work, he summarized his findings in an article he sent to the *Rheinischer Merkur*.[215] Independently of each other, Kafka and Adolph – Adolph's contacts with this budding researcher predated the Zahn controversy – got in touch with him. Both had recognized his work's potential for their campaign against the Chicago academic.[216] They dangled before him the possibility of defraying publishing costs for a book though subsidies from the Federal Press Office or the Morusverlag, the latter eventually publishing the work.[217] They also fortified him with a copy of Zahn's talk in German translation. Altmeyer proudly announced that he had discovered thirty-four errors of fact and reference, leading Adolph to boast that Altmeyer's work would be the death knell for Zahn's arguments: "Zahn's methodology – his lack of knowledge of the sources and literature – will be exposed in a way that will probably take the breath away from the Chicago sociologist, if he still has a scholarly conscience."[218]

At the urging of his backers, Altmeyer entered into the public fray with gusto.[219] He delivered a series of critical rebuttals in the fall of 1960 that in an exchange with Zahn on the pages of the *Badische Zeitung* crossed the line into vicious personal attacks.[220] A discussion about the failure of German Catholics under Hitler would be welcome, he opined in his opening lines, were not the "dubious figure of a Gordon Zahn" standing behind it. But no less than Kafka found that that the young Altmeyer's work was unduly apologetic, having whitewashed problematic figures like Rarkowski.[221] Its publication date was put off by more than two years, and it became largely a documentary history that awkwardly spliced together 242 letters, protests and meeting minutes from the Nazi era.[222] By this point, it was too late to influence the public clashes.[223]

The irony was not lost on Zahn. The controversy that had engulfed him for more than two years centered on a thirty-minute conference presentation. His 232-page monograph generated acerbic reviews here and there but nothing to rival the rancor of the preceding three years.[224] Thanks to his adversaries, his work reached an international audience, Catholic and Protestant alike. Had he been left to his own devices, his work would have appeared in niche Catholic publications, where it would likely have raised a few eyebrows but never generated anything approaching a scandal.

Zahn's Impact

What was the ultimate significance of Gordon Zahn's quixotic struggle against the hierarchy? It exposed core identities forged in personal experiences of dictatorship and war. Even though Zahn was a trained sociologist who had been taught that empirical observation requires personal detachment, details from his own experiences during the war continually surfaced in his own scholarly work; it is hard not to read his scholarly work as an extension of his life story.[225] The title of his book on Austrian conscientious objector Franz Jägerstätter, *In Solitary Witness*, applied equally well to himself, a voice in the wilderness. Zahn's quest against the hierarchy stemmed too from his own formidable but frankly less-than-existential ordeals in the 1940s, when he alternatively battled the American government, the Catholic hierarchy in Milwaukee and the administration of St. John's University in Collegeville, Minnesota. While more careful to excise personal references from their own accounts of the Catholic past under National Socialism, Adolph and other of Zahn's adversaries likewise felt compelled to put significant parts of their life stories to paper, sometimes under their own name, sometimes under pseudonyms.[226]

At the heart of their struggle were the different lessons they applied from their suffering during the Nazi era to the intense conflicts over rearmament and atomic weaponry at the height of the Cold War. Insisting that Catholic moral theology needed to be informed by modern social science and an empirical analysis of human behavior, Zahn called into question the viability of traditional Catholic teachings of war in a new era of total and atomic warfare.[227] Expressed on the eve of the Second Vatican Council, his criticisms of church leaders' conduct during World War II served as a scarcely veiled call for fundamental theological renewal and return to the core message of the New Testament, the Fifth Commandment and the early church. Ecclesiastical leaders, he stated explicitly, had lost sight of the reality that remaining faithful to true Christian teachings in times of extreme crisis such as the Second World War and the Cold War required nonconformity; being Christian meant "a return to the catacombs" and a church of martyrs.[228]

As with that of Ernst-Wolfgang Böckenförde, Zahn's criticism of German Catholics during the wartime years was intended as the first step in a larger intra-Catholic dialogue. At the Second Vatican Council, these issues were debated – but Zahn's position was not entirely embraced. A victory of sorts – and even this was partial – came only with the statement of the American bishops from 1983, "The Challenge of Peace," for which he was a ghostwriter.[229] This document granted Catholics the right to be pacifists and sought to place limits on the use of nuclear weapons. But his greatest triumph came in 2007 while he was eighty-nine and on his deathbed, his once-sharp mind ravaged by Alzheimer's. Given word that Franz Jägerstätter had just been beatified, he shed tears of joy.[230]

In the short term, Zahn's struggles to speak out freely in the Catholic public sphere about the conduct of the German hierarchy became a test case of sorts for progressive Catholics looking to exercise their right to critical dissent. In a display of open defiance, student journalists at Loyola University arranged for the medieval and church historian on the faculty, Raymond Schmandt, to review Zahn's book on the front page of the university newspaper one day after it officially appeared in print. In an obvious dig at the Loyola administration, Schmandt noted that "where better than in a Catholic university should that concern be manifested and discussed without fear of censorship."[231]

The saga of this American pacifist thus almost perfectly mirrored those of many Catholic nonconformists in Germany during this era – and some in the German episcopate saw it the same way. In 1963, Cardinal Döpfner added the American pacifist to a list of "nonconformist" Catholics that included Carl Amery, Ernst-Wolfgang Böckenförde, Heinrich Böll and Friedrich Heer, whose literature was "religiously zealous but not actually pious."[232] Not surprisingly, Zahn's work left its greatest mark during this time on a small group of scholars and intellectuals influenced by the nonconformist literature. Some of these would soon come into their own and become sensations of the international media. A young American political scientist and Jewish refugee from Nazi Germany, Guenter Lewy, discovered Zahn's findings tucked away in *The Catholic Worker* in 1958. This account inspired him to launch his own critical research into the conduct of the Catholic Church under National Socialism in the early 1960s.[233]

The onetime Communist Erwin Piscator, who directed *The Deputy* at its premiere in Berlin, took note of the appearance of Zahn's book, exclaiming that it could "naturally serve us very well."[234] Only then did the issue of martyrdom that underlay Zahn's efforts find a sympathetic ear in the press and mass media – but it did so from the unlikely mouthpieces of a former Communist, Erwin Piscator, and a nonpracticing Protestant, Rolf Hochhuth. Poised for a counter-strike were Walter Adolph, Robert Graham, SJ, and Julius Döpfner, all convinced that their hard-edged strikes against Gordon Zahn had proven successful. In returning to the same playbook, they were about to discover that things were not going to play according to script.

5   The Storm over *The Deputy*

On February 20, 1963, theatergoers at the Free People's Theater in West Berlin watched an epic confrontation unfold. Curtain up. Act I. Riccardo Fontana, SJ, a fictional hero, meets with Cesare Orsenigo, the papal nuncio to Germany. A uniformed SS officer forces his way inside the parlor. This is Kurt Gerstein, a devout Protestant. Frantically, he tells of the murder of a million Jews at Auschwitz and his unsuccessful attempts to sabotage the gas chambers. Fontana realizes that Pope Pius XII could end the mass killings through a public protest. He promises Gerstein that the Vatican will act. But he hears nothing from the pontiff, and his frustration mounts.

Act IV. In Rome to rouse the pope, Gerstein observes German troops rounding up the Jews of Rome for deportation in October 1943. But Pope Pius XII shows little sympathy for the plight of those hunted down under his very windows. His attention is drawn instead to the dreary state of Vatican finances. "We are filled with burning concern for our factories," he mutters in a cynical allusion to his immediate predecessor's famous encyclical of 1937 condemning National Socialism, "With Burning Concern."[1] Fontana implores the pontiff to protest. Momentarily embarrassed, Pius XII only grudgingly obliges. He pens a feeble text with the circumlocutions and diplomatic verbiage of a century earlier to be published in the October 25 issue of the Vatican newspaper *L'Osservatore Romano*: "The pope's mercy knows no limits, neither of nationality, nor of religion nor of race."[2]

When a seething Riccardo accuses him of issuing a blank check for Hitler, the visibly agitated pontiff loses his grip on his fountain pen and smudges his hand with ink. He calls on an assistant to fetch a water basin with which to wash his hands. Enraged by this gesture of Pontius Pilate, the young Jesuit does what the deputy of Christ on earth would not: he embraces martyrdom. He affixes the Jewish Star of David to his breast and directs searing words at the speechless pope: "God shall not destroy his Church only because a Pope shrinks from His summons."[3] He leaves to join Jews about to be deported in cattle cars to Auschwitz.[4] A voice

153

Figure 5.1 In the climactic scene of Rolf Hochhuth's play *The Deputy*, Pope Pius XII and Graf Fontana look on horrified as Riccardo Fontana, SJ, places the Star of David on his breast and leaves to join Roman Jews about to be deported to Auschwitz. Courtesy of the Archiv der Akademie der Künste, Berlin. Copyright Deutsches Theatermuseum München, Archiv Heinz Köster.

offstage reads the words of Ernst von Weizsäcker, the German ambassador to the Vatican: "The Pope has not allowed himself to be carried away into making any demonstrative statements against the deportation of the Jews." The mass murders, the voice continues, continued for more than a year, and the last prisoners were freed when the Soviet Army liberated Auschwitz two months later.[5] Curtain down.

The breathtaking indictment of Pope Pius XII by thirty-two-year-old playwright Rolf Hochhuth amounted to the smashing of an icon. Perhaps more than any contemporary ecclesiastical figure, Pius had been venerated by the faithful. Four years before Pius' death in 1958, his biographer, Prince Constantine of Bavaria, described how "time stood still" as he beheld the pontiff in his white raiment and "the Pope's eyes seemed to hold the promise of absolution for all mankind."[6] Many Bavarians saw him as one of their own, not least because of his years spent as nuncio in

Munich between 1917 and 1925. Many Germans regarded this Italian with exquisite German as the advocate for their beleaguered nation, for Pacelli had pleaded for a just peace and for mercy for many sentenced by Allied war crimes tribunals. But it was not only Germans who turned Pacelli into a figure of myth and legend. His unwavering condemnations of Communism garnered him nearly universal admiration from liberals and conservatives on both sides of the Atlantic. His tireless statesmanship and diplomacy earned him the epithet "the Pope of Peace." Even *Der Spiegel*, a voice increasingly critical of political Catholicism, paid homage to his diligent statesmanship upon his death in October 1958, duly noting the reverence he inspired inside and outside of the flock.[7]

Just as with Ernst-Wolfgang Böckenförde's reassessment of German Catholicism in 1933, Hochhuth's bold reappraisal caught the Catholic hierarchy completely off guard. And once again, there were stirrings beneath the surface that might have alerted astute observers to the reality of a coming reckoning with papal conduct during the Second World War. To be sure, some church critics, like devout Catholic literary giant Reinhold Schneider, had kept their misgivings private.[8] But as early as the Second World War, a surprisingly large number of individuals publicly expressed their frustration with Pius' unwillingness to issue bold condemnations of the atrocities committed by the Axis Powers.[9] In June 1945, the *Soviet Weekly*, a Communist newspaper in London, took Pius to task for having failed to speak out against the murder of millions.[10] In 1951, Jewish-French historian of anti-Semitism and pioneer of Holocaust research Léon Poliakov began analyzing the pope's "failure to issue that solemn and public declaration which the persecuted looked forward to so ardently."[11]

Hochhuth was initially unaware of most of these criticisms. He was a lone wolf, beholden to none of the networks and associations to which these critics belonged. He came up with the idea for his play on his own; putting Pius' silence center stage was his indisputable achievement. But in the course of his research, the young playwright encountered voices of opposition to papal conduct, some bold like the Austrian Friedrich Heer, others cautious like Poliakov. He discovered the essays, monographs and utterances of men like Gordon Zahn, Thomas Dehler and Ernst-Wolfgang Böckenförde, all critical of German Catholicism for its role in creating and sustaining the politics of the Federal Republic.

So why did Hochhuth's rendition of Pius stick when earlier criticisms had failed to gain traction? It was Hochhuth's masterstroke to have woven these threads of discontent into a coherent tapestry, one in which indictment found its ideal aesthetic. By subsuming it in the genre of a play and not an essay, he ensured that his criticism would be discussed by a broader audience and not just a coterie of intellectuals. In directing his fury at the pontiff and not those below in the hierarchy, he lent his creation greater narrative unity and dramatic power. But crucially, he brought his design to fruition at the most opportune time. The international mass media was in the midst of a fundamental structural transformation and, for reasons that will soon become clear, was increasingly receptive to voices of opposition and protest. His work found journalistic and literary champions who, skillfully navigating these changing waters, launched his creation.

The Deputy thus became the perfect storm. Its premiere marked the point when long-simmering controversies over the Catholic past finally boiled over in an explosion of surprising violence. The sound and fury of protests, death threats and riots as *The Deputy* journeyed from stage to stage in twenty countries during the coming six years guaranteed that the Catholic past was no longer the subject of brief articles on the back pages of newspapers. It was at center stage, splattered over front-page headlines, reprised on television and radio broadcasts and immortalized in glossy photo shoots for thriving illustrated magazines.[12]

This chapter will begin by examining the origins of *The Deputy*: how and why did a twenty-something editor for the Bertelsmann conglomerate with no formal high school degree decide to write such a play? Second: how did an aspiring playwright with no formal training as a historian find the raw materials for his work? Third, how did he find publishers and producers willing to shoulder its enormous risk? Fourth, how did he find the publicity to turn his papal indictment into a box office smash? Finally, why did his foes lose the public relations battles? This chapter argues that the counter-strikes by the defenders of the beleaguered pontiff transformed a debate about the silence of the wartime pope into something more injurious to their cause. This was a debate about freedom of expression, civil liberties and tolerance, when in the early to mid-1960s societal attitudes on these subjects were fundamentally shifting.

From Eschwege to Gütersloh: The Unlikely Journey of Rolf Hochhuth, 1931–1957

How did an aspiring twenty-something playwright from a forgotten region of central Germany come up with the idea in the late 1950s to castigate the head of the Catholic Church? As with Gordon Zahn and Ernst-Wolfgang Böckenförde, nearly unbroken lines of continuity led from formative experiences in childhood and youth to his critical reckoning with the church. Yet Hochhuth's journey was less intuitive than those of fellow critics. For one, he was raised Protestant like most of his classmates in his overwhelmingly Protestant hometown of Eschwege. He formally remained so, even if his religious upbringing was lax to the point where in the midst of confirmation he regarded himself as a "hypocrite" for no longer believing in doctrines like the resurrection of the body.[13] During the terrible years of dictatorship and war, this meant few to no encounters with individual Roman Catholic churchmen and lay leaders who might have soured him on the Church or conversely encouraged him to push for church reform. Identifying himself as a representative of this generation of 1945, Hochhuth once claimed that Hitler was his "father" – the father figure underlying his past and literary subject matter.[14] How do we make sense of his most unusual odyssey?

Certainly one part of the equation lies in the geographic isolation and palpable sense of insignificance pervading postwar Eschwege. Located on the eastern reaches of the state of Hesse, Eschwege slumbers in the scenic valley of the river Werra surrounded by idyllic hills, lakes and forests, a mecca for poets of a romantic ilk. Its harmonious mixture of half-timbered houses and turn-of-the-century bourgeois grace points to past prosperity. Its factories once kept the local populace well plied with shoes, leather goods and textiles. But with fewer than 20,000 inhabitants, it remains even today a picturesque provincial town too far off the beaten path to be known to most foreign tourists and even many Germans. The nearest cities lie in Kassel thirty miles to the northwest and Eisenach twenty miles to the east, and these are small to mid-sized. But contact to the latter became increasingly difficult or nearly impossible by the 1950s, as the Iron Curtain just kilometers away severed this regional hub from its rural hinterland to the east in Thuringia. East German state guard towers could easily be spotted from the eastern edge of the city. Authorities in the West eventually cut off rail service to the city center, forcing townspeople to rely on buses to reach forlorn rail platforms kilometers away. Straddling the zonal boundary and racked by high unemployment, Eschwege was dwindling into insignificance.

This very real sense of decline left an unmistakable imprint on the young Eschweger. He grew to loathe the first postwar chancellor, Konrad Adenauer, for having torn apart the German nation literally beneath his feet. Years later, he tarred the Roman Catholic chancellor as an "unteach-able separatist" and a "Rhenish League fanatic."[15] He condemned both Adenauer and East German leader Walter Ulbricht as "ideologues" and "high traitors" for dividing Germany.[16] Hochhuth, who after years of private art lessons from a local painter could draw skillfully, later doodled portraits of Pope Pius XII and Konrad Adenauer next to each other in the sketchbook containing the first draft of *The Deputy*.[17] Both men stood as symbols of the fervent anti-Communism that in his eyes had sundered

Germany. Hochhuth expressed his admiration instead for Bismarck, the grand architect of German unification.[18]

Though it would be too facile to suggest his condemnation of Pacelli's silence grew out of his hatred for Adenauer, the fact remains that the majority Protestant state of Hesse served as an incubator for critics of the church's role in politics and Adenauer's policies of Western integration. Hochhuth could look to precedents set by two Hessian Adenauer critics, Georg August Zinn and Gustav Heinemann, the CDU-turned-SPD delegate whose father and extended family hailed proudly from Eschwege.[19] Even more sharply than Zinn, Hochhuth sought to expose the claim that the Catholic Church had been a fount of resistance to National Socialism as a founding lie of the Federal Republic. Both liberals and socialists could make common cause against Adenauer's CDU. Elements of both ideologies also unmistakably found their way into the young Hochhuth, who would later be fascinated by Bismarck and yet also let his socialist heart excoriate capitalist excess.[20]

For such fears of decline were equally personal and informed the genesis of *The Deputy*, however indirectly.[21] Hochhuth was born in 1931 into a *gut bürgerlich* family.[22] This term is difficult to render precisely in English but denotes a respectable bourgeois family replete with manners, class, education and a powerful work ethic. His father ran – and lost – the family shoe factory in 1932. Even though his father regained both trade and status by running Eschwege's oldest grocery and seed company, lingering anxieties over finances, real and imagined, did not easily go away.[23] They may have been heightened by the unsettling professional circumstances in which the aspiring writer found himself in the late 1940s and 1950s. Despising mathematics and the natural sciences, he left his German academic high school without a degree in 1948 to pursue a career as a bookseller and expedite a literary career.[24] Telling his family and friends that he wanted to make a name for himself, the ambitious autodidact was nonetheless and predictably frustrated by his failure to advance.[25] In 1953, he wrote to a friend: "I move around on all fours and count the days that still remain in my attempt to rise literarily: one year is already wasted – the result is crippling."[26]

But his fortunes changed almost overnight. In 1955, he won a job as an assistant house editor at the rapidly growing Bertelsmann Publishing Company, famous for its Book Club. Reviewing and preparing manuscripts for publication, including works by Thomas Mann, Otto Flake and Erich Kästner, helped the aspiring literatus forge professional connections without which *The Deputy* never would have left the author's desk.[27] But Hochhuth still lacked the subject material to achieve a decisive breakthrough. A history aficionado, he found it through trial and error while sifting through the rich palette of materials offered by the immediate German past. Step by step, he extracted motifs out of traumatic experiences from his childhood and youth in Eschwege during the Nazi era. These themes ultimately laid the foundation for *The Deputy*, even if connections between his past and that depicted in his play were not obvious to theatergoers on the Kurfürstendamm in 1963.

That Hochhuth's immediate family did not buy into Nazi illusions, unlike most German liberals of the day, underlay some of these traumatic experiences. As befitting such a burgher family with formative roots in the German Empire, his mother and father were staunch national patriots. They nonetheless despised the Nazis' crudeness and brutal anti-Semitism.[28] Eschwege's Jewish community was larger than might be expected for a city its size, Jews outnumbering Catholics, Hochhuth claimed.[29] Some were merchants and manufacturers, others cattle merchants known for paying high prices and wages. Hochhuth's mother had befriended many Jews from the region, helping some in secret as the Nazis stepped up persecution.[30] She assisted the Jewish wife of a cousin who later poisoned herself after receiving an "invitation" to meet with the Gestapo.[31] But shortly after Kristallnacht, when the Jewish synagogue in Eschwege was burned down, a Jewish woman implored her to ask the local Nazi party leadership why her husband had been sent to Buchenwald. His mother refused to intervene. "Only an idiot can condemn her today for that," Hochhuth stated. No single citizen, he noted, could have stood openly against the terror of the Gestapo except those prepared for martyrdom.[32] Pius XII, in contrast, had had tremendous chances to warn unsuspecting Jews through public protests and perhaps even to intimidate Hitler.[33]

Firsthand reports of the murder of Jews scarred the young Hochhuth. One of his closest friend's father, a physician, was sent in 1942 to a military hospital near Smolensk.[34] He returned with blistering reports of how the German leadership was disposing of Jews. These reports left both boys overcome by shame, particularly since they had personally known Jews deported from Eschwege. From that point, it became a personal necessity to take up the subject material that led to *The Deputy*.[35] Portions of Acts III and V feature the arrests, deportations and murder of individual Jewish men, women and children. In early 1958, Hochhuth met a cabinetmaker in Southern Germany who while serving in the German army had been given an assignment in Auschwitz as punishment.[36] He told Hochhuth how he looked on as children miraculously surviving the gassing were pushed into the crematoria and burned alive. Hochhuth was later quoted in a Berlin newspaper as having subsequently asked himself not only "how something like that could happen" but also about the responsibility of "the Pope as the highest moral authority in Europe."[37]

Equally decisive in the genesis of *The Deputy* was the unexpected arrival in December 1943 in Eschwege of Marianne Heinemann, a quick-witted, blonde-haired, ponytailed orphan sitting in the front row of the class because her legs were too long. By his own admission a class clown, Hochhuth promptly developed a crush on her, in his words the "most beautiful girl in Eschwege."[38] In a partnership not unusual for artists and literati, she became not only his first wife but what Rolf later called his decisive literary coworker. Her mother, Rose Schlösinger, had been executed in August 1943 as a member of the Red Chapel resistance group, one with pronounced Communist and socialist roots.[39] Marianne introduced him to socialist ideas and literature. While on a walk with him, she came up with the idea for Act I, Scene II, in which leading Nazi villains, including Eichmann and the Doctor (a character loosely modeled on Josef Mengele), go bowling. She improvised and pantomimed the action for him.[40] A specialist in literature who published a book on German lyric poetry in 1963, she taught him the free verse in which *The Deputy* is written.[41] She discussed almost every line of his masterwork with him.[42]

The fate of Heinemann's mother both traumatized and inspired Hochhuth, who on at least one occasion laid flowers on her gravesite.[43] While working on *The Deputy*, he wrote a short novel (Novelle), *Berliner Antigone*, a moving epitaph for his deceased mother-in-law that should be read in tandem with his better-known play.[44] In her, he found a foil for the Pope. Here was a secular opponent of National Socialism unafraid of martyrdom – an act that, for Hochhuth, should have been the prerogative of Christ's deputy.

In lesser hands, these traumatic episodes would have remained mere memories. Channeling the moral outrage ensuing from such incidents into dramatic narratives is what became Hochhuth's stock-in-trade. One encounters the same pattern in almost all his major works: the playwright spots injustice, is overcome by outrage, identifies the evildoers to be held responsible, denounces them and holds to conviction even in the face of violent controversy or contrary evidence. Such moralism emerged out of his choleric temperament: Hochhuth was a pugilist who rarely shied from confrontation.[45] Recounting him as a young boy, one of his closest childhood friends observed: "When he didn't like something, he said so loudly."[46] Such insolence and impudence became essential ingredients in most of his literary creations. A personality with less temerity never would have dared to take on a figure as revered as the pope. At the same time, Hochhuth, who often displayed the sure hand of a public relations master, had a genius for discovering topics sure to send shock waves. Not inconveniently, the lists of his targets for moral outrage and of subject material guaranteeing the limelight easily overlapped.

Elucidating Hochhuth's personal idiosyncrasies, chance meetings and traumatic experiences merely shows how the stage was set for the young author to probe questions of ethical responsibility for the mass killing of Jews. Until the late 1950s, it was not clear that these ingredients would ever coalesce, let alone take the genre of a play. Hochhuth had been preoccupied with various writing projects, including an epistolary novel titled *Victoriastrasse 4* loosely based on his experience as a message runner for Eschwege's American occupiers in the summer and fall of 1945. *The Deputy* seems a bolt out of the blue, begun abruptly, most likely in late 1958, when he identified the pope's silence as a precise subject.[47]

What occasioned him to set aside other work and turn to Pope Pius XII? This query is inextricably bound up with this chapter's second question: how did a playwright with no formal training as a historian find his raw materials? The answer is straightforward. Ever since witnessing as a fourteen-year-old the collapse of Nazi Germany and the liberation of Eschwege by American soldiers, Hochhuth was determined to work through the history of the Third Reich. Like other members of the "generation of 1945," he was an avid reader of historical monographs and documentary editions. In the process, he encountered documents singling out the inaction of high-ranking Roman Catholic ecclesiastical leaders, including Pope Pius XII. Reading the glowing tributes after Pius XII's death in October 1958, Hochhuth was deeply unsettled.[48] To corroborate his *idée fixe* of papal silence, he dug more deeply into available evidence. *The Deputy* was generated by disgust.

From Gütersloh to Rome and Back: Hochhuth's Research into the Recent Papal Past, 1957–1962

Hochhuth was a voracious reader. He devoured classics of German literature, works by writers languishing in obscurity like Otto Flake, weekly newsmagazines including *Der Spiegel* and virtually all books exploring the recent German past and the Holocaust that came his way. Equipped with only rudimentary foreign language skills, he was, in general, reliant on works in the German language; he typically drew on salient literature from abroad only after it appeared in German translation.[49] Yet it was the work of foreign and émigré researchers that opened his eyes to papal conduct during the Holocaust. Most mainstream West German historians and academics had been unwilling to step into the minefields of anti-Semitism, Nazi occupation policies and genocide. Some had sullied their hands through their own enthusiastic work for Nazi wartime planning boards.[50]

The immediate trigger for Hochhuth's interest in the role of the high ecclesia was his discovery of an emotionally jarring testimony about mass gassings in Auschwitz by Kurt Gerstein. Hochhuth stumbled upon this report in a documentary volume compiled by Leon Poliakov and Josef Wulf, who had rendered it from its original broken French into German.[51] In this report, Gerstein described how he showed up at the door of the papal nuncio in Berlin, Cesare Orsenigo, to inform him about the ongoing exterminations. Asked whether he was a soldier, Gerstein was denied entry and told to leave, apparently by a subordinate priest.[52] Though the report did not indicate that this was indeed the case, Hochhuth assumed that the tenacious Gerstein would have forced his way through to meet with Orsenigo.[53] Mesmerized, Hochhuth attempted to write a Novelle but quickly realized that the enigmatic Gerstein was better suited for the stage than a short story.[54] Portions of the Gerstein report appear almost verbatim in the play's text with only slight changes to accommodate free verse.[55]

Hochhuth ran across more tangible links to the papacy when Poliakov and Wulf published a follow-up volume on the Third Reich. They unveiled seven documents about the role of Pius XII and the German ambassador to the Vatican, Ernst von Weizsäcker, during the roundup of Jews from Rome in October 1943.[56] These German Foreign Office documents featured telegrams between Berlin and Rome analyzing threats of a papal protest on behalf of the Jews. They also included the translation of an article from October 25–26 from the Vatican newspaper *L'Osservatore Romano* in which the pope declared that his mercy and charity knew "no boundaries of nationality, religion or race."[57] The concluding letter, in which Weizsäcker reported to his superiors in Berlin on October 28, 1943, that the pope would not issue a public protest, became the closing words of *The Deputy*.

For Hochhuth, this was the master find.[58] Here, at least on the surface, was foolproof evidence of the pope's inaction and complicity in the crimes of the Nazis. The final straw, it seems, came with Pope Pius' death in October 1958. Dozens of newspapers and magazines served up glowing tributes, immortalizing him as the "pope of peace," protector of the German nation, crusader against Communism and defender of the weak. Overcome by outrage, Hochhuth seems then to have embarked on his quest.[59] Beginning the historical legwork, he sent letter after letter to libraries, publishers and archives. He hauled in photos, a smattering of scholarly articles and the proceedings of the Wilhelmstrasse trials of German diplomats like Ernst von Weizsäcker.[60] Above all, he turned to books – on the Holocaust, the Vatican, Pius XII and, most crucially, the diaries, memoirs and "table talks" of the leading protagonists and villains from the day like Hitler, Goebbels, Count Ciano, Franz von Papen, Albrecht von Kessel and others.[61]

This task was not as daunting as it might seem today. In the late 1950s, research into the Holocaust and the Roman Catholic Church during the Nazi era was in its infancy. Scholarly bibliographies often amounted only to several pages, a sharp contrast to the wings of libraries that now house tens of thousands of suitable books and articles. Hochhuth further possessed the gift of being a quick study and fast writer. Even with the few hours in the day available to him mostly in the morning because of his three-quarter-time job at Bertelsmann, he wrote voluminously. He also received a stroke of good fortune. His edited editions of the nineteenth century caricaturist and poet Wilhelm Busch's work sold so many copies – more than a million – that his boss, Reinhard Mohn, granted him a paid three-month sabbatical on June 29, 1959, to devote to his literary pursuits.[62] This was the boon he needed. After a cumbersome search for housing, he and his wife headed to Rome in mid-September, the playwright out to determine whether Pius XII indeed had refused to issue a protest.[63]

Hochhuth's trip might seem quixotic. Lacking any sort of fluency in Italian, he could speak only with German-speaking officials at the Holy See willing to recount Pius' response to the deportation of Roman Jews in October 1943.[64] It also seems that Hochhuth arrived with only one connection, Dr. Gerd Kloeters, a recent fellowship recipient of the Görres Society charged with supporting Catholic academics.[65] He was in residence at the Collegio Teutonico along with another aspiring young German Catholic academic, Ludwig Hammermayer, who would become a history professor at the University in Munich.

In late October, Kloeters arranged for Hochhuth to meet with Monsignor Bruno Wüstenberg, a German prelate living in the same quarters.[66] But Wüstenberg was a problematic figure. He was well known - though not for the reasons he would have liked. He tore up the Roman streets in a red Porsche. He was also so notoriously short of stature that practical jokers changed his last name from Wüstenberg, or "desert mountain," to Wüsten*zwerg*, or "desert dwarf."[67] More importantly, he was consumed with hatred for Pacelli, whom he blamed for blocking his career. Pacelli was obviously not alone in his low regard. Pope Pius XII would send the stymied monsignor into exile as the pronuncio in Japan in 1966.

Kloeters may have facilitated Hochhuth's path to an even more problematic source, one whose letter of protest plays a pivotal role in the exchange between Fontana and Pius in Act IV of *The Deputy*. This was Alois Hudal, the notorious Austrian bishop, Nazi sympathizer and rector of the German church in Rome, Santa Maria dell'Anima. A consummate schemer, Hudal had an ax to grind even in his mid-seventies: Pius XII had cut off support for his German church in 1939.[68] Hudal is now the subject of opprobrium for his tireless efforts to reconcile National Socialism with Christianity and for organizing a "rat line" that steered the worst of the Nazi war criminals, including Adolf Eichmann and Franz Stangl, to safe havens in nations like Argentina.[69] Hochhuth, however, knew of him in a heroic light – as the author of a sharply worded letter to the commander of Rome's German forces. Excerpted by Poliakov and Wulf, Hudal's letter threatened a public papal protest should the arrests of Italian Jews not cease. Hochhuth could not have been aware that Hudal was not the real author. Higher-ups simply had Hudal sign it, believing that his well-known Nazi sympathies might lead to a better outcome.[70]

The young playwright's contacts were unaware of the extent of his ambitions.[71] In introducing himself, he told them that he was writing a literary work whose central protagonist was a young priest following the example of Berlin prelate Bernard Lichtenberg. Lichtenberg, Hochhuth told them, was planning "to let himself be deported to Poland to share the fate of the Jews" headed for the gas chambers.[72] Years later, Hochhuth admitted to having had a guilty conscience for deceiving Wüstenberg, who was "such a smart and nice man." But had he revealed his true intentions, he added, he never would have received any sort of an answer.[73]

What did Hochhuth get out of these interviews, two with Hudal and one with Wüstenberg? He received confirmation of what he sought: Pius had not issued a public protest. Both corroborated his suspicion: the Germans were not prepared to invade the Vatican and seize the pope as a prisoner, even had Pius protested. Hitler was not that "stupid," Hudal stated.[74] Such a move would have been "ridiculous," said Wüstenberg.[75] Hochhuth drew nearly verbatim from these quotations in his "Sidelines on History," an appendix of between forty and eighty pages depending on edition and font size.[76] In addition, one pivotal statement from Hochhuth's protocol of his first conversation with Hudal found its way into the main text. In his interview write-up, Hochhuth astutely noted that Hudal still seemed rather "infected" by the Nazi ideology: "Today, he still regrets that National Socialism and Christianity did not work together and cites a phrase of Molotov from around 1934, according to which Communism is finished if National Socialism and Christianity come to terms with each other."[77] Tendentiously, Hochhuth later put this piece of wishful thinking into the mouth of Cesare Orsenigo, the

Papal Nuncio in Berlin. In Act I, Hochhuth had Orsenigo opine: "Mr. Molotov grasped in 1934 that if the church in Germany should strike up an accord with the Hitler folks ... then Communism in Europe would be finished."[78]

Hochhuth later concluded that without his sabbatical in Rome, he never would have been able to bring his work to fruition.[79] He was given a desk at the top of St. Peter's Cathedral and from this perch gained a splendid view of the setting for Act IV, the Vatican and adjacent neighborhoods from which Roman Jews were arrested. Since the Vatican archives were closed to researchers of the post-1846 era, he had time to write. He began penning the first version of his play in the Vatican Library in a small bound notebook now preserved in the Swiss Literature Archives.[80] Yet one can also make the case that Hochhuth's sojourn in Rome – which appears to have lasted for between six and eight weeks and not the three months he claimed later – proved more critical for later public relations efforts.[81] He could credibly claim to have been in Rome and interviewed Vatican officials.

Upon his return to Gütersloh, the home base for Bertelsmann, Hochhuth found progress on the play stalled by the intense demands of his job as an editor. As his play took on greater dimensions than first envisioned, he was also forced to plunge into more extensive historical research.[82] This led him to individuals like Léon Poliakov, one of the first to systematically document the crimes of the Holocaust.[83] Corresponding frequently by phone and letter, Poliakov supplied Hochhuth with additional leads, contacts and source material, including the quotation from François Mauriac that gilds the opening pages to the paperback version of *The Deputy*.[84] Hochhuth later described Poliakov's assistance as "priceless."[85]

During this time, Hochhuth made significant changes. He added the famous handwashing scene, the climax of Act IV and, in many estimations, of the entire play.[86] This scene, he stated, "forced itself" upon him after he read through Pope Pius XII's address of June 2, 1945, extolling the church's resistance against National Socialism.[87] For Hochhuth, this address was little more than nauseating self-exculpation.

Hochhuth completed his draft in February 1961.[88] On May 23, 1961, he submitted it and sixty pages of documentation, the precursor to his "Sidelines on History," to the Rütten und Loening press.[89] The choice of publisher seemed ideal. Rütten und Loening had just made waves by publishing damaging documentation about the Nazi past of Hans Globke, one of Adenauer's closest advisers.[90] The press had just been purchased by Bertelsmann in 1960, and Hochhuth's boss, Reinhard Mohn, now oversaw its operations. By the end of August 1961,

Hochhuth had signed a contract and received an advance.[91] After he made the corrections to the page proofs in November, the advance copies went to print.[92] The play's publication seemed imminent, the last stage of a journey from Gütersloh to Rome and back.

From Gütersloh to Berlin, January 1962–February 1963

Yet *The Deputy* was not published by Rütten und Loening in 1962. In a dramatic twist, it was released as a paperback one day before its stage premiere in February 1963 by the Rowohlt Verlag, a rival publishing house with keen interests in theater and literature. Needless to say, there had been considerable backstage activity in two storied German publishing houses over the merits and dangers of placing such incendiary content under their mantle. Both sides saw the risks. Why did Rowohlt choose to assume them, knowing that Rütten und Loening had deemed the work too radioactive for publication? And how did this sudden development redound to the advantage of the playwright, who was shattered by news of betrayal?

These decisions were taken against a backdrop of business calculations, political interests and even backroom intrigues. Both Bertelsmann and Rowohlt consisted of interconnected subsidiaries and divisions.[93] As the CEO of the Bertelsmann conglomerate, Mohn apparently used the proceeds from the wildly successful Book Club to subsidize Rütten und Loening.[94] The fact of its new ownership was not commonly known, but it appears to have been decisive in Mohn's decision to break the contract with Hochhuth at the end of December 1961.[95] Hochhuth later recounted Mohn's justification: forty-seven percent of the subscribers to the Book Club consisted of Roman Catholics, and he could not afford to alienate such a wide segment of his base.[96] But, as Hochhuth noted, who in Germany even knew of the connections between the Bertelsmann Book Club and Rütten und Loening?[97] Hochhuth suspected that he had been the victim of sinister closed-door plotting. His typist, who worked on the manuscript in the evening to earn extra money, discovered surreptitious notes between two colleagues who were intending to sound the alarm to Mohn about the scandalous work going into print.[98] Mohn saw things differently. While conceding that he had indeed been influenced by the house personnel to whom Hochhuth referred, he insisted that he personally found Hochhuth's depiction tendentious and not "objective." Though Hochhuth had followed the best of intentions, the Book Club would have been saddled with too high a price to pay.[99]

Hochhuth was left high and dry with no publisher in sight. Few were willing to touch a work tarnished by rejection. His advance had to be paid back. In a letter to Mohn from 1968, he stated he would have sued Rütten und Loening for breach of contract had he had the money.[100] But unbeknownst to Hochhuth, an unexpected denouement was taking shape. Looking out for a cherished employee who had made so many valuable contributions, Mohn met with the senior editor of Rütten und Loening, Karl Ludwig Leonhardt. Leonhardt had been Hochhuth's supervisor at the Book Club and, more significantly, remained a close friend. Leonhardt took an unusual step: he forwarded the manuscript to Rowohlt and personally met with its representatives either with or without Mohn's authorization.[101] Rowohlt's chief editor, Fritz Raddatz, accordingly dubbed him *The Deputy's* "illegitimate producer."[102] Convinced that the recent past had to be overcome, Leonhardt had vocally championed *The Deputy* to Mohn and others at Bertelsmann.[103] Leonhardt was so angered by this turn of events that he quit his post at Rütten and Loening shortly after.[104]

This remarkable act of midwifery was one of three turning points in short succession that launched Hochhuth's literary career. Hochhuth later observed: "I am indebted to Leonhardt as to no one other than my parents" for having "forced" his work onto Rowohlt.[105] From its headquarters in the well-to-do outskirts of Hamburg, Rowohlt had carved out an international reputation as a left-liberal firm willing to take on challenging authors and embrace provocation. Its series of paperbacks, the "ro-ro-ro," was the largest and most prominent in Germany: its theater publishing wing had direct contact with stages and directors throughout the Federal Republic. Under Rowohlt's wings, *The Deputy* would have chances to fly unequaled by most other publishers.

But the acceptance at Rowohlt was also no sure thing. The readers at Rowohlt's Theater Division were initially critical.[106] Though its historical documentation was so rich that it could possibly be published as history, they saw "no chance of staging the play" on account of its excessive breadth, technical difficulties, incendiary content and excessive cast of twenty-four.[107] They considered publishing it as a cheap paperback or as a more expensive softcover but noted that its stylistic deficiencies left it below normal standards for acceptance.[108] The page proofs wound up in the rubbish bin of Klaus Juncker, head of the Rowohlt Theater Publishing Company.[109]

What followed was a second act of midwifery. Raddatz crept into Juncker's office and fished the manuscript out of the garbage can. He then handed it over to Heinrich Maria Ledig-Rowohlt, the head of Rowohlt, and "forced" him to peruse the manuscript overnight.[110] The next day, Ledig-Rowohlt telephoned Erwin Piscator for a verdict.[111] A veteran socialist, this venerable director was an institution in his own right. Famous for his "Political Theater" during the Weimar era, he spent the Nazi years in exile in Moscow, Paris and New York. Since his 1951 return to Germany he had worked with the Rowohlt Theater Division on a number of projects, including a recent stage adaptation of Tolstoy's *War and Peace*. He was set to take over the direction of the Free People's Theater in West Berlin in late 1962. And so Ledig-Rowohlt posed the question: did he wish to burden his debut with such an "explosive shock"?[112]

In less than twelve hours, Piscator agreed. He would premiere Hochhuth's play. Even though he was not fully convinced that "Hochhuth" was not a pseudonym for a more famous author, his reasons are not hard to discern.[113] Descended from a family of Protestant pastors, Piscator had a strong anticlerical streak, and *The Deputy* offered rich fruit for the picking, even if its author repeatedly took pains to argue that his work was a "pro-Catholic play" that retraced a young Jesuit's path to Golgatha.[114] This play was also, in part, a documentary, and by the 1960s, Piscator was keenly interested in launching documentary theater. This theater was to be a courtroom, the audience a jury.

For the third time, Hochhuth's play had been saved from a fate of dusty desk drawers or garbage bins by a *deus ex machina*.[115] With Piscator on board, Hochhuth's otherwise-unwieldy work was suddenly rendered stageable. Piscator cut its length from seven hours to two and a half, preventing it from becoming a critical and box office disaster.[116] All the same, the two men fought bitterly over the cuts right up to the premiere.[117] Against the vehement opposition of the playwright, Piscator insisted on excising virtually all of the fifth act, in which Fontana, Gerstein and the Doctor find themselves in a standoff in Auschwitz.[118] Less than ten days before opening night, Hochhuth grabbed a telephone out of the hands of Piscator's secretary and smashed it to the ground, leaving it in smithereens.[119]

Yet Hochhuth also repeatedly recognized his tremendous debt to Piscator.[120] Had *The Deputy* remained with Rütten und Loening, it would most likely have never been staged. Now under the aegis of Rowohlt, even financial difficulties were being ironed out. Ledig-Rowohlt came to a settlement of 1500 Deutschmark with Rütten und Loening, wiping out any advance for the author.[121] He agreed to risk a run of 7,000 copies.[122] The delay of nearly a year proved fortuitous. Anticlerical and anti-authoritarian attitudes in the critical German news media had hardened for reasons that will soon become clear.

Most significantly, Rowohlt's hand ensured access to the international press, directors, translators, prize committees and stages worldwide. On November 17, 1962, Hochhuth's work won the Gerhard-Hauptmann

Figure 5.2 Rolf Hochhuth and Erwin Piscator, the veteran theater director more than thirty years his senior, discuss their upcoming play, *The Deputy*. The senior playwright and director was forced to make substantial cuts into a play that would have otherwise lasted for seven hours. Courtesy of the Archiv der Akademie der Künste, Berlin. Copyright Deutsches Theatermuseum München, Archiv Ilse Buhs.

Prize of 1500 Deutschmark given by the Free People's Theater.[123] In bestowing the award, the jury explicitly took its hat off to "the angry young man of our dramatic literature."[124] With *The Deputy* now poised to receive top billing, the spotlight was ready to be turned on the author.

The Public Relations Battles before the Premiere,
January–February 22, 1963

Through many quirks of fate, Hochhuth's play found the right publisher, the right director, the right stage and the right timing. It lacked only one crucial ingredient: publicity. As with any debut, it needed the standard formal advertisements, announcements in the press and invitations to theater critics. As highly respected names, the Rowohlt Press and Piscator masterfully tapped into and exploited their network of international contacts in the realms of journalism, theater and literature. But even this was not necessarily enough, for even *The Deputy's* champions acknowledged its literary shortcomings – its clumsy use of free verse, excessive length, one-dimensional protagonists and lack of character development.[125] Though other scenes compensated in literary brilliance, no less than the author assumed until the very last minute that his brain-child would be a critical and box office failure.

But Hochhuth's play instead became an overnight box office hit. It enjoyed sixty sold-out performances in Berlin before the theater cut its run; tickets were found only through scalpers.[126] Its paperback version shot to number one on *Der Spiegel's* bestseller list in just six weeks.[127] Numerous theater companies, both in Germany and increasingly abroad, contacted Rowohlt for permission to stage it. Translations were hastily prepared into English, French, Swedish, Italian and more than six other languages.

So how did *The Deputy* defy even its author's expectations and become a smash hit? There is a deceptively simple answer: the hype – and not least Piscator's cuts – compensated for literary weaknesses. The new play became a commercial sensation because it was encased in controversy.[128] Rowohlt's literary team took it on knowing full well its scandalous potential – and arguably because of it. In introducing the manuscript to Piscator in February 1962, Ledig-Rowohlt stated that it contained "enormous explosive material and without a doubt would be strongly attacked and might even cause a scandal."[129]

But this answer falls short of a full explanation. The controversy first had to be created; the outrage had to be genuine. Slinging *The Deputy* into the public eye was the two-step performed by promoters and opponents in the frantic four-week lead-up to the premiere. The former dangled bait in front of the press, the latter overreacted through untoward expressions of outrage; rebuttals served as further bait. This *pas de deux* continued for months after the February 1963 premiere and when the play moved to new stages abroad.

For this dance to unfold, each side had to perform its part to perfection. The team at Rowohlt opted for precautions, shrouding the work in secrecy. Hochhuth was to retrieve copies of the page proofs from Rütten und Loening.[130] The book was to be released only on the day of the premiere. This was standard procedure for any savvy publisher interested in good sales. An earlier release, particularly for the work of an unknown author, could easily have cut into *The Deputy*'s take. Only one month before the premiere did Piscator invite international journalists including critics at *The New York Times*, *The Herald Tribune* and *The Sunday Times*.[131] In a masterful sleight of hand, he not only enclosed a foreword for the published version. With the hearings in Karlsruhe from 1956 still fresh, he told the journalists that "the play deals with the famous concordat of Pope Pius XII which had been signed by him and Herr Hitler." He concluded: "I would not have accepted this play because of its rather dangerous and sensitive substance would I not have believed that here is an extraordinary talent at work."[132] Dieter Borsche, the renowned actor playing Pius XII, described the work as "aggressive" in an interview with the Berlin newspaper *Der Abend*.[133] To pique the interest of the local press, those promoting the play directed attention to the fact that one of its dedicatees, the deceased Bernhard Lichtenberg, was a Berliner.[134]

By both happenstance and design, these measures hit a nerve for a group of Catholics in Berlin largely unknown to Hochhuth at the time. Possibly tipped off by the 1500 DM prize awarded to Hochhuth in November, the Catholic Committee in West Berlin managed to get its hands on one of the advance copies of the play, possibly one provided to the prize jury.[135] Among the twenty-five members of the Catholic Committee was Dr. Ernst-Alfred Jauch, the Berlin correspondent for the KNA, the Catholic wire-services agency. Also on the committee was Monsignor Erich Klausener Jr., the chief editor of Walter Adolph's old newspaper, the *Petrusblatt*. He was the son of Erich Klausener, the leader of Catholic Action murdered by the Nazis in 1934 and commemorated by Walter Adolph.[136] Overseeing measures was Walter Adolph, now serving as vicar general for the diocese and enraged by the dedication to Lichtenberg.

Their response set off a media scramble. Weeks before the premiere, *The Deputy* received the best publicity imaginable: a kitchen sink of enticing rumors and unrestrained animosity. Taking its cue from Borsche's interview, an initial KNA report from January 25 erroneously claimed that Hochhuth had studied documents in the Vatican archives.[137] Up next, Klausener fired his opening shots in the *Petrusblatt*.[138] Since the KNA and the *Petrusblatt* were in the habit of coordinating services, the latter made this blistering attack available on January 30 to the KNA, which passed it on to its subscribers. With hundreds of regional and local newspapers now in possession of it, one of the leading mainstream German wire-services agencies, the DPA, or German Press Agency, wrote up its own story about the *Petrusblatt*'s broadside and sent it down the wires to its hundreds of customers. "The *Petrusblatt* Attacks the Free People's Theater," ran a typical headline.[139] Hochhuth saw it necessary to issue a public defense. He handed over a written statement to the DPA, which it summarized and sent out. The subsequent headlines from February 3 zeroed in on the brewing conflict between Hochhuth and the *Petrusblatt*. "Controversy with the *Petrusblatt*," bellowed one caption.[140]

The KNA launched another round of attacks less than two weeks later. The premiere still more than a week away, Jauch put together a bruising critique. His title, "Take an Emetic, You Who Read This," echoed the words of Søren Kierkegaard.[141] Hochhuth, the KNA announced, was attempting to shift blame for the murder of six million Jews to the pope.[142] At the same time, Jauch sent out what at first glance appeared to be a standard "objective" news article. A closer read left little doubt that it was an attack on the playwright's methodology.[143] The KNA also printed a critical essay by Auxillary Bishop of Limburg Walter Kampe, who noted that Catholics felt obligated to defend the "maligned honor of a man whose memory is holy to us."[144] Incensed by the leak of the playbook and the coverage granted to aggressive critics, Piscator threatened all of the actors, stagehands and theater employees with a staggering fine of 10,000 DM were scripts, page proofs and advance copies to be passed on to third parties.[145]

Even if they did not print the KNA and DPA articles, editors at local and regional newspapers had been made aware. That bishops, religious newspapers and wire-services agencies were protesting so much and so soon suggested that the play must contain awful truths that the church did not want to come to light. To no surprise, daily newspapers throughout the Federal Republic began reporting on the coming sensation.[146] One DPA article from February 20 sent to hundreds of local and regional papers spoke of the "play which is eagerly awaited" and included a photo of Gerstein unsuccessfully beseeching Orsenigo to rescue Jews.[147] Their curiosity whetted, the most important national newspapers like the *Frankfurter Allgemeine Zeitung* as well as a surprisingly large number of local and regional papers sent their own journalists and theater critics to West Berlin to cover the premiere.[148] In bypassing the wire services, they denied the KNA the chance to provide its spin. These newspapers guaranteed *The Deputy* more detailed and prominent coverage – not the perfunctory blurb on the back pages reserved for out-of-town events.

The premiere was a resounding success. Newspapers reported that the feared scandal had failed to materialize.[149] Security did not intervene.

The appearance of Borsche on stage in the guise of the pope evoked only scattered whistles and yells.[150] A period of silence ensued as the curtain fell to be followed by five minutes of emphatic, prolonged applause, which drowned out isolated whistles and boos.[151] The young playwright and the old director emerged to take bows, the latter receiving the triumph eluding him during the turbulent Weimar years. The audience exited in silence.[152] The Catholic Action committee in Munich concluded that the "emotional" protests of the Berlin chancery had paved the way for Hochhuth's success.[153] In getting a large portion of the German population up in arms, it had turned the play into a "circus number."

Why Hochhuth Won the Public Relations Wars, February 1963–1966

It would seem that after this blaze of glory, the conflict had peaked and would fizzle out with time. Yet the conflict over *The Deputy* was revived over and over during the coming days, weeks, months and years. The Hochhuth phenomenon became a long-lasting wave that repeatedly crested before finally dissipating after a controversial run in Brussels in 1966. It would be easy to ascribe the protracted nature of this controversy to *The Deputy's* taboo-breaking effect. In toppling an icon, Piscator and Hochhuth allowed other critics of the church's past to come out of the closet and air their grievances publicly. Smelling both blood and profits, stages throughout the world embraced the new sensation. After Berlin, *The Deputy* moved to London, Basel, Paris, New York, Detroit – and the scandals inevitably spread, particularly when a large Catholic population was near enough and sufficiently focused to take action.

There were exceptions. These were overwhelmingly Protestant cities like Stockholm, Copenhagen, London and Helsinki. But a Catholic outlier, Munich, speaks volumes about the dynamics fueling this seemingly endless conflict. Upon learning of upcoming performances in February and March 1964, the Catholic Action committee for the Archdiocese of Munich and Freising launched "Operation Silence." This entailed refraining from any shows of public outrage and ignoring all letters, phone calls and personal pleas from hotheads.[154] Leading the mute was Auxillary Bishop Neuhäusler, who once again drew from the playbook honed in the Nazi and immediate postwar eras. His book from 1964, *The Seed of Evil*, put forward a vigorous defense of Pius – but without once mentioning Hochhuth or his play.[155] As his Catholic Action steering committee noted with pride, its silence had echoed. The play flopped, and SPD-led local trade unions hoping for a vigorous discussion were forced to offer tickets at half-priced discounts.[156]

These exceptions bore out what had already been discovered at Berlin. Protectors of Pius were playing an inordinate role in promoting the criticism of their adversaries. The dance between overzealous defenders and unapologetic critics was continuing. Starting just two days after the premiere, a revolving door of politicians, churchmen, theologians, intellectuals and academics entered the public arena to criticize, denounce and impugn. Their slings and arrows predictably prompted Hochhuth and members of the team at Rowohlt to repeatedly mount equally aggressive public defenses. Covered by the press, each skirmish raised new issues that went far beyond the historical accuracy of a playwright's portrayal of a deceased pontiff. Some centered on the need for theological reform, others on questions of civil liberties and tolerance for unpopular ideas.

So why did men like Adolph continue to turn on this work of a neophyte with open fury instead of greeting it with silence from their desks in Berlin, Bonn and Rome? For one, blasting away at foes was deeply rooted habit, a staple of the politicized journalism of the Weimar Republic, the lesson of Catholic failures in the Third Reich and the modus operandi in besieged wayposts like West Berlin. They were driven by the conviction that Hochhuth, in portraying Pius as beholden to financial interests, had parroted the anticlerical barbs of the East German regime. The inhabitants of "Central Germany," Adolph insisted, should not be hearing their own regime's propaganda from Western voices.[157]

Adolph also believed that hard-edged tactics had successfully quieted critics in the past. These had put Josef Fleischer's criticisms to rest in 1947, shamed Thomas Dehler in 1956 and muzzled Gordon Zahn in 1959 and 1960. Their criticisms had largely vanished, or so he thought, from the local, regional and national newspapers that were a staple of the German and American lay readership. He was badly mistaken. Dehler returned with words of approval, public and private, for his fellow papal critic.[158] Zahn published a lengthy analysis of *The Deputy*, critical of both playwright and pontiff.[159]

With the triumphant premiere of *The Deputy*, the genie was out of the bottle. It was not possible to abort the publication of a paperback already on the market or to stop future performances of a hit play. The challenge for Adolph and his fellow journalists and publicists lay in planting a corrective version of the papal past to counter distortions, half-truths and fabrications. And so the real battleground became the media. Most of the dozen or so discrete skirmishes over *The Deputy* between February 1963 and 1966 were fought by those with some expertise in public relations or journalism.

In opting for this strategy, Adolph and like-minded Catholic publicists did not recognize they were up against both a media culture and a public sphere undergoing a radical shake-up.[160] Even at the start, they were at a tremendous disadvantage. The Catholic press had never fully recovered from being silenced during the Nazi era. The circulation of the few Catholic daily local, regional and national newspapers lagged far behind that of secular competitors.[161] Though the weekly diocesan newspapers reached a peak readership in 1962, they could not consistently influence the twenty-four- to forty-eight-hour news cycle. They lacked modern layouts; their readership had become "unusually conservative," more progressive Catholics increasingly apt to disregard directives about which newspapers to read.[162]

This meant that the outcome of the public relations wars over *The Deputy* hinged on reporting in the nonreligious mainstream press – and on seismic shifts in the media landscape. By the second half of the 1950s, a younger generation, mostly men in their late twenties and early thirties, assumed positions as editors. These representatives of the "generation of 1945" were more likely to be secular – an astounding 40 percent were formally un-churched by the 1970s.[163] Many had spent months or years abroad, often in the United States and Great Britain, under the aegis of Allied reeducation and cultural exchange policies. While watching television, listening to the radio or reading newspapers, they encountered critical formats generally unknown in Germany – hard-hitting roundtables, open panel discussions and investigative reporting.

These younger journalists returned with more complex approaches to reporting. They were certainly not abandoning traditional reporting – telling stories deemed newsworthy. But they were augmenting them through new genres of celebrity reporting, investigative reporting and in-depth commentaries; they were enhancing them through better layouts, fonts and photo spreads. Crucially, they were bidding farewell to the models of consensus journalism that predominated in the 1950s. Instead of cavorting with leading politicians, they sought to muckrake and spark debate.

All of this helps explain why Catholic publicists lost their public relations battles. Increasingly suspicious of the intrusion of clerical might into politics, mainstream journalists and broadcasters were no longer going to identify with the champions of Pius in the CDU and the ecclesia, let alone socialize with them. Instead, they were critical of Catholic defense efforts – of the mash of street protests, denunciations, legal actions and pressure on broadcasters. They would make the Catholic reaction the story.

How then did new genres in journalism like the visual turn dispro-portionately benefit papal critics like Hochhuth? For many loyal

Catholics, the kneejerk response to Hochhuth's alleged act of blasphemy was to protest, just as they had done at many points in the past, such as upon the release in 1951 of the controversial film *Die Sünderin*, with its infamous shot of actress Hildegard Knef's exposed breast.[164] Some protests unfolded spontaneously; others were coordinated with chanceries and local clergy. But the result was usually the same: on the street level, demonstrations, marches, rallies, disruption of performances and riots; from laity and clerics above, sermons, press statements and press conferences that denounced. Where Catholics lived together in large enough numbers, the entire milieu was mobilized – the press, the hierarchy, youth organizations, social clubs and women's clubs – and sounded the voice of protest in chorus.[165] The call to arms came first from the chancery in Berlin; it was taken up by the hierarchy in Germany and, one by one, in a range of Swiss cities including Basel, Olten, Zofingen, Aarau and Soloturn before moving to New York, Paris and Italy.

It is not difficult to see why the secular media saw the ensuing street demonstrations and denunciations with reserve: they saw emotions and passions run wild. Eruptions of rage in Switzerland, France and the United States in the coming year dwarfed anything in the streets outside the Free People's Theater in Berlin. On September 24, 1963, nearly 6,000 Catholics picketed the theater in Basel and waved inflammatory signs; the next night, protestors disrupted the performance by setting off stink bombs and letting out howls of protest.[166] One shadowy Italian group threatened to bomb the theater, the synagogue and the Free Masons' Center, claiming that all three groups stood behind the production as part of a perfidious conspiracy.[167] For the premiere in Paris in mid-December 1963, protesters disrupted the performance not just with stink bombs but with sneezing powder.[168] A group of nearly thirty demonstrators garbed in paratrooper apparel let loose such a chorus of boos and whistles at the start of the act featuring Pius that the curtain was dropped. The militants stormed the stage, engaged in fisticuffs with the actors and threw the actor playing Pius to the ground before the police could handcuff and haul them off.[169] Rumor had it that they were members of the fanatical "Pro Pius Committee" that had reputedly made its first appearance in Basel; one of its ringleaders had purportedly been a member of the Franco-Algerian *pieds noirs* terrorist group, the OAS.[170] In New York, nearly 150 protestors blocked sidewalks and catcalled in front of the theater. Most were members of the "Ad Hoc Committee to Protest the Deputy," but fifteen, wearing swastikas, were members of the American Nazi Party, wielding signs such as "This is a hate play" and "Jews mock Pius XII."[171] At points, the protestors chanted so loudly that they could be heard inside the theater. One man bawled: "Don't picket, get in there and stop the show." The theater management was forced to lock the theater's doors during intermission to prevent the throngs of activists from staging an invasion.[172] After a production in Rome was banned in February 1965, the local theater company staged a clandestine performance. The police shut it down, and the brother of a lead actor took revenge several days later by planting two bombs at the Vatican's Saint Anne Gate, wakening Pope Paul VI from his nighttime slumber.[173] These attacks spelled trouble for the precarious coalition government of Aldo Moro.[174] The list of disruptions goes on and on – face slaps in the foyer and brawls in the tiers in Vienna, fistfights and riots in Brussels, a riot in the Swiss city of Olten and so on.[175]

It was not just that the laity didst protest too much, making for compelling television viewing, gripping radio reports, riveting headlines – and, of course, sold-out performances. It was that they put forward a message that was upended by the conduct of the messenger. Many protestors were demanding "tolerance" for injured Catholic sensibilities, which in this case meant the right to publicly express their outrage over Hochhuth's alleged act of blasphemy. Amid the melee that broke out with *The Deputy's* premiere in his archdiocese, Cardinal Feltin of Paris went on record as saying: "Who can fail to understand why a Catholic should be hurt by the wrong done to the memory of his Father?"[176] But it was extremely difficult for this message of tolerance to remain credible when some of its bearers were thuggish young men who stormed theaters. The militant protesters, as is usually the case, were a tiny, overzealous minority. In time, their actions would come to be seen as a problem by at least some of the chanceries.[177] But they bore the same message as more respected Catholic elders – Hochhuth's calumnious play was an intolerable provocation. And therein lay the problem. The Catholic leaders had hauled out their biggest guns in the cause of protest. Logically enough, these were mostly senior statesmen – politicians and distinguished churchmen delivering their own emotion-laden firsthand memories of Pius. Rightly or wrongly, their corrective version of the papal past became bound to images of intolerance.

No one could fail to note that these notables denounced in strong language. One week after the premiere, Cardinal Frings described portions of the play as "libelous."[178] In the first week of March, the German bishops issued a statement describing their shame at seeing Pius' reputation defiled by Germans in Germany.[179] Just before assuming the papal throne as Pope Paul VI, Cardinal Giovanni Battista Montini, a right-hand man of Pius XII, took to the pages of the leading English Catholic weekly, *The Tablet*, to express his displeasure at the "injustice" done to his

Figure 5.3 The police were forced to intervene at the premiere of
Rolf Hochhuth's play *The Deputy* in Basel, Switzerland,
on September 24, 1963. This was but one of scores of protests in
continental Europe and North America between 1963 and 1965.
Keystone AG,37503145 (RM).

deceased superior.[180] The nuncio, Corrado Bafile, sought to convert fury
into action. He sent a "note verbal" on March 15 to the German Foreign
Office urging the federal government to "exert its influence" to prevent an
ongoing defamation of Pius.[181] After governmental officials refused to
allow a high-ranking political figure to deliver a speech defending Pius'
character and honor, nineteen politicians in the CDU subsequently sent
a formal "small query" to the government.[182] They asked whether it was
not unsettling to the "friends of our people" that Pius XII had been
attacked "from the side of the Germans."[183] Commanding headlines

Figure 5.4 Crowds gathered in Basel, Switzerland, on September 24, 1963, for the premiere of Rolf Hochhuth's play *The Deputy*. The signs read: "Intolerance = Catholicism" and "Are you raising your hats because of Hochhuth?" The latter was a pun on Hochhuth's last name, which translates literally as "high hat." Keystone AG, 37503125 (RM).

for days, this statement extruded injured nationalism. Pius, they noted, not only had helped Jews during the Nazi persecution but also had "stood particularly close to the German people for the entire time."[184]

That heavyweights in the ecclesia and CDU were throwing their weight around had a decisive bearing on the mainstream secular media's coverage. Like journalists of every day and ilk, its correspondents and editorialists were itching for a good fight, a titillating story and grabbing headlines. But they proceeded to spin out the bout as the story of David and Goliath, but not in the way representatives of the religious press would have liked. For Walter Adolph, Catholics were the beleaguered David; Goliath consisted of the Protestant-dominated, liberal and socialist press in the West and, above all, the Communist colossus in the Eastern part of his Berlin diocese. The inheritors of a nearly 100-year old siege mentality, many Catholic commentators spoke of the Hochhuth affair as the resumption of the Kulturkampf of the 1870s.[185] But in the new take, the roles were precisely reversed. The youthful Hochhuth was David, his foes militant Philistine demonstrators, giants in the Catholic political and religious establishment, including a sitting pope and former advisor to Pius XII, Pope Paul VI.[186] In a coincidence unnoticed at the time, this story line in the media echoed the plot of the play. Hochhuth's main protagonist, a youthful Jesuit, defied the pontiff in a supreme act of nonconformity.

The narrative these journalists imposed made perfect sense in light of the premiere of February 20, 1963. In November 1962, Franz-Josef Strauss, the Catholic defense minister and head of the CSU, ordered the arrest of journalists, including *Der Spiegel* founder Rudolf Augstein, for allegedly leaking defense secrets. The Hochhuth controversy was the first major media scandal in the immediate aftermath of the *Spiegel* affair, and some reporters and commentators drew connections.[187] It was the first opportunity for Young Turks in the media world to fight back against an aggressive and undemocratic Catholic political establishment. Some embraced Hochhuth as one of their own, a poster child for generational change. Dozens of newspapers published flattering portraits extolling his sincerity, anti-Nazi convictions and anger at the unexpiated sins of his elders. According to this new gospel, youth alone was capable of sweeping away half-truths about the Nazi past.[188] The Berlin newspaper *Der Abend* praised Hochhuth's youthful courage, noting that "youth has the right to be radical and uncomfortable, to look not for partial answers but for the full truth, even if it is bitter."[189]

Hochhuth's youth allowed him to capitalize on the growing trend of celebrity reporting and the increased use of visual images. With a whirlwind but astoundingly successful premiere behind him, he and his theatrical brainchild received a flattering five-page spread in the glossy pages of the international edition of *Life* magazine.[190] Feature stories detailing his unlikely journey from obscurity to celebrity appeared in hundreds of Germany's daily and weekly newspapers. Readers learned of his interest in baroque furniture.[191] One embarrassingly saccharine article, "Chocolate for the Poet," observed

Figure 5.5 Under the headline "A Struggle with Rome," the young playwright Rolf Hochhuth graced the cover of Germany's leading newsmagazine, *Der Spiegel*. Courtesy of DER SPIEGEL 17/1963.

that "if he were to take a table with you in your pub on the corner, you would immediately feel at home with him."[192] Pictures and references to his attractive wife and their toddler appeared in the mass daily newspaper *Bild*.[193] He gilded the cover page of *Der Spiegel*.[194] That same issue and *Bild* published photos that became iconic, showing the young playwright wearing a suit riding his bicycle to work.[195] The contrast with his high-profile ecclesiastical and political nemeses, mostly unphotogenic men in their sixties, seventies and eighties, could not have been more marked.[196] Photos of aging, unsmiling wrinkled men attired in dark clerical garb evoked clerical closed-mindedness and the mustiness of a closed Catholic subculture, what Carl Amery derided in the same year as "the Catholic milieu" and which seemed to evoke the pope's silence.[197] They reinforced the message that a generational house cleaning was sorely in order.

The Hochhuth controversy also gave younger journalists the opportunity to make use of hard-hitting styles of reporting like investigative journalism they had encountered abroad. Their goal now was to puncture secrets, probe wrongdoing and expose evildoers. For Catholic apologists, these new genres were often nothing short of a disaster. For such journalists, Hochhuth was one of them – a master sleuth who had somehow penetrated the high walls of the Vatican to lay bare its crimes; his adversaries were cover-up agents. They accordingly cast their articles as detective and crime stories: how had Hochhuth accomplished this feat, and where had he found his sources?

Hochhuth's three-month sojourn in Rome inevitably became the subject of intense speculation.[198] He and others dropped tantalizing hints. In his "Sidelines to History," he explicitly noted that the Vatican archives refused to release documents for the period after 1846. But the main actor, Dieter Borsche, erroneously told a Berlin newspaper that Hochhuth had indeed used documents from the Vatican archives.[199] The newspaper of the Free People's Theater, moreover, claimed that Hochhuth had spent three months in the Vatican and used documentary material that was "in part difficult to access."[200] Hochhuth's appendix also contained numerous references to his conversations with Vatican officials. Who were they?

In attempting to put the kibosh on these claims, the KNA only gave the controversy new life. Its Rome bureau issued a press release shortly after the premiere stating that the young playwright was "completely unknown" to the "relevant parties" in Rome.[201] Its main source was Robert Leiber, SJ, a German Jesuit who had served as an adviser to Pope Pius XII. Leiber had a motive for jumping into the fray. Several years earlier, he had written the article "Pius and the Jews in Rome" in response to *The Yellow Star*, a documentary of graphic black-and-white photos of Holocaust victims published by Rütten und Loening.[202] Leiber had objected not to its gore but to its use of Ernst von Weizsäcker's quotation from the German ambassador with which Hochhuth closed

The Deputy. In any case, Hochhuth was not about to take the KNA attack sitting down. Two angry ripostes were handed over to the DPA, the rival wire-services agency. In the first, Hochhuth accused the KNA of "character assassination." In the second, the Rowohlt Press noted that Hochhuth had interviewed "numerous high clerics as well as nameless witnesses to the events of 1943" during his three months at the Vatican.[203] He had also been "received for an hour-long audience in the Secretariat of State of the Holy See."[204]

These scuffles in the press naturally led curious journalists to probe further. Hochhuth threw out more tantalizing hints. In an interview with the *Neue Rheinzeitung* approximately two weeks later, Hochhuth refused to divulge the names of his sources "until their deaths." But he then noted that one of them, a prelate, had just died – a reference to Hudal: "Perhaps I will decide to release his name at least."[205] In an extensive interview from late April, a hard-hitting journalist from *Der Spiegel* pushed him to reveal his source.[206] Hochhuth promptly clammed up. He told the journalists that he was remaining silent to protect his sources from recrimination. In any case, the controversy was prolonged, as the press, including the KNA, attempted to discern his informants' identities.[207] For sundry newspaper readers drawn to spy novels, how could the Catholic apology for Pius possibly compete with the cloak and dagger of Hochhuth's solo mission to Rome?[208]

The turn to investigative journalism gave Pius' critics an additional advantage. Journalists used to investigating crooked or despotic politicians now investigated a deceased pontiff. What did Pius know about the murder of Jews, and when did he know it? What did he do in response – and why? This had all of the elements of a compelling crime story – a crime, villains, motives, victims and concluding moral lessons. This was grist for hard-hitting younger journalists, a landmine for professional historians. Lacking expertise on the subject, the doyens of the West German historical profession remained reticent. Only a few historians like Wilhelm Alff and Hans Buchheim from the Institute for Contemporary History in Munich opted to jump into the raging waters.[209] The historian Rudolf Morsey reluctantly took part in a forum in Heidelberg only after learning that no other historian would take part.[210]

As a result, it was mostly diplomats, churchmen and statesmen from the 1930s and 1940s who attempted to fill the gaps in the historical register. Critical of *The Deputy* were Johannes Neuhäusler; Gustav Gundlach; Monsignore Alberto Giovannetti; Otto Dibelius, the Protestant bishop of Berlin; Robert Kempner, the famed German-Jewish prosecutor at the Nuremberg war crimes trials married to a devout Catholic; and Albrecht von Kessel, the German diplomat at the Vatican who had defended his superior, Ernst von Weizsäcker, at Nuremberg.[211] Sharing memories of Pius and the Nazi persecution of the churches, they argued that a public papal protest would have done little to save Jews. But they were also upstaged by illustrious names like Alsatian Lutheran missionary Albert Schweitzer and Confessing Church pastor Heinrich Grüber. Noting that he had been sent to prison in December 1940 after having twice attempted to join the Jews in ghettoes and prison camps, the latter argued that a pope who remained silent to save himself and disregarded the example of the Good Samaritan "had no right to call himself the successor of Jesus."[212] He accompanied Hochhuth to the United States for the run of *The Deputy* on Broadway. In the manner of an Old Testament prophet, he delivered talks at American universities and sermons at Protestant churches that excoriated churches' indifference to genocide: "We have all become guilty. All peoples and all churches remained silent." Christianity, he insisted, needed theological reform to purge itself of its anti-Semitism. Though adding little to the pontifical historical ledger, Protestant pulpiteers provided concluding lessons in good and evil, the finishing touches on these exercises in investigative journalism.

But investigative journalism was not the only critical format causing problems for Walter Adolph. The press was drawn to public forums springing up in scores of cities including Munich, Berlin, Duisburg, Heidelberg and Cologne. They quickly spread to virtually every nation where performances of *The Deputy* had electrified audiences and galvanized protestors to action.[213] They found a range of eager sponsors, including universities, Catholic fraternities and the Catholic Academy in Bavaria as well as the studios of radio and television stations.[214] Offering a chance for audience and speakers to pontificate about the past, most were set up in another relatively new journalistic genre – the "pro-con" format. Sponsors deployed speakers guaranteed to hold tightly to one side. Grüber appeared at public forums on *The Deputy* in Munich and Berlin. Even so, some hosts sought to stack the deck. The Catholic Academy in Bavaria invited only one critical voice to its forum, and its uniformity of opinion did not go unnoticed in the press.[215]

These public forums, intended as serious endeavors, grappled with moral, theological and existential questions that resisted easy answers: Did Pius XII have the duty to sacrifice himself for European Jews? Had Pius spoken out resoundingly against genocide, would the Nazis have retaliated, possibly arresting and executing him? Would a papal protest have led to stepped-up arrests and deportations, as it had after the Dutch bishops protested the roundup of Jews? Or would the Nazis have closed the gas chambers, as they seemingly had done after Bishop von Galen had protested against the euthanasia of the mentally and physically infirm in 1941? Above all: why did Pius remain silent?[216]

But the new public sphere was unpredictable, its forums a curious olio of the tribunal, confessional and carnival. In Munich in April 1963, hundreds had to be turned away from an auditorium that seated 600.[217] Just weeks earlier, Hochhuth, Piscator and Grüber had to be physically escorted to the podium because of a standing-room-only crowd of more than 1,000 in an auditorium designed for 600 at the Technical University in Berlin.[218] Radio Free Berlin, a prominent radio station, described the atmosphere as resembling the Bundestag debate about the *Spiegel* affair.[219] Following brief introductory remarks by Hochhuth and Grüber, who insisted that all, including the church, must own up to their own failures and forestall similar future tragedies, the more than two-hour discussion turned into an upwelling of passion and emotion.[220] Speakers from both the podium and audience were repeatedly interrupted by the applause, boos and catcalls of the restless crowd. In one instance, a young Germanist and historian from the audience who identified himself only as "Michel" went head-to-head with the playwright over what he called Hochhuth's one-sided "pseudo-historical sidelines." Though Hochhuth dished out masterful rebuttals, Michel refused to concede his points and yield the floor. The audience, finally, had enough, and his further protests were drowned out by the tumult from the crowd.[221]

Stonewalled by this spectacle of soul searching and Schadenfreude, Walter Adolph and his fellow fighters refused to participate in public discussions in the hopes that the issue of Pius' silence would die a natural death with no Catholic counterstrikes to resuscitate it. On March 18, 1963, Adolph visited the head of the broadcaster Radio Free Berlin to explain that no official Catholic representatives would take part in a planned live panel discussion.[222] Cardinal Frings, having already spoken out against Hochhuth three times, declined to issue a statement to be broadcast in a documentary about *The Deputy* on Hessian television.[223] As Limburger Auxillary Bishop Walter Kampe informed the television broadcaster, Frings' participation "would have served as further propaganda" for Hochhuth.[224] But in refusing to take part, they ceded the turf to their opponents, who suddenly had an open microphone. This meant that broadcasters were likely to turn to those more critical of the church's past. Ernst-Wolfgang Böckenförde appeared at one public forum. The publicist Carl Amery used his appearance at one forum to call for theological reform and for shedding the insularity of what he somewhat scornfully labeled the "Catholic milieu."

Figure 5.6 Rolf Hochhuth in conversation with the theater critic and journalist Friedrich Luft in 1965. The interest from the growing public sphere could scarcely be sated. Courtesy of Getty Images.

But more fundamental changes taking place in the public spheres in the West also rendered this strategy less viable. Adolph and other church leaders withdrew from the public sphere at precisely the time when participation in this "theater in modern societies" was dramatically increasing.[225] Throngs of men and women of all ages and confessions flocked to forums out of genuine interest in their web of interwoven theological, moral and historical questions. Fourteen months after the premiere in Berlin, a journalist from the West German radio remarked that no discussion since war's end had enjoyed such a broad resonance and found such attentive and critical listeners as the storm over *The Deputy*.[226]

The reasons for this surge of interest are not hard to discern. So many issues generating international headlines converged on the pages of *The Deputy*. For more than a decade, the media's interest in covering religious affairs – biblical criticism, church politics, the personalities of the church, theological reform – had been rising. The run of *The Deputy* on stages worldwide coincided with front-page headlines about the Second Vatican Council, the death of beloved Pope John XXIII and the election of Pope Paul VI. Hochhuth's play was germane to all of these stories.

Angelo Roncalli, as nuncio in Bulgaria, had rescued Jews, Giovanni Montini had worked closely with Pius XII, and the council by 1965 was wrestling with questions of Roman Catholic anti-Semitism. At the same time, the trial of Adolf Eichmann, the arrest of low-ranking concentration camp guards and the resumption of war crimes trials directed the spotlight back to *The Deputy*. Hochhuth was the first playwright to stage Auschwitz. What other work would allow the notorious Eichmann to go bowling with "The Doctor," his character loosely modeled after Josef Mengele?

Though originating out of genuine interest, these forums, open discussions and exchanges in the press came to serve another equally important function. They provided an ideal trial balloon to test the boundaries of the public sphere.[227] How were public discussions on hot-button topics to be carried out? Several commentators saw the debates triggered by *The Deputy* as the chance to broaden and democratize the public sphere, particularly since so many joined in these nationwide conversations.[228] And hence the paradox. As counterintuitive as it might seem in light of the fierce protests, Pope Pius XII was, in many ways, a safe choice for discussion. He was a citizen of none of the countries in which *The Deputy* was legally performed. Only for his contemporaries high in the Protestant and Catholic hierarchies and of a certain age was the conversation personal and immediate – and hence their often-anguished reactions. But for the overwhelming majority of those darting off to forums, there was little chance that the discussions of the sins of omission of a diplomat and worldwide spiritual leader could draw attention to the misconduct of one's fathers, brothers, cousins, friends and neighbors. Pius provided an ideal point of convergence for armchair moralists and a secure point of entry into the challenges posed by the recent German past.

But as safe as the topic was, it was this growing understanding of the public sphere as a forum for open debate, discursive exchange and deliberation that made it more difficult for men like Adolph to see their own corrective take root. The fate of two slim volumes about *The Deputy* controversy – one published by Adolph, the other by Rowohlt – neatly illustrate why Adolph's version failed to gain widespread currency. In September, Adolph published a 112-page volume, *Distorted History: Answer to Rolf Hochhuth*.[229] It regurgitated letters, apologies, position papers and polemics, including the defense of Pius XII mounted by Montini and excerpts from Robert Leiber's article in *Stimmen der Zeit*. It also tacked on more than forty pages of documents, mostly papal addresses and pastoral letters by the German bishops from 1941 through 1943. Scores of German newspapers duly noted the appearance of

Adolph's publications, but his apology preached to the choir.[230] In the course of its various editions, it sold fewer than 20,500 copies.[231] It received no foreign language translations.

By way of comparison, a similar venture by the Rowohlt Verlag met with astounding success. Rowohlt's chief editor, Fritz Raddatz, printed a compendium of reviews, exchanges between Hochhuth and critics, the text of the parliament's "small inquiry," numerous letters to the editor and letters to Hochhuth.[232] Within weeks of its publication, this slender 235-page paperback, *Summa Iniuria: Or Should the Pope Have Remained Silent?*, sold several hundred thousand copies and shot up to number six on *Der Spiegel's* best seller list. It served as a model for three additional anthologies in the coming two years, one published in Switzerland to coincide with the premiere in Basel and two, *The Storm over the Deputy* and *The Deputy Reader*, in New York.[233]

Why did Raddatz's volume prevail in this competition for sales and influence? It better met the spirit of the public sphere. Adolph's volume presented a chorus of like-minded voices, while Raddatz's volume at least claimed to be fair and balanced. Raddatz, for instance, reprinted portions of a withering review penned by Erich Klausener Jr. for the March 3 edition of the *Petrusblatt* because it, in Raddatz's words, "is important to the press to reproduce the objections to Hochhuth's play as well."[234] Its counterpoint of pro and con, however, masked the fact that Raddatz had shrewdly stacked the deck. Commentaries favorable to the playwright, including those written by Hochhuth himself, outnumbered the voices of the critics by approximately two to one.[235] Raddatz, moreover, manipulated the text of Klausener's critique. Raddatz had asked Klausener for permission, which Klausener explicitly denied, claiming that "the Rowohlt press itself is also all too committed to the Hochhuth discussion through the editing of this paperback."[236] Raddatz responded not only by appending this quotation to his header for Klausener's text. He cut and pasted from Klausener's review, not indicating where he made the majority of his cuts, no doubt since many of the lines cut were dismissive of Hochhuth's use of sources. Raddatz then printed this hatchet job under his own name. This seemed part of his larger public relations strategy. In unrelated instances, the Hungarian philosopher Georg Lukacs and the German Jesuit Karl Breuning, SJ, complained that their private letters to the author, which expressed support for the playwright's positions, were released to the press without their permission.[237]

But manipulation had no bearing on why Adolph's volume met with such disappointing sales. Like many Catholic responses to church critics before and after the controversy, his defense of Pius was predicated on the assumption that publishing contrary evidence, usually in the form of primary source documents, represented a foolproof way to counter the exaggerated claims of critics. Adolph's volume thus took on the tone of an angry fact checker. For *The Deputy*, as is true for almost any work bearing a provocative revisionist thesis, suffered from distinct methodological shortcomings. As critics, including even *Der Spiegel* magazine, pointed out at the time, Hochhuth had shunted aside contrary evidence. In the interview with the playwright, the *Spiegel* journalist confronted him on one fairly egregious "distortion."[238] On the front pages of the paperback edition, Hochhuth had provided a quotation critical of papal conduct from French novelist and Nobel laureate François Mauriac. Hochhuth, however, had cut Mauriac's observation that the pope also had the "horrible duty (through silence) to prevent worse evil."[239] In this vein, Hochhuth quoted directly in his "Sidelines to History" from a letter from Jan Ciechanowski, the former ambassador to Washington of the Polish government in exile. Ciechanowski confirmed that he had informed the Congress, the press, the White House, the cardinals and bishops of the extermination of the Jewish population in Poland. But Hochhuth ignored his assertion that "such a declaration (of protest) would have had no effect on Hitler."[240]

For Adolph and higher-ups in the Vatican, the strategy was simple – correct the errors, publish the documents and let the truth come to light. The most elaborate of these documentary editions, *Actes et documents du Saint-Siège relatifs à la période de la Seconde Guerre Mondiale* (*The Documents of the Holy See for the Period of the Second World War*), filled eleven volumes with documents in more than four languages. But even Adolph was aware of this strategy's shortcomings. He correctly recognized that issues of guilt and moral responsibility had displaced the question of whether Hochhuth had accurately depicted the pontiff's conduct.[241] But more broadly, what lay readers, let alone journalists, have the time to pore over thousands of pages – or even forty pages of documents in *Distorted History* – and distill these into short articles and eye-catching headlines? The pro-and-con format employed by some of Hochhuth's champions was a far better entry into a public sphere focused on morality than a compendium of desultory documentary evidence.

Clearly outmatched in light of these changes in the media and public sphere, the most determined of Hochhuth's opponents fought back with the only weapons left to them. They turned to hard-edged tactics that verged on censorship. The nuncio, Corrado Bafile, asked the Catholic Office in Bonn "to do all that it could to hinder performances of *The Deputy* from airing on radio and television."[242] As a coworker noted: "I must say that I have never seen the nuncio so personally engaged as in this question."[243] Each German state had its own television and radio committees, and representatives of the church were guaranteed several seats on these committees.[244] These representatives, and most likely Cardinal Frings himself, pressured the state television and radio networks into not giving air time either to Hochhuth, his supporters or the controversy itself. The Protestant head of the West German Radio and Television, Klaus von Bismarck, bowed to this pressure, issuing a directive forbidding his radio and television stations from presenting the text and the performance of *The Deputy*. "My personal considerations," he wrote, "have been co-determined by my own experience in already meeting many Catholic Christians, who have been deeply shaken in their personal faith and led to the point of doubt by the text and content of *The Deputy*."[245] Frings, it seems, was extremely satisfied with this outcome.[246] Yet other media directors in Berlin, Hesse and Bavaria refused.[247] Radio in the American Sector (RIAS) in Berlin, moreover, reported on the controversy almost from the outset.[248] As the controversy spread, even directors who had once yielded to ecclesiastical pressure changed their mind. Bismarck's own West German Radio even invited Hochhuth to its studios for an extensive interview in 1965.[249]

Making matters worse for those advocating harder-edged methods was the fact that their hard-edged tactics themselves became the story. Already in March 1963, some leading Berlin Catholics were considering a lawsuit against Hochhuth, Piscator and Ledig-Rowohlt for desecrating the memory of the deceased Bernhard Lichtenberg.[250] Nothing came of this effort, but similar considerations by the Catholic Office in Bonn blew up in their faces. At the end of March, the Catholic Office commissioned its leading lawyer, Karl Panzer, to determine whether a slander lawsuit by the sister of Pius XII would have any "chance of success."[251] His efforts were supposed to remain top secret, but Panzer boasted of them before an audience of young Catholic journalists.[252] One of those present apparently subscribed to the spirit of "aggiornamento" emanating from the ongoing Second Vatican Council and promptly leaked the news to the secular media. Although Panzer had, in fact, come to the conclusion that it would be best to stay away from any legal strategies, the very fact that such moves were even being considered created a secondary scandal that generated headlines for a number of days.[253]

Through such blunders, a debate originally about the silence of the pope was turned into a discussion about tolerance, freedom of speech and the boundaries of the public sphere. What were the limits to free speech? Who should be allowed to exercise that right? And here, the positions of many papal defenders and papal critics strikingly diverged. Just days after the premiere, Konrad Kraemer, the leader of the KNA, proclaimed that "freedom without truth sows the seeds of anarchy."[254] Without truth, he insisted, there is no freedom, for German Catholics "never allow that the reputation of Pius be defiled with dishonest infamy and agitation."[255]

As the conflict heated up, leading Catholics in Berlin resurrected an argument that had also been raised in the fight over denominational schools in the mid-1950s: they demanded "tolerance towards core Christian convictions."[256] In practice, this meant soft forms of censorship. Adolph protested a decision to distribute tickets to approximately 3,000 seventeen- and eighteen-year-old high schoolers.[257] In early April, he even appeared at the door of Adolf Arndt, now an SPD senator entrusted with cultural matters for Berlin.[258] Since the play was both tendentious and defamatory, the prelate told the senator following their ninety-minute meeting, granting schoolchildren tickets did not do justice to principles of tolerance.[259] His appeal was obviously in vain, for further protests were triggered by the Berlin Senate's decision to grant 22,000 schoolchildren free tickets to *The Deputy* in the fall of 1963.[260]

The KNA and the *Petrusblatt* also publicly denounced the awarding of a "young generation" prize to Hochhuth by a jury assembled by the Academy of Arts; the award was, they claimed, "5000 Marks for defamation."[261] As the cultural senator, Arndt was required to publicly administer the award. But he had misgivings, making no bones about the awkward dilemma "this explosive work" had placed him in.[262] He was required on the one hand to maintain good relations between church and state and on the other to uphold basic freedoms.[263] Though disagreeing with the jury's verdict, he was compelled to respect the artistic freedom of the jury.[264]

Under siege were models of old-school Catholicism, which asserted that there was no right to error. In 1959, the *Petrusblatt* published an article, "Where Tolerance Ends," that tidily summed up this traditional understanding – in cases of lies and defamation, the public sphere needed to be trimmed back.[265] But these were battles that Adolph and his supporters could no longer win in the mid-1960s, particularly after the *Spiegel* affair had steered public attention to questions of civil liberties. Angered at what they took to be censorship, opponents began calling attention to the lack of openness and the authoritarian spirit that in their eyes underlay the entire Catholic enterprise. The aggressive Catholic defense had thus become the story – and would continue to be so as protests unfolded in the coming years on both sides of the Atlantic.

The battles over *The Deputy* thus set the tone for ensuing public controversies about the Catholic past. It was not just that, once again, none of their combatants changed their mind after being confronted with – and vexed by – contrary evidence. Rather, the defenders of Pius XII repeatedly found themselves in a dilemma well known in the fields of social psychology and public relations. With proper publicity, those raising accusations almost always have the upper hand. If their opponents protest, they inadvertently redirect public attention to the original charges, thereby reinforcing them. But if those accused leave the charges uncontested, they leave the impression that the charges must have been valid. Otherwise, they would have protested.

The outcome of media battles between those hurling out iconic images of a pope washing his hands while Jews are deported and those trudging forward with corrections, protests, monographs and documentary editions was thus never in dispute. Even so, defenders of the church's past held to this strategy of correcting distortions and lies, even as the exposure to contrary evidence seems only to have intensified Rolf Hochhuth's hatred for Pope Pius XII. "If I had known how hard I would be attacked," he told a reporter in October 1963, "then I would have written some passages more sharply."[266] By the mid-2000s, he twisted the pope's verdict of National Socialism as a "satanic ghost" from his address to the College of Cardinals on June 2, 1945, into an epithet for the pontiff himself: Pius was now a "satanic coward."[267]

The Hochhuth controversy marked the fundamental turning point in the battles for the Catholic past. It represented the last gasp of the Catholic milieu, the final extraordinary mobilization of organizations, politicians and clerics. But this time, it was unable to prevent a fundamental taboo from being not just infringed but shattered. From this point on, criticism of the Catholic Church's past that had lain dormant or underground would be heaved into the public eye and received with open arms by the mainstream media. In typical Rhenish fashion, Cardinal Frings expressed his frustration with a joke. The Second Vatican Council, he noted, replaced the Latin liturgy with the vernacular. He could no longer refer to his liturgical headdress as a "mitre." He had to don a "high-hat," or what in German literally translates as a "Hochhuth."[268]

In 1964, German Catholic defenders of their church's conduct during the Third Reich found themselves ambushed by another critical attack. The alleged assailant was Guenter Lewy, a German-Jewish émigré born in the Lower Silesian capital of Breslau in 1923 and political scientist in central Massachusetts. Lewy had carried out groundbreaking research in Catholic archives in Germany between September 1961 and June 1962. In short order, he parlayed his findings into a book that told the story of Catholic support for National Socialism, *The Catholic Church and Nazi Germany*.[1]

Centuries of Christian anti-Judaism, Lewy argued, had "conditioned" a climate in which modern racially based anti-Semitism could flourish.[2] The number of Catholics prepared to oppose National Socialism was miniscule; they opposed the regime only when their direct interests were in jeopardy. Constrained by "reasons of state," they should instead have provided greater assistance and solace to the needs of victims of "an upsurge of monstrous barbarism."[3] As *The Deputy* continued to generate protests across the United States, Lewy's publisher, McGraw-Hill, recognized the potential of Lewy's findings to command attention and sales. It arranged for an extensive advertising campaign as well as a German translation. Once the latter appeared in print in early 1965, *Der Spiegel* chose to run an unprecedented eight-week series of excerpts, "With a Firm Step into the New Reich," beginning on its cover page of February 17, 1965.[4]

The Catholic Church and Nazi Germany created a storm of consternation among German Catholics, one that would prove as traumatic as Hochhuth's play *The Deputy*. It did so not only because its lucid account appeared first in America with a popular press and was certain to get a large following and the author's last name suggested he belonged to a racial minority that had been ruthlessly persecuted by the Nazis. It did so because Lewy had produced the first comprehensive scholarly account of the church's alleged failings during the entire Nazi era. Earlier critics had mostly produced chronologically narrow vignettes of ecclesiastical and papal conduct. In contrast, Lewy had constructed a 341-page picture into the entire twelve-year era of National Socialism. Even worse from the vantage point of beleaguered church defenders was that diocesan officials in Germany had granted him permission to use portions of their collections, not suspecting that he was out to write a critical history of the church's conduct in the Third Reich.

Lewy's coup cast a shadow over scholarship that lasted for decades. Decrying what one archivist described as his "misuse" of church documents, ecclesiastical officials began to restrict access to their holdings to those deemed sufficiently reliable – at least until their collections could be properly examined, inventoried and catalogued in full. Coming from an American Ph.D. in political science with the finest of credentials, his work exposed at the same time ongoing differences in historical methodology between the two sides of the Atlantic over how to approach the sensitive subject of the National Socialist past. Disagreements over methodology would come to comprise the heart of subsequent clashes, which from this point on moved from the streets to the more recondite pages of newspapers and historical quarterlies.

This chapter first retraces Lewy's unlikely journey from Breslau to central Massachusetts, one with formative experiences in British Palestine, Italy, the British occupation zone of Germany and New York City. Second, it examines his research strategies, which became a topic of controversy. Third, it delves into the battles that broke out immediately after his book appeared in print. Finally, it looks at the impact of his scholarship in the coming years and decades on the field of contemporary church history.

Guenter Lewy's Unlikely Journey, 1923–1961

Like Rolf Hochhuth's focus on Pope Pius XII, Guenter Lewy's interest in the support of the German Catholic Church for the National Socialist state did not stem from disillusioning youthful personal encounters with members of the ecclesia. For one, Roman Catholics were a minority in the overwhelmingly Protestant region of Lower Silesia.[5] For another, Lewy was not – nor would ever be – Christian. He was Jewish, the scion of a fairly well-off family from Breslau, one able as late as the early 1930s to afford a maid.[6]

Breslau was home to an exceptionally vibrant Jewish community, Germany's third largest, which numbered more than 24,000 in 1930.[7] But it was also a frontier town not far from Germany's disputed eastern border with Poland. Its politics had been veering sharply to the right in the 1920s and early 1930s.[8] Its voters cast a higher percentage of their ballots for the Nazis in the July elections of 1932 than compatriots in other large German cities.[9] Its Nazi police chief gained national fame and notoriety after 1933 for his zeal in persecuting minorities and political dissidents.

Battered by racial slurs, Lewy found solace in Jewish associations. At the age of nine, he joined the Breslau branch of *Die Greifen*, a close-knit group for Jewish boys in the spirit of the bourgeois youth movement. Jewish boys had often been barred from the mainstream youth movement, but in *Die Greifen* Lewy too was able to discover a sense of community through hikes in the countryside, campfires and singing. Its values and commitments were to be lifelong, and so they proved for Lewy, who more than sixty years later cited its undying influence in his decision to become an academic.[10]

The Zionist inclinations of *Die Greifen* also strengthened his resolve to leave for Palestine.[11] He began working on a small farm in Bavaria to prepare for work on a Palestinian kibbutz, having concluded already at the ages of thirteen and fourteen that there was no place for Jews in Nazi Germany. His fears were borne out when he was badly beaten up by an SA troop during the violence of Kristallnacht.[12] His father was sent to Buchenwald and released only when he could specify a site for emigration.[13] His mother and father gave up their floundering retail operation selling socks and stockings and left for Luxembourg. After the German invasion in May 1940, they made their way to the United States via France, Spain and Portugal. Several aunts and uncles were not so fortunate and perished in the Holocaust, the same fate awaiting more than 5,000 of Breslau's remaining Jews.[14]

Guenter Lewy left the kibbutz to join the Palestine Regime of the British Army in 1942 when Rommel stood at the gates of Alexandria.[15] This unit evolved into the core of the legendary Jewish Brigade, which fought alongside Montgomery's Eighth Army as it moved up the Italian peninsula in 1944 and 1945.[16] Lewy recalled being part of a combat patrol that took the first German prisoners. He had the delight of shouting to Wehrmacht soldiers in German: "Surrender, the Jews are here!"[17] His knowledge of German also came in handy after the war when he returned to Germany to serve as an interpreter for the British Army in Wuppertal.[18]

After his military discharge in 1946, Lewy joined his parents in the United States. A rich uncle who had made a fortune in Brazil after barely escaping the clutches of the police in Nazi Germany helped finance his undergraduate studies at City College in New York, a port of educational entry for ambitious Jewish immigrants and their children.[19] He studied psychology, sociology and government but also became interested in political science. He began auditing lectures at Columbia University by Franz Neumann, a German-Jewish émigré with ties to the Institute of

Social Research of the Frankfurt School and a keen interest in the political theory of the Reformation and Counter-Reformation.[20]

Lewy opted to pursue a graduate degree in political science with Neumann. Through his advisor, he came to investigate the theories of tyrannicide of the Spanish Jesuit Juan de Mariana. Mariana was a maverick sixteenth- and early-seventeenth-century scholastic and political theorist who noted that the king was responsible not only to God but to the people and the law of the land; unjust kings forfeited the loyalty of their subjects.[21] He made "irreverence against the Catholic faith" a defining characteristic of a tyrant.[22] He criticized the monarchy's seizure of church properties and valuables. But Mariana, unlike most thinkers of his day, did not make the pope the ultimate arbiter of the life and death of legitimate rulers.[23] He gave little heed to the indirect temporal powers of the papacy, or what was more commonly known as the *potestas indirecta*. If Mariana invoked an authority to legitimize resistance to the crown, it was the Spanish Cortes, or parliament.

Mariana's theories of tyrannicide from sixteenth- and seventeenth-century Spain thus handed Lewy an intellectual framework with which to reflect upon the conduct of the Catholic hierarchy in the first half of the twentieth century. For in Mariana's expostulations on tyrannicide, Lewy saw a rich scholastic tradition largely ignored in the coming centuries. To be sure, such traditions could be resurrected, as when the Spanish bishops openly supported General Franco's military revolt against the Spanish republic.[24] But the opposite seemed to have been the case in Nazi Germany, as Lewy discovered while reading an article by Gordon Zahn titled "Würzburg 1957" published in March 1958 in *The Catholic Worker* and easily available at New York newsstands.[25] Lewy read that the German hierarchy's near-total support for what was likely "history's most unjust war" had led to "the dead end of moral bankruptcy."[26] Contrary to conventional wisdom, the German churches had been reluctant to sanction resistance.

His interest piqued, Lewy wrote to Zahn in March 1960 to request a copy of his still-unpublished monograph, *German Catholics and Hitler's Wars*.[27] After reading through his manuscript in progress, Lewy decided to take on theoretical challenges Zahn had briefly articulated in his conclusion: why did so many Catholics accept the National Socialist state?[28] Here, Lewy turned to Mariana to invert the question: why did Catholics repudiate their own tradition of resistance to secular authority?[29]

Lewy's reflections took on a different tenor than those of Zahn, one consistent with his own religious proclivities and armed struggle against National Socialism. From early on, Lewy described himself as an atheist; this self-definition eventually softened into that of a "Jewish agnostic."[30]

Figure 6.1 Guenter Lewy, a Jewish refugee from Nazi Germany, drew on materials from German Catholic archives to put forward the first comprehensive and critical scholarly account of the German Catholic Church under Nazi rule. Courtesy of Guenter Lewy.

But he was no militant unbeliever with a knee-jerk hostility to religion. On the contrary, he later wrote a book arguing that secularism helped erode the moral fabric in the West; the title read "Why America Needs Religion."[31] The church, then, was a buttress of the societal and moral order, hence its importance in any analysis of the moral calamities wrought by the Third Reich.

Lewy's understanding of resistance was also fundamentally different from the calls for Christian martyrdom found in Zahn's pacifism. Resistance, for Lewy, did not exclude armed action. Had enough persons been steadfast in their commitment to tyrannicide, Lewy argued, National

Socialism might have been dealt a fatal blow. Think of the "possible beneficial consequence" that could have come from the assassination of a Stalin or Hitler, Lewy mused at the close of his chapter on resistance to tyranny.[32] He closed an article from 1960 on resistance to tyranny with a quotation from the German Jesuit Max Pribilla, SJ, who noted that "vigilance and determination" were the best "safeguards against the loss of liberty" and dictatorships. This credo was in keeping with a basic tenet of vital center liberalism: armed conflict was morally defensible and indeed even necessary under certain circumstances. True to this dictum, Lewy argued that the Vietnam War had been a morally defensible war and published striking criticisms of peace activists of that era.[33]

Lewy's Journey through German Catholic Archives, 1961–1962

Before setting out for Germany at the start of the 1961–1962 academic year, Lewy found himself confronted with a more pressing challenge: how would a non-Catholic scholar based in North America and with a critical agenda gain access to diocesan archives in Germany? The way in which this newly minted assistant professor of government at Smith College, a small women's college in Northhampton, Massachusetts, negotiated this challenge precipitated a swirl of allegations more than two years before his book was even published.

The furious reaction that Lewy's forays through ten German diocesan archives generated cannot be understood without recognizing that church archives, where they even existed, were in a state of disarray in the early 1960s.[34] Most manuscript collections had not been processed, organized and inventoried. Staffs lacked professionally trained archivists. Those overseeing collections, more often than not chancery officials, were themselves often unaware of their holdings' size and content. Access was granted, if at all, on the basis of word-of-mouth recommendations and letters of introduction. Official regulations did not yet exist.

Aware of the difficulties facing newcomers to this turf, Lewy contacted those more senior in the field like Zahn for advice.[35] Zahn specifically urged him to write Stasiewski and Neuhäusler.[36] He pointed out that "official historians" at many of the dioceses could "open doors that would otherwise remain closed." The sociologist from Chicago urged his junior colleague to refrain from mentioning his name but also asked him to pass back any information about the reaction his paper from Mundelein College had generated on the other side of the Atlantic.[37] Lewy eventually reported back to Zahn, albeit two years later, that the head of the KNA,

Konrad Kraemer, was erroneously claiming that Zahn was a "converted Jew" – and "that explains everything."[38]

Lewy used these tips and warnings to put together a strategy with which to shrewdly maneuver through the archives. He described his project to church and state archives in Germany in a manner less likely to raise suspicions. He was, he informed the chancery of the Archdiocese of Cologne in the spring of 1960, intending to write a book about "the fate of the Roman Catholic Church under Hitler." He was particularly interested in the "reaction of the church to the persecutions during the Third Reich and in the manner in which the church continued its ministry under these conditions."[39] He attached a brief letter from the secretary of the Board of Trustees at Smith College certifying that he was indeed a faculty member there.[40] He also procured a letter of introduction from the acting vicar general of the diocese of Springfield, Massachusetts, through the help of a Catholic friend of his wife.[41] The letter stated that Lewy was spending the 1961–1962 academic year in Germany carrying out research for a book on "the persecution of the Catholic Church under the Nazi regime" and added that any assistance would be "highly appreciated."

Lewy left for Germany in the second half of 1961 funded by a research fellowship from the Social Science Research Council and an additional grant from Smith College. Shortly after his arrival, he met for nearly an hour in the archdiocesan chancery with Neuhäusler, who was serving as the vicar general of Munich-Freising.[42] For once, it was the normally crafty veteran of Catholic resistance who seems to have been blindsided. He furnished his guest with three papal white books and promised to let him at a later point go through some of the material he had collected "at great daily risk to his life."[43] He reported that Lewy apparently left a "good impression."[44]

This "good impression" was what Neuhäusler mentioned in a memorandum to all of the Bavarian chanceries on November 9, 1961.[45] Prompting this communiqué was an inquiry from the vicar general of Passau. While paying him a visit to gain access to documentary collections on "the Church and National Socialism," Lewy dropped Neuhäusler's name as a reference.[46] Undoubtedly assuming that his American visitor would be stopping by other Bavarian archives and chanceries, Neuhäusler nonetheless wrote that chanceries needed to inspect any documents from the Nazi era before passing them on, his good impression notwithstanding. Correspondence between the bishops might not be suitable for publication. There was a tendency in the United States and in Bavaria to judge the statements of German bishops critically, as the writings of Zahn, Böckenförde

Figure 6.2 Auxiliary Bishop and Vicar General Johannes Neuhäusler met with Guenter Lewy in 1961, who left a "good impression" on his host. Courtesy of Das Archiv des Erzbistums Muenchen und Freising.

and a journalist from the *Süddeutsche Zeitung*, Karl Wucher, had made amply clear.[47]

Just one day later, Neuhäusler's opinion changed abruptly. Cardinal Döpfner informed him that Lewy had complained to a fellow in the Institute for Political Science in Munich that Neuhäusler had denied him use of the archdiocesan archives.[48] Neuhäusler was livid. Only Döpfner could authorize access, he fumed. The collections had yet to be inventoried. Lewy had failed to appreciate his own generosity in granting him use of his personal collection. He was now inclined not to provide any such assistance in the future even to the growing numbers of students and graduate students seeking dissertation topics.

Neuhäusler's mistrust grew as Lewy continued to make reference to his meeting with Neuhäusler during his round of visits to diocesan archives. A number of chanceries contacted him about their visitor's documentary requests. Neuhäusler responded with yet another memorandum on February 2, 1961, one now to all the chanceries in Germany and Austria.[49] Lewy's project, he wrote, was mutating far beyond its original scope. He was examining not only the Nazi war on the church but the conduct of the episcopate and of German Catholics toward National Socialism at the time of the Nazi seizure of power and the start of the Second World War. Diocesan officials needed to treat the correspondence between the bishops with special care. We cannot guarantee, he cautioned, that Lewy will not put himself in the camps of those like "professors of Loyola University" who "do not always provide interpretations in a purely objective manner and perhaps not least will put together a most displeasing critique of the conduct of the German bishops and Catholics."[50]

Some chanceries evidently heeded Neuhäusler's warning. In the preface to his book, Lewy pithily noted that the dioceses of Bamberg, Cologne, Freiburg im Breisgau, Rottenburg and Speyer had declined to cooperate "for reasons best known to themselves."[51] But such stonewalling did not derail his project. Nine other diocesan archives, including that of Paderborn, provided assistance.[52] Lewy also received unexpected aid. Ever since the publication of Böckenförde's article, inquiries to examine documents from the Weimar and Nazi eras were piling up at church archives.[53] The head of the Catholic Office in Bonn, Wilhelm Wissing, was aware that these requests were overstretching the capacities of overworked chanceries.[54] Wissing was about to join the board of trustees of the new Association for Contemporary History based out of the Catholic Academy in Bavaria.[55] The director of the latter was Karl Forster. Wissing, in turn, informed the bishops on February 20, 1962, that Forster would serve as the business director of the new historical association as well. All diocesan archives, he urged, should open their doors to users only upon a recommendation from this association or its director, Forster.[56]

Just nine days later, Lewy unexpectedly found himself in possession of a recommendation from Karl Forster. It is doubtful whether Lewy knew of Wissing's memorandum. In fact, Lewy asserted more than fifty years later that he had never met Forster.[57] Forster's letter nonetheless made clear that Lewy had "gotten in touch" with him "to gain a recommendation for the use of church archives."[58] Lewy, Forster wrote, was preparing a work about the church's "resistance" from 1933 to 1945. Archival materials germane to his project should be made available to him. Copies of Forster's letter of reference, in turn, made their way to German diocesan archives.[59] Lewy sent one copy to Berlin, where he also requested an interview with Vicar General Walter Adolph.[60] Adolph turned down his request, claiming that the pressures of his administrative duties made it impossible to take on "additional work of such a delicate nature."[61]

Lewy left Germany in late June 1962 with his work in progress poised to spark a controversy.[62] He had received enough support to ensure that his source base was sufficiently representative. But he had also aroused the misgivings of Adolph and Neuhäusler. The latter was so rankled that he resolved two years later to properly inventory the archdiocesan archive's collections in Munich and establish directives for use.[63]

For his part, Lewy showed remarkable diligence once back in the United States. He carried out additional research in the National Archives in Washington, DC. He worked in both the findings and the source material presented by all of the major works on the subject. He found time to serve as a television commentator on the Hochhuth controversy in the United States. He contacted the playwright to ask about a source that the Hessian native had used and even gave him a lecture tour at Columbia University before an audience of 1,700.[64] He wrote up his manuscript in less than eighteen months, thanks to a grant from the Rockefeller Foundation that freed him from teaching.[65] He secured publication with McGraw-Hill, a major trade publisher. *The Catholic Church and Nazi Germany* appeared in print in less than two years after his return from his former homeland. By any measure, this was a major feat, one that at this time would find no equal on the other side of the Atlantic.

The Attacks on Lewy's Scholarship

Lewy's book arrived with a splash on both sides of the Atlantic. Its dust jacket bore words of praise from the celebrated radio broadcaster turned historian William Shirer and the renowned Protestant theologian from Union Theological Seminary Reinhold Niebuhr.[66] Its publication on June 15, 1964, was accompanied by extensive advertisement in prominent venues like *The New York Times*.[67] *The New York Times* itself greeted it with a review not in the back pages normally reserved for light entertainment and the arts but on the politics pages under Section A news.[68] Sales did not disappoint. Lewy's book sold approximately 8,000 hardback copies in the English-speaking world over its two editions; ten paperback editions followed.[69]

With financial resources and a web of international contacts far superior to those at academic presses, McGraw-Hill arranged for a German translation in short order.[70] It allowed *Der Spiegel* to excerpt vast portions of the German manuscript. Its publisher, Rudolf Augstein, appended his own page-long commentary extolling Lewy's academic objectivity, even while granting that the author was no casual bystander to what had transpired between 1933 and 1945.[71]

Lewy's book appeared in American bookstores on June 15, 1964, while memories of the marches and demonstrations on Broadway triggered by *The Deputy* were still fresh.[72] The debates over his scholarship thus became a continuation of the Hochhuth controversy.[73] Lewy's findings were described as "support" for Hochhuth.[74] His writing style consisted of "Hochhuth prose."[75] He was the "Rolf Hochhuth of the academic fraternity." His book was "*The Deputy* of nonfiction."[76]

Lewy's book put defenders of the church's past who wished to answer this criticism in a difficult position. In light of their public relations fiascos over *The Deputy*, how exactly were they to respond? Lewy's book marked the moment when protests left the streets for the review and commentary pages of highbrow newspapers and academic quarterlies. Picketing a book release at thousands of stores or rallying against the release of a translation whose original had already been reviewed by German news outlets was out of the question.

Two alternatives were left. The first was to sue. No doubt recalling how threats of a lawsuit against Rolf Hochhuth had hurt their cause, those bringing the suit took care to make sure that it remained unpublicized. Lawyers for Cardinal Lorenz Jaeger, archbishop of Paderborn, threatened the German publisher of Lewy's book, the R. Piper Verlag, with damages should it not correct within two weeks one paragraph in all unsold and future editions.[77] They alleged that Lewy had falsified a quotation from Jaeger's Lenten pastoral letter from 1942 that Lewy argued had shown Jaeger's "sympathy for the Nazis' campaign of vilification against the Slavic *Untermenschen*."[78] Lewy had written that Jaeger had characterized Russia as a "country whose people 'because of their hostility to God and their hatred of Christ, had almost degenerated into animals.'"[79] The ensuing exchange between lawyers centered on questions of grammatical construction and on whether it was not the Russian people but rather their Communist overlords who "had almost degenerated into animals."[80] Lewy's publisher evidently believed that it was not likely to win this case, for it inserted small correction slips into existing copies and future editions.

The second alternative was to publish rebuttals in scholarly journals, daily newspapers and weekly newsmagazines.[81] The historian Rudolf Morsey penned a critical book review for the *Frankfurter Allgemeine Zeitung*.[82] Erich Klausener Jr., son of the murdered

Catholic Action leader, turned to the pages of the regional newspaper, *Rheinische Post*.[83]

But Lewy's critics suffered from the same structural drawbacks besetting defenders of Pope Pius XII. Not all secular venues of print journalism were available. *Der Spiegel* provided a forum only for Lewy and his champions. So too did *Stern*, another prominent weekly newsmagazine. It commissioned a commentary from Catholic writer and activist Carl Amery, who that year had authored a landmark book decrying the mustiness and closed-mindedness of the German "Catholic milieu."[84] Amery gladly seized this opportunity to call for church reform. A church wedded to authoritarianism, imperialism and nationalism, he wrote, had learned nothing from the catastrophe of 1933.[85] It continued to combat the achievements of the French Revolution, the culture of the left and the spirit of freedom.

Even worse from the vantage point of church defenders, other news outlets insisted on giving equal time to Lewy's champions. The prominent German highbrow weekly newspaper *Die Zeit* offered a formal counterpoint of pro and con on June 4, 1965, under the title "The Catholic Church under Hitler: Hochhuth Prose or Historical Research?" The pro was articulated by Hans Müller, the con by Ludwig Volk, SJ, a thirty-nine-year-old German Jesuit entering the field. Volk's response was a truncated version of a thirteen-page rebuttal he had just penned for the Jesuit journal *Stimmen der Zeit*.[86] Volk felt that the deck had been stacked against him, his arguments having been introduced as being "naturally of a different slant."[87]

The alternative was to publish only in reliably Catholic venues. Robert Graham, SJ, the American Jesuit who had made common cause with Walter Adolph against Gordon Zahn and Rolf Hochhuth, published his critique in *America* magazine, the Jesuit monthly.[88] But publishing in such venues meant reaching the like-minded instead of the undecided. Worse yet: it tempted some critics to deploy ad hominem attacks of the sort used freely against Zahn and Hochhuth.

For such attacks easily backfired. Lewy's critics could not accuse a refugee from National Socialism of lacking the understanding of life under a brutal dictatorship, the objection directed at Zahn.[89] At most, they could hint that his past during the Third Reich disqualified him from providing an objective analysis. Some specifically invoked his past, or at least what little of it could be gleaned from the snippets on his book's dust jacket. One review began with a staccato recitation of his biographical way stations – Breslau, Palestine, the United States.[90] The conclusion was expressed bluntly: Lewy was operating in the manner of a prosecutor delivering an indictment; he lacked impartiality; his findings were devoid of historical objectivity.

Figure 6.3 Ludwig Volk, SJ, entered the field of German Catholic history in the early 1960s while continuing to teach high school. Courtesy of the Archiv der Deutschen Provinz der Jesuiten, Abt. 800, Nr. 492.

It is hard not to hear in these courtroom semantics a reverberation of the mistrust from the immediate postwar years of the "thirty-niners," those Jews who had fled Germany for the United States in that year and returned as postwar occupation officials. But openly touching on his Jewish background was going to prove risky as cultural sensitivities shifted in the mid-1960s in response to growing public knowledge of the Holocaust. One reviewer from the Cologne archdiocesan newspaper directed ugly words at what he suspected to be Lewy's Jewish background only to find them exposed and pilloried in a subsequent issue of *Der Spiegel*.[91]

Since his critics could not launch a blitz of personalized attacks that had become almost standard in the campaigns against Gordon Zahn and Rolf Hochhuth, they had only one avenue left: accusations of poor scholarship. It is no small irony that some of those raising such allegations were themselves historical neophytes or relative newcomers to the craft. A native of Lower Franconia, Ludwig Volk, SJ, had first studied theology and philosophy, a course of study common for Jesuits.[92] He came to the historical profession only through a dissertation on the relationship between the church and National Socialism in Bavaria from 1930 to 1934, a topic first suggested to him by Ernst Deuerlein.

In what would become a recurring pattern, Volk would have the good fortune of being the first to view important collections from church archives. Not least thanks to a recommendation from Karl Forster, he received access to all of the Bavarian diocesan archives and the papers of Cardinal Faulhaber. While viewing collections that the Breslau native had also used, a fellow Jesuit in New York sent him a copy of Lewy's book that had just been released in bookstores in the United States and Great Britain.[93] Volk appears to have been affronted to the point where he altered his project. He changed his title from *The Bavarian Episcopate and Clergy in the Clashes with National Socialism, 1930–1934* to *The Bavarian Episcopate and National Socialism, 1930–1934*, in part so that his work could be seen as a response to Lewy.[94] He compared Lewy's use of primary sources with the originals and, in particular, those on "non-aryans and the Jewish question."[95]

Once Lewy's book appeared in German translation, Volk honed in on what he believed to be inaccurate or clumsy translations from the English original to the German.[96] The errors he believed to have found were picayune. Volk pedantically complained that the translator had rendered "ardent" as merely "eifrig." But he insisted that these were reflective of a spirit of dilettantism and accordingly passed these on to Morsey, who included a number of these in a largely negative review published in the *Frankfurter Allgemeine Zeitung* on November 4, 1965.[97]

But such criticism was mere window dressing. Lewy's critics raised a more fundamental methodological objection: his account was one-sided. Volk insisted that Lewy had chosen to see little more than accommodation, collaboration and ideological affinities.[98] Erich Klausener Jr. likewise took him to task for ignoring contrary evidence.[99] Lewy had accused the episcopate of silence, noting its seemingly tepid response to mass murder and to the cold-blooded killing of Klausener's father on June 30, 1934.[100] Klausener Jr. thus charged Lewy with having glossed over potentially exculpatory sources including a sharply worded sentence from a letter from the bishop of Berlin to Hitler. Historians, he averred, needed to include all of the evidence and not just that confirming pre-existing beliefs and interpretations.

But Lewy's critics reserved most of their fire for his comprehensive moral indictment of the church's conduct. Lewy's closing pages were indeed brimming with moralistic fervor. The church had "failed" by not "bearing witness to its moral cause," he concluded. It was "wrong" for church leaders to have been guided by reasons of state. They should have confronted evil by name and provided greater assistance to the victims of "an upsurge of monstrous barbarism."[101] The need for institutional survival had usurped the moral mission of the church. If ever again presented with moral challenges of a magnitude of those of Hitler's regime, mankind would need "better moral guidance."

Lewy's critics thus had no option but to insist that there was no place for moral judgment in the writing of professional history. Volk rebuked his adversary as an "absolute moralist" who could see in Hitler's regime only the incarnation of absolute evil. But these categories of demonic evil, as common sense as they were, were ahistorical. They presupposed moral omniscience on historical actors who lacked the benefit of hindsight.[102] For Volk, the descent into Nazi barbarism had unfolded not at once but step-by-step. Few could have foreseen that it would conclude with the horrors of Auschwitz. Were the "first expressions of the totalitarian use of power," including the abolition of civil liberties, the hostility toward religion and discriminatory measures against Jews, truly sufficient to have warranted Catholics to suspend their loyalty to the church back in 1933?

Volk pointed out that church leaders, like others with reservations about the regime, were constantly having to weigh the lesser of evils. Was submitting to state restrictions, albeit with a protest, worse than a rupture with the regime?[103] Any calculations ecclesiastical leaders made had to take into account the fact that the Nazis' foreign policy agenda included goals and "honorable motives" shared by virtually all patriotic Germans. The desire to revise the territorial settlements of the Treaty of Versailles was nearly universal. Germans had legitimate desires to reclaim territory taken away in 1919 and to protect German minorities living outside of national borders. Should Catholic Church leaders in Germany have foresworn all of these goals through a rupture with National Socialism?

For Volk, Lewy's transgression lay in his lack of "empathy." He would not empathize with the dilemmas faced by church leaders over the national question.[104] Volk's position was hardly unique. That a grave injustice had been inflicted on the German nation at the close of the First

World War remained a leitmotiv of a conservative and nationally oriented German historical profession well into the 1960s. Challenges to it, such as that launched by Fritz Fischer in 1964 in his revisionist account of German responsibility for the First World War, provoked angry outcries.[105] For demanding empathy carried advantages for defenders of church and nation. Historians with an empathetic understanding were less likely to cast stones. Or at least they could choose less jagged stones. Calls for empathy were particularly convenient when those alleged to have lacked it were critics from the far shores of the Atlantic and North Sea.

Yet there was an obvious tension between calls for empathy and the positivistic methodologies simultaneously championed by historians like Volk and Morsey. Was not empathy at odds with the rigorous detachment necessary for a strict reconstruction of the past? Positivism was based on a close and narrow read of that already articulated on paper. Empathy required imagination – imagining feelings not necessarily on the page. That this contradiction went unnoticed speaks volumes about the urgency with which these battles were fought in the 1960s.

The Rigorous Scholarship of the Association for Contemporary History

For those scholars coming together under the umbrella of the Association for Contemporary History, Lewy's book was the latest example of methodologically flawed critical scholarship. It reinforced their conviction that the handicraft of church history needed quality control. They developed standards that were a reaction against what they deemed the shoddy methodologies of contemporary church critics. An ethos of disciplinary excellence was certainly consistent with attempts within the high-ranking ecclesia to borrow from the tools of the modern social sciences to help with pastoral care.[106] But it was even more reminiscent of a deeper tradition. The new association was creating what was a guild in all but name. It was establishing a set of practices – rigorous training, expert craftsmanship, supervision of apprentices and control over documentary evidence – through which to hold historians to the codes and canons of "objective" historical scholarship.

Such high ideals of scholarship were deeply rooted in the Görres Society of Catholic academics, a loose association to which many of the association's members belonged.[107] The Görres Society had its origins in the confessional divisions of the Kulturkampf of the 1870s. Its Catholic scholars found themselves wrestling with how to distinguish themselves in a Protestant-dominated profession. Their solution was to appropriate the positivism of mainstream liberal scholarship while denouncing the failure of liberal Protestant scholars to live up to their own ideals of objectivity, impartiality and rigor.[108] A century later, the historians in the association responded similarly. They were to write their own history. They were to adhere to rigorous scholarly ideals from the nineteenth century, even where mainstream historians were distancing themselves from positivist approaches. They were dismissive of mainstream scholars who did not live up to these ideals. In sum, they were to write better history than their Protestant rivals.

The mantra of scholarly excellence undergirded the association's crowning achievement: two publication series that continue to the present day. Series A featured primary source anthologies with a level of detail and commentary more commonly found in biblical concordances or philological editions. Between 1965 and 1980, no fewer than twenty-seven documentary editions went to press, including six imposing volumes of documents on the church's history in the Third Reich.[109] Series B consisted of scholarly monographs, thirty of which were published between 1965 and 1980.[110]

Taking the name "the Blue Series" from the color of their bindings, these two series were all works of political and diplomatic history. They chronicled the choices of ecclesiastical, diplomatic and political elites during moments of crisis in church-state relations. For the Nazi era, the choices of subject matter were usually the flash points of the church struggle – the negotiations over the Reichskonkordat, the morality trials against priests in 1936 and 1937, state monitoring of the church, Catholic political exiles and the episcopate's response to state persecution. The methodology, originating in the Görres Society, showed an aversion to theory. It did not matter whether the theory came from Marxism, the social sciences, econometrics or social history. For these historians, and this was the central bone of contention with critics, facts had to precede theory. Comprehensive judgment was impossible until the facts had all been brought to light.

Association historian Dieter Albrecht summed up this credo in a letter of rejection to a well-meaning thirty-four-year-old amateur historian. The work in question was an ambitious but dilettantish popular history of the church struggle, a mix of documents and narrative.[111] For Albrecht, it was an awkward crossbreed, neither a purely documentary edition nor a scholarly monograph.[112] As such, it did not fit into either series. The association, he wrote the author, saw its first task as preparing documentary foundations; only then could interpretation follow and the sweeping judgments,

half-truths and hypotheses with no evidential support all too characteristic of the era be "corrected."[113]

This ethos meant that the alliance of historians in the association faced
a herculean task. It had to comb through the holdings of dozens of church
and state archives at home and abroad. These included twenty-one
diocesan archives in the Federal Republic; the archdiocesan archive in
Breslau, Poland, housing the papers of Cardinal Adolf Bertram; the
archives of ancillary organizations and Catholic political parties; the
German National Archives in Koblenz; captured Nazi records abroad;
and individual papers scattered throughout private homes, city and state
archives. Chanceries and archivists needed to inventory these collections
before research could even begin.

Recognizing that they would not be able to produce a comprehensive
one-volume work for the entire Nazi era, the historians in the association
chose instead a piecemeal approach, one with strengths and limitations.
Their monographs and documentary editions were so narrow in focus
that they verged on becoming microhistories. But they proved to be
uncompromisingly thorough, a stamp that gave them a decisive edge in
their competition with scholars from outside. What foreign academics or
even German graduate students with limited financial resources could
sustain multiyear document hunts in dozens of archives? Their ethos of
excellence was just as strongly reflected in their zeal for copyediting and
discussions over comma placement, the use of italics and line spacing.[114]
Here too what might come across as nit-picking was born out of a genuine
commitment to historical accuracy as well as the need to outdo adversaries in a Protestant-dominated profession.

Yet in one key respect the scholars in the association reversed course.
Catholic scholars had long been reluctant to write national history. This
had usually been the province of Protestant historians whose scholarship
bore the trademark nationalism and anticlericalism of the Kulturkampf
era. The historians in the new association were now willing to write
national history – but that of the Federal Republic. Between 1972 and
1974, Morsey and Repgen edited three volumes on Adenauer and his
politics.[115] A working group to which they belonged published six slender
edited volumes in paperback on the Adenauer era, most focusing on
church-state relations. The Federal Republic, they argued, was
a success story, not least because of the wisdom and foresight of
Catholic political leaders.

Restricting Access to the Archives

But the zeal of some guild masters in the Association for Contemporary History, almost all male historians in their thirties and forties, had a shadowy side. This too was born out of the struggles against church critics. They felt compelled to respond to how Guenter Lewy had gained entry into ecclesiastical archives and, in the words of the diocesan archivist in Limburg, "misused" documents.[116] In the coming decade, a few in the association sought to limit the entry of newcomers into the field. They did so by pulling levers of access to the archives. They could do so with some justification. Church archives were private archives, and their custodians were under no obligation to guarantee access to all aspiring users.

Of those Catholic historians resolved to keep potential users at bay, it was Ludwig Volk who did the most to convince well-placed officials in the ecclesia to put up barricades. That he was a relative latecomer to the field may well have been a motivating factor. Then as now, it was common for Jesuits in training to teach high school before or while pursuing an advanced degree. For years, Volk was forced to teach history and English to pupils at an academic high school and could work on his scholarship only part-time. Only in the fall of 1968 did his provincial reassign him to the Association for Contemporary History as a full-time researcher, editor and scholar.[117] His own scholarship delayed, Volk seems to have suffered particularly hard from the indignities of coming in second in the race against critics. Had Stasiewski's project appeared in print earlier, he seethed, attacks like those of Lewy never would have had the same impact.[118]

Almost as embittering was that Lewy had seemingly found it easier than he to gain entry to church archives. The Jesuit scholar was combing ecclesiastical collections for documents of the German bishops and Cardinal Faulhaber just as Neuhäusler was warning chanceries of Guenter Lewy. Some diocesan archivists and chancery officials responded with restrictions that affected him of all people. The vicar general of Hildesheim informed Volk that letters of recommendation now needed to contain not only a signature but an official stamp.[119] Lewy's letter from the vicar general of Springfield had not borne such a stamp. Volk also found himself in June 1965 shut out of the diocesan archive in Speyer, an archive that he had used back in September 1963. He was forced to appeal to the bishop.[120]

The more Volk learned about Lewy's apparent scholarly modus operandi, the angrier he became. A former colleague of Lewy's from Smith College and the University of Massachusetts, Amherst, whom Lewy had thanked in his introduction for her "detailed criticisms and suggestions," told Volk of her doubts regarding Lewy's technique of quotation and paraphrasing.[121] Lewy had held on to his "big picture" in spite of her objections. "As the warped picture which he then sketched of the church struggle showed," Volk wrote, "all of those who remained mistrustful of his wishes unfortunately turned out to be correct."[122]

Thoughts of Lewy seem to have solidified mistrust of outside scholars about whom little was known. In at least four instances, Volk worked to derail the archival aspirations of scholars fresh to the field or to partition off collections. In the first case, he helped prevent Stewart Stehlin, a young assistant professor at New York University, from drawing on sources in Rome and in German diocesan archives. Stehlin had received his Ph.D. in 1965 from Yale University under German émigré Hajo Holborn.[123] He had spent the 1962–1963 academic year in Hamburg under Fritz Fischer. The young American scholar was keenly interested in German foreign policy between 1914 and 1945 and German-Vatican relations.[124] While writing a book on Bismarck and the Guelph problem, Stehlin received a Guggenheim and Fulbright Senior Research Fellowship for the 1971–1972 academic year to travel to Germany, Rome and Poland to research German-Vatican relations for a scholarly monograph.[125]

Aware of the challenges in gaining access to ecclesiastical archives, Stehlin, a devout Catholic, secured a letter of recommendation from the cardinal of New York.[126] This letter no doubt helped him gain access to the papers of Cardinal Adolph Bertram, chairman of the Fulda Bishops Conference during the Third Reich. These papers were located in the archdiocesan archives in Wrocław, Poland, and no German scholar had yet been able to use them there. Volk had obtained a microfilmed copy but had been unable to make use of it for his dissertation.[127] Even better, a colleague in the foreign office introduced Stehlin to Ernst Deuerlein, who gave him a clandestine tour of the archdiocesan holdings in Munich.[128] Cardinal Döpfner's secretary hinted that the young American scholar might be able to view the papers of Cardinal Faulhaber.[129] Unfortunately for Stehlin, Deuerlein died unexpectedly of a stroke on November 26, 1971. Stehlin lost a pillar of support. Not suspecting any ill will, he met with Volk in early December, informed him of his successes in Breslau and asked about the location of materials in the Munich archdiocesan archives.[130] Volk, by his own admission, put up a front of reserve.[131] He disingenuously told Stehlin that he would not even know where to look.[132] When Stehlin told him of the tour of the archives and the materials that awaited him there, Volk's eyes, according to Stehlin, proceeded to bulge.[133]

From this point on, things did not go Stehlin's way. His forays were obviously too redolent of those of Lewy. He was a visiting scholar from the United States, bore a recommendation from a high-ranking American church official and was the first to view documents that had gone unused.

Volk admitted that he knew nothing "negative about the man as such." But as long as he remained a "blank slate," he needed to be approached with question – precisely because of the experiences with Lewy.[134] Being Catholic was "no protection from surprises."[135] In the coming days and weeks, Volk assumed the role of a gatekeeper. He sent out a flurry of letters to colleagues in his order, the ecclesia and the association with the unmistakable intent of preventing documents from reaching Stehlin's desk.[136]

One of the recipients was Angelo Martini, SJ, one of four Jesuit historians handpicked by Pope Paul VI in 1964 to prepare what turned out to be eleven volumes on Vatican diplomacy during the war.[137] It was impossible, Volk wrote Martini, to send Stehlin away from the archives completely empty-handed, but "his look inside is being quantitatively and thematically so limited that in any case no damage can be done."[138] Martini also did what he could to thwart the American scholar. One month later, he informed Volk that Stehlin had written to a long series of personae in Rome for help. It was "certain that he will receive nothing in these archives."[139] After Volk learned that Stehlin had mobilized a "swarm of intercessors" on his behalf in Rome, Martini again stepped in.[140] He ensured that Stehlin received nothing in the archives of the Secretariat of State and little at the Italian Ministry of Foreign Affairs.[141]

To block Stehlin's research in German diocesan archives, Volk prepared the template of a letter similar to that sent to Martini. It was intended to be sent to multiple recipients and presumably German chanceries.[142] Disclosing details of Stehlin's research, he urged them to drop an appropriate hint to the appropriate persons. They should do so internally, not mention his name ' and keep his letter confidential. The outcome was once again never in dispute. Stehlin received little of importance in German diocesan archives. With obvious satisfaction, Volk noted Stehlin's disappointment. "I have of course not made myself popular with him," he stated, "as he believes that I blocked him from a more liberal use" of these papers.[143] The irony ever eluded the suspicious Volk. Stehlin was, in fact, what he represented himself to be – a devout Catholic, a gentleman and a scholar. Stehlin's book on Weimar and the Vatican, published a decade later, proved to be a model of scholarly probity, one with no discernible animosities to the church or church officials.[144]

In two other instances, Volk's invisible hand made itself felt as he took it upon himself to improve upon and even reverse the decisions of archivists, chancery officials and even a cardinal. In January 1972, a graduate student of Karl Bosl, a Bavarian history professor in Munich, wrote to Konrad Repgen, the head of the association. The student was working on a dissertation on Cardinal Faulhaber.

He had received explicit approval from the archdiocesan office. Cardinal Döpfner would grant him partial use of Faulhaber's papers so long as his research did not stand in opposition to the work of the association. Repgen forwarded the student's letter to Volk, prompting exchanges by phone and letter over whether he should be allowed in. Rejecting Morsey's suggestion of a compromise solution, Volk insisted that the Faulhaber papers be closed to all graduate students.[145] The student, he pointed out, had taken on this project at his own risk – and with no guarantee of access. A blanket policy of rejecting all applicants would avoid a precedent: how could one justify turning down future applicants after having let in a graduate student?[146] The student was thus informed that in light of the numerous applications for use and the time-consuming nature of separating out personal, pastoral and personnel matters, the association was having to exercise extreme caution.[147] His recommendation could not be forwarded to Döpfner.

In the meantime, Volk began to draw up basic guidelines for the use of the Faulhaber papers.[148] The conditions for use were to be circumscribed.[149] At least until Volk had completed his own documentary editions on Faulhaber, permission for general use was not to be granted. Exceptions, however, could be granted by the archbishop of Munich-Freising but only after he had received a confidential recommendation from the head of the association.[150] One request that was not granted was from a nun from Oakland, California, with a Ph.D. seeking sources on the church and the Jewish question in the 1930s and 1940s.[151] Even though Volk had already published most of the relevant materials, the chancery turned down her request. In Volk's correspondence with Repgen about her case, her moralistic criticisms of the church's past, substandard German and refusal to wear a habit became topics of conversation.[152]

Volk, however, received an exception (presumably from Cardinal Döpfner of Munich) to view postwar ecclesiastical documents to present a paper at a conference for Catholic scholars of the postwar church. This conference had been convened following the publication of a modestly critical 416-page book, *The Churches and Politics in Germany*, by the American journalist Frederic Spotts.[153] Volk's successful bid was not without a certain irony. He had just worked to wall off portions of one postwar collection. In November 1972, the Catholic University Archives in Washington, DC, came into the possession of the papers of Aloisius Muench, who had passed away in 1963.[154] Though the papers were not completely inventoried until 1976, the archival staff made them available to Spotts, who was carrying out research for his study of the postwar religious landscape.[155] Because of sharp and "pointed theses" in his discussions of Catholic opposition to denazification and war crimes trials, this Protestant journalist quickly became a *bête noire* for many in the association and for Volk in particular.[156]

Spotts' book opened Volk's eyes to the fact that Muench's papers were now available to scholars.[157] And so in November 1975, the German Jesuit traveled to Washington, DC, for sixteen days under the aegis of the Secretariat of the German Bishops Conference to view the collection.[158] Once there, Volk discovered a striking contrast to West German ecclesiastical archives whose postwar collections were supposed to be off limits. An exception, he noted, had "regrettably" been made to Spotts in the archdiocesan archive in Cologne. At the Mullen Library of Catholic University, Muench's papers, which included sensitive documents about East Germany, were open for use with no strings attached. Such internal matters, Volk bristled, "do not belong to the public eye."[159] During one of his final days there, he urged the library director "to protect the interests of those people who could be comprised (as living under communist (sic) rule) by unrestricted use of the Muench-Papers."[160]

Volk subsequently urged both the secretary of the German Bishops Conference and its chairman, Cardinal Döpfner, to have the Secretariat of the Bishops Conference take up the matter.[161] But it did not need to intervene. Volk's conversation with the director and a follow-up letter from early December proved sufficient to persuade the staff in Washington to restrict the collection involving Germany while keeping open the materials from his ministry in the diocese of Fargo, North Dakota.[162] For guardians of the church's past and many diocesan officials and archivists, the lesson had been learned. Church archives needed to be exceptionally careful with whom they entrusted their treasured documents.

Conclusions

Guenter Lewy's book *The Churches in Nazi Germany* was the last major work on the Catholic Church's past to receive such attention-grabbing headlines in the mainstream secular print media on both sides of the Atlantic in the 1960s and 1970s.[163] Why did the author's feats cast such a long shadow over research into the Catholic Church's past? It was not because of any celebrity status. He rarely received its perks of prime-time television or radio appearances. His one appearance on West German television – he went head-to-head with Konrad Repgen – took place only in 1967, long after the public controversies had ebbed.[164] Too little was known about Lewy's biography save for tantalizing hints provided on his book's dust jacket, and these would have inhibited most fellow scholars in

Germany from personalizing criticism of his work. Few non-victims of National Socialism would have wished to go up against a bona fide Jewish victim of Nazi oppression. Debates about his claims thus tended to concentrate on his use of sources, paraphrasing and translations.

But in some quarters, the furious reaction ensued not necessarily because of its perceived scholarly deficiencies but because of its merits. Lewy had produced a panoramic, readable account of the church's past between 1933 and 1945 available to both German- and English-speaking audiences based on firsthand archival sources, something that no German Catholic scholar had been able to accomplish. That he had entered the archives under seemingly false pretenses – implying that he was writing a history of Catholic resistance rather than the reverse – only heightened outrage.

To no small extent, the response to Lewy was the story of frustration boiling over, and this shaped what was essentially a twofold agenda. Specifically citing the injury they believed wrought upon the church from this research sojourn from the 1961–1962 academic year, many chanceries as well as some of the historians in the Association for Contemporary History put brakes on the ability of outsiders to view further documents from the Nazi era from ecclesiastical collections.[165] It was not until 1988 that a comprehensive directive governing the use of diocesan archives would be put in place, and until then, decisions about whom to grant use of diocesan materials were made on a case-by-case basis.[166] Yet this network of historians also began producing unimpeachable documentary editions and monographs of the highest integrity, works clearly intended to take the wind out of their critics' sails.

Both approaches underscored the reality that the new Association for Contemporary History, or at least some of its members, was assuming the function of a guild. It drew on traditions of expert craftsmanship and professionalism long instilled by the Görres Society. But it also sought to exert a certain control of the raw materials and training of newcomers to the field. In so doing, members of the association provided an answer to a question that had been at the core of earlier debates but that had been skirted in the controversies involving Guenter Lewy's work: who had standing to carry out research into the Catholic past? Were they to be impartial scholars, firsthand witnesses or victims of Nazi persecution?

By the early 1970s, the Association for Contemporary History provided an answer. Those writing the church's history were to be scholars and of a certain type – attentive to detail, precise in every facet, relentless in the pursuit of sources, committed to ideals of scholarly objectivity and, above all, empathetic to the church's predicament in the 1930s and 1940s.

7   The Repgen-Scholder Controversy

On September 27, 1977, forty-seven-year-old Protestant church historian Klaus Scholder published in the *Frankfurter Allgemeine Zeitung* tantalizing excerpts from the first and forthcoming installment of what he intended to be his magnum opus.[1] *The Churches in the Third Reich* was to be a comprehensive, multivolume comparative history of both Catholic and Protestant churches under National Socialism. Its first volume alone for the year 1933 and the years leading up to it ran to more than 900 pages.[2] At the heart of both article and book lay a conjecture that most had thought a thing of the past. This was the "linkage argument" according to which the Center Party had signed off on the Enabling Act in exchange for the Reichskonkordat. The Center Party, Scholder insisted, was the "price" its leader, Ludwig Kaas, paid for his ultimate goal of achieving "peace with an authoritarian state" through the Reichskonkordat.[3]

To Catholic historian Konrad Repgen, Scholder's claims amounted to a second edition of Karl Dietrich Bracher's expert opinion to the Constitutional Court in 1956. Arousing his ire was the fact that his team of historians associated with the Association for Contemporary History had in the twenty years since the court's verdict carried out painstaking research into this treaty's origins. They had failed to uncover any smoking gun – or indeed any written or oral evidence that corroborated the link between the Center Party's capitulation in March 1933 and the Reichskonkordat. In fact, the historian, Rudolf Morsey, had just months earlier published a volume, *The Downfall of Political Catholicism*, in which he explicitly repudiated this hypothesis, the very one he had assiduously left open in his pioneering publications from the late 1950s and early 1960s.[4]

Repgen was thus unwilling to let the claims from Scholder's article, "The Capitulation of Political Catholicism: The Role of the Center Party Leader, Kaas, in Early 1933," go uncontested. He responded just four weeks later with a broadside in the Frankfurter daily that precipitated six exchanges over the next eighteen months.[5] The first exchanges took place in the *Frankfurter Allgemeine* in the fall of 1977, more elaborate ones in 1978 and early 1979 in Germany's leading contemporary historical quarterly, the *Contemporary History Quarterly*, published by the Institute for Contemporary History in Munich.[6] The audience for this controversy thus consisted both of professional German historians and the well-educated across Germany tackling the politics section of the *Frankfurter Allgemeine*. The exchanges centered on questions of historical methodology. Was it legitimate to conclude in light of the lack of a smoking gun that there had been a quid pro quo in March 1933 – the Reichskonkordat in exchange for the Enabling Act and annihilation of the Center Party?

Yet there were deeper issues at stake than whether it was warranted for historians to advance claims that were "possible" or "plausible" rather than "certain."[7] This chapter explores those factors that allowed the Reichskonkordat to become the crux of another major historical controversy, the last ideological battle rooted in the Adenauer era.[8] It begins by showing why Scholder opted to reignite the long-smoldering battle over the Reichskonkordat. It then explains why Konrad Repgen emerged as his chief adversary. It subsequently retraces their debate and concludes by assessing this controversy's long-term significance.

From FDP Functionary to Academic Historian: Klaus Scholder's Journey

Konrad Repgen and Klaus Scholder were perfect foils. One was a conservative Catholic, the other a Reformed Protestant. Repgen held a chair in history at the University of Bonn in a department known for its conservatism. Scholder was a professor in the Protestant seminary and department of Protestant theology in Tübingen, both wellsprings of Protestant theology and identity. Both were historians of not just the twentieth century but of the early modern era. Their political allegiances were unapologetic. Repgen was a CDU member who presided over the Association of Contemporary History and its network of supporters, several of whom were CDU officials. A functionary in the FDP, Scholder was determined to see the CDU in the "non-upholstered seats of the opposition."[9] Both were public intellectuals who, never shying from a good fight, found themselves in several fracases in the course of their academic careers.[10]

To no small measure, these pronounced ideological and political contrasts were rooted in upbringing. Scholder, born in Erlangen in 1930, was the son of a chemistry professor. But his roots and impossible-to-miss accent were Swabian. His liberal Protestant family was the embodiment of the *Bildungsbürgertum*, the social class of educated German families rooted in professions like law, education, medicine, journalism and the ministry. Such professions held an appeal for the young intellectual, and well into the late 1950s, he had not decided whether he would seek out a career in the ministry, the media, politics or the academy. Even his potential path in the university seemed unclear. His dissertation was in German studies, an analysis of the late classical and early romantic writer Jean Paul.[11]

Scholder eventually settled on a combination of them all, becoming a theologian, parish administrator, political functionary, church historian, university professor and not least a pundit and talking head for Germany's second television station, the ZDF. To these callings, he brought a certain joy in provocation as well as gifts as a communicator. Indeed, his knack for the bon mot and the perfectly sculpted sentence jumps off the page.[12] This talent enabled him to describe labyrinth events like those of the first half of 1933 with a verve few rivals could match. "I aim," he wrote, "to write academic books that are readable – or inversely, readable books that meet academic standards."[13]

That Scholder made the negotiations over the Reichskonkordat the centerpiece of his story and a cautionary tale was hardly surprising in light of formative experiences en route to a career in politics and the Protestant church. Scholder had long wrestled with how to make sense of the national calamities he had witnessed as a boy and teenager. The question of how to ascribe guilt – and indeed whether it could even be overcome – would remain at the center of his inquiry all the way to his death in 1985.[14] Like others in his immediate age bracket – and he too identified himself with the younger generation later dubbed the "generation of 1945" – he asked which of the old values should be retained.[15] What mistakes of his elders should be held up as cautionary tales? Which politicians, theologians and churchmen – the class of intellectuals and academics that remained his focus until the end – were worthy of emulation, and which had failed?

Already at the age of twenty-three as a student of history, theology and German in Tübingen, he had identified one such hero. This was Karl Barth, the Swiss-German theologian renowned for his theology of the transcendent and inscrutable God.[16] The influence of Barth's dialectical theology on the young student was so great (even if Scholder was no uncritical acolyte) that at least one of his theological contemporaries observed that his interest in the recent German past, and history more broadly, was derived from his Protestant theological convictions.[17] Barth's theological approach, Scholder later wrote in *The Churches and The Third Reich*, proved to be "one of the truly great theological models of Christian theology," particularly in the critical situation of 1933.[18] Ascribing to Barth the voice of prophecy, Scholder wrote that "this one voice" – one of Christian truth, faith, consolation and confidence – "was heard amid the tremendous din" of the political turmoil within the church.[19]

Less than a year later, Scholder found his political mentor. While attending a conference at the newly created Protestant Academy in Tutzing in July 1954, he met Karl Georg Pfleiderer, a liberal politician representing the FDP in the electoral district of Waibingen in Baden-Württemberg.[20] Between 1926 and 1945, Pfleiderer had served the German Foreign Ministry as an attaché in Peking, Moscow, Paris and Stockholm. Pfleiderer subsequently invited the young undergraduate to Bonn for a schooling in the ABCs of politics – how to write letters, forge contacts and prepare stump speeches. He tested his speeches and arguments against Adenauer on his protégé. Pleiderer, Scholder later wrote, taught him the mechanisms, significance and even greatness of politics; he imparted an understanding of the reach and centrality of diplomacy.[21] Such insights would inform his explorations into the tangled movements of statesmen and politicians between Berlin and the Holy See in 1933.

Just as significantly, Pfleiderer put him on the fast track toward a political career in the FDP. That path took him to the FDP headquarters in Bonn in the same southside neighborhood where Böhler's Catholic Office was located. In late 1956, Scholder became the political and cultural desk officer for West Germany's third-largest party. He was hired by one of its two titans, Thomas Dehler, and worked with its other, Reinhold Maier, who like Scholder was a native of Baden-Württemberg.[22] He collated documents, analyzed public statements and prepared commentaries on a host of issues pertaining to education and the churches. When the Constitutional Court announced its verdict in the case of the Reichskonkordat at the end of March 1957, Scholder even interrupted a vacation to evaluate commentaries in the press and a public statement by Maier.[23] The precocious twenty-seven-year-old was one of three architects of the party's Berlin Program from January 1957, the first comprehensive manifesto in the party's brief ten-year history. They developed this platform to bring unity to the party's unruly factions, including veterans of the old Weimar-era liberal parties and newcomers looking for alternatives to the CDU and SPD.[24]

As pragmatic as Scholder was in steering the party agenda, in his think pieces on political responsibility, cultural and educational policy and the ideal relationship between Christianity and liberalism he bore rigid attitudes miles apart from those of the CDU.[25] Public schools, he wrote during the school controversy, should be interdenominational. If the churches wished for parochial education, they should establish private schools.[26]

An article three years later, "Christianity and Liberalism," in the FDP magazine *Liberal* spelled out the reasons for such claims.[27] It was not the prerogative of the church to establish itself as an authority over the world. It was to be in it – but not ruling over it. It had long been the prerogative of liberals, Scholder insisted, to combat any forces that presumed to be acting as the moral, spiritual or political guardians of society. Liberalism, he insisted, rested on three pillars – that the free human being was also the most perfected, that the world was structured around principles of reason and that human beings of goodwill were agents of reason and freedom. For a long time, this meant combating the church. But it was now necessary to move on from the ideological warfare of the past century. Using the same catchphrases as had Böckenförde three years earlier in his first article in *Hochland*, Scholder argued that the parties and church were to act as "sentinels" (*Wächter*) vis-à-vis each other. The parties were to make sure that the church refrained from acting on "pseudo-political" claims to serve as a guardian of nation and society; the church was to keep the parties from implementing "pseudo-religious" visions. Scholder did not need to specify what he meant by the latter; any educated reader would instantly have discerned that he was referring to both Communism and National Socialism.

Nowhere in Scholder's political writings will one find overtly anti-Catholic rhetoric or passages, at least about the church's role in the present. In fact, the goal of this ordained churchman, who left his job at the FDP in Bonn in 1958 to serve first as a parish administrator in the Swabian city of Bad Überkingen and then as a lecturer at the renowned Protestant seminary and his spiritual home in Tübingen, was to find common ground between Christianity and modernity; he believed that separating church and state was the best way to pursue this goal and, in turn, strengthen both institutions. However absent in his analysis of the German religious present, the anticlerical spirit that so infused liberal Protestant identity of earlier eras nonetheless seeped into his writings probing the Catholic Church's less liberal past. "We would be foolish," he wrote in 1960 in an echo of nineteenth-century liberal prejudice, if we did not acknowledge that liberals' "mistrust" of the church had been exceptionally well justified.

In contrast, Scholder took pride in Protestant accomplishments from earlier centuries – or at least, those from its more progressive, non-Lutheran wings. Such pride poured forth from the opening lines of his *Habilitation*, the second dissertation required to assume a German professorship. He wrote that the development of historical-critical methods – which any theologically literate reader would have understood to be largely a Protestant phenomenon – represented "without a doubt" one of the most "important" events in the history of modern theology.[28] Initially, all three major confessions, Lutherans, Reformed and Catholics alike, had beginning in the seventeenth century opposed the findings and claims of the Copernicans, Socinianins and the Pre-Adamites who were challenging the received view of the cosmos on which the understanding of the bible rested. This criticism, indeed, ultimately shattered the trust people had placed in the literal truth of the bible and spelled an end to the rule of the church of the Middle Ages. But it was primarily non-Lutheran Protestant theologians who beginning in the nineteenth century embraced historical-critical methods, their potential to undermine faith notwithstanding.[29] It was now the task of Protestant theology to see these critical tools of modernity not solely as an impoverishing loss but also as a source of enrichment that would bring "freedom" in their wake.[30]

Scholder published his slim 172-paged scholarly account of seventeenth-century biblical criticism in 1966, but it was not until 1968 that he secured a professorship to his liking. He turned down an offer from the University of Bonn (where he ironically might have become a colleague of Konrad Repgen) to assume a chair instead at his beloved university in Tübingen.[31] He began as the Professor of Church Offices and Administration. But he seized the opportunity to expand what in most hands would have remained a narrow post into one of contemporary church history; in 1971, he succeeded in having his chair transferred into the history department.[32]

These maneuvers make clear that Scholder had his eye on a monumental scholarly undertaking, one requiring all the perks – a steady income, research funds and, not least, undergraduate assistants and graduate researchers – of a chair in contemporary church history. This was initially intended to be a critical history of the Protestant churches in Nazi Germany, in which motifs and vignettes from his work as a church historian, politician and churchman would converge. Already as a twenty-something, he had placed questions of moral and political responsibility at the center of a lengthy lecture delivered at the Institute for European History in Mainz in 1959.[33] He had previously addressed the topic of Christianity in the Third Reich only through a smattering of articles and political thinkpieces. These had been restricted to brief portraits of well-known resisters like the Scholl siblings and Dietrich Bonhoeffer. But over the course of the 1960s, he began to hone in on the Protestant capitulation in 1933, the same chronological point of entry for chroniclers of Catholicism in the 1950s and early 1960s.[34] Interwoven with his discussion of Protestant blunders was an analysis of the dialectical theologies of the 1920s of Karl Barth and Friedrich Gogarten, which he saw as the antivenin for the racism and ultranationalism of the German Christians.

Scholder's approach represented a frontal assault on what had long been a consensus on the Protestant church struggle in Germany. The sundry volumes being churned out by the Protestant Association of the History of the Church Struggle continued to cast their subject as Manichean tales of good versus evil: heroic resisters in the Confessing Church, inspired by the teachings of the Gospel, took on the satanic legions of National Socialism.[35]

And so already in the early 1960s, well before receiving his professorship, Scholder began the spadework for his excavations into the checkered past of the twenty-eight Protestant state churches.[36] But if shattering the orthodoxies about the Protestant church struggle were not enough, Scholder embarked on an even more herculean endeavor. He decided to widen his critical lens to take in the pasts of *both* German churches. In his foreword, he claimed that the necessity of doing so had become clear to him while wading through the materials for a regional history of the church struggle in Baden in 1970.[37] The history of the two churches, he had discerned, were much more tightly linked to each other than "we had previously assumed."[38]

But Scholder's biconfessional feat was not as new as he would later claim it to be.[39] Something similar had just been accomplished by Anglo-Canadian historian John Conway, whose groundbreaking 474-paged multiconfessional tome *The Nazi Persecution of the Churches, 1933–1945*, appeared in print in the United Kingdom and North America in 1968 and in German translation a mere one year later.[40] While Conway was carrying out his research in Germany during the 1964–1965 academic year, the two historians had met to discuss their respective projects. "I won't say that we agreed to divide the spoils," Conway stated, "but obviously he had some concern that I was trying to latch on to what he was up to."[41] Conway assured Scholder that he was not writing first and foremost about the churches but rather about state policies toward the churches. Scholder's fears, it seems, never quite subsided. He did not review Conway's book, though it had been lauded in the Anglo-Saxon historical world.[42] Scholder, in fact, cited Conway's work only twice – once to make reference to a document the Anglo-Canadian historian had included in the appendices to the English edition and once to tear apart his claim that Hitler never had a coherent plan for how to manage the churches politically.[43]

As Conway knew, writing a biconfessional history of this era was a daunting and seemingly insurmountable task. Scholder's familiarity with the minutiae of the Reichskonkordat negotiations from his desk job at the FDP notwithstanding, this was *terra incognita*. As Scholder noted in the introduction to his landmark book, Germany was – and remains – a confessionally divided land.[44] This fact alone was hardwired into the self-understandings of both churches. Historians were no exception, and Scholder was perfectly aware that especially in the rarefied world of the academy, Catholic and Protestant church historians operated in parallel universes. Departments of Protestant theology were distinct from their counterparts of Catholic theology, and rarely did the twain meet, particularly in the hallowed halls of the Protestant Seminary in Tübingen, that beacon of Protestant identity in southwest Germany.[45] Conway discovered this during a lecture on Nazi policies toward the churches he delivered in Tübingen in 1965 at the invitation of Scholder. He asked his host whether Catholic theologians would be present. "They haven't been invited!" came the reply.[46]

Consistent with this divide, Scholder was not in regular contact with Catholic scholars from the Association of Contemporary History as he carried out research.[47] Nor did he possess the ecclesiastical connections necessary to breach diocesan archives now under lock and key. Even if he had, few diocesan officials would have granted entry to a card-carrying member of the FDP and ordained clergyman from the Protestant seminary in Tübingen, particularly with the debacle involving Guenter Lewy fresh in many minds.

This left Scholder with few options for his research. The first was to draw from the wellspring of documentary editions being put together by the Association for Contemporary History. He described the nearly twenty dense volumes in print by the time he was completing his manuscript as "without equal" in contemporary history in their "comprehensiveness, richness (of content) and editorial quality."[48] The second option was to make use of the labors of his students in mining state archives. Back then, it was much more acceptable for German professors to employ talented graduate students not just as collators and proofreaders but as researchers and even ghostwriters. In keeping with custom, Scholder drew on the assistance of two prize students, Gerhard Besier and Leonore Siegele-Wenschkewitz. Besier would go on to complete Scholder's lifelong project after his untimely death in 1985 and enjoy a renowned, if controversial, career in the academy and in politics. Siegele-Wenschkewitz would also enjoy a celebrated career as not only an ordained clergywoman but a researcher of anti-Jewish tendencies within Christianity and feminist theology.

Their contributions went completely unacknowledged in Scholder's book except for a pithy two sentences thanking unnamed "librarians, archivists, co-workers and friends, colleagues and students."[49] It was Siegele-Wenschkewitz's suspected influence on his project that raised eyebrows for Scholder's critics and, in turn, injected extra fuel to the controversy between Scholder and Repgen.[50] She completed her dissertation under Scholder in 1972 on the religious politics of the National Socialist party and state. Like her adviser, she provided a parallel account of both churches. As Scholder's research assistant (Mitarbeiter), she analyzed copies of documents that her adviser had collected from his research stint financed by the German Research Council; she also worked these into her dissertation, supplementing them with documents found in other archives.

Scholder did not even list Siegele-Wenschkewitz's scholarship in his bibliography, even though it had been published as a book in 1974 and featured a thirty-three-page chapter on the Reichskonkordat.[51] She had suggested that the Lateran Accords of 1929 between the Holy See and Fascist Italy had increased the likelihood of a concordat with Nazi Germany. No less than Hitler had noted already in 1929 that the Vatican was willing to deal with authoritarian states; when compared with recalcitrant liberal or enemy Communist states, such states represented the lesser of evils.[52] She had also claimed, bolstered by quotations from Catholic leaders like Ludwig Kaas, that certain ideological affinities between the church and Fascism expedited negotiations; both were authoritarian and hierarchical.[53] These were themes that Scholder raised in his massive tome and in his exchanges with Repgen. Critics like Ludwig Volk, noting similarities to Scholder's work, suspected correctly that the student may have taught the master – or that cross-fertilization had been at work.[54]

Whatever the contributions of Scholder's students may have been, the result was the same: a brilliantly written 900-page monograph that made use of primary sources from fourteen state or secular archives, fourteen Protestant or Protestant-affiliated archives – and zero Catholic archives. Its content decisively skewed toward the Protestant church struggle. Fifteen chapters were devoted exclusively to the Protestant churches, six to the Catholic Church, and four covered both or changes affecting both. This asymmetry stemmed, Scholder insisted in his foreword, not from his confessional loyalties but from the confusion and chaos tearing apart the Protestant churches in 1933.[55]

Scholder had a point, even though he admitted to Morsey while writing his book in the summer of 1976 that his main focus was on Protestantism.[56] Illustrating the byzantine administrative structures of the twenty-eight Lutheran, Reformed or United state churches – to say nothing of their tensions, rivalries and schisms – certainly required a larger canvas than did an administrative portrait of the one true church. Protestants, moreover, were a majority in the German Reich.

The proportion of pages he devoted to Protestantism was not out of line with the confessional ratio from that time – 64 percent to 34 percent.

But this was not apparent from the promotional excerpts run in the *Frankfurter Allgemeine Zeitung* on September 27, 1977. This teaser was part of a public relations blitz by the media-savvy Scholder, who also had 179 copies of his book dispatched to higher-brow daily newspapers, weekly newspapers, magazines, radio stations and television stations. He even suggested having Karl Dietrich Bracher and Rolf Hochhuth review his book.[57] His article, "The Capitulation of Political Catholicism: The Role of the Center Party Leader, Kaas, in Early 1933" was red meat for highbrow critics of the church's past. It focused exclusively on the ignominious role played by Catholic politicians and ecclesiastical leaders in the catastrophe of 1933. Nowhere was the Protestant past from 1933 to be found in either headline or article.[58]

Worse yet, Scholder resurrected the notorious "linkage argument." Incorrectly informing his readers that this claim had been first raised by Bracher in his expert opinion for the Constitutional Court, Scholder gave it renewed life by reintroducing what he called a new "principal witness."[59] This was Heinrich Brüning, the disgraced former Center Party Chancellor from 1930 to 1932, whose posthumous memoirs appeared in print in 1970.[60] Brüning claimed that the chief culprit behind the Center Party's ignominious demise was his rival, Ludwig Kaas, whose "resistance" to National Socialism had allegedly weakened "when Hitler spoke of a concordat and Papen guaranteed that such a concordat was as good as guaranteed." Yet even here Scholder had to frame his argument as conjecture. Why was Brüning's testimony credible thirty-seven years after the fact? Because the former Center Party leader had "undoubtedly" been in possession of excellent sources of information.[61] "If one is clear about the entire situation," Scholder concluded in a statement that aroused Repgen's ire, "everything speaks for the credibility of this representation, even if it is not specifically provable."[62]

That Scholder was disguising what should have been labeled a "hypothesis" as a "thesis" was the immediate cause for offense.[63] Just two days after Scholder's article had appeared in print, the historian from Bonn fired off a letter to the *Frankfurter Allgemeine* requesting the opportunity to publish a rebuttal. It would take the form of excerpts from a forthcoming chapter on the Reichskonkordat set to appear later that year in a handbook for church history.[64] Repgen's rationale was simple: Scholder was putting forward an interpretation that squared away neither with the state of the field nor the findings from the sources themselves. The editor for political books responded favorably. He suggested, however, that Repgen might tailor his rebuttal more precisely to

Scholder's assertions rather than duplicating excerpts from a forthcoming publication.[65] Repgen obliged. His rebuttal, equally scholarly and school-masterish, straddled two whole newspaper pages.

The Roots of Konrad Repgen's Rigor

Of those dismayed by Scholder's resuscitation of the old claim that the Center Party had been the "price" for the Reichskonkordat, why was it Konrad Repgen who rose to shoulder a public challenge? To be sure, the pool of potential respondents sufficiently versed in the diplomatic intricacies of the Reichskonkordat negotiations was miniscule. Of the historians in the Association for Contemporary History, only a small coterie – Ludwig Volk, Rudolf Morsey and Dieter Albrecht – was up to the task.[66]

Just about everything made Repgen the obvious candidate to take on Scholder: a pugilistic temperament, uncompromising political and confessional loyalties, an intimate familiarity with the documentary evidence, a more than passing acquaintance with key players from 1933 and, not least, an almost puritanical methodological rigor. He was, in the words of political historian Hans-Peter Schwarz, "a Christian knight" and a "fanatic of empirical detail-research."[67]

This everything was consistent with values drummed into him in childhood, and therein lay another contrast with Scholder. For liberal Protestant families like Scholder's, a career in the academy, the clergy or education was the norm. Repgen, in contrast, was the upwardly mobile striver. His was a Horatio Alger story, a boy from a comparatively less privileged family pulling himself up by his bootstraps and closing a notorious "educational gap" with Protestants through hard work.

Born in 1923, Konrad Repgen came by deeply rooted values of thrift and education as a child in Friedrich-Wilhelms-Hütte. This was a highly industrialized satellite community of what is now Troisdorf, a medium-size blue-collar Catholic city less than ten kilometers east of the Rhine and a moderate streetcar ride from Bonn. His strong-willed but loving mother was a farm girl, his father an elementary school teacher and illustration of self-reliance.[68] An autodidact who taught himself literature and the piano, the Repgen patriarch repeatedly stressed that social advancement could come only through education. Paying no heed to the daily commute, he sent his son to an academic high school in Bonn to learn the Latin, Greek, German and mathematics that were the hallmark of a classical education. Adamantly opposed to the Nazis, he refused to sign off on paperwork allowing his son to break off his schooling before turning seventeen to enlist in the army.[69] And so unlike his classmates, Repgen

Figure 7.1 The young Catholic historian Konrad Repgen became the
first director of the Association for Contemporary History and the
leading critic of Klaus Scholder's account of the Catholic Church in
1933. Courtesy of Rudolf Morsey.

received his high school degree before entering the army. He returned
from four years of frigid winters and scorching summers on the Eastern
front battle-hardened and mentally toughened. "We were in Russia," he
would later tell colleagues in the Association for Contemporary History,
putting any academic tempests-in-teapots in their proper perspective.[70]

The trait that became most evident in Repgen's approach to history was
one instilled in youth: the desire not just to do one's best but to do it better
than the rest. On his path to the highest tiers of the academy, he had
always had more to prove than historians like Scholder from the educated
Protestant upper-middle class. The few Catholic historians entering
tenured positions in German universities through the 1960s, and not
least the holders of chairs reserved by law for Catholics, had to battle

perceptions that they were second-rate. The way to overcome stereotypes was to overcompensate. Repgen's curriculum vitae reveals not just a stupendous productivity vastly greater than that of Scholder: he published more than 160 massive books, edited volumes and articles between 1950 and 1987.[71] It also reveals a rarely found expertise in multiple fields chronologically far afield – the early modern era, the nineteenth century and the twentieth century.

Repgen specifically attributed his rigor to an ethos of Catholic scholarship.[72] The Catholic historian, Repgen averred, used the same methodological instruments as the non-Catholic but possessed an extra motivation.[73] He had a religious duty to fulfill his earthly duties as well as possible, being compelled religiously to always "pull the best out of himself." It was his duty to pay more attention to "methodological things" than others, who "as non-Christians" lacked this "motivation." One cannot help but hear in this a swipe at doctrines of salvation held by the Reformed Protestant Scholder.

Repgen extended this credo to the politics of the Federal Republic, pointing out that German Catholics through their representatives in the CDU-CSU had performed far more ably than their predecessors. Since 1945, the Catholic minority had steered its nation away from the darkness of the recent past. It did so not through novels or impassioned pleas in the arts sections of newspapers but through its commitment to a constitutional democracy – to the values it helped enshrine in the West German Basic Law, to the nuts and bolts of running a parliament effectively and to ensuring that the social obligations of the state were upheld.[74] "That was and that is," he asserted, "the actual and best overcoming of the past" brought about by Germans.[75] Bonn was not Weimar.

Though at least five years older than most intellectuals of the so-called "generation of 1945" like Scholder and Böckenförde keenly interested in the recent German past, in a certain sense Repgen also belonged to this cohort. He too had formative educational experiences in the postwar era; instrumental in his growth were, as they were to be for Böckenförde and Morsey, Catholic student fraternities and campus ministers. By his own admission, he was something of an idealist, seeking answers to the most basic of questions in the war's aftermath. Why did things have to come to such a cataclysmic end? What can we learn from the past? Can we avoid a repetition of the past?[76]

The answer he found most convincing was provided by the church: the actual cause for the German catastrophe lay in the German people's turning away from Christianity.[77] There was only one solution: rechristianization, and this ambition had appropriately, he noted, been at the heart of the early platforms of the Christian Democratic Union. This antidote differed strikingly from that of Scholder who sought to separate church and state. So too did Repgen's politics. Repgen, whose parents had been staunch Center Party voters until its dissolution in 1933, joined the CDU in 1958. He retained active ties to the CDU, and above all, to the Konrad Adenauer Foundation in St. Augustin located none too far from his childhood home. He remained wary of the anticlerical agendas of the other parties. Shortly after reading Scholder's account of the Reichskonkordat in the morning newspaper, he sent off a lapidary comment to the Secretary of the German Bishops Conference, Josef Homeyer: "Scholder is an FDP-man."[78]

In his scholarly pursuits, Repgen never strayed far from questions of revolution, war and peace. His focal point was the statesmanship of princes, monarchs, tyrants, parliamentarians, diplomats and pontiffs during eras of upheaval and catastrophe. Like his dissertation and Habilitation adviser, the renowned Bonn historian Max Braubach, Repgen showed his mettle as an old-school political and diplomatic historian.[79] After completing a dissertation on the 1848 revolution, he jumped back two centuries to scrutinize papal diplomacy toward the close of the Thirty Years' War. His herculean analysis of why the papacy rejected the peace treaties of 1648 showed some of the same characteristics of the work of association members about the Reichskonkordat: it too was detective work of the highest order. Repgen showed how papal archivists on three separate occasions were forced to issue reports showing how the papacy had protested earlier peace accords. To do so, he had to trace these treaties' prehistory back to the 1520s. Just like the research on Vatican diplomacy in 1933, Repgen's project grew far beyond all initial expectations. Instead of requiring three to four years to research and write, he needed nine. He spent three of these at the Vatican archives and library and the German Historical Institute in Rome.[80] His 934 pages of findings straddled two encyclopedic volumes published in 1962 and 1965.[81]

The connections between his work on the papal diplomacy of the Thirty Years' War and on the Reichskonkordat lay not only in methodology. Two summers before leaving for Rome in 1953, Repgen had the opportunity to discuss ecclesiastical questions with Robert Leiber, SJ, who had spent the wartime years in Rome.[82] He again encountered Leiber in Rome, confirming his impression of him as a fact-driven, trustworthy and exemplary member of a religious order. As we have seen, Leiber had taken issue with Morsey's reconstruction of some of the events in 1933 on the pages of the Jesuit magazine *Stimmen der Zeit*.[83] Some of the founding members of the Association for Contemporary History, not surprisingly, were skeptical of Leiber's accounts.[84]

In contrast, others had expressed mounting frustration that Leiber had not been forthcoming with all that he knew about 1933 or Pope Pius XII's wartime activities.

Repgen too was initially skeptical but changed his mind after 1963. He could not dispel his impression of Leiber as upright. He began to delve into the documents himself only to discover that newly released documents from the Vatican archives corroborated the senior Jesuit's account. Leiber had relied not on his memory but on Vatican documents themselves: his account was entirely credible. The trust Repgen placed in his source would factor into his controversy with Scholder, who would accuse him – "correctly," as Repgen would later note – of towing Leiber's line.[85]

As the successor to Braubach's professorship at the University of Bonn from 1967 through 1988 and the director of the Association for Contemporary History, Repgen would repeatedly return to the Reichskonkordat.[86] He oversaw work on four documentary editions that directly touched on its origins and implantation.[87] He corrected page proofs, pointed out typographic errors, and subjected Volk's monograph on the Reichskonkordat to a vigorous overhaul. With Repgen now a recognized expert on the subject (more so than Scholder), the stage was thus set for two diplomatic and political historians with clashing politics to collide. One was a devout profane historian, the other an ordained Protestant church historian.

And both were throwbacks to an earlier era. Both faiths were witnessing in the late 1960s and 1970s an outpouring of new forms of religiosity and a questioning of orthodoxies.[88] During this time of ferment, both Repgen and Scholder harbored particularist understandings of their respective faiths that were not necessarily shared by the majority of their co-religionists. With his strong personal and professional commitment to Reformed Protestantism, Scholder looked askance at the radical currents within the faith gaining in profile. Repgen was a conservative Catholic critical of progressive movements within the fold.[89] Even though both were at odds with the radical intellectual culture permeating the German academy in the 1970s, these particularist understandings shaped how each man viewed the other and provided fuel for the controversy to come.[90]

The Points of Controversy

As the two elaborated on their points of disagreement, it quickly became apparent that their debate was going to center exclusively on Catholic complicity from 1929 through 1933. Repgen never raised his pen to challenge Scholder's analysis of Protestant responsibility for the cataclysmic events of 1933. Their debate thus bore out an old pattern. As critical as they were of the conduct of their co-religionists during the Third Reich, Protestant critics like Scholder felt compelled to highlight Catholic culpability. In fact, Scholder's attacks on the hagiographies produced by confessional contemporaries (and especially the Lutherans) gave him the moral cover to cast stones at the Reichskonkordat, a treaty he believed would forever remain "morally disputed."[91] In contrast, Repgen, like many prominent Catholic intellectuals, chose not to preach openly about the sins of the Protestant past. He either did not believe it his place to do so or did not deem himself sufficiently competent to analyze the intrigues and schisms bedeviling Protestant theologians and churchmen.

A similar pattern emerged in how each framed the positions of his adversary. Repgen never once implied that Scholder's Protestant commitments had shaped his arguments. Nor did he let slip that Scholder was Protestant. For Repgen, a hypothesis stood or fell on the strength of the weight of evidence that could be marshalled on its behalf; ad hominem attacks cut into the seriousness of the historical enterprise. For Scholder, in contrast, the personal was the methodological. Repgen was, first and foremost, a Catholic historian. His positions were representative of what he repeatedly characterized as "Catholic research."[92]

However *ad hominem* these claims, in one sense, Scholder was right. In his style of argumentation, Repgen made deft use of the tools of scholastic disputation. This approach, German historian Hubert Wolf notes, repeatedly forced Scholder to lay claim to positions that went far beyond those originally formulated. This was what the Dominican Johannes Eck had masterfully done to Martin Luther during the Leipzig Disputation in 1519, conniving his adversary into embracing positions raised by Jan Hus, the Bohemian priest burned at the stake in 1415 for heresy.[93]

Why did Scholder fall into the trap? Very likely because his position was difficult to defend. Lacking definitive written proof for his quid pro quo, he could only make the case that such a deal was "possible," "probable" or "plausible." In his response of October 27, 1977, Repgen methodically pummeled his adversary with five objections.[94] As Volk and Morsey had done years earlier, he cast doubt on the accuracy of Brüning's memoirs and their account of 1933. He cited the absence of proof for his claims of a quid pro quo. It is, he concluded, not "convincing to hold fast to such a problematic hypothesis."

Repgen's rejoinder clearly got under Scholder's skin. The same day it appeared in print, a representative from his publisher dashed off an aggrieved response to Paul Mikat, a member of the Association for Contemporary History who was serving as president of the Görres Society.[95] The cause for offense: Herr Professor Repgen had written a "polemically exaggerated response" to Scholder's article without having read his entire book. A rebuttal would soon be coming, and indeed one ran on November 19, 1977, in the *Frankfurter Allgemeine*.[96]

In his opening lines, Scholder cried foul. Konrad Repgen was merely regurgitating what he had written back in his articles of 1967 and 1970. That he could with "such conviction and objectivity" state little more than this was because he had read only the advance excerpts and "not my book," which had been available in bookstores since October 21. "Once again, it is shown," he added sarcastically, "how much easier it is to refute a book when one does not read it at all, because one knows in advance that its theses are wrong."

In contrast, he, Scholder, had new arguments. He would have been a "fool" otherwise. Previous research, and therein lay its weakness, had focused all too narrowly on the negotiations leading up to the Reichskonkordat. Yet its true antecedents were not the series of treaties with the states of Bavaria, Baden and Prussia, as Volk maintained, but the Lateran Accords of 1929. What made this claim new? Scholder had discovered – and for the first time he credited his graduate assistant, Leonore Siegele-Wenschkewitz, for a find – a speech from Hitler published just eleven days after the Lateran Accords had been signed.[97] In it, Hitler stated that the best way to solve the problem of relations with the Vatican was through a treaty similar to Mussolini's. Scholder also claimed to have discovered something that "the entire Catholic literature on the concordat" had not cited even once, let alone analyzed. This was an article written by the Center Party leader Ludwig Kaas in the middle of 1932 and published in early 1933 that also "left no doubt" that the Lateran Accords offered a model solution.

From these opening salvos, it was clear that an undercurrent of anger was seeping into their exchanges. For Scholder, this manifested itself in snipes and barbs; for Repgen, in stridency. Scholder found himself consciously ratcheting up more cautious formulations from just two months earlier.[98] In his article from September, he had summed up his case for a quid pro quo as "credible" or "plausible"; he now formulated it as, "in his eyes, a certainty."[99] In September, he had noted that "it is certainly correct, that until today no hard and fast proof has been found in either state or church archives for plans for a concordat in March 1933." He now stated that "we are not quite without evidence, as Repgen claims." He pointed to a letter to Paul von Hindenburg from March 23, 1933, from the president of the Protestant Church Federation, who described unconfirmed reports about possible negotiations with the Vatican and asked the senior statesman to step in, if necessary, to ensure Protestant interests.

But most indicative of Scholder's growing indignation was his dismissal of Repgen's methodological *idée fixe*: one needed "positive, stringent proof from the sources." Scholder responded below the belt. Was this not, he queried, a "trump card" similar to that played by British historian David Irving? Long before he jumped into outright Holocaust denialism, Irving was gaining ignominy for claims that Hitler, whose signature was nowhere to be found on orders for genocide, lacked knowledge of the Final Solution.[100]

This was an assault on Repgen's professional integrity, and he had little choice but to issue a rebuttal once again in the *Frankfurter Allgemeine*. He did so on December 7 with a terse four-paragraph letter to the editor, responding to allegations of questionable "scholarly ethics."[101] Of course, he pointed out, he had discussed only the arguments excerpted in the *Frankfurter Allgemeine*. Scholder's book had not yet even come on the market on the date he handed over his article to the editor. Both Morsey and Deuerlein had already used Kaas' article from 1933, even if the latter had made the same interpretative errors as Scholder.

But Repgen would not let the matter rest there. A daily newspaper, he informed readers, was not the ideal medium to delve into the methods and rules of the historical discipline. He would continue the discussion later in a more suitable venue. The sequels were not long in coming. Already by early February 1978 word had spread of Scholder's intent to publish a follow-up article that fall.[102] By April 1978, the two combatants had agreed to carry out the next round in the *Contemporary History Quarterly* as well as on rules and deadlines.[103] Their papers were to be of equal length (both clocked in at approximately thirty-five pages) and were to be synchronized with one another for the October issue. Repgen, however, found himself at a disadvantage. His deadline came approximately six weeks earlier in order for Scholder to have the last word. Possibly because he was hoping to expand his critique into a full-fledged book the following year, Repgen accepted these terms with no grumbling.[104]

Both sides immediately began scrambling for new documents to bolster their case. Volk approached his Jesuit colleague in Rome, Angelo Martini, SJ, for help. As one of the four editors of the eleven documents of papal documents pertaining to the Second World War, Martini had access to the Vatican archives.[105] To find new sources from the Italian Foreign Ministry, Scholder enlisted the aid of a colleague at the German Historical Institute in Rome as well as a left-wing Italian professor, Giampiero Carocci.[106] Tellingly, Scholder had to rely on a translator to render Carocci's documents into German, leading Repgen to suspect (and not without good reason) that his opponent's Italian was not up to snuff.[107]

These were not Scholder's only new pieces of evidence. A Catholic journalist, Dr. Antonius John, having just read Scholder's tome, called to tell him of a record that had been in his hands since 1958.[108] It was his protocol of a conversation in 1953 with former Center Party delegate August Christian Winkler.[109] Winkler had told him of a remarkable meeting between him and Kaas in the latter's residence in Berlin shortly after March 5, 1933. The doorbell had suddenly rung, when in strode Papal Nuncio Orsenigo at the behest of Cardinal Secretary of State Eugenio Pacelli. Winkler left the room and learned from Kaas that "something important had taken place." The first contacts had been made toward a concordat, and the Holy See was accordingly going to order the Center Party to sign off on the Enabling Act. Orsenigo then expressed his belief that the church was indifferent to the form of political system as long as "the freedom of the church" was guaranteed.[110]

Once Scholder received what seemed to be a smoking gun, the situation seemed to change "very unfavorably," Ludwig Volk observed with consternation.[111] How to respond was on the agenda of a meeting of the Association for Contemporary History on April 15, 1978, that addressed Scholder's book. Since Winkler had died in 1961, there was no possibility of questioning the source.[112] Repgen announced that he would deal with this "pseudo-historical statement" in his article for the *Contemporary History Quarterly*. Before doing so, Repgen sent Scholder a copy of the same protocol in his possession. This account was, he asserted, "altogether non-credible."[113] If Scholder was of the same opinion, he stated, he would make a note of it in a short footnote. Otherwise, he would expand and expound upon its deficiencies as a credible source.[114] Scholder nonetheless opted to make use of it, believing that at its core it "bore the stamp of truth." Before he did so, he sent Morsey a copy of the protocol and asked his opinion of it.[115]

Morsey promptly dispatched to him two pages expressing skepticism.[116] Winkler's account, Morsey wrote, was error-ridden. Kaas, for instance, lived in a hospital in Berlin that lacked a doorbell. That Kaas would have revealed such crucial and sensitive information to a backbencher like Winkler stretched credulity. John's written account, coming on the heels of the fight before the Constitutional Court, may well have been influenced by Bracher's depiction of events. Scholder was not dissuaded. It was improbable, he insisted, that Winkler would have made up the story altogether.[117]

This pro and con made its way to the pages of the *Contemporary History Quarterly*, where it underscored a central feature of their exchange: both historians could look at the same documents and draw entirely opposite conclusions about their meaning. For Repgen,

Winkler's story told over lunch to an impressionable young man twenty-five years later was a source absolutely unsuited to reconstruct the events of 1933.[118] Scholder, while conceding that Winkler might have fabricated the story, pointed out that something similar might actually have transpired. Based on his considerations of "the bigger picture" and the current state of knowledge, the latter was a "more probable" conclusion.[119]

This bone of contention became the capstone of their debate, their conflicting interpretations of one central document: Kaas' diary-like jottings from 1935 that Morsey had helped bring to light in 1960. Kaas had detailed how he had gone to Rome on March 24, 1933, one day after the signing of the Enabling Act. On his return trip to Berlin, he changed trains in Munich on the morning of April 8, 1933. By chance, he encountered Franz von Papen and his wife in the dining car. What Kaas wrote down next led Repgen and Scholder to diametrically opposed conclusions. In this disputed passage, one difficult to render syntactically into idiomatic English, Kaas had stated: "In the course of a conversation which he (Papen) initiated in his compartment, I determined that the intention to conclude a potential Reichskonkordat, an intention that had also been repeatedly discussed in public, was a done deal."

For Repgen, the meaning was self-evident: Kaas was reporting that he had hitherto only heard rumors of a possible Reichskonkordat.[120] In the course of his conversation with von Papen, he discovered for the first time that these intentions were now reality. For Scholder, on the other hand, the document indicated the reverse: Kaas had known of these plans long before April 8, 1933. If one reads the sentence carefully, Scholder noted, nowhere did Kaas state that he had been uninformed of the regime's intent to conclude a potential treaty. Rather, he was admitting that he was aware of this; otherwise, the phrase "an intent that had *also* (italics mine) been repeatedly discussed in public" would have made no sense. The plans for a Reichskonkordat, in other words, had already been discussed with Kaas and publicly before Kaas learned in the train compartment that von Papen had been the one entrusted with carrying them out.[121]

Whose interpretation was correct? With both adversaries agreeing that Kaas was one to weigh his words carefully, their dispute centered on the syntactical placement of the word "also." More broadly, it rested on how to explain a chain of events for which written sources were in short supply. Repgen asserted that which was supposedly empirically verifiable had to take priority over hypothetical alternatives, those "might haves" or "could haves."[122] What irked Scholder was Repgen's Olympian certainty.[123] Repgen had peppered his rejoinders to Scholder with phrases like "his letter cannot be understood differently" and "the conclusion is unavoidable." Scholder hurled at his opponent the dangerous charge of being a positivist who believed that empirically verifiable evidence alone provided the path to historical truth. This, Scholder insisted, could "only lead to error."[124] Repgen was trying to use documents to prove what was actually unprovable – the claim that there had been no concrete plans for a Reichskonkordat before the start of April 1933. Just because no written records had yet been found did not mean that such negotiations had not taken place. After all, the first half of 1933 was a time of revolution; state authorities and political parties were no longer operating under standard procedures. Should one at least not consider scenarios for which the leading players, either by design or necessity, left no written records?

As significant as they were, these methodological disagreements did not serve as the true cornerstone of this controversy. The feuding pair actually had more in common with each other methodologically than the harsh exchanges might lead one to suspect. Both were old-school political and diplomatic historians, focusing narrowly on the maneuvers of churchmen, politicians and the theologies that drove them. Both eschewed the social history gaining in vogue in the 1970s, Repgen vocally so.[125] Both had made the acquaintance of politicians, diplomats, churchmen and journalists who like Leiber featured prominently in their accounts. They were, in other words, writing about a world they knew firsthand and well.

At the center of their strife was something else: the opposing moral judgments they cast on these statesmen and their decisions. Unleashing a torrent of words was Scholder's claim that the Reichskonkordat represented the triumph of political expediency over morality.[126] For a church determined to attain security from such a treaty, Scholder argued, the Reichskonkordat was unavoidable but morally problematic.[127] Repgen took umbrage. He not only noted that Scholder had labeled the Catholic response to the National Socialist challenge a "capitulation" while neutralizing his criticism of the Protestant capitulation by titling his chapter "The Seizure of Power and Protestantism."[128] He also insisted that the church's response had been the morally correct course of action. The pope had not been negligent. This treaty represented the only possibility for defense against the Nazi police state: Under a totalitarian system, simply preserving the church's independence and administering the sacraments was a form of resistance.[129] The Reichskonkordat gave bishops, the papacy and the church abroad the means to protest: violations were met with protests. The Reichskonkordat, Repgen thus concluded, was the exact opposite of a capitulation: it was the legal form of nonconformity (*Nichtanpassung*).

Scholder chose to duck these issues of ecclesiastical resistance in his response. They were, he alleged, too "complex" to allow for a satisfactory reply in this forum.[130] But tellingly, neither historian denied that it was legitimate for historians otherwise schooled in objectivity to pass moral judgment on their subjects. Scholder, in fact, introduced his book by asserting he would call out "blindness, lies, arrogance, stupidity and opportunism by name, even when it was clothed in clerical garb and spoke the language of the churches."[131] He saw it as a moral calling to come to terms with questions of guilt, both of the churches and of the nation.[132] Repgen's defense of the church also rested on moral grounds. Allowing the church to carry out its sacramental mission, he implied, was a theological and moral imperative: souls hung in the balance were baptism, communion and the last rites not to be administered.

For both scholars, history served the moral and religious needs of the present. The Christian scholar, Repgen wrote several years later, had the particular obligation to recognize the import that his findings would have on the faithful. History, he wrote, creates identity: it tells us "who I am and we are."[133] As keepers of collective identity, Catholic historians bore tremendous responsibility. Mistakes of fact or interpretation could have "calamitous" consequences for the entire community, as these historical controversies had made clear.[134] The unstated conclusion: untoward and dishonest criticism could shake faith.

Since Repgen and Scholder were in apparent agreement that historians were entitled to raise moral claims, each had to search for other ways to discredit the moral judgments passed by his adversary. Each did so by claiming that confessional and political biases had left his adversary unable to serve as an impartial moral arbiter. This was not difficult for either to do. Repgen linked his opponent to the chain of concordat critics beginning with Georg August Zinn and Thomas Dehler. In doing so, he took liberties with his opponent's positions, often giving them a more extreme formulation than his adversary.[135] He claimed that Scholder's "major argument" (Scholder had never put this claim in such terms) resembled that from Zinn's address to the Parliamentary Council on January 20, 1949. For Repgen, such similarities showed how historical judgments about this treaty and present-day politics were intertwined.[136]

Scholder also looked for ways to diminish Repgen's moral standing. At the heart of Repgen's argumentation, he saw an effort to "exculpate the Vatican for any involvement in the prehistory of the concordat and at the same time accordingly for any complicity in Hitler's seizure of power."[137] That Scholder now hinted at Vatican machinations – an echo, perhaps, of liberal suspicion of ultramontanism from the late nineteenth and early twentieth centuries – showed how far the parameters of the debate had shifted. Scholder was no longer directing his criticisms solely at Kaas, as he had done in his article in the *Frankfurter Allgemeine*, but – like Hochhuth – at the apex of the Vatican hierarchy.

Hanging over this analysis – as Scholder's choice of the word "exculpate" (*entlasten*) makes clear – was the question of ecclesiastical guilt. For Scholder, guilt required contrition, confession and expiation. But even here, his reflections were infused by the denominational divide from the 1950s. Scholder had a way to explain why the Catholic Church was more in need of having a mirror held up to it, and it was a line of argumentation that had been used by Protestant church leaders since the fight over the Reichskonkordat from the mid-1950s.[138] The Protestant church had shown contrition, while the Roman Catholic Church had not.[139] In his last published interview from 1985, Scholder elaborated on this claim. Protestant church leaders, he noted, had issued a remarkable declaration of guilt in Stuttgart on October 19, 1945.[140] In contrast, those at the top of the Catholic hierarchy like Pope Pius XII had done no such thing. In his widely publicized address before the College of Cardinals on June 2, 1945, Pope Pius XII had refused to cede a millimeter of ground to those who had sought an acknowledgment that the church might have resisted more courageously.[141] Ever since, Scholder implied, church leaders had remained so convinced of their own rectitude that they could not own up to their own sins.

Part of the blame, Scholder intimated, lay in the Association for Contemporary History of which Repgen had been the director.[142] This Catholic historical association, he alleged, had come to enjoy a scholarly "monopoly." Its position was not dissimilar to the stranglehold exerted by veterans of the Confessing Church, the Dahlemites, over the historiography of the Protestant Church struggle.[143] While the association's documentary editions were of the highest quality – and in fact unequaled in the entire field of contemporary history – he insisted that its groupthink needed to be challenged. Trust busting was necessary not only so that outsiders would be able to provide competing histories but for moral and religious renewal. To avoid repeating past errors, the churches needed to account openly for their failures, a task for which insiders with ties to high-ranking figures in the ecclesia were ill suited. This was, for Scholder, the confessional elephant in the room.

The two men's formal exchanges came to a close in early 1979 when Scholder simply refused to answer his opponent's charges any longer. Repgen, it seems, bombarded his nemesis into silence. In his "epilogue" published in the *Contemporary History Quarterly*, Repgen pointed to a whopping seventy points – "if I count correctly" – in which Scholder had failed to "convince" him; of these seventy, the Bonn historian contented himself with sketching out a mere ten.[144] Scholder contended himself with a pithy one-paragraph reply. Finding nothing new in Repgen's ten theses, he had nothing further to add.[145]

Epilogue

Yet this was not quite the end. An epilogue of sorts to this controversy underscored a peculiar dynamic. Confessional tensions on the whole had significantly eased by the late 1970s – but not for the small circles of professional historians writing about the churches under Nazism. They naturally assumed that Scholder was going to remain a decisive presence in the field and, for the members of the Association for Contemporary History, a powerful adversary. He was gearing up for his second installation of his multivolume history of the churches in the Third Reich. In the fall of 1980, he published an article critical of the German episcopate and the head of the Fulda Bishops Conference, Adolf Bertram, in the *Frankfurter Allgemeine*.[146] No one could have anticipated his struggles with the cancer that would claim his life in 1985.

This alone explains the aggrieved reactions of many in the association to a film aired on November 4, 1980, on Germany's second television station, the ZDF. This controversy underscored the futility of the defense strategies that had been deployed ever since the Hochhuth affair. The film, *Like Fate . . . Like a Disaster . . . the Catholic Church in the Third Reich*, had been scripted by two young intellectuals seeking to teach younger Germans about the Catholic Church's troubling role in the Third Reich.[147] The most prominent of this duo, Michael Albus, had received a Ph.D. in theology, had a background in church history and had led the office of public relations for the Central Committee of German Catholics. Klaus Scholder, the longstanding commentator for the ZDF, served as a consultant to the filmmakers. Their hour-and-fifteen-minute-long film featured interviews with witnesses from the era of National Socialism, who, according to the somewhat-misleading press release for the film, "had been in important positions back then."[148] "Can we learn anything from the history back then?" the youthful filmmakers, sporting vintage late-1970s haircuts, queried at the close.[149]

Though the film was shown only once on television before being consigned to the filing cabinet, several of the middle-aged historians on the board of the Association for Contemporary History, including Repgen, Albrecht and Volk, wrote harsh letters of protest to the ZDF. They cited the film's alleged conceptual muddles and lack of objectivity. Repgen enumerated nine specific objections.[150] But tellingly, their criticisms did not mention Scholder's role as a consultant. Nor could they, for the film's one-sidedness had, in part, come about through a unilateral act of disarmament. In the early stages of planning, Albus had invited Scholder *and* Volk, both internationally recognized experts, to serve as consultants. From the outset, however, Volk had made his participation conditional on the Association for Contemporary History's receipt of a synopsis of the broadcast. This was tantamount, Albus later complained, to requiring its approval.[151] Shortly into production, Volk opted out.

To Albus, this incident had revealed a confessional pettiness that he was surprised to find in a person of Volk's "intellectual capacity."[152] Making the letters of protest from three members of the association more inexplicable for Albus was that a church representative on the committee of the ZDF, Father Eberhard von Gemmingen, SJ, had screened the film, apparently finding it unobjectionable. A member of the German Bishops Conference had even testified to the filmmakers' objectivity.[153]

What Albus and Scholder were experiencing firsthand was something that would have been unthinkable during the Hochhuth controversy back in 1963. The most persistent and furious denunciations were coming not from the bishops but from Catholic historians ensconced for more than a decade in the Association for Contemporary History. The bishops were either giving their seal of approval to more critical accounts or refraining from commentary altogether. Left-wing Catholics like Karl Otmar von Aretin from the generation of 1945 had openly sided with the Protestant Scholder. Adding to the cacophony were the voices of younger Catholics coming of age in the second half of the 1960s. What was left of the onetime Catholic milieu – the network of ancillary organizations and political action groups – was ideologically and politically fragmented. Many prominent Catholic lay organizations had lurched to the left in the late 1960s and 1970s. They were no longer in lockstep with the bishops, who themselves lacked the political and moral gravitas of their predecessors in the immediate postwar era. Indeed, Repgen would take umbrage with reforms introduced by the Second Vatican Council and Volk with the direction his own order had taken.[154]

Those critical of the church's past were thus far less likely to complain about how the bishops had constrained research. Like Scholder, they pointed the finger at the Association for Contemporary History instead. Its alleged scholarly hegemony served as a call to arms. Looking for an alternative nexus for contemporary church history, those disgruntled with the state of research created an alternative working group in the late 1980s with an annual conference in the Ruhr city of Schwerte.[155]

But the association's critics in some ways gave their *bête noire* too much credit. Its alleged stranglehold over scholarly research never translated into a decisive advantage outside the highbrow conservative print media. While professional historians like Repgen could take their case to the politics and review sections of the *Frankfurter Allgemeine*, they could not produce films or like Scholder become regular television commentators.

And so Volk was left on the sidelines to ponder the confessional biases that still punctuated the intellectual landscape of the late 1970s and early 1980s. It was strange, Volk wrote, that public attention was so consumed by the Reichskonkordat's origins when those from "the Protestant camp" should, in fact, have been much more outraged by Scholder's claims.[156] When a Catholic professor speaks "in unfriendly tones about the great reformer, Martin Luther," he ruefully concluded, "that is a scandal." But when a Protestant professor "takes aim at Cardinal Bertram, that is completely acceptable."[157] As much as this was polemical overreach, it was also an accurate barometer of the confessional asymmetries emerging out of the politics and ideologies of the 1950s and persisting decades later.

Conclusions

Why did the responses by prominent figures in the ecclesia to twelve years of dictatorship, war and genocide turn the Catholic Church into such a clear target for moral censure in the postwar era?

In the immediate aftermath of the Second World War between 1945 and 1949, what little public criticism there was of the German churches for their alleged sins of commission and omission during the years of National Socialism tended to be directed evenly at the Catholic and Protestant churches. To be sure, Communist propagandists decrying "clerico-Fascism" disproportionately targeted the Catholic Church. Pacifists and conscientious objectors like Josef Fleischer aired specific grievances against their *bêtes noires*, mostly Catholic chaplains and bishops in whom they had been personally disappointed.

But even their moral reckoning with the Catholic Church in the press represented the departure from the rule in more ways than one. Facing a severe paper shortage and Allied restrictions over the German airwaves and print media, most harboring reservations about the churches' conduct during the Third Reich, including even the future chancellor, Konrad Adenauer, expressed them privately (if at all). Not wishing to further damage Germany's reputation abroad at a time when talk of collective guilt, war crimes trials, denazification and reparations remained in the air, most saw it by the late 1940s as in the national interest to lapse into silence. This fact alone elevated to orthodoxy the picture of the church triumphant, of clear-headed leaders valiantly resisting and the faithful unflinchingly following. This was just as true for the Protestant clergy, who while ensconcing themselves in leadership positions in the new Protestant Church of Germany extolled their own courageous witness behind the cross of the Confessing Church during the years of idolatry and persecution.

But beginning in early 1949 during the deliberations in the Parliamentary Council and even more so by 1956, the year that the question of the Reichskonkordat's validity went before the West German Constitutional Court, such symmetry gave way. The critical pendulum swung fiercely – and almost entirely in the direction of the Catholic Church. Doubts about the moral fitness of Catholic bishops, Cardinal Secretary of States and pontiffs of the Nazi era were cascaded before the public. They screamed from front-page headlines, the magazine covers of the most influential newsweeklies, the glossy pages of illustrated magazines and the best-seller lists in Germany and the United States. Protests, riots and boycotts served as a magnet for the lenses and recording devices of newspaper, radio and television journalists from both sides of the Atlantic. By comparison, similar criticisms of the moral righteousness of Protestant church officials came with a mute. More often than not the province of specialty scholars and dissident theologians, only occasionally could they be heard over the din accompanying the critical assault on the personae of the Catholic ecclesia and their pasts.[1]

Why did the alleged sins of the Catholic Church ring so much louder than those of their Protestant brethren? This has been a guiding question for this book, since by almost all objective yardsticks, the German Protestant leadership left behind a more troubling record of collaboration than their Catholic counterparts.[2] Between 10 and 20 percent (in some states far more than half!) of Protestant clergy, and not just members of the German Christians, had formally joined the Nazi Party or ancillary organizations like the SA, and many of these took pains to express their solidarity with Nazi values.[3] Even celebrated resisters in the oppositional Confessing Church, we now know, had bought into much of the ideology and anti-Semitism of the Nazi regime. By contrast, less than 1 percent of Catholic clergy joined the Nazi party, and the worst of the "brown priests" were often reprimanded for their excess zeal.[4]

There is a simple answer to why the majority opted to focus on the past of Germany's religious minority, whose sins in marked contrast to those of the Protestant majority were more frequently deemed to be of omission than of commission. It was (and remains) easier to make sense of the Catholic Church's apparent moral failings. Everyone could play the expert. It was a universal church. Its structures were tidily hierarchical; its bishops, cardinals and pontiffs were household names, celebrities even, and archetypes of authority. By way of comparison, the Protestant churches of Germany were paragons of opacity. Even vested church officials could not easily explain to neophytes the theological and historical differences between their Reformed, United and Lutheran brethren, the jumbled structures of the twenty-eight Protestant state churches and the internal fissures tearing apart committees, emergency leagues and dissident church bodies in the 1930s. There was no Protestant pope to command public attention. How then could the media distill Protestant conduct into 2,000-word articles, let alone encapsulate it in attention-grabbing headlines?

But there were also Protestant churchmen from the years of persecution like Martin Niemöller who were well known to the faithful around the world for their resistance but also for their misplaced nationalism. Why did their conduct during the Third Reich not spark greater imbroglios internationally from the 1950s through the 1970s? Here too there is a deceptively simple explanation rooted in a template that still largely remains true to this day. Protestant politicians, churchmen, journalists, playwrights and scholars were willing to enter into or launch public discussions about the Catholic past in the Third Reich, while their Roman Catholic counterparts in the press, ecclesia, intelligentsia and academy rarely, if ever, spoke out openly about the Protestant past. To be sure, not all Protestants who went on record with their judgments were critical of the Catholic Church's record; some defended it. By dint of sheer volume, though, newspaper readers and radio listeners were far more likely to hear about the records of Catholic clergymen, those both good and ill, during the Third Reich than those of their Protestant counterparts.

But it was more than the numbers of voices that contributed to this confessional imbalance: it was the fact that in these controversies Protestant churchmen, politicians and intellectuals sounded theological chords of sin, confession, absolution and forgiveness that they knew would not – nor could not – be as easily directed against their own churches. Klaus Scholder was but one of many Protestant church officials who over more than three decades insisted that the Stuttgart Confession of Guilt from October 19, 1945, had served as proof of repentance and that the Catholic Church, lacking an equivalent statement, was now in greater need of contrition.[5]

Well-respected Protestant theologians also pointed to differences in the respective structures of the ecclesia to argue that the Catholic Church had a greater guilt to expunge. As the celebrated Alsatian medical missionary and Lutheran theologian Albert Schweitzer argued in a letter that generated headlines across Germany when published in September 1963, the Catholic Church bore the greater guilt because it was a "well-organized supranational power capable of having done something" – and certainly more than the "unorganized, powerless and national" Protestant church body.[6] In this vein, Berlin church official and onetime Confessing Church member Heinrich Grüber argued in 1963 and 1964 that the centralized hierarchical structure of the Catholic Church made it more capable of mobilizing the faithful: "Catholics in the smallest villages thought and did that which came down to them through the directives of the Vatican."[7]

In sum, the Catholic Church, according to this view, had better weapons than the Protestants – legions of priests and lay followers, an ethos of obedience, an unmistakable chain of command and a pope at the top. It could have – and should have – done more.

Yet it is tempting here to recite the old adage that this array of self-proclaimed Protestant moralists and truth-tellers was pointing out the mite in their neighbors' eyes while failing to see the log in their own, and there would certainly be more than a grain of truth to this. But can they be forgiven for not seeing the log? In noting that outright collaboration was more prevalent among Protestant church leaders, we have the benefit of hindsight – and specifically of painstaking research into the failures of German Protestantism that appeared on the shelves of academic libraries in the form of dozens of scholarly articles and monographs starting in the mid-1980s.[8] Those weighing the moral responsibility of the churches during the Adenauer era, however, had a lopsided picture at their finger-tips. As a rule, they had in one hand Protestant hagiography – the self-confident volumes by and about the onetime leaders of the Confessing Church.[9] In the other they held the increasingly critical public statements, books and articles into the Catholic Church's responsibility for the Nazi seizure of power that were appearing in print already by mid-1956 and finding an echo in the media as a result of the widely publicized hearings before the Constitutional Court in Karlsruhe over the validity of the Reichskonkordat.

Was the verdict by some Protestants that the Catholic Church was more deserving of censure, then, the result of simple ignorance? The answer is "yes" and "no." Younger intellectuals, those like Rolf Hochhuth born between the late 1920s through the early 1930s and for the purposes of our story coalescing into the cohort of public intellectuals now put into the pigeon-hole of "the generation of 1945," certainly lacked knowledge of what had transpired within Protestant church councils, bishoprics, committees and leagues not known for their transparency – but the insiders from the 1930s and 1940s did not. Eager as some of these were to demythologize the conduct of confessional rivals, to no surprise they showed less interest in deconsecrating the hagiographies that they or their brethren in the Confessing Church had helped create.[10]

Many Catholics once again put on the defensive thus suspected (and sometimes with good reason) that public criticisms of Catholic conduct aired by those like Grüber represented the resurfacing of rank anti-Catholic prejudice from a Protestant-dominated cultural establishment and news media. Yet such suspicions of a renewed Kulturkampf, made however plausible by the confessional strife of the 1950s and 1960s, overlooked one crucial factor: faithful Catholics, including converts, non-conformists and progressives, were just as involved in formulating and disseminating this reappraisal of their church's past as onetime confessional enemies like Protestants, Jews and atheists. For critical or nonconformist Catholics, the schisms, factions and capitulations of Protestants were simply irrelevant to their story. Their belief in the need for church reform in no way hinged on and might even have been diminished by comparisons with the Protestant church struggle. Their moral activism, at least for those who had lived through the terrible years of dictatorship and war, often stemmed from traumatic personal recollections of what had been done to them – or not done for them – by their church. Their adversaries were driven on by memories of a completely different nature, of what had been done to their church by the National Socialist state and how the church had come to the aid of those in need.

But pointing to how memories of tribulation resurfaced does not entirely explain our conundrum. After all, why did survivors disappointed with the conduct of Protestant church officials not air their criticisms publicly as well? The major reason lies in the fact that for many political activists, the Catholic Church was a far greater source of day-to-day grumblings than the Protestant Church.[11] As a rule, these nonconformist and critical Catholics tended to share with Protestant pundits a mistrust of the Catholic Church's seemingly singular role in the politics of the Federal Republic. Such misgivings, expressed both viscerally through tirades against the "clericalization" of West German politics and in the form of meticulous reflections about the need to redraw lines between church and state, explain better than any other factor the disproportionate focus in the early decades of the fledgling republic on the apparent sins of the Catholic Church.

Triggering their ire were issues for which it was seemingly impossible to hold the new Protestant Church of Germany culpable: public reminders to the faithful to vote "Christian," the bid to maintain and expand denominational schools segregated by confession by insisting on the validity of the Reichskonkordat from 1933 and clerical pronouncements on war and peace that seemed to echo perfectly Adenauer's pro-Western alignment in the Cold War. When read aloud from the pulpit as pastoral letters, such statements of principle and purpose were cast as religious duty and moral necessity, the fate of Christian Germany even on occasion alleged to be hanging in the balance. It was easy to draw a simple conclusion: the Catholic Church had overstepped its rightful boundaries in politics and society.

Between 1949 and 1962, those unhappy with this course steered by Konrad Adenauer's Christian Democratic Union experienced one defeat after another. The federal parliamentary elections of 1953 and 1957 tipped the scales decisively in favor of the Christian Democratic parties who, in spite of diminishing electoral returns from 1961 on, continued to wield power until 1969. Frustrated with the seemingly unstoppable advance of the CDU in the late 1950s, a party inter-confessional in theory but in practice supported disproportionately by faithful Catholics, an unlikely smattering of opposition politicians, Catholic nonconformists and young public intellectuals became increasingly perturbed by the church's unwillingness to tolerate dissent. As hearings over the Reichskonkordat and the guilt of Nazi camp guards and bureaucrats directed their gaze back to the Nazi era, some critics began to see continuity between ecclesiastical mentalities from the 1920s and the 1960s. Were not church positions on war and peace in the Cold War the same as they had been during the Nazi era? Had not the church, still reluctant to embrace an ethos of democracy, always had greater affinities with authoritarian regimes? The target thus inevitably broadened. No longer just the church's role in the politics of the present, it came to include its values and priorities from Weimar to Bonn and the moral claims of Christian Democracy to have been born out of religiously inspired resistance against the Third Reich. Demythologizing the past thus became a way to reverse the unfavorable political tides of the Federal Republic.

But there was an irony behind the efforts of these Catholic and Protestant fellow travelers to diminish the moral legitimacy of church and party. In taking the Christianizing zeal of leaders in church and party at face value, they imagined the links between them to be vaster than they in fact were. The CDU was not the old Weimar-era Center Party, the overheated rhetoric of hardliners like Bishop Michael Keller of Münster or the entreaties of CDU politician Adolf Süsterhenn notwithstanding. Its leader, Konrad Adenauer, though a devout Catholic, was not a cleric – nor a tool of the clergy. He sought to reduce the dependence on the church and clergy, not the reverse.

Critics would thus have been innocent of the reality that even Adenauer's decision to legally contest Lower Saxony's new school law placing limits on denominational schools – ultimate proof of collusion for ideological adversaries of the CDU – had been undertaken reluctantly. Documents released by church and party archives since the 1980s accordingly tell a less partisan and more nuanced story. But to those on the front lines of politics, such a story would have been belied by the pronouncements of clerical hardliners and the harsh judgments of critics seeking greater separation of church and state. Only after these conflicts over how to position the church in the culture and society of the Federal Republic had been put to rest and portions of the neoscholastic edifice anchoring moral and political orthodoxies abandoned could this reality be made plausible. These wars over the Catholic past, often begun as proxy wars, stemmed at least in part from misperceptions of how lines between church and state were changing – and ironically often in the way that critics sought.

Pointing to the fractured political landscape of the Adenauer era thus helps explain why the past of the Catholic and not the Protestant Church became the lightning rod for critics frustrated with the slow pace of reform. But directing attention to specific political battles of the Adenauer era like those over the validity of the Reichskonkordat does not account for a second puzzle. Why did the ensuing controversies, still asymmetrically focused on the alleged misdeeds of one church, prove so enduringly explosive, persisting years and even decades after the storms igniting them had passed by?

The persistence of political fault lines from the first two decades of the Federal Republic's existence well into the 1970s certainly provides part of the explanation here. Though many of the confessional storms from the mid-1950s had long dissipated, not all the political allegiances that had fueled them had.[12] The young cohort of public intellectuals of "the generation of 1945" had invariably found themselves schooled by these struggles, reacting viscerally to both the ideological, religious and political currents of Adenauer's Germany and the responses, laudatory and excoriating, that their words, plays and deeds evoked. Combatants like Protestant historian Klaus Scholder and Catholic historian Konrad Repgen, young men in their twenties and thirties during the confessional strife of the Adenauer era, remained card-carrying members of the rival FDP and CDU, respectively, and ardent defenders of their parties' worldviews. To no surprise, the suspicions and prejudices generated during the struggles of the late 1950s and 1960s over the Catholic Church's past during National Socialism resurfaced during the renewed exchanges of the late 1970s.

As professors in the 1970s, moreover, both Repgen and Scholder were working within an academic and intellectual culture increasingly polarized, even balkanized, by the ascendency of - isms, old and new alike. Fundamentally dividing many students, graduate students and professors was no longer just the question of how to account for the origins and crimes of National Socialism but the extent to which its spirit had permeated the political, cultural and religious institutions of the Federal Republic. Critics notably pointed out that politicians, statesmen and civil servants tainted because of their misdeeds during the Nazi era had returned to their seats of power, a metaphor for a larger illiberal restoration after 1949. All of Germany's major political parties had rehabilitated politicians with compromised pasts, but as Germany's largest party and with a self-understanding of having been born out of the resistance against Hitler, Adenauer's CDU bore the sharpest scrutiny. As long, then, as the political and moral legacy of the CDU remained contested, so too did the church's past in the Third Reich.

Bearing the stamp of battles over church and state, the controversies over the Catholic past during the National Socialist era invariably retained their explosive character. Not only had combatants harnessed the energy and passions of politics. Some also drew upon the infrastructures of politics and the ecclesia to launch and finance teams for research like the association of Catholic scholars that Repgen had headed since 1962, the Association for Contemporary History. Those with strong political inclinations thus had found solidarity with kindred spirits, and the existence of networks of the seemingly like-minded inevitably kept controversies about the church's past at a boiling point. Ensuing controversies were no longer just about what had happened between 1933 and 1945. They were about the networks themselves and their political pedigrees. They were, above all, about whether ideological adversaries on "the other side" had stifled the free exchange of ideas or distorted the truth.

Making these parameters of debate plausible was more than the fact that closed-door networks almost always appear to be more homogeneous and malevolent to outsiders (and especially to adversaries) than they are in reality. It was the timing: the discussions about the Catholic Church's past followed on the heels of national debates that repeatedly reached parliamentary floors about the need for greater tolerance in society. Schoolchildren in denominational schools, religious dissidents, political mavericks and investigatory journalists were among those deemed to have suffered at the hands of those wielding power and, by extension, the tyranny of the majority. Allegations that public schools and political parties closely linked to the Catholic Church were agents of intolerance were thus etched into debates about the National Socialist past just as journalists with new self-understandings as guardians of dissent were drawing attention to censorship. The hard-hitting response by Catholic apologists like Walter Adolph to the criticisms of Gordon Zahn and Rolf Hochhuth made allegations of intolerance increasingly credible. The press honed in on how Catholic leaders in Berlin sought to deny tickets to *The Deputy* to sixteen- and seventeen-year-old high school students. Critics saw such actions as little more than crude censorship. Catholic defenders, in contrast, believed that their religious liberty was at stake: had they not the right to practice their faith freely and speak out against that which infringed on their beliefs and freedom of conscience?

That researchers like Ludwig Volk, SJ, prevented outside researchers from reaching documents detailing the church's past meant that even into the 1970s, the debates about the church's past during the Third Reich in Germany functioned as a referendum on Catholic intolerance. The irony of this was certainly lost on Protestant critics like Klaus Scholder who saw the historians in the Association for Contemporary History as the face of "Catholic research."

What outsiders like Scholder did not see was something not immediately apparent. Traditionalists like Volk, as influential as they might have been in the narrow circles of historians researching the Catholic past during the era of National Socialism, were out of step with the changing currents in German Catholicism in the 1970s and 1980s. Some in the hierarchy were willing to entertain and sanction more critical accounts of their church's past. In a notable instance, theologian Johannes Baptist Metz drafted a resolution titled "Our Hope" for the Würzburger Synod, a gathering between 1972 and 1975 convened by the German Bishops Conference to implement the resolutions of the Second Vatican Council.[13] Metz's resolution was open about the guilt of the Catholic Church during the Third Reich. In a passage that echoed Guenter Lewy's criticism of ecclesiastical conduct, Metz wrote that the church had been too narrowly fixated on its own institutional survival and had stood by silently as the regime – and Christians – committed one crime after another against the Jews.[14] Remarkably, Metz's resolution was approved by a vote of 225 to 25, with a mere 15 abstaining.[15]

But there was something else that for decades kept these debates about the church's past during the Third Reich at the point of combustion. It was the fact that the exposure to contrary claims and evidence, rather than leading to more balanced conclusions, seems to have entrenched combatants even more firmly in their original views. Between 1945 and 1980, countless books, articles, editorials, radio broadcasts and television documentaries appeared about the church during the era of National Socialism. Yet it appears that only one participant in the debates of this era, Rudolf Morsey, altered his position on a point that might be considered fundamental. Having in the 1950s and 1960s left open the possibility that the Center Party might have signed off on the Enabling Act in exchange for the Reichskonkordat, by the late 1970s he concluded that the evidence unearthed in the intervening decades did not support claims of a causal link between the two. For so many other combatants, the rule held: the exposure to contrary claims and/or evidence tended to inflame rather than temper.

Describing the range of tactics, from sophisticated to crude, with which these culture warriors dealt with claims and evidence that ran contrary to their message has provided much of the substance for this book. In most cases, there was abundant contrary evidence – and how could there not have been, even within a church best known as a bastion of conservatism and anti-modernism? The Catholic Church was home to just under 21 million faithful in twenty-four dioceses in Germany alone in 1930, and approximately 210 million additional believers were scattered across the rest of the vast European continent.[16] Within a fold this large and diverse, there were going to be agents of resistance, equivocation and collaboration – and this for all sorts of reasons, sacred and profane. And the earliest chroniclers knew this. Johannes Neuhäusler and Walter Adolph were firsthand witnesses to the vacillations of ecclesiastical superiors like Cardinal Adolf Bertram and Cardinal Michael Faulhaber, the latter alternatively condemning National Socialist racial heresies and praising Hitler in exceptional terms. So too did those returning to the subject in the coming decades. If they had not come across contrary evidence and views in their excursions through the documents, they were certainly made aware of them by their outraged critics.

And hence the paradox: almost all of these partisans took pains to insist that their findings rested on an unshakable foundation of objectivity. They purported to write history in the spirit of Leopold Ranke, history allegedly "as it actually had been." They published documentary collections or appendixes, the very epitome of objectivity at least to those not intimately familiar with the events as they had actually unfolded. Yet at the same time, some resorted to questionable tactics designed to uphold the purity of their position but that were, in fact, incommensurate with the spirit of letting the truth come to light. Calls to gather documentary evidence were issued but in such a way that only writings and papers of the right ilk would make their way to the table. Problematic sentences or paragraphs were excised from documentary anthologies. Adversaries' evidence was dismissed as unrepresentative, inaccurately translated or ripped out of context. And the messenger was shot. Ad hominem attacks became the norm. Present-minded agendas, political loyalties and religious and national biases were all cited as grounds for why the accounts of adversaries lacked legitimacy. Legal actions were considered and on occasion pursued. Attempts were made to have opponents dismissed from their jobs.

To be sure, not every participant stooped to such depths; most shied away from more extreme steps, contenting themselves with assailing their adversaries' methodologies and credentials. Explaining this striking disjunction between professed creeds and actual behavior nonetheless remains the unanswered puzzle in this book. Why did the exposure to contrary evidence and points of view so often lead to the closing of ranks and minds instead of the reverse? Why did it, at least in the short run, embitter and prolong rather than enlighten and refine? Certainly to those watching the irresistible ebbs and flows of historical currents, the battles over the Catholic past would illustrate how the writing of history can easily proceed dialectically. Overstated theses generate equally overwrought antitheses. But at least through the 1980s, a synthesis was never wrung out of the ensuing struggles, not as long as the original participants in the controversies were bracing to defend their claims. Each round of accusations thus triggered little more than a fusillade of counter-accusations. Even the entry of newcomers did not fundamentally alter this pattern, for even some of these simply took up the mantles of polemic from their predecessors.

The dynamic thus became self-sustaining: the more sweeping and unsparing the criticisms, the less likely the combatants were to change their minds. Part of this stemmed from the politics of German defeat. Reassessments of the church and its leading personae arose as war crimes tribunals were generating headlines and resentment well into the 1970s. Parlance from the courthouse easily seeped into the writings of those making their case about the church's conduct between 1933 and 1945 before the courtroom of public opinion. Historical verdicts were presented as indictments or pleas for acquittal, conclusions couched in categories of guilt and innocence. In this spirit, Cardinal Faulhaber used examples of ecclesiastical resistance to rebut claims of the collective guilt of the German people in his preface to Johannes Neuhäusler's *Cross and Swastika*, while Rolf Hochhuth let his major character, Riccardo Fontana, SJ, inculpate Pope Pius XII as a "criminal." And hence the imperviousness to contrary evidence: how many prosecutors and defense attorneys publicly change their mind about the guilt or innocence of those facing them in the docket, even in the wake of new evidence?

But examples of those who hold tightly to claims in the face of contrary evidence cut across all lines of generation, nationality, religion and era. The culprit, a vast and growing literature from the realm of cognitive neuroscience has argued, is something more universal: cognitive biases that shape how humans arrive at judgments and hold onto them. Such biases, this literature insists, are pervasive, since human cognitive faculties are not models of perfect rationality.[17] As Nobel Prize–winning psychologist Daniel Kahneman has argued, thinking is mostly rationalization, all pretenses at rationality and objectivity notwithstanding. Emotions drive and form human judgments long before rational facilities are even aware of it. Rational facilities, in fact, often do little more than scour for evidence to support judgments already made at the gut level: they embrace arguments and reasoning that in more sober circumstances would be dismissed as unsound. The more emotion-laden the subject, the more likely distortions and biases are to enter in.[18] Coming under fire for one's beliefs, moreover, leads most humans to defend them all the more tenaciously; hearing contrary arguments on issues laden with emotion leads partisans to dig in their heels. Humans are spurred to action by that which they most dislike.[19]

If such cognitive biases were not enough to allow partisans to dismiss contrary findings, social pressures certainly were. Putting like-minded persons in a group to discuss a partisan topic, study after study has shown, is apt to turn their convictions even more strident.[20] As groups close ranks, the critical question becomes who is admitted to or excluded from the group: who is friend, and who is foe? Should these groups become formalized – should they turn into working groups, networks, associations or think tanks – orthodoxies emerge from which individual members only rarely depart. In turn, the experience of shared combat – of plotting strategies, battling critics and experiencing victory – strengthens these convictions and orthodoxies. Challenging groupthink thus becomes too risky, particularly when money, reputation, careers, social prestige, collegiality and friendships are at stake.

This list of cognitive biases and social pressures amounts to a recipe for how to keep partisans from backing off from their views. It adeptly accounts for the striking partisanship in the United States from the 1990s onward, as those pioneering research into questions of "attitude polarization" and "biased assimilation" intended it to do. But it just as easily applies to those reconstructing the church's history for the cataclysmic era of the Third Reich and Second World War, since virtually every one of these ingredients was in place. The political battles of the Adenauer era were bitterly partisan, discussions of the Third Reich intensely personal and fraught with emotion. Those entering this terrain were thus more likely to form snap moral judgments before weighing all the available evidence. When thumbing through evidence, they often did so selectively, looking for that which confirmed what they already believed – and disregarding that which suggested a different set of conclusions.

Waging these fights was also bound to put combatants under pressure from members of their own tribe. With so many tasks involved – finding qualified scholars to carry out research, unearthing relevant documents, gaining access to those still under lock and key, compiling source collections, publishing exposés and scoops, wooing journalists, holding press conferences, arranging television and radio appearances, taking part in formal debates, writing devastating critiques, defanging enemies and, not least, financing every one of these steps – it was only a matter of time before informal collaborations would coalesce into working groups and formal networks. From the mid-1950s onward, then, the like-minded came together to tell the story of the church under National Socialism and battle adversaries on "the other side." Almost by definition, these were partisan lineups that, internal differences notwithstanding, were keen on presenting a public facade of unanimity. Openly departing from the party line or views of the group risked the wrath of friends and fellow soldiers, a step few were willing to take lightly for reasons both personal and professional. For some, and this seems to be a regular feature of partisan politics, the tribe was more important than the truth.

What lends these insights from social psychology and cognitive neuroscience additional plausibility is one fact: the lines between historical analysis and moral judgment were so loose that the two at times were inseparable. Characteristic was a blurring of distinctions between the analysis of primary source documents (based on empirical "proof" of "what had happened"), the raising of counterfactual claims (resting on uncertain foundations of probability, expressed as "might haves") and moral judgments (phrased as "should haves" and "ought to haves"). Pius XII "should have" issued a public protest, since it "could have" saved the lives of many Jews. And hence the quagmire in which the historians taking part in these debates found themselves: no amount of historical evidence could shake deep and genuine moral convictions since the moral and historical categories used were not designed to accomplish the same tasks. For cognitive researchers, this is to be expected: the mind processes complex logical problems differently than emotional "gut-level" judgments, the former requiring effort, the latter automatic.[21] But it also put those historians eschewing moral judgment at a disadvantage: they could not easily respond with the tools of their craft. Any counterfactual arguments they raised in response could by definition claim only probability, not actuality. Even the most smoking of smoking guns could not resolve the question of whether Pius "should have" spoken out more forcefully against Nazi genocide.

Historians entering into debates about the Catholic Church during the Nazi era faced a related challenge. The rules for their profession were seemingly obvious. Most, citing credos of historical objectivity, believed, however quaintly or naively this might seem to later generations steeped in postmodern hermeneutics, in letting the sources speak for themselves. When put together properly, they would tell the story of the church under National Socialist rule – and hence the emphasis on publishing documentary editions. But the rules for moral inquiry were much less fixed. Participants in these debates drew indiscriminately from a trough of ethical theories and principles, even those seemingly incompatible or mutually exclusive. In making their claims, they could simultaneously cite categorical imperatives, utilitarian calculations and natural law ethics. Was the greater good served when the church worked for its own survival, ensuring that the sacraments could continue to be administered and souls not put in jeopardy? Would a public protest by Pope Pius XII against Nazi genocide, even one that would have put the survival of the papacy in jeopardy, have saved more lives and provided the greatest good? Was it his categorical duty to have issued a more ringing public denunciation of National Socialism regardless of the consequences?

What made these questions inescapable – and all the more charged – was the fact that the Christian tradition had provided frequently conflicting answers, all easily corroborated by stories, parables and historical evidence from the centuries and millennia. These questions had, in fact, animated and sustained the tradition itself – precisely because they went to the heart of what it meant to be Christian. The conflict between the non-Christian state and the faith is as old as Christianity itself. The earliest Christians had been forced to wrestle with questions of martyrdom, the act of sacrifice central to the new faith.[22] Three of the gospels, after all, quoted Jesus as telling the crowd that those who truly wished to be his disciple should deny themselves, take up their cross and follow him: "for whoever wishes to save his life will lose it but whoever loses his life for my sake and the gospel will save it." The stories of the lives of the saints too told of suffering and gruesome deaths that preceded the bliss of martyrdom.

It is little wonder that stories of sacrifice provoked so much soul-searching in the aftermath of the Third Reich. The reflections on the cost of discipleship by Johannes Neuhäusler and Walter Adolph on the one hand, Gordon Zahn and Rolf Hochhuth on the other – and the opposing answers they provided were part of this larger struggle within the tradition itself. The hostility between the church and modern secular nation-states, particularly after 1789, had reopened old wounds and problems of identity. Not all Catholics during the twelve years of the Third Reich found themselves forced into choosing whether to take up their cross, nor certainly did all ecclesiastical leaders. Were they nonetheless obliged to have become saints and martyrs? And yet the Nazi state demanded similar sacrifices in the service of its ideals, as had not only other secular states but also the pagan Roman Empire. Was the church's purpose, then, primarily sacramental, its task ensuring that the faithful would continue to receive the seven sacraments during an era of tribulation? If so, the Catholic Church would by definition be held to different standards than the Protestant churches, which had few or no sacraments to administer and accordingly different ecclesiastical structures. Or was it to live the life of Christ at the time of trial, even unto death, a sacrifice for all of humanity?[23]

Such moral and theological questions were taken up by theologians both during and in the wake of the Second Vatican Council. Theologians and churchmen ranging from Hans Küng, Heinrich Grüber, Albert Schweitzer, Johann Baptist Metz, Giovanni Montini (the future Pope Paul VI) and Pope John Paul II all added to the commentary, each in his own way. And here, we are arriving at one of the most remarkable features of these controversies about the past, one that has only just recently begun to be explored.[24] Neither the theologians nor the historians ever achieved a consensus, either moral or historical, about how to come to terms with the Catholic past. They operated instead in parallel universes. They employed different vocabularies and, to no surprise, repeatedly talked at cross-purposes. Theologians like Metz openly spoke of guilt and responsibility, while the historians in the Association for Contemporary History eschewed such moral categories. For the latter, what better way for those not trained in theology to shut down a non-historian than by providing irrefutable documentary evidence to the contrary and highlighting an allegedly superior historical methodology?

But for Metz, such evidence ultimately counted for little. What historical verdict about the church's past, he asked rhetorically on November 21, 1975, was so definitive that no contrary evidence could be mustered against it?[25] And yet just eight years later in late January 1983, Joseph Höffner, archbishop of Cologne and chairman of the German Bishops Conference, sent out the opposite message. While issuing a joint declaration from the bishops fifty years after Hitler's appointment as chancellor, he published a detailed letter from Konrad Repgen, the association's head.[26] The association received financing from the German Bishops Conference, and in this twelve-page letter, Repgen painted a largely flattering portrait of the Catholic Church between 1933 and 1945 and of the efforts of his association to bring this truth to light. Only the entire truth, Repgen wrote, can make one free. For Repgen and Höffner, history still mattered.

And hence, with only some exaggeration, reflections on the church's past from the 1980s onward came to resemble a Tower of Babel. Simultaneously speaking were professional and amateur historians. The former included loyal Catholics in the Association for Contemporary History, critical Catholics in Germany, Protestants, Jews and those from abroad. The latter included publicists, filmmakers, journalists and not least contemporary witnesses by then in their fifties, sixties and seventies. But also speaking were theologians, bishops and popes, each with different perspectives on how the church was to come to terms with questions of guilt in the aftermath of the Shoah. Metz, Höffner and Pope John Paul II each brought different understandings to the table. John Paul II sought to get rid of a distinction, deeply rooted in pre-Vatican II understandings of the church, between the church as an institution free of sin and the conduct of individual Christians who went astray.[27] It had become impossible, even for the church, to speak with one voice. The diversity of opinion, however, did not diminish the moral and theological weight of these issues: it only made them more urgent. This fact alone significantly explains why so many engaging in a comprehensive moral and theological reckoning with the church's past during the Third Reich were reluctant to let contrary evidence undercut the purity of their positions.

That is why it is necessary to step back from the debates to see how they arose. This book has chosen the path of historicizing – that is, showing how the moral, theological and historical questions about the church's past were shaped by personal experiences, religious convictions, political agendas, social pressures and partisan conflicts. The questions posed, the hypotheses ventured and the calls for evidence issued were the choices of individual sculptors who often presupposed the conclusions to be drawn through how they formulated their queries. These first lines of inquiry, in turn, set the parameters for debates continuing until this day.

But will seeing how present-minded agendas colored the pursuit of the past help us discover and restore the breadth and messiness of European Catholic responses to right-wing dictatorships and totalitarianism? A historicization may have appeal to disinterested scholars willing to embrace complexity. But it will undoubtedly have no impact on the larger need to use the experience of the churches under National Socialism as a lesson in morality, a set of Aesop's fables updated for the twenty-first century.[28] This story raises too many universal themes hardwired into human experience. It contains basic narratives and plotlines easily recognizable to humans all across the world and the centuries. For defenders, the struggle had been Manichean: it had been between Christian truth and Nazi paganism, cross and swastika and two competing lords – and the church had emerged triumphant, a host of saints and martyrs bearing witness to the struggle. For critics, the story was of betrayal – of their fellow human beings and of the faith itself. Churchmen had ignored centuries-old prohibitions on unjust war. They had ignored or even mocked the lessons of the Good Samaritan, refusing to help the least of their brethren, the victims of Nazi oppression, because of their race, ethnicity or politics. They had refused to take up their cross and sacrifice themselves or their institution. In seeking instead the favor of the new state and to protect their own, they had betrayed their ideals.

These versions of the story show that many harbor a deeply rooted desire for heroes and villains to be pure – and seek the historical proof to reassure themselves of this. Many want that emotional clarity that comes with viewing the institution of the church and its leading personae in a moment of rupture and crisis as steadfast either in their heroism or their failure. Many have thus desperately wanted a different story – one either of perfect resistance or of a "church that failed." The former, of course, brings solace for the faithful and, for some, sustains belief untroubled by doubt. The latter vindicates those seeking ecclesiastical reform or those striving to give historical legitimacy to their unbelief, particularly for those aligning themselves with the so-called "New Atheism" since the turn of the twenty-first century.[29] For those not desiring the moral complexity and potential challenge to faith, including that of unbelief, there is an easy solution: cutting out the inconvenient facts that stand in the way.

And that is why the battles over the Catholic past during the twelve years of the Third Reich are unlikely to ever be completely resolved, even if all questions of historical evidence were miraculously to be answered once and for all through the release of documents from the pontificate of Pope Pius XII. As long as Christianity remains a vibrant presence in the lives of billions worldwide and Christians look not just to the early church but to ecclesiastical leaders of the modern era for succor and inspiration, these battles will continue to flare up. Catholics, Protestants, Jews and increasingly those of little or no faith will, for their own array of reasons, challenge the self-understanding and theologies of Catholic Church leaders from the era of totalitarianism. They will question whether churchmen lived up to the ideals of their faith.

Such probes are likely to remain centered around the extent to which the church had lived up to that dictum voiced so succinctly in the Book of James: "What good is it, my brothers, if he says he has faith but does not have works?" Insisting that faith had to be unceasingly lived out and acted upon, this verse distills the essence of these battles over the past that had begun over Catholic just war teachings, public schools segregated by confession, pastoral letters urging voters to vote for Christian candidates, a disputed treaty from the summer of 1933 and a pope's response to the Holocaust. These controversies were – and are likely to remain – about the church's place in the world.

Notes

Introduction

1. Rolf Hochhuth, *Der Stellvertreter* (Reinbek: Rowohlt Verlag, 1963).
2. On the tax advantages of Switzerland, see: HAWDR, #05790, Kreuzfeuer mit Herrn Hochhuth am 15.6.65.
3. For literature on the CDU's origins, see Hans-Otto Kleinmann, *Geschichte der CDU: 1945–1982* (Stuttgart: Deutsche Verlags-Anstalt, 1993); Noel Cary, *The Path to Christian Democracy* (Cambridge, MA: Harvard University Press, 1996); Frank Bösch, *Die Adenauer-CDU: Gründung, Aufstieg, und Krise einer Erfolgspartei, 1945–1969* (Stuttgart: Deutsche Verlags-Anstalt, 2001); Maria Mitchell, *The Origins of Christian Democracy: Politics and Confession in Modern Germany* (Ann Arbor: The University of Michigan Press, 2012), 44–53; Jörg-Dieter Gauger, Hanns Jürgen Küsters and Rudolf Uertz, ed., *Das Christliche Menschenbild: Zur Geschichte, Theorie und Programmatik der CDU* (Freiburg: Herder, 2013).
4. For the statistical information, see Statistisches Bundesamt, ed., *Bevölkerung und Wirtschaft, 1872–1972* (Stuttgart: Kohlhammer Verlag, 1972), 97.
5. Wolfgang Kraushaar, *Die Protest-Chronik 1949–1959. Eine illustrierte Geschichte von Bewegung, Widerstand und Utopie* (Hamburg: Verlag Rogner & Bernhard bei Zweitausendeins, 1996).
6. For examples, see the 1,700-page set of volumes: Friedrich Giese and Friedrich August Frhr. von der Heydte, ed., *Der Konkordatsprozess, 4 Bde.* (München: Isar Verlag, 1957–1959).
7. For reflections on the Catholic historiography, see Ulrich von Hehl and Konrad Repgen, ed., *Der deutsche Katholizismus in der zeitgeschichtlichen Forschung* (Mainz: Grünewald, 1988); Mark Edward Ruff, "Integrating Religion into the Historical Mainstream: Recent Literature on Religion in the Federal Republic of Germany," in: *Central European History* 42 (2009), 307–337; Heinz Hürten, "50 Jahre Kommission für Zeitgeschichte. Überlegungen zu Problemen der Katholizismusforschung," in: Markus Raasch and Tobias Hirschmüller, ed., *Von Freiheit, Solidarität und Subsidiarität. Staat und Gesellschaft der Moderne in Theorie und Praxis. Festschrift für Karsten Ruppert zum 65. Geburtstag* (Berlin: Duncker & Humblot, 2013), 753–760; Wilhelm Damberg and Karl-Joseph Hummel, ed., *Katholizismus in Deutschland. Zeitgeschichte und Gegenwart* (Paderborn: Schöningh, 2015).

8. On the absence of an era of silence, see David Cesarini and Eric J. Sundquist, *After the Holocaust: Challenging the Myth of Silence* (London: Routledge, 2011).

9. These events included the vandalizing of a Cologne synagogue in 1959; the trial of the notorious architect of the Final Solution, Adolf Eichmann, in 1961; the trial of Auschwitz personnel between 1963 and 1965; the wave of protests and student rebellions in the late 1960s; and the screening of the American television miniseries *Holocaust* in 1979.

10. A complete bibliography would run to more than thirty pages. For some of the most important recent literature, see James Diehl, *The Thanks of the Fatherland: German Veterans after the Second World War* (Chapel Hill: University of North Carolina Press, 1993); Norbert Frei, *Vergangenheitspolitik Vergangenheitspolitik. Die Anfänge der Bundesrepublik und die NS-Vergangenheit* (Munich: Beck, 1996); Jeffrey Herf, *Divided Memory: The Nazi Past in the Two Germanys* (Cambridge, MA: Harvard University Press, 1997); Aleida Assmann and Ute Frevert, *Geschichtsvergessenheit – Geschichtsversessenheit. Vom Umgang mit deutschen Vergangenheiten nach 1945* (Stuttgart: DVA, 1999); Rudy Koshar, *From Monuments to Traces: The Artifacts of German Memory, 1870–1990* (Berkeley: University of California Press, 2000); Gavriel Rosenfeld, *Munich and Memory: Architecture, Monuments and the Legacy of the Third Reich* (Berkeley: University of California Press, 2000); S. Jonathan Wiesen, *West German Industry and the Challenge of the Nazi Past* (Chapel Hill: University of North Carolina Press, 2001); Robert G. Moeller, *War Stories: The Search for a Usable Past in the Federal Republic of Germany* (Berkeley: University of Carolina Press, 2001); Peter Reichel, *Vergangenheitsbewältigung in Deutschland: Die Auseinandersetzung mit der NS-Diktatur von 1945 bis heute* (Munich: Beck, 2001); Nicolas Berg, *Der Holocaust und die westdeutschen Historiker: Erforschung und Erinnerung* (Göttingen: Wallstein, 2003); Gavriel Rosenfeld, *The World Hitler Never Made: Alternate History and the Memory of Nazism* (Cambridge, UK: Cambridge University Press, 2005); Dagmar Herzog, *Sex after Fascism: Memory and Morality in Twentieth-Century Germany* (Princeton: Princeton University Press, 2005); Constantin Goschler, *Schuld und Schulden: Die Politik der Wiedergutmachung für NS-Verfolgte seit 1945* (Göttingen: Wallstein Verlag, 2005); Norbert Frei, *1945 und Wir: Das Dritte Reich im Bewusstsein der Deutschen* (München: Beck C.H., 2005); Wulf Kansteiner, *In Pursuit of German Memory: History, Television, and Politics after Auschwitz* (Athens: Ohio University Press, 2006); Bill Niven, ed., *Germans as Victims: Remembering the Past in Contemporary Germany* (Houndmills: Palgrave MacMillan, 2006); Torben Fischer and Matthias N. Lorenz, ed., *Lexikon der "Vergangenheitsbewältigung," in Deutschland. Debatten- und Diskursgeschichte des Nationalsozialismus nach 1945* (Bielefeld: Transcript, 2007); Gavriel Rosenfeld and Paul B. Jaskot, ed., *Beyond Berlin: Twelve German Cities Confront the Nazi Past* (Ann Arbor: University of Michigan Press, 2008); Stephan Alexander Glienke, Volker Paulmann and Joachim Perels, ed., *Erfolgsgeschichte Bundesrepublik? Die Nachkriegsgesellschaft im langen Schatten des Nationalsozialismus* (Göttingen: Wallstein, 2008); Bill Niven and Chloe Paver, ed., *Memorialization in Germany since 1945* (Basingstoke: Palgrave

MacMillan, 2010); Gavriel Rosenfeld, *Building after Auschwitz: Jewish Architecture and the Memory of the Holocaust* (New Haven: Yale University Press, 2011); Mark Wolfgram, *"Getting History Right": East and West German Collective Memories of the Holocaust and War* (Lanham: Bucknell University Press, 2011); Arnd Bauerkämper, *Das umstrittene Gedächtnis: Die Erinnerung an Nationalsozialismus, Fascismus und Krieg in Europa seit 1945* (Paderborn: Schöningh, 2012) and his bibliography, 487–514; Kristina Meyer, *Die SPD und die NS-Vergangenheit* (Göttingen: Wallstein, 2015).

11. The literature on the history of memory is too enormous to cite fully here. For overviews, see Maurice Halbwachs, *Les cadres sociaux de la memoire* (Paris: F. Alcan, 1925); Pierre Nora, *Les lieux de mémoire*, 7 vols. (Paris: Gallimard, 1984–1992); Jan Assmann and Tonio Holscher, *Kultur und Gedächtnis* (Frankfurt: Suhrkamp, 1988); Peter Burke, "History as Social Memory," in: Thomas Butler, ed., *Memory: History, Culture and the Mind* (Oxford: Basil Blackwell, 1990), 97–113; Jan Assmann, *Das kulturelle Gedächtnis: Schrift, Erinnerung und politische Identität in frühen Hochkulturen* (Munich: Beck Verlag, 1992); Iwona Irwin-Zarecki, *Frames of Remembrance: The Dynamics of Collective Memory* (New Brunswick: Transaction, 1994); Alon Confino, "Collective Memory and Cultural History: Problems of Method," in: *American Historical Review* 105 (1997), 1386–1403; Jay Winter and Emmanuel Sivan, ed., *War and Remembrance in the Twentieth Century* (Cambridge: Cambridge University Press, 1999); Jan-Werner Müller, "Introduction: The Power of Memory, the Memory of Power and the Power over Memory," in: Jan-Werner Müller, ed., *Memory and Power in Postwar Europe: Studies in the Presence of the Past* (New York: Cambridge University Press, 2002), 1–35; Alon Confino, *Germany as a Culture of Remembrance: Promises and Limits of Writing History* (Chapel Hill: University of North Carolina Press, 2006); Jay Winter, *Remembering War: The Great War between Memory and History in the Twentieth Century* (New Haven: Yale University Press, 2006); Richard Ned Lebow, Wulf Kansteiner and Claudio Fogo, *The Politics of Memory in Postwar Europe* (Durham: Duke University Pres, 2006); Gavriel Rosenfeld, "A Looming Crash or a Soft Landing? Forecasting the Future of the Memory 'Industry,'" in: *Journal of Modern History*, 81 (2009), 122–158.

12. Several prominent church critics, like Catholic radio commentator and publicist Walter Dirks and the writers Karlheinz Deschner, Carl Amery and Heinrich Böll, receive short shrift here. They primarily drew on the research and expertise of others for their claims. The latter two laid the groundwork instead for debates about the alleged insularity of the Catholic milieu and the role of the church in the Federal Republic. For a brief sketch of Dirks, see Walter Kettem, "Walter Dirks," in: Friedrich Wilhelm Bautz and Traugott Bautz, ed., *Biographisch-Bibliographisches Kirchenlexikon, Band 18* (Hamm: Herzberg, 2001), 360–367; Ulrich Bröckling, "Walter Dirks," in: Friedrich Georg Hohmann, ed., *Westfälische Lebensbilder, Bd 17* (Münster: Aschendorff Verlag, 2005), 241–254. On Amery, see Götz Fenske, "Begegnungen mit Carl Amery und Herbert Gruhl," in: Herbert-Gruhl-Gesellschaft e.V., ed., *Naturkonservativ. 2008/2009* (Bad Schüssenried:

Gerhard Hess Verlag, 2009), 90–110. For several portraits of Böll, see Klaus Schröter, ed., *Heinrich Böll* (Reinbek: Rowohlt, 1987); Jochen Schubert, *Heinrich Böll* (Paderborn: Fink, 2011); see Karlheinz Deschner's numerous works, including *Abermals krähte der Hahn: Eine kritische Kirchengeschichte von den Anfängen bis zu Pius XII* (Stuttgart: H.E. Günther, 1962) and *Ein Jahrhundert Heilsgeschichte. Die Politik der Päpste im Zeitalter der Weltkriege*. 2 Bände (Cologne: Kiepenheuer & Witsch, 1982–1983).

13. Joseph Bottum and David G. Dalin, ed., *The Pius Wars: Responses to the Critics of Pius XII* (Lanham, MD: Lexington Books, 2010).

1   The First Postwar Anthologies, 1945–1949

1. For historiographical analyses, see Ulrich von Hehl, "Kirche und Nationalsozialismus: Ein Forschungsbericht," in: Geschichtsverein der Diözese Rottenburg-Stuttgart, ed., *Kirche im Nationalsozialismus* (Sigmaringen: Thorbecke, 1984), 11–29; Christian Schmidtmann, "'Fragestellungen der Gegenwart mit Vorgängen der Vergangenheit beantworten': Deutungen der Rolle der Kirche und Katholiken in Nationalsozialismus und Krieg vom Kriegsende bis in die 1960er Jahre," in: Andreas Holzem and Christoph Holzapfel, ed., *Zwischen Kriegs-und Diktaturerfahrung. Katholizismus und Protestantismus in der Nachkriegszeit* (Stuttgart: Kohlhammer Verlag, 2005), 167–201 and, in particular, 175–176; Karl-Josef Hummel, "Gedeutete Fakten: Geschichtsbilder im deutschen Katholizismus 1945–2000," in: Karl-Joseph Hummel/Christoph Kösters, ed., *Kirchen im Krieg: Europa 1939–1945* (Paderborn: Schöningh, 2007), 507–567 and, in particular, 509.

2. For examples: Emil Kaim, *Der Bischof ist wieder da, Verbannung und Heimkehr des Bischofs von Rottenburg, Dr. Johannes Baptista Sproll* (Rotthenburg: Verlag des Bischöflichen Ordinariats Rottenburg, 1945); Alfons Erb, *Bernhard Lichtenberg, Dompropst von St. Hedwig zu Berlin* (Berlin: Morus Verlag, 1946); Max Bierbaum, *Die letzte Romfahrt des Kardinals von Galen* (Münster: Aschendorff Verlag, 1946); Peter Tritz, S.J., *Die Katholische Kirche in Deutschland, 1933–1945* (Frankfurt: Michael Verlag Fr. Borgmeyer, 1946); Friedrich Muckermann, *Der Deutsche Weg* (Zurich: N.Z.N. Verlag, 1946); Alois Natterer, *Der Bayerische Klerus in der Zeit dreier Revolutionen 1918–1933–1945* (Munich: Verlag Katholische Kirche Bayerns, 1946); Johannes Steiner, *Propheten wider das Dritte Reich, aus den Schriften des Dr. Fritz Gerlich und des Paters Ingbert Naab, O.F.M. Cap.* (Munich: Verlag Dr. Schnell und Dr. Steiner, 1946); John S. Steward, *Sieg des Glaubens* (Zurich: Thoman-Verlag, 1946); Ferdinand Strobel, *Christliche Bewährung, 1933–1945* (AG Otten: Verlag Otto Walter, 1946); *Josef Moersdorf, August Froehlich, Pfarrer von Rathenow* (Berlin: Morus Verlag, 1947); Max Bierbaum, *Kardinal von Galen* (Münster: Regensberg, 1947); Alfred P. Delp, S.J., *Im Angesicht des Todes* (Frankfurt: Josef Knecht, 1949); Matthias Laros, ed., *Dr. Max Josef Metzger (Bruder Paulus), Gefangenschafts-Briefe* (Augsburg: Kyrios Verlag, 1947).

3. For examples from the Protestant side: Dietrich Bonhoeffer, *Auf dem Wege zur Freiheit* (Geneva: World Council of Churches, 1946); Willy Jannasch, *Deutsche Kirchendokumente* (Zollikon: Evangelischer Verlag, 1946); Fritz Klinger, ed.,

Dokumente zum Abwehrkampf der deutschen evangelischen Pfarrerschaft gegen Verfolgung und Bedrueckung 1933–1945 (Nuernberg: Verlag Jacob Mendelsohn, 1946); Werner Koch, *Bekennende Kirche Heute* (Stuttgart: W. Kohlhammer Verlag, 1946); Erik Wolf, *Zeugnisse der Bekennenden Kirche of Das Christliche Deutschland 1933–1945* (Freiburg: Herder Verlag, 1946); Walter Künneth, *Der grosse Abfall* (Hamburg: Fritz Wittig Verlag, 1947); Hanns Lilje, *Im finstern Tal* (Nuernberg: Laetare Verlag, 1947); Edmund Schlink, *Der Ertrag des Kirchenkampfes* (Gütersleh: Bertelsmann Verlag, 1947); Joachim Beckmann, *Kirchliches Jahrbuch, 1933–1944* (Gütersloh: Bertelsmann Verlag, 1948); Hanns Lilje, ed., *Begegnungen* (Nürnberg: Laetare Verlag, 1949).

4. Johannes Neuhäusler, *Kreuz und Hakenkreuz, Zweiter Teil* (Munich: Katholische Kirche Bayerns, 1946), 10; Peter Pfister, ed., *Zeuge der Wahrheit: Johannes Neuhäusler: Ein Leben im Zeichen des Kreuzes. Herausgegeben anläßlich der 100. Wiederkehr des Geburtstags von Weihbischof Johannes Neuhäusler* (Dachau: Kuratorium für Sühnemal KZ Dachau, 1988).

5. AEM, NL Johannes Neuhäusler, VN N 240, Johannes Neuhäusler an das Kath. Pfarramt Pattensee (Leine), March 21, 1947; Bayerisches Hauptstaatsarchiv, StK Bayer. Verdienstorden 129, Staatsministerium für Unterricht und Kultus, Vorschlag auf Verleidung des Bayerischen Verdienstordens, München, den March 31, 1959, Gez: Prof. Dr. Maunz, Staatsminister.

6. AEM, NL Johannes Neuhäusler, VN N 240, Bestell-Liste für Kreuz und Hakenkreuz (no date).

7. Wilhelm Corsten, ed., *Kölner Aktenstücke* (Cologne: J.P. Bachem, 1949).

8. For the literature on the American occupation, see Christoph Weisz, ed., *OMGUS-Handbuch. Die amerikanische Militärregierung in Deutschland, 1945–1949* (Munich: Oldenbourg, 1994); Thomas W. Maulucci and Detlev Junker, ed., *GIs in Germany: The Social, Economic, Cultural and Political History of the American Military Presence* (New York: Cambridge University Press, 2013).

9. For literature on the Catholic Church's often-troubled relationship to occupation officials in the immediate postwar period, see Frederic Spotts, *The Churches and Politics in Germany* (Middletown: Wesleyan University Press, 1973); Ludwig Volk, SJ, "Der Heilige Stuhl und Deutschland, 1945–1949," in: *Stimmen der Zeit* 194 (1976), 795–823; Frank M. Buscher, *The U.S. War Crimes Trial Program in Germany, 1946–1955* (Westport: Greenwood Press, 1989), 93–97; Norbert Trippen, *Josef Kardinal Frings (1887–1978), Bd. I: Sein Wirken für das Erzbistum Köln und für die Kirche in Deutschland* (Paderborn: Schöningh Verlag, 2003); Suzanne Brown-Fleming, *The Holocaust and Catholic Conscience: Cardinal Aloyisius Muench and the Guilt Question in Germany* (South Bend: University of Notre Dame Press, 2006); Ulrich Helbach, "'Schuld' als Kategorie der Vergangenheitsbewältigung der katholischen Kirche nach 1945," in: Thomas Brechenmacher and Harry Oelke, ed., *Die Kirchen und die Verbrechen im nationalsozialistischen Staat* (Göttingen: Wallstein Verlag, 2011), 245–255; Steven M. Schroeder, *To Forget it all and Begin Anew: Reconciliation in Occupied Germany, 1944–1954* (Toronto: University of Toronto Press, 2013).

10. For one example, see NA, RG 260, Religious Affairs Branch, Box 178, File: Faulhaber, Memorandum of the Bishops of the American Occupied Zone of Germany in accordance with the Chairman of the Fulda Bishop's Conference, H.H. Cardinal Frings, submitted to the Chief of the American Military Government in Germany, General Lucius D. Clay, July 27, 1947.

11. On Bell, see Edwin Robertson, *Unshakeable Friend. George Bell and the German Churches* (London: CCBI, 1995); Andrew Chandler, *Brethren in Adversity: Bishop George Bell, The Church of England and the Crisis of German Protestants, 1933–1939* (Suffolk: Woodbridge, 1997). On Pope Pius XII's involvement in these plots, see Mark Riebling, *Church of Spies: The Pope's Secret War against Hitler* (New York: Basic Books, 2015).

12. For a full list, see www.cambridge.org/9781107190665.

13. Wilhelm Jussen, SJ, ed., *Gerechtigkeit schafft Frieden, Reden und Enzykliken des Heiligen Vaters Pius XII* (Hamburg: Hansa Verlag Josef Toth, 1946), 93–114. Pius insisted that only individual guilt could be punished.

14. For the text of this address, see www.vatican.va/holy_father/pius_xii/spee ches/1945/documents/hf_p-xii_spe_19450602_accogliere_it.html (accessed April 16, 2014).

15. Marshall Knappen, *And Call It Peace* (Chicago: University of Chicago Press, 1947), 96; Konrad Repgen, "Die Erfahrung des Dritten Reiches und das Selbstverständnis der deutschen Katholiken," in: Victor Conzemius, Martin Greschat and Hermann Kocher, ed., *Die Zeit nach 1945 als Thema kirchlicher Zeitgeschichte* (Göttingen: Vandenhoeck und Ruprecht, 1988), 127–179; Harold Marcuse, *Legacies of Dachau: The Uses and Abuses of a Concentration Camp* (Cambridge: Cambridge University Press, 2001), 50; Ulrich Helbach, "'Schuld' als Kategorie der Vergangenheitsbewältigung der katholischen Kirche nach 1945." On the debates about Allied allegations of collective guilt, see Norbert Frei, "Von deutscher Erfindungskraft," in: *Rechtshistorisches Journal* 16 (1997), 621–634; Karl-Joseph Hummel, "Umgang mit der Vergangenheit: Die Schulddiskussion," in: Karl-Joseph Hummel and Michael Kißener, ed., *Die Katholiken und das Dritte Reich: Kontroversen und Debatten* (Paderborn: Schöningh Verlag, 2010), 217–235; Karl-Joseph Hummel, "Die Schuldfrage," in: Christoph Kösters and Mark Edward Ruff, ed., *Die katholische Kirche im Dritten Reich. Eine Einführung* (Freiburg: Herder Verlag, 2011), 154–170.

16. "Entwurf Jaegers für eine Eingabe der westdeutschen Bischöfe an Pius XII. Zur Kollektivschuldfrage," in: Ulrich Helbach, ed., *Akten deutscher Bischöfe seit 1945, Westliche Besatzungszonen 1945–1947, I* (Paderborn: Schöningh Verlag, 2012), 115–120. For an analysis, see Ulrich Helbach, "'Schuld' als Kategorie der Vergangenheitsbewältigung der katholischen Kirche nach 1945," 245–255.

17. "Hirtenwort des deutschen Episkopates vom 22 August 1945," in: Ludwig Volk, ed., *Akten deutscher Bischöfe über die Lage der Kirche 1933–1945, Bd. VI, 1943–1945* (Mainz: Matthias-Grünewald Verlag, 1985), 688–694 and, in particular, 689.

18. Ibid., 689. For larger analyses of how the church dealt with the question of guilt in this pastoral letter, see Konrad Repgen, "Die Erfahrung des Dritten Reiches," 147–154 and, in particular, 161; Günter Baadte, "Grundfragen der politischen

und gesellschaftlichen Neuordnung in den Hirtenbriefen der deutschen Bischöfe 1945–1949," in: *Jahrbuch für christliche Sozialwissenschaften* 27 (1986), 95–113 and, in particular, 99–100; Vera Bücker, *Die Schulddiskussion im deutschen Katholizismus nach 1945* (Bochum: Brockmeyer, 1989).

19. "Protokoll der Plenarkonferenz des deutschen Episkopats, Fulda, 21–23 August 1945," in: Ludwig Volk, *Akten deutscher Bischöfe über die Lage der Kirche 1933–1945, Bd. VI, 1943–1945*, 673; Reimund Haas, "Zum Verhältnis von Katholischer Kirche und Nationalsozialismus im Erzbistum Köln. Stationen der Bewältigung und Erfoschung in der Erzdiözese, 1945–1981," in: *Schulinformationen*, 13/81, 5 Heft, November 15, 1981, 57–73, 60.

20. "Protokoll der Plenarkonferenz des deutschen Episkopats, Fulda, 21–23 August 1945," 673.

21. HAEK, Gen II 23, 23a, 5, Fragebogen betr. Erhebungen über die Verhältnisse während der Kriegszeit (no date); HAEK, WuV, 9, Vorläufige Erfassung der Verfolgungspolitik des Dritten Reiches gegen die Katholische Kirche (no date).

22. Nr. 64, "Materialsammlung zur Geschichte des Erzbistums Köln während des "Dritten Reiches," in: *Kirchlicher Anzeiger, Köln*, October 10, 1945; Nr. 135, Materialsammlung zur Geschichte des Erzbistums Köln während des "Dritten Reiches," in *Kirchlicher Anzeiger, Köln*, April 5, 1946; Nr. 152, Opfer des Nationalsozialismus," in: *Kirchlicher Anzeiger, Köln*, April 25, 1946.

23. Ansprache von Bischofsvikar Prälat Dr. Joseph Teusch aus Anlaß der Promotion zum Ehrendoktor der Nanzan-Universität, Presseamt des Erzbistums Köln, PEL, Dokumente, Nr. 94, March 18, 1975, 4–11.

24. For an overview of Stasiewski, see Raimund Haas, *Bernhard Stasiewski (1905–1995): Osteuropahistoriker und Wissenschaftsorganisator* (Münster: Monsenstein und Vennerdat, 2007).

25. Ludwig Volk, *Akten deutscher Bischöfe über die Lage der Kirche 1933–1945, Bd. VI*; Ulrich von Hehl, Christoph Kösters, Petra Stenz-Maur, *Priester unter Hitlers Terror: Eine biographische und statistische Erhebung* (Paderborn: Schöningh Verlag, 1998).

26. For examples of their respective use in war crimes trials, restitution cases, the Reichskonkordat case and the Frankfurt euthanasia trials of 1967, see ACSP, NL Josef Müller, S89 Kirche, Neuhäusler, 1945–1971, Abschrift, Dr. Kurt Kauffmann, Internationaler Militärgerichtshof Nürnberg, Verteidigung an Domkapitular Martin Grassl, September 5, 1946; IFZG, ID 105, Band 2, 1113/53, Hans Buchheim, "Gutachten über die Kollektivverfolgung der katholischen Kirche in der Nationalsozialistischen Zeit," München, May 12, 1953; Friedrich Giese and Friedrich August Frhr. v.d. Heydte, ed., *Der Konkordatsprozess, I Band* (Munich: Isar Verlag, 1957), 366; HAEK Gen II, 2.13, 29, Joseph Teusch to Johannes Neuhäusler, March 11, 1967.

27. *Mit brennender Sorge. Das päpstliche Rundschreiben gegen den Nationalsozialismus und seine Folgen in Deutschland, Das christliche Deutschland 1933 bis 1945, Dokumente und Zeugnisse, Katholische Reihe: Heft 1* (Freiburg: Herder, 1946); *Zeugnis und Kampf des deutschen Episkopats. Gemeinsame Hirtenbriefe und Denkschrifte. Das christliche Deutschland 1933 bis 1945. Dokumente und Zeugnisse. Katholische Reihe: Heft 2* (Freiburg: Herder,

1946); Heinrich Portmann, *Bischof von Galen spricht! Ein apostolischer Kampf und sein Widerhall. Das christliche Deutschland 1933 bis 1945, Dokumente und Zeugnisse, Katholische Reihe: Heft 3* (Freiburg: Herder, 1946); Franz Büchner, *Der Eid des Hippokrates, Die Grundsätze der ärztlichen Ethik, Das christliche Deutschland, 1933 bis 1945, Dokumente und Zeugnisse, Katholische Reihe: Heft 4* (Freiburg: Herder, 1945); Max Müller, *Das christliche Menschenbild und die Weltanschauungen der Neuzeit, Das christliche Deutschland 1933 bis 1945, Katholische Reihe: Heft 5* (Freiburg: Herder, 1945); Phillipp Dessauer, *Das Bionome Geschichtsbild. Hintergründe und Konsequenz einer Geschichtsideologie, Das Christliche Deutschland 1933 bis 1945, Katholische Reihe: Heft 6* (Freiburg: Herder, 1946); Konrad Hofmann, ed., *Hirtenrufe des Erzbischofs Gröber in die Zeit, Das christliche Deutschland 1933 bis 1945, Katholische Reihe: Heft 7* (Freiburg: Herder, 1947); Konrad Hofmann, *Schlaglichter: Belege und Bilder aus dem Kampf gegen die Kirche, Das christliche Deutschland 1933 bis 1945, Katholische Reihe: Heft 8* (Freiburg: Herder, 1947).

28. Franz Büchner, *Der Eid des Hippokrates*.
29. Franz Büchner, *Pläne und Fügungen: Lebenserinnerungen eines deutschen Hochschullehrers* (München: Urban & Schwarzenberg, 1965), 96–97.
30. Ibid.
31. Ibid.
32. Julius Dorneich, "Die Sammlung 'das christliche Deutschland,'" in: *Familien-Blätter DORNEICH*, Heft 11, Privatdruck, Freiburg, 1974, 8–10.
33. On Schneider and conscience, see Joseph Ratzinger, "Das Gewissen in der Zeit," in: Peter Thiede, ed., *Über Reinhold Schneider* (Frankfurt am Main: Suhrkamp, 1980), 99–113. For two overviews of the literature on Schneider, see Walter Schmitz, "Reinhold Schneider: Ein katholischer Intellektueller im Zeitalter der Weltkriege," in: Hans-Rüdiger Schwab, ed., *Eigensinn und Bindung. Katholische deutsche Intellektuelle im 20. Jahrhundert. 39 Porträts* (Kevelaer: Verlag Butzon und Bercker, 2009), 341–359; Walter Schmitz, "Reinhold Schneider (1903–1958): Geschichtspoetik und Reichsidee," in: Thomas Pittrof and Walter Schmitz, ed., *Freie Anerkennung übergeschichtlicher Bindungen. Katholische Geschichtswahrnehmung im deutschsprachigen Raum des 20. Jahrhunderts. Beiträge des Dresdener Kolloquiums vom 10. bis 13. Mai 2007* (Freiburg i. Br./Berlin, Wien: Rombach Verlag, 2010), 273–298.
34. For examples, see Reinhold Schneider, *Die Sonette von Leben und Zeit, dem Glauben und der Geschichte* (Köln: Jakob Hegner Verlag, 1954); Reinhold Schneider, *Las Casas vor Karl V.: Szenen aus der Konquistadorenzeit* (Wiesbaden: Insel Verlag, 1946).
35. Cordula Koepcke, *Reinhold Schneider, Eine Biographie* (Würzburg: Echter Verlag, 1993), 183.
36. Ibid., 184; Franz Büchner, *Pläne und Fügungen*, 97.
37. For the text, "Unaufgeforderter Hirtenwortentwurf des Schriftstellers Reinhold Schneider für die Fuldaer Bischofskonferenz im August 1945," see Ulrich Helbach, "Quellenanhang," in: Thomas Brechenmacher and Harry Oelke, ed., *Die Kirchen und die Verbrechen im nationalsozialistischen Staat* (Göttingen: Wallstein Verlag, 2011), 256–259.

38. "Reinhold Schneider an Albert Stohr, August 7, 1945," in: Ulrich Helbach, *Akten deutscher Bischöfe seit 1945: Westliche Besatzungszonen, 1945–1947, I* (Paderborn: Schöningh Verlag, 2012), 202–204. See also Karl-Joseph Hummel, "Gedeutete Fakten: Geschichtsbilder im deutschen Katholizismus," in: Karl-Joseph Hummel and Christoph Kösters, ed., *Kirchen im Krieg: Europa 1933–1945* (Paderborn: Schöningh, 2007), 512–513.
39. Franz Büchner, *Pläne und Fügungen*, 97.
40. Ibid.
41. Reinhold Schneider, *Geleitwort für die Sammlung "Das christliche Deutschland 1933–1945"* (Freiburg: Herder Verlag, 1946).
42. Ibid.
43. Konrad Hofmann, ed., *Schlaglichter, Das Christliche Deutschland 1933 bis 1945* (Freiburg: Herder Verlag, 1947), 92–98. Hofmann included the last testaments of Max Ulrich Graf von Drechsel, Alois Grimm, SJ, Pastor Josef Mueller and Nikolaus Gross.
44. Hans Maier, *Böse Jahre, gute Jahre. Ein Leben 1931* (München: Beck Verlag, 2011), 39; Christoph Schmider, "Erzbischof Conrad Gröber (1872–1948)" in: Christoph Schmider, *Die Freiburger Bischöfe: 175 Jahre Erzbistum Freiburg. Eine Geschichte in Lebensbildern* (Freiburg: Herder, 2002), 148.
45. On Gröber, see Erwin Keller: *Conrad Gröber 1872–1948. Erzbischof in schwerer Zeit* (Freiburg: Herder, 1982); Hugo Ott, "Conrad Gröber (1872–1948)," in: Jürgen Aretz, Rudolf Morsey and Anton Rauscher, ed., *Zeitgeschichte in Lebensbildern. Aus dem deutschen Katholizismus des 19. und 20. Jahrhunderts. Band 6* (Mainz: Matthias-Grünewald-Verlag, 1984); Bruno Schwalbach, *Erzbischof Conrad Gröber und die deutsche Katastrophe. Sein Ringen um eine menschliche Neuordnung* (Karlsruhe: Badenia Verlag, 1994).
46. EAF, Nb8/17, Conrad Gröber to Ivo Zeiger, September 4, 1946.
47. Mark Riebling, *Church of Spies*, 19, 267.
48. On Gerst, see Ekkehard Blattmann, "Über den 'Fall Reinhold Schneider' im Lichte von Reinhold Schneiders Kollaboration mit den Kommunisten," in: Ekkehard Blattmann and Klaus Hönig, ed., *Über den "Fall Reinhold Schneider"* (Munich: Schnell & Steiner, 1990), 88–94.
49. For one example, see Wilhelm Karl Gerst, "Die Predigt in Telgte," in: *Frankfurter Rundschau*, October 26, 1945. For examples of the controversy generated, see Bistumsarchiv Münster (BAM), A0–2, Bischöfliches Sekretariat – Neues Archiv, Wilhelm Karl Gerst to Kaplan Heinz Wolf, December 31, 1945.
50. Wilhelm Karl Gerst, "Um den 'Ehrenplatz in der Geschichte der nationalen Revolution,'" in: *Frankfurter Rundschau*, August 20, 1946, 5; EAF, Nb8/17, Conrad Gröber to Ivo Zeiger, September 4, 1946.
51. Konrad Hofmann, *Hirtenrufe des Erzbischofs Gröber in die Zeit*, 8.
52. Ibid.
53. Ibid., 8–9.
54. Ibid., 9, 11, 15.
55. Ibid., 9, 14.
56. Ibid., 8.

57. For examples: Johannes Neuhäusler, *Kreuz und Hakenkreuz, Band I*, 95; *Band II*, 164–167, 338; USHMM, RG 76.001 M, Reel 6, 432, Protokoll über 2 Unterredungen vom H.H. Domkapitular Johann Neuhäusler München mit Herrn Staatsminister Esser, bayer. Staatskanzlei, 1. Unterredung, October 27, 1933, 2. Unterredung, October 28, 1933; USHM RG 76.001 M, Reel 3, 198, Abschrift, Promemoria über die neuerliche Beschränkung von Versammlungen katholischer Vereine, January 3, 1933; USHMM RG 76.001, Reel 6, 48, Ludwig Siebert to Vassallo di Torregrossa, January 17, 1934; Vassallo di Torregrossa to Johannes Neuhäusler, January 18, 1934; Roman Bleistein, *Rupert Mayer: Der verstummte Prophet* (Frankfurt am Main: Verlag Josef Knecht, 1993), 279–281, 288–297, 317–332. See also Ludwig Volk, SJ, *Der bayerische Episkopat und der Nationalsozialismus, 1930–1934* (Mainz: Matthias-Grünewald Verlag, 1974).

58. Johannes Neuhäusler, *Amboß und Hammer: Erlebnisse im Kirchenkampf des Dritten Reiches* (Munich: Manz, 1967), 131, 153–154.

59. Archiv der KZ Gedenkstätte Dachau, 36.609/9, Michael Höck, "Ein Brückenbauer zur Dritten Welt. Weihbischof Dr. Johannes B. Neuhäusler in der Reihe: Berühmte Schüler des Freisinger Domgymnasiums." No date, but probably December 1973.

60. AEMF, NL Johannes Neuhäusler, VN N 414, Newspaper Clipping, Anton Maier, "Ein frommer Bischof – ein grosser Mensch," in: *Deutsche Tagespost*, December 18, 1973, 5.

61. ACSP, NL Josef Müller, C84111, Bayerischer Rundfunk, Abteilung Kirchenfunk, Kirche und Welt. Wilhelm Sandfuchs, "Den Armen die Frohbotschaft künden." Zum Tode von Weihbischof Dr. Johannes Neuhäusler, December 17, 1973, 17:45–18:00, 2; "German Cardinal Arrives Incognito: Archbishop of Munich was Reported Here Saturday – Won't Answer to Title – Met at Pier by Delegation – Only Captain and Pursuer of the Albert Bailin Knew He Was Michael von Faulhaber," in: *The New York Times*, June 15, 1926, 5.

62. Peter Pfister, *Zeuge der Wahrheit*, 5; Archiv der KZ Gedenkstätte Dachau, 36.609/9, Michael Höck, "Ein Brückenbauer zur Dritten Welt," 2.

63. Johannes Neuhäusler, *Amboß und Hammer*, 14–15.

64. Peter Pfister, *Zeuge der Wahrheit*, 7.

65. USHMM, RG 76.001M, Reel 2, 190, Giovanni Tomico to Eugenio Pacelli, June 19, 1933.

66. Syracuse University Library, Dorothy Thompson Papers, Box 102, Folder Heading: MSS, untitled, Subject Headings N. This was undoubtedly a reference to internal conflicts at the monastery at Ettal.

67. USAHEC, Harold C. Deutsch Papers, Series III, Box 1, Folder 7, Müller interviews, 7–8.

68. Ibid., 12.

69. Johannes Neuhäusler, *Amboß und Hammer*, 130–140; USAHEC, Harold C. Deutsch Papers, Series III, Box 1, Folder 7, Müller interviews, 6.

70. KAB, Tonband, Rolf Hochhuth, Der Stellvertreter, 22. 4. 1963, Podiumsgespräch unter Teilnahme von Dr. Buchheim; Johannes Neuhäusler, *Amboß und Hammer*, 135.

71. These included Pater Rupert Mayer, SJ, Andreas Rohracher, Weihbischof in Gurk, Austria and, after 1939, the Archbishop of Salzburg Corbinian Hofmeister, the abbot of Metten, the Dominican priest Laurentius Siemer and Father Johannes Albrecht of Ettal, a Benedictine monastery close to Oberammergau and a center of resistance activities. For a brief description of Neuhäusler's contacts with Rohracher, see AES, NL Andreas Rohracher, 19/29, Korr. mit Bischöfen im Ausland, 1950–1958, Johannes Neuhäusler to Andreas Rohracher, September 26, 1953. One notable exception was Thea Graziella Schneidhuber, the sister-in-law of the Munich police president murdered on June 30, 1934. But she was also a Jewish convert to Christianity and for that reason gassed at Ravensbrück. On her ties to Neuhäusler, see Johannes Neuhäusler, *Amboß und Hammer*, 131. On her marriage, see J. Répin, *Freiheit und Arbeit: Ein Dichterbuch* (Zürich: Füßli Verlag, 1910), 110. See also Bayerisches Hauptstaatsarchiv, MKK 38233, Akten des Bayer. Staatsministeriums für Unterricht und Kultur, Mappe: Johannes Neuhäusler, Weihbischof, 41–45, Abschrift zu II 3240/41, Der Chef der Sicherheitspolizei und des SD, Berlin den June 27, 1941, IV 1–554/41, Betrifft: Neuhäusler, Johann, Domkapitular.

72. USAHEC, Harold Deutsch Papers, Interview with Josef Müller, March 24, 1966, 1–2. See Harold C. Deutsch, *The Conspiracy against Hitler in the Twilight War* (Minneapolis: University of Minneapolis Press, 1968), 113.

73. Josef Müller, *Bis zur letzten Konsequenz: Ein Leben für Frieden und Freiheit* (München: Süddeutscher Verlag, 1975), 63–64; Harold C. Deutsch, *The Conspiracy against Hitler in the Twilight War*, 112; Friedrich Hermann Hettler, *Josef Müller ("Ochsensepp"): Mann des Widerstandes und erster CSU-Vorsitzender* (München: Kommissionsverlag, 1991), 36–46; USAHEC, Harold C. Deutsch Papers, Series III, Box 1, Folder 7, Müller interviews, 10.

74. On Müller's connection to the conspirators, see Eberhard Bethge, *Dietrich Bonhoeffer: A Biography* (Minneapolis: Fortress Press, 2000), 672–675; Marikje Smid, *Hans von Dohnanyi, Christine Bonhoeffer: Eine Ehe im Widerstand gegen Hitler* (Gütersloh: Gütersloher Verlagshaus, 2002), 235–242; Klaus-Jürgen Müller, *Generaloberst Ludwig Beck. Eine Biographie* (Paderborn: Schöningh, 2008), 410–418; see the letter from Dietrich Bonhoeffer to Eberhard Bethge, January 19, 1941, in: Mark S. Brocker, ed., *Dietrich Bonhoeffer Works, Volume 16, Conspiracy and Imprisonment, 1940–1945, Translated from the German Edition* (Minneapolis: Fortress Press, 2012), 110.

75. ACSP, NL Josef Müller, F65 Kriegsfolgen, Spruchkammerverfahren gegen Josef Müller, 1946–7, Abschrift, Abteilung Information, Vernehmung Johannes Neuhäusler, December 19, 1946.

76. Unnamed British official referring to Pius' role, as quoted in Harold C. Deutsch, *The Conspiracy against Hitler in the Twilight War*, 349. For accounts of this conspiracy, see Marikje Smid, *Hans von Dohnanyi, Christine Bonhoeffer*, 234–266; Robert Ventresca, *Soldier of Christ: The Life of Pope Pius XII* (Cambridge, MA: Harvard University Press, 2013), 162–164; Mark Riebling, *Church of Spies*.

77. On the plotters and their failures, see Sigismund Payne Best, *The Venlo Incident* (New York: Hutchison, 1950); Peter W. Ludlow, "Papst Pius XII, die britische Regierung und die deutsche Opposition im Winter 1939/40," in: *Vierteljahrshefte für Zeitgeschichte* 22 (1974), 299–341; Lothar Kettenacker, "Die britische Haltung zum deutschen Widerstand während des Zweiten Weltkriegs," in: Lothar Kettenacker, ed., *Das "Andere Deutschland" im Zweiten Weltkrieg. Emigration und Widerstand in internationale Perspektive* (Stuttgart: Klett, 1977); Peter Hoffmann, "Peace through Coup d'etat: The Foreign Contacts of the German Resistance, 1933–1944," in: *Central European History* 19 (1986), 3–44 and, especially, 18–21; Klaus-Jürgen Müller, *Der deutsche Widerstand und das Ausland* (Berlin: Gedenkstätte deutscher Widerstand, 1986), 13; Patricia Meehan, *The Unnecessary War: Whitehall and the German Resistance to Hitler* (Oxford: Clardendon, 1992); M.R.D. Foot, "Britische Geheimdienste und deutscher Widerstand 1939–1945," in: Klaus-Jürgen Müller and David N. Dilks, ed., *Großbritannien und der deutsche Widerstand, 1933–1944* (Paderborn: Schöningh, 1994), 161–168 and, in particular, 163; Eberhard Bethge, *Dietrich Bonhoeffer*, 671–675; Reinhard Doerries, *Hitler's Last Chief of Foreign Intelligence: Allied Interrogations of Walter Schellenberg* (London: Cass, 2003). Neuhäusler told the Bavarian minister of state, Anton Pfeiffer, in December 1946 that he had intentionally refused to be drawn into the anti-Nazi activities of Müller's circles. ACSP, NL Josef Müller, F65 Kriegsfolgen, Spruchkammerverfahren gegen Josef Müller, 1946–1947, Abschrift; Johannes Neuhäusler to Herrn Staatsminister Dr. Anton Pfeiffer, December 13, 1946. But this claim was undermined by his confidential statement to the denazification tribunal itself. ACSP, NL Müller, F65, Kriegsfolgen, Spruchkammerverfahren gegen Josef Müller, 1946–7, Abschrift, Abteilung Information 19. 12. 46, Vernehmung.
78. ACSP, NL Josef Müller, F65 Kriegsfolgen, Spruchkammerverfahren gegen Josef Müller, 1946–7, Abschrift, Abteilung Information, Vernehmung Johannes Neuhäusler, December 19, 1946.
79. AEMF, NL Johannes Neuhäusler, VN N 238, Prof. Dr. Florent Peeters to Kardinal Faulhaber, January 5, 1947; Johannes Neuhäusler, *Amboß und Hammer*, 134.
80. Walter Mariaux, *The Persecution of the Catholic Church in the Third Reich. Facts and Documents translated from the German* (London: Burns Oates, 1940). The original was titled *Todfeind des Christentums. Tatsachen und Dokumente aus dem Kampf des Nationalsozialismus gegen die katholische Kirche*. See Roman Bleistein, "Walter Mariaux und der Kirchenkampf des Dritten Reiches," in: *Stimmen der Zeit* 212 (1994), 793–805.
81. Johannes Neuhäusler, *Amboß und Hammer*, 134–135.
82. USHMM, RG 76.001 M, Reel 3, 198, Buchwieser to den Ministerrat des Landes Bayern, December 3, 1933; Alberto Vassallo-Torregrossa to Eugenio Pacelli, December 28, 1933.
83. Neuhäusler learned from his nephew that the Gestapo had resolved to "neutralize" (kaltstellen) him. BHSA, MKK 38233, Akten des Bayer. Staatsministeriums für Unterricht und Kultur, Mappe: Johannes

Neuhäusler, Weihbischof, 41–45, Neuhäusler to das Bayerische Kultusministerium, München, July 2, 1945.

84. Johannes Neuhäusler, *Amboß und Hammer*, 153–163; USHMM, ITS Tracing Service, Document ID 43991762; NA, RG 338, Records of U.S. Army Command, United States versus Martin G. Weiss et al., November 15–December 17, 1945, M1174, 1, Statement of Neuhäusler Johann, Capri, May 28, 1945.

85. ITS Archives, Doc. No 90421799#1.

86. For details, see Neuhäusler's testimony from November 1945 in the trial of Martin Weiss et al. The transcript can be found at AGD, Mappe: Johannes Neuhäusler. The Gestapo had learned that Niemöller was considering converting to Catholicism. Placing him next to two articulate Catholics, it believed, might hasten the process and drive a wedge through the heart of the Confessing Church. The opposite, not surprisingly, proved to be the case. Surrounded by two Bavarian Catholics, Niemöller decided to remain Protestant. See Martin Niemöller, "Gedanken zu dem Thema: Evangelisch oder Katholisch (1939)," in: *Sinn und Form* 52 (2001), 449–459; "Niemoeller's Friends Deny His Conversion. Say Imprisoned Pastor Is Only Studying Catholic Doctrine," in: *The New York Times*, February 5, 1941, 3; Jürgen Schmidt, *Martin Niemöller im Kirchenkampf* (Hamburg: Leibniz Verlag, 1971); Gerhard Niemöller, Leserbrief, in: *Frankfurter Allgemeine Zeitung*, Nr. 276, November 27, 2000.

87. ITS Archives, Doc. No. 43991762; Hans-Günter Richardi, *SS-Geiseln in der Alpenfestung. Die Verschleppung prominenter KZ-Häftlinge aus Deutschland nach Südtirol* (Bozen: Edition Raetia, 2006); Johannes Neuhäusler, *Amboß und Hammer*, 190–201.

88. Johannes Neuhäusler, *Amboß und Hammer*, 209.

89. Ibid., 205–209; "Freed Priest Sees Pope: Neuhaeusler Reports in Niemoeller, a Fellow Prisoner," in: *The New York Times*, May 24, 1945, 4; Friedrich Hermann Hettler, *Josef Müller ("Ochsensepp")*, 201–202; USHMM, U.S. Relations with the Vatican and the Holocaust, 1940–1950, Collection, NARA II, Gale Doc.#: SC5001107660, J. B. (illegible last name) to Myron Taylor, May 30, 1945.

90. Johannes Neuhäusler, *Amboß und Hammer*, 209.

91. These included Dr. Gustav Goerdeler and Dr. Hermann Pünder, head of the Reich Chancellory until January 30, 1933. Former Austrian Chancellor Kurt von Schnussnigg was present but did not take part. "For What I Am," in: *Time*, June 18, 1945, 28; "A Hero with Limitations," in: *The New York Times*, June 7, 1945, 18; "War News Summarized," in: *The New York Times*, June 6, 1945, 1.

92. Johannes Neuhäusler, *Amboß und Hammer*, 209.

93. Sam Pope Brewer, "Niemoeller Asks Iron Rule of Reich: Freed Pastor Says Germany Is Unfit for Democracy – Four Anti-Nazis Agree," in: *The New York Times*, June 6, 1945; "Francis S. Harmon: Notes No. 19 (Bericht über eine Unterredung mit Martin Niemöller am 6. Juli 1945," in: Clemens Vollnhals, ed., *Die evangelische Kirche nach dem Zusammenbruch: Berichte ausländischer Beobachter aus dem Jahre 1945* (Göttingen: Vandenhoeck & Ruprecht, 1988),

35–40. See the conference paper by Matthew Hockenos, "Martin Niemöller in America, 1946–1947: A Hero with Limitations," http://contemporary churchhistory.org/2012/06/conference-paper-martin-niemoeller-in-america/ (accessed January 31, 2013).

94. Marshall Knappen, *And Call It Peace*, 112.

95. ITS Archive, Sonderfall, Inhaftierungsbescheingung, Johannes Neuhäusler, May 7, 1957.

96. Johannes Neuhäusler, *Kreuz und Hakenkreuz, Teil I*, 7.

97. Johannes Neuhäusler, *Saat des Bösen, Kirchenkampf im Dritten Reich* (München: Manz Verlag, 1964), 7.

98. AEMF, NL Johannes Neuhäusler, N242, Abschrift, Niemöller, Sonderdruck aus dem "Basler Kirchenboten," Reformationssonntag, 1945, gezeichnet Professor Karl Barth.

99. AEMF, Kardinal Faulhaber Archiv, 8305, Abschrift, Faulhaber an Bischof Heinrich Wienken, September 26, 1941; SAM, STAnw M II VSG 25/2, Beschuldigtenvernehmungsprotokoll: Edgar Stiller vom August 18, 1951, im Verfahren gegen Edgar Stiller; Hans-Günter Richardi, *SS-Geiseln in der Alpenfestung*, 135–137; AGD, File, Johannes Neuhäusler, Interrogation by American military officials of Neuhäusler.

100. Neuhäusler contradicted this account in 1967 when he claimed that he dictated the first twelve pages to the daughter of Jakob Kaiser in the days immediately after the press conference in Naples on June 5. Kaiser was also a concentration camp survivor and a future co-founder of the CDU. Johannes Neuhäusler, *Amboß und Hammer*, 210. Are these accounts irreconcilable? Coming twenty-one years later, his account from 1967 may be less plausible. Alternatively, he may have dictated to Kaiser's daughter lines that he had committed to memory or carried with him in the form of shorthand notes.

101. Johannes Neuhäusler, *Kreuz und Hakenkreuz, Teil II*, 405–411.

102. Johannes Neuhäusler, *Kreuz und Hakenkreuz, Teil I*, 7–8.

103. Ibid.

104. Johannes Neuhäusler, "Wie Pius XII. 1945 über Deutschland sprach," in: *Münchener Katholische Kirchenzeitung*, March 4, 1956, 184–185; Friedrich Hermann Hettler, *Josef Müller ("Ochsensepp")*, 201–202; USHMM, U.S. Relations with the Vatican and the Holocaust, 1940–1950, Collection, NARA II, Gale Doc. #: SC5001107660, J. B. (illegible last name) to Myron Taylor, May 30, 1945.

105. For this address, see www.vatican.va/holy_father/pius_xii/speeches/1945/do cuments/hf_p-xii_spe_19450602_accogliere_it.html (accessed February 26, 2013).

106. Johannes Neuhäusler, *Amboß und Hammer*, 209–210; *Kreuz und Hakenkreuz, Teil I*, 7; *Kreuz und Hakenkreuz, Teil II*, 10.

107. Johannes Neuhäusler, *Kreuz und Hakenkreuz, Teil I*, 7. For write-ups, see "War News Summarized," in: *The New York Times*, June 6, 1945, 1; "For What I Am," in: *Time*, June 18, 1945, 28.

108. Johannes Neuhäusler, *Kreuz und Hakenkreuz, Teil II*, 10. In a retelling of this story from 1967, however, he put them on record as asking specifically about not just the "German resistance" but also "the resistance from the

churches." Defending an aggrieved national honor, the same goal of Pope Pius XII, was clearly at the center of Neuhäusler's agenda in 1946. Two decades later, his priority was defending his church, which had just come under fire from Guenter Lewy and others for its alleged paucity of resistance. The journalists could, of course, have raised both questions, but Neuhäusler obviously chose to report their questions differently. Johannes Neuhäusler, *Amboß und Hammer*, 209.

109. Mildly nationalistic tones had crept even into his "Atlas of Catholic World Missions" from 1932. Johannes Neuhäusler, ed., *Atlas der katholischen Weltmission, Zusammengestellt und mit erläuterndem Text versehen durch die internationale Fideskorrepondenz in Rom unter Verwertung kartographischen und statistischen Materials des Archisv der Hilfskongregation der Glaubensverbreitung, als Jahrbuchfolge 1932 des Priestermissionsbundes im deutschen Sprachgebiet* (München: Fischer, 1932), 104–105; Staatsarchiv München, 34475/2, Auszug aus dem Tagebuch seiner Exzellenz des Herrn Weihbischof Dr. Neuhäusler: (Geführt im KZ-Dachau für die Jahre 1943–1945), 5. SAM, 34475/2, Auszug aus dem Tagebuch seiner Exzellenz des Herrn Weihbischof Dr. Neuhäusler (Geführt im KZ-Dachau für die Jahre 1943–1945), 5.

110. Bundesarchiv, B 305/140, Schreiben von Neuhäusler vom 15.1. 1950 as cited in Ernst Klee, Persilscheine und falsche Pässe: Wie die Kirchen den Nazis halfen (Frankfurt am Main: Fischer Verlag, 1991), 51,170.

111. USHMM, U.S. Relations with the Vatican, Nara II, 1940–1945, Gale Doc. # SC5001112675, Segregetaria di Stato di sua Santita (no author) to Harold Tittmann, November 24, 1945. For a clear statement of his opposition to denazification, see "Weihbischof Dr. Joh. Neuhäusler nimmt Stellung zur Entnazifizierung," in: *Münchener Katholische Kirchenzeitung*, March 28, 1948, 94.

112. The transcript can be found at AGD, Mappe: Johannes Neuhäusler.

113. USHMM, U.S. Relations with the Vatican, 1940–1945, Gale Doc. # SC5001112675, document number 106297/SA, Segretaria di Stato di sua Santita to Harold Titmann, November 24, 1945.

114. Johannes Neuhäusler, *Kreuz und Hakenkreuz, Teil I*, 4.

115. Hans-Günter Richardi, *Lebensläufe: Schicksale von Menschen, die im KZ Dachau waren, Dachauer Dokumente, Band 2* (Dachau: Books on Demand, 2001). Neuhäusler's assistant was his twenty-six-year-old nephew and the future esoteric theologian and professor of philosophy Anton Neuhäusler, better known later through his pseudonym, Franz Ringseis. AEMF, NL Johannes Neuhäusler, VN N238, Toni (Anton Neuhäusler) to Johannes Neuhäusler, January 6, 1946. For examples of his output, see Anton Neuhäusler, *Telepathie, Hellsehen, Präkognition* (Bern: Francke Verlag, 1957); *Begriffe der philosophischen Sprache* (Munich: Ehrenwirth, 1963).

116. For accounts of Neuhäusler's opposition to war crimes trials, see James J. Weingartner, *Crossroads of Death: the Story of the Malmedy Massacre and Trial* (Berkeley: University of California Press, 1979), 188–189; Frank M. Buscher, *The U.S. War Crimes Trial Program in Germany, 1946–1955* (Westport: Greenwood Press, 1989), 93–97; Ernst Klee, *Persilscheine und*

falsche Pässe: Wie die Kirchen den Nazis halfen, 79–82, 95, 105, 107–108; James
J. Weingartner, *A Peculiar Crusade: Willis M. Everett and the Malmedy Massacre*
(New York: New York University Press, 2000), 156–157, Norbert Frei,
Vergangenheitspolitik: Die Anfänge der Bundesrepublik und die NS-Vergangenheit
(Munich, Verlag C.H. Beck, 1996), 141–163; AEMF, NL Neuhäusler, VN
N31, Neuhäusler to Captain Sigismund Payne Best, June 19, 1969. On the
prisoners' lack of true penitence, see AES, NL Andreas Rohracher, 19/29,
Korr. mit Bischöfen im Ausland, 1950–1958, Johannes Neuhäusler to
Andreas Rohracher, December 28, 1953.

117. Johannes Neuhäusler, *Kreuz und Hakenkreuz II*, 407–408.
118. Johannes Neuhäusler, *Amboß und Hammer*, 183–184.
119. On the trial of Wilhelm Schubert and Gustav Sorge from October 13, 1958,
     to February 6, 1959, see Hendrik George Van Dam and Ralph Giordano,
     ed., *KZ-Verbrecher vor deutschen Gerichten. Dokumente aus den Prozessen, 2
     volumes* (Frankfurt: EVA, 1962, 1966), Vol. I, 151–510. On Schubert's
     vicious beating of Neuhäusler, see Winfried Meyer, *Emil Büge: 1470 KZ-
     Geheimnisse. Heimliche Aufzeichnungen aus der Politischen Abteilung des KZ
     Sachsenhausen, Dezember 1939 bis April 1943* (Berlin: Metropol, 2010), 127.
     Tellingly, Neuhäusler made no mention of this beating in *Amboß und
     Hammer*. See also Weihbischof J(ohannes) Neuhäusler, "Neuzugang –
     Beruf: Pfaffe. Wie ich den "Pistolen Schubert" (im KZ Sachsenhausen)
     erlebte," in: *Petrusblatt*, Nr. 49, December 7, 1958; KNA Archiv,
     Neuhäusler File, KNA Informationsdienst Nr. 8, February 21, 1959, 163.
120. Johannes Neuhäusler, *Kreuz und Hakenkreuz, Teil II*, 10.
121. Ibid., 11.
122. Ibid.
123. Ibid., 19–21.
124. Ibid., 406–408.
125. For examples: see Neuhäusler's transcriptions of Michael Faulhaber's
     Pastorale Anweisungen für den Klerus from April 5, 1933, *Kreuz und
     Hakenkreuz, II*, 51–52. For the original, see Bernhard Stasiewski, *Akten
     deutscher Bischöfe, I*, 35–38; *Kreuz und Hakenkreuz, II*, 52–55; for the
     original, Bernhard Stasiewski, *Akten deutscher Bischöfe über die Lage der Kirche,
     1933-1945, I*, 239–248; *Kreuz und Hakenkreuz, II*, 55–62; for the original, see
     Bernhard Stasiewski, *Akten über die Lage der Kirche, II* (Mainz: Grünewald,
     1976), 331–341; *Kreuz und Hakenkreuz, II*, 63–67; for the original, Ludwig
     Volk, *Akten deutscher Bischöfe, Bd. IV*, 555–564; *Kreuz und Hakenkreuz, II*,
     111; for the original, Ludwig Volk, *Akten Kardinal Michael von Faulhaber II*,
     228–233. A full listing would require many additional pages.
126. For examples, see Johannes Neuhäusler, *Kreuz und Hakenkreuz, II*, 52, 53,
     61, 62, 67, 69, 71, 78, 103, 113, 114, 118, 124, 132, 133, 134, 135, 136,
     137, 138, 139, 140, 143, 145, 150, 151, 152, etc.
127. Hans Müller, "Zur Behandlung des Kirchenkampfes in der
     Nachkriegsliteratur," in: *Politische Studien* 12 (1961), 474–481. On his
     piety, see AEMF, NL Neuhäusler, VN N 12, Hans Müller to Johannes
     Neuhäusler, November 27, 1964. On this point, see also Donald J. Dietrich,
     Catholic Citizens in the Third Reich: Psycho-Social Principles and Moral

Reasoning (New Brunswick: Transaction Publishers, 1988), 174, footnote 20. Müller had, in fact, significantly undercounted the number of documents that had been cleansed by Neuhäusler. For more on Müller, see Chapters 3 and 6.

128. AEMF, NL Neuhäusler, VN N 12, Johannes Neuhäusler to Hans Müller, November 24, 1964.

129. Johannes Neuhäusler, *Saat des Bösen*, 7–8.

130. Neuhäusler, for instance, described only two couriers, his "most courageous" – Müller and Schneidhuber. Johannes Neuhäusler, *Amboß und Hammer*, 131. An SD report from 1941 described an additional accomplice, an unnamed "white-collar worker in sales" accused of high treason by the People's Court in Berlin. BHSA, MKK 38233, Akten des Bayer. Staatsministeriums für Unterricht und Kultur, Mappe: Johannes Neuhäusler, Weihbischof, 41–45, Abschrift zu II 3240/41, Der Chef der Sicherheitspolizei und des SD, Berlin den June 27, 1941, IV 1–554/41, Betrifft: Neuhäusler, Johann, Domkapitular. Neuhäusler never mentioned that Schneidhuber was a Jewish convert to Christianity – and had been gassed for precisely that reason.

131. Müller's intraparty foes, battling with him over the ideological direction of the CSU, cited his shadowy work as a lawyer in the summer of 1933 on the financial liquidation of the Leohaus, the headquarters of Catholic social welfare, cinema and workers organizations. Friedrich Hermann Hettler, *Josef Müller ("Ochsensepp")*, 34–44, 274–290. ACSP, NL Josef Müller, F6412, Zeitungsausschnitte, "Dr. Josef Müller – ein Koalitionspartner Hitlers. Enthüllungen der "Süddeutschen Zeitung" – Er ging mit der nationalsozialistischen Fraktion," Würzburg, November 12, 1946 (no newspaper name given), "Enthüllungen über den Landesvorsitzenden der CSU: Dr. Josef Müller – Koalitionspartner Hitlers, Aus den Akten der Bayerischen Politischen Polizei, 'Ich bejahe die nationalsozialistische Bewegung,'" München, November 12, 1946 (no newspaper name given); "Diskussion um Dr. Josef Müller. Vorsitzender der bayerischen CSU weist Anklagen zurück – Das Protokoll der Gestapo," in: *Die Neue Zeitung*, November 15, 1946; ACSP, NL Josef Müller, F6413, Zeitungsausschnitt, "Spruchkammerverfahren gegen Dr. Josef Müller. Kandidatur Dr. Müllers für den Posten des Ministerpräsidenten damit unmöglich," in: *Der Allgauer - Kempten*, Nr. 99, December 14, 1946.

132. Thomas Brechenmacher and Michael Wolffsohn, *Geschichte als Falle. Deutschland und die jüdische Welt* (Neuried: Ars Una, Neuried 2001), 19.

133. Karl-Ulrich Gelberg, "Josef Müller (1898–1979)," in: Jürgen Aretz, Rudolf Morsey and Anton Rauscher, ed. *Zeitgeschichte in Lebensbildern. Aus dem deutschen Katholizismus des 19. und 20. Jahrhunderts, Band 8* (Mainz: Matthias-Grünewald Verlag, 1997), 155–172 and, in particular, 158.

134. Harold H. Tittmann III, ed., *Inside the Vatican of Pius XII: The Memoir of an American Diplomat during World War II, Harold H. Tittmann Jr.* (New York: Image Books, 2004), 212–213. It seems beyond doubt that Müller would have shared this information with his close friend and confidante, particularly since both flew back from Rome to Capri together.

135. ACSP, NL Josef Müller, S89 Kirche, Neuhäusler, 1945–1971, G84/11, Josef Müller to Johannes Neuhäusler, January 26, 1973.
136. Wilhelm Leibusch, *Einer aus der Lausitzer Strasse: Eine katholische Jugend in Berlin-Kreuzberg zu Anfang des Jahrhunderts* (Berlin: Morus Verlag, 1968); Walter Adolph, "Erinnerungen 1922–1933," in: *Wichmann Jahrbuch für Kirchengeschichte im Bistum Berlin, 1970–1975* (Berlin: Morus Verlag, 1976), 34–85. Adolph used fictionalized names throughout, but the *Wichmann Jahrbuch* provided a glossary translating the fictionalized names into their real-life equivalents.
137. Erich Klausener Jr., "Erinnerung an Walter Adolph," in: *Wichmann Jahrbuch für Kirchengeschichte im Bistum Berlin, 1970–1975*, 10–11.
138. Wilhelm Leibusch, *Einer aus der Lausitzer Strasse*, 187–192.
139. Ibid., 216–222.
140. Ibid., 224–226.
141. Erich Klausener Jr., "Erinnerung an Walter Adolph," 12–13; on Klausener Sr., see Klaus Große Kracht, "Erich Klausener (1885–1934). Preußentum und Katholische Aktion zwischen Weimarer Republik und Drittem Reich," in: Richard Faber and Uwe Puschner, ed., *Preußische Katholiken und katholische Preußen im 20. Jahrhundert* (Würzburg: Königshausen & Neumann, 2011), 271–296. For an uncritical account, see Tilman Pünder, "Erich Klausener (1885–1934)," in: Jürgen Aretz, Rudolf Morsey, and Anton Rauscher, ed., *Zeitgeschichte in Lebensbildern. Aus dem deutschen Katholizismus des 19. und 20. Jahrhunderts, Bd 10* (Münster: Aschendorff, 2001), 43–59.
142. On Sonnenschein, see Werner Krebber, ed., *Den Menschen Recht verschaffen. Carl Sonnenschein – Person und Werk* (Würzburg: Echter Verlag, 1996); Friedel Doért, *Carl Sonnenschein: Seelsorger, theologischer Publizist und sozialpolitischer Aktivist* (Münster: Aschendorff, 2012).
143. It also included the journalist Emil Dovifat. On Dovifat, see Klaus-Ulrich Benedikt, *Emil Dovifat: Ein katholischer Hochschullehrer und Publizist* (Mainz: Matthias-Grünewald-Verlag, 1986); Otto Köhler, *Unheimliche Publizisten: Die verdrängte Vergangenheit der Medienmacher* (Munich: Knaur, 1995); Bernd Sösemann, "Auf dem Grat zwischen Entschiedenheit und Kompromiß," in: Bernd Sösemann, ed., *Emil Dovifat. Studien und Dokumente zu Leben und Werk* (Berlin: Walter de Gruyter, 1998), 103–159.
144. For examples of the friendship with the Klausener family, see KZG, NL Walter Adolph, WA5i, Adolph to Frau Klausener, May 17, 1946; Adolph to Erich Klausener Jr., September 18, 1946.
145. Erich Klausener Jr., "Erinnerung an Walter Adolph," 13.
146. On the first seven years of the *Petrusblatt*, see Wolfgang Tischner, *Katholische Kirche in der SBZ/DDR 1945–1951* (Paderborn: Schöningh, 2001), 485–508. On Lichtenberg, see Gotthard Klein, "Bernhard Lichtenberg und die Berliner Blutzeugen, 1933–1945," in: *Wie im Himmel so auf Erden. 90. Katholikentag vom 3. bis 27. Mai 1990 in Berlin. Dokumentation, Teil II* (Paderborn: Bonifatius, 1991), 1691–1721; Gotthard Klein, *Seliger Bernhard Lichtenberg* (Regensburg: Schnell & Steiner, 1997); Ursula Prubeta, "Seliger Dompropst Bernhard Lichtenberg," in:

Helmut Moll, ed., *Zeugen für Christus. Das deutsche Martyrologium des 20. Jahrhunderts* (Paderborn: Schöningh, 1999), 104–109; Kevin Spicer, "The Propst from St. Hedwig: Bernhard Lichtenberg as a Paradigm for Resistance," in: Sharon Leder and Milton Teichman, ed., *The Burdens of History: Post Holocaust Generations in Dialogue* (Merion Station, PA: Merion Westfield, 2000), 25–40; Kevin Spicer, C.S.C., "Totalitarianism: Last Years of a Resister in the Diocese of Berlin. Bernhard Lichtenberg's Conflict with Karl Adam and his Fateful Imprisonment," in: *Church History* 70 (2001), 248–270.

147. For examples, most not written by Adolph, see: *Petrusblatt*: "Berliner Priester im Konzentrationslager," December 23, 1945, 9–10; "Weihnachten in der Prinz-Albrecht-Strasse," December 30, 1945, 4; "Ich sterbe um 3 Uhr!" January 6, 1946, 5–6; "Wie sie starben," February 17, 1946, 3; "In Kürze: Berlin," February 17, 1946, 7; "Der Weg zur Vollendung: Pfarrer Albert Hirsch zum Gedächnis," March 10, 1946; "Der Fall Stettin," April 28, 1946, 5–6; "Der Fall Stettin (Fortsetzung)," May 5, 1946, 18; "Der Fall Stettin (Fortsetzung)," May 12, 1946, 5; "Der Fall Stettin (Schluss)," May 19, 1946; "Der letzte Brief," May 26, 1946, 3–4; "'Das ist der Mann, was sein Wille ist,'" June 30, 1946, 5; "Ein Märtyrer des Friedens," July 7, 1946, 2–3; "Das ewige Gesetz," July 7, 1946, 5; "Bernhard Lichtenberg," September 8, 1946, 3–4; "Klausener, Blutzeuge der Katholischen Aktion," September 22, 1946, 3; P. L. de Coninck, SJ, "Priestergespräche in Dachau," October 6, 1946, 3; "Priestergespräche in Dachau (1. Fortsetzung)," October 13, 1946, 2; "Priestergespräche in Dachau (2. Fortzsetzung)," October 20, 1946; "Priestergespräche in Dachau (3. Fortsetzung)," October 27, 1946, 2–3; "Priestergespräche in Dachau (4. Fortsetzung)," November 3, 1946, 2; "Priestergespräche in Dachau (5. Fortsetzung)," November 10, 1946, 2; "Priestergespräche in Dachau (Schluss)," November 17, 1946, 2; Johannes Maria Höcht, "Eine Weihnacht in Gestapohaft," December 2, 1946, 2; "Aus dem Bistum: Dr. Erich-Klausener-Gedenkstunde," July 11, 1948, 7. For books on martyrs, see Walter Adolph, *Wilhelm Wagner: Domvikar bei St. Hedwig zu Berlin* (Berlin: Morus Verlag, 1947); Heinz Kühn, *Blutzeugen des Bistums Berlin* (Berlin: Morus Verlag, 1950); Walter Adolph, *Im Schatten des Galgens. Zum Gedächtnis der Blutzeugen in der national-sozialistischen Kirchenverfolgung* (Berlin: Morus Verlag, 1953); Walter Adolph, *Erich Klausener* (Berlin: Morus Verlag, 1955). On the early years of the Morus Verlag, see Wolfgang Tischner, *Katholische Kirche in der SBZ/DDR*, 508–523.

148. See the extensive collection of correspondence in DAB III/6–14, II, Maria Regina Martyrum. See also Franz Pfeifer, ed., *Gedenkkirche Maria Regina Martyrum Berlin. Zu Ehren der Märtyrer für Glaubens-und Gewissensfreiheit* (Lindenberg: Fink, 2013).

149. *Hirtenworte in ernster Zeit; Kundgebungen des Bischofs von Berlin, Konrad Kardinal von Preysing in den Jahren 1945–1947* (Berlin: Morus-Verlag, 1947).

150. "Der Kampf der kath. Kirche gegen den Nationalsozialismus," in: *Petrusblatt*, December 30, 1945, 5.

151. "Dokumente klagen," in: *Petrusblatt*, July 21, 1946.
152. For one brief correspondence, see DAB, III/6–14–1, Walter Adolph to Johannes Neuhäusler, August 9, 1958.
153. KZG, NL Walter Adolph, 4e, Manuskript, Erich Klausener, 32. I would like to thank Klaus Große Kracht for pointing me to this manuscript.
154. Ibid., 36–37.
155. Walter Adolph, *Erich Klausener*, 147.
156. Bischöfliches Ordinariat Berlin, ed., *Dokumente aus dem Kampf der katholischen Kirche im Bistum Berlin gegen den Nationalsozialismus* (Berlin: Morus Verlag, 1946), 6.
157. Ulrich von Hehl, ed., *Walter Adolph: Geheime Aufzeichnungen aus dem nationalsozialistischen Kirchenkampf, 1935–1943* (Mainz: Matthias-Grünewald Verlag, 1979), XXIV.
158. Bischöfliches Ordinariat Berlin, ed., *Dokumente aus dem Kampf der katholischen Kirche im Bistum Berlin gegen den Nationalsozialismus*, 6.
159. On Von Preysing, see Wolfgang Knauft, *Konrad von Preysing. Anwalt des Rechtes. Der erste Berliner Kardinal und seine Zeit* (Berlin: Morus Verlag, 1998); Kevin Spicer, *Resisting the Reich: The Catholic Clergy in Hitler's Berlin* (Dekalb: Northern Illinois University Press, 2004).
160. Ulrich von Hehl, *Walter Adolph: Geheime Aufzeichnungen*, xxv.
161. Walter Adolph, *Kardinal Preysing und zwei Diktaturen: Sein Widerstand gegen die totalitäre Macht* (Berlin: Morus Verlag, 1971), 73–79.
162. See Martin Georg Goerner, *Die Kirche als Problem der SED: Strukturen kommunistischer Herrschaftsausübung gegenüber der evangelischen Kirche, 1945 bis 1958* (Berlin: Akademie Verlag, 1997); Wolfgang Tischner, *Katholische Kirche in der SBZ/DDR: Die Formierung einer Subgesellschaft im entstehenden sozialistischen Staat* (Paderborn: Schöningh, 2001); Sean Brennan, *The Politics of Religion in Soviet-Occupied Germany: The Case of Berlin-Brandenburg, 1945–1949* (New York: Lexington Books, 2011).
163. Bernd Schaefer, *The East German State and the Catholic Church, 1945–1989* (New York: Berghahn Books, 2010), 21; Wolfgang Tischner, *Katholische Kirche in der SBZ/DDR*, 496–500.
164. On Stasiewski, see Reimund Haas and Stefan Samerski, ed., *Bernhard Stasiewski (1905–1995) – Osteuropahistoriker und Wissenschaftsorganisator* (Münster: MV Wissenschaft, 2007). The other was Professor Curt Brienitzer-Kleinschmidt, who was kidnapped by Russian security forces in the late 1940s and deported to his death in a Russian work camp. KZG, NL Walter Adolph, WA5, Ein Opfer der Gewalt (no date, no author).
165. NL Bernhard Stasiewski, Folder: Auslandsreisen, Bericht, Narzissa Stasiewski, September 11, 1946; Marya Tahörnder an das Polizeipräsidium Berlin, March 29, 1947; interview with Narzissa Stasiewski.
166. On the Thälmann cults, see Rüdiger Schmidt, "Sieger der Geschichte? Antifascismus im 'anderen Deutschland,'" in: Thomas Großbölting, ed., *Friedensstaat, Leseland, Sportnation? DDR-Legenden auf dem Prüfstand* (Berlin: Christoph Links Verlag, 2009), 208–229; Jon Berndt Olsen, *Tailoring Truth: Politicizing the Past and Negotiating Memory in East Germany, 1945–1990* (New York: Berghahn Books, 2015), 87–96.

167. "Dompropst Lichtenberg, ein Kämpfer Christi," in: *Petrusblatt*, December 2, 1945, 3–5.
168. Walter Adolph, *Im Schatten des Galgens*, 12.
169. "Lüge als politische Waffe. Wir meinen dazu …, " in: *Petrusblatt*, September 25, 1949, 1; "Der Kampf gegen die Kirche," in: *Petrusblatt*, September 25, 1949, 2.
170. For examples, "Der Kampf der katholischen Kirche gegen den Nationalsozialismus, 1933–1945," in: *Petrusblatt*, December 16, 1945, and "Fortsetzung: Der Kampf der katholischen Kirche gegen den Nationalsozialismus," December 23, 1945, 7–8. See the four-part series in the *Petrusblatt* by Propst Ernst Daniel, "Der Fall Stettin." The articles appeared as follows in the *Petrusblatt*: April 28, 1946, 5; May 5, 1946, 6; May 12, 1946, 5; May 19, 1946, 6. See also, "Zwischenbilanz, 1933–1945," September 1, 1946, 3–4.
171. AKM, NL Werthmann, I Pers. Dok, Der Fall "Fleischer" III, Mitteilungen des Rechtsanwalts Dr. Felix Fleischer, Berlin-Charlottenburg 5, Herbertsstrasse 16, über seinen Bruder, Josef Fleischer, June 10, 1940.
172. Ibid. For a fuller exposition of Josef Fleischer's pacifism, see UNDA, Gordon Zahn Papers, CZHN, 13264–13360, Record of my Fulbright Year, 125–131.
173. AKM, NL Werthmann, Der Fall Fleischer II, Aktenvermerk, June 2, 1956.
174. HAEK, CR II 25.2.5, Dr. Josef Fleischer, Kriegsdienstverweigerung und Militärseelsorge, no date.
175. HAEK, Gen II 23.23a, 11, Zeitungsausschnitt; Johannes Fleischer, "Schuldbekenntnis der versäumten Pflichten. Die andere Konsequenz," in: *Der Tagesspiegel, Berlin*, January 12, 1947.
176. Walter Adolph, "Dolchstoss-Legende in neuer Form," in: *Petrusblatt*, January 26, 1947.
177. Wilhelm Corsten, *Kölner Aktenstücke* (Cologne: Bachem Verlag, 1949).
178. HAEK, GEN II 22.13, 14, Das Erzbischöfliche Generalvikariat an das Hochwürdigste Bischöfliche Generalvikariat in Fulda, March 22, 1962, Betr: Corsten, Kölner Aktenstücke.
179. HAEK, Gen II 23, 23a, 9, Susanne Schoelkens to das General Vikariat, August 27, 1946.
180. On opposition to Allied policies, see, in particular, Jörg Friedrich, *Die Kalte Amnestie: NS-Täter in der Bundesrepublik* (Berlin: List Verlag, 2007). For literature on victimization, see Robert G. Moeller, "Germans as Victims? Thoughts on a Post-Cold War History of World War II's Legacies," *History and Memory* 17 (2005), 1–35; Gilad Margalit, *Guilt, Suffering, and Memory: Germany Remembers Its Dead of World War II* (Bloomington: Indiana University Press, 2010); Helmut Schmitz and Annette Seidel-Arpacı, *Narratives of Trauma: Discourses of German Wartime Suffering in National and International Perspective* (Amsterdam: Rodopi, 2011).
181. Johannes Neuhäusler, *Wie war das in Dachau: ein Versuch, der Wahrheit näherzukommen* (Dachau: Kuratorium für Sühnemal KZ, 1960); Johannes Neuhäusler, *Saat des Bösen*; Johannes Neuhäusler, *Amboß und Hammer*.
182. "KZ Pater Roth Schwarzer Winkel," in: *Der Spiegel*, February 14, 1962.

183. AEMF, NL Johannes Neuhäusler, N176, Neuhäusler to die geehrten
     Schriftleitungen der Katholischen Kirchenzeitungen, Betreff: Kurat
     Roth – Dachau (no date but the first half of 1961).
184. Norbert Göttler, *Die Akte Pater Leonhard Roth: sein Leben und Sterben im
     Einsatz für Gerechtigkeit und historische Wahrheit* (Dachau: Verein Zum
     Beispiel Dachau, 2004); Harold Marcuse, *Legacies of Dachau*, 230–233.
185. "OSS-Report: Interview with Pastor Niemöller (18 Juni 1945)," in:
     Clemens Vollnhals, ed., *Die evangelische Kirche nach dem Zusammenbruch*,
     21–24.
186. See Heinz Kühn, "Quo vadis, Reinhold Schneider?," in: *Blick in die Zeit.
     Beilage zum Petrusblatt*, 19, May 13, 1951; Ekkehard Blattmann and
     Klaus Mönig, ed., *Über den "Fall Reinhold Schneider"* (München: Verlag
     Schnell, 1990); Ekkehard Schneider, *Militarisierung oder Passion. Ein Beitrag
     zum "Fall Reinhold Schneider"* (Frankfurt am Main: Peter Lang, 1992);
     Ekkehard Blattmann, *Reinhold Schneider im Roten Netz. Der "Fall Reinhold
     Schneider" im kryptokommunistischen Umfeld* (Frankfurt am Main: Peter
     Lang, 2001).

2   The Battles over the Reichskonkordat, 1945–1957

1. "Der Antrag der Bundesregierung vom 12. März 1955," in: Friedrich Giese
   and Friedrich August Frhr. v.d. Heydte, ed., *Der Konkordatsprozess. 1. Teilband*
   (München: Isar Verlag, 1957), 20–29.
2. "Das Gesetz über das öffentliche Schulwesen in Niedersachsen vom 14.
   September 1954," in: Friedrich Giese and Friedrich August Frhr. v.d.
   Heydte, ed., *Der Konkordatsprozess. 1. Teilband*, 12–19.
3. "Der Antrag der Bundesregierung vom 12. März 1955," 26. The German
   terms were *Bekenntnisschule* and *Simultanschule*.
4. Friedrich Giese and Friedrich August Frhr. v.d. Heydte, ed., *Der
   Konkordatsprozess. 4. Teilband* (München: Isar Verlag, 1959), 1566.
5. "Der Antrag der Bundesregierung vom 12. März 1955."
6. "Die Antragserwiderung der niedersächsischen Landesregierung vom 14. mai
   1955," in: Friedrich Giese and Friedrich August Frhr. v.d. Heydte, ed., *Der
   Konkordatsprozess. 1. Teilband*, 41.
7. "Die Beitrittserklärung von Bremen vom 25. Juni 1955," in: Friedrich Giese
   and Friedrich August Frhr. v.d. Heydte, ed., *Der Konkordatsprozess. 1.
   Teilband*, 98–104; "Die Beitrittserklärung von Hessen vom 15. Juli 1955,"
   in: Friedrich Giese and Friedrich August Frhr. v.d. Heydte, ed., *Der
   Konkordatsprozess. 1. Teilband*, 135–137.
8. www.1000dokumente.de/index.html?c=dokument_de&dokument=0006_er
   m&object=facsimile&l=de (accessed June 11, 2015).
9. "Die Beitrittserklärung von Bremen vom 25. Juni 1955," in: Friedrich Giese
   and Friedrich August Frhr. v.d. Heydte, ed., *Der Konkordatsprozeß. 1.
   Teilband*, 101–102; "Die Beitrittserklärung von Hessen vom 15. Juli 1955,"
   in: Friedrich Giese and Friedrich August Frhr. v.d. Heydte, ed., *Der
   Konkordatsprozeß. 1. Teilband*, 135.

10. For a summary of the linkage argument, see Carsten Kretschmann, "Eine Partei für Pacelli? Die Scholder-Repgen-Debatte," in: Thomas Brechenmacher, ed., *Das Reichskonkordat 1933* (Paderborn: Schöningh Verlag, 2007), 13–24 and, especially, 19. See also Konrad Repgen, "P. Robert Leiber SJ, der Kronzeuge für die vatikanische Politik beim Reichskonkordat 1933. Anmerkungen zu meiner Kontroverse mit Klaus Scholder, 1977–1979," in: Thomas Brechenmacher, ed., *Das Reichskonkordat 1933*, 13–24, 24–37.

11. Rebecca Ayako Bennette, *Fighting for the Soul of Germany: The Catholic Struggle for Inclusion after Unification* (Cambridge, MA: Harvard University Press, 2012), 132–133; Margaret Lavinia Anderson, *Windthorst: A Political Biography* (Oxford: Clarendon Press, 1981), 134; Ellen Lovell Evans, *The German Center Party, 1870–1933: A Study in Political Catholicism* (Carbondale: Southern Illinois University Press, 1981), 39–41.

12. Rebecca Ayako Bennette, *Fighting for the Soul of Germany*, 133; Marjorie Lamberti, "State, Church and the Politics of School Reform during the Kulturkampf," in: *Central European History* 19 (1986), 63–81 and, especially, 76–77.

13. For an excellent overview, see Kristian Buchna, *Ein klerikales Jahrzehnt? Kirche, Konfession und Politik in der Bundesrepublik während der 1950er Jahre* (Baden-Baden: Nomos Verlag, 2014), 88–123.

14. See Horst Groschopp, ed., *"Los von der Kirche": Adolph Hoffmann und die Staat-Kirche-Trennung in Deutschland: Texte zu 90 Jahre Weimarer Reichsverfassung* (Aschaffenburg: Alibri Verlag, 2009).

15. See Articles 146 and 174. www.documentarchiv.de/wr/wrv.html#VIERTER_ABSCHNITT02 (accessed June 11, 2015). On the reaction by the churches, see Klaus Scholder, *Die Kirchen und das Dritten Reich, Band I, Vorgeschichte und Zeit der Illusionen 1918–1934* (Frankfurt am Main: Propyläen Verlag, 1986), 19–23.

16. Frederic Spotts, *The Churches and Politics in Germany* (Middletown: Wesleyan University Press, 1973), 211; Robert Ventresca, *Soldier of Christ: The Life of Pope Pius XII* (Cambridge, MA: Harvard University Press, 2013).

17. Article 11 stipulated that diocesan border changes that extended beyond the borders of Germany would have to be approved by the Reich government. After 1945, the Reichskonkordat emerged as a means to contest the postwar territorial settlements under which Germany had lost territory – and the German bishops portions or all of their dioceses – to Poland, the Soviet Union and a rival German state.

18. Ernst-Wolfgang Böckenförde, "Der deutsche Katholizismus im Jahre 1933. Eine kritische Betrachtung," in: *Hochland* 53 (1961), 215–239.

19. www.kathpedia.com/index.php?title=Reichskonkordat_%28Text%29 (accessed June 11, 2015).

20. USHMM, RG76.001M, Reel 3, 198, Newspaper Clipping, "Die Schule des katholischen deutschen Kindes ist die im Reichskonkordat vom Führer gewährleistete Konfessionsschule," in: *Bayerische Volkszeitung*, January 15, 1934.

21. Ernst-Wolfgang Böckenförde, "Der deutsche Katholizismus im Jahre 1933. Eine kritische Betrachtung."

22. USHMM, R676.001M, Reel 3, 198, Newspaper Clipping, "Zur Schulanmeldung: Was jeder Nationalsozialist wissen muss" (no date, but most likely early January 1934).

23. The number of students attending interconfessional public elementary schools, in fact, rose only modestly from 15 to 24 percent between 1931 and 1937. Peter Lundgreen, *Sozialgeschichte der deutschen Schule im Überblick: Teil II: 1918–1980* (Göttingen: Vandenhoeck und Ruprecht, 1981), 42. For accounts of the Nazis' Schulpolitik, see Rolf Eilers, *Die nationalsozialistische Schulpolitik* (Cologne: Westdeutscher Verlag, 1963); Uwe Schmidt, *Hamburger Schulen im "Dritten Reich"* (Hamburg: Verlag der Staats- und Universitätsbibliothek Hamburg, 2010); Lisa Pine, *Education in Nazi Germany* (New York: Berg, 2010).

24. Wilhelm Damberg, *Der Kampf um die Schulen in Westfalen, 1933–1945* (Mainz: Matthias-Grünewald Verlag, 1986), 88.

25. Wilhelm Damberg, "Die Säkularisierung des Schulwesens am Beispiel der Bekenntnisschule in Westfalen 1906–1968," in: Matthias Frese and Michael Prinz, ed., *Politische Zäsuren und Gesellschaftlicher Wandel: Regionale und vergleichende Perspektiven* (Paderborn: Schöningh, 1996), 631–647 and, especially, 636.

26. See Wilhelm Damberg, *Der Kampf um die Schulen in Westfalen*; Wilhelm Damberg, "Die Säkularisierung des Schulwesens am Beispiel der Bekenntnisschule in Westfalen 1906–1968."

27. Wilhelm Damberg, *Der Kampf um die Schulen in Westfalen*, 215–231.

28. Robert Ventresca, *Soldier of Christ*, 83.

29. Neuhäusler provided significant excerpts from a protest from the German Bishops Conference in Fulda to the Reich Ministry for Church Affairs on January 13, 1937, in which the bishops cited specific violations article by article. Johannes Neuhäusler, *Kreuz und Hakenkreuz, Teil II* (Munich: Katholische Kirche Bayerns, 1946), 94–98.

30. Robert Ventresca, *Soldier of Christ*, 83–85.

31. http://w2.vatican.va/content/pius-xii/it/speeches/1945/documents/hf_p-xii_s pe_19450602_accogliere.html (accessed June 14, 2014).

32. "Bericht Zeigers, Rom, 20 September 1945," in: Ludwig Volk, ed,. *Akten deutscher Bischöfe über die Lage der Kirche 1933–1945, Band VI* (Mainz: Matthias-Grünewald Verlag, 1985), 768.

33. "Pius XII an den deutschen Episkopat, 18 January 1947," in: Ulrich Helbach, ed., *Akten deutscher Bischöfe seit 1945, Westliche Besatzungszonen, 1945–1947, II* (Paderborn: Schöningh Verlag, 2012), 963–961, 970.

34. Quoted in Frederic Spotts, *The Churches and Politics in Germany* (Middletown: Wesleyan University Press, 1973), 211. See also Ludwig Volk, "Der Heilige Stuhl und Deutschland, 1945–1949," in: Anton Rauscher, ed., *Kirche und Katholizismus, 1945–1949* (Paderborn: Schöningh, 1977), 53–87 and, in particular, 69.

35. PAAA, B130, 5445A, Jaenicke, Botschaft der Bundesrepublik Deutschland an das Auswärtige Amt, Bonn, Betr: Einstellung des Papstes zur Verzögerung des Urteils des Bundeverfassungsgerichts, Bezug: Drahtbericht Nr. 53 vom December 12, 1956.

36. "Frings an die Bischöfe der britischen Besatzungszone, 10 September 1945," in: Ludwig Volk, ed,. *Akten deutscher Bischöfe, Band VI*, 736. On Zeiger, see Robert Ventresca, *Soldier of Christ*, 238–239.
37. For examples, see "Denkschrift [Jaegers oder Bernings] für Griffin zur Bekenntnisschule, o.O., vor 28 September 1945," "Protokoll über Gespräch Frings mit Asbury, 5 Juli 1946," "Machens an das Oberpräsidium der Provinz Hannover, 29 Juli 1946" and "Erklärung des Episkopats zur Bekenntnisschule, 20–22 August 1946," in: Ulrich Helbach, ed., *Akten deutscher Bischöfe seit 1945, Westliche Besatzungszonen, 1945–1947, I* (Paderborn: Schöningh Verlag, 2012), 259–264, 601–603, 631–634, 728.
38. On the origins of the term, see Hermann Sacher, ed, *Staatslexikon: Vierter Band: Papiergeld bis Staatsschulden* (Freiburg: Herder Verlag, 1931), 829–834.
39. "Denkschrift [Jaegers oder Bernings] für Griffin zur Bekenntnisschule, o.O., vor 28 September 1945," in: Ulrich Helbach, ed., *Akten deutscher Bischöfe seit 1945, Westliche Besatzungszonen, 1945–1947, I*, 263–264.
40. Wilhelm Damberg, *Abschied vom Milieu? Katholizismus im Bistum Münster und in den Niederlanden 1945–1980* (Paderborn: Schöningh, 1997), 430–432.
41. Kristian Buchna, *Ein klerikales Jahrzehnt?*, 176–187.
42. Angela Bauer-Kirsch, Herrenchiemsee. Der Verfassungskonvent von Herrenchiemsee – Wegbereiter des Parlamentarischen Rates (Ph.D diss., University of Bonn, 2005).
43. For an overview, see Wolfgang Benz, *Von der Besatzungsherrschaft zur Bundesrepublik: Stationen einer Staatsgründung, 1946–1949* (Frankfurt am Main: Fischer, 1985), 200–235; Michael F. Feldkamp, *Der Parlamentarische Rat, 1948–1949: Die Entstehung des Grundgesetzes* (Göttingen: Vandenhoeck & Ruprecht, 1998).
44. Klaus Gotto, "Die katholische Kirche und die Entstehung des Grundgesetzes," in: Anton Rauscher, ed., *Kirche und Katholizismus, 1945–1949* (Paderborn: Schöningh Verlag, 1977), 88–108.
45. Wilhelm Damberg, *Abschied vom Milieu?*, 429.
46. Ibid.; Wolfgang Tischner, *Die Katholische Kirche in der SBZ/DDR 1945–1951* (Paderborn: Schöningh Verlag, 2001), 275.
47. HAEK, CR II, 16.10.4, Bericht über die Verhandlungen, die am Dienstag, den 14. Dezember zwischen Vertretern der Kirchen und des Parlamentarischen Rates stattfanden.
48. For opposing retrospectives, see Bernhard Bergmann and Josef Steinberg, ed., *In Memoriam Wilhelm Böhler: Erinnerungen und Begegnungen* (Cologne: Bachem Verlag, 1965); Frederic Spotts, *The Churches and Politics in Germany*, 175–176; Burkhard van Schewick, *Die Katholische Kirche und die Entstehung der Verfassungen in Westdeutschland, 1945–1950* (Mainz: Schöningh, 1980), 30; Burkhard van Schewick, "Wilhelm Böhler (1891–1958)," in: Jürgen Aretz, Rudolf Morsey and Anton Rauscher, ed., *Zeitgeschichte in Lebensbildern. Aus dem deutschen Katholizismus des 19. und 20. Jahrhunderts, Band 4* (Mainz: Matthias-Grünewald Verlag, 1980), 197–207; Konrad Repgen, "Der Konkordatsstreit der fünfziger Jahre. Von Bonn nach Karlsruhe (1949–1955/57)," in: *Kirchliche Zeitgeschichte 3* (1990), 201–245; Kristian

Buchna, *Ein klerikales Jahrzehnt?*, 336–342. On Roman opposition to Böhler's political activities, see HAEK, NL Frings II, Nr. 1, Addenda 1, Josef Frings to Aloisius Muench, December 6, 1956.

49. On Süsterhenn and natural law, see Winfried Baumgart, "Adolf Süsterhenn (1905–1974)," in: Jürgen Aretz, Rudolf Morsey and Anton Rauscher, *Zeitgeschichte in Lebensbildern, Aus dem deutschen Katholizismus des 19. und 20. Jahrhunderts, Band 6* (Mainz: Matthias Grünewald Verlag, 1984), 189–199; Christoph von Hehl, *Adolf Süsterhenn (1905–1974): Verfassungsvater, Weltanschauungspolitiker, Föderalist* (Düsseldorf: Droste Verlag, 2012); Kristian Buchna, *Ein klerikales Jahrzehnt?*, 156–160.

50. www.vatican.va/holy_father/pius_xi/encyclicals/documents/hf_p-xi_en c_31121929_divini-illius-magistri_en.html (accessed June 14, 2016).

51. HAEK, CRII, 16.10.4, Josef Frings to Konrad Adenauer, January 17, 1949.

52. Marquette University Archives, John Riedl Papers, C-1.12 Series, Jor -2.5, Box 3, School Reform, Robert Murphy to John Taylor, November 4, 1946.

53. See Maria Mitchell, "Materialism and Secularism: CDU Politicians and National Socialism, 1945–1949," in: *The Journal of Modern History* 67, 2 (1995), 278–308.

54. Dorothee Buchhaas-Birkholz, *Gesetzgebung im Wiederaufbau. Schulgesetz in Nordrhein-Westfalen un Betriebsverfassungsgesetz. Eine vergleichende Untersuchung zum Einfluß von Parteien, Kirchen und Verbänden in Land und Bund, 1945–1952* (Düsseldorf: Droste Verlag, 1985); Maria Mitchell, "Materialism and Secularism," 278–308.

55. Wolfgang Tischner, *Die Katholische Kirche in der SBZ/DDR*, 275, 293.

56. "Das Gutachten von Prof. Dr. Hans Peters (Köln)," in: Friedrich Giese and Friedrich August Frhr. v.d. Heydte, *Der Konkordatsprozeß. 2. Teilband* (München: Isar Verlag, 1957), 648–669; Friedrich Giese and Friedrich August Frhr. v.d. Heydte, ed., *Der Konkordatsprozeß. 4. Teilband*, 1455–1462, 1468–1476, 1478–1499, 1546–1555, 1558–1560.

57. Burkhard van Schewick, *Die Katholische Kirche und die Entstehung der Verfassungen.*

58. HAEK, CR II, 16.10.4, Wilhelm Böhler, Bericht über die Verhandlungen, die am Dienstag, den 14. Dezember zwischen Vertretern der Kirchen des Parlamentarischen Rates stattfanden, December 17, 1948.

59. HHSTA, ABT 502, 6288. Streitgespräch über das Thema, Elternrecht zwischen Justizminister Zinn (SPD), OLG-Präs Dr. Dehler (FDP), Stud. Rat. Dr. Finck (CDU), Frau Helene Wessel (Zentrum), Von Radio München am 8. 3.49, 1800 Uhr übertragen.

60. HAEK, 502–6288, Newspaper Clipping, Herbert Borris, "Eltern oder Staat – ist das die Frage? Bemerkungen zu einer Diskussion bei Radio Frankfurt," in: *Frankfurter Rundschau*, March 28, 1949; R., Eig. Bericht, report of a radio broadcast from Radio Frankfurt, no date, but probably on or around March 28, 1949.

61. HAEK, CR II, 16.10.4, Wilhelm Böhler, Bericht über die Verhandlungen, die am Dienstag, den 14. Dezember zwischen Vertretern der Kirchen des Parlamentarischen Rates stattfanden, December 17, 1948.

62. Kristian Buchna, *Ein klerikales Jahrzehnt?*, 217.

63. Clemens Vollnhalls, "Das Reichskonkordat von 1933 als Konfliktfall im Allierten Kontrollrat," in *Vierteljahrshefte für Zeitgeschichte* (1987), 677–706.

64. "Bericht Virrions über sein Gespräch mit Gröber, 8 August 1946," in: Ulrich Helbach, ed., *Akten deutscher Bischöfe seit 1945, Westliche Besatzungszonen, 1945–1947, I*, 663–669.

65. CUA, NL Muench, Box 43, Folder 22, Muench to Hochwürdigste Exzellenz, September 19, 1947. It is not clear to which of the bishops this was sent.

66. On Keller, see Heinz Hürten, "Michael Keller (1896–1961)," in: Jürgen Aretz/Rudolf Morsey/Anton Rauscher, ed., *Zeitgeschichte in Lebensbildern. Aus dem deutschen Katholizismus des 19. und 20. Jahrhunderts, Band 4* (Mainz: Matthias-Grünewald Verlag, 1980), 208–224; Wilhelm Damberg, *Abschied vom Milieu?*, 73–106.

67. HAEK, CR II, 16.10.4, Wilhelm Böhler, Bericht über die Verhandlungen, die am Dienstag, den 14. Dezember zwischen Vertretern der Kirchen des des Parlamentarischen Rates stattfanden, December 17, 1948, 7.

68. HAEK, CR II, 16.10.5, Konrad Adenauer to Josef Frings, February 7, 1949.

69. AEMF, NL Johannes Neuhäusler, N266, Abschrift, Visitator Apostolicus, Kronberg, den January 13, 1949, Nr. 1431/49, C. Rossi to Josef Frings und Wilhelm Böhler.

70. "Bonn und die christlichen Kirchen," in: *Die Zeit*, Nr. 1, January 6, 1949. For an earlier, more neutral position, see: Hermann Höpker-Aschoff, "Das Reichskonkordat," in: *Die Hilfe. Zeitschrift für Politik, Wirtschaft und geistige Bewegung 39*, Nr. 14, 1933, 396–400.

71. ADL, NL Thomas Dehler, N1–3086, Dehler befürwortet neuen Konkordatsabschluss (fdk), no date, but probably 1956. Dehler cited Höpker – Aschoff's speech from 1948 in this address, which was summarized through the wire service, FDK. For an account of the Hauptausschuss des Parlamentarischen Rates, see Michael Feldkamp, ed., *Der Parlamentarischer Rat, 1948–1949: Hauptausschuß: 14* (München: Oldenbourg Wissenschaftsverlag, 2010).

72. On education in Hesse, see James F. Tent, *Mission on the Rhine: Reeducation and Denazification in American-Occupied Germany* (Chicago: University of Chicago Press, 1982), 167.

73. There is still no biography of Zinn. The closest is a catalogue for an exhibition on Zinn put together by the main Hessian State Archives. See "Georg August Zinn – Ministerpräsident, 1950–1969. Katalog zur Ausstellung des Hessischen Hauptstaatsarchivs im Auftrag der Hessischen Landesregierung," 2001.

74. On Arndt, see Dieter Gosewinkel, *Adolf Arndt: Die Widerbegründung des Rechtstaats aus dem Geist der Sozialdemokratie (1945–1961)* (Bonn: Dietz Verlag, 1991).

75. Specifically, he was referring to Articles 137, 138, 139 and 141. For the text of his report, see AEMF, NL Johannes Neuhäusler, N266, Dr. Jenuschat, Parlamentarischer Rat, Hauptausschuss, 46 Sitzung, Donnerstag, den 20. Januar 1949, 10 Uhr, Auszug; BAK B136/5845, Fiche 8, Abschrift, Parlamentarischer Rat, Hauptausschuss, 46. Sitzung, Donnerstag, den 20. Januar, 1949, 10 Uhr.

76. Ibid.
77. HHSTA, 502-6288, "Das Reichskonkordat. Von Dr. theol. Dr. rer. pol. Paul Jungblut, Hinterzarten/Schwarw" (no date); HAEK, Bestand Katholisches Büro I, #81, Staat und Reichskonkordat, Wilhelm Böhler to Konrad Adenauer, January 21, 1949.
78. This was the phrase used by the CDU-protocoller. Sitzungsprotokoll vom January 20, 1949, 12 Uhr, in: Rainer Salzmann, ed, *Die CDU/CSU im Parlamentarischen Rat. Sitzungsprotokolle der Unionsfraktion* (Stuttgart, Klett-Cotta Verlag, 1981), 349; BAK, B122/2182.Fiche 2, Abschrift, Anlage 2, Zinn to die Redaktion der "Ruhr-Nachrichten," Dortmund, April 1, 1949. On the Catholic response, see Norbert Trippen, *Josef Kardinal Frings (1887–1978), Bd. I: Sein Wirken für das Erzbistum und für die Kirche in Deutschland* (Paderborn: Schöningh Verlag, 2003), 373; Christoph von Hehl, *Adolf Süsterhenn*, 409.
79. HAEK, CR II, 16.10.5, Fritz Stricker, Die Niederlage von Bonn! Münster, March 12, 1949; Parlamentarischer Rat, Hauptauschuß, Bonn 1948/49, 46. Sitzung, Donnerstag, den January 20, 1949, 501.
80. HHSTA, 502–6288, Newspaper Clipping, "Scharfe Kritik an der Katholischen Kirche. Justizminister Zinn zum Reichskonkordat. Gegen 'Privilegien' der Kirchen," in: *Süddeutsche Zeitung*, January 22, 1949; "'Mißdeutung des Reichskonkordates': Das Erzbischöfliche Ordinariat München erwidert auf die Bonner Kritik," in: *Süddeutsche Zeitung*, January 25, 1949; HHSTA, 502, 6288, Rede von G. A. Zinn, January 28, 1949; Wilhelm Karl Gerst, "Reichskonkordat und Kriegsächtung. Kann das "totalitäre Reichskonkordat bestehenbleiben?" This typed manuscript was likely printed in the *Frankfurter Rundschau*.
81. Johannes Meerfeld, "Die streitende Kirche," in: *Rheinische Zeitung (Bonn Stadt)*, February 23, 1949; Wilhelm Böhler, "Die streitende Kirche" in: *KND* 50, 25 February 1949; Wilhelm Böhler, "Die streitende Kirche," in: *KND* 64, March 18, 1949; Johannes Meerfeld, "Schlußwort einer Fehde," in: *Rheinische Zeitung (Bonn Stadt)*, April 23, 1949; Kristian Buchna, *Ein klerikales Jahrzehnt?*, 173–174.
82. HAEK, Gen II 22.13, 10, Gustav Kafka to Joseph Teusch, March 11, 1960.
83. This was Georg Smolka, who between 1959–1969 was Professor an der Hochschule für Verwaltungswissenschaften in Speyer. KAS, NL Heinrich Krone, 028–014/1, Heinrich Krone to Johannes Schauff, September 22, 1952.
84. Rudolf Morsey, "Gründung und Gründer der Kommission für Zeitgeschichte, 1960–1962," in: *Historisches Jahrbuch* 115 (1995), 458–459; DAB, I/4–20a, Kirche und Staat, Generalvikar Puchowski to Heinrich Krone, May 20, 1954.
85. See also Burkhard van Schewick, *Die Katholische Kirche und die Entstehung der Verfassungen in Westdeutschland*, 118–127.
86. On Adenauer's skepticism of natural law, see Christoph von Hehl, *Adolf Süsterhenn*, 410. See also LHA, 700, 177, Nr. 478. On how the bishops came around to Adenauer's strategy, see Burkhard van Schewick, *Die Katholische Kirche und die Entstehung der Verfassungen in Westdeutschland*, 119–120; Ludwig Volk, "Der Heilige Stuhl und Deutschland, 1945–1949,"

in: Dieter Albrecht, ed., *Katholische Kirche und Nationalsozialismus. Ausgewählte Aufsätze* (Mainz: Grünewald Verlag, 1987), 144–174.

87. HAEK, CR II, 16.10.5, Konrad Adenauer to Josef Frings, February 7, 1949. Tellingly, Adenauer failed to note that an exception known as the Bremer Klausel was being granted to the state of Bremen in apparent violation of the Reichskonkordat.

88. Behind this effort were Böhler and Süsterhenn. See Konrad Repgen, "Der Konkordatsstreit der fünfziger Jahre," 218–220.

89. On the origins of Article 123, see Alexander Hollerbach, "Zur Entstehungsgeschichte des staatskirchenrechtlichen Artikel des Grundgesetzes," in: Dieter Blumenwitz, ed., *Konrad Adenauer und seine Zeit: Politik und Persönlichkeit des ersten Bundeskanzlers* (Stuttgart: Deutsche Verlags-Anstalt, 1976), 367–382.

90. "Geheime Freuden," in: *Der Spiegel*, June 13, 1956.

91. This is the official translation of the Basic Law. https://www.btg-bestellservice.de/pdf/80201000.pdf. For an example of subsequent confusion, see HAEK, Bestand Katholisches Büro Bonn I, #108, Stellungnahmen zum Reichskonkordat, Prof. Dr. jur. Küchenhoff to Adolf Süsterhenn, March 10, 1949.

92. "Das Gutachten von Profesor Dr. Walter Schätzel (Bonn): Transformation, Partnerschaft und sonstige Probleme des Reichskonkordats von 1933," in: Friedrich Giese and Friedrich August Frhr. v.d. Heydte, *Der Konkordatsprozeß, III Teilband* (München: Isar Verlag, 1958), 1094–1123.

93. Ibid., 1108.

94. Konrad Repgen, "Der Konkordatsstreit der fünfziger Jahre," 219.

95. "Bericht Böhlers, Köln, 9 Mai 1949," and "Frings an Adenauer, Köln, 1 Mai 1949," in: Annette Mertens, ed., *Akten deutscher Bischöfe seit 1945. Westliche Besatzungszonen und Gründung der Bundesrepublik Deutschland 1948/1949* (Paderborn: Schöningh Verlag, 2010), 623–632, 612–613. For a description of the final discussion over the Elternrecht in the Parliamentary Council, see Christoph von Hehl, *Adolf Süsterhenn*, 416–418.

96. "Pius XII. an die deutschen Bischöfe," in: *Kirchlicher Anzeiger Köln*, 1949, 195–200.

97. HHSTA, 502–6288, Abschrift, "Papst Pius XII. zum Bonner Grundgesetz," in: *Allgemeine Kölnische Rundschau*, May 2, 1949.

98. Quoted in Burkhard van Schewick, *Die Katholische Kirche und die Entstehung der Verfassungen in Westdeutschland*, 124.

99. "Erklärung und Hirtenwort der Bischöfe zum Grundgesetz, 23 May 1949," in: Annette Mertens, *Akten deutscher Bischöfe*, 657–671 and, in particular, 668. For an account of this pastoral letter's origins, see Norbert Trippen, *Josef Kardinal Frings (1887–1978)*, Bd. I, 382–384.

100. "Erklärung und Hirtenwort der Bischöfe zum Grundgesetz, 23 May 1949," in: Annette Mertens, *Akten deutscher Bischöfe*, 657–671 and, in particular, 667.

101. "Die Beitrittserklärung von Bremen vom 25. Juni 1955," in: Friedrich Giese and Friedrich August Frhr. v.d. Heydte, ed., *Der Konkordatsprozess. 1. Teilband*, 125–126.

102. Norbert Frei, *Vergangenheitspolitik: Die Anfänge der Bundesrepublik und die NS-Vergangenheit* (Munich: Beck Verlag, 1996), 24–25; Udo Wengst, *Thomas Dehler (1897–1967): Eine politische Biographie* (Munich: R. Oldenbourg Verlag, 1997), 56–75.

103. ADL, NL Thomas Dehler, N1–41, Rede des Landesvorsitzenden der FDP, Dr. Dehler in Bayreuth, am July 11, 1949.

104. Hans-Joachim Dörger, *Religion als Thema in Spiegel, Zeit und Stern* (Hamburg: Furche Verlag, 1973), 74.

105. BAK, B122/2182.Fiche 2, Abschrift, Anlage 2, Zinn to the Redaktion der "Ruhr-Nachrichten," Dortmund, April 1, 1949.

106. "Briefe an 'die Zeit,' Antwort an Höpker-Aschoff," in: *Die Zeit*, January 20, 1949, 12; "Dr. Dehler erlaubt sich Angriffe gegen die Kirche," in: *St. Heinrichsblatt*, 28, July 10, 1949, 4.

107. HHSTA, 502–6288. R., Eig. Bericht, Report of a radio broadcast from Radio Frankfurt, no date but probably on or around March 28, 1949.

108. Rudolf Hars, *Die Bildungsreformpolitik der Christlich-Demokratischen Union in den Jahren 1985 bis 1954: ein Beitrag zum Problem des Konservatismus in der deutschen Bildungspolitik* (Frankfurt am Main: Peter Lang, 1981).

109. Reinhold Maier, *Erinnerungen, 1948–1953* (Tübingen: Rainer Wunderlich Verlag, 1966), 527.

110. See the testimony by Hans Peters and Ekhard Koch in: Friedrich Giese and Friedrich August Frhr. v.d. Heydte, ed., *Der Konkordatsprozeß. 4 Teilband*, 1471–1476, 1505–1509.

111. ASD, NL Karl Bechert, Box 51, Mappe 140, Karl Bechert, Reichskonkordat, June 30, 1955.

112. NLA, NDS 400, ACC 165/94, Nr. 74, Newspaper Clipping, "Eine Bekenntnisschule mit drei Kindern: In Quelle bei Bielefeld gab es Tränen und Proteste," in: *Ostfriesische Rundschau*, May 9, 1955.

113. Twenty-eight percent had only one classroom and one teacher; 24 percent two classrooms and teachers. Peter Lundgreen, *Sozialgeschichte der deutschen Schule*, 43–44.

114. ASD, NL Karl Bechert, Box 51, Mappe 137, Speech by Dr. Dahlem (no date).

115. ASD, NL Karl Bechert, Box 51, Mappe 132, Niederschrift über die Gründungsversammlung der Vereinigung zur Erhaltung und Förderung der Christlichen Simultanschulen in Rheinland-Pfalz am 19.6. 1954 in Mainz, Gaststätte Neubrunnenhof; Newspaper Clipping, "Für Zusammenleben der Konfessionen: Eine Vereinigung zur Erhaltung der Simultanschulen gegründet," in: *Allgemeine Zeitung, Ingelheimer Ausgabe*, June 21, 1954; Newspaper Clipping, "Menschenwürde in Gefahr! 'Die Furcht geht um in Rheinland-Pfalz': Neue Beweise der intoleranten, unchristlichen und gegen das Grundgesetz verstößenden Schulpolitik des rheinland-pfälzischen Kultusministeriums," in: *Die Freiheit*, November 2, 1954; ASD, NL Karl Bechert, Box 51, Mappe 131, Karl Bechert to Herrn Lehrer Sarg, Gau-Algesheim, April 16, 1953; Box 54, Mappe 140, "Ich sage nein zum Reichskonkordat," in: *Blatt 2 der Lehrer-Korrespondenz* Nr. 13 (no date, but most likely July 1955).

116. ASD, NL Karl Bechert, Box 51, Mappe 132, Niederschrift über die Gründungsversammlung der Vereinigung zur Erhaltung und Förderung der Christlichen Simultanschulen in Rheinland-Pfalz am 19.6. 1954 in Mainz, Gaststätte Neubrunnenhof.

117. Frank Bösch, *Die Adenauer-CDU: Gründung, Aufstieg und Krise einer Erfolgspartei, 1945–1969* (Stuttgart: Deutsche Verlagsanstalt, 2001), 132.

118. ASD, NL Karl Bechert, Box 51, Mappe 131, Abschrift aus "Die Freiheit," Mainz, 13. Mai 1953, "Pfarrer aus dem Zimmer gewiesen. Kein Raum für den evangelischen Religionsunterricht in der katholischen Konfessionsschule Drais."

119. ASD, NL Karl Bechert, Box 51, Mappe 137, Gebetbuch und Gesangbuch für das Bistum Speyer, "Die Beichte des Erwachsenen, Pflichten der Eltern," 69; Box 51, Mappe 132, Niederschrift über die Gründungsversammlung der Vereinigung zur Erhaltung und Förderung der Christlichen Simultanschulen in Rheinland-Pfalz am 19.6. 1954 in Mainz, Gaststätte Neubrunnenhof.

120. ASD, NL Karl Bechert, Box 51, Mappe 133, Rede in Mainz am 26.4.1955, "Kulturpolitik noch unduldsamer?"

121. HAEK, CR II 2.19, 43, Josef Frings, Entwurf für die Mitglieder der Fuldaer Bischfskonferenz, Einiges zur Situation der katholischen Kirche in Deutschland Herbst 1953 bis Sommer 1954; Norbert Trippen, "Interkonfessionelle Irritationen in den ersten Jahren der Bundesrepublik Deutschland," in Karl Dietrich Bracher, Paul Mikat, Konrad Repgen, Martin Schumacher and Hans-Peter Schwarz, ed., *Staat und Parteien: Festschrift für Rudolf Morsey zum 65. Geburtstag* (Berlin: Duncker & Humblot, 1992), 345–378; Kristian Buchna, *Ein klerikales Jahrzehnt?*, 348–368 and, especially, 367–368.

122. Frank Bösch, *Die Adenauer-CDU*, 132.

123. ASD, NL Karl Bechert, Box 51, Mappe 132, Newspaper Clipping, "Konfessionalisierung der Universitäten und der Höheren Schulen bleibt das Ziel!," in: *Die Freiheit*, Mainz, November 19, 1954; "Konfessionalisierung soll weitergehen: Regierungsdirektor von den Driesch wies auf die höheren Schulen hin," in: *Ingelheimer Zeitung*, November 18, 1954; "Konfessionstrennung auch auf dem Friedhof? Ein bedenklicher Vorgang in Unterfranken," in: *Die Freiheit*, Mainz, December 8, 1954.

124. "Konfessionsstreit: Aus einem Napf," in: *Der Spiegel*, 29, July 15, 1953.

125. ASD, NL Karl Bechert, Box 51, Mappe 137, Speech by Dr. Dahlem (no date).

126. ASD, NL Karl Bechert, Box 51, Mappe 132, Evangelischer Bund, Konfessionskundliches Institut, Konfessionskundliche Mitteilungen 1/1954, Inhalt: Toleranz in Italien, Das Marianische Jahr, Bensheim, February 18, 1954; HHSTA, 502–6272, Entschliessung des Pfarrer-Konvents in Ingelheim am April 29, 1955.

127. HHSTA, 502–6279, Lilje as quoted in Matthäus Ziegler, "Gültigkeit und Zweckmäßigkeit des Reichskonkordates," in: *Stimme der Gemeinde zum kirchlichen Leben, zur Politik, Wirtschaft und Kultur, Sonderheft*, March 1956, 1. For others' fears of Catholic "theocracy" see NHSA, NDS 400, ACC 165/ 94, Nr. 57, Abschrift, Evangelischer Bund, Konfessionskundliches Institut

Bensheim, *Konfessionskundliche Mitteilungen*, 3/1956 and, in particular, the article by Pfarrer D. Sucker, "Evangelisches Interesse am Reichskonkordat," May 15, 1956.

128. NHSA, VVP 10 (Dep.), Nr. 125II, Ulrich Scheuner to Ministerialrat Dr. Konrad Müller, April 25, 1955. Ironically, Scheuner was one of the authors of the expert opinions submitted on behalf of the government, even though he apparently concurred in the decisions made by the EKD to give no support to the government's position.

129. "Das Gesetz über das öffentliche Schulwesen in Niedersachsen vom 14. September 1954," in: Friedrich Giese and Friedrich August Frhr. v.d. Heydte, ed., *Der Konkordatsprozess. 1. Teilband*, 13.

130. For an overview of many of Staatsekretär Dr. Bojunga's actions pertaining to the fight over the schools and the Reichskonkordat, see the extensive collections of documents in NSLA, Hannover, NDS.400, ACC 165/94, Nr. 74, 75.

131. Frank Bösch, *Die Adenauer-CDU*, 133; HAEK, Bestand Katholisches Büro I, #108, Stellungnahmen zum Reichskonkordat, Dr. Günter Schultz, Hamburg, in: *MDR* Heft 7 (1956), 398.

132. Wilhelm Damberg, *Der Kampf um die Schulen in Westfalen*, 230–231; "NS-Schulen?," in: *Die Zeit*, February 11, 1954.

133. BAK, B141, 6447, Newspaper Clipping, Adolf Süsterhenn, "Reichskonkordat und Elternrecht: Das niedersächsische Schulgesetz entfesselt den Kulturkampf," in: *Rheinischer Merkur*, December 3, 1954; NSLA, NDS.400, ACC 165/94, Nr. 79, Newspaper Clipping, *Oldenburger Volkszeitung*, December 4, 1954.

134. NSLA, NDS, ACC 165/94, Nr. 76, Abschrift, Wilhelm Berning, Joseph Machens, Michael Keller and Lorenz Jaeger to Hinrich Kopf, February 7, 1954.

135. HAEK, Bestand Katholisches Büro I (Amtzeit Böhler), #109, Walter Kampe to Wilhelm Böhler, 20 April 1956; Wihelm Böhler to Walter Kampe, April 23, 1956.

136. NSLA, VVP 10 (DEP), Nr 125 II, D. Hermann Diem to Landesbischof D. Haug, May 21, 1956; NSLA, VVP 10 (DEP), Nr. 128 I, Vertrauliche Besprechung über den Verfassungsstreit zum Reichskonkordat zwischen der Bundesregierung und den Landesregierungen von Niedersachsen, Hessen und Bremen, no date, but the meeting took place on November 15, 1955. Attending were Präsident D. Brunotte, Oberkirchenrat Ranke, Oberkirchenrat Dr. Dr. Niemeier, Frau Oberkirchenrätin Dr. Schwarzhaupt, MdB, Pfarrer D. Dr. Sucker, Prof. Dr. Scheuner, Ministerialdirektor Osterloh, Ministerialrat Dr. Konrad Müller.

137. Konrad Repgen provided a different interpretation: Adenauer's steps were not reluctant but deliberate. Konrad Repgen, "Der Konkordatsstreit der fünfziger Jahre," 240–243.

138. Frank Bösch, *Die Adenauer-CDU*, 132–138.

139. BAK, B141, 6447, Konrad Adenauer to Hinrich Wilhelm Kopf, March 5, 1954; Aloisius Muench to Konrad Adenauer, February 17, 1954; Alfons Kupper, "Um die Probleme des Reichskonkordats," in:

Bernhard Bergmann and Josef Steinberg, ed., *In Memoriam Wilhelm Böhler*, 94.

140. On the petition by the Katholische Elternschaft Niedersachsens, see Konrad Repgen, "Der Konkordatsstreit der fünfziger Jahre," 240.

141. For the early history of the "Katholisches Büro," see Kristian Buchna, *Ein klerikales Jahrzehnt?*, 315–347.

142. HAEK, Bestand Katholisches Büro Bonn I, #108 Stellungnahmen zum Reichskonkordat, Wilhelm Böhler to Joseph Kaiser, May 11, 1949; Bestand Katholisches Büro Bonn I, #81 Staat und Reichskonkordat, "Bedürfen Länderkonkordate der Zustimmung der Bundesregierung? Rechtsgutachten erstattet von Dr. jur. Joseph H. Kaiser, Lehrbrauftragter an der Universität Tübingen," May 16, 1949; Bestand Katholisches Büro Bonn I, #108 Stellungnahmen zum Reichskonkordat, Wilhelm Böhler to Joseph Kaiser, September 24, 1949; Bestand Katholisches Büro Bonn I, #108 Stellungnahmen zum Reichskonkordat, Abschrift, Joseph Kaiser to Wilhelm Böhler, October 26, 1949; Konrad Repgen, "Der Konkordatsstreit der fünfziger Jahre," 226.

143. Konrad Repgen, "Der Konkordatsstreit der fünfziger Jahre," 238.

144. LHA, 700,177, Nr. 285, Adolf Süsterhenn to Joseph Machens, February 2, 1955; Christoph von Hehl, *Adolf Süsterhenn*, 458–459.

145. For examples of Leibholz's ties to Reichskonkordat critics, see NSLA, VVP 10 (Dep.), Nr. 125H, Gerhard Leibholz to Konrad Müller, April 11, 1957.

146. See the text of an unsent letter to several bishops. HHSA, 502–6265, Georg August Zinn to Albert Stohr, J.B. Dietz (Fulda), Wilhelm Kempf (Limburg), November 1955.

147. Christoph von Hehl, *Adolf Süsterhenn*, 462.

148. HHSA, 502–6265, Georg August Zinn to Albert Stohr, J.B. Dietz (Fulda), Wilhelm Kempf (Limburg), November 1955.

149. "Georg August Zinn – Ministerpräsident, 1950–1969. Katalog zur Ausstellung des Hessischen Hauptstaatsarchivs im Auftrag der Hessischen Landesregierung," 2001, 68.

150. Dieter Gosewinkel, *Adolf Arndt*, 388–390.

151. Adolf Süsterhenn, "Reichskonkordat und Elternrecht: Das niedersächsische Schulgesetz entfesselt den Kulturkampf," in: *Rheinischer Merkur*, December 3, 1954; Adolf Arndt, "Süsterhenn und das Konkordat: Eine Stellungnahme von Dr. Arndt," in: *Neuer Vorwärts*, December 10, 1954; Adolf Arndt, "Reichskonkordat noch Gültig?," in: *Neuer Vorwärts*, Nr. 46, November 19, 1954.

152. NSLA, NDS.400, ACC 165/94, Nr. 74, Friedemann Pitzer to Helmut Bojunga, July 24, 1955.

153. HSTA, 502–6265, Adolf Arndt to Georg August Zinn, February 1, 1956.

154. HSTA, 502–6265, Adolf Arndt to Georg August Zinn, January 21, 1956; Dieter Gosewinkel, *Adolf Arndt*, 483, footnote 217. On the significance of his marriage, see Eckhard Jesse, "Karl Dietrich Bracher (geboren 1922)," in: Eckhard Jesse and Sebastian Liebold, ed., *Deutsche Politikwissenschaftler – Werk und Wirkung* (Baden-Baden: Nomos Verlag, 2014), 143–158. See also Annedore Leber, with the assistance of Willy Brandt and Karl

Dietrich Bracher, ed., *Das Gewissen steht auf. 64 Lebensbilder aus dem deutschen Widerstand 1933–1945* (Berlin: Hase & Koehler, 1954).

155. Ulrike Quadbeck, *Karl Dietrich Bracher und die Anfänge der Bonner Politikwissenschaft* (Baden Baden: Nomos Verlag, 2008), especially 102–106, 122. Bracher had delivered lectures for the Hessische Hochschulwochen für staatswissenschaftlicher Fortbildung in the 1950s. The contact to Zinn undoubtedly arose there.

156. See Werner Conze's ambivalent review of Bracher, in: *Historische Zeitschrift* 183 (1957), 378–382 and his modified assessment in: *Historische Zeitschrift* 187 (1959), 407–408. For the controversy between Conze and Bracher, see Ulrike Quadbeck, *Karl Dietrich Bracher*, 192–202; Horst Möller, "Die Weimarer Republik in der zeitgeschichtlichen Perspektive der Bundesrepublik Deutschland während der fünfziger und frühen sechziger Jahre: Demokratische Tradition und NS-Ursachenforschung," in: Ernst Schulin, ed., *Deutsche Geschichtswissenschaft nach dem Zweiten Weltkrieg (1945–1965)* (München: R. Oldenbourg Verlag, 1989), 157–180 and, in particular, 164–169.

157. Karl Dietrich Bracher, *Die Auflösung der Weimarer Republik: Eine Studie zum Problem des Machtverfalls in der Demokratie* (Stuttgart: Ring Verlag, 1955).

158. HHSTA, 502–6273, Barwinski to die Abteilung III im Hause, May 5, 1956; Karl Dietrich Bracher to Barwinski, June 18, 1956; 502–6278, Hans Schneider to Barwinski (without a date, but probably July 1956).

159. Astrid Eckert, *Kampf um die Akten. Die Westalliierten und die Rückgabe von deutschem Archivgut nach dem Zweiten Weltkrieg* (Stuttgart: Steiner Verlag, 2004).

160. PAAA, B80, 288, Jaenicke to das Auswärtige Amt, Bonn, June 10, 1955; Botschaft der Bundesrepublik Deutschland, London to das Auswärtige Amt, London, June 28, 1955.

161. Auskunfterteilung, Holger Berwinkel, Politisches Archiv des Auswärtigen Amtes to the author, April 9, 2014.

162. BAK, B136/5848, Fiche 10, "Kleine Anfrage zu Reichskonkordatsakten," Bonn (fdk) (no date), Kleine Anfrage 203 der Fraktion der FDP betr. Akten zum Reichskonkordat, Deutscher Bundestag, 2. Wahlperiode, 1953, November 8, 1955; George O. Kent, "The German Foreign Ministry's Archives in Whaddon Hall, 1948–1958," in: *The American Archivist*, 1961 24 (1), 43–54.

163. BAK, B136/5848, Fiche 10, Heinrich von Brentano an den Herrn Präsidenten des Deutschen Bundestages Betr.: Akten zum Reichskonkordat, November 25, 1955.

164. HHSA, 502–6265, Der Vizepräsident des Bundesverfassungsgerichts als Vorsitzender des Zweiten Senats to die Regierung des Landes Hessen vertreten durch den Herrn Ministerpräsidenten, January 25, 1956.

165. Auskunfterteilung, Holger Berwinkel, Politisches Archiv des Auswärtigen Amtes to the author, April 9, 2014.

166. HHSTA, 502–6261, Barwinski to Dr. Wehrhahn, February 16, 1956; Georg August Zinn to Rudolf Laun, February 16, 1956; Barwinski to Adolf Schüle, February 16, 1956.

167. HHSTA, 502–6287a, Barwinski to den Herrn Bundesminister des Innern, March 29, 1956.

168. HHSTA, 502–6261, Barwinski to Adolf Schüle, February 16, 1956; "Der Schriftsatz der hessischen Landesregierung vom 30. April 1956," in: Friedrich Giese and Friedrich August Frhr. v.d. Heydte, ed., *Der Konkordatsprozess. 2. Teilband*, 587; ADL, NL Dehler, N1–3086, Prof. Dr. Karl Bechert to Thomas Dehler.

169. HHSTA, 502–6261, Georg August Zinn to Rudolf Laun, February 16, 1956.

170. "Der Schriftsatz der hessischen Landesregierung vom 30. April 1956," in: Friedrich Giese and Friedrich August Frhr. v.d. Heydte, ed., *Der Konkordatsprozess. 2. Teilband*, 610–614. For articles, see, Hans Henrich, "Hitler auf der Suche nach Anerkennung. Die Tragödie des Reichskonkordats. Wie der Vatikan betrogen wurde," in: *Göttinger Presse*, May 31, 1956; "Gott erhalte unseren Reichskanzler. Die Tragödie des Reichskonkordats. Großer Jubel bei den Bischöfen," in: *Göttinger Presse*, June 1, 1956.

171. "Das Gutachten von Priv-Doz. Dr. Karl Dietrich Bracher (Berlin)," in: Friedrich Giese and Friedrich August Frhr. v.d. Heydte, ed., *Der Konkordatsprozess. 3. Teilband*, 947–992 and, in particular, 969.

172. "Der Schriftsatz der hessischen Landesregierung vom 30. April 1956," in: Friedrich Giese and Friedrich August Frhr. v.d. Heydte, ed., *Der Konkordatsprozess. 2. Teilband*, 609–610; "Das Gutachten von Priv.-Doz Dr. Karl Dietrich Bracher," in: Friedrich Giese and Friedrich August Frhr. v.d. Heydte, ed., *Der Konkordatsprozess. 1. Teilband*, 984–985. For a rebuttal, see "Die wörtliche Niederschrift über die Verhandlung am 4., 5., 6., 7., und 8. Juni 1956 vor dem Bundesverfassungsgericht. 2. Verhandlungtag (5. Juni 1956)," in: Friedrich Giese and Friedrich August Frhr. v.d. Heydte, ed., Der *Konkordatsprozess. 3. Teilband*, 1281.

173. HAEK, Bestand Katholisches Büro I, #109, Allgemeine Korrespondenzen zur Konkordatsfrage; Wilhelm Böhler to Helene Weber; Wilhelm Böhler to Georg Schreiber; Wilhelm Böhler to Franz Graf von Galen; Wilhelm Böhler to Joseph Joos, May 3, 1956.

174. HAEK, Bestand Katholisches Büro Bonn I, #109, Allgemeine Korrespondenzen zur Konkordatsfrage, R. an Deuerlein, May 12, 1956; Christoph von Hehl, *Adolf Süsterhenn*, 462.

175. HAEK, Bestand Katholisches Büro Bonn I, #108 Stellungnahmen zum Reichskonkordat, Herbert Groppe an Westhoff, February 17, 1952, Herbert Groppe to Wilhelm Böhler, March 7, 1952; Herbert Groppe to Wilhelm Böhler, April 24, 1952; Herbert Groppe to Wilhelm Böhler, May 16, 1952; Herbert Groppe to Wilhelm Böhler, May 20, 1952; Herbert Groppe to Wilhelm Böhler, September 3, 1952; Wilhelm Böhler to Walter Kampe, October 5, 1952; Walter Kampe to Wilhelm Böhler, November 20, 1952; Herbert Groppe to Wilhelm Böhler, November 21, 1952.

176. HAEK, Bestand Katholisches Büro Bonn I, #108 Stellungnahmen zum Reichskonkordat, Herbert Groppe to Wilhelm Böhler, December 8, 1952, Anlage.

177. On Deuerlein's temperament, see HAEK, Bestand Katholisches Büro I, #95, Rechtsgutachten zum Reichskonkordat, Josef Held to Wilhelm Böhler, October 25, 1955.

178. HAEK, Kath. Büro Bonn I, #93, Ernst Deuerlein, "Das Reichskonkordat – eine Hitleridee? Der Vertrag mit dem Heiligen Stuhl war schon ein Ziel der Weimarer Republik," in: *Rheinischer Merkur*, July 17, 1953.

179. Ernst Deuerlein, *Das Reichskonkordat* (Düsseldorf: Patmos Verlag, 1956).

180. Böhler reiterated this argument after the decision by the court had been released. See Wilhelm Böhler, "Zur Karlsruher Entscheidung über das Reichskonkordat," in: *Echo der Zeit*, April 7, 1957, 7.

181. HAEK, Bestand Katholisches Büro Bonn I, #95, Rechtsgutachten zum Reichskonkordat, Ernst Deuerlein to Adolf Süsterhenn, March 31, 1956.

182. HAEK, Gen II 3.3a, 45, Katholisches Büro Bonn, Tätigkeitsbericht für das Jahr 1955/1956, erstattet für die Fuldaer Bischofskonferenz 1956, September 1956.

183. HAEK, Bestand Katholisches Büro I, #109 Allgemeine Korrespondenzen zur Konkordatsfrage, Alfons Kupper to Wilhelm Böhler, January 5, 1956; R. (Böhler's secretary) to Ernst Deuerlein, January 5, 1956.

184. BSB, NL Ernst Deuerlein, Ana 463.I, 1, Morsey, Rudolf, Ernst Deuerlein to Rudolf Morsey, November 20, 1955.

185. This was a point made by Rudolf Morsey in his review in: *Theologische Revue* 53 (1957), 19–23; Rudolf Morsey, "Gründung und Gründer der Kommission für Zeitgeschichte," 453–485 and, in particular, 455, footnote 10. I; Interview with Rudolf Morsey, June 9, 2016; Rudolf Morsey's private archive contains an original copy of Deuterlein's book, one not turned to pulp.

186. BSB, NL Deuerlein, Ana 463.1.1 Rudolf Morsey, Ernst Deuerlein to Rudolf Morsey, May 30, 1956.

187. HAEK, Bestand Katholisches Büro Bonn I, #90, Rechtsgutachten zum Reichskonkordat, Konkordatstagung in Honnef, 12–14 April 1956. For Böhler's request to the Franciscan sisters, see HAEK, Katholisches Büro I, #126, Schwester Ms. Aloysa, Generalsekretärin to Wilhelm Böhler, June 19, 1956.

188. Alfons Kupper, "Um die Probleme des Reichskonkordats," 96.

189. For discussions of the "linkage argument," see Friedrich Stampfer, "Zur Vorgeschichte des Konkordats: Die Zustimmung des Zentrums zum Ermächtigungsesetz erschwindelt," in: *Badische Allgemeine Zeitung*, April 12, 1956; K.A., "Wie das Konkordat zustande kam: Die Auflösung des Zentrums 1933 und der Weg zum Einparteien-Staat," in: *Deutsche Zeitung*, May 19, 1956; Hans Henrich, "Adolf Hitler auf der Suche nach Anerkennung: Die Tragödie des Reichskonkordats. Wie das Dritte Reich den Vatikan betrog," in: *Frankfurter Rundschau*, May 12–13, 1956.

190. HAEK, Bestand Katholisches Büro I (Amtszeit Böhler), #109, Allgemeine Korrespondenzen zur Konkordatsfrage, Walter Kampe to Wilhelm Böhler, April 20, 1956.

191. ASD, NL Karl Bechert, Box 54, Mappe 141, Newspaper Clipping, "Konkordat war Hitlers Waffe gegen Juden. Hessen: Reichskonkordat

kann in Bundesrepublik nicht aufrechterhalten werden," in: *Hessische Zeitung*, May 7, 1956.

192. On publication plans: BSB, NL Ernst Deuerlein, Ana 463, I, I, Böhler, Wilhelm, Ernst Deuerlein to Wilhelm Böhler, November 23, 1955; Ernst Deuerlein to Wilhelm Böhler, May 28, 1956; HAEK, Bestand Katholisches Büro I, #95, Rechtsgutachten zum Reichskonkordat, Ernst Deuerlein to Wilhelm Böhler, March 20, 1956. For publications, see Herbert Groppe, *Das Reichskonkordat vom 20. Juli 1933: Eine Studie zur staats- und völkerrechtlichen Bedeutung dieses Vertrages für die Bundesrepubik Deutschland* (Köln: Verlag J.P. Bachem, 1956).

193. HAEK, Bestand Katholisches Büro Bonn I, #95, Rechtsgutachten zum Reichkskonkordat, Forschbach, Presse-und Informationsamt der Bundesregierung to Adolf Süsterhenn, March 29, 1956.

194. HAEK, Bestand Katholisches Büro Bonn I, #94 Rechtsgutachten zum Reichskonkordat, R. an Herrn Pribil, Verlag Schwann, Düsseldorf, May 26, 1956; HAEK, Bestand Katholisches Büro Bonn, I, #95, Rechtsgutachten zum Reichskonkordat, Wilhelm Böhler to Alfons Kupper, May 24, 1956.

195. CUA, NL Muench 37, Box 59, Folder 8, KNA Sonderbeilage, Überblick über die Geschichte des Reichskonkordats vom July 20, 1933, May 1958; BSB, NL Deuerlein, Ana 463., I, i, Böhler, Wilhelm, Ernst Deuerlein to Wilhelm Böhler, May 28, 1956.

196. Dieter Gosewinkel, *Adolf Arndt*, 482.

197. IFZG, ED 94–305–75, Deutscher Bundestag, 2. Wahlperiode, 1953, Drucksache 2258, Große Anfrage der Abgeordneten Melles, Dr. Reif, Petersen und Genossen betr. Verfassungsklage wegen des Reichskonkordats, March 23, 1956.

198. 2. Deutscher Bundestag – 146 Sitzung, Bonn, Mitwoch, den 30. May 1956, 7758.

199. Ibid., 7752. Cilien's musings on the Reichskonkordat were made possible by materials provided to him in great haste by Böhler and his team from the Katholisches Büro. HAEK, Gen II 3.3a, 45, Katholisches Büro Bonn, Tätigkeitsbericht für das Jahr 1955/1956, erstattet für die Fuldaer Bischofskonferenz 1956, September 1956.

200. 2. Deutscher Bundestag – 146 Sitzung, Bonn, Mitwwoch, den May 30, 1956, 7766.

201. Ibid., 7761.

202. PAAA, B130, Nr. 4700A, Abschrift, Hans Berger, Aufzeichnung Betr: Äußerungen Dr. Dehlers zum Reichskonkordat, April 30, 1955.

203. Frank Bösch, *Die Adenauer-CDU*, 174–194; Udo Wengst, *Thomas Dehler*, 279–291.

204. The accounts of Dehler's speech vary since he delivered it partially extemporaneously and it was repeatedly interrupted by applause, laughter and cries. For different accounts, see ADL, NL Dehler, N1–3086, Auszug aus der Hamburger Rede Dr. Dehlers, gehalten am March 4, 1956; ADL, NL Dehler, N1–2598. "Das Unergründliche in Herrn Thomas Dehler: FDP-Chef verteilt Kinnhaken nach allen Seiten," in: *Hamburger Echo*,

March 5, 1956. For additional reactions, see Jürgen Fröhlich, ed., Wolfgang Schollwer, *"Gesamtdeutschland ist uns Verpflichtung": Aufzeichnungen aus dem FDP-Ostbüro 1951–1957* (Bremen: Die deutsche Bibliothek, 2004), 177–178.

205. ADL, NL Dehler, N1–3086, Thomas Dehler to Georg August Zinn, January 18, 1956; Georg August Zinn to Thomas Dehler, January 24, 1956; Barwinski to Thomas Dehler, February 7, 1956. In this correspondence, Zinn and Dehler addressed each other with their first names and with the familiar form. For his these quotations, see ADL, NL Thomas Dehler, N1–2598, "'Ich gebe keine Antwort': Dehler besteht auf Verdächtigungen des Vatikans und Reichskonkordats," in: *Kirchenzeitung für das Erzbistum Köln*, March 11, 1956.

206. "Scharfe Attacke Dehlers gegen den Bundeskanzler: Rede im überfüllten Curiohaus," in: *Hamburger Abendblatt*, March 5, 1956; "Wieder scharfe Angriffe Dehlers. Rede auf dem Parteitag in Hamburg. 'Verbrecherisches Konkordat,'" in: *Frankfurter Allgemeine Zeitung*, March 5, 1956; "Ehrenbürger Dehler: Von Thomas und Caesar," in: *Der Spiegel*, March 21, 1956; Udo Wengst, *Thomas Dehler*, 7.

207. HAEK, Bestand Katholisches Büro I, #107, Presseberichte zu Thomas Dehler, Bundesjustizminister, bzgl. des Reichskonkordat, (no name or date but underneath, 7 März, Papstfeier der deutschen Gemeinde in Rom).

208. "Werkvolk-Präses rettet Dehler-Versammlung: Bayern protestieren auf ihre Art gegen Beleidigung der Katholiken – Msgr. Maier als 'Salomon,'" in: *Echo der Zeit*, March 11, 1956; "Dehler in München ausgepfiffen: Tumulte um eine Wahlrede – Katholischer Geistlicher rettet Versammlung," in: *Bonner Rundschau*, March 13, 1956; "Schwerer Tumult um Dehler: Politische Gegner schrien den FDP-Vorsitzenden nieder," in: *Die Welt*, March 13, 1956; "In München bekam Dehler eine Quitting," in: *Deutsche Tagespost*, March 16–17, 1956. For one super-charged letter, see ADL, NL Thomas Dehler, N1 – 1556, Päpstlicher Hausprälat Karl Nissl to Thomas Dehler, March 11, 1956.

209. "Reichskonkordat: Geheime Freuden," in: *Der Spiegel*, June 13, 1956.

210. *Der Spiegel* wrote: "Am 30. April 1920 überreichte Diego von Bergen, bis dahin preußischer Gesandter beim Vatikan, dem Papst sein Beglaubigungsschreiben als Botschafter des Deutschen Reiches." Deuerlein had written: "Am 30. April überreichte der erste Botschafter des Deutschen Reiches beim Hl. Stuhl, Diego von Bergen, sein Beglaubigungsschreiben." CUA, NL Muench, Box 59, Folder 8, Mai 1956, KNA-Sonderbeilage Reichskonkordat, Ernst Deuerlein, Überblick über die Geschichte des Reichskonkordats vom 20. Juli 1933.

211. HHSTA, 504–7559b, Newspaper Clipping, No author, "Ein unsichtbarer Angeklagter: Der Rechtsstreit um die Gültigkeit des Konkordats," in: *Deutsche Zeitung*, June 9, 1956.

212. ASD, NL Karl Bechert, Mappe 141, Karl Bechert to Barwinski, June 19, 1956.

213. HHSTA, 502–6283, Barwinski, Bericht über den Konkordatsstreit, March 30, 1957.
214. BSB, NL Deuerlein, ANA 463, I, I, Böhler, Wilhelm, Ernst Deuerlein to Wilhelm Böhler, April 1, 1957.
215. HHSTA, 502–7559b, Newspaper Clipping, "Prälat Böhler: Konkordat entspricht Weimarer Verfassung," in: *Offenbach Post*, July 26, 1956; HHSTA, 502–6288, Staatskanzlei, Pressestelle, Wiesbaden, Pressenotiz, July 26, 1956; HHSTA 504–7559b, Newspaper Clipping, "Hessische Staatskanzlei: Ansicht Prälat Böhlers in krassem Gegensatz zu Aktenmaterial," in: *Offenbach Post*, July 28, 1956; newspaper clipping, "Hessen lehnt Böhlers Thesen ab: Stellungnahme der Staatskanzlei zur Gültigkeit des Konkordats," in: *Die Welt*, July 28, 1956.
216. Konrad Repgen, "Der Konkordatsstreit der fünfziger Jahre," 205–206.
217. BSB, NL Deuerlein, Ana 463.I, i, Böhler, Wilhelm, Ernst Deuerlein to Wilhelm Böhler, July 14, 1956.
218. On Hennecka's role, see Konrad Regpen, "Bundesverfassungsgerichts-Prozesse als Problem der Zeitgeschichtsforschung," in: Karl Dietrich Bracher, Paul Mikat, Konrad Repgen, Martin Schumacher and Hans-Peter Schwarz, ed., *Staat und Parteien: Festschrift für Rudolf Morsey zum 65. Geburtstag* (Berlin: Duncker & Humblot, 1992), 863–881 and, in particular, 875–876.
219. BSB, NL Deuerlein, Ana 463.I, i, Böhler, Wilhelm, Ernst Deuerlein to Wilhelm Böhler, July 14, 1956.
220. Ibid.
221. BSB, NL Deuerlein, Ana 463.I, i, Böhler, Wilhelm, Ernst Deuerlein to Wilhelm Böhler, October 24, 1956.
222. PAAA, B130, 5445A, Abschrift, Aufzeichnung, Betr: Besuch bei Pro-Staatssekretär Tardini, R. Salat, Rom, den December 12, 1956.
223. PAAA, B130, 5445A, Telegramm, Jaenicke to das Auswärtige Amt in Bonn, December 12, 1956; see also, Abschrift, Aufzeichnung, R. Salat, December 12, 1956.
224. PAAA, B130, 5445A, Proposed letter to Dr. Rudolf Katz, no author or date, but this was clearly written between December 12, 1956 and January 15, 1957.
225. Ibid.
226. PAAA, B130, 5445A, Vermerk, Hans Berger, Abteilung 5, Bonn, den January 16, 1957.
227. CUA Archives, Muench Papers, Box 1, Folder 20, Muench diary entry from March 22, 1957. For another but not entirely accurate account, see Frederic Spotts, *The Churches and Politics in Germany*, 218, footnote.
228. CUA Archives, Muench Papers, Box 1, Folder 20, Muench diary entry from March 26, 1957. For press coverages, see HHSTA, 504–7559b, Newspaper Clipping, "Kulturhoheit der Länder trotz Konkordat. Der Vertrag mit dem Vatikan gültig/Entscheidung des Bundesverfassungsgericht," in: *Frankfurter Allgemeine Zeitung*, March 27, 1957.
229. "Das Urteil des Bundesverfassungsgerichts vom 26. März 1957," in: Friedrich Giese and Friedrich August Frhr. v.d. Heydte, ed., *Der Konkordatsprozeß. 4. Teilband* (München: Isar Verlag, 1958), 1685.

230. Ibid., 1686.
231. Ibid., 1685–1686.
232. Ibid., 1712.
233. HAEK, Bestand Katholisches Büro Bonn, I, #125, Korrespondenz zum Prozess über die Geltung des Reichskonkordats, Böhler to die Redaktionen der Kirchenblätter, March 20, 1957.
234. www.vatican.va/roman_curia/secretariat_state/archivio/documents/rc_seg-st_ 19650226_concordato-sassonia-inf_ge.html (accessed June 15, 2016).
235. Frederic Spotts, *The Churches and Politics in Germany*, 218.
236. For the text of this dissent, see "Abweichende Meinung- gemeinsam mit BVerfR Prof. Friesenhahn und BVerfR Dr. Federer ausgearbeitet – zum Urteil des Bundesverfassungsgericht vom 26. März 1957 in dem Verfassungsrechtstreit zwischen der Bundesregierung und der Landesregierung des Landes Niedersachsen betreffend die Vereinbarkeit des Niedersächsichen Schulgesetzes mit dem Reichskonkordat – 2 BvG 1/ 55," in Willi Geiger, ed., *Abweichende Meinungen zu Entscheidungen des Bundesverfassungsgerichts* (Tübingen: J.C.B. Mohr Verlag, 1989), 75–112. On this dissent, see Konrad Repgen, "Der Konkordatsstreit der fünfziger Jahre," 203–204.
237. Frederic Spotts, *The Churches and Politics in Germany*, 218. Though Spotts did not indicate his sources, this information presumably came from the individuals he interviewed for his book.
238. CUA Archives, Muench Papers, Box 1, Folder 20, Muench diary entry from March 30, 1957.
239. For an indirect reference to this, see NSLA, VVP 10 (Dep.= Nr. 125H, Gerhard Leibholz to Konrad Müller, April 11, 1957.
240. The dissent was finally published in 1979. Ernst Friesenhan, "Zur völkerrechtlichen und innerstaatlichen Geltung des Reichskonkordats," in: Gerd Kleinheyer and Paul Mikat, ed., *Beiträge zur Rechtsgeschichte. Gedächtnisschrift für Hermann Conrad* (Paderborn: Schöningh, 1979), 151–180.
241. Klaus Scholder, *Die Kirchen und das Dritte Reich, Band 1: Vorgeschichte und Zeit der Illusionen 1918–1934* (Frankfurt a.M.: Propyläen/Ullstein 1977), *Band 2: Das Jahr der Ernüchterung 1934. Barmen und Rom* (Berlin: Siedler, 1985).
242. William Patch, *Heinrich Brüning and the Dissolution of the Weimar Republic* (New York: Cambridge University Press, 2006); Robert Ventresca, *Soldier of Christ*, 79.

3 Generation Gaps and the Böckenförde Controversy

1. This was the phrase used by Konrad Repgen, as quoted in: Ernst-Wolfgang Böckenförde, *Der deutsche Katholizismus im Jahre 1933. Kirche und demokratisches Ethos. Mit einem historiographischen Rückblick v. Karl-Egon Lönne* (Freiburg: Herder, 1988), 14.
2. Ernst-Wolfgang Böckenförde, "Der deutsche Katholizismus im Jahre 1933. Eine kritische Betrachtung," in: *Hochland* 53 (1961), 215–239.

3. Ibid. These incriminating quotations came from Franz von Papen, Ildefons Herwegen, Conrad Gröber, Adolph Bertram, Joseph Lortz, Karl zu Löwenstein, Michael von Faulhaber and Clemens August Graf von Galen.

4. "Drittes Reich: Führers Prälaten," in: *Der Spiegel*, May 24, 1961.

5. Ernst-Wolfgang Böckenförde, *Der deutsche Katholizismus im Jahre 1933. Kirche und demokratisches Ethos*, 9–10. On the generation of 1945, see A. Dirk Moses, "The Forty-Fivers: A Generation between Fascism and Democracy," in: *German Politics and Society* 17 (1999), 105–127; A. Dirk Moses, *German Intellectuals and the Nazi Past* (New York: Cambridge University Press, 2007), especially 55–73; Franz-Werner Kersting, Jürgen Reulecke and Hans-Ulrich Thamer, "Aufbrüche und Umbrüche: Die zweite Gründung des Bundesrepublik 1955–1975. Eine Einführung," in: Franz-Werner Kersting, Jürgen Reulecke and Hans-Ulrich Thamer, ed., *Die zweite Gründung der Bundesrepublik. Generationswechsel und intellektuelle Wortergreifungen 1955–1975* (Stuttgart: Franz Steiner, 2010), 7–18.

6. Gebriele Rosenthal, *Die Hitler-Jugend Generation: Biographische Thematisierung als Vergangenheitsbewältigung* (Essen: Die blaue Eule, 1986), 97–99.

7. HAEK, Bestand Katholisches Büro I, #108, Freiherr von der Heydte to Wilhelm Böhler, June 2, 1956.

8. Ibid. On von der Heydte, see "Friedrich August Freiherr von der Heydte: ein katholischer Adeliger im "Reich" – ein Wehrmachtsgeneral im 'Großraum,'" in: Vanessa Conze, ed., *Das Europa der Deutschen. Ideen von Europa in Deutschland zwischen Reichstradition und Westorientierung (1920–1970)* (München: Oldenbourg-Verlag, 2005). The other editor was Friedrich Giese, a law professor and liberal Protestant. Giese passed away in 1958, more than a year before the final volume could be published.

9. HAEK, Bestand Katholisches Büro I, #108, Stellungnahmen zum Reichskonkordat, Adolf Süsterhenn to Friedrich August Freiherr von der Heydte, November 11, 1955; HAEK, Bestand Katholisches Büro I, #109, Allgemeine Korrespondenzen zur Konkonkordatsfrage, Wilhelm Böhler to Günter Olzog, June 1, 1957; HAEK, CR II, 1.17a, 5, Alfons Kupper to Joseph Teusch, October 8, 1958.

10. "Der Schriftsatz der hessischen Landesregierung vom 30. April 1956," in: Friedrich Giese and Friedrich August Frhr. v.d. Heydte, ed., *Der Konkordatsprozess. 2. Teilband* (München: Isar Verlag, 1957), 609–610; "Das Gutachten von Priv.–Doz Dr. Karl Dietrich Bracher," in: Friedrich Giese and Friedrich August Frhr. v.d. Heydte, ed., *Der Konkordatsprozess. 3. Teilband* (München: Isar Verlag, 1958), 984–985.

11. Friedrich Giese and Friedrich August Frhr. v.d. Heydte, ed., *Der Konkordatsprozess, 4 Teilbände* (Munich: Isar Verlag, 1957–1959).

12. Erich Matthias, "Die Sitzung der Reichstagsfraktion des Zentrums am 23. März 1933," in: *Vierteljahrshefte für Zeitgeschichte* 4 (1956), 302–307.

13. HAEK, Bestand Katholisches Büro I, #95, Rechtsgutachten zum Reichskonkordat, Ernst Deuerlein to Anton Böhm, July 19, 1956. On Matthias's publication, see Rudolf Morsey, "Das Ende der Zentrumspartei 1933: Forschungsverlauf und persönliche Erinnerungen an

die Zusammenarbeit mit Zeitzeugen," in: Thomas Brechenmacher, ed., *Das Reichskonkordat, 1933* (Paderborn: Schöningh Verlag, 2007), 41–45.

14. HAEK, Bestand Katholisches Büro I, #95, Rechtsgutachten zum Reichskonkordat, Ernst Deuerlein to Wilhelm Böhler, September 8, 1956.

15. Karl Dietrich Bracher, Wolfgang Sauer and Gerhard Schulz, *Die nationalsozialistische Machtergreifung: Studien zur Errichtung des totalitären Herrschaftssystems in Deutschland, 1933/34* (Cologne: Westdeutscher Verlag, 1960); Erich Matthias and Rudolf Morsey, ed., *Das Ende der Parteien: 1933* (Düsseldorf: Droste Verlag, 1960).

16. Nicolas Berg, *Der Holocaust und die westdeutschen Historiker: Erforschung und Erinnerung* (Göttingen: Wallstein Verlag, 2003).

17. Rudolf Morsey, "Gründung und Gründer der Kommission für Zeitgeschichte, 1960–1962," in: *Historisches Jahrbuch* 115 (1995), 453–485 and, in particular, 466. See NL Bernhard Stasiewski, KFZG, Rudolf Morsey, Vorschlag für eine Klausurtagung von Historikern und Politikern zum Thema "Kirche und Staat am Ausgang der Weimarer Zeit" (no date).

18. IFZG, München, ED 346/4, NL Johannes Schauff, Heinrich Brüning to Heinrich Krone, November 16, 1960; see also the concluding chapters of William Patch, *Heinrich Brüning and The Dissolution of the Weimar Republic* (New York: Cambridge University Press, 1998); Heinrich Brüning, *Memoiren, 1918–1934* (Stuttgart: DVA, 1970).

19. Papen's reappointment was widely covered in the media. For one example, "Ehrentitel: Katholisches Ärgernis," in: *Der Spiegel* (46), November 11, 1959. *Spiegel's* article (and its title) quoted heavily from an impassioned critique of the reappointment by the Catholic publicist and journalist Otto Roegele: "Ein Ärgernis," in: *Rheinischer Merkur*, Nr. 44, October 30, 1959. See also Oskar Neisinger, "Wegbereiter der Tyrannei: Die deutschen Katholiken haben Franz v. Papens politische Vergangenheit nicht vergessen," in: *Die Allgemeine Sonntagszeitung*, November 8, 1959, 1; HAEK, Gen II 23.23a, 52, Dr. Hugo Poth to Josef Frings, November 3, 1959.

20. Wolfgang Weber, *Priester der Klio. Historisch-sozialwissenschaftliche Studien zur Herkunft und Karriere deutscher Historiker und zur Geschichte der Geschichtswissenschaft, 1800–1970* (Frankfurt am Main: Peter Lang, 1984), 54, 83–93.

21. HAEK, Bestand Katholisches Büro Bonn I, #109, Allgemeine Korrespondenzen zur Konkordatsfrage, Entwurf, Wilhelm Böhler to Georg Schreiber, Münster. This draft was never sent; a final version was sent on July 6, 1957.

22. For examples, see Privatbesitz Rudolf Morsey, Kupper, Denkschrift betreffend Inangriffnahme der wissenschaftlichen Erforschung der Geschichte des Katholizismus in Deutschland zur Zeit der Weimarer Republik und des Dritten Reiches (1918–1945), May 1961.

23. KAB, BI/9, Denkschrift betr. Errichtung eines Instituts zur Erforschung der Geschichte des deutschen Katholizismus im 19. Jahrhundert (Entwurf), no date indicated, but undoubtedly September 12, 1956.

24. KAB, A1/1, Stellungnahme von Dr. Ibach zur Denkschrift Just, Deuerlein, Kupper, September 12, 1956.

25. Oliver Schütz, *Begegnung von Kirche und Welt. Die Gründung Katholischer Akademien in der Bundesrepublik Deutschland 1945–1975* (Paderborn: Schöningh, 2004).

26. KAB, BI/9, Denkschrift betr. Errichtung eines Instituts zur Erforschung der Geschichte des deutschen Katholizismus im 19. Jahrhundert (Entwurf), no date indicated, but undoubtedly September 12, 1956.

27. BAK, NL Hans Peters, N1220, 54, Abschrift, Alfons Kupper to Braubach, Buchheim, Conrad, Just, Schwarz, Deuerlein and Ibach, January 8, 1957. Arbeitsplan für die Besprechung des Arbeitskreises Reichskonkordat am February 22, 1957, in Bonn. Rudolf Morsey to the author, March 4, 2012.

28. Privatbesitz, Rudolf Morsey, Alfons Kupper to Rudolf Morsey, February 6, 1957.

29. See Rudolf Morsey, "Das Ende der Zentrumspartei 1933," 37–39.

30. Georg Schreiber, *Zwischen Demokratie und Diktatur: Persönliche Erinnerungen an die Politik und Kultur des Reiches von 1919 bis 1944* (Münster: Regensberg, 1949); Wilhelm Damberg, "Georg Schreiber und Joseph Lortz in Münster 1933–1950," in: Leonore Siegele-Wenschkewitz and Carsten Nicolaisen, ed., *Theologische Fakultäten im Nationalsozialismus* (Göttingen: Vandenhoeck und Ruprecht, 1993), 145–167; Rudolf Morsey, "Georg Schreiber (1882–1963)," in: Rudolf Morsey, ed., *Zeitgeschichte in Lebensbildern. Band 2* (Münster: Aschendorff Verlag, 2000), 177–185; Robert Krieg, *Catholic Theologians in Nazi Germany* (New York: The Continuum International Publishers Group, 2004), 73–74.

31. Rudolf Morsey, "Das Ende der Zentrumspartei 1933," 38.

32. When discussing the disappearance of democratic substance in the Center Party, for instance, Morsey cautioned that this suggestion could not be depicted in all its details because of still-missing sources about intraparty conflicts. Rudolf Morsey, "Die Deutsche Zentrumspartei," in: Rudolf Morsey and Erich Matthias, ed., *Das Ende der Parteien*, 415.

33. HAEK, Bestand Katholisches Büro Bonn I, #109, Allgemeine Korrespondenzen zur Konkordatsfrage, Abschrift, Rudolf Morsey to Alfons Kupper, June 3, 1956; BSB, NL Deuerlein, Ana 463, I, i., Böhler, Wilhelm, Ernst Deuerlein to Wilhelm Böhler, June 22, 1956.

34. Rudolf Morsey, *Der Untergang des politischen Katholizismzus. Die Zentrumspartei zwischen christlichem Selbstverständnis und "Nationaler Erhebung": 1932/1933* (Stuttgart: Belser Verlag, 1977), 132, 196.

35. Privatbesitz Rudolf Morsey, Report of Morsey, February 22, 1957.

36. Alfons Kupper, "Zur Geschichte des Reichskonkordats: Ein Beitrag zur Geschichte des Verhandlungsablaufs zwischen Ostern 1933 und der Ratifikation des Konkordats," in: *Stimmen der Zeit* 163 (1959), 278–302; Alfons Kupper, "Zur Geschichte des Reichskonkordats: Die Verhandlungsperiode bis zur Unterzeichnung (5.–20. Juli 1933)," in: *Stimmen der Zeit* 163 (1959), 354–375; "Zur Geschichte des Reichskonkordats," in: *Stimmen der Zeit* 171 (1962), 25–50. For his future plans, see HAEK, CR II, 1.17a.5, Alfons Kupper to Josef Frings, January 5, 1959.

37. Privatbesitz Rudolf Morsey, Akten-Notiz, Wilhelm Wissing, Betr.: Konkordatsarbeit Dr. Kupper, March 13, 1959 (this document originally came from the archive of das Katholische Büro). See also Rudolf Morsey, "Gründung und Gründer der Kommission für Zeitgeschichte," 468.
38. On the controversies surrounding Conze's past during the Nazi era, see Götz Aly, "Theodor Schieder, Werner Conze oder die Vorstufen der physischen Vernichtung," in: Winfried Schulze and Otto Gerhard Oexle, ed., *Deutsche Historiker im Nationalsozialismus* (Frankfurt am Main: Fischer Verlag, 1999), 163–214; Jan Eike Dunkhase, *Werner Conze: ein deutscher Historiker im 20. Jahrhundert* (Göttingen: Vandenhoeck & Ruprecht, 2010).
39. Erich Matthias, "Der Untergang der Sozialdemokratie," in: *Vierteljahrshefte für Zeitgeschichte* 4 (1956), 179–226, 250–286. Morsey and Matthias had collaborated on several documentary editions. See Morsey and Matthias, *Der Interfraktionelle Ausschuß 1917/18* (Düsseldorf: Droste Verlag, 1959); *Die Regierung des Prinzen Max von Baden* (Düsseldorf: Droste Verlag, 1962). See also Martin Schumacher, "Gründung und Gründer der Kommission für Geschichte des Parlamentarismus und der politischen Parteien," in: Karl Dietrich Bracher, Paul Mikat, Konrad Repgen, Martin Schumacher and Hans-Peter Schwarz, ed., *Staat und Parteien: Festschrift für Rudolf Morsey zum 65. Geburtstag* (Berlin: Duncker & Humblot, 1992), 1029–1054 and, in particular, 1054. See Wolfgang Weber, *Biographisches Lexikon zur Geschichtswissenschaft in Deutschland, Österreich und der Schweiz. Die Lehrstuhlinhaber für Geschichte von den Anfängen des Faches bis 1970* (Frankfurt am Main: Peter Lang, 1984), 397. Matthias, though he had close ties to the SPD, was not a formal member of the party. Rudolf Morsey to the author, March 4, 2012.
40. Erich Matthias and Rudolf Morsey, *Das Ende der Parteien: 1933* (Düsseldorf: Droste Verlag, 1984).
41. Martin Schumacher, ed., *Annotierte Bibliographie 2002. Die Veröffentlichungen der Kommission für Geschichte des Parlamentarismus und der politischen Parteien seit 1952* (Düsseldorf: Droste Verlag, 2004), 258–259; Erich Matthias and Rudolf Morsey, *Das Ende der Parteien: 1933.*
42. Rudolf Morsey, "Tagebuch 7.–20. April 1933. Aus dem Nachlaß von Prälat Ludwig Kaas," in: *Stimmen der Zeit* 166 (1960), 12, 422–430.
43. Dieter Marc Schneider, *Johannes Schauff (1902–1990): Migration und "Stabilitas" im Zeitalter der Totalitarismen* (Munich: R. Oldenbourg Vorlag, 2001), 190.
44. Ibid., 189.
45. Rudolf Morsey, "Gründung und Gründer der Kommission für Zeitgeschichte," 460.
46. Dieter Marc Schneider, *Johannes Schauff*, 192; Rudolf Morsey to the author, March 4, 2012.
47. Rudolf Morsey, "Tagebuch 7.–20. April 1933."
48. "Reichskonkordat: Hitler klatschte," in: *Der Spiegel*, December 7, 1960.
49. For a profile of Sontheimer, see Alfons Söllner, "Kurt Sontheimer (1928–2005)," in: Eckard Jesse and Sebastian Liebold, ed., *Deutsche Politikwissenschaftler – Werk und Wirkung. Von Abendroth bis Zellentin*

(Baden-Baden: Nomos Verlagsgesellschaft, 2014), 711–724. On Broszat, see Klaus-Dietmar Henke and Claudio Natoli, *Mit dem Pathos der Nüchternheit. Martin Broszat, das Institut für Zeitgeschichte und die Erforschung des Nationalsozialismus* (Frankfurt: Campus Verlag, 1991).

50. Christian Schmidtmann, *Katholische Studierende: Ein Beitrag zur Kultur- und Sozialgeschichte der Bundesrepublik Deutschland* (Paderborn: Schöningh, 2005), 223–224.

51. Nikolai Hannig, *Die Religion der Öffentlichkeit. Kirche, Religion und Medien in der Bundesrepublik, 1945–1980* (Göttingen: Wallstein Verlag, 2010), in particular, 234–239.

52. On war crime trials, see Devin Pendas, "Seeking Justice, Finding Law: Nazi Trials in Postwar Europe," in: *Journal of Modern History* 81 (2009), 352–354. On the Ulm trial, see Claudia Fröhlich, *Wider die Tabuisierung des Ungehorsams: Fritz Bauers Widerstandbegriff und die Aufarbeitung von NS-Verbrechen* (Frankfurt am Main: Campus Verlag, 2005); Patrick Tobin, "No Time for 'Old Fighters': Postwar West Germany and the Origins of the 1958 Ulm Einsatzgruppen Trial," in: *Central European History* 4 (2011), 684–710. On the mostly hostile reception of Shirer's book in Germany, see Gavriel Rosenfeld, "The Reception of William L. Shirer's *The Rise and Fall of the Third Reich* in the United States and Germany, 1960–1962," in: *Journal of Contemporary History* 29 (1994), 95–128.

53. ACDP, NL Heinrich Krone, 1–028–014/1, Heinrich Brüning to Heinrich Krone, November 16, 1960; Robert Leiber, SJ, "Reichskonkordat und Ende der Zentrumspartei," in: *Stimmen der Zeit* 167 (1960), 213–223; Rudolf Morsey, "Gründung und Gründer der Kommission für Zeitgeschichte," 464.

54. ACDP, NL Heinrich Krone, 1–028–014/1, Heinrich Brüning to Heinrich Krone, November 16, 1960.

55. Robert Leiber, SJ, "Reichskonkordat und Ende der Zentrumspartei," 213–223.

56. See Rudolf Morsey, "Gründung und Gründer der Kommission für Zeitgeschichte," 467.

57. Ibid.

58. Friedrich Heer, "Der Linkskatholizismus," in: *Zeitschrift für Politik* 5 (1958), 134–161; Martin Stankowski, *Linkskatholizismus nach 1945* (Köln: Pahl Rugenstein, 1974); Gerd-Rainer Horn and Emmanuel Gerard, *Left-Catholicism, 1943–1955. Catholics and Society in Western Europe at the Point of Liberation* (Leuven: Leuven University Press, 2001); Josef P. Mautner, "Dekonstruktion des Christentums: Linkskatholizismus und Gegenwart," in: Richard Faber, ed., *Katholizismus in Geschichte und Gegenwart* (Würzburg: Königshausen & Neumann, 2005), 227–256.

59. Heinrich Böll, *Ansichten eines Clowns* (Berlin: Kiepenheuer & Witsch, 1963).

60. See the following two obituaries of Müller (1928–2005): www.mein-dortmund.de/professor-hans-mueller.pdf and www.mein-dortmund.de/professor-hans-mueller.html (accessed June 15, 2016).

61. AKAB, BI/9, Hans Müller to Karl Forster, April 14, 1961; Hans Müller, *Katholische Kirche und Nationalsozialismus* (Munich: Nymphenburger Verlag, 1963).

62. Hans Müller, *Katholische Kirche und Nationalsozialismus*, 12.

63. Hans Müller, "Zur Behandlung des Kirchenkampfes in der Nachkriegsliteratur," in: *Politische Studien* 12, Heft 135 (1961), 474–481.

64. Hans Müller, "Zur Vorgeschichte der Kundgebung der Fuldaer Bischofskonferenz vom 28.3.1933," in: *Werkhefte katholischer Laien* 15 (August 1961), 258–264; Hans Müller, "Zur Interpretation der Kundgebung der Fuldaer Bischofskonferenz vom 28.3.1933," in: *Werkhefte katholischer Laien* 16 (May 1962), 196–200. On the *Werkhefte katholischer Laien*, see BAK, NL Böckenförde, #575, Rudolf Morsey to Ernst-Wolfgang Böckenförde, August 16, 1961; Friedhelm Boll, "Die 'Werkhefte katholischer Laien' 1947–1963," in: Michel Grunewald, ed., *Das Katholische Intellektuellenmilieu in Deutschland, seine Presse und seine Netzwerke (1871–1963)* (Bern: Peter Lang, 2006), 507–536.

65. See Paul Weinberger, "Der ungelöste Pakt: Kirche und Drittes Reich – im Jahre 1958," in: *Werkhefte katholischer Laien* (1958), 178–187.

66. Ibid., 181.

67. For examples, see the report by Gustav Kafka, ZDK, 4100, Bericht für die Hauptkommission der deutschen Bischöfe, Bad Godesberg, March 1, 1960; ZDK, 4100, Zum Phänomen des Linkskatholizismus, Bericht für die Hauptkommission der deutschen Bischöfe, April 1961; Gustav Kafka, "Nonkonformisten, Linkskatholiken und andere Katholiken," in: *Wort und Wahrheit*, January 14, 1959.

68. For one example, see Otto Semmelroth, SJ, "Kritik an der Kirche?" in: *Stimmen der Zeit* 173 (1964), 4, 241–254 and, in particular, 254.

69. For the best overview of Böckenförde, see the nine essays in Hermann-Josef Große Kracht and Klaus Große Kracht, ed., *Religion. Recht. Republik. Studien zu Ernst-Wolfgang Böckenförde* (Paderborn: Schöningh, 2014). See also Mark Edward Ruff, "Ernst-Wolfgang Böckenförde und seine kirchenpolitischen Schriften," in: Hans-Rüdiger Schwab, ed., *Eigensinn und Bindung: Katholische deutsche Intellektuelle im 20. Jahrhundert: 39 Porträts* (Kevalaer: Verlag Butzon und Bercker, 2009), 599–616.

70. KZG, NL Walter Adolph, WA25C3, Abschrift, Der Erzbischof von München und Freising, Bedenkliche ekklesiologische Tendenzen im Schrifttum "nonkonformistischer" Katholiken, München, August 24, 1963.

71. Böckenförde met Spaemann through the seminar in philosophy at Münster offered by the distinguished philosopher Joachim Ritter. Ernst-Wolfgang Böckenförde and Robert Spaemann, "Die Zerstörung der naturrechtlichen Kriegslehre: Erwiderung an Pater G. Gundlach SJ," in: Rudolf Fleischmann, ed., *Atomare Kampfmittel und christliche Ethik. Diskussionsbeiträge deutscher Katholiken* (München: Kösel Verlag, 1960), 161–196; Markus Drüding, "Das philosophische Seminar in Münster," in: Hans-Ulrich Thamer and Daniel Droste, ed., *Die Universität Münster in der Zeit des Nationalsozialismus* (Münster: Aschendorff, 2012), 569–602; Dirk von Laak, *Gespräche in der Sicherheit des Schweigens. Carl Schmitt in der politischen Geistesgeschichte der frühen Bundesrepublik* (Oldenbourg: Akademieverlag, 2002), 192–200.

72. Dieter Gosewinkel, "'Beim Staat geht es nicht allein um Macht, sondern um die Staatliche Ordnung als Freiheitsordnung': Biographisches Interview mit Ernst-Wolfgang Böckenförde," in: Ernst-Wolfgang Böckenförde and Dieter Gosewinkel, ed., *Wissenschaft, Politik, Verfassungsgericht. Aufsätze von Ernst-Wolfgang Böckenförde* (Berlin: Suhrkamp, 2011), 317.

73. Christian Schmidtmann, *Katholische Studierende*, 465.

74. Knud von Harbou, *Wege und Abwege. Franz-Josef Schöningh, Mitbegründer der Süddeutschen Zeitung. Eine Biographie* (München: Allitera Verlag, 2013).

75. Christian Schmidtmann, *Katholische Studierende*, 465.

76. Ernst-Wolfgang Böckenförde, *Der deutsche Katholizismus im Jahre 1933. Kirche und demokratisches Ethos*, 9–10.

77. Dietmar Klenke, *Schwarz, Münster, Paderborn: Ein antikatholisches Klischeebild* (Münster: Waxmann Verlag, 2008).

78. Michael Keller, "Neugestaltung der Arbeitswelt aus christlichem Geist. Ansprache auf der KAB-Tagung in Rheinhausen am 2. Juni 1957," in: Michael Keller, *Iter para tutum* (Münster: Aschendorff Verlag, 1961).

79. AES, NL Andreas Rohracher, 19/29, Korr. mit Bischöfen im Ausland, 1950–1958, Michael Keller to Andreas Rohracher, June 11, 1957.

80. Christian Schmidtmann, *Katholische Studierende*, 465; Ernst-Wolfgang Böckenförde, "Begegnungen mit Adolf Arndt," in: Claus Arndt, ed., *Adolf Arndt zum 90. Geburtstag. Dokumentation der Festakademie in der Katholischen Akademie Hamburg* (Bonn: Friedrich Ebert Stiftung, 1995), 32–39.

81. Adolf Arndt, "Christentum und freiheitlicher Sozialismus," in: *Christlicher Glaube und politische Entscheidung. Eine Vortragsreihe der Arbeitsgemeinschaft Sozialdemokratischer Akademiker München* (Munich: Isar Verlag, 1957), 133–164; Rudolf Uertz, "Annäherungen: Christliche Sozialethik und SPD," in: *Historisch-Politische Mitteilungen* 13 (2006), 93–120.

82. Dieter Gosewinkel, *Adolf Arndt. Die Wiederbegründung des Rechtsstaats aus dem Geist der Sozialdemokratie (1945–1961)* (Bonn: Dietz, 1991), 559ff.

83. Ernst-Wolfgang Böckenförde, *Kirche und christlicher Glaube in den Herausforderungen der Zeit: Beiträge zur politisch-theologischen Verfassungsgeschichte* (Münster: LIT Verlag, 2004), 8.

84. ASD, NL Adolf Arndt, Box 5, Mappe 13, Ernst-Wolfgang Böckenförde to Adolf Arndt, December 15, 1957; ASD, NL Peter Nellen, 6b, Abschrift, Ernst-Wolfgang Böckenförde to Adolf Arndt, December 28, 1960.

85. Interview with Ernst-Wolfgang Böckenförde, Freiburg im Breisgau, 2006.

86. Felix Dirsch, "Das 'Hochland' – Eine katholisch-konservative Zeitschrift zwischen Literatur und Politik 1903–1941," in: Hans-Christof Kraus, ed., *Konservative Zeitschriften zwischen Kaiserreich und Diktatur. Fünf Fallstudien.* (Berlin: Duncker & Humblot, 2003); Knud von Harbou, *Wege und Abwege*, 290.

87. Knud von Harbou, *Wege und Abwege*.

88. Franz-Josef Schöningh, "Zum 50. Jahrgang: Ein Wort des Herausgebers," in: *Hochland* 50 (1957/1958), 3.

89. Dieter Gosewinkel, "Beim Staat geht es nicht allein um Macht," 392; UBEI, VA 1, Kösel Archiv, VII 3.1, Hochland Korrespondenz, Mappe 9, Franz-Josef Schöningh to Ernst-Wolfgang Böckenförde, July 16, 1957.

90. UBEI, VA 1, Kösel Archiv, VII 3.1, "Hochland"-Korrespondenz, Mappe 9, Ernst-Wolfgang Böckenförde to Franz-Josef Schöningh, July 15, 1957.

91. Ernst-Wolfgang Böckenförde, "Das Ethos der modernen Demokratie und die Kirche," in: *Hochland* 50 (1957/1958), 4–19.

92. Thomas Ellwein, *Klerikalismus in der deutschen Politik* (Munich: Isar Verlag, 1955).

93. UBEI, VA 1, Kösel Archiv, VII 3.1 "Hochland"-Korrespondenz, Mappe 9, Franz-Josef Schöningh to Dr. Werner Böckenförde, September 24, 1957.

94. UBEI, VA 1, Kösel Archiv, VII 3.1 "Hochland"-Korrespondenz, Mappe 9, Ernst-Wolfgang Böckenförde to Franz-Josef Schöningh, October 17, 1957.

95. Dieter Gosewinkel, "Beim Staat geht es nicht allein um Macht," 396.

96. ZDK, Referat für Staatsbürgerliche Angelegenheiten, 4231/2, Gustav Kafka to Heinrich Tenhumberg, October 29, 1957. On Schmitt's influence on Böckenförde, see Jan-Werner Müller, *A Dangerous Mind. Carl Schmitt in Postwar European Thought* (New Haven: Yale University Press, 2003), 166ff and 118ff; Klaus Große Kracht, "Unterwegs zum Staat. Ernst-Wolfgang Böckenförde auf dem Weg durch die intellektuelle Topographie der frühen Bundesrepublik, 1949–1964," in: Hermann-Josef Große Kracht and Klaus Große Kracht, ed., *Religion. Recht. Republik*, 40 and, especially, 16–22; Ernst-Wolfgang Böckenförde, "Der Begriff des Politischen als Schlüssel zum staatsrechtlichen Werk Carl Schmitts," in: Ernst-Wolfgang Böckenförde, *Recht, Staat, Freiheit. Studien zur Rechtsphilosophie, Staatstheorie und Verfassungsgeschichte* (Frankfurt a. M.: Suhrkamp Verlag, 1991), 344–366; Ernst-Wolfgang Böckenförde, "Politische Theorie und politische Theologie. Bemerkungen zu ihrem gegenseitigen Verhältnis," in: Jacob Taubes, ed., *Religionstheorie und politische Theologie. Bd. 1: Der Fürst dieser Welt. Carl Schmitt und die Folgen* (München: W. Fink, 1983), 16–25.

97. ZDK, Referat für Staatsbürgerliche Angelegenheiten, 4231/2, Gustav Kafka to Heinrich Tenhumberg, October 29, 1957.

98. ZDK, Referat für Staatsbürgerliche Angelegenheiten, 4231/2, Heinrich Tenhumberg to Gustav Kafka, October 31, 1957.

99. Hermann-Josef Spital, in: *Echo der Zeit*, January 12, 1958.

100. UBEI, VA I, Kösel Archiv, VII 3.1, Mappe 26, Heinrich Wild to Hermann-Josef Spital, January 29, 1958; UBEI, VA I, Kösel Archiv, VII 3.1, Hochland-Korrespondenz, Mappe 17, Heinrich Wild to Ernst-Wolfgang Böckenförde, January 29, 1958; Ernst-Wolfgang Böckenförde to Heinrich Wild, January 31, 1958; Franz-Josef Schöningh to Ernst-Wolfgang Böckenförde, February 5, 1958; Ernst-Wolfgang Böckenförde to Franz-Josef Schöningh, February 8, 1958; Franz-Josef Schöningh to Ernst-Wolfgang Böckenförde, February 19, 1958; UBEI, VA I, Kösel Archiv, VII 3-1. Mappe 26, Franz-Josef Schöningh to Hermann-Josef Spital, February 5, 1958, Franz-Josef Schöningh to Hermann-Josef Spital, February 19, 1958; Ernst-Wolfgang Böckenförde, *Kirche und christlicher Glaube*, 8.

101. "Arbeitskreis: Staatspolitische Arbeit," in: *Zentralkomitee der Deutschen Katholiken, Arbeitstagung Saarbrücken, 16–19 April 1958* (Paderborn:

Verlag Bonifacius-Druckerei, 1958), 223–260 and, in particular, 240, 244–245.

102. Hermann-Josef Spital, "Noch einmal: Das Ethos der modernen Demokratie und die Kirche," in: *Hochland* 50 (1957/1958), 409–421.

103. Franz-Josef Schöningh, "Zum 50. Jahrgang. Ein Wort des Herausgebers," 3.

104. Kirchlicher Anzeiger für die Erzdiözese Köln, December 2, 1957, Nr. 454 (Die katholischen Organisationen in der Zeit des Nationalsozialismus).

105. Heinrich Roth, *Katholische Jugend in der NS-Zeit unter besonderer Berücksichtigung des Katholischen Jungmännerverbandes. Daten und Dokumente* (Düsseldorf: Verlag Haus Altenberg, 1959).

106. Editor's note, "Der deutsche Katholizismus im Jahre 1933," 391–392.

107. Ernst-Wolfgang Böckenförde, *Der deutsche Katholizismus im Jahre 1933. Kirche und demokratisches Ethos*, 12–13.

108. Ernst-Wolfgang Böckenförde, *Kirche und christlicher Glaube*, 113.

109. Paul Weinberger, "Kirche und Drittes Reich im Jahre 1933," in: *Werkhefte katholischer Laien* (1958), 91–100.

110. Rudolf Morsey, "Die Deutsche Zentrumspartei," in: Rudolf Morsey and Erich Matthias, ed., *Das Ende der Parteien*, 405.

111. Ernst-Wolfgang Böckenförde, "Der deutsche Katholizismus im Jahre 1933. Eine kritische Betrachtung," in: *Hochland* 53 (1961), 215–239.

112. Ernst-Wolfgang Böckenförde, *Kirche und christlicher Glaube*, 113.

113. Dieter Gosewinkel, "Beim Staat geht es nicht allein um Macht," 363.

114. UBEI, VA1, Kösel-Archiv, Autorenkorrespondenz, Ernst-Wolfgang Böckenförde, Heinrich Wild to Ernst-Wolfgang Böckenförde, November 8, 1960.

115. UBEI, VA1, Kösel Archiv, Autorenkorrespondenz, Ernst-Wolfgang Böckenförde, Ernst-Wolfgang Böckenförde to Heinrich Wild, December 23, 1960.

116. UBEI, VA1; Kösel Archiv, Autorenkorrespondenz, Ernst-Wolfgang Böckenförde, Ernst-Wolfgang Böckenförde to Heinrich Wild, December 23, 1960; Ernst-Wolfgang Böckenförde to Heinrich Wild, January 3, 1961.

117. UBEI, VA1, Kösel Archiv, Autorenkorrespondenz, Ernst-Wolfgang Böckenförde, Ernst-Wolfgang Böckenförde to Heinrich Wild, January 18, 1961; Ernst-Wolfgang Böckenförde to Heinrich Wild, February 2, 1961.

118. BAK, NL Böckenförde, 575, Ernst-Wolfgang Böckenförde to Julius Döpfner, February 18, 1961; Ernst-Wolfgang Böckenförde to Michael Keller, February 8, 1961.

119. UBEI, VA1, Kösel Archiv, Autorenkorrespondenz, Ernst-Wolfgang Böckenförde, Ernst-Wolfgang Böckenförde to Heinrich Wild, January 3, 1961; BAK, NL Böckenförde, #575, Rudolf Morsey to Ernst-Wolfgang Böckenförde, February 16, 1961.

120. Dieter Gosewinkel, "Beim Staat geht es nicht allein um Macht," 404.

121. Ernst-Wolfgang Böckenförde, "German Catholicism in 1933," translated by Raymond Schmandt, in: *Cross Currents* (Summer 1961), 283–304. Schmandt was a colleague of Gordon Zahn at Loyola University.

122. For a complete list, see Ernst-Wolfgang Böckenförde, "Der deutsche Katholizismus im Jahre 1933: Stellungnahme zu einer Diskussion," in: *Hochland* 54 (1962), 217–245, in particular, footnote 1.

123. Hans Peters, "Die Scheinwahrheit des Jahres 1933. Die katholischen Bischöfe nach der Machtergreifung des Nationalsozialismus," in: *Kölnische Rundschau, Bonner Rundschau*, March 26, 1961, 11.

124. IFZG, München, Archiv, ID 105, Band 2, Hans Buchheim, Gutachten über die Kollektivverfolgung der katholischen Kirche in der Nationalsozialistischen Zeit, May 12, 1953.

125. Hans Buchheim, *Totalitäre Herrschaft. Wesen und Merkmale* (Munich: Kösel Verlag, 1962); Hans Buchheim, *Die SS. Das Herrschaftsinstrument Befehl und Gehorsam* (Olten: Walter Verlag, 1965); Nicolas Berg, *Der Holocaust und die westdeutschen Historiker*, especially 313–318, 409–419.

126. Phillip Stelzel, "Working toward a Common Goal? American Views on German Historiography and German-American Scholarly Relations during the 1960s," in: *Central European History* 41 (2008), 639–671, 654.

127. Hans Buchheim, "Der deutsche Katholizismus im Jahr 1933. Eine Auseinandersetzung mit Ernst-Wolfgang Böckenförde," in: *Hochland* 54 (1961/1962), 497–515.

128. BAK, NL Böckenförde, #575, Ernst-Wolfgang Böckenförde to Michael Keller, May 3, 1961; Michael Keller to Ernst-Wolfgang Böckenförde, May 27, 1961. Keller's dart was triggered by a letter from Böckenförde complaining about the decision, possibly from the bishop himself, to reprint substantial portions of Hans Peters' blistering critique in the Münster diocesan newspaper.

129. Paul Weinberger, "Der ungelöste Pakt: Kirche und Drittes Reich – im Jahre 1958," 178–187.

130. Rudolf Morsey, "Die Deutsche Zentrumspartei," 415, footnote 11. In this footnote, Morsey quoted directly from Böckenförde. "Ernst-Wolfgang Böckenförde spricht von einer 'inneren Affinität der Kirche zu autoritären Regimen, sofern sie der Ansicht ist, daß diese auf christlicher Grundlage stehen'; Das Ethos moderner Demokratie und die Kirche," in: *Hochland* 50, 1957/1958, S. 18.

131. Ernst-Wolfgang Böckenförde, "Der deutsche Katholizismus im Jahre 1933," 216.

132. There were exceptions. See Rudolf Morsey, "Die Deutsche Zentrumspartei," 405–406.

133. HAEK, Gen II 22.13, 12, Zeitungsausschnitt, Deutsche Tagespost, Nr. 108, September 8–9, 1961.

134. Friedrich Heer, "Die Tabus im Katholizismus," in: *Magnum*, June 1961, as cited in: BAK, NL Böckenförde, #475, Alfred Kröner to Ernst-Wolfgang Böckenförde, April 9, 1962.

135. For one example, see Josef Paulus, "Eine 'Hochland'-Legende," in: *Rheinischer Merkur*, March 10, 1961, 9.

136. BAK, NL Böckenförde, #575, Ernst-Wolfgang Böckenförde to Jakob Hommes, July 16, 1961; Heinrich Wild to Michael Schmaus, February 1, 1961.

137. AKAB, B I/9, Rudolf Morsey to Karl Forster, March 29, 1961.
138. Rudolf Morsey, *Görres-Gesellschaft und NS-Diktatur. Die Geschichte der Görres-Gesellschaft 1932/33 bis zum Verbot 1941* (Paderborn: Schöningh Verlag, 2002), 224–225.
139. Ernst-Wolfgang Böckenförde, *Kirche und christlicher Glaube*, 166–167.
140. Ernst-Wolfgang Böckenförde, *Der deutsche Katholizismus im Jahre 1933. Kirche und demokratisches Ethos*, 48.
141. Ernst-Wolfgang Böckenförde, *Kirche und christlicher Glaube*, 166–167.
142. Ibid., 62.
143. Hans Peters, "Die Scheinwahrheit des Jahres 1933."
144. Ernst-Wolfgang Böckenförde, "German Catholicism in 1933," 284.
145. Rudolf Morsey, "Die Deutsche Zentrumspartei," 417.
146. Ernst-Wolfgang Böckenförde, *Kirche und christlicher Glaube*, 143.
147. BAK, NL Böckenförde, #575, Julius Döpfner to Ernst-Wolfgang Böckenförde, March 29, 1961.
148. BAK, NL Böckenförde, #575, Michael Keller to Ernst-Wolfgang Böckenförde, May 27, 1961.
149. Rudolf Morsey, *Der Untergang des politischen Katholizismzus*, 140.
150. Richard Heinzmann, "Michael Schmauss in Memorarium," in: *Münchener Theologische Zeitschrift: Vierteljahrsschrift für das Gesamtgebiet der katholischen Theologie* (1994), 123–127.
151. BAK, NL Böckenförde, #575, Ernst-Wolfgang Böckenförde to Herbert Wehner, February 8, 1961.
152. "Führers Prälaten," in: *Der Spiegel*, May 24, 1961.
153. Interview with Rudolf Morsey, March 15, 2007, Bonn.
154. Privatbesitz Rudolf Morsey, Rudolf Morsey to Heinrich Krone, March 9, 1959, Anlage.
155. Ibid.
156. Rudolf Morsey, "Das Ende der Zentrumspartei 1933," 46.
157. KAB, BI/9, "Das Ende der Parteien: Ein Werk der Kommission für Geschichte des Parlamentarismus und der politischen Parteien," Das Zentrum, Bulletin des Presse/und Informationsamtes der Bundesregierung, January 18, 1961, 109–112.
158. KAB, A16/5, Pressedienst des Sekretariats der Deutschen Bischofskonferenz, 15. November 1978. Ansprache des Vorsitzenden der Wissenschaftlichen Kommission, "Kommission für Zeitgeschichte," Professor Dr. Rudolf Morsey, aus Anlaß des Erscheinens des 50. Bandes der "Veröffentlichungen der Kommission für Zeitgeschichte" am 15. November 1978.
159. Interview with Rudolf Morsey, March 15, 2007, Bonn.
160. Rudolf Morsey, "Gründung und Gründer der Kommission für Zeitgeschichte," 461.
161. Ibid.; KAS, NL Krone, I-028–014/7, Johannes Schauff to Heinrich Krone, February 2, 1960.
162. Rudolf Morsey, "Gründung und Gründer der Kommission für Zeitgeschichte," 461, 465; KAB, BI/9, List of participants. (No name, no title, no date).

163. KAS, NL Krone, I-028–014/7, Heinrich Krone to Johannes Schauff, February 2, 1961.
164. KAB, B I/9, Christine Teusch to Karl Forster, April 13, 1961.
165. Dieter Marc Schneider, *Johannes Schauff*, 195.
166. Rudolf Morsey, "Gründung und Gründer der Kommission für Zeitgeschichte," 472.
167. Ibid., 468–469.
168. NL Bernhard Stasiewski, KFZG, Vorschlag für eine Klausurtagung von Historikern und Politikern zum Thema "Kirche und Staat am Ausgang der Weimarer Zeit"; KAB BI/9, Einladungsschreiben, Karl Forster, March 24, 1961; Privatbesitz Rudolf Morsey, Alfons Kupper, Denkschrift betreffend Inangriffnahme der wissenschaftlichen Erforschung der Geschichte des Katholizismus in Deutschland zur Zeit der Weimarer Republik und des Dritten Reiches (1918–1945), May 1961.
169. KAB, BI/9, Einladung von Karl Forster, March 24, 1961.
170. KAB, BI/9, Karl Forster to Christine Teusch, April 19, 1961.
171. KAB, BI/9, Alfons Kupper to Karl Forster, April 10, 1961.
172. KAB, A16/1, Karl Frings to Johannes Schauff, August 29, 1962.
173. KAB, BI/9, Hans Müller to Karl Forster, April 14, 1961.
174. KAB, BI/9, Karl Forster to Christine Teusch, April 19, 1961.
175. Rudolf Morsey, "Gründung und Gründer der Kommission für Zeitgeschichte," 472.
176. ACDP, NL Krone, I-028–014/7, Johannes Schauff to Heinrich Krone, April 17, 1961; ACDP, NL Krone, I-028–014/1, Johannes Schauff to Christine Teusch, April 17, 1961. (This was sent out only on May 1, 1961).
177. KAB, BI/9, Karl Forster to Heinrich Krone, March 20, 1961; Heinrich Krone to Karl Forster, May 10, 1961; Karl Forster to Heinrich Krone, May 12, 1961.
178. Rudolf Morsey, "Gründung und Gründer der Kommission für Zeitgeschichte," 470, 473.
179. The others were delivered by Karl Buchheim (the father of Hans Buchheim), Johannes Hirschmann, SJ, and Repgen. KAB, BI/9, Einladung von Karl Forster, March 24, 1961.
180. Interview with Rudolf Morsey, Neustadt an der Weinstrasse.
181. Konrad Repgen was a Privatdozent, a title for which there is no equivalent in English. It denotes an aspiring academic who has completed his second dissertation, or Habilitation, but has yet to receive a formal appointment to be a professor.
182. KAB, BI/9, Invitation and Program, Karl Forster, March 24, 1961. See Rudolf Morsey, "Gründung und Gründer der Kommission für Zeitgeschichte," 469.
183. Rudolf Morsey, "Gründung und Gründer der Kommission für Zeitgeschichte," 469.
184. KAB, BI/9, Rudolf Morsey to Karl Forster, March 9, 1961.
185. Rudolf Morsey, "Gründung und Gründer der Kommission für Zeitgeschichte," 469. For the text of the lecture, see: KAB BI/9,

Privatdozent Dr. Konrad Repgen, Bonn, "Die Staatskrise ab 1930 und die deutschen Katholiken."

186. See KAB BI/9, Abschrift aus dem Brief von Herrn Dr. A.H. Berning, Aachen, Capitelstr.1 vom 12.5.61.
187. Heinrich Krone, *Tagebücher. Erster Teil: 1945–1961* (Düsseldorf: Droste Verlag, 1995), 492.
188. Ibid.
189. Rudolf Morsey, "Gründung und Gründer der Kommission für Zeitgeschichte"; IFZG, NL Schauff, ED 346/24, Rundschreiben Forster, July 26, 1962.
190. IFZG, NL Schauff, ED 346/24, Rundschreiben Karl Forster, July 26, 1962.
191. Rudolf Morsey, "Gründung und Gründer der Kommission für Zeitgeschichte," 481. The academic board of directors included Dieter Albrecht, Clemens Bauer, Karl Bosl, Karl Buchheim, his son Hans Buchheim, Ernst Deuerlein, Gustav Gundlach, SJ (the Catholic social theorist and confidant of Pope Pius XII whose defense of the use of atomic weapons had been starkly criticized by Böckenförde), Josef Höfer, Hubert Jedin, Paul Mikat, Rudolf Morsey, Konrad Repgen, Otto Roegele, Max Spindler, Bernhard Stasiewski and Bernhard Zittel.
192. KAB A/10/2 Niederschrift über die Sitzung des Kuratoriums der Kommission für Zeitgeschichte bei der Katholischen Akademie in Bayern am Montag, 17. Dezember 1962, im Katholischen Büro Bonn.
193. Members included Hans Berger, Forster, Schauff, Peters, Joseph Ernst Fürst Fugger von Glött (who was a CSU delegate), Prelate Bernhard Hanssler (who served as one of the directors of the Central Committee of German Catholics), Wilhelm Wissing (who had succeeded Böhler as head of the Catholic Office in Bonn), Bundesminister Fritz Schäffer, Joseph Fonk and, not least, Karl Theodor Freiherr zu Guttenberg, a CSU politician. For a more critical description of this network, see Olaf Blaschke, "Geschichtsdeutung und Vergangenheitspolitik. Die Kommission für Zeitgeschichte und das Netzwerk kirchenloyaler Katholizismusforscher 1945–2000," in: Thomas Pittrof and Walter Schmitz, ed., *Freie Anerkennung übergeschichtlicher Bindungen. Katholische Geschichtswahrnehmung im deutschsprachigen Raum des 20. Jahrhunderts* (Freiburg: Rombach Verlag, 2010), 479–521.
194. Rudolf Morsey, "Das Ende der Zentrumspartei 1933," 40.
195. See Dieter Albrecht, *Der Notenwechsel zwischen dem Heiligen Stuhl und der deutschen Reichsregierung, Bd I: Von der Ratifizierung des Reichskonkordats bis zur Enzyklika "Mit brennender Sorge"* (Mainz: Matthias-Grünewald Verlag, 1965); Ludwig Volk, *Der bayerische Episkopat und der Nationalsozialismus* (Mainz: Matthias-Grünewald Verlag, 1965); Bernhard Stasiewski, *Akten deutscher Bischöfe über die Lage der Kirche 1933–1945, Bd I: 1933–1934* (Mainz: Matthias-Grünewald Verlag, 1968); Rudolf Morsey, *Die Protokolle der Reichstagungfraktion und des Fraktionsvorstandes der Deutschen Zentrumspartei, 1926–1933* (Mainz: Matthias-Grünewald Verlag, 1969); Ludwig Volk, *Kirchliche Akten über die Reichskonkordatsverhandlungen 1933* (Mainz: Matthias-Grünewald Verlag, 1969); Alfons Kupper, *Staatliche*

Akten über die Reichskonkordatsverhandlungen 1933 (Mainz: Matthias-Grünewald Verlag, 1969).

196. IFZG, ID103-6-101, Clemens Bauer, Ernst Deuerlein, Rudolf Morsey and Ernst Walter Zeeeden to das Bundesministerium des Innern, February 1962, Eingegangen am March 14, 1962.

197. KAB A/10/2, Niederschrift über die Sitzung des Kuratoriums der Kommission für Zeitgeschichte bei der Katholischen Akademie in Bayern am Montag, December 17, 1962, im Katholischen Büro Bonn; Rudolf Morsey, "Gründung und Gründer der Kommission für Zeitgeschichte," 483.

198. Alfons Kupper, *Staatliche Akten über die Reichskonkordatsverhandlungen 1933*; Rudolf Morsey, "Gründung und Gründer der Kommission für Zeitgeschichte," 468; NLBS, KFZG, Schriftwechsel A-K, Alfons Kupper to Bernhard Stasiewski, December 22, 1968.

199. Privatbesitz Rudolf Morsey, Akten-Notiz, Wilhelm Wissing, Betr.: Konkordatsarbeit Dr. Kupper, March 13, 1959 (this document originally came from the archive of das Katholische Büro). See also NLBS, KFZG, Schriftwechsel A-K, Alfons Kupper to Bernhard Stasiewski; Alfons Kupper to Bernhard Stasiewski, December 20, 1960.

200. KAB A/10/2, Niederschrift über die Sitzung des Kuratoriums der Kommission für Zeitgeschichte bei der Katholischen Akademie in Bayern am Montag, 17. Dezember 1962 im Katholischen Büro Bonn.

201. Bernhard Stasiewski, *Akten deutscher Bischöfe über die Lage der Kirche 1933–1945, Bd I.*

202. IFZG, ID 103-6-106, Krausnick to das Bundesministerium des Innern, z. Hd. Herrn Oberregierungsrat Dr. Petersen, April 2, 1962.

4   Gordon Zahn versus the German Hierarchy

1. KZG, NL Adolph, WA 16a, "The Catholic Press and the National Cause in Nazi Germany, Gordon Zahn," Presented before the American Catholic Sociological Society Convention, Mundelein College, September 2, 1959.

2. UNDA, Gordon Zahn Papers, 13231–13263, Journal Record of a Controversial Research Report, 3.

3. Ibid., 4.

4. For a transcription of the press release, see KZG, NL Adolph, WA 16a, Abschrift, Mundelein College Public Relations Office, Peggy Roach, Press Release, American Catholic Sociological Convention for Release Wednesday PM, Sept. 2 (1959).

5. KZG, NL Walter Adolph, WA 16a, Abschrift, Mundelein College Public Relations Office, Peggy Roach, American Catholic Sociological Convention, for Release Wednesday PM, August 31, 1959; "Bishops Backed Hitler, Study Finds," in: *Chicago Daily News*, September 2, 1959; "Catholic Clergy in Nazi Germany Draws Criticism," in: *Chicago Sun-Times*, September 2, 1959; "Hitler Backed by Catholics, Scholar Says: Professor at Loyola Traces Trend," in: *Chicago Daily Tribune*, September 3, 1959.

6. UNDA, Gordon Zahn Papers, 13231–13263, Journal Record of a Controversial Research Report, 5.

7. See Gordon Zahn, "Würzburg 1957," in: *The Catholic Worker*, March 1958, 3; Gordon Zahn, "German Pacifists," in: *America*, May 18, 1957, 232–233; Gordon Zahn, "He Would Not Serve," in: *America*, July 5, 1958, 388–389.

8. Interview with Michael Hovey.

9. Interview with Susan Kalmer and Geraldine Ogren, November 6, 2009.

10. Interview with Michael Hovey. Zahn was later to label his family background as "upper lower-class." See Gordon Zahn, *Another Part of the War: The Camp Simon Story* (Amherst: University of Massachusetts Press, 1979), 17.

11. Interview with Susan Kalmer.

12. Gordon Zahn, *Another Part of the War*, 4–5.

13. Interview with Michael Hovey; Gordon Zahn, *Another Part of the War*, 5.

14. Interview with Susan Kalmer.

15. Gordon Zahn, *Another Part of the War*, 4.

16. Gordon Zahn, *Vocation of Peace* (Eugene: Wipf and Stock, 1992), viii; Gordon Zahn, *Another Part of the War*, 5.

17. Gordon Zahn, *Vocation of Peace*, 6.

18. Ibid., 5–6.

19. Interview with Michael Hovey.

20. Gordon Zahn, *Another Part of the War*, 5.

21. For a fine bibliography on this enormous literature, see Allan Fitzgerald, ed., *Augustine through the Ages: An Encyclopedia* (Grand Rapids: Eerdmans, 1999), 875–876.

22. Gordon Zahn, *Another Part of the War*, 6; Gordon Zahn, *War, Conscience and Dissent* (New York: Hawthorn Books, 1967), 145–176.

23. See Mel Piehl, *Breaking Bread: The Catholic Worker and the Origin of Catholic Radicalism in America* (Philadelphia: Temple University Press, 1982), 205.

24. Gordon Zahn, *Vocation of Peace*, dedicatory page.

25. Mark and Louise Zwick, *The Catholic Worker Movement: Intellectual and Spiritual Origins* (Mahwah, New Jersey: Paulist Press, 2005), 19; Mel Piehl, *Breaking Bread*, 134; James T. Fisher, *The Catholic Counterculture in America, 1933–1962* (Chapel Hill: University of North Carolina Press, 1989).

26. Gordon Zahn, *Another Part of the War*, 81.

27. Ibid., 246.

28. Gordon Zahn, "Memories of Camp Warner," in: *The Catholic Worker*, October–November 1977.

29. www.catholicdemocrats.org/MA/2008/01/remembering_gordon_zahn_co foun.php (accessed June 17, 2016).

30. UNDA, Gordon Zahn Papers, 3314, Rev. Baldwin Dworshak to Gordon Zahn, September 2, 1947.

31. St. John's University Archives, St. John's University Yearbook, 1945.

32. For descriptions of St. John's in the 1930s, see Colman Berry, *Worship and Work: Saint John's Abbey and University, 1856–1956* (Collegeville: Saint John's Abbey, 1956); Dominic Sandbrook, *Eugene McCarthy: The Rise and Fall of Postwar American Liberalism* (New York: Knopf, 2004), 8–13. See

"Miss Dorothy Day Visits St. John's," in: *The Record: Official Newspaper of St. John's University and Organ of the Alumni*, October 24, 1946, 1.

33. Gordon Zahn, "Germany through American Eyes" in: *The Record: Official Newspaper of St. John's University and Organ of the Alumni*, January 16, 1947, 2.

34. Interview with Susan Kalmer.

35. Sylvester Theisen to the author, October 22, 2009. Theisen was a close friend of Zahn who also studied at St. John's University; he served in Germany between January 1955 and February 1958 as a special representative for intellectual and cultural affairs in West Germany for the American Catholic Bishops. See also David Klingeman, OSB, "The Military Chaplains of St. John's," in: *The Abbey Banner: Magazine of St. John's Abbey* 3, 2 (2003), 10–11.

36. Interview with Michael Hovey. On this point, see Colman J. Barry, OSB, *The Catholic Church and German-Americans* (Milwaukee: Catholic University of America Press, 1953), 277.

37. UNDA, Gordon Zahn Papers, 3314, Rev. Baldwin Dworshak to Gordon Zahn, September 2, 1947.

38. The obituary in the *London Times* erroneously claims that Zahn slept in his car. Zahn never even owned an automobile, having failed his driver's license test multiple times. www.catholicdemocrats.org/MA/2008/01/remembering_gordon_zahn_cofoun.php (accessed June 17, 2016).

39. UNDA, Gordon Zahn Papers, 3314, Rev. Baldwin Dworshak to Gordon Zahn, September 2, 1947. Dworshak served as prior of St. John's.

40. Dominic Sandbrook, *Eugene McCarthy*, 18.

41. Michael Gallagher's beautifully written paean to Zahn contains several factual errors. Gallagher claims that Zahn encountered McCarthy at St. John's and that as a senator he procured them jobs in Washington. Zahn met McCarthy at St. Thomas, where McCarthy was a sociology instructor. McCarthy joined Congress, in fact, as a member of the House of Representatives and not the Senate. See Michael Gallagher, "Let Us Now Praise Gordon Zahn," at www.catholicpeacefellowship.org/downloads/gordon_zahn.pdf.

42. On Furfey, see Loretta Morris, "Celebration of a Life: Paul Hanly Furfy," in: *Sociology of Religion* 54 (1993), 219–220; Bronislaw Misztal, Francesco Villa and Eric Sean Williams, *Paul Hanly Furfey's Quest for a Good Society* (Washington: Department of Sociology and the Life Cycle Institute, The Catholic University of America, The Council for Research in Values and Philosophy, 2005). For Furfey's appraisal of Zahn's dissertation, see UNDA, Gordon Zahn Papers, 3696, Paul Hanly Furfey to C.J. Nuesse, July 1, 1952.

43. Paul Sullins, "Paul Hanly Furfey and the Catholic Intellectual Tradition," in: Bronislaw Misztal, Francesco Villa and Eric Sean Williams, ed., *Paul Hanly Furfey's Quest for a Good Society*, 125–147. Gordon Zahn, *Readings in Sociology: Selected with Introduction and Commentary, The College Readings Series, No. 3* (Westminster, Maryland: the Newman Press, 1958);

Gordon Zahn, *What Is Society? Volume 147 of the Twentieth century Encyclopedia of Catholicism* (New York: Hawthorn Books, 1964).

44. UNDA, Gordon Zahn Papers, 3700, Gordon Zahn to Reverend Damian Reid, C.P., Literary Editor, The Sign, March 19, 1953; Gordon Zahn, "McCarthyism: A 'Catholic Issue.'" See also Donald F. Crosby, *God, Church and Flag: Senator Joseph McCarthy and the Catholic Church, 1950–1957* (Chapel Hill: University of North Carolina Press, 1978).

45. For a lucid summary of this Catholic world, see James O'Toole, *The Faithful: A History of Catholics in America* (Cambridge: Harvard University Press, 2008), 145–198.

46. Gordon Zahn, *German Catholics and Hitler's Wars: A Study in Social Control* (New York: Sheed and Ward, 1962), 3–5.

47. Gordon Zahn, *German Catholics and Hitler's Wars*, 5–6.

48. Anselm Doering-Manteuffel, *Katholizismus und Wiederbewaffnung: die Haltung der deutschen Katholiken gegenüber der Wehrfrage 1948–1955* (Mainz: Matthias-Grünewald Verlag, 1981); Anselm Doering–Manteuffel, "Die Kirchen und die EVG: Zu den Rückwirkungen der Wehrdebatte im westdeutschen Protestantismus und Katholizismus auf die politische Zusammenarbeit der Konfessionen," in: Hans-Erich Volkmann and Walter Schwengler, ed., *Die Europäische Verteidigungsgemeinschaft: Stand und Probleme der Forschung* (Boppard am Rhein: Harald Boldt Verlag, 1985), 317–340; David Clay Large, *Germans to the Front: West German Rearmament in the Adenauer Era* (Chapel Hill: University of North Carolina Press, 1996).

49. UNDA, Gordon Zahn Papers, 13264–13360, Record of my Fulbright Year. A more complete list includes: Dr. and Mrs. Jaeuber, Prof. Dr. Berthold, Professor Franz Rauhut, Dr. Nehring, Father Stratmann, Frau Schmidtmann, Rappich, Dr. Johannes Hessen, Dr. Koch, Mr. Hüpgens, Dr. Salzbacher, Peter Nellen, Dr. Geck, Dr. Antz, Werthmann, Paulus Lenz, Prof. Dr. Hasenfuss, Domkapitular Kramer, Dr. Heinz Fleckenstein, Baronin von Guttenberg, Dr. Rheinfelder, Abbott Hugo Lang, Father Sieben, SJ, Sr. Getrudis, Kaspar Mazer, Archbishop Dr. Franz König, Prof. Dr. Johannes Ude, Prof. Dr. Ulrich Noack, Dr. Dietrich Wendland, Manfred Höhhammer, Dr. Anton Scharnagl, Alfons Erb, Msgr. Baumeister, Domkapitular Stehlin, Generalvikar Simon Hirt, Hans Lukashek, Francis Keller, Dr. Karl Färber, Dr. Josef Knecht, Johannes Fleischer, Josef Fleischer, Hans Wirtz, Friedrich Ferber, Walter Ferber, Charles Froehlicher, Dr. Hans Bauer, Dr. Fauber, Dr. Rudolf Gunno, Dr. Leo Weismantel, Nikolaus Fries, Prälat Peter Buchholz, Sr. Maria Murtha, Pfarrer Felix Heinz, Bernhard Stasiewski, Melchoir Grunsey, M. Laros, Fr. Paul, Pfarrer Josef Karobatt, Dr. Holzapfel, Walter Dirks, Walter Adolf, Johannes Neuhäusler and Gustav Gundlach, SJ. On Stratmann: P. Franziskus Maria Stratmann O.P., *In der Verbannung: Tagebuchblätter 1940 bis 1947* (Frankfurt am Main: Europäische Verlagsanstalt, 1962); Rainer Maria Groothius, *Im Dienste einer überstaatlichen Macht: Die deutschen Dominikaner unter der NS-Diktatur* (Münster: Verlag Regensberg, 2002), 405–420.

50. See Wilhelm Meier-Dörnberg, "Die Auseinandersetzung um die Einführung der Wehrpflicht in der Bundesrepublik Deutschland," in: Roland G. Foerster, ed., *Die Wehrpflicht: Entstehung, Erscheinungsformen und politisch-militärische Wirkung* (Munich: Oldenbourg Verlag, 1994), 107–118.

51. ASD, NL Peter Nellen, Box 7, Deutscher Bundestag, Stenographischer Dienst, Stenographisches Protokoll (Sonderprotokoll) der 94. Sitzung des Ausschusses für Verteidigung, Bonn, Freitag, den 1. Juni 1956, Tagesordnung: Entgegennahme der Stellung von Vertretern der Evangelischen und Katholischen Kirche zur Frage der Kriegsdienstverweigerung, 37, 43.

52. On these topics, see Patrick Bernhard, *Zivildienst zwischen Reform und Revolte: Eine bundesdeutsche Institution im gesellschaftlichen Wandel, 1961–1982* (München: Oldenbourg Verlag, 2005), especially 32–33; Volker Möhle and Christian Rabe, *Kriegsdienstverweigerer in der BRD: Eine empirisch-analytische Studie zur Motivation der Kriegsdienstverweigerer in den Jahren 1957–1971* (Opladen: Westdeutscher Verlag, 1972).

53. For an overview, see Frank Buchholz, *Strategische und militärpolitische Diskussionen in der Gründungsphase der Bundeswehr, 1949–1960* (Frankfurt am Main: Peter Lang, 1991), especially 201–241.

54. AKMB, NL Werthmann, I Pers. Dokumente, "Der Fall 'Fleischer I,'" Erklärung des Weltfriedensbundes katholischer Kriegsgegener zum päpstlichen Veto gegen die Kriegsdienstverweigerung aus Gewissensgründen, January 1957.

55. For one example, see DAB, V/7–25–2, Karl Peters, Walter Rest and Walter Dirks to Julius Döpfner, May 9, 1958.

56. DAB, 17–25–1, Erklärung, no date, but probably May 6 or 7, 1958.

57. UNDA, Gordon Zahn Papers, 13264–13360, Record of my Fulbright Year in Germany, October 26, 1956.

58. AKMB, Berlin, NL Georg Werthmann, Der Fall Fleischer I, Franz Rauhut to Georg Werthmann, no date, but probably summer 1956. According to Zahn, Rauhut's wife was Protestant.

59. UNDA, Gordon Zahn Papers, CZHN, 13264–13360, Record of my Fulbright Year, December 19, 1956.

60. HAEK, Gen II, 23.23a, 11, Zeitungsausschnitt, Johannes Fleischer, "Schuldbekenntnis der versäumten Pflichten. Die andere Konsequenz," in: *Der Tagesspiegel*, Berlin, January 12, 1947; Walter Adolph, "Dolchstoss-Legende in Neuer Form," in: *Das Petrusblatt*, January 26, 1947.

61. AEMF, Kardinal Faulhaber Archiv, 5010, Johannes Fleischer to das Erzbischöfliche Ordinariat München, January 30, 1946. In this enclosure, he enclosed two essays, "Die neue Welt," and "Der dreifache Verrat"; Johannes Fleischer, "Schuldbekenntnis der versäumten Pflichten"; Johannes Fleischer, "Was lehrt der Papst über den totalen Krieg"; Johannes Fleischer, "Der päpstliche Bankrott: Was ist von der Weihnachtsansprache Pius XII. zu halten?," in: *Die Andere Zeitung*, January 24, 1957, 2.

62. UNDA, Gordon Zahn Papers, CZHN, 13264–13360, Record of my Fulbright Year, February 22, 1957.

63. Most of these complaints and requests for information were sent to the pastor in Donaueschingen, where Fleischer had settled. Pfarrarchiv Donaueschingen,

Matthias Defregger, Sekretär des Erzbischofs, München to das Katholische Stadtpfarramt Donaueschingen, February 12, 1954; Stadtpfarrer, Donaueschingen to das Hochw. Erzbischöfliches Sekretariat (München-Freising), February 15, 1954; Verlag für kirchliches Schrifttum im Verlag Wort und Werk, Köln to Pfarrer Held, Donaueschingen, April 20, 1954; Dr. Tuschen, Generalvikar, Erzbischöfliches Generalvikariat, Paderborn, October 30, 1954; Dr. Eugen Seiterich, Erzbischof von Freiburg to Herrn Geistl. Rat Dekan K. Held, November 10, 1954; Geheimsekretär, Der Bischof von Aachen to das katholische Pfarramt, Donaueschingen, January 14, 1955; Bistumskonservator, Trier and das Katholische Pfarramt, St. Johann-Baptista, Donaueschingen, January 21, 1955; Konrad Held to den Erzbischof von Freiburg, April 12, 1957; HAEK, CR II 25.2.5, Matthias Defregger, Erzbischöflicher Sekretär to Wilhelm Böhler, February 17, 1954.

64. Pfarrarchiv, Donaueschingen, Katholisches Pfarramt, Donaueschingen to das Hochw. Erzb. Ordinariat, Freiburg i. Br, January 16, 1957, Leumundszeugnis (No author, but most likely Konrad Keld); KZG, NL Adolph, WA34a, Andreas Hermes to Emil Dovifat, January 31, 1947.

65. AKMB, NL Georg Werthmann, I, Persönliche Dokumente, Der Fall, "Fleischer," I, Josef Fleischer to Heinrich Höfler, March 28, 1956.

66. HAEK, CR II, 25.2.5, Dr. Josef Fleischer, Kriegsdienstverweigerung und Militärseelsorge, no date, but undoubtedly February 1956.

67. AKMB, NL Georg Werthmann, I, Persönliche Dokumente, Der Fall, "Fleischer," I, Betr.: "Bericht des Herrn Verteidigungsministers zu den Angriffen gegen H.H. Generalvikar Werthmann" (3. Punkt der Tagesordnung der 95. Sitzung des Verteidigungsausschusses am 4.6. 1956), June 6, 1956.

68. AKMB, NL Georg Werthmann, I, Persönliche Dokumente, Der Fall, "Fleischer," I, Josef Fleischer to Heinrich Höfler, March 28, 1956; Bestätigung, Dr. Paul Fleischer, February 27, 1956.

69. BAM, AO-798, Generalvikariate, Bischöfe, Georg Werthmann to Michael Keller, May 29, 1955.

70. Biographisches-Bibliographisches Kirchenlexikon, Georg Werthmann, to be found at www.kirchenlexikon.de/w/werthmann_g.shtml (Accessed: October 15, 2016).

71. Johannes Güsgen, "Die Bedeutung der Katholischen Militärseelsorge," in: Rolf-Dieter Müller and Hans-Erich Volkmann, ed., *Die Wehrmacht: Mythos und Realität* (München: Oldenbourg Verlag, 1999), 503–524; Lauren Faulkner, *Wehrmacht Priests: Catholics Priests and the Nazi War of Annihilation* (Cambridge, MA: Harvard University Press, 2015). For an account of Werthmann directly inspired by Zahn's work, see Guenter Lewy, *The Catholic Church and Nazi Germany* (New York: McGraw-Hill, 1964), 236–242.

72. Gordon Zahn, *German Catholics and Hitler's Wars*, 152–153.

73. AKMB, Sammlung Werthmann, SW 1010/VII, 1, Aktenvermerk, ohne Name, April 27, 1952.

74. See Johannes Güsgen, *Die katholische Militärseelsorge in Deutschland zwischen 1920 und 1945: Ihre Praxis und Entwicklung in der Reichswehr der Weimarer*

Republik und der Wehrmacht des nationalsozialistischen Deutschlands unter besonderer Berücksichtigung ihrer Rolle bei den Konkordatsverhandlungen (Cologne: Böhlau Verlag, 1989).

75. UNDA, Gordon Zahn Papers, 13264–13360, Record of my Fulbright Year, June 25, 1957.

76. Biographisches-Bibliographisches Kirchenlexikon, Georg Werthmann.

77. AKMB, NL Georg Werthmann, I, Persönliche Dokumente, Der Fall "Fleischer," I, Betr.: "Bericht des Herrn Verteidigungsministers zu den Angriffen gegen H.H. Generalvikar Werthmann" (3. Punkt der Tagesordnung der 95. Sitzung des Verteidigungsausschusses am 4.6. 1956), June 6, 1956.

78. For evidence of the consternation that this reporting in the East German press brought to high-ranking Catholic officials, see AKMB, NL Georg Werthmann, I, Persönliche Dokumente, Der Fall "Fleischer," III, Johannes Neuhäusler to Josef Wendel, München, April 13, 1956.

79. AKMB, NL Georg Werthmann, I, Persönliche Dokumente, Der Fall "Fleischer," III, SPD-Presse Korrespondenz, SPD-Landesverband Bayern, "Restaurative Kräfte auch in der Militärseelsorge," April 12, 1956.

80. AKMB, NL Georg Werthmann, I, Persönliche Dokumente, Der Fall "Fleischer," I, Betr.: "Bericht des Herrn Verteidigungsministers zu den Angriffen gegen H.H. Generalvikar Werthmann" (3. Punkt der Tagesordnung der 95. Sitzung des Verteidigungsausschusses am 4.6. 1956), June 6, 1956.

81. UNDA, Gordon Zahn Papers, 13264–13360, Record of my Fulbright Year, February 27, 1957.

82. AKMB, NL Georg Werthmann, I, Persönliche Dokumente, Der Fall "Fleischer," I, Betr.: "Bericht des Herrn Verteidigungsministers zu den Angriffen gegen H.H. Generalvikar Werthmann" (3. Punkt der Tagesordnung der 95. Sitzung des Verteidigungsausschusses am 4.6. 1956), June 6, 1956, 2.

83. AKMB, NL Georg Werthmann, I, Persönliche Dokumente, Der Fall "Fleischer," III, W. Rieß to Heinz Göhler, April 24, 1956; Heinz Göhler to W. Riess, April 26, 1956; W. Rieß to das Erzbischöfliche Sekretariat, z.Hd. v. H.H. Erzbischöfliches Sekretar Matthias Defregger; W. Rieß to Heinz Göhler, June 20, 1956.

84. AKMB, NL Georg Werthmann, I, Persönliche Dokumente, Der Fall "Fleischer," I, Erklärung, Würzburg, June 3, 1956; Franz Rauhut to Georg Werthmann, May 19, 1956; Der Fall, "Fleischer," III, W. Rieß to Franz Rauhut, July 9, 1956.

85. AKMB, NL Georg Werthmann, I, Persönliche Dokumente, Der Fall "Fleischer," III, Georg Werthmann to Frau Becker, June 18, 1956.

86. UNDA, Gordon Zahn Papers, 13264–13360, Record of my Fulbright Year, 23, February 27, 1957.

87. AKMB, NL Georg Werthmann, I, Persönliche Dokumente, Der Fall "Fleischer," III, Georg Werthmann to Gordon Zahn, July 24, 1957.

88. Gordon Zahn, *German Catholics and Hitler's Wars*, 147.

89. UNDA, Gordon Zahn Papers, 13264–13360, Record of my Fulbright Year, November 13, 1956.

90. Gordon Zahn, *In Solitary Witness: the Life and Death of Franz Jägerstätter* (New York: Holt, Rinehart and Winston, 1964).

91. AKMB, Sammlung Werthmann, SW 1010/VII, I, Gordon Zahn to Georg Werthmann, stamped, December 17, 1961; Gordon Zahn to Georg Werthmann, August 25, 1961. Zahn referred to these controversies in his first letter to Werthmann, who continued to send him materials.

92. Gordon Zahn, *German Catholics and Hitler's Wars*, 7–8, 147.

93. AKMB, Sammlung Werthmann, SW 1028/VIII, 5, Georg Werthmann to Matthias Defregger, June 15, 1957.

94. Gordon Zahn, *German Catholics and Hitler's Wars*, 161–162.

95. These three Würzburg professors were Rauhut, Noack and Schneider. See UNDA, Gordon Zahn Papers, 3147, Zahn to Father Belfield, April 21, 1960. On Catholic peace movements in the Federal Republic, see Daniel Gerster, *Friedensdialoge im Kalten Krieg: eine Geschichte der Katholiken in der Bundesrepublik, 1957–1983* (Frankfurt: Campus Verlag, 2012). On Zahn's reserve: UNDA, Gordon Zahn Papers, 13264–13360, Record of my Fulbright Year, October 26, 1956; February 23, 1957 (morning).

96. ZDK, #4231/7, Gustav Kafka to Professor Dr. Heinz Fleckenstein, September 11, 1959, and ZDK #4231/7, Aktennotiz (from Kafka), Bad Godesberg, September 11, 1959.

97. Bayerischer Rundfunk, Hörfunkarchiv, Kirchenfunk, "Katholische Welt: Vor 30 Jahren – Bayerns Klerus sagt 'Nein.' Von Weihbischof Dr. Johannes Neuhäusler," Sendezeit: Sonntag, den July 24, 1966, 08.00–08.30/ II. Pr. The last page of this transcript is devoted to Neuhäusler's meeting with Zahn. The actual radio broadcast, however, left out the lines about this visit. Tellingly, this recollection appears nowhere in Zahn's record of the same meeting.

98. KZG, NL Adolph, WA 16a, Walter Adolph, "Bemerkungen zu dem Vortrag von Gordon C. Zahn, Die Katholische Presse und die nationale Frage im nationalsozialistischen Deutschland" (no date given). Tellingly, Zahn's extremely detailed journal notes on these two meetings do not mention these scoldings. It seems likely that Adolph and Neuhäusler had taken retrospective liberties in their accounts addressed to Bavarian radio listeners and American newspaper readers ten and three years later, respectively. See UNDA, 13264–13360, Record of my Fulbright Year, May 2, 1957; July 8, 1957.

99. HAEK, CRII 2.5,2.5, Predigtskizze, Erster Standortgottesdienst in Köln am October 10, 1956, in St. Gereon.

100. Gordon Zahn, "Würzburg 1957," in: *The Catholic Worker*, March 1958, 3. Found in KNA Archiv, Bonn, Gordon Zahn, "Der Kardinal und die 'Bundeswehr,'" in: *Neue Zeit*, Berlin-Ost, November 28, 1956.

101. ZDK, 4231/7, Abschrift, Nicholas Bakony to Otto Roegele, September 2, 1959.

102. ZDK, 4231/7, Otto Roegele to Heinrich Koeppler, September 7, 1959.

103. ZDK, 4930, Referat für staatsbürgerliche Angelegenheiten – Berichte – Schriftverkehr, 1952–1965 - Lebenslauf, Gustav Kafka (ohne Datum).

104. KZG, NL Walter Adolph, WA16a, Gustav Kafka to Gordon Zahn, November 6, 1959.

105. ZdK, 4930, Referat für staatsbürgerliche Angelegenheiten – Berichte – Schriftverkehr, 1952–1965 - Lebenslauf, Gustav Kafka (ohne Datum).

106. KZG, NL Walter Adolph, WA16a, Gustav Kafka to Gordon Zahn, December 18, 1959.

107. UNDA, Gordon Zahn Papers, 13231–13263, Journal Record of a Controversial Research Report, 6–7.

108. KZG, NL Walter Adolph, WA16a, Gordon Zahn to Regina Kühn, no date, but clearly early September 1959.

109. William J. Gleeson, "Support of Hitler by Catholic Bishops Is Labeled 'Untrue'. Dr. Zahn's Findings Contested," in: *The New World*, September 11, 1959, 1.

110. Heinz R. Kühn, *Mixed Blessings: An Almost Ordinary Life in Hitler's Germany* (Athens: University of Georgia Press, 1988), 8–15.

111. Ibid., 188.

112. DAB, I/ 5–12 – Kühn, Heinz, Dompropst Msgr. Piossek, Berlin to Heinz Kühn, August 6, 1945; Bonaventure Rebstock OSB to Piossek, July 2, 1945.

113. Heinz R. Kühn, *Mixed Blessings*, 183–189; Heinz R. Kühn, *Blutzeugen des Bistums Berlin* (Berlin: Morus Verlag, 1952).

114. Heinz R. Kühn, *Mixed Blessings*, 188–189; KZG, NL Walter Adolph, WA5L3, Heinz Kühn to Walter Adolph, April 26, 1952.

115. Heinz R. Kühn, "We Will Bear True Faith," in: *America*, September 14, 1957, 618–620.

116. NL Walter Adolph, WA 5L3, Walter Adolph to Heinz Kühn, August 10, 1957; Heinz Kühn to Walter Adolph, September 8, 1957; Heinz R. Kühn, "We Will Bear True Faith," 618–620.

117. Interview with Angelika Kühn.

118. "Dr. Gordon Zahn's Letter," in: *The New World*, November 13, 1959; William J. Gleeson, "Support of Hitler by Catholic Bishops Is Labeled 'Untrue': Dr. Zahn's Findings Contested," 1.

119. KZG, NL Walter Adolph, Heinz Kühn to Gerhard Fittkau, September 27, 1959.

120. UNDA, Gordon Zahn Papers, 13231–13263, Journal Record of a Controversial Research Report, 19–21.

121. Interview with Angelika Kühn.

122. KZG, NL Walter Adolph, WA 16a, Gerhard Fittkau to Walter Adolph, December 15, 1959; PAAA, B92, Band 104, Abschrift, Gerhard Fittkau to Johannes Neuhäusler, December 22, 1959; DAB V17–25–2, Aus einem Brief von Msgr. Gerhard Fittkau, Direktor des Amerikanischen Bonifatiusvereins, 1050 East, 233rd Street, New York, vom Januar 25, 1960, an Kardinal Bea; AKMB, Sammlung Werthmann, SW 1010/VII, 1; Gerhard Fittkau to Franz Hengsbach, February 2, 1960; KZG NL

Walter Adolph, WA 16a, Gerhard Fittkau to Walter Adolph, April 6, 1960; UNDA, Gordon Zahn Papers, 8370, Gerhard Fittkau to Dorothy Day, April 13, 1960.

123. UNDA, Gordon Zahn Papers, 13152, Dorothy Day to Gordon Zahn, May 16, 1960.

124. See Fittkau's defense of Rarkowski, "Noch einmal: Feldbischof Franz Justus Rarkowski," in: *Kirchenzeitung für das Bistum Aachen*, February 2, 1969, Nr. 5, 12/13.

125. Gerhard Fittkau, *Mein dreiunddreissigstes Jahr* (München: Kösel Verlag, 1957); Gerhard Fittkau, *My Thirty-Third Year: A Priest's Experience in a Russian Work Camp* (New York: Farrar, Strauss and Cudahy, 1958). Fittkau was beloved by his parishioners. See Hans Poschmann, 60 Jahre unser guter Hirte: Ein Nachruf auf Prälat Professor Dr. Gerhard Fittkau, June 3, 2006, available at www.visitator-ermland.de/arch-ebr/20041fitt kau2.htm. (accessed June 17, 2016).

126. KZG, NL Walter Adolph, WA 5b2, Gerhard Fittkau to Walter Adolph, February 26, 1954; Gerhard Fittkau to Walter Adolph, March 22, 1954.

127. KZG, NL Walter Adolph, WA 5b2, Gerhard Fittkau to Walter Adolph, March 22, 1954.

128. ZDK, 4231/7, Georg Bitter, Paulus Verlag Recklinghausen, to Gustav Kafka, March 21, 1960.

129. KZG, NL Adolph, WA 16a, Erwin Stindl to Julius Döpfner, March 21, 1960; Sylvester Theisen to the author, December 20, 2009.

130. Wolfgang Tischner, *Katholische Kirche in der SBZ/DDR, 1945–1951* (Paderborn: Schöningh, 2001), 496–500.

131. KZG, NL Adolph, WA 16a, Walter Adolph to Max Jordan, November 14, 1959.

132. Gerd Horten, *Radio Goes to War: The Cultural Politics of Propaganda during World War II* (Berkeley: University of California Press, 2003), 30.

133. UNDA, Gordon Zahn Papers, 3140, Gordon Zahn to Francis Connell, March 28, 1960.

134. ZDK, 4231/1, Grundsätzliches Gespräch über die Religionspolitik in der DDR, April 6, 1961. For an account of the SED's *Kirchenpolitik*, see Bernd Schaefer, *The East German State and the Catholic Church, 1945–1989* (New York: Berghahn Books, 2010), 64–84.

135. No author, *Prediger des Atomtodes* (Berlin: Verlag des Ministeriums für Nationale Verteidigung, 1959).

136. KZG, NL Adolph, WA 16a, Walter Adolph to Gordon Zahn, March 11, 1960.

137. ZDK 4231/7 Referat für staatsbürgerliche Angelegenheiten, Abschrift, Heinz Fleckenstein to Gustav Kafka, September 12, 1959.

138. UNDA, Gordon Zahn Papers, 13152, Dorothy Day to Gordon Zahn, May 16, 1960.

139. Gordon Zahn, "Würzburg 1957," 3–4.

140. Gordon Zahn, *War, Conscience and Dissent*, 47.

141. Gordon Zahn, *In Solitary Witness*, 6.

142. KZG, NL Adolph, WA 16a, Walter Adolph, Bemerkungen zu dem Vortrag von Gordon C. Zahn, Die katholische Presse und die nationale Frage im nationalsozialistischen Deutschland, 8.

143. PAAA, B92, Band 104, Telegram, December 7, 1959; PAAA, B92, Band 104, Abschrift, Gerhard Fittkau to Johannes Neuhäusler, December 22, 1959.

144. KZG, NL Adolph, WA 16a, Gustav Kafka to Walter Adolph, October 15, 1959.

145. UNDA, Gordon Zahn Papers, 13152, Dorothy Day to Gordon Zahn, May 16, 1960.

146. Interview with Susan Kalmer.

147. UNDA, Gordon Zahn Papers, 13125, J. Manuel Espinosa to Gordon Zahn, June 20, 1960.

148. ZDK 4231/7 Referat für staatsbürgerliche Angelegenheiten, Gustav Kafka to Karl Fürst zu Löwenstein, October 16, 1959.

149. Kafka had contacted Sylvester Theisen, an American sociologist at St. John's University in Minnesota whom he knew from Theisen's days as a special representative for intellectual and cultural affairs in West Germany for the American Catholic Bishops between 1955 and 1958. Kafka knew nothing of the close friendship between Theisen and Zahn. Theisen dutifully forwarded Kafka's letter to Zahn, who obliged the request and sent Kafka a copy of his paper. See ZDK, 4231/7 Referat für staatsbürgerliche Angelegenheiten, Gustav Kafka to Sylvester Theisen, September 9, 1959; Sylvester Theisen to the author, December 17, 2009; UNDA, Gordon Zahn Papers, 13231–13263, Journal Record of a Controversial Research Report, 18; ZDK, 4231/7 Referat für staatsbürgerliche Angelegenheiten, Sylvester Theisen to Gustav Kafka, September 14, 1959; Sylvester Theisen to Gordon Zahn, September 14, 1959; Gordon Zahn to Gustav Kafka, September 16, 1959.

150. ZDK, 4231/7, Gustav Kafka to Karl Fürst zu Löwenstein, October 16, 1959; KZG, NL Walter Adolph, WA 16a, Gerhard Fittkau to Walter Adolph, November 25, 1959; Anmerkungen zum Schreiben Seiner Eminenz August Kardinal Bea vom February 11, 1960.

151. DAB, NL Döpfner, V/7–25–2, Lorenz Jaeger to Julius Döpfner, November 2, 1959; KZG, NL Walter Adolph, WA 16a, Walter Adolph to Julius Döpfner, October 28, 1959; DAB, NL Döpfner, V/7–25–2, Augustin Bea to Julius Döpfner, February 11, 1960.

152. AEM, NL Johannes Neuhäusler, VN N13, Johannes Neuhäusler to Herrn Dr. Zöller, Presse und Informationsamt der Bundesregierung in Bonn, November 25, 1959.

153. ZDK, #4237/7, Karl Fürst zu Löwenstein to Gustav Kafka, September 19, 1959; Gustav Kafka to Karl Fürst zu Löwenstein, September 19, 1959; Gustav Kafka to Karl Fürst zu Löwenstein, October 16, 1959.

154. UNDA, Gordon Zahn Papers, 13231–13263, Journal Record of a Controversial Research Report, 8–9; KZG, NL Walter Adolph, WA 16a, Copy, Gordon Zahn to John R. Kelly, September 18, 1959; Gordon Zahn to John Kelly, September 21, 1959.

155. KZG, NL Walter Adolph, WA 16a, Gerhard Fittkau to Walter Adolph, November 25, 1959.
156. UNDA, Gordon Zahn Papers, 13231–13263, Journal Record of a Controversial Research Report, 9–10.
157. Gordon Zahn, "Catholic Support of Hitler's Wars," and Walter Adolph, "Monsignor Adolph's Reply," in: *The New World*, November 13, 1959.
158. UNDA, Gordon Zahn Papers, 13231–13263, Journal Record of a Controversial Research Report, 10; Paul Mundy, "Dr. Paul Mundy's Letter," and Placidus Jordan, "Father Jordan's Letter," in: *The New World*, November 20, 1959.
159. KZG, NL Walter Adolph, WA 16a, Gerhard Fittkau to Walter Adolph, November 25, 1959.
160. KZG, NL Walter Adolph, WA 16a, "'Catholicism Aided Hitlerism,' Says Loyola Professor," in: *Voice of Freedom: Keep Them Free, A Nondenominational, Nonsectarian Publication Devoted to the Cause of Religious Freedom and Our American Way of Life*, November 1959; Gerhard Fittkau to Walter Adolph, November 25, 1959.
161. KZG, NL Walter Adolph, WA 16a, Gerhard Fittkau to Walter Adolph, November 25, 1959; ZDK, #4231/7, Gerhard Fittkau to Gustav Kafka, December 10, 1959.
162. KZG, NL Walter Adolph, WA 16a, Gerhard Fittkau to Walter Adolph, November 25, 1959.
163. Ibid.
164. KZG, NL Walter Adolph, WA 16a, Gerhard Fittkau to James Maguire, December 1, 1959.
165. KZG, NL Walter Adolph, WA 16a, Gerhard Fittkau to Walter Adolph, November 25, 1959.
166. Ibid; Walter Adolph to Gerhard Fittkau, December 10, 1959.
167. UNDA, Gordon Zahn Papers, 13231–13263, Journal Record of a Controversial Research Report, 26–27.
168. KZG, NL Walter Adolph, WA 16a, Anmerkungen zum Schreiben Seiner Eminenz August Kardinal Bea vom 11. Februar 1960.
169. DAB V17–25–2, Aus einem Brief von Msgr. Gerhard Fittkau, Direktor des Amerikanischen Bonifatiusvereins, 1050 East, 233rd Street, New York, vom 25. Januar 1960, an Kardinal Bea.
170. For one example, see the copy of a letter from Bea to an unnamed professor from July 10, 1950. Günter J. Ziebertz, *Berthold Altaner (1885–1964): Leben und Werk eines schlesischen Kirchenhistorikers* (Cologne: Böhlau Verlag, 1997), 337–339.
171. "200-Per-Cent Patriotism?," in: *America*, September 26, 1959, 755; "Correspondence," in: *America*, October 24, 1959.
172. DAB, NL Döpfner, V/7–25–2, Augustin Bea to Julius Döpfner, February 11, 1960.
173. DAB, NL Döpfner, V/7–25–2, Augustin Bea to Julius Döpfner, February 20, 1960.
174. DAB, NL Döpfner, V/7–25–2 Augustin Bea to Julius Döpfner, April 8, 1960.

175. DAB, NL Döpfner, V/7–25–2, Thurston N. Davis, SJ to Julius Döpfner, May 18, 1960.

176. DAB, V/7–25–2, NL Döpfner, James Maguire to Julius Döpfner, May 18, 1960.

177. UNDA, Gordon Zahn Papers, 13231–13263, Journal Record of a Controversial Research Report, 26–27.

178. UNDA, Gordon Zahn Papers, 13231–13263, Journal Record of a Controversial Research Report, 36–41, 56–69; Loretta Morris, "Defining Prudence," Annual Meeting, Society for the Scientific Study of Religion, Albuquerque, New Mexico, November 4–6, 1994. Zahn's paper was published instead in *Cross Currents* through contacts provided by the editor at Helicon Press. UNDA, Gordon Zahn Papers, 8382, Gordon Zahn to David McManus, January 25, 1961; Gordon Zahn, "The German Catholic Press and Hitler's Wars," in: *Cross Currents*, Fall 1960, 337–351.

179. Interview with Peter Steinfels.

180. "Die katholische Presse und der Nationalismus im Nazi-Deutschland. Eine Erwiderung auf das Gutachten von Prof. Zahn, Chikago," in: *Kirchenzeitung für das Bistum Aachen*, 17, April 24, 1960; "'Bischöfe und Hitlers Feldzüge': Gordon Zahn hat ein neues Buch geschrieben," in *KNA – Informationsdienst*, Nr. 37, September 23, 1962; Robert Graham, SJ., *Review of German Catholics and Hitler's Wars: A Study in Social Control*, in: *America*, April 28, 1962, 145–146; "State of the Question: Dialogue in a Dilemma," in: *America*, June 9, 1962, 377–378; "Ein unqualifizierter Angriff: Zu einem Buch von Gordon Zahn," in: *KNA: Der Buchbrief*, Nr. 2, July 1, 1962; "Zwischen Schwarz-Weiss und historischer Wahrheit: Zu Büchern von Guenter Lewy und Gordon C. Zahn über die Katholische Kirche im Dritten Reich," in: *Deutsche Tagespost*, July 13, 1965; P.A.N. "Gordon Zahn vs. The Hierarchy," in: *The Wanderer Forum*. This was a reprint found at: Catholic University Archives, NL Muench, Box 60, Folder 2. For a positive review: "Das Dilemma der Katholiken: Ihre Wertordnung und der Patriotismus streiten miteinander," in: *Die Zeit*, September 18, 1964.

181. Gordon Zahn, *Die deutschen Katholiken und Hitlers Kriege* (Graz: Styria Verlag, 1965).

182. UNDA, Gordon Zahn Papers, 13231–13263, Journal Record of a Controversial Research Report, 74; Michael Gallagher, "Let Us Now Praise Gordon Zahn," at www.catholicpeacefellowship.org/downloads/gordon_zahn.pdf (accessed June 17, 2016).

183. DAB, NL Döpfner, V/7–25–2, Augustin Bea to Julius Döpfner, April 8, 1960.

184. KZG, NL Walter Adolph, WA 16a, The Catholic Press and the National Question in National-Socialist Germany: Remarks on a Paper by Dr. Gordon Zahn, By Msgr. Walter Adolph. This was the "official" English-language version of Adolph's remarks, as translated and edited by Heinz Kühn.

185. KZG, NL Walter Adolph, WA 16a, Max Jordan to Walter Adolph, November 22, 1959.

186. KZG, NL Walter Adolph, WA 16a, Heinz Kühn to Walter Adolph, November 11, 1959; for the original, see HAEK, Gen II 22.13, 10, Walter Adolph, Bemerkungen zu dem Vortrag von Gordon Zahn, Die katholische Presse und die nationale Frage in nationalsozialistischen Deutschland.

187. AEMF, NL Johannes Neuhäusler, VN N13, Johannes Neuhäusler to Zöller, Presse und Informationsamt der Bundesregierung in Bonn, November 25, 1959.

188. PAAA, B92, Band 104, Telegram, December 7, 1959; Generalkonsulat der Bundesrepublik Deutschland, Chicago and das Auswärtige Amt, Bonn, Betr: Vortrag von Professor Dr. Gordon Zahn, Loyola University, Chicago, über Haltung der katholischen Kirche in Deutschland gegenüber dem Nationalsozialismus, December 10, 1959.

189. PAAA, B92, Band 104, Abschrift, Gerhard Fittkau to Johannes Neuhäusler, December 22, 1959; AEMF, NL Johannes Neuhäusler, VN N 13, Zöller to Johannes Neuhäusler, January 13, 1960; PAAA, B 92, Band 104, Kunisch to das Generalkonsulat der Bundesrepublik Deutschland, Chicago, February 1, 1960.

190. ZDK, #4231/7, Auswärtiges Amt to das Zentralkomitee der Deutschen Katholiken, Bezug: Bericht des Generalkonsulats Chicago vom 7. März 1960, Bonn, March 19, 1960; Deutsches Generalkonsulat Chicago, Lupin to das Auswärtige Amt, Bonn, March 7, 1960.

191. ZDK, 4231/7, Aktenvermerk, March 4, 1960.

192. ZDK, 4231/7, Programm für den Informationsbesuch der Arbeitsgemeinschaft Kirchliche Presse e.V. in Bonn am 9. und 10. Märy 1960.

193. Privat Sammlung Narzissa Stasiewski, NL Bernhard Stasiewski, KFZG, Arbeitsgemeinschaft Kirchliche Presse, E.V., Betr: Erfahrungen der katholischen Kirchenpresse in der NS-Zeit, March 22, 1960.

194. AEMF, NL Johannes Neuhäusler, VN N13, Zöller to Johannes Neuhäusler, March 11, 1960.

195. HAEK, Gen II 22.13, 10, Gustav Kafka to Joseph Teusch, March 18, 1960; ZDK, 4231/7, Gustav Kafka to Gerhard Fittkau, March 22, 1960.

196. KZG, NL Walter Adolph WA 16a, Erwin Stindl to Julius Döpfner, March 21, 1960.

197. HAEK, Gen II 22.13, 10, Paul Böhringer to die Redaktion DER SPIEGEL Abteilung Kultur, April 11, 1960. For unclear reasons, *Der Spiegel* never ran its article.

198. HAEK, Gen II 22.13, 10, Paul Böhringer to Julius Döpfner, August 11, 1960; UNDA, Gordon Zahn Papers, CZHN 8329, Gordon Zahn to Father Reinhold, June 10, 1960.

199. UNDA, Gordon Zahn Papers, 13231–13263, Journal Record of a Controversial Research Report, 32.

200. See the extensive correspondence between Zahn and the Helicon editor, David McManus. UNDA, Gordon Zahn Papers, 4006, 4034; 4041, including Gordon Zahn to David McManus, May 24, 1959. McManus, Helicon's founder, had married a German immigrant.

201. "Bericht des Zentralkomitees für die Hauptkommission der Fuldaer Bischofkonkerenz, Bad Godesberg, 1. März 1960," in: Heinz Hürten, ed., *Akten deutscher Bischöfe seit 1945. Bundesrepublik Deutschland 1956–1960* (Paderborn: Schöningh, 2012), 878; DAB, V/7-25-2, Julius Döpfner to Paul Böhringer, L. Schwann Verlag, May 2, 1960.

202. UNDA, Gordon Zahn Papers, 13231–13263, Journal Record of a Controversial Research Paper, 29–30; 4006, Gordon Zahn to David McManus, January 25, 1961; 8382, David McManus to Paul Böhringer, Schwann Verlag, March 9, 1961.

203. HAEK, Gen II 22.13,10, Abschrift, Dr. P. Böhringer to Bischof Döpfner, March 28, 1960.

204. UNDA, Gordon Zahn Papers, 8382, David McManus, Helicon Press, to Paul Bohringer, L. Schwann Verlag, March 9, 1961.

205. UNDA, Gordon Zahn Papers, 4020, Philip Scharper, Editor, Sheed & Ward, to Gordon Zahn, October 18, 1960; 4021, Gordon Zahn to Philip Scharper, September 21, 1960; 4020, Philip Scharper to Gordon Zahn, November 16, 1960; 4006, Gordon Zahn to David McManus, January 25, 1961.

206. David Meconi, SJ, *Spiritual Writings: Frank Sheed and Maisie Ward* (Maryknoll: Orbis Books, 2010).

207. Robert Graham, SJ, "Review of German Catholics and Hitler's Wars: A Study in Social Control," 145–146.

208. "State of the Question: Dialogue on a Dilemma," in: *America*, June 9, 1962, 377–379.

209. UNDA, Gordon Zahn Papers, 4023, Gordon Zahn to Louise Wijnhausen, November 11, 1963.

210. Ibid.; UBEI, VA 1, Köselarchiv, Autorenkorrespondenz, E-W, Ernst-Wolfgang Böckenförde, Ernst-Wolfang Böckenförde to Heinrich Wild, September 2, 1962; Heinrich Wild to Ernst-Wolfgang Böckenförde, January 8, 1963; MLB, NL Carl Amery (Anton Mayer), Gordon Zahn to Carl Amery (Anton Mayer), January 28, 1964.

211. ADTK, NL Franziskus Stratmann, Franziskus Stratmann to Gordon Zahn, January 3, 1965; Franziskus Stratmann to Schreckenberg, January 19, 1965; Franziskus Stratmann to Schreckenberg, February 1, 1965; Franziskus Stratmann to Gordon Zahn, February 2, 1965.

212. "Das Klerusblatt ein 'Hilfsorgan der NS-Propagandamaschine'? Anklagen, die sich selbst das Urteil sprechen. Ein Diskussionsbeitrag von Paul Hümmelink, München," in: *Klerusblatt*, München, 40, Nr. 10, May 15, 1960; "Die deutschen Katholiken und Hitlers Krieg: Scharfe Kritik eines amerikanischen Jesuiten-Professors an der Haltung der Kirchenfürsten," in: *Die Abendzeitung München*, May 28, 1962. For articles by and about Zahn in the *Werkhefte katholischer Laien*, see Gordon Zahn, "Die deutsche katholische Presse und Hitlers Kriege," (1961), 180–182, 204–206; Gerd Hirschauer,"Keine Aussicht auf Einsicht: Gordon Zahns Untersuchung und die heutige katholische Presse," (1961), 215–217, 265–270; Carl Amery, "Der Bohrer des Dr. Zahn," (1962), 346–349; Hans Müller,

"Zum Thema: Die katholische Presse im Dritten Reich," (1962), 25–28; "Das Gewissen und die rechtmäßige Obrigkeit," (1962), 335–338.

213. KNA Archiv, Gordon Zahn, Gordon Zahn to Konrad Kraemer, September 12, 1962; "Ein unqualifizierter Angriff: Zu einem Buch von Gordon C. Zahn," 1–4.

214. ZDK, 4231/7, Gustav Kafka to Karl-Aloys Altmeyer, March 7, 1960; Karl-Aloys Altmeyer to the author, May 28, 2009. For Altmeyer's earlier contacts with Adolph, see KZG, NL Walter Adolph, WA 16f, Karl-Aloys Altmeyer to the Morus-Verlag, no date, but probably January 1959; Karl-Aloys Altmeyer to Walter Adolph, March 6, 1959; Karl-Aloys Altmeyer to Walter Adolph, May 12, 1959.

215. KZG, NL Walter Adolph, WA 16f, Karl-Aloys Altmeyer to Walter Adolph, March 12, 1960.

216. KZG, NL Walter Adolph, WA 16f, Karl-Aloys Altmeyer to den Morus-Verlag, no date, but probably 1959; Karl-Aloys Altmeyer to Walter Adolph, March 6, 1959; Karl-Aloys Altmeyer to Walter Adolph, May 12, 1959.

217. ZDK, 4231/7, Gustav Kafka to Karl-Aloys Altmeyer, March 11, 1960. The Schwaben-Verlag had intended to publish the work but decided against it, citing the risk; KZG, NL Walter Adolph, WA 24e, Walter Adolph to Konrad Kraemer, KNA, June 1, 1962.

218. HAEK, Gen II 22.13, 10, Abschrift, Karl Aloys Altmeyer to Gustav Kafka, March 16, 1960; KZG, NL Walter Adolph, WA16a, Walter Adolph to Gerhard Fittkau, April 5, 1960.

219. ZDK 4231/7, Karl-Aloys Altmeyer to Gustav Kafka, April 13, 1960.

220. Karl Aloys Altmeyer, "Versagten die deutschen Katholiken im Dritten Reich? Versuch einer kurzen Antwort auf eine Verurteilung vom grünen Tisch aus," in: *Deutsches Volksblatt*, September 15, 1960 and September 16, 1960. This piece was also printed in the *Badische Zeitung*. See Gordon Zahn's response: "Versagten die deutschen Katholiken im Dritten Reich? Professor Gordon C. Zahn antwortet auf die Erwiderungen von Karl Aloys Altmeyer," in: *Badische Volkszeitung*, November 3, 1960; Karl Aloys Altmeyer, "Versagten die deutschen Katholiken im Dritten Reich? Der Wahrheit einen Schritt näher – Offener Antwortbrief auf das gestern abgedruckte Schreiben Professor Zahns," in: *Badische Zeitung*, November 4, 1960; Karl-Aloys Altmeyer to the author, May 28, 2009.

221. ZDK, 4231/7, Gustav Kafka to Karlheinz Schmithüs, July 15, 1960. Twenty-four years later, Gottfried Beck also noted the apologetic character of Altmeyer's work as well as a number of errors in the edition. See Beck, *Die Bistumspresse in Hessen und der Nationalsozialismus, 1930–1941* (Paderborn: Schöningh Verlag, 1996), 12, 15. Tellingly, Beck's work continued to wrestle with Zahn's challenge.

222. Karl Aloyius Altmeyer, *Katholische Presse unter NS-Diktatur: die katholischen Zeitungen und Zeitschriften Deutschlands in den Jahren 1933 bis 1945: Eine Dokumentation* (Berlin: Morus Verlag, 1962).

223. UNDA, Gordon Zahn Papers, 13231–13263, Journal Record of a Controversial Research Report, 73–74.

224. On this point, see Arthur A. Cohen, "Review of Gordon Zahn, *German Catholics and Hitler's Wars*," in: *Worldview* 6, Nr. 9, September 1963, 10–11.

225. See Gordon Zahn, *Vocation of Peace*, vii; *In Solitary Witness*, 4–6; *Another Part of the War; Chaplains in the RAF: A Study in Role Tension* (Manchester: Manchester University Press, 1969), 36; *German Catholics and Hitler's Wars*, 3–11.

226. See Heinz R. Kühn, *Mixed Blessings*; Johannes Neuhäusler, *Amboß und Hammer: Erlebnisse im Kirchenkampf des Dritten Reiches* (München: Manz Verlag, 1967), Gerhard Fittkau, *Mein dreiunddreissigstes Jahr*; Wilhelm Leibusch, *Einer aus der Lausitzer Straße: Eine katholische Jugend in Berlin-Kreuzberg zu Anfang des Jahrhunderts* (Berlin: Morus Verlag, 1968).

227. Gordon Zahn, "Social Science and the Theology of War," in: William J. Nagle, ed., *Morality and Modern Warfare: The State of the Question* (Baltimore, Helicon Press, 1960).

228. Gordon Zahn, *War, Conscience and Dissent*, 46.

229. UNDA, Gordon Zahn Papers, 13231–13263, Journal Record of a Controversial Research Report, 74–75.

230. Interview with Michael Hovey.

231. "Study Moral Implications of War in Zahn's Book on Hitler: Reviewed by Raymond Schmandt, Ph.D., Associate Professor, Department of History," in: *The Loyola News* XLI, Nr. 21, March 29, 1962. Interview with Peter Steinfels. Steinfels was the editor at the time for the Loyola student newspaper. For additional coverage of Zahn, see Tom Philpott, "German Catholics and Hitler's Wars: Catholic Self-Criticism in Zahn Talk," in: *The Loyola News* XLII, Nr. 19, March 21, 1963.

232. KZG, NL Walter Adolph, Julius Döpfner, WA25 C3, "Nr. 3 – Bedenkliche ekklesiologische Tendenzen im Schrifttum 'nonkonformistischer' Katholiken, Fuldauer Bischofskonferenz 28–29. August 1963," August 24, 1963, 7–8.

233. Interview with Guenter Lewy.

234. ADK, Archiv Theater der Freien Volksbühne, Schnellhefter, der Schnellvertreter, Vorkorrespondenz, Erwin Piscator to Rolf Hochhuth, September 25, 1962.

5   The Storm over *The Deputy*

1. Rolf Hochhuth, *Der Stellvertreter, Mit einem Vorwort von Erwin Piscator und Essays von Karl Japsers, Walter Muschg und Golo Mann, 35. Auflage, April 2002* (Reinbek bei Hamburg: Rowohlt Verlag, 1963, 1998), 258.

2. Ibid., 283.

3. Rolf Hochhuth, *The Deputy. With a Preface by Albert Schweitzer. Translated by Richard and Clara Winston* (Baltimore: The Johns Hopkins University Press, 1963, 1997), 220.

4. Rolf Hochhuth, *Der Stellvertreter*, 258, 288–293.

5. Ibid., 378–379. The stage version premiered in Berlin cut out almost the entirety of Act V, which features a different ending. The final scene featured Fontana imprisoned in Auschwitz, pitted against his archnemesis,

"The Doctor," a diabolic incarnation of absolute evil loosely modeled after Josef Mengele, the so-called "Angel of Death."

6. Prince Constantine of Bavaria, *The Pope: A Portrait from Life*, translated by Diana Pyke (London: Allan Wingate, 1954), 32–33.

7. *Der Spiegel*, October 15, 1958. See René Schlott, *Papsttod und Weltöffentlichkeit seit 1878: Die Medialisierung eines Rituals* (Paderborn: Schöningh, 2013), 139–155, especially 152–155.

8. Karl-Josef Kuschel, Macht und Gewissen: Kirchenkritik als Machtkritik bei Reinhold Schneider, Katholische Akademie Freiburg, April 5, 2008. www .theologie-und-literatur.de/fileadmin/user_upload/Theologie_und_Literatur/ MachtundGewissen.pdf (accessed June 13, 2015).

9. Muriel Guittat-Neudin, "'Les Silences de Pie XII': Entre Mémoire et Oubli, 1944–1958," in: *Revue D'Historie Ecclésiastique* 105 (2011), 215–239.

10. HAEK, Gen II 23, 23a, 5, Der "Sowjet Weekly" (London) gegen den Papst, translation and excerpt of the article, "Quo Vadis, Vatican?" from June 16, 1945.

11. Léon Poliakov, *Bréviere de la Haine* (Paris: Calmann-Lévy, 1951). For the English translation, see Léon Poliakov, *Harvest of Hate: The Nazi Program for the Destruction of the Jews of Europe* (Westport: Greenwood Press, 1954), 296; Léon Poliakov, *Mémoires* (Paris: Jacques Grancher Éditeur, 1999).

12. For examples of coverage in glossy magazines, see "The Play That Rocked Europe," in: *The Saturday Evening Post*, February 29, 1964, 36–39; Tom Prideaux, "Homage and Hate for 'The Deputy,'" in: *Life*, March 13, 1964, 28D.

13. Rolf Hochhuth, "Der Mensch sollte so leben, als gäbe es Gott," in: Karl-Josef Kuschel, *'Ich Glaube nicht, dass ich Atheist bin': Neue Gespräche über Religion und Literatur* (Munich: Piper, 1992), 169–193, 175–176; Birgitt Lahann, *Hochhuth – Der Störenfried* (Bonn: Dietz Verlag, 2016), 27, 372–373.

14. "Mein Vater heißt Hitler: Fritz J. Raddatz im Gespräch mit Rolf Hochhuth," in: *Die Zeit*, April 9, 1976.

15. SLA, NL Hochhuth, #302, Friedhofs-Ordnung und Eiserner Vorhang: Notizen über Eschwege.

16. Rolf Hochhuth, "Friedhöfe und Eiserner Vorhang: Notizen in meiner Vaterstadt Eschwege an der Werra," in: York-Egbert König and Karl Kollmann, ed., *Eschwege: Ein Lesebuch* (Husum: Husum Druck-und Verlagsgesellschaft, 1996), 97–116, and in particular, 112.

17. On Hochhuth's artistic instruction, see SLA, NL Hochhuth, #302, no date, no name, no title. For the drawing, see SLA, NL Hochhuth, #1, loses Blatt.

18. For one of several examples, see Rolf Hochhuth, "Der Mensch sollte so leben, als gäbe es Gott."

19. It is tempting to draw a parallel between Hochhuth and Rudolf Augstein, the pugnacious founder of *Der Spiegel*. Augstein, who equally esteemed Bismarck's statesmanship, also relished in bringing down the high and mighty. During the notorious *Spiegel* affair of November 1962, he was the subject of a campaign by his enemies. As unlikely as it might seem, both

Augstein and Hochhuth fused elements of national liberalism with a withering capitalist critique. They regarded each other, it seems, with a critical reserve.

20. Rolf Hochhuth, *Der Klassenkampf ist nicht zu Ende* (Reinbek: Rowohlt, 1965). For his interest in Bismarck, see Rowohlt Theater Verlag, Magazine Clipping, "Hochhuth ... Unverzeihliches über Gott," in: *Littera* 1/IV, 4. Jahrg., 1964.

21. This theme of decline was one expressed in the novel *Buddenbrooks* by one of Hochhuth's literary heroes, Thomas Mann, whose rich, labyrinthical prose style bears more than a passing resemblance to that of his devotee. On his admiration for Thomas Mann, see SLA, NL Rolf Hochhuth, #396, Lebenslauf, no date, but most likely late 1963 or 1964, 4.

22. Heinz Puknus and Norbert Göttler, *Rolf Hochhuth: Störer im Schweigen. Der Provokateur und seine Aktionsliteratur* (München: Herbert Utz Verlag, 2011), 12.

23. SLA, NL Rolf Hochhuth, #250, Rolf Hochhuth to Dieter (no last name given), June 11, 1953; Birgit Lahann, *Hochhuth – Der Störenfried* (Bonn: Dietz Verlag, 2016), 24.

24. On his dislike for mathematics and physics, see KNA Archive, Berlin, Newspaper Clipping, "Hochhuth wird nicht hochmütig. "Von der Kunst kann man nicht leben." 'Nacht-depesche' interviewte Autor des 'Stellvertreter,'" in: *Nachtdepesche*, February 22, 1963; Birgit Lahann, *Hochhuth – Der Störenfried* 22–23.

25. SLA, NL Rolf Hochhuth, #396, Lebenslauf.

26. SLA, NL Rolf Hochhuth, #250, Hochhuth to Dieter, June 6, 1953.

27. SLA, NL Rolf Hochhuth, Schachtel 269, Rolf Hochhuth to die Redkation, DIE ZEIT, Hamburg (no date given, but most likely April 4, 1963).

28. Interview with Hans Heinrich Koch, Eschwege.

29. Anna Maria Zimmer, "Zur Geschichte der jüdischen Gemeinden in Eschwege," in: Karl Kollmann, ed., *Geschichte der Stadt Eschwege* (Eschwege: Selbstverlag der Stadt Eschwege, 1993), 341–357; Birgit Lahann, *Hochhuth – Der Störenfried*, 19.

30. Interview with Hans Heinrich Koch, Eschwege.

31. UNDA, CZHN, 3066, Interview with Rolf Hochhuth in *Ramparts*, February 13, 1964; Birgit Lahann, *Hochhuth – Der Störenfried*, 26. In Lahann's account, it was Hochhuth's Jewish aunt who poisoned herself.

32. SLA, NL Rolf Hochhuth, #396, Lebenslauf, 2.

33. Ibid.

34. Interview with Hans Heinrich Koch, Eschwege.

35. Interview with Hans Heinrich Koch: According to Koch "Wir haben uns kaputt geschämt ... Ich habe die Juden doch gekannt ... Es war ein Bedürfnis von ihm, sich um den Stellvertreter zu kümmern."

36. "Die Frage wurde dem Papst 1943 gestellt," in: *Werra-Rundschau*, March 23, 1963.

37. KZG, NL Walter Adolph, WA 16D1, Newspaper Clipping, "Rolf Hochhuth arbeitet an zwei neuen Stücken," in: *Die Welt am Sonntag*, March 10, 1963.

38. Heinz Puknus and Norbert Göttler, *Rolf Hochhuth: Störer im Schweigen*, 19; Birgit Lahann, *Hochhuth – Der Störenfried*, 36.
39. Birgit Lahann, *Hochhuth – Der Störenfried*, 38–39.
40. Marianne Heinemann-Sideri to the author, December 30, 2011.
41. Ibid; Marianne Hochhuth, *Das Buch der Gedichte. Deutsche Lyrik von den Anfängen bis zur Gegenwart* (Gütersloh: Bertelsmann, 1963).
42. "Wer ist das eigentlich, dieser Rolf Hochhuth?," in: *Werra Rundschau*, March 7, 1963.
43. On the significance of his mother-in-law's death, see Fritz J. Raddatz, *Tagebücher, 1982–2001* (Reinbek: Rowohlt, 2010), 89; Marianne Heinemann-Sideri to the author, December 30, 2011.
44. Rolf Hochhuth, *Die Berliner Antigone: Erzählung und Fernsehspiel* (Paderborn: Schöningh Verlag, 1980).
45. Birgit Lahann, *Hochhuth – Der Störenfried*, 9. Reporters also noticed his choleric temperament. See Felix Schmidt, "Wieder zielt Hochhuth auf ein Tabu," in: *Bild*, April 14, 1963. Even the critic for the *Frankfurter Allgemeine Zeitung* gave his review the title: "Fragments of a Great Anger." Dieter Hildebrandt, "Bruchstücke eines großen Zorns," in: *Frankfurter Allgemeine Zeitung*, February 22, 1963.
46. Interview with Hans Heinrich Koch.
47. Heinz Puknus and Norbert Göttler, *Rolf Hochhuth: Störer im Schweigen*, 25; "'Ein Satanischer Feigling': Dramatiker Rolf Hochhuth über die neuen Kontroversen zu seinem Papst-Stück 'Der Stellvertreter' und Pius XII," in: *Der Spiegel*, May 26, 2007.
48. "Die Frage wurde dem Papst 1943 gestellt," in: *Werra-Rundschau*, March 23, 1963.
49. Birgit Lahann, *Hochhuth – Der Störenfried*, 30.
50. Götz Aly, "Theodor Schieder, Werner Conze oder die Vorstufen der physischen Vernichtung," in: Winfried Schulze and Otto Gerhard Oexle, ed., *Deutsche Historiker im Nationalsozialismus* (Frankfurt am Main: Fischer-Taschenbuchverlag, 1999), 163–214; Ingo Haar, *Historiker im Nationalsozialismus. Deutsche Geschichtswissenschaft und der "Volkstumskampf" im Osten* (Göttingen: Vandenhoeck und Ruprecht, 2000); Jan Eike Dunkhase, *Werner Conze. Ein deutscher Historiker im 20. Jahrhundert* (Göttingen: Vandenhoeck & Ruprecht, 2010).
51. Kurt Gerstein, "Augenzeugenbericht über Massenvergasungen," in: Léon Poliakov and Josef Wulf, *Das Dritte Reich und die Juden* (Berlin: Arani, 1955), 101–115; for Hochhuth's discovery of this, see ADK, Erwin-Piscator Center, 182, F66, From: Paul Moor, Berlin stringer, filing through Bonn Bureau, February 19, 1963.
52. Kurt Gerstein, "Augenzeugenbericht über Massenvergasungen."
53. Rolf Hochhuth, *Der Stellvertreter* (1998), 387.
54. ADK, Erwin-Piscator Center, 182, F66, from Paul Moor, Berlin stringer, filing through Bonn Bureau, February 19 1963.
55. For two examples: the Gerstein report contains the lines: "Dann setzt sich der Zug in Bewegung. Voran ein bildhübsches junges Mädchen, so gehen sie die Allee entlang, alle nackt, Männer, Frauen, Kinder, ohne Prothesen."

Hochhuth wrote: "Und die Kinderleichen. Ein junges Mädchen ging dem Zug voran, nackt wie alle. Mütter, alle nackt." The report contains the lines: "Wie Basaltsäulen stehen die Toten aufrecht aneinander gepreßt in den Kammern. Es wäre auch kein Platz hinzufallen oder auch nur sich vorüber zu neigen. Selbst im Tode noch kennt man die Familien. Sie drücken sich, im Tode verkrampft, noch die Hände, so daß man Mühe hat, sie auseinander reißen, um die Kammern für die nächste Charge freizumachen." Hochhuth wrote: "Wie Basaltsäulen stehn die nackten Leichen da, im Tode noch erkennt man die Familien. Sie haben sich umarmt, verkrampft – mit Haken reißt man auseinander." Rolf Hochhuth, *Der Stellvertreter* (1963, 1998), 37, 38; Kurt Gerstein, "Augenzeugenbericht über Massenvergasungen," 101–115.

56. Léon Poliakov and Josef Wulf, *Das Dritte Reich und seine Diener: Dokumente* (Berlin: Arani, 1956), 79–86.
57. Ibid., 86.
58. Birgit Lahann, *Hochhuth – Der Störenfried*, 51.
59. SLA, NL Rolf Hochhuth, #396, Rolf Hochhuth, Lebenslauf.
60. SLA, NL Rolf Hochhuth, #296, Rolf Hochhuth to den Verlag Volk und Welt, June 16, 1959; #5, Frau Dr. S. Noller, Institut für Zeitgeschichte to Rolf Hochhuth, July 9, 1959; Rolf Hochhuth to das Bayrische Staatsarchiv z. Hd. Herrn Prof. Memmsen, August 24, 1959; #269, Rolf Hochhuth to Elfriede Gerstein, August 26, 1959; #5, Elfriede Gerstein to Rolf Hochhuth, March 17, 1960; #269, Rolf Hochhuth to Ilse Wolf, Wiener Library, June 13, 1961.
61. Rolf Hochhuth, *Der Stellvertreter* (1963, 1998), 381–469.
62. SLA, NL Rolf Hochhuth, #396, Rolf Hochhuth to Reinhard Mohn, June 9, 1959; #296, Reinhard Mohn to Herrn Dr. Boeck z.H. Herrn Leonhardt, June 29, 1959.
63. SLA, NL Rolf Hochhuth, #269, Rolf Hochhuth to die Kulturabteilung des Auswärtigen Amtes z.Hd. Herrn Staatssekretär, Dr. Dieter Sattler, July 10, 1959; Dieter Sattler to Rolf Hochhuth, July 16, 1959; E. Minewegen, Legationsrat to Rolf Hochhuth, August 7, 1959; Rolf Hochhuth to Dieter Sattler, August 31, 1959.
64. On his lack of fluency, see the translations he made in pencil on a document written in Italian. SLA, NL Rolf Hochhuth, #1, Bombe sul Vaticano.
65. Interview with Ludwig Hammermayer, Eichstätt.
66. SLA, NL Rolf Hochhuth, #5, Rolf Hochhuth to Bruno Wüstenberg, October 23, 1959. For the protocol of Hochhuth's interview, see #5, Rolf Hochhuth to Marianne (Hochhuth), October 26, 1959.
67. Interview with Ludwig Hammermayer, Eichstätt.
68. Michael Phayer, *Pius XII, The Holocaust and the Cold War* (Bloomington: Indiana University Press, 2007), 195–196; AES, NL Andreas Rohracher, 20/99, Dr. Jakob Weinbacher to Andreas Rohracher, September 1, 1952.
69. Michael Phayer, *Pius XII, The Holocaust and the Cold War*, 195–207; Gerald Steinacher, *Nazis auf der Flucht: wie Kriegsverbrecher über Italien nach Übersee entkamen* (Innsbruch: Studienverlag, 2008).
70. Michael Phayer, *Pius XII, The Holocaust and the Cold War*, 76–79.

71. SLA, NL Rolf Hochhuth, #269, Rolf Hochhuth to Ludwig Hammermeier (sic), March 12, 1960.
72. SLA, NL Rolf Hochhuth, #5, Rolf Hochhuth to Bruno Wüstenberg, October 23, 1959. Birgit Lahann asserts that Hochhuth told both that he was planning to write about Maximilian Kolbe. While this may also have been the case, the written correspondence refers to Lichtenberg – and not Kolbe. Birgit Lahann, *Hochhuth – Der Störenfried*, 44.
73. Birgit Lahann, *Hochhuth – Der Störenfried*, 44–45.
74. SLA, NL Rolf Hochhuth, #5, Handwritten Protocol of Hochhuth's Interview with Alois Hudal, October 22, 1959.
75. SLA, NL Rolf Hochhuth, #5, Rolf Hochhuth to Marianne Hochhuth, October 26, 1959; Rolf Hochhuth to Bruno Wüstenberg, October 23, 1959.
76. Rolf Hochhuth, *Der Stellvertreter* (1963, 1998), 428.
77. SLA, NL Rolf Hochhuth, #5, Handwritten Protocol of Hochhuth's Interview with Alois Hudal, October 22, 1959.
78. Rolf Hochhuth, *Der Stellvertreter* (1963, 1998), 32.
79. Unternehmensarchiv, Berthelsmann, 0046/48, Rolf Hochhuth to Reinhard Mohn, March 21, 1968.
80. SLA, NL Rolf Hochhuth, Schachtel Ausstellung, Ringbuch mit Recherchenmaterial.
81. Letters looking for housing indicate that he only planned to spend from September 15 to October 30, 1959, in Rome itself. SLA, NL Rolf Hochhuth, #1, Rolf Hochhuth to Signora Ciancio, no date, but probably the first half of August; E. Minwegen to Rolf Hochhuth, August 7, 1959; Signora Caterinici to Rolf Hochhuth, August 14, 1959. An identification card from the Biblioteca Apostolica Vaticana bears the date 21.10.1959; a Benutzungskarte from the Institut für Zeitgeschichte in Munich shows that it had been extended from 28.10.59 through 18.1.60, indicating that he may well have returned to Germany by late October. SLA, NL Rolf Hochhuth, #396.
82. SLA, NL Rolf Hochhuth, #5, Rolf Hochhuth to Bruno Wüstenberg, February 18, 1960.
83. Léon Poliakov, "Le centre de Documentation Juivre, ses archives ses publications," in: *Cahiers D'histoire de la Guerre* 2 (1949), 39–44; Laura Jockusch, *Collect and Record! Jewish Holocaust Documentation in Early Postwar Europe* (New York: Oxford University Press, 2012), 63–65, 169–171.
84. See SLA, NL Rolf Hochhuth, #5, Léon Poliakov to Rolf Hochhuth, April 27, 1961; Léon Poliakov to Rolf Hochhuth, May 26, 1961. For the quote by Mauriac, see Rolf Hochhuth, *Der Stellvertreter* (1963), 6.
85. SLA, NL Rolf Hochhuth, #5, Rolf Hochhuth to Léon Poliakov, May 24, 1961.
86. SLA, NL Rolf Hochhuth, Schachtel Ausstellung, Ringbuch mit Recherchenmaterial. The first version of the fourth Act lacks this climactic scene. He later added the following instructions in a bright blue pen: "Die Pilatusszene: vielleicht – ein Waschbecken, das ihm gebracht wird, weil er sich beim Unterschreiben seiner (illegible word) die Finger bekleckert hat" and "Hände waschen."

87. Rolf Hochhuth, *Der Stellvertreter* (1963), 273. For the text of this address, see Ludwig Volk, *Akten deutscher Bischöfe über die Lage der Kirche, 1933–1945, Band VI, 1943–1945* (Mainz: Grünewald Verlag, 1985), 884–893.

88. SLA, NL Rolf Hochhuth, #352, Rolf Hochhuth to Dr. Eric Bentley, December 5, 1964.

89. SLA, NL Rolf Hochhuth, #6, Rolf Hochhuth to Herrn Leonhardt, May 23, 1961. These dates for completing and printing the manuscript proofs do not correspond to those of Birgit Lahann, who puts them at 1959 and 1960, respectively. Lahann's account is based on interviews with the playwright; this timeline is based on the written correspondence from Hochhuth's papers. Birgit Lahann, *Hochhuth – Der Störenfried*, 56.

90. Reinhard-Maria Strecker, ed., *Dr. Hans Globke. Aktenauszüge, Dokumente* (Hamburg: Rütten & Loening, 1961).

91. ÖLA, NL Friedrich Heer, Rolf Hochhuth to Friedrich Heer, January 23, 1962, ohne Signatur.

92. On his advance, see Unternehmensarchiv, Bertelsmann, 0046/48, Rolf Hochhuth to Reinhard Mohn, March 21, 1968; SLA, NL Rolf Hochhuth, #352, Rolf Hochhuth to Eric Bentley, December 5, 1964.

93. Fritz J. Raddatz, *Jahre mit Ledig: Eine Erinnerung* (Reinbek: Rowohlt, 2015), 85–86.

94. Unternehmensarchiv, Bertelsmann, 0046/48, Rolf Hochhuth to Reinhard Mohn, March 21, 1968.

95. For the date of the break of contract, see ÖLA, Wien, NL Friedrich Heer, Rolf Hochhuth to Friedrich Herr, January 23, 1962, ohne Signatur.

96. Interview with Rolf Hochhuth.

97. Ibid.

98. Unternehmensarchiv, Bertelsmann, 0046/48, Rolf Hochhuth to Reinhard Mohn, March 21, 1968.

99. Unternehmensarchiv, Bertelsmann, 0046/48, Reinhard Mohn to Rolf Hochhuth, March 25, 1968.

100. Unternehmensarchiv, Bertelsmann, 0046/48, Rolf Hochhuth to Reinhard Mohn, March 21, 1968.

101. It is not clear whether Mohn was informed about this step. Mohn's letter to Hochhuth from 1968 seems to indicate that he was on board with this step, but this cannot be determined conclusively. Unternehmensarchiv, Bertelsmann, 0046/48, Reinhard Mohn to Rolf Hochhuth, March 25, 1968; SLA, NL Rolf Hochhuth, #396, Rowohlt Verlag, unknown to Karl Ludwig Leonhardt, February 26, 1962.

102. Fritz J. Raddatz, *Jahre mit Ledig*, 85.

103. Interview with Margaret Osthus.

104. SLA, NL Rolf Hochhuth, #352, Rolf Hochhuth to Eric Bentley, December 5, 1964.

105. Bestand Margaret Osthus, Rolf Hochhuth to Herrn Pfarrer Jürgen Ehlers, July 29, 2007.

106. ADK, Archiv Theater der Freien Volksbühne Berlin, Schnellhefter, Der Stellvertreter, Vorkorrespondenz, Heinrich Maria Ledig-Rowohlt to Erwin

Piscator, February 26, 1962; SLA, NL Rolf Hochhuth, #396, Rowohlt Verlag, unknown to Karl Ludwig Leonhardt, February 26, 1962.

107. ADK, Archiv Theater der Freien Volksbühne Berlin, Schnellhefter, Der Stellvertreter, Vorkorrespondenz, Heinrich Maria Ledig-Rowohlt to Erwin Piscator, February 26, 1962.

108. SLA, NL Rolf Hochhuth, #396, unknown to Karl Ludwig Leonhardt, February 26, 1962. The German terms are Taschenbuch and Kartonierte Buchausgabe.

109. Fritz J. Raddatz, *Jahre mit Ledig*, 87.

110. Ibid., 87–88.

111. Ibid.; ADK, Archiv Theater der Freien Volksbühne Berlin, Schnellhefter, Der Stellvertreter, Vorkorrespondenz, Heinrich Maria Ledig-Rowohlt to Erwin Piscator, February 26, 1962.

112. ADK, Archiv Theater der Freien Volksbühne Berlin, Schnellhefter, Der Stellvertreter, Vorkorrespondenz, Heinrich Maria Ledig-Rowohlt to Erwin Piscator, February 26, 1962.

113. On Piscator's belief that "Hochhuth" was a pseudonym, see Birgit Lahann, *Hochhuth – Der Störenfried*, 54–62.

114. HAEK, Gen II, 22.13, 35, KNA, Nr. 36, Donnerstag, February 21, 1963/B, "Hochhuth: 'Ungeheuerliche Behauptung.'"

115. Hochhuth himself admitted this publicly. HAEK, GEN II, 22.13, 35, Newspaper Clipping, "NRZ-Gespräch mit Bühnen-Autor Rolf Hochhuth, 'Ich hasse Papst Pius XII nicht,'" in: *Neue Rheinzeitung*, March 9, 1963.

116. HAEK, GEN II, 22.13, 35, Newspaper Clipping, "Zahmer Piscator gab nur ein Fragment: Uraufführung von Hochhuths 'Der Stellvertreter,'" in: *Kölner Stadt-Anzeiger*, February 22, 1963.

117. For a cut made right before the premiere, see ADK, Schnellhefter, Der Stellvertreter, Vorkorrespondenz, Erwin Piscator to Erhart Stettner, March 20, 1963.

118. For discussions on the fifth act, see ADK, Schnellhefter, Der Stellvertreter, Vorkorrespondenz, Kleinselbeck to Hochhuth, August 16, 1962; Rolf Hochhuth to Kleinselbeck and Erwin Piscator, August 18, 1962; Rolf Hochhuth to Erwin Piscator, August 28, 1962.

119. "Die Frage wurde dem Papst 1943 gestellt," in: *Werra-Rundschau*, March 22, 1963.

120. KZG, NL Walter Adolph, WA 16 D1, Newspaper Clipping, "Nach der Premiere," in: *Berliner Morgenpost*, February 22, 1963.

121. Rolf Hochhuth, "L'Impromptu de Madame Tussaud," in Siegfried Unseld, ed., *Heinrich Maria Ledig-Rowohlt zuliebe. Festschrift zu seinem 60. Geburtstag am 12 März 1968* (Reinbek: Rowohlt, 1968), 31–57, 33.

122. Ibid.

123. SLA, NL Rolf Hochhuth, #269, Freie Volksbühne e.V. to Rolf Hochhuth, November 2, 1962.

124. HABF, HF/5462B, Zeittheater und Zeitgeschichte. Marginalien zu Rolf Hochhuths Schauspiel "Der Stellvertreter," Sendung: 2.5.63, 21: 15–22:00 Uhr, 6.

125. SLA, NL Rolf Hochhuth, #5, Hans Egon Holthusen to Rolf Hochhuth, February 19, 1962.

126. "Rolf Hochhuth: Ein Kampf mit Rom," in: *Der Spiegel*, (17), April 24, 1963.

127. Ibid.

128. For one example: "Shattering," in: *Newsweek* (63), March 9, 1964, 78–79. The author wrote: "'The Deputy' is a botch – crude, unshapely, and strident – but it is also a theatrical experience so shattering that it makes the usual yardsticks seem piffling and irrelevant."

129. ADK, Archiv Theater der Freien Volksbühne Berlin, Schnellhefter, Der Stellvertreter, Vorkorrespondenz, Heinrich Maria Ledig-Rowohlt to Erwin Piscator, February 26, 1962.

130. ADK, Erwin Piscator Center, 2150, Heinrich Maria Ledig-Rowohlt to Erwin Piscator, March 8, 1962.

131. ADK, Archiv Theater der Freien Volksbühne Berlin, Schnellhefter, Der Stellvertreter, Vorkorrespondenz, Erwin Piscator to Brooks Atkinson, January 21, 1963; Erwin Piscator to Kenneth Tinen, January 21, 1963; Erwin Piscator to Tom Curtis, January 21, 1963; Erwin Piscator to John Crosby, January 21, 1963; Erwin Piscator to Howard Taubmann, January 22, 1963; Leo Kerz to Erwin Piscator, January 16, 1963.

132. ADK, Archiv Theater der Freien Volksbühne Berlin, Schnellhefter, Der Stellvertreter, Vorkorrespondenz, Erwin Piscator to John Crosby, January 21, 1963.

133. For a report on this interview, see KZG, NL Adolph WA 16D1, Newspaper Clipping, KNA, "Borsche spielt 'Pius XII.' Erstlingswerk von Hochhuth: 'Der Stellvertreter,'" January 25, 1963.

134. ADK, Archiv Theater der Freien Volksbühne Berlin, Schnellhefter, Der Stellvertreter, Vorkorrespondenz, Rolf Hochhuth to Erwin Piscator, March 12, 1962.

135. DAB, NL Erich Klausener Jr., V/12–6–2–2, Korr.–Klausener, 62–64, Katholiken-Ausschuss der Bistums Berlin, Fachausschuss "Öffenliches Leben," Minutes of the meeting taken by Dr. Ernst Alfred Jauch, March 14, 1963.

136. Ibid.

137. KZG, NL Adolph WA 16D1, Newspaper Clipping, KNA, "Borsche spielt "Pius XII.", January 25, 1963.

138. Erich Klausener, "Auge auf Berlin: Papst bei Piscator," in: *Petrusblatt*, February 3, 1963.

139. DRA, "'Petrusblatt' greift die Freie Volksbühne an. Unfaires Stück über Pius XII," in: *Der Tagesspiegel*, January 31, 1963; DPA, "Petrusblatt zur nächsten Piscator-Premiere," in: *Telegraf*, January 31, 1963.

140. DRA, "Kontroverse mit dem Petrusblatt. Ein Autor nimmt Stellung," February 3, 1963; "Schauspiel-Autor antwortet dem Petrusblatt," in: *Der Tagesspiegel*, February 3, 1963; "Die Antwort," in: *Der Abend*, February 2, 1963; "Nicht Pius XII: Hochhuth antwortet dem Petrusblatt," in: *Der Tag*, Berlin, February 3, 1963.

141. KNA Archive, File: Rolf Hochhuth, Ernst-Alfred Jauch, "Nimm ein Brechmittel ... du, der du dies liesest," February 12, 1963.

142. Ibid.

143. Ernst-Alfred Jauch, "Theater-Angriff auf Papst Pius XII. Rolf Hochhuths Schauspiel, Der Stellvertreter. Piscator bereitet Uraufführung vor," in: *Mühlheimer Tageblatt*, February 13, 1963.

144. KNA Archive, Bonn, Folder: Rolf Hochhuth, Walther Kampe, "Das Schweigen des Papstes. Hätte Pius XII die Juden retten können?," in: *KNA*, February 15, 1963.

145. ADK, Archiv Theater der Freien Volksbühne Berlin, Schnellhefter, Der Stellvertreter, Vorkorrespondenz Piscator to alle Schauspieler und Mitarbeiter des Theaters am Kurfürstendamm, February 12, 1963.

146. H. G. Sellenthin, "Querschüsse vor der Premiere. Piscator entfesselt Debatten," in: *Neue Rhein-Zeitung*, February 19, 1963; Hans-Ulrich Kersten, "Die katholische Kirche und die KZ-Gasöfen. Zu einer bevorstehenden Piscator-Inszenierung," in: *Kölner Stadt-Anzeiger*, February 19, 1963.

147. KNA Berlin, Newspaper Clipping, DPA, No name or title, in: *Tagesblatt Bersenbrück, Osnabrück*, February 20, 1963.

148. Heinz Ritter, "Der Wille zur Wahrheit: Erregender Abend im Theater am Kurfürstendamm," in: *Der Abend, Berlin*, February 21, 1963; Walter Kaul, "Eifernde Reportage mit Tendenz," in: *Der Kurier, Berlin*, February 21, 1963; Georg Groos, "Piscator handhabe den Rotstift," in: *Düsselerdorfer Nachrichten*, February 22, 1963; Dieter Hildebrandt, "Bruchstücke eines großen Zorns: Erwin Piscator inszeniert 'Der Stellvertreter' von Hochhuth," in: *Frankfurter Allgemeine Zeitung*, February 22, 1963; "Papst Pius an den Pranger gestellt. Rolf Hochhuths Stück, 'Der Stellvertreter' in Piscators Fassung, von unserem zur Uraufführung nach Berlin entsandten Redakteur," in: *Kölnische Rundschau*, February 22, 1963; Friedrich Luft, "Der Christ in der Hölle der Barbarei," in: *Die Welt, Essen*, February 22, 1963; Dora Fehling, "Die entsetzlichen Umwege des Herrn," in: *Telegraf, Berlin*, February 22, 1963; Werner Fiedler, "Fragwürdig in der Zielrichtung," in: *Der Tag, Berlin*, February 22, 1963; Walther Karsch, "Jüngste Geschichte auf der Bühne," in: *Der Tagesspiegel, Berlin*, February 22, 1963; Hans Fabian, "Großes Zeitstück," in: *Berliner Stimme*, February 23, 1963; Hellmuth Karasek, "Hintertreppe zum Vatikan," in: *Deutsche Zeitung*, February 23, 1963.

149. KZG, NL Adolph, WA 16 D1, Newspaper Clipping, "Eifernde Reportage mit Tendenz. 'Der Stellvertreter' von Rolf Hochhuth im Theater am Kurfürstendamm," in: *Der Kurier, Berlin*, February 21, 1963; "Der Christ in der Hölle der Barbarei. 'Der Stellvertreter': Rolf Hochhuths 'christliches Trauerspiel' von Piscator uraufgeführt," in: *Die Welt, Berlin*, February 22, 1963; "Papst Pius an den Pranger gestellt. Rolf Hochhuths Stück 'Der Stellvertreter' in Piscators Fassung," in: *Kölnische Rundschau*, February 22, 1963; "Zahmer Piscator gab nur ein Fragment. Uraufführung von Hochhuths 'Der Stellvertreter'" in: *Kölner Stadt-Anzeiger*, February 22,

1963; "Erwarteter Theaterskandal blieb aus," in: *Der Mittag*, Düsseldorf, February 22, 1963.

150. RTVA, RIAS, Berlin, Kulturelles Wort, Manuskript, Friedrich Luft, "Rolf Hochhuth 'Der Stellvertreter,'" February 24, 1963.
151. KZG, NL Adolph, WA16 D1, Newspaper Clipping, "Die Tragödie der Gewissensnot. Rolf Hochhuths 'Stellvertreter' war auch ein großer Sieg für Piscator," in: *Berliner Morgenpost*, February 22, 1963.
152. "Drama That Rocks Germany," in: *Life International*, March 11, 1963, 14–15.
153. AEMF, Dokumentation Pressestelle, 1958a (Der Stellvertreter, 1964), document with no name or date, but most likely a speech from the K.A. Ausschuss des Erzbistums München-Freising from late January or early February 1964.
154. Ibid.
155. Johannes Neuhäusler, *Saat des Bösen: Kirchenkampf im Dritten Reich* (Munich: Manz Verlag, 1964).
156. AEMF, Dokumentation Pressestelle, 1957a, "Der Stellvertreter" I, 1963, "Des Fischers vergeblicher Fischzug oder: Die Macht des Schweigens." An abridged version with a truncated ending is to be found in: *Münchener Kirchenzeitung*, April 19, 1964.
157. KZG, NL Adolph, WA 25C3, Aktennotiz, Anlage 6, Protokoll Diöz Ref. Tagung, 1963, March 19, 1963.
158. Thomas Dehler, "Sie zuckten mit der Achsel," in: Fritz Raddatz, ed., *Summa Iniuria oder Durfte der Papst schweigen? Hochhuths "Stellvertreter" in der öffentlichen Kritik* (Reinbek: Rowohlt, 1963), 231–232; ADL, NL Thomas Dehler, N1–1895, Thomas Dehler to Rolf Hochhuth, June 19, 1963.
159. KZG, NL Adolph, WA 16 D2, Gordon Zahn, "'The Vicar': A Controversy and a Lesson," in: *The Critic*, 42–47 (no date indicated).
160. Karl Christian Führer, Knut Hickethier and Axel Schildt, "Öffentlichkeit – Medien – Geschichte. Konzepte der modernen Öffentlichkeit und Zugänge zu ihrer Erforschung," in: *Archiv für Sozialgeschichte*, 41 (2001), 1–38; Daniela Münkel, *Willy Brandt und die "Vierte Gewalt." Politik und Massenmedien in den 50er bis 70er Jahren* (Frankfurt: Campus Verlag, 2005); Christina von Hodenberg, *Konsens und Krise. Eine Geschichte der westdeutschen Medienöffentlichkeit 1945–1973* (Göttingen: Wallstein, 2006); Frank Bösch, "Mediengeschichte im 20. Jahrhundert. Neue Forschungen und Perspektiven," in: *Neue Politische Literatur* 52 (2007), 409–429.
161. ZDK, VV Sitzungen 1958–1966 (2), 2306 Schachtel 2, 1742, Referat von Dr. Josef Knecht, "Der Deutsche Katholizismus in der gegenwärtigen publizistischen Situation," Vollversammlung des Zentralkomitee der deutschen Katholiken, November 5–6, 1964, Bensberg, 10.
162. Ibid.
163. Christina von Hodenberg, *Konsens und Krise*, 245–292; Nicolai Hannig, *Die Religion der Öffentlichkeit: Kirche, Religion und Medien in der Bundesrepublik 1945–1980* (Göttingen: Wallstein Verlag, 2010), 106–108.

164. Heide Fehrenbach, *Cinema in Democratizing Germany: Reconstructing National Identity after Hitler* (Chapel Hill: University of North Carolina Press, 1995), 92–117.
165. HAEK, Gen II 22.13, 39, "Der Katholische, Deutsche Frauenbund in Bayern 'Wir protestieren,'" March 9, 1963.
166. Nadine Ritzer, *Alles nur Theater? Zur Rezeption von Rolf Hochhuths "Der Stellvertreter" in der Schweiz, 1963/1964* (Fribourg: Academic Press Fribourg, 2006), 61–62.
167. Ibid., 60.
168. Siegfried Broesicke, "Stinkbomben gegen den 'Stellvertreter': Pariser Hochhuth-Skandal ohne Ende," in: *Abendzeitung,* December 16, 1963.
169. HAEK, Gen II 22.13, 44, Newspaper Clipping, AP, "Tumulte und Prügel um Hochhuth," in: *Berliner Zeitung,* December 13, 1963.
170. Siegfried Broesicke, "Stinkbomben gegen den 'Stellvertreter.'"
171. "'Deputy' Opening Picketed by 150. Laymen of 3 Faiths and U.S. Nazis March Peacefully," in: *The New York Times,* February 27, 1964, 24; Dolores Schmidt and Earl Schmidt, *The Deputy Reader: Studies in Moral Responsibility* (Glenview: Scott, Foresman and Company, 1965), i.
172. "Shattering," in: *Newsweek,* March 9, 1964, 78–79; John Chapman, "Despite all the Commotion, 'the Deputy' Is Interesting and Challenging Theater," in: *Chicago Tribune,* March 8, 1964, F14.
173. Rowohlt Theater Verlag, Archiv, Hochhuth, Newspaper Clipping, "Hochhuths Papstdrama in Rom verboten," in: *Frankenpost,* February 18, 1965; "Schauspieler legte Bombe am Vatikan: Volonte spielt in Hochhuths 'Stellvertreter' mit," in: *Westdeutsche Rundschau,* Wuppertal, February 20, 1965; "Italiens Linke gegen den Papst. 'Der Stellvertreter' und ein Bombenanschlag in Rom," in: *Der Tagesspiegel,* February 23, 1965.
174. "Furor over Play 'Deputy' called Threat to Moro," in: *Chicago Tribune,* February 15, 1965, B20.
175. Nadine Ritzer, *Alles nur Theater?,* 78–85, Rowohlt Theaterverlag, str. "Krawall und Schlägerei in Brüssel bei Hochhuths 'Stellvertreter'", in: *Süddeutsche Zeitung,* February 16, 1966.
176. "'The Deputy' in Paris," in: *America,* January 4, 1964, 9.
177. AEMF, Dokumentation Pressestelle, 1958a (Der Stellvertreter, 1964), document with no name or date, but most likely a speech from the K.A. Ausschuss des Erzbistums München-Freising from late January or early February 1964.
178. HAEK, GEN II, 22.13, 35, Newspaper Clipping, "Erzbischof: Künstler sollen für Christentum streiten. Gäste aus vielen Ländern beim 'Aschermittwoch der Künstler,'" in: *Neue Rheinzeitung an Rhein und Ruhr,* February 28, 1963; "Kardinal Frings: Hochhuths Vorwurf gegen Papst Pius XII. ist eine Verleumdung," in: *KNA,* February 28, 1963.
179. "Erlasse der Bischofskonferenz der Diözesen Deutschlands, Nr. 117, Erklärung zum Schauspiel, 'Der Stellvertreter,'" in: *Kirchlicher Anzeiger für die Erzdiözese Köln,* April 1, 1963, 93–94.
180. Giovanni Battista Montini, "Pius XII and the Jews," in: *The Tablet,* July 6, 1963; reprinted in: *Commonweal,* February 28, 1964, 651–652.

181. PAAA, B26, 186, Verbalnote, March 15, 1963. KAS, NL Gerhard Schröder, I 483–287–2, Korr. Brentano, Aufzeichnung, April 11, 1963; PAAA, D26, 186, Verärgerung des Vatikans über Hochhuths "Stellvertreter," no date, but probably May or June 1963.

182. PAAA, B26, 182, Aufzeichnung, Dr. Jansen, Bonn, April 2, 1963.

183. BT, Parlamentsarchiv, 4. Wahlperiode, Drucksache IV/1216, Kleine Anfrage der Abgeordneten Majonica, Lemmer und Genossen, May 2, 1963. For a draft of this statement, see KAS, NL Gerhard Schröder, I 483–287–2, Korr. Brentano, Entwurf der Antwort der Bundesregierung.

184. Ibid.

185. HAWDR, 02393, 38/D51, Zur Diskussion steht Hochhuths "Stellvertreter" – Ein Bericht über Aufführungen, Kritiken und Kontroversen, April 28, 1964, 4–5.

186. For examples, see the extensive report on the controversy prepared by the international biographical press service. Already in its first paragraph, it honed in on the vast forces arrayed against Hochhuth, including church leaders, theologians, publicists and some politicians. It noted that only a "minority of voices saw in Hochhuth the courageous man of the pen, who broke a taboo in the name of freedom of expression." See HAWDR 02188, Interpress: Internationaler biographischer Pressedienst, Rolf Hochhuth, Großer Wurf aus Gütersloh, Steckbrief des Autors und seines Erstlings, Nr. 73, April 19, 1963.

187. See DRA, Personalia Hochhuth, St.R.K, Abteilung Information, SFB, Das Thema, April 3, 1963.

188. For one example, see DRA, Inszenierung, Der Stellvertreter, #333, Newspaper Clipping, "Vor der neuen Piscator-Premiere: Gespräch mit einem jungen Bühnenautor," in: *Telegraf*, February 17, 1963.

189. "Der Wille zur Wahrheit: Erregender Abend im Theater am Kurfürstendamm. Hochhuths 'Der Stellvertreter,'" in: *Der Abend*, Berlin, February 21, 1963.

190. "Drama That Rocks Germany," in: *Life International*, 34, Nr. 4, March 11, 1963, 12–16.

191. Felix Schmidt, "Wieder zielt Hochhuth auf ein Tabu," in: *Bild*, April 14, 1963.

192. ADK, Archiv Theater der Freien Volksbühne Berlin, Schnellhefter, Der Stellvertreter, Newspaper Clipping, Eve Stolze, "Schokolade für den Dichter," in *GZ*, February 25, 1963.

193. Ibid.; Marianne Koch, "Rolf Hochhuth freut sich auf den Alltag," in: *Bild-Zeitung*, February 28, 1963.

194. "Rolf Hochhuth: Ein Kampf mit Rom," in: *Der Spiegel*, April 24, 1963.

195. Such photos ironically masked the fact that the *Spiegel* reporting was, in fact, not uncritical of its subject. A similar photo appeared in *Bild*. Felix Schmidt, "Wieder zielt Hochhuth auf ein Tabu," in: *Bild*, April 14, 1963.

196. "Ein Kampf mit Rom," in: *Der Spiegel*, April 24, 1963. To be fair, *Spiegel* also produced images of the aging men – Piscator, Ledig-Rowohlt, etc. – who had supported Hochhuth.

197. Carl Amery, *Die Kapitulation oder Deutscher Katholizismus heute* (Reinbek: Rowohlt, 1963).

198. To this day, Hochhuth's use of sources has a source of controversy. Former intelligence operative Ion Pacepa alleged that Hochhuth's success was actually a masterstroke by the KGB, which had infiltrated the Vatican. According to his account, in February 1960 Nikita Khrushchev signed off on "a super-secret plan for destroying the Vatican's moral authority in Western Europe." The deceased Pacelli was to be "the main target" in a mission that had been given the code name "Seat-12." A Vatican representative working for the KGB, Agostino Casaroli, allegedly gave Pacepa access to the Vatican archives, and "hundreds of documents connected in any way with Pope Pius XII" were smuggled out of the Vatican Archives and the Apostolic Library. At some point in 1963 after the operation had been wrapped up – Pacepa did not give the precise date – he was told in Bucharest by General Ivan Agayants, the "famous chief of the KGB's disinformation department," that these efforts "had materialized into a powerful play attacking Pope Pius XII." For this account, see Ion Pacepa, "Moscow's Assault of the Vatican," in: *National Review*, January 2007. For arguments rebutting these claims, see: Thomas Brechenmacher, "Hochhuths Quellen. War 'Der Stellvertreter' vom KGB inspiriert?," in: *Frankfurter Allgemeine Zeitung*, April 26, 2007; Mark Edward Ruff, "Rolf Hochhuth and the KGB: Debunking Claims of a Conspiracy" (article in progress).
199. KZG, NL Adolph WA16D1, Newspaper Clipping, "Borsche spielt 'Pius XII.' Erstlingswerk von Hochhuth: 'Der Stellvertreter,'" in: *KNA*, January 25, 1963; KNA Archiv, File: Rolf Hochhuth, "Papst bei Piscator. Zu Rolf Hochhuths 'Stellvertreter,'" in: *KNA*, February 4, 1963. Both articles referred to an interview between Borsche and the Berlin newspaper *Der Abend* from January 15, 1963.
200. HAEK, Gen II, 22.13, 35, Newspaper Clipping, "'Der Stellvertreter' ausgeliefert. Einzelne 'Spitzen' gegen Papst und Kurie eliminert," in: *KNA* (no date). This article quoted from the FVB newspaper.
201. "'Stellvertreter'-Autor spricht von Rufmord. Kontroverse um die neue Berliner Piscator-Inszenierung spitzt sich immer mehr zu," in: *Freie Presse, Bielefeld*, February 25, 1963.
202. Robert Leiber, "Pius XII und die Juden in Rom, 1943–1944," in: *Stimmen der Zeit*, 167 (1960–1961), 428–436, as cited on 427, 429, 433, 435, 436; Gerhard Schoenberner, *Der gelbe Stern. Die Judenverfolgung in Europa 1933 bis 1945* (Hamburg: Rütten und Loening Verlag, 1960), 108; SLA, NL Rolf Hochhuth, #269, Rolf Hochhuth to Robert Kempner, 14 June 1963. In this letter, Hochhuth noted that he had given assistance to Schoenberner, but it is not clear to what extent since he was not thanked by name.
203. "Weiter heftiger Streit um 'Stellvertreter': Schauspiel-Autor Hochhut (sic) spricht von 'Rufmord,'" in: *Rundschau am Sonntag*, February 24, 1963.
204. Hdt, "Hochhuth klärt Vorwürfe," in: *Frankfurter Allgemeine Zeitung*, February 26, 1963.
205. Helmut Kotschenreuther, "NRZ-Gespräch mit Bühnen-Autor Rolf Hochhuth, 'Ich hasse Papst Pius XII. nicht,'" in: *Neue Rheinzeitung*, March 9, 1963.
206. "Mein Pius ist keine Karikatur: SPIEGEL-Gespräch mit Dramatiker Rolf Hochhuth," in: *Der Spiegel*, Nr. 17, April 24, 1963, 90.

207. For attempts by the KNA to discern their identities, see HAEK, Gen II 22, 13, 34, Presse-und Informationsamt der Bundesregierung, Spiegel der Katholischen Kirchenpresse, March 30, 1963, 5.

208. In a phone call to Wolfgang Knauft, a member of the Catholic Committee in Berlin, Hochhuth let slip that Hudal had served as one of his informants. Knauft passed this information to Adolph and Klausener, who forwarded it to Cardinal Frings. But they did not reveal publicly Hudal's identity. HAEK, Gen II 22.13, 32, Erich Klausener Jr. to Joseph Frings, April 26, 1963, Betreff: Telefonat Rolf Hochhuth – Kuratus Knauft am 3. März von 20.30 Uhr bis 21.15 Uhr.

209. "Aktuelle Diskussion bis halb elf: VHS-Gespräch über Hochhuths 'Stellvertreter' ging Thema auf den Grund," in: *Neue Rheinzeitung*, May 17, 1963; KNA Archiv, File: Rolf Hochhuth, KNA-Informationsdienst Nr. 15, "Vernichtende Kritik Prof. Bussmanns an Hochhuths 'Stellveteter' – D. Dr. Dibelius," April 11, 1963; Wilhelm Alff, "Richtige Einzelheiten – verfehltes Gesamtbild," in: *Frankfurter Allgemeine Zeitung*, May 11, 1963; Rolf Hochhuth, "Ein Gesamtbild gibt es nicht: Antwort an Wilhelm Alff," in: *Frankfurter Allgemeine Zeitung*, May 30, 1963.

210. Morsey showed a reluctance to participate in such forums, citing the need for a stronger basis of source material. DAB, V/12–6–2–2, NL Erich Klausener Jr., V/12 Korr. Klausener 62–64, Rudolf Morsey to Erich Klausener Jr., May 31, 1963.

211. DAB, NL Erich Klausener Jr., V/12, Korr. Klausener 62–64, Robert Kempner, Brief an die Frankfurter Zeitung, March 15, 1963; HAEK, Gen II 22.13, 38, Albrecht von Kessel, "Der Papst und die Juden," in: *Die Welt*, April 6, 1963; KNA Archiv, File: Rolf Hochhuth, Alberto Giovannetti, "Geschichte, Theater und Geschichten: zu Hochhuth: Verhältnisse von damals nicht mit heutigem Maßstab messen," April 10, 1963; KAB, B1/17, Newspaper Clipping, "Stellvertreter des Stellvertreters: Eine Diskussion in der Katholischen Akademie über Hochhuths Schauspiel," in: *Münchener Merkur*, April 24, 1963; HAEK, Gen II 22.13, 37, Newspaper Clipping, "'Der Stellvertreter' – in München diskutiert: Umstrittenes Drama vor der Katholischen Akademie," in: *Augsburger Allgemeine*, April 25, 1963; KNA Archiv, KNA, File: Rolf Hochhuth, "Kein Bewältigen durch Vergessen: Ansprache von Weihbischof Dr. Johannes Neuhäusler bei der Grundsteinweihe für den 'Karmel Heilig Blut Dachau' am 28. April 1963"; HAEK Gen II 22.13, 38, Newspaper Clipping, dpa, "M.W.Kempner verteidigt Pius XII," in: *Kölner Stadt-Anzeiger*, May 25–26, 1963.

212. ADK, Archiv Theater der Freien Volksbühne Berlin, Schnellhefter, Der Stellvertreter, Vorkorrespondenz, Heinrich Grüber to Erwin Piscator, March 4, 1963; HAEK, Gen II 22.13, 38, Newspaper Clipping, "Die Meinung von Propst Grüber: Entscheidend ist nur, was laut gesagt wurde," in: *Freiheit und Recht, Düsseldorf*, May 1963; RTVA, "Schweitzer über Hochhuths Drama," in: *Frankfurter Allgemeine Zeitung*, September 25, 1963.

213. RTVA, Bayerischer Rundfunk München, Der Stellvertreter, Vorspann zur Diskussion am April 29, 1963; KZG, HAEK, Gen II 22.13, 37, Newspaper

Clipping, "Hochhuth sammelte Minuspunkte. 'Stellvertreter'-Diskussion im Kölner 'Kongreß für die Freiheit der Kultur,'" in: *Kölnische Rundscharu*, April 29, 1963; NL Walter Adolph, WA 16D1, "'Rhythmisierte Dokumente': Podiumsdiskussion mit Rolf Hochhuth in Köln," in: *KNA*, May 3, 1963; RTVA, Rolf Hochhuth, Newspaper Clipping, D, "Aktuelle Diskussion bis halb elf: VHS-Gespräch über Hochhuths 'Stellvertreter' ging Thema auf den Grund," in: *Neue Rheinzeitung*, May 17, 1963; HAEK, Gen II 22.13, 38, Newspaper Clipping, "Gericht über Hochhuth? Zu einem Podiumsgespräch in München," in: *Berliner Allgemeine Wochenzeitung der Jugend in Deutschland*, May 24, 1963; RTVA, hfn, "Hochhuth – Anti-Hochhuth," in: *Abendzeitung*, July 27–28, 1963.

214. For examples at universities, see KNA Archiv, File: Rolf Hochhuth, KNA, Bayerischer Dienst, "War des Papstes Schweigen ein 'Verbrechen?'. Studenten diskutieren über Hochhuths "Stellvertreter," July 29, 1963. For examples of television discussions, see HAEK, Gen II 22.13, 38, "Pius XII. und die Juden: Fernseh-Diskussion über Rolf Hochhuths Drama, 'Der Stellvertreter,'" in: *Der Abend, Berlin*, May 20, 1963; "Durfte Pius XII. schweigen? Eine Fernsehdiskussion über Hochhuths 'Stellvertreter,'" in: *Flensburger Tageblatt*, May 31, 1963. For a detailed description of a two-hour program on the second channel of Sender Freies Berlin, see KZG, NL Adolph, WA 16D2, Aktennotiz, August 25, 1963.

215. HAEK, Gen II 22.13, 37, Newspaper Clipping, "'Der Stellvertreter' – in München diskutiert: Umstrittenes Drama vor der Katholischen Akademie," in: *Augsburger Allgemeine*, April 25, 1963; KAB, B1/17, Newspaper Clipping, "Stellvertreter des Stellvertreters: Eine Diskussion in der Katholischen Akademie über Hochhuths Schauspiel," in: *Münchener Merkur*, April 24, 1963. For comments regarding the absence of contrary positions, see HA-WDR, 02188, Newspaper Clipping, "Pius XII. und die Pforten der Hölle. Die Katholische Akademie in Bayern veranstaltet eine Diskussion über Hochhuths 'Stellvertreter,'" in: *Münchener Kulturberichte* 16, April 24, 1963.

216. Several of these questions formed the basis for a forum in Cologne. See KZG, NL Adolph, Wa 16D1, "'Rhythmisierte Dokumente': Podiumsdiskussion mit Rolf Hochhuth in Köln," in: *KNA*, May 3, 1963.

217. KAB, B 1/17, Newspaper Clipping, Alfred Hoentzsch, "Der Stellvertreter: Bericht über ein Podiumsgespräch um das gleichnamige Schauspiel von Rolf Hochhuth in der Katholischen Akademie in München" (no newspaper names given; no date indicated, but probably April 24, 1963).

218. DRA, Pressearchiv, Personalia, Hochhuth, St.R.K., Abteilung Information, SFB, Das Thema, April 3, 1963; KNA Archiv, File: Rolf Hochhuth, "'Stellvertreter' weiter im Mittelpunkt der Diskussionen: Lebhafte Aussprachen in Berlin – Antikatholische Ressentiments," April 3, 1963.

219. DRA, Pressearchiv, Personalia, Hochhuth, St.R.K., Abteilung Information, SFB, Das Thema, April 3, 1963.

220. HAEK, Gen II 22.13, 34, Newspaper Clipping, "Es geht um Dich persönlich. Neue Diskussion um den 'Stellvertreter,'" in: *Berliner Stimme*, March 30, 1963.

221. DRA, Pressearchiv, Personalia, Hochhuth, St.R.K., Abteilung Information, SFB, Das Thema, April 3, 1963.

222. NL Adolph, WA 25C3, Aktennotiz, Anlage 6, Ptokoll Diöz Ref. Tagung, 1963, March 19, 1963.

223. HAEK, Gen II 22.13, 32, Hanke and Seibt, Hessischer Rundfunk to Joseph Frings, March 7, 1963, Schöller to den Hessischen Rundfunk, Abt. FS-Zeitgeschehen, May 10, 1963.

224. DAL, D, Publizistik, II, Rundfunk, 1963–1964, Walter Kampe to Herrn Intendant Werner Heß, Frankfurt/Main, Hessicher Rundfunk, May 20, 1963.

225. Nancy Fraser, "Rethinking the Public Sphere: A Contribution to the Critique of Actually Existing Democracy," in: *Social Text* 26 (1990), 56–80.

226. WDR Archiv, 03293, 38/D51, "Zur Diskussion steht Hochhuths 'Stellvertreter' – Ein Bericht über Aufführungen, Kritiken und Kontroversen," April 28, 1964.

227. This topic was the subject of Habermas' landmark Habilitation. Jürgen Habermas, *Strukturwandel der Öffentlichkeit. Untersuchungen zu einer Kategorie der bürgerlichen Gesellschaft* (Neuwied: Luchterhand, 1962).

228. WDR Archiv, 03293, 38/D51, "Zur Diskussion steht Hochhuths "Stellvertreter" – Ein Bericht über Aufführungen, Kritiken und Kontroversen," April 28, 1964.

229. Walter Adolph, *Verfälschte Geschichte: Antwort an Rolf Hochhuth* (Berlin: Morus Verlag, 1963)

230. KZG, NL Adolph, WA 16D2, KNA, "Verfälschte Geschichte als Grundlage der Verdammung," July 10, 1963; "'Antwort an Rolf Hochhuth': Eine Schrift des Berliner Generalvikars Walter Adolph," in: *Deutsches Volksblatt, Stuttgart*, July 11, 1963; "'Antwort an Rolf Hochhuth': Berliner Generalvikar Walter Adolph zu dem Stück 'Der Stellvertreter,'" in: *Aachener Volkszeitung*, July 16, 1963; "Antwort an Hochhuth," in: *Nürtinger Zeitung*, July 19, 1963; "Antwort an Hochhuth," in: *Hamburger Echo*, July 19, 1963; "Adolphs Kapitulation," in: *Kölner Stadtanzeiger*, July 23, 1963; HAEK, Gen II 22.13, 41, "Hochhuth und kein Ende," in: *Der Kurier*, Berlin, July 22, 1963.

231. DAB, IV/54 – 183, Bestände des Morus Verlags, Verfasser: Walter Adolph, Titel: Verfälschte Geschichte; Walter Adolph, *Verfälschte Geschichte*.

232. Fritz Raddatz, ed., *Summa Iniuria oder Durfte der Papst Schweigen? Hochhuths "Stellvertreter" in der öffentlichken Kritik* (Reinbek: Rowohlt, 1963).

233. Joachim Günter, *Der Streit um Hochhuths "Stellvertreter"* (Basel: Basilius Presse, 1963); Eric Bentley, ed., *The Storm over the Deputy* (New York: Grove Press, 1964); Dolores Barracano Schmidt and Earl Robert Schmidt, ed., *The Deputy Reader: Studies in Moral Responsibility* (Glenview: Scott, Foresman and Company, 1965).

234. Fritz Raddatz, *Summa Iniuria*, 163.

235. By my reckoning, fifty contributions were extremely supportive of the playwright, twenty-six were critical or condemnatory, five were mixed, and eleven were neutral in their orientation, simply reporting on the positions raised.

236. DAB, NL Erich Klausener Jr., V/12 Korr. Klausener, 62–64, Fritz. Raddatz to Erich Klausener Jr., June 25, 1963; Erich Klausener Jr. to Fritz Raddatz, July 17, 1963; NL Adolph, WA 513, Erich Klausener Jr. to Walter Adolph, July 18, 1963.
237. SLA, NL Hochhuth, #271, Georg Lukacs to Rolf Hochhuth, August 9, 1963; Karl Breuning to Rolf Hochhuth, May 13, 1963.
238. "Mein Pius ist keine Karikatur: SPIEGEL-Gespräch mit Dramatiker Rolf Hochhuth," in: *Der Spiegel*, Nr. 17, April 24, 1963, 90.
239. Ibid.
240. SLA, NL Rolf Hochhuth, #5, Jan Ciechanowski to Rolf Hochhuth, December 18, 1961.
241. Walter Adolph, *Verfälschte Geschichte*, 8.
242. HAEK, Katholisches Buro, ZUG 862 #126, Prälat (no name given) to Franz Hermann, March 15, 1963.
243. Ibid.
244. Heinz Glässgen, *Katholische Kirche und Rundfunk in der Bundesrepublik Deutschland 1945–1962* (Berlin: Spiess Verlag 1983); Nicolai Hannig, "Religion gehört. Der Kirchenfunk des NWDR und WDR in den 1950er und 60er Jahren," in: *Geschichte im Westen* 22 (2007), 113–137.
245. HAWDR, #13006, Klaus von Bismarck to Herrn. Dr. Brühl, Dr. Lange, Dr. Zons, Dirks, Wiegenstein, Waltermann, Dr. Oxenius, April 9, 1963.
246. HAWDR, #02188, Aktennotiz zur Frage "Der Stellvertreter," gez. Walter Dirks, April 11, 1963.
247. HAWDR, #13006, Dr. Zons to Klaus von Bismarck, Betr: Hochhuth "Der Stellvertreter," March 20, 1963; RTVA, Hessischer Rundfunk, Frankfurt-Main, Zur Diskussion um Rolf Hochhuths "Stellvertreter," Manuskript: Hans Kühner, April 7, 1963; RTVA, Bayerischer Rundfunk in München, Der Stellvertreter, Vorspann zur Diskussion am April 29, 1963.
248. ADK, Theater der Freien Volksbühne, "Der Stellvertreter von Rolf Hochhuth," Band 15, RIAS, Berlin, Kulturelles Wort, Unkorrigierte Manuskript Kopie, March 3, 1963.
249. HAWDR #05790, Kreuzfeuer mit Herrn Hochhuth am 15.6.65.
250. DAB, V/1–3, Vermerk: Möglichkeiten für ein gerichtliches Vorgehen gegen Hochhuth, Rowohlt-Verlag und das Theater am Kurfürstendamm wegen der Nennung des Namens von Dompropst Lichtenberg. Berlin, den March 11, 1963.
251. HAEK, Katholisches Büro, ZUG 862, #126, Dr. Jur. Karl Panzer to Wilhelm Wissing, Köln, March 29, 1963; Aktenvermerk, Betr: "Der Stellvertreter" von Hochhuth, April 5, 1963.
252. HAEK, Katholisches Büro, ZUG 862, #126, Aktenvermerk, Dr. Erning, Betr: Dr. Panzer.
253. ACDP, NL Gerhard Schröder, I 483–287–2, Korr. Heinrich von Brentano, Newspaper Clipping, "Gezielte Aktion gegen Hochhuth? Indiskretion nährt Gerüchte über geplanten Boykott des 'Stellvertreters,'" in: *Frankfurter Rundschau*, May 9, 1963.

254. KNA Archiv, File: Rolf Hochhuth, Nr. 38, Montag, February 25, 1963, "Freiheit ohne Wahrheit ist Anarchie" (KNA – 63/II/319 – FS-Voraus); KNA Archiv, Dr. K. Kraemer, "Der Würde ins Gesicht geschlagen! Ohne Wahrheit keine Freiheit," February 25, 1963.

255. KNA Archiv, File: Rolf Hochhuth, Konrad Kraemer, "Der Würde ins Gesicht geschlagen! Ohne Wahrheit keine Wahrheit," February 25, 1963.

256. LAB, B/002, Nr. 10583, Eduard Bernoth, Katholiken-Ausschuss des Bistums Berlin to die Mitglieder des Senats von Berlin und des Abgeordetenhauses von Berlin, May 30, 1961.

257. KZG, NL Walter Adolph, WA 16D1, Newspaper Clipping, "Protest gegen Schüleraufführung," in: *Der Tagesspiegel Berlin*, March 21, 1963.

258. ASD, NL Adolf Arndt, Box 102, Mappe 343, Vermerk, April 4, 1963; DPA, "Vorstellung jeden Abend ausverkauft: 3000 Schüler wollen Hochhuth-Drama sehen – Bischöfliches Ordinariat protestiert," in: *Hanauer Anzeiger*, March 23, 1963.

259. ASD, NL Adolf Arndt, Box 102, Mappe 343, Walter Adolph to Adolf Arndt, April 25, 1963.

260. PAAA, B26, 186, Dienststelle des Auswärtigen Amtes to das Auswärtige Amt, Bonn, October 16, 1963.

261. KZG, NL Adolph, WA 16D1, "Ins Geschicht geschlagen: Kritik an Preis für Hochhuth," in: *KNA*, April 25, 1963; Ernst-Alfred Jauch, "5000 Mark für die Verleumdung auf der Bühne," in: *KNA*, April 26, 1963.

262. LAB, B Rep 014, Nr. 2247, text of Arndt's speech.

263. KZG, NL Adolph, WA 16D1, KNA, Ernst-Alfred Jauch, "5000 Mark für die Verleumdung auf der Bühne," in: *KNA*, April 26, 1963.

264. ASD, NL Adolf Arndt, Box 102, Mappe 343, Arndt to Joseph Zörlein, July 22, 1963.

265. "Wo die Toleranz endet," in: *Petrusblatt*, July 19, 1959.

266. HAEK, Gen II, 22.13.43, Newspaper Clipping, "Eva Stolze sprach mit Rolf Hochhuth – Der Autor des 'Stellvertreter,'" in: *B.Z.*, October 14, 1963.

267. "'Ein Satanischer Feigling': Dramatiker Rolf Hochhuth über die neuen Kontroversen zu seinem Papst-Stück 'Der Stellvertreter' und Pius XII," in: *Der Spiegel*, May 26, 2007.

268. CUA, NL Muench, Box 60, Folder 5, transcript of Colman Barry's Interview with Josef Frings, 1965.

6   Guenter Lewy and the Battle for Sources

1. Guenter Lewy, *The Catholic Church and Nazi Germany* (New York: McGraw-Hill, 1964).

2. Ibid., 269.

3. Ibid., 340–341.

4. Guenter Lewy, *Die katholische Kirche und das Dritte Reich* (Munich: Piper Verlag, 1965); Guenter Lewy, "Mit festem Schritt ins neue Reich," in: *Der Spiegel*, February 17, 1965, Cover Photo. Excerpts from his book continued on February 24, March 3, March 10, March 17, March 24, March 31, and April 7, 1965.

5. See Abraham Ascher, *A Community under Siege: The Jews of Breslau under Nazism* (Stanford: Stanford University Press, 2007), in particular 60–65; Till van Rahden, *Juden und andere Breslauer: Die Beziehungen zwischen Juden, Protestanten und Katholiken in einer deutschen Großstadt von 1860 bis 1925* (Göttingen: Vandenhoeck & Ruprecht, 2000).
6. Guenter Lewy to the author, June 8, 2013.
7. Estimates of the size of the pre-1933 population vary between 23,000 and 24,500. Abraham Ascher, *A Community under Siege*, 3; Robert Conrads, ed., *No Justice in Germany: The Breslau Diaries, 1933–1941, Willy Cohn* (Stanford: Stanford University Press, 2012), xi.; Michael A. Meyer, ed., *German-Jewish History in Modern Times, Volume 4, Renewal and Destruction, 1918–1945* (New York: Columbia University Press, 1998), 236.
8. Abraham Ascher, *A Community under Siege*, 50–61.
9. Ibid., 60.
10. Ibid., 54. For a description of the Jewish youth groups in Breslau, see Walter Laqueur, *Thursday's Child has far to go: A Memoir of the Journeying Years* (New York: Scribner, 1992), 77–86.
11. Abraham Ascher, *A Community under Siege*, 190; Michael A. Meyer, ed., *German-Jewish History in Modern Times, Volume 4, Renewal and Destruction*, 299–301, 315–316.
12. Guenter Lewy to the author, June 8, 2013.
13. Ibid.
14. Ibid. See also Robert Conrads, ed., *No Justice in Germany: The Breslau Diaries.*
15. Guenter Lewy to the author, June 8, 2013.
16. Morris Beckman, *The Jewish Brigade: An Army with Two Masters, 1944–45* (Rockville: Sarpedon, 1998); Howard Blum, *The Brigade: An Epic Story of Vengeance, Salvation, and WWII* (New York: Harper Collins, 2001).
17. Guenter Lewy to the author, June 8, 2013.
18. Ibid.
19. Ibid.
20. On Neumann, see Joachim Rückert, "Franz Leopold Neumann (1900–1954) – ein Jurist mit Prinzipien," in: Marcus Lutter, Ernst C. Stiefel and Michael H. Hoeflich, ed., *Der Einfluß deutscher Emigranten auf die Rechtsentwicklung in den USA und in Deutschland* (Tübingen: J.C.B. Mohr Verlag, 1993), 437–474; William E. Scheuermann, *Between the Norm and the Exception: The Frankfurt School and the Rule of Law* (Cambridge, MA: The MIT Press, 1994); Rolf Wiggershaus, *The Frankfurt School: Its History, Theories and Political Significance*, translated by Michael Robertson (Cambridge, MA: MIT Press, 1995), 223–230, 470. On Lewy's undergraduate studies, see Guenter Lewy to the author, June 8, 2013.
21. Guenter Lewy, *Constitutionalism and Statecraft during the Golden Age of Spain: A Study of the Political Philosophy of Juan de Mariana, SJ* (Geneva: Librairie E. Droz, 1960), 65, 78.
22. Ibid., 79.
23. Ibid., 77.

24. Guenter Lewy, "Resistance to Tyranny: Reasons, Right or Duty?," in: *The Western Political Quarterly* 13, Nr. 3 (1960), 581–596, especially 589.
25. Guenter Lewy to the author, June 8, 2013.
26. Gordon Zahn, "Würzburg 1957," in: *The Catholic Worker*, March 1958, 3.
27. UNDA, Gordon Zahn Papers, CZHN 13172, Guenter Lewy to Gordon Zahn, March 10, 1960.
28. UNDA, Gordon Zahn Papers, CZHN 13177, Guenter Lewy to Gordon Zahn, April 30, 1960.
29. Ibid.
30. Guenter Lewy to the author, June 8, 2013.
31. Guenter Lewy, *Why America Needs Religion: Secular Modernity and Its Discontents* (Grand Rapids: Eerdmans, 1996).
32. Guenter Lewy, *Constitutionalism and Statecraft*, 81.
33. Guenter Lewy, *America in Vietnam* (New York: Oxford University Press, 1978), vi. It was probably no accident that Reinhold Niebuhr, the political theorist and theologian often associated with so-called vital center liberalism from the late 1940s and 1950s, was summoned to write a laudatio for the dust jacket.
34. See Toni Diederich, "Zur Geschichte des Archivwesens der katholischen Kirche in Deutschland nach dem Zweiten Weltkrieg," in: Bundeskonferenz der kirchlichen Archive in Deutschland, ed., *Führer durch die Bistumsarchive der katholischen Kirche in Deutschland* (Siegburg: Schmitt, 1991), 17–34. There was no Catholic archive for West Berlin and East Berlin until 1970 and 1980, respectively; the plans for the archive in West Berlin dated back only to 1966. Gotthard Klein, "25 Jahre Diözesanarchiv Berlin. Eine Zwischenbilanz," in: *Wichmann-Jahrbuch* 32/33 (1993), 157–175, 160.
35. For examples of the contacts, see UNDA, Gordon Zahn Papers, 13177, Guenter Lewy to Gordon Zahn, April 30, 1960; NL Bernhard Stasiewski, KFZG, Unsorted Material, Dr. Müller, Bundesarchiv to Bernhard Stasiewski, July 5, 1960, Az: 9712 b/Lewy.
36. UNDA, Gordon Zahn Papers, 13178, Gordon Zahn to Guenter Lewy, May 6, 1960.
37. Ibid.
38. UNDA, Gordon Zahn Papers, 03265, Guenter Lewy to Gordon Zahn, March 29, 1962.
39. HAEK, Gen II 22.13, 12, Guenter Lewy to die Erzdiözese Köln, May 20, 1960.
40. HAEK Gen II 23.13, 13, Florence McDonald, Secretary of the Board of Trustees, Smith College, June 6, 1961.
41. HAEK, Gen II 23.13, 13, Walter C. Connell, Acting Vicar General, Diocese of Springfield, To Whom it may Concern, February 18, 1961. Lewy sent this letter to a number of diocesan archives. Johannes Neuhäusler transcribed it and included it in the addenda he sent to all of the German and Austrian chanceries. See also Guenter Lewy to the author, June 8, 2013.
42. AEMF, NL Johannes Neuhäusler, VN N12, Johannes Neuhäusler to Dr. Heinz Laufer im Institut für politische Wissenschaften, München, November 10, 1961. In a letter to the author from June 8, 2013, Lewy

denied having met Neuhäusler. Neuhäusler's recollection of the meeting (from either September or October 1961) was so detailed that it is hard to escape the conclusion that a meeting did indeed take place. See AEMF, NL Johannes Neuhäusler, VN N12, Johannes Neuhäusler to Ernst Deuerlein, March 20, 1964.

43. AEMF, NL Johannes Neuhäusler, VN N12, Johannes Neuhäusler to Dr. Heinz Laufer, November 10, 1961.

44. AEMF, NL Johannes Neuhäusler, VN N12, Johannes Neuhäusler to die Hochwürdigsten Erzbischöflichen und Bischöflichen Ordinariate von Bayern, November 6, 1961.

45. Ibid.

46. Ibid.

47. Ibid.

48. AEMF, NL Johannes Neuhäusler, VN N 12, Johannes Neuhäusler to Heinz Laufer, November 10, 1961.

49. HAEK, Gen II 22.13, 13, Ordinariat des Erzbistums München und Freising an die Hochwürdigsten Erzbischöflichen und Bischöflichen Ordinariate von Deutschland und Österreich, Betr: Dr. Guenter Lewy – Archivforschungen über das 3. Reich, February 2, 1962.

50. Ibid.

51. Guenter Lewy, *The Catholic Church and Nazi Germany*, xiv.

52. Ibid. These archives were those of Passau, Regensburg, Eichstätt, Hildesheim, Paderborn, Aachen, Trier, Mainz and Limburg.

53. DAL, 551B, Wilhelm Wissing, Katholisches Büro Bonn to die Hochwürdigsten Herren Erzbischöfe und Bischöfe in der Bundesrepublik Deutschland, February 2, 1962.

54. Ibid.

55. This decision had been made on January 24, 1962. See Rudolf Morsey, "Gründung und Gründer der Kommission für Zeitgeschichte (1960–1962)," in: *Historisches Jahrbuch* 115 (1995), 478.

56. DAL, 551B, Wilhelm Wissing, Katholisches Büro Bonn to die Hochwürdigsten Herren Erzbischöfe und Bischöfe in der Bundesrepublik Deutschland, Febuary 2, 1962.

57. Guenter Lewy to the author, June 8, 2013.

58. DAB, Lewy, I/4–20a, Photocopy, Empfehlung, Dr. Karl Forster, München, March 1, 1962.

59. Ibid.

60. DAB, I/4–20a, Guenter Lewy to Walter Adolph, June 19, 1962.

61. DAB, I/4–20a, Walter Adolph to Guenter Lewy, June 22, 1962.

62. DAB, I/4–20a, Guenter Lewy to Walter Adolph, June 19, 1962.

63. AEMF, NL Johannes Neuhäusler, VN N 12, Johannes Neuhäusler to Ernst Deuerlein, March 20, 1964.

64. SLA, NL Rolf Hochhuth, #271, Guenter Lewy to Rolf Hochhuth, June 5, 1963; #352, Rolf Hochhuth to Walter Busse, May 26, 1964; #421, Rolf Hochhuth to Fritz Raddatz, March 15, 1964.

65. Guenter Lewy, *The Catholic Church and Nazi Germany*, xv.

66. Guenter Lewy, *The Catholic Church and Nazi Germany*, dust jacket.

67. Display Ad 29, No Title, in: *The New York Times*, June 16, 1964, 34.

68. Foster Hailey, "Dispute over Pius Reopened by Book: New Study of Church and Nazis cites Pope's Role," in: *The New York Times*, June 15, 1964, 26.

69. Guenter Lewy to the author, June 27, 2013.

70. Interview with Guenter Lewy. The translation appeared as Guenter Lewy, *Die Katholische Kirche und das Dritte Reich. Aus dem amerikanischen von Hildegard Schulz* (Munich: Piper Verlag, 1965).

71. Rudolf Augstein, "Lieber Spiegel-Leser," in: *Der Spiegel*, February 17, 1965, 41.

72. Lewy's article in the February 1964 issue of *Commentary* led the journal to publish no fewer than nine reader letters. Guenter Lewy, "Pius XII, the Jews, and the German Catholic Church," in: *Commentary* 37 (2), (1964), 23–35. Letters from Readers, in: *Commentary* 37 (6), (1964), 6–14.

73. For three examples, see Rowohlt Theater Verlag, Archiv, no author, "Papstbild bewußt verzerrt? Prof. Lewy legt Ergebnisse seiner geschichtlichen Forschungsarbeit vor," in: *Die Freiheit, Mainz*, December 18, 1964; HAEK, Gen II 22,13, 24, Newspaper Clipping, "Die Katholiken im Hitler-Staat," in: *Frankfurter Allgemeine Zeitung*, December 5, 1964; Robert A. Graham, SJ, "A Return to Theocracy: The Latest Attack on the Vatican Reveals the Irony of Its Author's Demands," in: *America*, July 18, 1964, 70–72.

74. Rowohlt Theater Verlag, Archive, Newspaper Clipping, Max Bogner, "Schützenhilfe für Hochhuth: Aufsehenerregende Studie über Kirche und Nazi-Deutschland," in: no newspaper title given, but one from Munich, June 6, 1964.

75. Ludwig Volk, SJ, "Zwischen Geschichtsschreibung und Hochhuthprosa: Kritisches und Grundsätzliches zu einer Neuerscheinung über Kirche und Nationalsozialismus," in: *Stimmen der Zeit*, 176 (1965), 29–41; Ludwig Volk, SJ, "Ein unhistorischer Historiker," in: *Die Zeit*, June 4, 1965.

76. Robert A. Graham, SJ, "A Return to Theocracy," in: *America*, July 18, 1964, 70.

77. Privatbesitz Guenter Lewy, Dr. Anton Roesen, Dr. Waldowski, Michael Rossen, Rechtsanwälte to den Verlag R. Piper & Co., October 8, 1965.

78. Guenter Lewy, *The Catholic Church and Nazi Germany*, 231.

79. Ibid.

80. The original passage from Jaeger read: "Schaut hin auf Rußland! Ist jenes arme unglückliche Land nicht der Tummelplatz von Menschen, die durch ihre Gottfeindlichkeit und durch ihren Christushaß fast zu Tieren entartet sind?" The German version of Lewy's text read: "Erzbischof Jaeger bekundete sogar seine Sympathie für die Verleumdungskampagne der Nationalsozialisten gegen die slawischen 'Untermenschen' und bezeichnete Rußland als ein Land, dessen Menschen "durch ihre Gottfeindlichkeit und durch ihren Christushaß fast zu Tieren entartet sind." (Guenter Lewy, *Die Katholische Kirche und das Dritte Reich*, 255). The English version read: "Archbishop Jäger even showed sympathy for the Nazis' campaign of vilification against the Slavic *Untermenschen* (subhumans) and characterized Russia as a country whose people 'because of their hostility to God and their hatred of Christ, had almost degenerated into animals.'" Guenter Lewy,

The Catholic Church and Nazi Germany, 231. For the ensuing discussions, see Privatbesitz Guenter Lewy, Dr. Anton Roesen, Dr. Waldowski, Michael Rossen, Rechtsanwälte to den Verlag R. Piper & Co., October 8, 1965. For examples of ensuing grammar discussions, see Privatbesitz Guenter Lewy, Rechtsanwälte Ferdinand Sieger, Guido Lehmbruck, Stuttgart to Rechtsanwälte Anton Koesen, Waldowski and Michael Rossen, Betr: S.E. Lorenz Kardinal Jaeger/Guenter Lewy "Die katholische Kirche und das Dritte Reich" R. Piper & Co Verlag München, December 7, 1965; Anton Roesen, Waldowski, Michael Rossen to Ferdinand Sieger and Guido Lehmbruck, December 10, 1965.

81. For one example of a lawsuit that was withdrawn, see, DAB, I/4–20a, Wilhelm Wissing to das Bischöfliche Ordinariat, z.Hd. Walter Adolph, July 26, 1965.

82. Rudolf Morsey, "Kirche im Dritten Reich," in: *Frankfurter Allgemeine Zeitung*, November 4, 1965.

83. Erich Klausener Jr., "Angeklagter: Katholische Kirche. Erich Klausener antwortet Lewy," in: *Rheinische Post*, June 17, 1965.

84. Carl Amery, *Die Kapitulation oder Deutscher Katholizismus heute* (Reinbek: Rowohlt, 1963); Carl Amery, "Hitler und der Klerus," in: *Stern* 31, October 11, 1964.

85. Carl Amery, "Hitler und der Klerus."

86. Hans Müller, "Die Katholische Kirche unter Hitler: Hochhuthprosa oder Historische Forschung?," in: *Die Zeit*, Nr. 23, June 4, 1965; Ludwig Volk, SJ, "Ein unhistorischer Historiker," in: *Die Zeit*, Nr. 23, June 4, 1965; Ludwig Volk, SJ, "Zwischen Geschichtsschreibung und Hochhuthprosa," 29–41.

87. ADPJ, NL Ludwig Volk, 771–2/Ib, Ludwig Volk to Paul Sethe, June 27, 1965; Paul Sethe to Ludwig Volk, July 14, 1965.

88. Robert Graham, SJ, "A Return to Theocracy: The latest attack on the Vatican reveals the irony of its Author's Demands," in: *America*, July 18, 1964, 70–72. For correspondence between Graham and Adolph about Lewy, see KZG, NL Walter Adolph, WA 5L2, Walter Adolph to Robert Graham, December 16, 1964; Robert Graham to Walter Adolph, February 6, 1965; Walter Adolph to Robert Graham, February 17, 1965; Walter Adolph to Robert Graham, February 26, 1965.

89. Ludwig Volk, SJ, "Zwischen Geschichtsschreibung und Hochhuthprosa," 29.

90. HAEK Gen II 23.13, 31, Newspaper Clipping, Enno Wolters, "Angeklagter: Katholische Kirche. Kläger – Hart – aber befangen," in: *Rheinische Post*, May 22, 1965.

91. Excerpts from "'Die Kirche steht im Feuer falscher Angriffe': Katholische Stimmen zur SPIEGEL-Serie, 'Mit festem Schritt ins Neue Reich,'" in: *Kirchenzeitung für das Erzbistum Köln*, as quoted in: *Der Spiegel*, April 7, 1965.

92. Christoph Kösters and Petra von der Osten, "Ludwig Volk (1926–1984) – ein katholischer Zeithistoriker," in: Ronald Lambrecht and Ulf Morgenstern, ed., *"Kräftig vorangetriebene Detailfoschungen": Aufsätze für Ulrich von Hehl zum 65. Geburtstag* (Leipzig und Berlin: Kirchhof & Franke, 2012), 27–56.

93. ADPJ, NL Volk, 771–2/Ia, Ludwig Volk to Hochw. Pater, lieber Mitbruder, Munich, July 9, 1964.
94. ADPJ, NL Volk, 771–2/Ib, Ludwig Volk to Karl Bosl, München, March 7, 1965; Christoph Kösters and Petra von der Osten, "Ludwig Volk (1926–1984) – ein katholischer Zeithistoriker," 33.
95. ADPJ, NL Volk, 771–2/Ia, Ludwig Volk to Hochw. Pater, lieber Mitbruder, Munich, July 9, 1964; Ludwig Volk to Rudolf Morsey, July 11, 1964; AEMF, NL Johannes Neuhäusler, VN N12, Bischöfliches Ordinariat, Limburg/Lahm to Johannes Neuhäusler, October 6, 1964.
96. ADPJ, NL Volk, 771–2/Ib, Ludwig Volk to Rudolf Morsey, May 29, 1965.
97. Rudolf Morsey, "Kirche im Dritten Reich," in: *Frankfurter Allgemeine Zeitung*, November 4, 1965. Morsey made use of several of Volk's examples, including the rendition of "ardent" as "eifrig." See ADPJ, NL Volk, 771–2/Ib, Rudolf Morsey to Ludwig Volk, Bonn, June 1, 1965.
98. Ludwig Volk, SJ, "Zwischen Geschichtsschreibung und Hochhuthprosa," 33.
99. HAEK, Gen II 22.13, 29, Newspaper Clippings, Hans Asmussen, "Die Kirche und das Dritte Reich: Zu einer Artikelserie von Guenter Lewy im 'Spiegel'" in: *Rheinischer Merkur*, no date given; Erich Klausener Jr., "Angeklagter: Katholische Kirche. Erich Klausener antwortet Lewy," in: *Rheinische Post*, June 17, 1965.
100. Guenter Lewy, *The Catholic Church and Nazi Germany*, 169–171.
101. Ibid., 340–341.
102. Ludwig Volk, SJ, "Zwischen Geschichtsschreibung und Hochhuthprosa," 36.
103. Ibid., 39.
104. Ibid., 35.
105. For a bibliographical summary of works responding to Fischer, see Helmut Böhme, "'Primat' und 'Paradigmata-'. Zur Entwicklung einer bundesdeutschen Zeitgeschichtsschreibung am Beispiel des Ersten Weltkrieges," in: Hartmut Lehmann, ed., *Historikerkontroversen* (Göttingen: Wallstein Verlag, 2000), footnote 1, 89–92; on empathy, see Phillip Stelzel, "Working toward a Common Goal? American Views on German Historiography and German-American Scholarly Relations during the 1960s," in: *Central European History* 41 (2008), 639–671 and, especially, 654.
106. Benjamin Ziemann has called this process "Verwissenschaftlichung." See Benjamin Ziemann, *Katholische Kirche und Sozialwissenschaften, 1945–1975* (Göttingen: Vandenhoeck & Ruprecht, 2007).
107. On the Görres Gesellschaft, see Wilhelm Spael, *Görres-Gesellschaft, 1876–1941* (Paderborn: Schöningh, 1957).
108. Rebecca Ayako Bennette, *Fighting for the Soul of Germany: The Catholic Struggle for Inclusion after Unification* (Cambridge, MA: Harvard University Press, 2012), 135–156. See also Christopher Dowe, *Auch Bildungsbürger: Katholische Studierende und Akademiker im Kaiserreich, Kritische Studien zur Geschichtswissenschaft* (Göttingen: Vanderhoeck & Ruprecht, 2006).
109. Three bore the name of Stasiewski, though it took the assistance of Repgen, Volk and Morsey to bring them to fruition. Volk assumed the leading role on the remaining three, and he died of cancer shortly after completing work on the last volume.

110. www.kfzg.de/Publikationen/publikationen.html (accessed August 18, 2013).
111. HAEK, Gen II 22.13, 24, Klaus Szymichowski to das Katholische Büro z. Händen von Herrn Dr. Niemeyer, May 15, 1964.
112. HAEK, Gen II 22.13, 24, Kommission für Zeitgeschichte, Prof. Dr. D. Albrecht to Klaus Szymichowski, April 25, 1964.
113. Ibid.
114. For one example, see ADPJ, NL Volk, 771–2/Ib, Konrad Repgen to Ludwig Volk, June 7, 1965.
115. Konrad Repgen and Rudolf Morsey, ed., *Adenauer Studien I* (Mainz: Matthias-Grünewald Verlag, 1971), *Adenauer Studien II: Wolfgang Wagner: Die Bundespräsidentenwahl 1959* (Mainz: Matthias-Grünewald Verlag, 1972), *Adenauer Studien III: Untersuchungen und Dokumente zur Ostpolitik und Biographie* (Mainz: Matthias-Grünewald Verlag, 1974).
116. AEMF, NL Johannes Neuhäusler. VN N12, Generalvikar i.V. Lun, Bischöfliches Ordinariat, Limburg to Johannes Neuhäusler, October 6, 1964.
117. ADPJ, NL Volk, 771–2/IIIb, Gestellungsvertrag zwischen der Kommission für Zeitgeschichte bei der katholischen Akademie in Bayern vertreten durch das geschäftsführende Mitglied des Kuratoriums Msgr. Dr. Karl Forster und dem Provinzialrat der Oberdeutschen Provinz der Gesellschaft Jesu, München, vertreten durch den HH Provinzial Pater Heinrich Krauss, October 11, 1968.
118. ADPJ, NL Volk, 771–2/Ib, Volk to the Bishop of Speyer, June 26, 1965. He wrote: "Wäre sie früher erschienen, wären Angriffe wie die von Lewy nicht in dieser Weise möglich gewesen."
119. ADPJ, NL Volk, 771–2/Ib, Sendker, Generalvikar, Hildesheim, to Ludwig Volk, March 5, 1965.
120. ADPJ, NL Volk, 771–2/Ib, Volk to the Bishop of Speyer, June 26, 1965.
121. ADPJ, NL Volk, 771–2/IIIc, Beate Ruhm von Oppen to Ludwig Volk, April 23, 1969.
122. Ibid.
123. Interview with Stewart Stehlin, August 19, 2007. Curriculum Vitae, Stewart Stehlin, available at http://history.fas.nyu.edu/attach/13995 (accessed June 21, 2016).
124. Stewart Stehlin, "Bismarck and the New Province of Hanover," in: *Canadian Journal of History* 4, Nr. 2 (1969), 67–94. Stewart Stehlin, "Bismarck and the Secret Use of the Guelph Fund," in: *The Historian*, 33 (1970), 21–39; Stewart Stehlin, "The Publication of the 'Akten zur deutschen auswärtigen Politik, 1918–1945,'" in: *Central European History* I (1968), 193–199; Stewart Stehlin, "Documents on German Foreign Policy," in: *AHA Newsletter*, 6 (1967), 12–14.
125. Stewart Stehlin, *Bismarck and the Guelph Problem, 1866–1890* (The Hague: Martinus Nijhoff, 1973).
126. ADPJ, NL Volk, 771–2/IVb, Ludwig Volk to P. Angelo Martini, December 19, 1971.
127. Christoph Kösters and Petra von der Osten, "Ludwig Volk (1926–1984) – ein katholischer Zeithistoriker," 41–42.
128. ADPJ, NL Volk, 771–2/IVb, Ludwig Volk to P. Angelo Martini, December 19, 1971; Interview with Stewart Stehlin.

129. Ibid.
130. Interview with Stewart Stehlin.
131. ADPJ, NL Volk, 771–2/IVb, Ludwig Volk to P. Angelo Martini, December 19, 1971.
132. Interview with Stewart Stehlin.
133. Ibid.
134. ADPJ, NL Volk, 771–2/IVc, Volk to unnamed recipient, January 14, 1972.
135. ADPJ, NL Volk, 771–2/IVb, Ludwig Volk to P. Angelo Martini, December 19, 1971.
136. Volk informed Morsey of the situation, but Morsey, who had met Stehlin years ago in Bonn, made it clear that he did not view the American historian as competition. ADPJ, NL Ludwig Volk, 771–2/IVb, Ludwig Volk to Rudolf Morsey, December 19, 1971; Rudolf Morsey to Ludwig Volk, December 23, 1971. For his flurry of letters, see ADPJ, NL Volk, 771–2/IVc, Volk to unnamed recipient, January 14, 1972.
137. ADPJ, NL Volk, 771–2/IVb, Ludwig Volk to P. Angelo Martini, December 19, 1971.
138. Ibid.
139. ADPJ, NL Volk, 771–2/IVc, Angelo Martini, SJ, to Ludwig Volk, January 25, 1972.
140. ADPJ, NL Volk, 771–2/IVc, Ludwig Volk to Rudolf Morsey, January 31, 1972; Angelo Martini to Ludwig Volk, February 25, 1972.
141. ADPJ, NL Volk, 771–2/IVc, Angelo Martini, SJ, to Ludwig Volk, February 25, 1972.
142. ADPJ, NL Volk, 771–2/IVc, Volk to unnamed recipient, January 14, 1972; Ludwig Volk to Schlund, Generalvikar von Freiburg, March 13, 1972.
143. ADPJ, NL Volk, 771 – 2/IVc, Ludwig Volk to Angelo Martini, February 18, 1972; Ludwig Volk to Angelo Martini, March 13, 1972.
144. Stewart Stehlin, *Weimar and the Vatican, 1919–1933: German-Vatican Diplomatic Relations in the Interwar Years* (Princeton: Princeton University Press, 1983).
145. ADPJ, NL Volk, 771–2/IVc, Ludwig Volk to Konrad Repgen, January 28, 1972; Ludwig Volk to Rudolf Morsey, January 31, 1972.
146. Ibid. The editions appeared in print as Ludwig Volk, ed., *Akten Kardinal Michael von Faulhabers 1917–1945, Bd. I: 1917–1934* (Mainz: Matthias-Grünewald Verlag, 1975) and *Akten Kardinal Michael von Faulhabers 1917–1945, Bd. II: 1935–1945* (Mainz: Matthias-Grünewald Verlag, 1978).
147. ADPJ, NL Volk, 771–2/IVc, Zur Antwort an Herrn Sawatzki (no date); Ludwig Volk to Karl Forster, February 3, 1972.
148. See Christoph Kösters and Petra von der Osten, "Ludwig Volk (1926–1984) – ein katholischer Zeithistoriker," 43–45.
149. ADPJ, NL Volk, 771–2/IVc, Ludwig Volk to Karl Forster, February 3, 1972.
150. Ibid.; Ludwig Volk, Empfehlungen zur Benutzung des Faulhaber-Archivs, June 26, 1972.

151. ADPJ, NL Ludwig Volk, 771–2/VIIIa, Sister Ethel Mary Tinnemann, SNJM, to Ludwig Volk, February 1, 1979; Bruno Fink to Ludwig Volk, July 2, 1979; Sister Ethel Mary Tinnemann to Ludwig Volk, September 3, 1979. On Sister Ethel Mary Tinnemann, see www.snjmca.org/sister-ethel-mary (accessed June 21, 2016).

152. ADPJ, NL Ludwig Volk, 771–2/VIIIa, Ludwig Volk to Konrad Repgen, September 15, 1979; Konrad Repgen to Sister Ethel Mary Tinnemann, March 21, 1979.

153. ADPJ, NL Volk, 771–2/VIb, Ludwig Volk to Julius Döpfner, June 21, 1976; Frederic Spotts, *The Churches and Politics in Germany* (Middletown: Wesleyan University Press, 1973).

154. http://archives.lib.cua.edu/findingaid/muench.cfm (accessed June 21, 2016).

155. Frederic Spotts, *The Churches and Politics in Germany*.

156. ADPJ, NL Volk, 771–2/VIa, Ludwig Volk, Bericht über den Archivbesuch in Washington zur Einsichtnahme in den Nachlaß Muench (November 5–20, 1975), München, December 4, 1975. For a withering review of Frederic Spotts' work, see Ludwig Volk, in: *Theologische Revue* 73, (1977), 232–234. For additional words of excoriation, see Burkhard van Schewick, *Die Katholische Kirche und die Entstehung der Verfassungen in Westdeutschland, 1945–1950* (Mainz: Matthias-Grünewald Verlag, 1980).

157. CUA, Muench Accession File, Ludwig Volk to the Catholic University of America Archives, August 12, 1975.

158. CUA, Muench Accession File, Ludwig Volk to Catholic University of America, Archives, September 25, 1975. ADPJ, NL Volk, 771–2/VIa, Ludwig Volk, Bericht über den Archivbesuch in Washington, December 4, 1975.

159. ADPJ, NL Volk, 771–2/VIa, Ludwig Volk, Bericht über den Archivbesuch in Washington, December 4, 1975.

160. CUA, Muench Accession File, Ludwig Volk to Lloyd Wagner, December 8, 1975; ADPJ, NL Volk, 771–2/VIa, Ludwig Volk to Julius Döpfner, November 30, 1975.

161. ADPJ, NL Volk, 771–2 /VIa, Ludwig Volk to Julius Döpfner, November 30, 1975; Ludwig Volk, Bericht über den Archivbesuch in Washington, December 4, 1975; Ludwig Volk to Josef Homeyer, December 11, 1975; Ludwig Volk to Josef Homeyer, December 17, 1975.

162. CUA Muench Accession File, Ludwig Volk to Lloyd Wagner, December 8, 1975; Memorandum, Lloyd Wagner to George Hruneni Jr., December 12, 1975; George Hruneni Jr. to Ludwig Volk, January 7, 1976.

163. Saul Friedlaender, *Pius XII and the Third Reich: A Documentation* (New York: Knopf, 1966).

164. KNA Archive, Guenter Lewy, Westdeutsches Fernsehen, Sonntag, February 19, 1967, 20:30 Horizonte: Vatikan und Nationalsozialismus. Gespräch zwischen Guenter Lewy und Konrad Repgen.

165. AEMF, NL Johannes Neuhäusler. VN N12, Generalvikar i.V. Lun, Bischöfliches Ordinariat, Limburg to Johannes Neuhäusler, October 6, 1964.

166. For the text of the Catholic archival regulations, see www.archive-bw.de/six cms/media.php/44/katholische_kirche_rechtsgrundlagen.pdf (accessed June 21, 2016).

7   The Repgen-Scholder Controversy

1. Klaus Scholder, "Die Kapitulation des politischen Katholizismus. Die Rolle des Zentrums-Vorsitzenden Kaas im Frühjahr 1933," in: *Frankfurter Allgemeine Zeitung*, September 27, 1977, 9.

2. Klaus Scholder, *Die Kirchen und das Dritte Reich, Band 1: Vorgeschichte und Zeit der Illusionen 1918–1934* (Frankfurt a.M.: Propyläen/Ullstein, 1977); *Band 2: Das Jahr der Ernüchterung 1934. Barmen und Rom* (Berlin: Siedler, 1985).

3. Klaus Scholder, "Die Kapitulation des politischen Katholizismus," 9.

4. Rudolf Morsey, *Der Untergang des politischen Katholizismus. Die Zentrumspartei zwischen christlichem Selbstverständnis und "Nationale Erhebung" 1932–33* (Stuttgart: Belser, 1977).

5. Konrad Repgen, "Konkordat für Ermächtigungsgesetz? Gegen die Hypothese von einem Tauschgeschäft zwischen Hitler und dem Vatikan," in: *Frankfurter Allgemeine Zeitung*, October 24, 1977, 10–11.

6. Klaus Scholder, "'Ein Paradigma von säkularer Bedeutung': Hitler, Kaas und das Ende des politischen Katholizismus in Deutschland. Eine Antwort auf Konrad Repgen," in: *Frankfurter Allgemeine Zeitung*, November 19, 1977, 11–12; Konrad Repgen, "Repgen zu Scholders' Antwort," in: *Frankfurter Allgemeine Zeitung*, December 7, 1977, 9; Konrad Repgen, "Über die Entstehung der Reichskonkordats-Offerte im Frühjahr 1933 und die Bedeutung des Reichskonkordats. Kritische Bemerkungen zu einem neuen Buch," in: *Vierteljahrshefte für Zeitgeschichte* 26, Nr. 4 (1978), 499–534; Klaus Scholder, "Altes und Neues zur Vorgeschichte des Reichskonkordats. Erwiderung auf Konrad Repgen," in: *Vierteljahrshefte für Zeitgeschichte* 26, Nr. 4 (1978), 535–570; Konrad Repgen and Klaus Scholder, "Nachwort zu einer Kontroverse," in: *Vierteljahrshefte für Zeitgeschichte* 27, Nr. 1 (1979), 159–161.

7. For examples, see Konrad Repgen, "Ein Merkblatt für Seminararbeiten," in: *Geschichte in Wissenschaft und Unterricht* 33 (1982), 704–706, 705; Konrad Repgen, "Reichskonkordats-Kontroversen und historische Logik," in: Manfred Funke, Hans-Adolf Jacobsen, Hans-Helmuth Knütter, and Hans-Peter Schwarz, ed., *Demokratie und Diktatur: Geist und Gestalt politischer Herschaft in Deutschland und Europa. Festschrift für Karl Dietrich Bracher* (Düsseldorf: Droste Verlag, 1987), 158–177.

8. For a comprehensive historicization of this debate, see Hubert Wolf, "Reichskonkordat für Ermächtigungsgesetz? Zur Historisierung der Scholder-Repgen-Kontroverse über das Verhältnis des Vatikans zum Nationalsozialismus," in: *Vierteljahrshefte für Zeitgeschichte* 60, Nr. 2 (2012), 169–200.

9. BAK, NL Klaus Scholder, Klaus Scholder to Hans Roos, October 6, 1969.

10. On Repgen's battles in the academy, see Wolfgang Tischner, "Konrad Repgen wird 90 Jahre," May 5, 2013, available at www.kas.de/wf/de/33 .34255/ (accessed June 20, 2016).

11. His dissertation was titled "Die Verwirklichung des Imaginativen in den Romanen Jean Pauls."

12. For an example of his joy in provocation, see the following letter in which he described with obvious relish attending a forum at the Thomas-Morus-Akademie in Bensberg, "wo mich 80 kampfbereite Katholiken erwarteten nebst Herrn Morsey und Herrn Repgen." BAK, NL Klaus Scholder, #422, Klaus Scholder to Wolf Jobst Siedler, January 30, 1978.

13. BAK, NL Klaus Scholder, #422, Klaus Scholder to Wolfgang Richter, January 7, 1981.

14. On this point, see Jürgen Moltmann, "Die politische Relevanz der Theologie: Fortsetzung eines theologisch-politischen Gesprächs mit Klaus Scholder und ein Versuch, ihn zu verstehen," in: *Evangelische Theologie* 47 (1987), 498–504 and, in particular, 502–504; Heiko A. Oberman, "Klaus Scholder, 1930–1985," in: *Zeitschrift für Kirchengeschichte* 96 (1985), 295–300 and, in particular, 296.

15. For one example, see Klaus Scholder, "Die Jugend und das Vaterland," in: *Deutsche Universitätszeitung* 8, Nr. 23, December 7, 1953, 3–5.

16. Ibid. For one of many works on Barth, see Gerhard Wehr, *Karl Barth. Theologe und Gottes fröhlicher Partisan* (Gütersloh: Gütersloher Verlagshaus, 1985).

17. Gerhard Schulz, "Im Gedenken an Klaus Scholder," in: *Evangelische Theologie* 47 (1987), 477–485 and, in particular, 478–479; Heiko A. Oberman, "Klaus Scholder, 1930–1985," 295–300.

18. Klaus Scholder, *The Churches and the Third Reich, Volume One, Preliminary history and the Time of Illusions, 1918–1934* (Philadelphia: Fortress Press, 1988), 440.

19. Ibid. For the original, see Klaus Scholder, *Die Kirchen und das Dritte Reich*, 559.

20. Klaus Scholder, *Karl Georg Pfleiderer: Der liberale Landrat, Politiker und Diplomat, Heft 6, Schriftenreihe der Reinhold-Maier-Stiftung zur Geschichte* (Stuttgart: Reinhold-Maier-Stiftung, 1979), 5.

21. Ibid.

22. Hildegard Hamm-Brücher, "Erinnerungen an einen christlichen, liberalen und süddeutschen Demokraten. Klaus Scholder zum Gedenken," in: *Liberal*, 29, 2 (1987), 97–103 and, in particular, 97.

23. ADL, Bestand Kulturpolitischer Bundesausschuß, A7–13, Kulturpolitisches Referat, Freie Demokratische Partei, Werbung und Information, Indecipherable name to Klaus Scholder, March 27, 1957.

24. Hildegard Hamm-Brücher, "Erinnerungen an einen christlichen, liberalen und süddeutschen Demokraten," 97.

25. Klaus Scholder, *Kulturpolitik – Warum und Wie? Schriftenreihe der Freien Demokratischen Partei* (Detmold: Hermann Bösmann GmbH, 1957); Klaus Scholder, *Die Problematik der politischen Verantwortung in unserer jüngsten Geschichte* (Wiesbaden: Franz Steiner Verlag, 1959); Klaus

Scholder, "Christentum und Liberalismus," in: *Liberal* (1960), 12–18; Klaus Scholder, "Der Geist des Staates als Aufgabe der Kulturpolitik," in: *Liberal* (1961), 7–16; Klaus Scholder, "Zwanzig Jahre danach," in: *Liberal* (1963), 5–8.

26. Klaus Scholder, *Kulturpolitik – Warum und Wie?*, 10.
27. Klaus Scholder, "Christentum und Liberalismus." Scholder did not specify whether he was referring to either the Catholic or Protestant churches. But his claims would have been understood virtually everywhere as singling out the Catholic Church.
28. Klaus Scholder, *Ursprünge und Probleme der Bibelkritik im 17. Jahrhundert. Ein Beitrag zur Entstehung der historisch-kritischen Theologie* (München: Kaiser Verlag, 1966), 7.
29. This was not a point that Scholder made explicitly; he did not need to do so.
30. Klaus Scholder, *Ursprünge und Probleme der Bibelkritik*, 172.
31. Friedrich Wilhelm Graf, "Klaus Scholder," in: *Neue Deutsche Biographie (NDB). Band 23* (Berlin: Duncker & Humblot, 2007), 440–441. To have become a colleague of Repgen in Bonn, however, he would have had to switch over to the history department, as he indeed did in Tübingen. For the reasons why he turned down the position in Bonn, see BAK, NL Klaus Scholder, #245, Klaus Scholder to Hans Roos, October 6, 1969.
32. Gerhard Besier to the Author, June 6, 2014; Friedrich Wilhelm Graf, "Klaus Scholder," 440–441.
33. Klaus Scholder, *Die Problematik der politischen Verantwortung*.
34. Klaus Scholder, "Die evangelische Kirche und das Jahr 1933," in: *Geschichte in Wissenschaft und Unterricht* (1965), 700–714; Klaus Scholder, "Die evangelische Kirche in der Sicht der nationalsozialistischen Führung bis zum Kriegsausbruch," in: *Vierteljahrshefte für Zeitgeschichte* 16 (1968), 15–35; Klaus Scholder, "Die Kapitulation der evangelischen Kirche vor dem nationalsozialistischen Staat," in: *Zeitschrift für Kirchengeschichte* 81 (1970), 183–206.
35. For a complete list, see www.ekd.de/zeitgeschichte/publikationen/kirchen kampf.html (accessed June 20, 2016).
36. Klaus Scholder, *Die Kirchen und das Dritte Reich, Band 1*, vii. Scholder wrote: "Die Vorarbeiten für dieses Buch reichen fast zehn Jahre zurück." Assuming that he completed his foreword at some point in early to mid-1977, this would have placed the origins of his research between 1967 and 1968, just before assuming his professorship in Tübingen.
37. Ibid.
38. BAK, NL Klaus Scholder, #246, Klaus Scholder to Johann Baptist Metz, October 22, 1970.
39. KZG, NL Ludwig Volk, #306, Klaus Scholder, *Die Kirchen und das Dritte Reich*, 6. Punkte zum Inhalt, die möglicherweise besonderes Interesse beanspruchen werden. The promotional blurb stated: "Dies ist nun die erste Gesamtdarstellung, in der beide Kirchen zusammen in ihrem Nebeneinander, Miteinander und Gegeneinander behandelt werden."

40. John Conway, *The Nazi Persecution of the Churches, 1933–1945* (London: Weidenfeld and Nicholson, 1968); John Conway, *Die nationalsozialistische Kirchenpolitik 1933–1945: Ihre Ziele, Widersprüche und Fehlschläge* (Munich: Kaiser Verlag, 1969).

41. Interview with John Conway, June 24, 2014.

42. Richard Hunt, Review of *The Nazi Persecution of the Churches, 1933–1945*, in: *Annals of the American Academy of Political and Social Sciences* 385 (1969) 195–196; David Schoenbaum, Review of *The Nazi Persecution of the Churches, 1933–1945*, in: *The Journal of Modern History* 42 (1970), 485–461; Beate Ruhm von Oppen, Review of *The Nazi Persecution of the Churches, 1933–1945*, in: *The Catholic Historical Review* 55 (1970), 631–632; R.G.L. Waite, Review of *The Nazi Persecution of the Churches, 1933–1945*, in: *The American Historical Review* 75 (1969), 152–154; James Hastings Nichols, Review of The Nazi Persecution of the Churches 1933–1945, in: *Church History* 39 (1970), 130. Conway's book, however, later received a withering critique from Ludwig Volk. Ludwig Volk, SJ, "Hitlers Kirchenminister: Zum Versuch einer Gesamtdarstellung des Kirchenkampfes im NS-Staat," in: Dieter Albrecht, ed., *Katholische Kirche und Nationalsozialismus: Ausgewählte Aufsätze von Ludwig Volk* (Mainz: Schöningh, 1987), 348–353. Volk's essay originally appeared in: *Stimmen der Zeit* 190 (1972), 277–281.

43. Klaus Scholder, *Die Kirchen und das Dritte Reich, Band 1*, 207, 782, ff. 77, 804, ff. 73.

44. Ibid., vii.

45. Scholder was a Stiftsrepetent. For reflections on the Protestantischer Stift, see Joachim Hahn and Hans Mayer, *Das Evangelische Stift in Tübingen. Geschichte und Gegenwart – zwischen Weltgeist und Frömmigkeit* (Stuttgart: Theiss, 1985); Friedrich Hertel, ed., *In Wahrheit und Freiheit. 450 Jahre Evangelisches Stift in Tübingen* (Stuttgart: Calwer, 1986).

46. Interview with John Conway; John Conway to the author, November 20, 2014.

47. He contacted Ludwig Volk in 1970 and Morsey in 1976. See BAK, NL Klaus Scholder, #245, Klaus Scholder to Ludwig Volk, March 23, 1970; Ludwig Volk to Klaus Scholder, March 24, 1970; Klaus Scholder to Ludwig Volk, April 2, 1970; Klaus Scholder to Ludwig Volk, June 15, 1970; Privatsammlung Rudolf Morsey, Rudolf Morsey to Klaus Scholder, June 15, 1976; Klaus Scholder to Rudolf Morsey, July 6, 1976; Rudolf Morsey to Klaus Scholder, July 17, 1976.

48. Klaus Scholder, *Die Kirchen und das Dritte Reich, Band 1*, viii.

49. Ibid., ix.

50. ADPJ, NL Ludwig Volk, 47, 771–2/VII a, Rudolf Morsey to Ludwig Volk, December 12, 1977.

51. Leonore Siegele-Wenschkewitz, *Nationalsozialismus und Kirchen. Religionspolitik von Partei und Staat bis 1935* (Düsseldorf: Droste Verlag, 1974), 90–123.

52. Ibid., 91–92, 108.

53. Ibid., 104–108.

54. ADPJ, NL Ludwig Volk, 47, 771–2/VII a, Rudolf Morsey to Ludwig Volk, December 12, 1977.
55. Klaus Scholder, *Die Kirchen und das Dritte Reich, Band 1*, viii.
56. Scholder did state that he would attempt to have a running secondary focus on Catholicism. Privatsammlung Rudolf Morsey, Klaus Scholder to Rudolf Morsey, July 6, 1976.
57. BAK, NL Klaus Scholder, #422, Frau Kiwit, Buchexpedition, Scholder, Die Kirchen und das 3. Reich (Westdeutschland & Ausland), October 14, 1977. The publicity clearly worked because Scholder's book received widespread critical attention both in the popular and scholarly press. For examples, "Gott oder Führer," in: *Der Spiegel*, January 16, 1978; Peter Forster, "Die Kirchen und das Dritte Reich," in: *Neue Zürcher Zeitung*, April 28, 1978; Barbara Beuys, "Grüß Gott: Heil Hitler: Wie deutsche Kirchenführer sich mit den Nazis arrangiert haben, enthüllt ein Tübinger Wissenschaftler in einer neuen Untersuchung," in: *Stern*, May 31, 1978; Wolf Scheller, "Kirchen an der Schwelle zum Nazistaat: Klaus Scholders Werk über den Sündenfall der Amtskirchen/Prolingheuer über 'Fall Barth,'" in: *Frankfurter Rundschau*, December 12, 1978.
58. Scholder did mention how Protestant leaders had reacted to the signing of the Enabling Act but only to shore up his claim of a quid pro quo between the Enabling Act and the Reichskonkordat. He also proposed printing excerpts from two chapters on the "Jewish question" and "Theological Decisions in the Summer of 1933" that would have directed the spotlight on Protestants. BAK, NL Klaus Scholder, #422, Klaus Scholder to Wolf Jobst Siedler, July 5, 1977.
59. Klaus Scholder, "Die Kapitulation des politischen Katholizismus. Die Rolle des Zentrums-Vorsitzenden Kaas im Frühjahr 1933," in: *Frankfurter Allgemeine Zeitung*, September 27, 1977, 9.
60. Heinrich Brüning, *Memoiren. 1918–1934* (Stuttgart: DVA, 1970). On the authenticity of these, see Rudolf Morsey, *Entstehung, Authentizität und Kritik von Brünings Memoiren 1918–1934.* (Opladen: Westdeutscher Verlag, 1975).
61. Klaus Scholder, "Die Kapitulation des politischen Katholizismus," 9.
62. Ibid.
63. Konrad Repgen, "Konkordat für Ermächtigungsgesetz?," 10–11.
64. Privatsammlung, Thomas Brechenmacher, Konrad Repgen to Die Frankfurter Allgemeine Zeitung, September 29, 1977. Repgens's article "Reichskonkordat" was to appear in Hubert Jedin and Konrad Repgen, ed., *Handbuch der Kirchengeschichte, Band VII* (Freiburg: Herder-Verlag, 1979), 36–96.
65. Privatsammlung Thomas Brechenmacher, Dr. Hermann Rudolph to Konrad Repgen, October 5, 1977; Alfred Rapp to Konrad Repgen, October 13, 1977.
66. These were mentioned by Scholder as potential reviewers with little good to say about his work. BAK, NL Klaus Scholder, Klaus Scholder to Wolf Jobst Siedler, September 6, 1977.
67. As quoted in "Konrad Repgen 80, Glückwunsch," in: *Die Welt*, May 5, 2003; www.welt.de/print-welt/article692161/Konrad-Repgen-80.html (accessed June 20, 2016).

68. Konrad Repgen, "Dank und Rückblick," in: Joachim Scholtyseck, Klaus Borchard, Georg Rudinger, Maximilian Lanzinner, Hans Günter Hockerts, Jürgen Aretz and Konrad Repgen, ed., *Fünf Jahrzehnte Geschichtswissenschaft in Bonn. Konrad Repgen zum 80. Geburtstag*, Bonner Akademische Reden 87 (Bonn: Bouvier, 2003), 39.

69. Ibid.; Interview with Rudolf Morsey, Neustadt an der Weinstrasse, June 9, 2016.

70. Ibid.

71. "Schriftenverzeichnis Konrad Repgen. Zusammengestellt von Helene Thiesen," in: Klaus Gotto and Hans Günter Hockerts, ed., *Von der Reformation zur Gegenwart: Beiträge zu Grundfragen der neuzeitlichen Geschichte* (Paderborn: Schöningh, 1988). 349–359. Scholder's list of publications was a fraction of that of Repgen. See BAK, NL Klaus Scholder, #330, Schriftenverzeichnis von Klaus Scholder (no date, but probably 1968 or 1969).

72. He used the term "Christian" scholarship – but it is clear that he meant "Catholic" scholarship. Konrad Repgen, "Christ und Geschichte," in: *Jahres- und Tagungsbericht der Görres-Gesellschaft 1981* (Cologne, 1982), 18–34, reprinted in: Klaus Gotto and Hans Günter Hockerts, ed., *Von der Reformation zur Gegenwart: Beiträge zu Grundfragen der neuzeitlichen Geschichte* (Paderborn: Schöningh, 1988), 319–334.

73. Ibid., 330–331.

74. Konrad Repgen, "Dank und Rückblick," 42. This was a jab at critics like the author Heinrich Böll and the writer Carl Amery.

75. Ibid.

76. Ibid., 45.

77. Ibid., 45–46.

78. Privatsammlung Thomas Brechenmacher, Konrad Repgen to Josef Homeyer, September 29, 1977.

79. Braubach would leave a powerful imprint on Repgen. See Konrad Repgen, "In Memoriam Max Braubach, " in: *Historische Zeitschrift* 224 (1977), 82–91; Konrad Repgen, "Max Braubach. Leben und Werk," in: *Annalen des Historischen Vereins für den Niederrhein, insbesondere das alte Erzbistum Köln* 202 (1999), 9–41; Konrad Repgen, *Max Braubach. Person und Werk*, in: Ulrich Pfeil, ed., *Das Deutsche Historische Institut Paris und seine Gründungsväter* (München: Oldenbourg, 2007), 104–117.

80. Konrad Repgen, "P. Robert Leiber SJ, Der Kronzeuge für die vatikanische Politik beim Reichskonkordat 1933. Anmerkungen zu meiner Kontroverse mit Klaus Scholder, 1977–1979," in: Thomas Brechenmacher, ed., *Das Reichskonkordat 1933* (Paderborn: Schöningh, 2007), 28, footnote 13; Konrad Repgen, *Papst, Kaiser und Reich, 1521–1644, I Teil, Darstellung* (Tübingen: Max Niemeyer Verlag, 1962), xiii.

81. Konrad Repgen, *Papst, Kaiser und Reich, xiii*; Konrad Repgen, *Die römische Kurie und der westfälische Friede. Idee und Wirklichkeit des Papsttums im 16. und 17. Jahrhundert. 2. Teil: Analekten und Register* (Tübingen: Max Niemeyer Verlag, 1965).

82. Konrad Repgen, "P. Robert Leiber SJ," 28.

83. Robert Leiber, SJ, "Reichskonkordat und Ende der Zentrumspartei," in: *Stimmen der Zeit* 167 (1960), 213–223.

84. Konrad Repgen, "P. Robert Leiber SJ," 27–28. For other accounts by Leiber, see Robert Leiber, SJ, "Pius XII," in: *Stimmen der Zeit* 163 (1958), 81–100; Robert Leiber, SJ, "Der Vatikan und das Dritten Reich," in: *Politische Studien* 14 (1963), 293–298. He also delivered a lecture at a conference in Munich on September 18, 1962.

85. Klaus Scholder, "Altes und Neues zur Vorgeschichte des Reichskonkordats," 535; Konrad Repgen, "P. Robert Leiber SJ," 27.

86. Konrad Repgen, *Hitlers Machtergreifung und der deutsche Katholizismus. Versuch einer Bilanz. Festvortrag gehalten am 13. November 1963 anläßlich der feierlichen Eröffnung des Rektoratsjahres 1963/4, von Dr. phil. Konrad Repgen, ordentlicher Professor für Neuere und Neueste Geschichte an der Universität des Saarlandes* (Saarbrücken: Saarbrücker Zeitung Verlag + Druckerei, 1967); Klaus Scholder, "'Ein Paradigma von säkularer Bedeutung,'" 11–12.

87. Bernhard Stasiewski, ed., *Akten deutscher Bischöfe über die Lage der Kirche 1933–1945, Band I, 1933–1934* (Mainz: Matthias-Grünewald Verlag, 1968); Dieter Albrecht, *Der Notenwechsel zwischen dem Heiligen Stuhl und der deutschen Reichsregierung. Von der Ratifizierung des Reichskonkordats bis zur Enzyklika "Mit brennender Sorge"* (Mainz: Matthias-Grünewald Verlag, 1969); Alfons Kupper, ed., *Staatliche Akten über die Reichskonkordatsverhandlungen 1933* (Mainz: Matthias-Grünewald Verlag, 1969); Rudolf Morsey, ed., *Die Protokolle der Reichstagsfraktion und des Fraktionsvorstands der Deutschen Zentrumspartei, 1926–1933* (Mainz: Matthias-Grünewald Verlag, 1969).

88. The literature here is too enormous to summarize. For fine introductions and overviews, see Steve Bruce, *Religion in the Modern World: From Cathedrals to Cults* (Oxford: Oxford University Press, 1996); Siegfried Hermle, Claudia Lepp and Harry Oelke, ed., *Umbrüche. Der deutsche Protestantismus und die sozialen Bewegungen in den 1960er und 70er Jahren* (Göttingen: Vandenhoeck & Ruprecht, 2007); Callum Brown, *The Death of Christian Britain: Understanding Secularization, 1800–2000* (London: Routledge, 2009); Klaus Fitschen, Siegfried Hermle, Katharina Kunter, Claudia Lepp and Antje Roggenkamp-Kaufmann, ed., *Die Politisierung des Protestantismus. Entwicklungen in der Bundesrepublik Deutschland während der 1960er und 70er Jahre* (Göttingen: Vandenhoeck & Ruprecht, 2011); Katharina Kunter and Annegreth Schilling, *Globalisierung der Kirchen. Der Ökumenische Rat der Kirchen und die Entdeckung der Dritten Welt in den 1960er und 1970er Jahren* (Göttingen: Vandenhoeck & Ruprecht, 2014); Stefan Voges, *Konzil, Demokratie und Dialog. Der lange Weg zur Würzburger Synode (1965–1971)* (Paderborn: Schöningh, 2015).

89. See the following think piece critical of progressive theologians, liturgical innovations and movements to democratize the church: KZG, NL Walter Adolph, WA 35b, Konrad Repgen and Hubert Jedin to Julius Kardinal Döpfner, September 16, 1968. For a published version without Repgen's name, see Konrad Repgen, ed., *Hubert Jedin, Lebensbericht. Mit einem Dokumentenanhang* (Mainz: Matthias-Grünewald Verlag, 1984), 266–272.

90. Nikolai Wehrs, *Protest der Professoren: Der "Bund der Freiheit der Wissenschaft" in den 70er Jahren* (Göttingen: Wallstein, 2014).

91. Klaus Scholder, *Die Kirchen und das Dritte Reich, Band 1*, 523.

92. Klaus Scholder, "Altes und Neues zur Vorgeschichte des Reichskonkordats," 531, 551.

93. Hubert Wolf, "Reichskonkordat für Ermächtigungsgesetz?," 187.

94. Konrad Repgen, "Konkordat für Ermächtigungsgesetz?," 10–11.

95. Privatsammlung Thomas Brechenmacher, Wolf Jobst Siedler to Paul Mikat, October 27, 1977.

96. Klaus Scholder, "'Ein Paradigma von säkularer Bedeutung,'" 11–12.

97. Ibid.

98. Klaus Scholder, "Altes und Neues zur Vorgeschichte des Reichskonkordats," 541.

99. Klaus Scholder, "'Ein Paradigma von säkularer Bedeutung,'" 11–12.

100. Ibid.

101. Konrad Repgen, "Repgen zu Scholders' Antwort," in: *Frankfurter Allgemeine Zeitung*, December 7, 1977, 9.

102. ADP, NL Ludwig Volk, 47, 771–2/VII b, Rudolf Morsey to Ludwig Volk, February 9, 1978.

103. The intermediaries were the editor, Karl Dietrich Bracher; Hans-Peter Schwarz; and the managing editor (Geschäftsführender Redakteur), Hermann Graml. See Privatsammlung Brechenmacher, Hans-Peter Schwarz to Konrad Repgen, February 28, 1978; Hermann Graml to Konrad Repgen, March 15, 1978; Konrad Repgen to Hermann Graml, April 10, 1978.

104. On Repgen's plans to respond to Scholder in book form, see ADPJ, NL Ludwig Volk, 47, 771–2/VII b, Ludwig Volk to Konrad Repgen, June 23, 1978.

105. ADPJ, NL Ludwig Volk, 47, 771–2/VII b, Ludwig Volk to Angelo Martini, April 30, 1978; Angelo Martini to Ludwig Volk, May 11, 1978; Ludwig Volk to Angelo Martini, May 14, 1978; Ludwig Volk to Konrad Repgen, June 23, 1978.

106. ADPJ, NL Ludwig Volk, 47, 771–2/VII b, Ludwig Volk to Angelo Martini, September 21, 1978; Angelo Martini to Ludwig Volk, October 21, 1978; Klaus Scholder, "Altes und Neues zur Vorgeschichte des Reichskonkordats," 561, footnote 78. The relevant documents came from the Archivio Storico Ministero Affari Esteri.

107. Klaus Scholder, "Altes und Neues zur Vorgeschichte des Reichskonkordats," 561, footnote 78. Konrad Repgen, "P. Robert Leiber SJ," 26. As Besier put it, foreign languages were not Scholder's strength. Gerhard Besier to the author, June 6, 2014.

108. Klaus Scholder, "Altes und Neues zur Vorgeschichte des Reichskonkordats," 566, footnote 97; ADPJ, NL Ludwig Volk, 47, 771–2/VII b, Ludwig Volk to Angelo Martini, April 30, 1978.

109. Privatsammlung Rudolf Morsey, Aufzeichnung, Antonius John vom 18.5.1958 (no date on the document).

110. Ibid.

111. ADJP, NL Ludwig Volk, 47, 771–2/VI b, Ludwig Volk to Angelo Martini, April 30, 1978.

112. Konrad Repgen, "Über die Entstehung der Reichskonkordats-Offerte im Frühjahr 1933," 525–526, footnote 98.

113. Privatsammlung Brechenmacher, Konrad Repgen to Klaus Scholder, June 8, 1978.

114. Ibid.

115. Privatsammlung Rudolf Morsey, Klaus Scholder to Rudolf Morsey, July 28, 1978.

116. Privatsammlung Rudolf Morsey, Klaus Scholder to Rudolf Morsey, August 7, 1978.

117. Privatsammlung Rudolf Morsey, Klaus Scholder to Rudolf Morsey, August 10, 1978.

118. Konrad Repgen, "Über die Entstehung der Reichskonkordats-Offerte im Frühjahr 1933," 525.

119. Klaus Scholder, "Altes und Neues zur Vorgeschichte des Reichskonkordats," 567.

120. Konrad Repgen, "Über die Entstehung der Reichskonkordats-Offerte im Frühjahr 1933," 518.

121. Klaus Scholder, "Altes und Neues zur Vorgeschichte des Reichskonkordats," 555.

122. Konrad Repgen, "Über die Entstehung der Reichskonkordats-Offerte im Frühjahr 1933," 500–501.

123. Klaus Scholder, "Altes und Neues zur Vorgeschichte des Reichskonkordats," 537.

124. Ibid.

125. BAK, NL Klaus Scholder, #246, Klaus Scholder to Konrad Raiser, November 26, 1970.

126. Klaus Scholder, Die Kirchen und das Dritte Reich, Band 1, 523.

127. Konrad Repgen, "Über die Entstehung der Reichskonkordats-Offerte im Frühjahr 1933," 529.

128. Ibid., 530–531.

129. Ibid., 532.

130. Klaus Scholder, "Altes und Neues zur Vorgeschichte des Reichskonkordats," 567–568.

131. Klaus Scholder, Die Kirchen und das Dritte Reich, Band 1, ix.

132. Klaus Scholder, "Lässt sich Schuld bewältigen? Ein Gespräch mit Klaus Scholder über den 8. Mai," in: Herder Korrepondenz 3 Heft (1985), 115–120.

133. Konrad Repgen, "Christ und Geschichte," 30.

134. Ibid.

135. Hubert Wolf, "Reichskonkordat für Ermächtigungsgesetz?", 187.

136. Konrad Repgen, "Über die Entstehung der Reichskonkordats-Offerte im Frühjahr 1933," 530.

137. Klaus Scholder, "Altes und Neues zur Vorgeschichte des Reichskonkordats," 536.

138. See Heinrich Grüber's comments on the subject, Rowohlt Theater-Verlag, Archive, text of Wilhelm Unger, "'Entscheidend ist, was ausgesprochen

wird.' Propst Grüber stellt sich vor Rolf Hochhuth," in: *Kölner Stadt-Anzeiger*, March 14, 1963.

139. The apparent absence of a Catholic declaration of guilt in 1945 has been the subject of historical controversy. For contrasting views, some of which focus on the first pastoral statement by the Fulda Bishops Conference in August 1945, see Karl-Joseph Hummel, "Gedeutete Fakten: Geschichtsbilder im deutschen Katholizismus," in: Karl-Joseph Hummel and Christoph Kösters, ed., *Kirchen im Krieg: Europa, 1939–1945* (Paderborn: Schöningh, 2007), 507–568 and, in particular, 509–512; Karl-Joseph Hummel, "Umgang mit der Vergangenheit: Die Schulddiskussion," in: Karl-Joseph Hummel and Michael Kißener, ed., *Die Katholiken und das Dritte Reich: Kontroversen und Debatten* (Paderborn: Schöningh, 2009), 217–235. For a contrasting view, see Antonia Leugers, "Forschen und Forschen Lassen: Katholische Kontroversen und Debatten zum Verhältnis Kirche und Nationalsozialismus," in: *theologie.geschichte beiheft* 2/2010, Universitätsverlag Saarbrücken, 89–109.

140. Klaus Scholder, "Lässt sich Schuld bewältigen?," 115–120.

141. Ibid.

142. Klaus Scholder, "Altes und Neues zur Vorgeschichte des Reichskonkordats," 535–540. He specifically mentioned Morsey and Volk.

143. Ibid., 540.

144. Konrad Repgen und Klaus Scholder "Nachwort zu einer Kontroverse," in: *Vierteljahrshefte für Zeitgeschichte* 27, Nr. 1 (1979), 159–161.

145. Ibid., 161.

146. Klaus Scholder, "Ein Requiem für Hitler. Kardinal Bertram und der deutsche Episkopat im Dritten Reich," in: *Die Frankfurter Allgemeine Zeitung*, October 25, 1980.

147. ZDFUA, Bestand, Programmdirektor, Allgemeine Korrespondenz, 1.9.80 – bis 30.1.81, 5/0890, Dieter Stolte to Konrad Repgen, December 11, 1980.

148. ADPJ, NL Ludwig Volk, 47, 771–2/IX a, Pressetext, "Wie ein Schicksal … wie ein Verhängnis … Katholische Kirche im Dritten Reich, Fragen von Michael Albus und Franz Stepan," Zweites Deutsches Fernsehen, Sendezeit: 04.11.1980, 21.25–22.40.

149. ZDF Unternehmensarchiv, *Wie ein Schicksal … wie ein Verhängnis … Katholische Kirche im Dritten Reich*. Those interviewed included Oskar Neisinger, Erwin Keller, Marianne Pünder and Bernhard Welte.

150. ADPJ, NL Ludwig Volk, 47, 771–2/IX a, Ludwig Volk to Michael Albus, November 8, 1980; Repgen to den Herrn Intendanten des Zweiten Deutschen Fernsehens, November 11, 1980; Dieter Albrecht to das Zweite Deutsche Fernsehen, November 13, 1980; ZDFUA, Bestand, Programmdirektor, Allgemeine Korrespondenz, 1.9.80 – bis 30.1.81, 5/0890, Konrad Repgen to Dieter Stolte, November 11, 1980; Konrad Repgen to Dieter Stolte, December 19, 1980; Konrad Repgen to Dieter Stolte, January 15, 1981.

151. ADPJ, NL Ludwig Volk, 47, 771–2/IX a, Michael Albus to Ludwig Volk, December 10, 1980.

152. Ibid.

153. Ibid.

154. Christoph Kösters and Petra von der Osten, "Ludwig Volk. Ein katholischer Zeithistoriker," in: Roland Lambrecht and Ulf Morgenstern, ed., *Kräftig vorangetriebene Deitailforschungen. Aufsätze für Ulrich von Hehl zum 65. Geburtstag* (Leipzig – Berlin: Kirchhof & Franke, 2012), 27–56; KZG, NL Walter Adolph, WA 35b, Konrad Repgen and Hubert Jedin to Julius Kardinal Döpfner, September 16, 1968.

155. Olaf Blaschke, "Geschichtsdeutung und Vergangenheitspolitik. Die Kommission für Zeitgeschichte und das Netzwerk kirchenloyaler Katholizismusforscher, 1945–2000," in: Thomas Pittrof and Walter Schmitz, ed., *Freie Anerkennung übergeschichtlicher Bindungen. Katholische Geschichtswahrnehmung im deutschsprachigen Raum des 20. Jahrhunderts* (Freiburg: Rombach Verlag, 2010), 517.

156. ADPJ, NL Ludwig Volk, Ludwig Volk to Beate Ruhm von der Oppen, 47–771–2 VII, May 15, 1978.

157. ADPJ, NL Ludwig Volk, 47, 771–2/IX a, Ludwig Volk to P. Robert Graham, SJ, November 8, 1980.

Conclusions

1. See the two slender booklets by Friedrich Baumgärtel, the forty-page booklet *Wider die Kirchenkampflegenden* (Neuendettelsau: Freimund Verlag, 1959) and the expanded ninety-one-page version (Neuendettelsau: Freimund Verlag, 1959); Dietrich Goldschmidt and Hans-Joachim Kraus, ed., *Der ungekündigte Bund. Neue Begegnung von Juden und christlicher Gemeinde. Im Auftrag der deutschen Arbeitsgemeinschaft Juden und Christen beim deutschen evangelischen Kirchentag* (Stuttgart: Kreuz Verlag, 1963); Wolfgang Gerlach, *Als die Zeugen schwiegen: Bekennende Kirche und die Juden* (Berlin: Institut Kirche und Judentum, 1987).

2. For this case, see Manfred Gailus, "Keine gute Performance. Die deutschen Protestanten im 'Dritten Reich,'" in: Manfred Gailus and Armin Nolzen, ed., *Zerstrittene "Volksgemeinschaft". Glaube, Konfession und Religion im Nationalsozialismus* (Göttingen: Vandenhoeck & Ruprecht, 2011), 96–121.

3. Clemens Vollnhals, *Evangelische Kirche und Entnazifizierung: Die Last der nationalsozialistischen Vergangenheit, 1945–1949* (München: R. Oldenbourg, 1989), 226. According to American denazification yardsticks, 95 percent of the clergy in the state church of Bremen were tainted.

4. Kevin Spicer, *Brown Priests: Catholic Clergy and National Socialism* (Dekalb: Northern Illinois University Press, 2008), 233, 240. Spicer puts 138 priests, including members of religious orders, on his list of brown priests. Of these, fifty-three joined the Nazi Party. It should be pointed out that while the worst of the brown priests received reprimands, most did remain in the priesthood.

5. Klaus Scholder, "Lässt sich Schuld bewältigen? Ein Gespräch mit Klaus Scholder über den 8. Mai," in: *Herder Korrepondenz*, 3 Heft (1985), 115–120.

6. SLA, NL Rolf Hochhuth, 269, Abschrift, Albert Schweitzer to den Rowohlt Verlag, June 30, 1963. For its printed version, see ag, "Schweitzer über Hochhuths Drama," in: *Frankfurter Allgemeine Zeitung*, September 25, 1963.

7. HAEK, Gen II, 22.13, 35, Newspaper Clipping, Wilhelm Unger, "'Entscheidend ist, was ausgesprochen wird.' Propst Grüber stellt sich vor Rolf Hochhuth," in: *Kölner Stadt-Anzeiger*, March 14, 1963.

8. For an overview of the Protestant historiography, see Rudolf von Thadden, "Kirchengeschichte als Gesellschaftsgeschichte," in: *Geschichte und Gesellschaft* 9 (1983), 598–614; Joachim Mehlhausen, "Zur Methode kirchlicher Zeitgeschichtsforschung," in: *Evangelische Theologie* 48 (1988), 508–521; Norbert Friedrich, "Die Erforschung des Protestantismus nach 1945. Von der Bekenntnisliteratur zur kritischen Aufarbeitung," in: Norbert Friedrich and Traugott Jähnichen, ed., *Gesellschaftspolitische Neuorientierungen des Protestantismus in der Nachkriegszeit* (Münster: LIT, 2002), 9–35; Jochen-Christoph Kaiser, "Tendenzen und Probleme der kirchlichen Zeitgeschichte seit 1945," in: *Mitteilungen der Evangelischen Arbeitsgemeinschaft für Zeitgeschichte* 55 (2006), 51–68; Klaus Fitschen, "Die Kirchen und das Dritte Reich. Überlegungen zu Entwicklungen, Tendenzen und Desideraten der Forschung im Bereich des Protestantismus," in: *Mitteilungen zur Kirchlichen Zeitgeschichte* 6 (2012), 113–123; Hartmut Ludwig, "Deutung und Umdeutung des Kirchenkampfes. Geschichtsinterpretation als Kampf um die Deutungshoheit," in: Reinhard Höppner and Joachim Pereles, ed., *Das verdrängte Erbe der Bekennenden Kirche* (Stuttgart: Radius, 2012), 39–81. For examples of seminal works of revisionist historiography, see Robert Ericksen, *Theologians under Hitler: Gerhard Kittel/Paul Althaus/Emanuel Hirsch* (New Haven: Yale University Press, 1985); Almuth Meyer-Zollitsch, *Nationalsozialismus und evangelische Kirche in Bremen* (Bremen: Staatsarchiv der freien Hansestadt Bremen, 1985); Wolfgang Gerlach, *Als die Zeugen schwiegen: Bekennende Kirche und die Juden* (Berlin: Institut Kirche und Judentum, 1987); Jochen-Christoph Kaiser and Martin Greschat, ed., *Der Holocaust und die Protestanten: Analysen einer Verstrickung* (Frankfurt am Main: Athenäum, 1988); Clemens Vollnhals, *Evangelische Kirche und Entnazifizierung, 1945–1949. Die Last der nationalsozialistischen Vergangenheit* (München: R. Oldenbourg Verlag, 1989); Victoria Barnett, *For the Soul of the People: Protestant Protest against Hitler* (New York: Oxford University Press, 1992); Doris Bergen, *Twisted Cross: The German Christian Movement in the Third Reich* (Chapel Hill: University of North Carolina Press, 1996); Manfred Gailus, *Protestantismus und Nationalsozialismus. Studien zur nationalsozialistischen Durchdringung des protestantischen Sozialmilieus in Berlin* (Köln: Böhlau Verlag, 2001); Martin Greschat, *Die evangelische Christenheit und die deutsche Geschichte nach 1945. Weichenstellungen in der Nachkriegszeit* (Stuttgart: Kohlhammer Verlag, 2002); Matthew Hockenos, *A Church Divided: German Protestants confront the Nazi Past* (Bloomington: Indiana University Press, 2004); Susannah Heschel, *The Aryan Jesus: Christian Theologians and the Bible in Nazi Germany* (Princeton: Princeton University Press, 2008).

9. See the first thirty volumes in the series "Arbeiten zur Geschichte des Kirchenkampfes" from 1958–1984, along with the Ergänzungsreihe, Volumes 1–15 from 1964–1990: www.ekd.de/zeitgeschichte/publikationen/ki rchenkampf.html as well as www.ekd.de/zeitgeschichte/publikationen/kirchen kampf_ergaenzungsreihe.html (accessed June 20, 2016).

10. For two examples, see the angry responses by Wilhelm Niemöller to criticism by Friedrich Baumgärtel and John Conway. See BAK, NL Klaus Scholder #330, Wilhelm Niemöller to Heinz Brunotte (Auszugsweise Abschrift), July 17, 1965; #73, Wilhelm Niemöller to John Conway, November 10, 1969.

11. Kristian Buchna, *Ein klerikales Jahrzehnt? Kirche, Konfession und Politik in der Bundesrepublik während der 1950er Jahre* (Baden-Baden: Nomos Verlag, 2014).

12. On the diminishing of confessional strife, see Kristian Buchna, *Ein klerikales Jahrzehnt?*, 516–522.

13. Stefan Voges, *Konzil, Demokratie und Dialog. Der lange Weg zur Würzburger Synode (1965–1971)* (Paderborn: Schöningh, 2015).

14. "Beschluss: Unsere Hoffnung," in: L. Bertsch, SJ, Ph. Boonen, R. Hammerschmidt, J. Homeyer, F. Kronenberg, K. Lehmann unter Mitarbeit von P. Imhof, SJ, ed., *Gemeinsame Synode der Bistümer in der Bundesrespublik Deutschland. Beschlüsse der Vollversammlung, Offizielle Gesamtausgabe I* (Freiburg: Herder Verlag, 1976), 108–109.

15. L. Bertsch, SJ, Ph. Boonen, R. Hammerschmidt, J. Homeyer, F. Kronenberg, K. Lehmann unter Mitarbeit von P. Imhof, SJ, ed., *Gemeinsame Synode der Bistümer in der Bundesrespublik Deutschland*, 74.

16. Die amtliche Zentralstelle für kirchliche Statistik des katholischen Deutschlands, ed., *Das Kirchliche Handbuch für das Katholische Deutschland, Band 18: 1933-1934* (Cologne, 1934), 25–49; Große Brockhaus, *Handbuch des Wissens in 20 Bänden, 15 völlig neubearbt. Aufl.*, Bd. 5 (Leipzig, 1930), 744.

17. Daniel Kahneman, *Thinking, Fast and Slow* (New York: Farrer, Straus and Giroux, 2011). For criticisms, see Gerd Gigerenzer, "How to make Cognitive Illusions Disappear," in: *European Review of Social Psychology* 2 (1991), 83–115.

18. On the power of negative emotions to influence judgments, see Paul Rozin and Edward B. Royzman, "Negativity Bias, Negativity Dominance and Contagion," in: *Personality and Social Psychology Review* 5 (2001), 296–320. See also Roy F. Baumeister, Ellen Batslavski, Catrin Dinkenauer and Kathleen D. Vohs, "Bad Is Stronger than Good," in: *Review of General Psychology* 5 (2001), 323–370.

19. The pioneering study was C. G. Lord, L. Ross and M. R. Lepper, "Biased Assimilation and Attitude Polarization: The Effect of Prior Theories on Subsequently Considered Evidence," in: *Journal of Personality and Social Psychology* 37 (1979), 2098–2109. Their findings have been replicated in a number of subsequent studies, including A. G. Miller, J. W. McHoskey, C. M. Bane and T. G. Dowd, "The Attitude Polarization Phenomenon: Role of Response Measure, Attitude Extremity, and Behavioral Consequences of Reported Attitude Changes," in: *Personality and Social Psychology Bulletin* 64 (1993), 561–574; J.W. McHoskey, "Case Closed? On the John F. Kennedy Assassination: Biased Assimilation of Evidence and Attitude Polarization," in: *Basic and Applied Social Psychology* 17 (1995), 395–409; G. D. Munro and P. H. Ditto, "Biased Assimilation, Attitude Polarization, and Affect in

Reactions to Stereotype-Relevant Scientific Information," in: *Personality and Social Psychology Bulletin* 23 (1997), 636–653; G.D. Munro, S. P. Leary and T. P. Lasane, "Between a Rock and a Hard Place: Biased Assimilation of Scientific Information in the Face of Commitment," in: *North American Journal of Psychology* 6 (2004), 431–444; Guy A. Boysen and David L. Vogel, "Biased Assimilation and Attitude Polarization in Response to Learning about Biological Explanations of Homosexuality," in: *Sex Roles* 57 (2007), 755–762.

20. Prashant Bordia and Nicholas DiFonzo, "Psychological Motivations in Rumor Spread," in: Gary Alan Fine, Véronique Campion-Vincent and Chip Heath, ed., *Rumor Mills: The Social Impact of Rumor and Legend* (New York: Aldine, 2005), 87–101; Nicholas DiFonzo, *The Watercooler Effect: The Indispensible Guide to Understanding and Harnessing the Power of Rumor* (New York: Avery, 2009).

21. Daniel Kahneman, *Thinking, Fast and Slow*, 29. See Jonathan St. B. T. Evans and Keith Frankish, ed., *In Two Minds; Dual Process and Beyond* (New York: Oxford University Press, 2009); Keith Stanovich and Richard West, "Individual Differences in Reasoning: Implications for the Rationality Debate," in: *Behavioral and Brain Sciences* 23 (2000), 645–665.

22. On the diversity of Christian identity in the early Christian world, see Douglas Boin, *Coming Out Christian in the Roman World: How the Followers of Jesus Made a Place in Caesar's Empire* (New York: Bloomsbury Press, 2015).

23. On these points, see Jacques Kornberg, *The Pope's Dilemma: Pius XII Faces Atrocities and Genocide in the Second World War* (Toronto: University of Toronto Press, 2015).

24. Wilhelm Damberg, "Die Schuld der Kirche in der Geschichte," in: Karl-Joseph Hummel and Christoph Kösters, ed., *Kirche, Krieg und Katholiken: Geschichte und Gedächtnis im 20. Jahrhundert* (Freiburg: Herder Verlag, 2014), 148–171.

25. Metz, quoted in Wilhelm Damberg, "Die Schuld der Kirche in der Geschichte," 161–162.

26. Konrad Repgen to Joseph Kardinal Höffner, January 11, 1983; Sekretariat der Deutschen Bischofskonferenz, ed., *Erinnerung und Verantwortung. 30. Januar 1933 – 30. Januar 1983. Fragen, Texte, Materialien*, January 24, 1983.

27. Wilhelm Damberg, "Die Schuld der Kirche in der Geschichte," 167.

28. For a sense of how black-and-white narratives continue to be overrepresented in scholarship, see the following work and its hundred-page bibliography: Joseph Bottum and David Dalin, *The Pius War: Responses to the Critics of Pius XII* (New York: Lexington Books, 2004).

29. See Sam Harris, *The End of Faith: Religion, Terror, and the Future of Reason* (New York: Norton, 2005), 100–107.

Glossary of Names

Adolph, Walter (1902–1975) priest and journalist from the working-class neighborhood of Kreuzberg in Berlin, right-hand man to Bishop von Preysing between 1936 and 1939, head of the Morus Verlag and *Petrusblatt*, chronicler of Catholic martyrs during the Third Reich and vicar general for the diocese of Berlin from 1961 through 1969.

Arndt, Adolf (1904–1974) house lawyer of the SPD, born in Königsberg in East Prussia, joined the SPD in 1946, helped the Hessian government make its case before the Constitutional Court from June 4–8, 1956, over the validity of the Reichskonkordat and served as the senator for science and art in Berlin from March 11, 1963, through March 31, 1964.

Bea, Augustin (1881–1968) German Jesuit priest and later cardinal born in 1881 in Riedböhring bei Donaueschingen, rector at the Pontifical Biblical Institute in Rome from 1924 through 1949, cardinal deacon at St. Saba from December 1959 through June 1960, served as an ecumenical advocate in the years thereafter, including the Second Vatican Council, helped draft *Nostra Aestate*, the landmark statement of 1965 disavowing anti-Semitism and died in Rome.

Böckenförde, Ernst-Wolfgang (1930–present) renowned Catholic German constitutional theorist, justice on Germany's Constitutional Court from 1983 to 1996, historian and author of "German Catholicism in 1933."

Böhler, Wilhelm (1891–1958) Catholic priest and prelate, liaison between the bishops and the CDU and leader of the Catholic Office in Bonn until his death in 1958.

Bracher, Karl Dietrich (1922–2016) political scientist and historian who taught at the University of Bonn from 1959 to 1987, specialist in the collapse of the Weimar Republic and Nazi seizure of power in 1933 and author of an expert opinion from 1956 about the validity of the Reichskonkordat.

Corsten, Wilhelm (1890–1970) Catholic priest, theologian and author of *Cologne Documents* (1949).

Dehler, Thomas (1897–1967) liberal politician, Reichskonkordat critic and leader of the FDP from 1954 to 1957.

Deuerlein, Ernst (1918–1971) German historian, veteran of Stalingrad, author of *Das Reichskonkordat* (1956) and founding member of the Association for Contemporary History.

Döpfner, Julius (1913–1976) bishop of Würzburg from 1948 through 1957, bishop of Berlin from 1957 through 1961, appointed cardinal in 1958, archbishop of Munich-Freising from 1961 through 1976 and chairman of the German Bishops Conference from 1965 until his death in 1976.

Faulhaber, Michael von (1869–1952) archbishop of Munich-Freising from 1917 until 1952 and elevated to the rank of cardinal in 1921.

Fittkau, Gerhard (1912–2004) priest from Ermland in East Prussia, ordained in 1937, served as secretary to Bishop Maximilian Kaller of Ermland, installed as pastor in Süssenberg in East Prussia, sent to a Soviet penal camp in the Arctic in March 1945, returned to Germany in September 1945 and served in New York as the director of the St. Boniface Society from 1949 through 1960.

Fleischer, Josef (1912–1998) Catholic pacifist from Berlin and the sole surviving Catholic conscientious objector in Germany during the Second World War, resided in Basel and Freiburg im Breisgau.

Forster, Karl (1928–1981) Catholic theologian and first director of the Catholic Academy in Bavaria from 1957 through 1967.

Frings, Josef (1887–1978) archbishop of Cologne from 1942 until 1969, appointed cardinal in 1946 and served as chairman of the Fulda Bishops Conference from 1945 through 1965.

Gerst, Wilhelm Karl (1887–1968) Communist journalist, practicing Catholic and critic of the church's conduct during the Third Reich.

Hochhuth, Rolf (1931–present) German playwright and author of *The Deputy* (1963).

Höpker-Aschoff, Hermann (1883–1954) German liberal politician, member of the FDP, member of the Parliamentary Council from 1948 to 1949 and first president of the Constitutional Court from 1951 until his death in 1954.

Jordan, Max (1895–1977) German-American radio pioneer who took the name Placidus Jordan after entering the Benedictine order in 1954 and published critiques of Gordon Zahn's work.

Kafka, Gustav (1907–1974) German-Austrian academic, jurist, Jewish convert to Catholicism imprisoned because of his racial background from 1940 to 1945, specialist in legal and political questions for the Zentralkomitee der deutschen Katholiken from 1956 to 1961 and opponent of Gordon Zahn.

Keller, Michael (1896–1961) bishop of Münster from 1947 through 1961.

Klausener, Erich (1885–1934) leader of Catholic Action in Berlin murdered by the Nazis on June 30, 1934.

Klausener, Erich Jr. (1917–1988) Catholic priest, son of Erich Klausener and editor of the *Petrusblatt* after 1953.

Krone, Heinrich (1895–1989) Center Party and CDU politician and leader of the CDU-CSU caucus in the Bundestag from 1956 to 1961.

Kühn, Heinz R. (1919–2006) Catholic journalist for the Morus Verlag in Berlin, suffered in the Third Reich because of his half-Jewish status, emigrated to the United States in 1951 under a cultural exchange program and worked in public relations, communications and education in Chicago.

Kupper, Alfons (1917–1978) Catholic historian who worked as Wilhelm Böhler's assistant for the hearings in Karlsruhe in 1956 over the validity of the Reichskonkordat and authored articles and an edited volume on the treaty's history.

Leonhardt, Karl Ludwig (1922–2007) editor and business director at Rütten und Loening publisher who forwarded a copy of *The Deputy* to the Rowohlt press.

Lewy, Guenter (1923–present) German-American political scientist of Jewish background, author of *The Catholic Church and Nazi Germany* (1964).

Mohn, Reinhard (1921–2009) German entrepreneur and head of the Bertelsmann publishing house from 1971 to 1981.

Morsey, Rudolf (1927–present) German historian, scholar of political Catholicism and the Center Party and founding member of the Association for Contemporary History.

Muench, Aloisius Joseph (1889–1962) German-American bishop of Fargo, North Dakota, from 1935 to 1959, liaison between OMGUS and the Catholic church from 1946 to 1949, papal nuncio to Germany from 1951 to 1959 and appointed cardinal in 1959.

Müller, Hans (1928–2005) historian, author of a documentary history from 1963 of the Catholic Church from 1930 to 1935 and professor in Dortmund from 1975 through 1993.

Müller, Josef (1898–1979) Bavarian lawyer, politician, resistance agent, liaison to Eugenio Pacelli, concentration camp survivor and cofounder of the CSU.

Neuhäusler, Johannes (1888–1973) cathedral canon and auxiliary bishop in the archdiocese of Munich-Freising and author of books on the persecution of the Catholic Church in the Third Reich, including *Cross and Swastika* (1946) and *Anvil and Hammer* (1967).

Niemöller, Martin (1892–1984) Protestant churchman, theologian, leader in the Confessing Church, concentration camp survivor, drafter of the Stuttgart Confession of Guilt and president of the Protestant Church of Hessen-Nassau from 1947 through 1965.

Pacelli, Eugenio (1876–1958) papal nuncio to Germany from 1920 through 1929, cardinal secretary of state from 1930 through 1939 and pontiff (Pius XII) from 1939 until his death in 1958.

Papen, Franz von (1879–1969) Center Party politician from 1921 through 1932, chancellor of Germany from June–December 1932, helped to engineer plot to bring Hitler to power on January 30, 1933 and vice chancellor from 1933 through 1934.

Piscator, Erwin (1893–1966) theater director, former Communist and director of *The Deputy* in Berlin in 1963.

Poliakov, Léon (1910–1997) French historian and early chronicler of the Holocaust.

Raddatz, Fritz (1931–2015) German essayist, biographer and chief editor at the Rowohlt Press from 1960 until 1969.

Repgen, Konrad (1923–2017) German historian, cofounder of the Association for Contemporary History and critic of Klaus Scholder.

Schauff, Johannes (1902–1990) Center Party politician at the close of the Weimar era, German emigré in Rome and Brazil and driving force behind the creation of the Association for Contemporary History.

Schneider, Reinhold (1903–1958) German-Catholic writer and church critic who between 1945 and 1948 helped compile the ten-volume series on the Catholic Church in the Third Reich for the Herder Verlag.

Scholder, Klaus (1930–1985) Protestant church official, church historian, FDP politician, author of *The Churches in the Third Reich* (1977, 1985) and critic of Konrad Repgen.

Schreiber, Georg (1882–1963) prelate, theologian, Catholic church historian and former Center Party politician from the Weimar era based in Münster after 1945.

Sideri (née Heinemann), Marianne (1932–present) first wife of Rolf Hochhuth, author of a book on German lyric poetry and daughter of Rose Schlösinger executed on August 5, 1943, for her role in the Red Chapel resistance movement.

Spital, Hermann-Josef (1925–2007) German theologian and bishop of Trier from 1981 until 2001.

Stasiewski, Bernhard (1905–1995) priest, professor in Bonn, church historian and Eastern European specialist commissioned in 1953 to put together a history of the Catholic Church under National Socialism.

Stehlin, Stewart (1936–present) American historian and author of *Weimar and the Vatican, 1918–1933* (1983).

Volk, Ludwig, SJ (1926–1984) German Jesuit and historian who wrote and edited volumes on the Reichskonkordat and the Catholic Church in the Third Reich.

Werthmann, Georg August (1898–1980) Feldgeneralvikar in the Wehrmacht from 1936 to 1945 and Generalvikar in the Bundeswehr from 1956 through 1962.

Zahn, Gordon (1918–2007) American Catholic pacifist and sociologist from Chicago and author of *German Catholics and Hitler's Wars* (1962) and *In Solitary Witness: The Life and Death of Franz Jägerstätter* (1964).

Zinn, Georg-August (1901–1976) lawyer and SPD politician who served as the Ministerpräsident of Hesse from 1950 through 1969.

Bibliography

The secondary sources on the topic of the Catholic Church and the National Socialist past easily fill a library annex; a comprehensive listing would require a separate volume. For that reason, you may find a listing at www.cambridge.org/9781107190665. Below is a list of collections used for this work. The archival abbreviations indicated are used in the endnotes.

Archdiocese of Chicago, Archives (ACA)
    Albert Meyer Papers
Archiv der Deutschen Provinz der Jesuiten, München (ADPJ)
    NL Ludwig Volk
Archiv der Dominikanerprovinz Teutonia, Köln (ADTK)
    NL Franziskus Stratmann
Archiv der Erzdiözese Salzburg (AES)
    NL Andreas Rohracher
Archiv des Erzbistums München und Freising (AEMF)
    Dokumentation Pressestelle
        499
        1506
        2080
        1957–1960, Der Stellvertreter
    Kardinal Faulhaber Archiv
    NL Johannes Neuhäusler
    PA – P III 1454 Roth Leonhard
    Registratur des Generalvikars: Kirche und Drittes Reich
    Registratur des Generalvikars: Lager-Seelsorge
Archiv der Gedenkstätte, Dachau (AGD)
Archiv der Akademie der Künste, Berlin (ADK)
    Archiv Theater der Freien Volksbühne Berlin
        Band, 186–189
        FVB, I–VIII
        Schnellhefter, Der Stellvertreter, Vorkorrespondenz
        Schnellhefter, Der Stellvertreter, Berlin
    Erwin-Piscator-Center
    Piscator Sammlung
Archiv der Sozialen Demokratie der Friedrich-Ebert-Stiftung, Bonn (ASD)

Depositum, Christel Beilmann
NL Adolf Arndt
NL Willy Brandt
NL Walter Dirks
NL Peter Nellen
NL Georg August Zinn
Sammlung, "Linkskatholizismus," Martin Stankowski
Archiv des Katholischen Militärbischofs, Berlin (AKMB)
    Sammlung Werthmann
        SW 998, 1010, 1028
    NL Werthmann
        Der "Fall Fleischer," I–III
Archiv des Liberalismus, Gummersbach (ADL)
    Biographische Sammlung, Klaus Scholder
    Bestand Thomas Dehler, N1, 3086, 3088, 3089
    Bestand Erika Fischer, N14–29
    Bestand Clara von Simson, N88–117
    Bestand Wolfgang Mischnick, A38–127
    Bestand Reinhold Maier, A34–74, 75
    Bestand Kulturpolitischer Bundesausschuß, A10, 13, 37, 93, 94
    Bestand Bundeshauptausschuß, 1964, A12ß49,
Archiv für Christlich-Soziale Poliitk, Munich (ACSP)
    NL Alois Hundhammer
    NL Richard Jaeger
    NL Josef Müller
Bayerisches Hauptstaatsarchiv, München (BHA)
    MKK 38233, MK 49229
    StK Bayer. Verdienstorden, 129
Bayerische Staatsbibliothek, München (BSB)
    NL Ernst Deuerlein
Bistumsarchiv Münster (BAM)
    A O, 2–6 Bischöfliches Sekretariat, Neues Archiv
    A O, 798, Generalvikariat, Wehrmachtseelsorge
    A101, 3–5 Materialsammlung, Drittes Reich
    A101, 48, Bischöfliches Generalvikariat, Neues Archiv, Presse/
        Zeitungen, April 1944–Okt. 1950
    A101, 325–327
Bistumsarchiv Osnabrück (BAO)
Bundesarchiv Koblenz (BAK)
    NL Ernst-Wolfgang Böckenförde
    NL Paul-Egon Hübinger
    NL Hans Peters
    NL Klaus Scholder
    B122 Bundespräsidialamt, 2069, 2180–2182, 4924, 5156, 5609,
        5556, 5557
    B136 Bundeskanzleramt, 2032, 5843, 5844, 5854, 5857
    B138 Bundesinnenministerium, 5845–5848, 6880, 6941

B141 Bundeskanzleramt, 6447–6456
B144 1112
Catholic University Archives, Washington (CUA)
    Alois Muench Accession Papers
    Alois Muench Papers
    Paul Furfey Papers
Deutscher Bundestag, Referat ID 2, Parlamentsarchiv (BT)
    94 Sitzung des Verteidigungsausschusses vom 1. Juni 1956
    Bundestagsdrucksachen IV/1216 und IV/1221
        Kleine Anfrage der CDU-Abgeordneten Majonica und Lemmer
Deutsches Rundfunkarchiv, Babelsberg (DRA)
    Inszenierung, Der Stellvertreter, 333
    Pressearchiv, Personalia, Rolf Hochhuth
    Pressearchiv, Personalia, Erwin Piscator
    SFB, 375, Korrespondenz zum "Stellvertreter"
Deutschlandradio Kultur, Abt. Dokumentation und Archive, Berlin
    Audioaufnahme, "Die Zeit im Feuer"
    Audioaufnahme, "Kalenderblatt v. 20.2.63"
    Audioaufnahme,   "Pressekonferenz,   Rolf   Hochhuth: Der
    Stellvertreter"
Diözesanarchiv Berlin (DAB)
    I/1–58, Betreuungen Kl–Ku
    I/4–20a, Nationalsozialismus
    I/4–35, Wiedergutmachung (Entnazifierung)
    I/4–39, Apostolischer Stuhl, Nuntiatur
    I/4–72, Katholisches Büro, Bonn, 1963
        I/4–413–1, 2, Maria Regina Martyrum
    I/5–12, Kühn, Heinz
    I/12, 19–20, Morus Verlag
    III/6–14, 16, 17, Maria Regina Martyrum
    IV/63–268, 269, Katholiken-Ausschuß des Bistums Berlin
    IV/54–83, Kartei Morus Verlag
    NL Walter Adolph
        V/1-1 Schriftlicher Nachlass, Einzelvorgänge
        V/1-3 Der Stellvertreter
        V/1-5-2 Presse zu Hochhuth, Der Stellvertreter
        V/1-7, 8 Korrespondenz
    NL Alfred Bengsch
        V/5-6, 1-2 Nuntiatur
    NL Julius Döpfner
        V/7-25-1 Bundesrepublik Deutschland und Berlin (West)
        V/7-25-2 Prof. Gordon Zahn
    NL Erich Klausener Jr.
        V/12–4–7 Kirchliche Medienarbeit
        V/12–6–2–2 Hochhuth, Der Stellvertreter
        V/12–11 Korrespondenz

NL Wilhelm Weskamm
  V/24-4 Allgemeine Korrespondenz
  V/24-11 Priester
Diözesanarchiv Limburg (DAL)
  209 B
  551 B
  NL Walter Kampe,
    D Publizistik, II, Rundfunk, 1963–1964
Diözesanarchiv Rottenburg (DAR)
  G1.1, 16.1zb, Friedensbund Deutscher Katholiken, 1950–1958
  G1.1, 16.1zm, Friedensbund Deutscher Katholiken, 1950–1958
  G1.5.156, Erhebungen zur Frage der Kollektivverfolgung der Katho-
    lischen Kirche in der NS Zeit (1938–1944), 1952–1953
  G1.5.157, Negativ von Kopien wichtiger Dokumente, die sich Dr.
    Stasiewski aus dem Bestand "NS-Akten" des Diözesanarchives für
    sein Forschungsverhalten "Katholische Kirche und NS"
    zusammenstellte
Erzbischöfliches Archiv Freiburg (EAF)
  NL Conrad Gröber
Evangelisches Zentralarchiv, Berlin (EZA)
  2/1005, 2/1696, 2/1807, 2/1808, 2/1939–1942, 2/1958, 2/2264
  4/15
  7/4072, 7/5927
  87/265, 87/267
  631/29, 631/97, 631/98
  686/939, 686/940, 686/941, 686/942
  743/168
Geheimes Staatsarchiv Preußischer Kulturbesitz (GStA)
  NL Heinrich Grüber
Hauptstaatsarchiv Nordrhein-Westfalen, Düsseldorf (HANR)
  NL Christine Teusch
Herder Verlag, Freiburg, Archiv
Hessisches Hauptstaatsarchiv, Wiesbaden (HHSA)
  502 Ministerpräsident-Staatskanzlei, 6247–6288
  504 Hessisches Kultusministerium, 7558 -7559
Historisches Archiv des Bayerischen Rundfunks, München (HABR)
Historisches Archiv des Erzbistums Köln (HAEK)
  CR II 1.9 Erzdiözese München und Freising
  CR II 1.17a, 4–5
  CR II 2.19, 2–4 Bischofskonferenzen
  CR II 2.3, 1–5, Hirtenworte der Bischöfe
  CR II 14.1.2–6, Verwaltung des Kirchenvermögens und
    Rechnungswesens
  CR II 16.10, 1–8 Deutsche Reichsverfassungen, Landesverfassungen
  CR II 25.18, 3–4 Militaria
  CR II 25.2, 4–8 Militärseelsorge
  CR II 27.30.1

Gen II 22.13, 1–48, Auseinandersetzungen des Christentums mit jeweils neuen Weltanschaungen

Gen II 23.23a, 4–62, Politische Akten

Gen II 23.23e, 1–5, Entnazifizierung

Gen II 22.59, 8–9, Friedensbund deutscher Katholiken

Katholisches Büro, ZUG 862 #126, Der Stellvertreter, Korrespondenz

Katholisches Büro Bonn I (Amtszeit Böhler), 81, 90, 91, 93, 94, 95, 105, 107, 108–111, 113, 117, 121, 125, 126, 131, 188, 254

Dienstakten Wilhelm Böhler, 315–320

WUV 9, 101, Widerstand und Verfolgung

Historisches Archiv der Stadt Köln (HASK)

NL Christine Teusch

Historisches Archiv des Westdeutschen Rundfunks, Köln (HAWDR)

02188, 03293, 04745, 05119, 05790, 07574, 11424, 12911, 12985, 13006

Institut für Zeitgeschichte, München (IFZ)

ID 34/2, Hausarchiv, Alff, Wilhelm

ID 34/23, Hausarchiv, Buchheim, Hans, Allgemein

ID 102/12, Hausarchiv

ID 103/6, Hausarchiv

ID 103/21, Hausarchiv

ID 103/30, Hausarchiv

ID 105/2, Gutachten, Hans Buchheim

ED 94/305 Staatssekr. Dr. W. Strauß

ED 107/2, Olef

ED 120/175, Sammlung Wilhelm Hoegner

ED 346, NL Johannes Schauff

ED 369/320, NL Ludz, Peter Christian

International Tracing Service, Bad Arolsen (ITS)

Documents on Johannes Neuhäusler

Jugendhaus Hardehausen, Dokumentationsstelle (JHH)

NL Christel Beilmann

NL Gerd Hirschauer

Katholische Akademie Bayern (KAB)

A 1/1 Gründung –Katholische Akademie in Bayern

A 16/1-5, Kommission für Zeitgeschichte

BI Tagungen

BI/9 Die Deutschen Katholiken und das Schicksal der Weimarer Republik, Würzburg 1961

BI/11 Bewältigung historischer und politischer Schuld, München 1961

BI/15 Gibt es ein deutsches Geschichtsbild?, 1960 Würzburg

BI/17 Podiumsgespräch, Der Stellvertreter, München 1963

BI/18 Der Katholische Widerstand gegen den Nationalsozialismus, München 1963

Katholische Nachrichtenagentur, Berlin, Archiv (KNA, Berlin), now located in the Kommission für Zeitgeschichte in Bonn

Katholischen Nachrichtenagentur, Bonn, Archiv (KNA Archive), now
   located in the Kommission für Zeitgeschichte in Bonn
   Amery, Carl
   Böckenförde, Ernst-Wolfgang
   Hochhuth, Rolf
   Lewy, Günter
   Neuhäusler, Johannes
   Zahn, Gordon
Kommission für Zeitgeschichte, Bonn (KZG)
   NL Walter Adolph
   NL Ludwig Volk
Konrad Adenauer Stiftung, Sankt Augustin (KAS)
   NL Odilo Braun
   NL Heinrich Köppler
   NL Heinrich Krone
   NL Ernst Lemmer
   NL Ernst Majonica
   NL Gerhard Schröder
Landesarchiv Berlin (LAB)
   B Rep 002, Nr. 7349, #1, 2a
   B Rep 002, Nr. 10583
   B Rep 014, Nr. 2247–8
   C Rep 104, Nr. 607
Landeshauptarchiv Koblenz (LHAK)
   NL Adolf Süsterhenn
Loyola University, Chicago, Archives (LUC)
   James Maguire Papers
   Ralph Gallagher Papers
Marquette University Archives (MUA)
   Dorothy Day Papers
   John Riedl Papers
Memorial de la Shoah, Centre de documentation juive contemporaine,
   Paris
   CDLXVII-84a
   DLVI (1) -64b
Monacensia, Literaturarchiv und Bibliothek München (MLB)
   NL Carl Amery (Anton Mayer)
   NL Friedrich Schnack
National Archives, College Park (NA)
   RG 260, Religious Affairs Branch
   RG 319, Records of the Office of the Assistant Chief of Staff, G-2
      Intelligence, Records of the Investigative Records Repository,
      Personnel Name File, Rudolf Aschenver (sic)
   RG 549, Records of U.S. Army Europe, Judge Advocate Division,
      War Crimes Branch, Records Relating to Post-Trial Activities,
      1945–1957
Niedersächsisches Landesarchiv, Hannover (NSLA)

NDS, 50, ACC.2000/100, 315, 321
NDS, 52, 54/91, 100
NDS, 400, ACC. 165/94, 54–58/2, 73–79, 31/86, 473
VVP, 10, 125 I, 125 II, 126 I, 126 II, 128 I
Österreichisches Literaturarchiv der Österreichischen Nationalbibliothek, Wien (ÖLA)
    NL Friedrich Heer
Pfarrarchiv, Donaueschingen (PAD)
    Sammlung, Josef Fleischer
Politisches Archiv des Auswärtigen Amtes, Berlin (PAAA)
    B26, Band 50, 186
    B80, Band 286, 288
    B92, Band 104
    B130, 3756A, 4700A, 5433A, 5445A, 5600A
Privatsammlung, Thomas Brechenmacher
Privatsammlung, Guenter Lewy
Privatsammlung, Rudolf Morsey
Privatsammlung, Rudolf Pawelka, Puchheim bei München
Privatsammlung, Germaine Poliakov-Rousso, Massy, France
Privatsammlung, Narzissa Stasiewski, Ittenbach bei Königswinter
    Kommission für Zeitgeschichte
    Schriftwechsel, Bernhard Stasiewski, 1945–1970
Regent College, Vancouver, Canada, Library
    John Conway Papers
Rheinische Friedrich-Wilhelms-Universität Bonn, Archiv
    NL Paul Egon Hübinger
Rowohlt Theater Verlag, Archiv, Reinbek bei Hamburg (RTVA)
Rowohlt Verlag, Pressearchiv, Reinbek bei Hamburg (RVPA)
St. John's University Archives, Collegeville, Minnesota (SJUA)
Schweizerisches Literaturarchiv, Bern (SLA)
    NL Rolf Hochhuth
Staatsarchiv München (SAM)
    Staatsanwaltschaften 34698, 34699, 34474/2
Stadtarchiv Freiburg im Breisgau (SAF)
    Einwohner Meldekartei
Stadtarchiv Eschwege (SAE)
    Einwohner Meldekartei
    Materialsammlung 73–2 Literatur, Rolf Hochhuth
Syracuse University Archives (SUA)
    Dorothy Thompson Papers
United States Army Heritage and Education Center, Carlisle, PA (USAHEC)
    Harold C. Deutsch Papers
United States Holocaust Memorial Museum, Archive (USHMM)
    NL Theophil Wurm
    RG76.001M, Selected Records from the Vatican Archives, 1865–1939

United States Relations with the Vatican and the Holocaust, 1940–1950

Universitätsbibliothek, Eichstätt – Ingolstadt (UBEI)

VA 1, Köselarchiv

    Autorenkorrespondenz Hans Buchheim

    Autorenkorrespondenz Ernst-Wolfgang Böckenförde

    VII 3.1, "Hochland"-Korrespondenz, Mappe 9

    VII 3.1, "Hochland"-Korrespondenz, Mappe 17

    VII 3.1, "Hochland"-Korrespondenz, Mappe 26

University of Notre Dame, Archives (UNDA)

    Gordon Zahn Papers

Unternehmensarchiv, Bertelsmann, Gütersloh (UAB)

    ZDF-Archiv, Mainz

Zentralarchiv der Evangelischen Kirche in Hessen und Nassau, Darmstadt (ZAEK)

    NL Martin Niemöller

Zentralarchiv zur Erforschung der Geschichte der Juden in Deutschland, Heidelberg (ZEGJD)

    NL Josef Wulf

Zentralkomitee der deutschen Katholiken, Bad Godesberg, Archiv (ZdK)

    1740

    1741

    1742

    2202/1a

    2202/1b

    2302/1a

    2306/2a

    3211

    4100

    4100 (Duplikate)

    4230 Referat für staatsbürgerliche Angelegenheiten

    4231 Reden und Aufsätze von Dr. Gustav Kafka

    4231/1– VS-Unterlagen, Dr. Prauss

    4231/2 Privatdienstliches Schriftverkehr

    4231/7 Referat Gordon Zahn über die Rolle der Kirche im 3. Reich

    4930

    8058/8

    KT Berlin, 1, Arbeitstagung Saarbrücken

    KT Berlin, 5, Korrespondenz, Fürst zu Löwenshtein

Interviews

Ernst-Wolfgang Böckenförde, Freiburg

John Conway, Vancouver

Rolf Hochhuth, Berlin

Ludwig Hammermayer, Ingolstadt
Hans-Heinrich Koch, Eschwege
Marianne Hochhuth-Sideri (née Heinemann), Basel
Heinz Hürten, Eichstätt
Michael Hovey, Detroit
Angelika Kühn, Oak Park
Guenter Lewy, Washington
Rudolf Morsey, Bonn
Margaret Osthus, Gütersloh
Germaine Poliakov-Rousso, Massy
Narzissa Stasiewski, Ittenbach bei Königswinter
Stewart Stehlin, New York
Peter Steinfels, New York
Heinz-Dietrich Thiel, Berlin
Norbert Trippen, Köln

Index